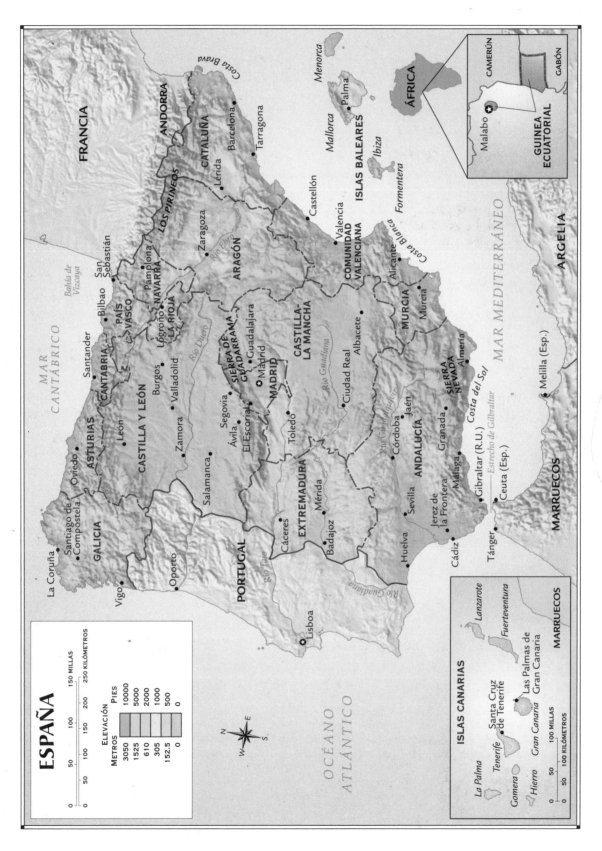

ESPAÑA

ELEVACIÓN

METROS	PIES
3050	10000
1525	5000
610	2000
305	1000
152.5	500
0	0

FRANCIA

ANDORRA

Costa Brava

CATALUÑA

Barcelona

Tarragona

Lérida

Menorca

Palma

Mallorca

ISLAS BALEARES

Ibiza

Formentera

LOS PIRINEOS

Castellón

San Sebastián

Pamplona

NAVARRA

Zaragoza

Río Ebro

ARAGÓN

Valencia

COMUNIDAD VALENCIANA

Costa Blanca

Bilbao

PAÍS VASCO

Logroño

LA RIOJA

Alicante

Bahía de Vizcaya

Santander

CANTABRIA

MAR CANTÁBRICO

Burgos

SIERRA DE GUADARRAMA

Guadalajara

Madrid

MADRID

CASTILLA-LA MANCHA

MURCIA

Murcia

Almería

SIERRA NEVADA

Valladolid

Río Duero

Segovia

Ávila

El Escorial

Albacete

Río Guadiana

Ciudad Real

León

ASTURIAS

Oviedo

CASTILLA Y LEÓN

Zamora

Toledo

Jaén

Granada

Córdoba

Málaga

Costa del Sol

MAR MEDITERRÁNEO

Melilla (Esp.)

ARGELIA

GALICIA

Santiago de Compostela

La Coruña

Vigo

Oporto

Salamanca

Cáceres

EXTREMADURA

Mérida

Badajoz

Río Tajo

PORTUGAL

Sevilla

Jerez de la Frontera

Huelva

ANDALUCÍA

Río Guadalquivir

Río Guadiana

Cádiz

Tánger

Gibraltar (R.U.)

Ceuta (Esp.)

Estrecho de Gibraltar

MARRUECOS

Lisboa

OCÉANO ATLÁNTICO

N
E
W
S

50 100 150 200

0 50 100 150 MILLAS

0 50 100 150 250 KILÓMETROS

ÁFRICA

CAMERÚN

GABÓN

Malabo

GUINEA ECUATORIAL

ISLAS CANARIAS

La Palma

Tenerife

Gomera

Hierro

Santa Cruz de Tenerife

Gran Canaria

Las Palmas de Gran Canaria

Lanzarote

Fuerteventura

MARRUECOS

0 50 100 MILLAS

0 50 100 KILÓMETROS

DEDICATION

This book is lovingly dedicated to Tracy D. Terrell (1943–1991). Tracy left us an enduring legacy and a methodology that has had a significant impact on second language teaching and on the evolution of textbook materials. He also envisioned this book and guided us, the co-authors, to its fruitful completion. Tracy was our inspirational mentor. His kind spirit and brilliant vision infuse every page. His ever-generous heart touched many of us—friends, colleagues, teachers, students—in an indelible way. We miss him. And we hope he is proud of our work on this new edition of *Dos mundos*.

Dos mundos

SEVENTH EDITION

Comunicación y comunidad

Tracy D. Terrell
Late, University of California, San Diego

Magdalena Andrade
Irvine Valley College

Jeanne Egasse
Irvine Valley College

Elías Miguel Muñoz

 Higher Education

Boston   Burr Ridge, IL   Dubuque, IA   New York   San Francisco   St. Louis
Bangkok   Bogotá   Caracas   Kuala Lumpur   Lisbon   London   Madrid   Mexico City
Milan   Montreal   New Delhi   Santiago   Seoul   Singapore   Sydney   Taipei   Toronto

Higher Education

Published by McGraw-Hill, an imprint of The McGraw-Hill Companies, Inc., 1221 Avenue of the Americas, New York, NY 10020. Copyright © 2010, 2006, 2002, 1998, 1994, 1990, 1986. All rights reserved. No part of this publication may be reproduced or distributed in any form or by any means, or stored in a database or retrieval system, without the prior written consent of The McGraw-Hill Companies, Inc., including, but not limited to, in any network or other electronic storage or transmission, or broadcast for distance learning.

This book is printed on acid-free paper.

2 3 4 5 6 7 8 9 0 WCK/WCK 0 9

ISBN: 978-0-07338521-1 (Student's Edition)
MHID: 0-07-338521-2 (Student's Edition)
ISBN: 978-0-0730476-9 (Instructor's Edition)
MHID: 0-07-730476-4 (Instructor's Edition)

Editor in Chief: *Michael Ryan*
Editorial Director: *William R. Glass*
Sponsoring Editor: *Katherine K. Crouch*
Director of Development: *Scott Tinetti*
Development Editor: *Jennifer Kirk*
Editorial Coordinator: *Janina Tunac Basey*
Marketing Manager: *Jorge Arbujas*
Production Editor: *Carey Eisner*
Design Manager: *Preston Thomas*
Cover Designer: *Lisa Buckley*
Text Designer: *Linda Robertson*
Senior Photo Research Coordinator: *Nora Agbayani*
Photo Researcher: *Gene Fitzer*
Illustrator: *Dave Bohn*
Senior Production Supervisor: *Richard DeVitto*
Composition: *10/12 Warnock Pro by Aptara®, Inc.*
Printing: *45# Pub Matte Plus, Quebecor World*

Front Cover: NASA—digital copyright Science Faction/Getty Images
Back Cover: Andrew Paterson/Getty Images

Credits: The credits appear at the end of the book and are considered an extension of the copyright page.

Library of Congress Cataloging-in-Publication Data

Dos mundos / Tracy Terrell . . . [et al.]. — 7th ed.
   p. cm.
  English and Spanish.
  Includes index.
   ISBN-13: 978-0-07-338521-1 (alk. paper)
   ISBN-10: 0-07-338521-2 (alk. paper)
   1. Spanish language—Textbooks for foreign speakers—English.   I. Terrell, Tracy D.   II. Title: 2 mundos.
PC4129.E5D67 2009b
468.2'421—dc22

2008052459

The Internet addresses listed in the text were accurate at the time of publication. The inclusion of a Web site does not indicate an endorsement by the authors or McGraw-Hill, and McGraw-Hill does not guarantee the accuracy of the information presented at these sites.

www.mhhe.com

Contents

PASO A
La clase y los estudiantes 1

PASO B
Las descripciones 21

PASO C
Mi familia y mis amigos 37

CAPÍTULO 1
Los datos personales y las actividades 56

CAPÍTULO 2
Mis planes y preferencias 84

CAPÍTULO 3
Las actividades y los lugares 118

CAPÍTULO 6
La residencia 214

CAPÍTULO 7
Hablando del pasado 244

CAPÍTULO 8
La comida 274

CAPÍTULO 9
La niñez y la juventud 310

CAPÍTULO 10
Nuestro planeta 340

CAPÍTULO 11
De viaje 372

CAPÍTULO 12
La salud y las emergencias 410

CAPÍTULO 13
De compras 444

To the Instructor

Welcome to the Seventh Edition of *Dos mundos*! Those of you already familiar with our textbook know that this is a special kind of text. Through its communicative methodology, *Dos mundos* offers an exciting alternative to the many Spanish-language textbooks available today. Our program allows instructors to do what they have always wanted to do as educators: help students enjoy the process of learning to communicate in a second language.

Our main objectives have not changed since the First Edition. The **Actividades de comunicación** continue to play a primary role, while grammar serves as an aid in the language acquisition process. The core of our program is communication. But over the years, we have made several changes to *Dos mundos*. With each new edition we bring in fresh, practical ideas from the field of second-language teaching. And we listen to you, the instructors who use *Dos mundos*.

We are excited about the expanded cultural content and the literature in *Dos mundos*. Before going any further, we invite you to flip through the pages of our textbook. Note the variety of photos, authentic materials, and literary selections. Every chapter opens with a work of fine art and a new section called **¡Conozca... !,** both tied to one or more of the twenty-one Spanish-speaking countries. We are pleased with our renewed emphasis on the art, history, and cultures of the Hispanic world as the textbook we envisioned with Tracy Terrell continues to evolve. It is our hope that you continue to benefit from all that *Dos mundos* has to offer.

Seventh Edition: An Overview

The subtitle of our book—*Comunicación y comunidad*—reflects the main goals of the program: achieving communicative competence in Spanish and establishing community connections both inside the classroom and within the larger Spanish-speaking world.

The Seventh Edition of the main text and its accompanying *Cuaderno de actividades* both begin with three preliminary **Pasos** and have fifteen regular chapters. These chapters are divided into three main sections:

Actividades de comunicación y lecturas: Communicative activities and readings

Vocabulario: Vocabulary introduced in the communicative activities

Gramática y ejercicios: Grammar explanations and verification exercises

We have kept the cultural magazine, **Vida y cultura,** which appears after **Capítulos 4, 9,** and **15.** The first magazine now features an article on Paraguayan harp music, and there is also a new article on **son jarocho,** the traditional music of Veracruz, Mexico, in the third magazine. We have expanded the cultural readings in the regular chapters with new **Ventanas culturales** and **Ventanas al pasado.** Several of the literary selections from the previous edition continue to appear in the Seventh Edition, now under the heading **Enlace a la literatura.** But we have added two new types of **Enlace** on music and film: **Enlace a la música** and **Enlace al cine.**

Guided Tour

Entrada al Capítulo

Each regular chapter begins with two pages that orient you to the themes and activities of the chapter. On the left-hand page, a **Metas** feature provides a brief overview of the objectives, and fine art from the Spanish-speaking world illustrates the chapter theme. **Sobre el artista** introduces the artist and his or her place in the culture of the Spanish-speaking world.

At the top of the right-hand page is a new feature in this edition, **¡Conozca... !**, with interesting information about each Spanish-speaking country. Next, three columns detail the communicative activities, readings, culture topics, and grammar exercises included in the chapter. In addition, icons on this page highlight the multimedia materials that accompany the chapter.

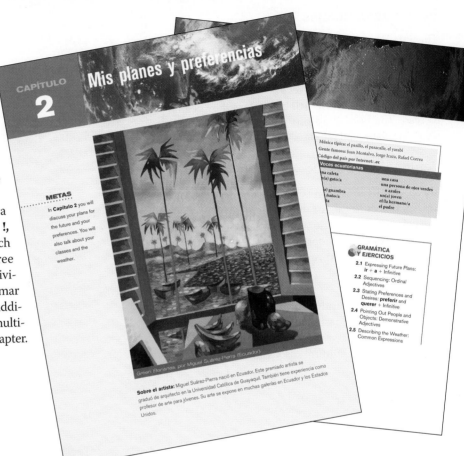

CAPÍTULO 2

Mis planes y preferencias

METAS
In **Capítulo 2** you will discuss your plans for the future and your preferences. You will also talk about your classes and the weather.

Green Bananas, por Miguel Suárez-Pierra (Ecuador)

Sobre el artista: Miguel Suárez-Pierra nació en Ecuador. Este premiado artista se graduó de arquitecto en la Universidad Católica de Guayaquil. También tiene experiencia como profesor de arte para jóvenes. Su arte se expone en muchas galerías en Ecuador y los Estados Unidos.

Música típica: el pasillo, el pasacalle, el yaraví
Gente famosa: Juan Montalvo, Jorge Icaza, Rafael Correa
Código del país por Internet: .ec

Voces ecuatorianas

una caleta	una casa
un(a) gato/a	una persona de ojos verdes o azules
un(a) guambra	un(a) joven
ñaño/a	el/la hermano/a
ta	el padre

GRAMÁTICA Y EJERCICIOS

2.1 Expressing Future Plans: **ir + a** + Infinitive

2.2 Sequencing: Ordinal Adjectives

2.3 Stating Preferences and Desires: **preferir** and **querer** + Infinitive

2.4 Pointing Out People and Objects: Demonstrative Adjectives

2.5 Describing the Weather: Common Expressions

Actividades de comunicación y lecturas

Los planes

✴ Lea Gramática 2.1.

Andrea Ruiz habla de los planes de su familia para el fin de semana

El sábado Pedro y las niñas van a lavar el carro.

El sábado por la tarde, Pedro y yo vamos a dar una fiesta.

También vamos a bailar en un club de jazz.

El domingo por la mañana, vamos a ir a misa con las niñas.

✴ El viernes por la noche Pedro y yo vamos a ver una película.

El domingo por la tarde Pedro va a escribir una carta.

Luego vamos a almorzar en un restaurante.

Actividades de comunicación y lecturas

These activities and readings are the core of *Dos mundos*. Each chapter is divided into three or four themes, each introduced with color art illustrating structures and vocabulary. At the top of each art display you will see the instructions **Lea Gramática... ,** directing students to read or review the grammar point that corresponds to that particular theme. Following the display are the communicative activities. Students participate in these activities with their instructor and/or their classmates in order to develop listening and speaking skills.

Reading and Cultural Materials

Every chapter contains a variety of reading and cultural materials: **Ventanas culturales, Ventanas al pasado, Enlaces** and **Lectura.**

Ventanas culturales

These cultural readings focus on four aspects of life in the Spanish-speaking world: **Nuestra comunidad, Las costumbres, La vida diaria,** and **La lengua.** Students should review the new vocabulary in the **Vocabulario útil** box before they begin to read. The brief questions in **Comprensión** can also stimulate general class discussion.

Ventanas al pasado

These cultural readings focus on aspects of the social, cultural, or political history of the Spanish-speaking world. Again, the **Vocabulario útil** box acquaints students with unfamiliar vocabulary, and the **Comprensión** questions test students' understanding of the material.

The **Ventanas culturales** and **Ventanas al pasado** readings may be assigned for homework, but their cultural content makes them ideal for in-class reading and cultural discussion.

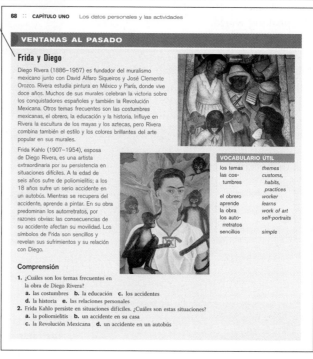

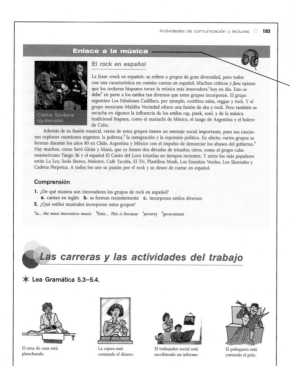

Enlace a la literatura / a la música / al cine

This segment is a link to Hispanic literature, music, and cinema, thus the name **Enlace.** The **Enlace a la literatura** consists of poetry and fiction by well-known Spanish, Latin American, and U.S. Latino writers. New to this edition are the **Enlace a la música** and **Enlace al cine,** short readings that present exciting information about the music and cinema of the Spanish-speaking world. New or difficult vocabulary is glossed, and each **Enlace a la literatura** is followed by a creative writing activity, allowing students to develop their writing skills in Spanish and encouraging them to associate the reading of literature with active participation in the creative process. All **Enlaces a la música** and **al cine** are followed by a comprehension activity. The **Enlace** segments are also available in audio format on the Audio Program. You can also find a link to an iTunes iMix on the *Dos mundos* Online Learning Center: **www.mhhe.com/ dosmundos7.**

Lectura

The **Lecturas** present a variety of topics, such as sports, leisure activities, regional foods, and interesting cities or regions of the Spanish-speaking world. These materials may be read in class or may be given as homework. Students should review the reading hints in **Pistas para leer** and the new vocabulary words in the **Vocabulario útil** box before they begin to read. Follow-up questions include **Comprensión,** which assesses general understanding of the material, and either **Un paso más... ¡a escribir!,** a creative writing activity related to the topic of the reading, or **Un paso más... ¡a conversar!,** a whole-class discussion activity. Selected readings from the **Lectura** sections are also available in audio format on the Online Learning Center and also on a special audio CD that is part of the Audio Program.

En resumen

This section includes activities that summarize the chapter material. **De todo un poco** features one or more communicative activities for students to do in groups. **¡Dígalo por escrito!** is an individual writing activity that requires students to use chapter themes and grammar in a creative

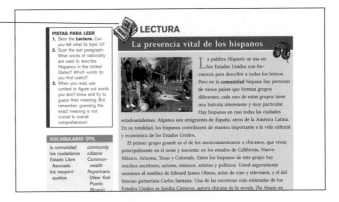

way. **¡Cuéntenos usted!** gives students a series of guided questions related to the chapter theme and then asks them to tell their own story.

Vocabulario

At the end of every chapter, before the blue grammar pages, is a one- or two-page list of all the new vocabulary words from the **Actividades de comunicación.** All vocabulary words are available in audio format on the Online Learning Center and on special audio CDs in the Audio Program.

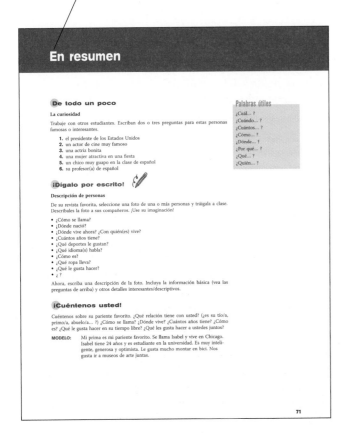

Gramática y ejercicios

The blue grammar pages include explanations of the basic grammar and follow-up exercises. **¿Recuerda?** sidebars call attention to previously relevant grammar points. Brief margin notes provide additional information about Spanish grammar. The explanations and the exercises are designed to be done as homework, using the Answer Key in Appendix 4 to make corrections.

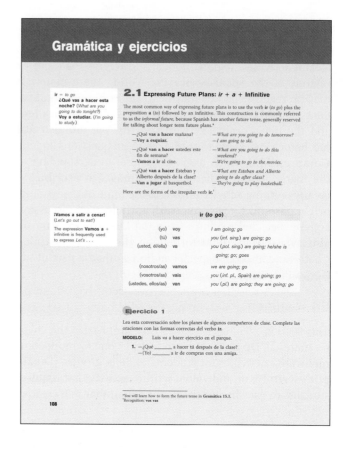

Vida y cultura

Vida y cultura follows **Capítulos 4, 9,** and **15.** This cultural magazine section includes articles on various aspects of Hispanic culture from several countries. Footnotes are provided to clarify unfamiliar vocabulary.

Features and Changes in the Textbook

■ **Chapter Themes:** We have retained all communication themes from the previous edition, while updating activities and cultural information.

■ **Chapter Openers:** Each two-page opener features a piece of fine art from one of the twenty-one Spanish-speaking countries and a new feature called **¡Conozca… !** that provides country-specific data on holidays, typical food and music, famous people and other areas of interest.

■ **Actividades de comunicación:** The communicative activities have been updated to reflect current issues and student interests. Each of the **Actividades de comunicación** is categorized under one of seventeen different types (see under *Dos mundos* Methodology: **Specifics,** toward the end of this *To the Instructor* section). All activities are sequenced from input to output in order to promote comprehension before production. The **Diálogo** activities are included only in the **Pasos** and in **Capítulo 1.** Their purpose is to provide controlled practice in using formulaic conversational expressions.

■ **En resumen:** These review sections support the chapter themes. The **¡Dígalo por escrito!** sections are individual writing activities suitable for assigning as homework or extra credit. The **¡Cuéntenos usted!** activity is designed to develop oral narrative ability and may be used at the end of a chapter or later in the course as a review activity. **Capítulos 12, 13, 14,** and **15** also include a service-learning activity called **Conexión a la comunidad,** which encourages students to use their Spanish in real-life volunteer settings.

■ **Vocabulario:** The end-of-chapter vocabulary lists include all the vocabulary from the **Actividades de comunicación.**

■ **Reading Materials:** The Seventh Edition of *Dos mundos* continues to emphasize reading and literacy. It features a wide variety of cultural topics, exciting literature, and realia-based materials. The two main categories of readings are **Lecturas** and **Enlaces.**

• **Lectura:** This reading segment focuses on many aspects of Hispanic culture such as sports, holiday celebrations, leisure activities, and regional foods. The **Pistas para leer** box provides pre-reading questions, clues, and useful strategies such as scanning and cognate recognition.

• *Enlace:* This material is presented in the segments **Enlace a la literatura, Enlace a la música,** and **Enlace al cine.** As in the previous edition, the **Enlace a la literatura** consists of poetry and fiction selections by well-known Spanish, Latin American, and U.S. Latino writers. Some of the writers featured are José Martí, Octavio Paz, María Elena Walsh, Rosario Castellanos, Tomás Rivera, and Federico García Lorca. Each selection is preceded by an introduction to the author.

Students will be encouraged by their enjoyment of these literary works; we are confident that literature can be understood and appreciated early in the language acquisition process. New to the Seventh Edition are the **Enlace a la música** and **Enlace al cine,** short readings that present exciting information about the music and cinema of the Spanish-speaking world. Some of the topics highlighted are Andean and Cuban music, as well as Mexican, Spanish, Argentine, and Chilean cinema.

■ **Culture:** In addition to the cultural content described in the preceding section on reading materials, the Seventh Edition includes other cultural features.

• **Vida y cultura:** An attractive magazine section (after **Capítulos 4, 9,** and **15**) that presents articles on high-interest topics such as music, history, cuisine, and art.

• **Ventanas culturales:** As the title suggests, these are windows into the culture and society of the Hispanic world. There are four categories of **Ventanas culturales: Nuestra comunidad, La lengua, La vida diaria,** and **Las costumbres.** The Seventh Edition features topics such as **flamenco** music, the **Diablada de Oruro** celebration in Bolivia, and the **Ballet Folklórico de México.**

• **Ventanas al pasado:** focus on some historical aspect of Hispanic culture. Some of the topics include the art of Diego Rivera and Frida Kahlo, Arabic contributions to the field of medicine, and the work of Spanish architect Antoni Gaudí.

• **¡Ojo!:** Brief descriptions of customs in and points of interest about the Hispanic world.

• **¡Conozca… !:** This feature, new to the Seventh Edition, includes country-specific data on cities, population, holidays, typical foods and music, famous people, and colloquial language. This information can serve as a starting point for a more in-depth discussion of many aspects of daily life and culture in Spanish-speaking countries.

■ **Grammar:** Here are features of note in the Seventh Edition.

• **Explanations:** Clear and concise explanations and the Answer Key provided in Appendix 4 allow the grammar component to be used by students outside the classroom. A simple overview of basic grammar, **Some Useful Grammatical Terms,** introduces the grammar of **Paso A.** A simple introduction to direct object pronouns has been added to **Capítulo 3.** This concept is re-entered in more detail in **Capítulo 6, Capítulo 8,** and **Capítulo 13. Gramática 11.2,** Softening Commands, The Present Subjunctive following **querer,** has been expanded to include the verb **sugerir.** This will allow students to practice the use of the present subjunctive in more contexts before additional uses of the subjunctive are presented in subsequent chapters.

- **Margin Notes:** These give students quick hints and brief overviews of grammar points for review purposes.

- **Illustrations:** Many complex grammar concepts are illustrated with a drawing, called **Gramática ilustrada,** to help students visualize the grammatical structure.

- **Review:** The **¿Recuerda?** feature reminds students to review previous relevant grammar sections.

- **Helpful Hints:** **¡Ojo!** and other marginal boxes in the grammar section provide helpful hints for doing the grammar exercises.

- **Verbs:** Simple presentations of **-ar** and **-er/-ir** verbs are in **Paso C** and **Capítulo 1.** The present tense is reexamined more completely in **Capítulos 3** and **4.**

Features and Changes in the *Cuaderno de actividades* (Workbook / Laboratory Manual)

The *Cuaderno de actividades* is intended for use primarily outside the classroom. This combined workbook / laboratory manual features **Actividades escritas, Actividades auditivas, Resumen cultural, Pronunciación y ortografía, Videoteca,** and **Lecturas.** The Preface in the *Cuaderno de actividades* provides a detailed description of all sections and types of activities.

- **Actividades escritas:** These writing activities echo the chapter themes and allow students to express themselves more freely than in the verification exercises of the **Gramática y ejercicios.**

- **Actividades auditivas:** These listening passages correspond to the chapter themes and give students the opportunity to hear Spanish speakers interacting using the vocabulary and structures featured in the chapter. Brief comprehension questions accompany these passages.

- **Resumen cultural:** These questions review the cultural content of the main text.

- **Pronunciación y ortografía:** Explanations of pronunciation and spelling are followed by audio exercises.

- **Videoteca:** Includes **Los amigos animados** and **Escenas en contexto.** Each section contains corresponding comprehension questions.

- **Lecturas:** New readings have been added, including several **Notas culturales.**

Although the **Actividades escritas** and the **Actividades auditivas** are in separate sections, they coordinate with the chapter themes. We suggest that instructors assign the **Actividades escritas** as they are working through the chapter and that they assign the **Actividades auditivas** toward the end of the chapter, when students have had

ample exposure to comprehensible input in class. Additional advanced grammar concepts, along with verification exercises, are in a section of the *Cuaderno* called **Expansión gramatical.** These additional grammar topics and others are also available on the Online Learning Center.

Supplements

As a full-service publisher of quality educational products, McGraw-Hill does much more than just sell textbooks to students. We create and publish an extensive array of print, video, and digital supplements to support instruction on your campus. Orders of new (versus used) textbooks help us defray the cost of developing such supplements, which is substantial. Please consult your local McGraw-Hill representative to learn about the availability of the following supplements that accompany this edition of *Dos mundos: Comunicación y comunidad.*

For Instructors and for Students

 McGraw-Hill has partnered with Quia™, the leading developer of online tools for foreign language instruction and learning, to create CENTRO, a comprehensive learning management system that allows you to manage your course with robust communication tools, record-keeping that can be imported to Blackboard and other CMS platforms, integration of instructor resources such as Digital Transparencies and PowerPoint™ slides, as well as the ability to customize or add your own content.

- CENTRO includes a fully interactive digital version of the textbook that has a real-time voice chat feature, integrated audio and video, an integrated gradebook, and many other resources that make this a truly innovative online system for the teaching and learning of Spanish.

- CENTRO is also home to the Quia™ online *Cuaderno de actividades.* This digital alternate version of the printed *Cuaderno* is easy for students to use and ideal for instructors who want to manage students' coursework online. Identical in practice to the print version, the online *Cuaderno* contains the full Audio Program as well as segments from the DVD. The online *Cuaderno* also provides students with automatic feedback and scoring of their work.

- Also featured in CENTRO is a new collection of minidocumentaries and interviews from Yabla™, delivered in a player that allows students to view a transcript of the clips as well as to slow down the pace of the speaking, if they so desire. Interactive games are embedded in the player for additional comprehension and practice.

Please contact your local McGraw-Hill sales representative for more information. (**http://dosmundos.mhcentro.com**)

- The *Cuaderno de actividades,* described earlier, offers additional practice with vocabulary, grammar, and skill development.

■ The Audio Program, coordinated with the **Actividades auditivas** from the *Cuaderno de actividades,* is available in audio CD format and also on the Online Learning Center. Additionally, an audio recording of the **Enlace a la literatura** passages and selected **Lecturas** from the textbook are included in special audio CDs as part of the Audio Program. The audio recordings for the **Lecturas** can also be found on the Online Learning Center. An audio icon identifies these readings in the textbook.

■ Each chapter of the DVD consists of two animated dialogues (**Los amigos animados**), and the **Escenas en contexto** (a two- to three-minute functional vignette filmed on location in Costa Rica, Ecuador, Mexico, Peru, and Spain). The Yabla™ videos, mentioned on the previous page, are also available on the DVD. The activities for these two segments are found in the **Videoteca** sections of the *Cuaderno de actividades.*

■ The Online Learning Center (**www.mhhe.com/dosmundos7**) provides students with a wealth of activities specially created for use with *Dos mundos.* The Online Learning Center includes additional vocabulary and grammar practice quizzes, cultural activities (including new cultural PowerPoint™ slides), the Laboratory Audio Program, the Textbook Audio recordings, the Flash Grammar Tutorials, and more.

■ A downloadable musical playlist, designed by the *Dos mundos* authors to coordinate with the text, is available for purchase through iTunes®. See the Online Learning Center for details.

For Instructors Only

■ The annotated *Instructor's Edition* of *Dos mundos* provides notes that offer extensive pre-text activities, teaching hints, and suggestions for using and expanding materials, as well as references to the supplementary activities in the Instructor's Manual and the Instructor's Resource Kit.

■ Instructors have password-protected access to all portions of the Online Learning Center, which includes such resources as the Instructor's Manual and the Instructor's Resource Kit, Digital Transparencies, Cultural PowerPoint™ presentations, the Testing Program, the Audioscript, and more. For password information, please contact your McGraw-Hill sales representative.

■ The Picture File contains fifty color photographs, designed to stimulate conversation in the classroom.

■ The Instructor's Manual provides a general introduction to communicative language teaching and to the types of activities found in the program. It also offers step-by-step instructions for teaching the **Pasos** and **Capítulo 1.** There are suggestions for pre-text activities, TPR (Total Physical Response) sequences, and many additional activities for each chapter.

■ The Instructor's Resource Kit contains supplementary activities and games that correspond to chapter themes.

The Seventh Edition also includes Internet activities (also available on the *Dos mundos* Online Learning Center) and a **Lotería cultural** for each chapter.

■ A set of Digital Transparencies displays drawings, color maps, and other illustrations, mostly from the main text.

■ The Testing Program contains listening comprehension (with Testing Audio CD), reading, vocabulary, and grammar tests. It also includes suggestions for testing oral production and writing skills. The Seventh Edition provides nine sample exams (one for each two-chapter segment), as well as a variety of alternative activities/exercises for all three **Pasos** and fifteen chapters that can be recombined to create different versions of the tests.

■ The Audioscript is a transcript of all recorded materials in the Audio Program.

Other Materials Available

■ The *¡A leer! Easy Reader Series* features two short readers, *Cocina y comidas hispanas,* on regional Hispanic cuisines, and *Mundos de fantasía,* which contains fairy tales and legends.

■ The *Storyteller's Series* offers high-interest fiction designed for advanced beginning or intermediate students. Three books are available: *Viajes fantásticos, Ladrón de la mente,* and *Isla de luz.*

■ The *El mundo hispano* reader features five major regions of the Hispanic world, as well as a section on Hispanics in the United States.

■ CourseSmart is a new way to find and buy eTextbooks. At CourseSmart you can save up to 50 percent off the cost of a print textbook, reduce your impact on the environment, and gain access to powerful web tools for learning. CourseSmart has the largest selection of eTextbooks available anywhere, offering thousands of the most commonly adopted textbooks from a wide variety of higher education publishers. CourseSmart eTextbooks are available in one standard online reader with full text search, notes and highlighting, and email tools for sharing notes between classmates. For further details contact your sales representative or go to **www.coursesmart.com.**

Second-Language Acquisition

Dos mundos is designed to work well with a variety of communicative approaches. The program is primarily based on Tracy D. Terrell's research, James Asher's Total Physical Response (TPR), and elements of Stephen D. Krashen's theoretical model of second-language acquisition.[1] Krashen posits that we have two ways of developing language ability: acquisition and learning. *Language acquisition* is a subconscious or automatic process; that is,

---

[1]Portions of this section (and the next) are quoted by permission of Stephen D. Krashen, *Fundamentals of Language Acquisition*, Laredo Publications, 1992.

we are not focused on form and we are usually not aware that it is happening. Research supports the view that adults can and do acquire language subconsciously, even if not as naturally as children do. *Language learning* is a conscious or controlled process: it occurs when we are focused on form and aware that we are learning. When you talk about grammar rules, you are usually talking about learning.

We normally produce language using our acquired or implicit linguistic competence, whereas we use our learned system—our knowledge of explicit rules—to monitor or edit our output. Current theories of language acquisition posit that we acquire language best when we understand messages or receive *comprehensible input,* either aural or written: reading is an excellent source of comprehensible input.

These theories also suggest that attitudes and feeling can influence language acquisition. If students are overly anxious or do not perceive the target culture in a positive light, they may understand the input but a psychological block (the Affective Filter) will prevent their acquisition of the new language.[2]

Dos mundos: From Theory to Action

Our goal is to make language acquisition theory work in the classroom. Here is how we do it.

1 Aiming for Meaning

The primary goal of the *Dos mundos* classroom is to provide aural and written input that is both interesting and comprehensible. This input helps students take in meaning and integrate it within their developing language system. *Dos mundos* helps students create meaning from the new language through both comprehensible input (listening) and guided output (speaking).

2 I'm Listening!

Comprehension precedes production in both first- and second-language acquisition. Thus, students' ability to use new vocabulary and structures is directly related to the opportunities they have had to interact aurally, orally, and visually in meaningful and relevant contexts with the new language. Students need many opportunities to interact in meaningful contexts before they can express their own meaning successfully.

3 Taking Our Time

Because speech emerges in stages, *Dos mundos* allows for three stages of language development: comprehension, early speech, and speech emergence.

The activities in **Paso A** are designed to give students the opportunity to develop initial comprehension ability while producing only minimal fixed expressions (see **Diálogos** in the section **Los saludos** in **Paso A**). The activities in **Paso B** encourage the transition from comprehension to the ability to respond naturally in single words. By the end of **Paso C** and through **Capítulo 1,** most students are making the first transitional steps from short answers to longer phrases and complete sentences. This is accomplished through guided output activities such as **Diálogos abiertos, Descripción de dibujos, Intercambios,** and **Entrevistas.** Students will continue to pass through these same three stages with the new material of each chapter. It is important to keep in mind that the vocabulary and structures presented in **Capítulo 1** may not be fully acquired until **Capítulo 5** or later.

The pre-text activities, the **Actividades de comunicación,** and the **Actividades auditivas** in the *Cuaderno de actividades* all provide opportunities for understanding Spanish before more developed production is expected. The Instructor's Manual includes additional activities for each chapter to provide further opportunities for comprehensible input and guided production. As students gradually become more fluent listeners and speakers, *Dos mundos* challenges their skills with higher level language and more open-ended output activities: **Entrevistas, Narración, ¡Cuéntenos usted!** This process helps students continue to acquire higher level lexical and grammatical structures.

4 We All Make Mistakes

Errors in form are not corrected in classroom activities that are aimed at communication. We anticipate that students will make many errors as speech emerges. Given sufficient exposure to Spanish, these early errors do not usually affect students' future language development nor do they impede basic interpersonal communication with native speakers. While doing the **Actividades de comunicación** in class, we recommend correcting only factual errors and responding naturally to students' communication, expanding or restating when it feels normal and natural to do so and when the correction or expansion can be woven easily into the conversational thread.

In contrast, students can and should correct their responses to the self-study **Gramática y ejercicios** using the Answer Key in Appendix 4 and to the **Actividades auditivas** and the **Actividades escritas** using the Answer Key at the back of the *Cuaderno de actividades.*

5 Relax and Let it Happen!

Students acquire language best in a low-anxiety environment and when they are truly engaged with the material. Such an atmosphere is created when the instructor: (1) provides

---

[2]For more detailed information, see the section on Second-Language Acquisition Theory in the Instructor's Manual.

students with truly interesting, comprehensible input; (2) does not focus excessively on form; and (3) lets students know that communicating in a new language is possible. Student motivation to acquire Spanish will be higher if he/she has enjoyable and meaningful experiences in the new language. The *Dos mundos* program creates a positive classroom atmosphere by sparking student interest and encouraging involvement in two sorts of activities: those that relate directly to students and their lives and those that relate to the Hispanic world. Hence, the **dos mundos** referred to in the title. Input and interaction in these two areas—along with the expectation from the instructor that students will be able to communicate their ideas—create a classroom environment wherein the instructor and the students feel comfortable listening and talking to one another.

6 It Takes a Community

People acquire both first and second languages as part of a larger language community. Group work in a *Dos mundos* classroom provides valuable oral interaction in Spanish and creates a classroom community that facilitates communication. Students are also encouraged to integrate themselves into the larger Hispanic community through cultural readings, Internet activities, and service opportunities.

7 Speak Your Mind!

Speaking helps language acquisition in several ways. It encourages comprehensible input via conversation, and it provides feedback on communicative accuracy (Was the listener able to understand the speaker?). Speaking also allows students to engage in real language use as the instructor and students share opinions and information about themselves. *Dos mundos* provides students with many opportunities for meaningful production in Spanish.

8 A Place for Grammar

Although *Dos mundos* focuses on acquiring communicative competence through oral, listening, and written activities, there are also practical reasons for grammar study. Formal knowledge of grammar helps students edit their written work; it also gives students confidence about their progress with the new language. Some language students derive great satisfaction when they learn about what they are acquiring and when they are able to utilize grammatical knowledge to make the input they hear and read more comprehensible. In addition, a gentle focus on form may help some students to recognize gaps in their developing language and thereby achieve more accuracy in their output.

9 Language with a Purpose

The goal of a *Dos mundos* Spanish class is proficiency in basic communication skills: listening, reading, speaking, and writing. Proficiency is defined as the ability to understand and convey information and/or feelings in a particular situation for a particular purpose. Grammatical accuracy is one part of communicative proficiency, but it is not the primary goal. The activities in *Dos mundos* support different aspects of language acquisition.

COMPREHENSIBLE INPUT	OUTPUT	EXPLICIT KNOWLEDGE OF RULES
Pre-text activities	**Actividades de**	**Gramática y ejercicios**
Actividades de	**comunicación**	
comunicación		
Ventanas culturales	**¡Dígalo por escrito!**	**Ejercicios de pronunciación**
Ventanas al pasado	**¡Cuéntenos usted!**	**y ortografía**
Enlaces	**Un paso más...**	
Lecturas	**¡a escribir!**	
	Un paso más...	
	¡a conversar!	
	Actividad creativa	
Actividades auditivas	**Actividades escritas**	
Videoteca		

Dos mundos materials fully support the National Standards for Foreign Language Education.[3]

STANDARD	*DOS MUNDOS* MATERIALS
Communication	**Actividades de comunicación, En resumen, ¡Cuéntenos usted!, Actividades auditivas**
Cultures	Opener page fine art, **Sobre el artista, ¡Conozca... !** sections on opening pages, **¡Ojo!** side bars, **Ventanas culturales, Ventanas al pasado, Video (Escenas en contexto)**
Connections	**Ventanas culturales, Ventanas al pasado, Enlaces literarios, Lecturas, Video (Escenas en contexto)**
Comparisons	**Gramática y ejercicios, Pronunciación y ortografía, Ventanas culturales, Ventanas al pasado, Lecturas, Video (Escenas en contexto)**
Communities	**Ventanas culturales, Conexión a la comunidad, Video (Escenas en contexto),** Internet activities from the IRK

Dos mundos Methodology: Specifics

Each of the fifteen regular chapters of *Dos mundos* opens with the **Actividades de comunicación y lecturas,** which stimulate the acquisition of vocabulary and grammar. The following types of communicative activities appear in most chapters.

Student-centered input (pre-text oral activities in Instructor's Edition)

Photo-centered input (Pre-text oral activities in Instructor's Edition)

Definitions (**Definiciones**)

Association activities (**Asociaciones**)

Discussions (**Conversación, Un paso más... ¡a conversar!**)

Realia-based activities (**Del mundo hispano**)

Description of drawings (**Descripción de dibujos**)

Interactions (**Intercambios**)

Narration series (**Narración**)

Dialogues (**Diálogos, Diálogos abiertos**)

Identification activities (**Identificaciones**)

Personal opinion activities (**Preferencias**)

Interviews (**Entrevistas**)

Polls (**Encuestas**)

Culminating activities (**En resumen**)

Storytelling activity (**¡Cuéntenos usted!**)

Creative writing activities (**Un paso más... ¡a escribir!, ¡Dígalo por escrito!, Actividad creativa**)

In addition, the Instructor's Manual contains TPR (Total Physical Response) and additional activities, all of which provide comprehensible input.

The **Vocabulario** list that follows each **Actividades de comunicación y lecturas** section contains most of the new words that have been introduced in the vocabulary displays and activities. Students should recognize these words when they are used in a clear, communicative context. Many will also be actively used by students in later chapters and as the course progresses.

The readings in *Dos mundos* are by no means exhaustive; we recommend that instructors read aloud to students and when students are ready for independent reading, allow them to select material of interest to them. The *¡A leer! Series,* the *El mundo hispano* reader, or the *Storyteller's Series* are appropriate for second-, third-, or fourth-semester accompaniment to *Dos mundos.*

The **Gramática y ejercicios** sections (the blue pages) at the end of each chapter are designed for quick reference and ease of study. The purpose of the grammar exercises is for students to verify that they have understood the explanation: we do not believe that students acquire grammar by doing exercises. Students may self-check their work using the Answer Key found in Appendix 4 of the textbook.

Most new topics in the **Actividades de comunicación y lecturas** sections begin with references (marked **Lea Gramática...**) to the pertinent grammar section(s) of the chapter. The **Actividades de comunicación** are designed to be done in a purely communicative way, with both instructor and students focusing on the message being conveyed. Although all activities can be done without previous grammar study, most students will find it helpful to review the associated grammar points before doing the **Actividades de comunicación.**

[3]See the Instructor's Manual for more detail.

Acknowledgments

A special note of gratitude is due to Stephen D. Krashen for his research on second-language acquisition theory. Dr. Krashen has given us many valuable insights into creating more natural activities and providing comprehensible input for students. We also remain grateful to Dr. Joseph Goebel for his help in writing the section **¡Dígalo por escrito!**

We would like to thank Dr. Karen Christian for her contributions to the first Instructor's Resource Kit (with the Third Edition). And our heartfelt thanks go to Beatrice Tseng (Irvine Valley College) for her creative work on the Fourth, Fifth, Sixth, and Seventh Editions of the Instructor's Resource Kit and for her tireless quest to update the Internet activities.

The authors would like to express their gratitude to the many members of the language-teaching profession whose valuable suggestions through reviews and user diaries contributed to the preparation of the Seventh Edition. The appearance of their names here does not necessarily constitute an endorsement of the text or its communicative methodology.

User Diarists

Tania Garmy, University of Tulsa
Nancy Shearer, Cuesta College

Reviewers

Beatriz Gómez Acuña, Carthage College

Pilar Ara, Pasadena City College

Carolina Ávila, Mexican American Cultural Center

Edward Baranowski, California State University, Sacramento

Geoffrey Ridley Barrow, Purdue University, Calumet-Hammond

Luis Belaustegui, University of Missouri, Kansas City

Linda Burgess-Getts, Thomas Nelson Community College

Fernando Burgos, University of Memphis

Rosa Campos-Brito, Loyola College of Maryland

Lina Castellanos, Carthage College

An Chung Cheng, University of Toledo

Candace J. Chesebro, Chapman University

Edgar Cota-Torres, University of Colorado, Colorado Springs

Patricia Crespo-Martín, Foothill College

Michael F. Dillon, Piedmont College

Concepcio Domenech, Front Range Community College

Andrés Xavier Echarri, University of West Georgia

Paul Eckhardt, Mt. Hood Community College

Ezekiel J. Flannery, Purdue University, Calumet-Hammond

Ruston C. Ford, Indian Hills Community College

Christina Fox-Ballí, Eastfield College

Paola Galeano, Carthage College

Kathleen Gallivan, West Virginia University

Joseph J. Goebel Jr., The College of New Jersey

Ana B. Fernández González, West Virginia University

Bridgette W. Gunnels, University of West Georgia

Polly J. Hodge, Chapman University

Alex Idavoy, Brookdale Community College

Robert Jacques, Georgian Court College

Barbara Kruger, Finger Lakes Community College

Linda Elizabeth Lassiter, Southern University and A&M College

Ornella Lepri Mazzuca, Dutchess Community College

Ellis B. Long, Thomas Nelson Community College

Rebecca López, Mexican American Cultural Center

Teresita López, Camden County College

Elvia Macías de Pérez, Folsom Lake College

Richard McCallister, Delaware State University

Carlos Molina, Mexican American Cultural Center

Gerry Monroy, Brookdale Community College

Thelma Montoya, Mexican American Cultural Center

Regina Morín, The College of New Jersey

Rebekah L. Morris, Wake Forest University

Stacie Munger, Cochise College

Daniel J. Nappo, University of Tennessee, Martin

Eduardo Negueruela, University of Miami

Nancy Nieman, Santa Monica College

Michelle Renee Orecchio, University of Michigan

Arturo Ortiz, Lenoir-Rhyne College

Linda Patton, Central Oregon Community College

Teresa Pérez-Gamboa, University of Georgia

Loknath Persaud, Pasadena City College

Jesús R. Pico-Argel, Wake Forest University

Ana Piffardi, Eastfield College

Kristina Primorac-Waggoner, University of Michigan

Kathryn Quinn-Sánchez, Georgia Court University

Callie Rabe, Finger Lakes Community College

Alister Ramírez, Hunter College, CUNY

Elsy Ramírez-Monroy, Brookdale Community College

Lea Ramsdell, Towson University

Tony Rector-Cavagnaro, Cuesta College

Sofía Hurón Reyes, Mexican American Cultural Center

Pascal Rollet, Carthage College

Marcos Romero, Aquinas College

Leticia Romo, Wake Forest University

Linda Ann Roy, Tarrant County College

Lilia Ruiz Debbe, SUNY-Stony Brook

Eric Sakai, Community College of Vermont, Montpelier

Fernando Salcedo, Riverside Community College District

Annette Sánchez, Nashville State Community College

Elizabeth Buckley Sánchez, University of Tulsa

Robert Sanders, Portland State University

Arthur J. Sandford, Ventura College

Terry D. Sellars, Nashville State Technical Community College

Virginia Serna, Texas State Technical College

Nancy Shearer, Cuesta College

James Smolen, Bucks County Community College

Craig Stokes, Dutchess Community College

Silvia Teodorescu, Hartnell College

Jasmina Terzioska, Purdue University, Calumet-Hammond

Beatrice Tseng, Irvine Valley College

María-Encarna Moreno Turner, Wake Forest University

Titiana Vargas, Carthage College

Ferdinand Vélez, Eastern Washington University

Clara Vélez-Graham, Phoenix College

Gloria Vélez-Rendón, Purdue University, Calumet-Hammond

Celinés Villalba, University of California, Berkeley

Susan Walter, University of Denver

Suzanne Ward, Davidson County Community College

Susan Zárate, Santa Monica College

Many other people participated in the preparation of the Seventh Edition of *Dos mundos*. We feel indebted to Dr. Thalia Dorwick for the guidance and opportunities she has given to us throughout the years. We are grateful to Dr. William Glass, our Editorial Director for this project, who encouraged us to strengthen the cultural and literary content of *Dos mundos* and who continues to advise us on aspects of second-language acquisition. Our sponsoring editor, Katie Crouch, helped us to envision the design of this edition and brought a wealth of fresh ideas to our project. Our Seventh Edition editor, Jenni Kirk, was immensely helpful. We thank her for her patience, care, and support for helping us to realize all of our new ideas and for the great photos she found!

We are grateful to the following McGraw-Hill staff for tireless work and assistance on this edition: Scott Tinetti (Director of Development & Media Technology), Janina Tunac-Basey (Editorial Coordinator), Carey Eisner (Production Editor), Nora Agbayani (Photo Research Coordinator), Gene Fitzer (Photo Researcher), Preston Thomas (Design Manager), Richard DeVitto (Production Supervisor), and Allison Hawco (Senior Media Producer).

We would also like to acknowledge the sales and marketing support we have received from McGraw-Hill over the years, and specifically from Jorge Arbujas (Marketing Manager).

Special thanks go to Sally Richardson, the gifted artist who made our Cast of Characters come to life in previous editions and to Daryl Slaton, the artist on the Seventh Edition who also created our exciting animation segments. In addition we would like to thank Laura Chastain (El Salvador) for her help with questions of language usage and cultural content.

Finally, we thank each other for many years of moving *Dos mundos* from idea to print. We hope our contributions continue to be worthwhile in the 21st century.

To the Student

The course you are about to begin is designed to help you develop your ability to understand and speak everyday Spanish, and to help you learn to read and write in Spanish.

Researchers distinguish two ways of developing ability in another language: (1) through a subconscious process called language acquisition—like "picking up" Spanish while living in Mexico or Spain; and (2) through a conscious process called language learning, which has to do with memorizing and applying grammar rules. *Language acquisition* gives us our fluency, much of our accuracy in speaking, and our ability to understand language when we hear it. You know you've acquired a word when it "feels" and sounds right in a given context. *Language learning* is not as useful in oral communication, but it helps us edit our speech and writing. You know you've *learned* a rule when, for example, you can recall it in order to produce the right form of a verb.

The **Actividades de comunicación y lecturas** of *Dos mundos* will help you acquire Spanish through listening to your instructor and interacting with your classmates; the **Actividades auditivas** of the *Cuaderno de actividades* also provide opportunities to practice your listening comprehension skills. The **Gramática y ejercicios** section of the text and many sections of the *Cuaderno* will offer opportunities for learning Spanish and for applying the rules you have learned. Our goal in *Dos mundos* is to make it possible for you to *acquire* the language, not just *learn* it. Keep in mind that language acquisition takes place when we understand messages; that is, when we comprehend what we read or what we hear. The most effective ways for you to improve your Spanish are to listen to it, read it, and interact with native speakers of the language as much as possible!*

Classes that use *Dos mundos* provide you with a great deal of language you can understand. Your instructor will speak Spanish to you and will use gestures, photos, real objects, and sound effects to make himself or herself understood. You only need to focus on what your instructor is saying; that is, on *the message*. You do not have to think *consciously* about grammar or try to remember all the vocabulary that is being used.

---

*For a more in-depth understanding of the terms *acquisition* and *learning* you may wish to read the To the Instructor section of this text.

You will also have plenty of opportunities for reading. The more you read, the better your Spanish will become. When you are reading, pay attention to the message. You don't have to know every word or figure out every grammatical structure in order to understand what you read!

You will be speaking a lot of Spanish in the classroom, both with your instructor and with your classmates. And when you speak, you will make mistakes. Don't be overly concerned about these mistakes; they are a natural part of the language acquisition process. The best way to eliminate your errors is not to worry or think hard about grammar when you talk but to continue to get more language input through listening, conversation, and reading. In time, your speech will become more accurate.

Getting Started with the *Pasos*

Understanding a new language is not difficult once you realize that you can comprehend what someone is saying without knowing every word. The key to communication is *understanding the ideas* and *the message* the speaker wants to convey.

Several techniques can help you develop good listening comprehension skills. First and most important, *you must guess at meaning!* In order to improve your ability to guess accurately, pay close attention to the context. If someone greets you at 3:00 P.M. by saying **Buenas tardes,** chances are they have said *Good afternoon,* not *Good morning* or *Good evening.* You can make a logical guess about the message being conveyed by focusing on the greeting context and time of day.

In class, ask yourself what you think your instructor has said even if you haven't understood most—or any—of the words. What is the most likely thing to have been said in a particular situation? Be logical in your guesses and try to follow along by paying close attention to the flow of the conversation. *Context, gestures, and body language will all help you guess more accurately.*

Another strategy for good guessing is to *listen for key words.* These are the words that carry the basic meaning of the sentence. In the class activities, for example, if your instructor points to a picture and says in Spanish, **¿Tiene el pelo castaño este hombre?** (*Does this man have brown hair?*), you will know from the context and intonation that a question is being asked. By focusing on the key words **pelo** (*hair*), **castaño** (*brown*), and **hombre** (*man*), you will be able to answer the question correctly.

Remember: *You do not need to know grammar rules* to understand much of what your instructor says to you. For example, you wouldn't need to know the words **Tiene, el,** or **este** in order to get the gist of the previous question. Nor would you have needed to study verb conjugations. However, if you do not know the meaning of the key vocabulary words, **pelo, castaño,** and **hombre,** you will not be able to make good guesses about what is said.

Vocabulary

Because comprehension depends on your ability to *recognize the meaning of key words* used in the conversations you hear, the preliminary chapters of *Dos mundos*—the **Pasos**—will help you become familiar with many new words in Spanish, probably several hundred of them. *You should not be concerned about pronouncing these words perfectly;* saying them easily will come with more exposure to spoken Spanish.

Review key vocabulary frequently: Look at the Spanish and try to *visualize the person* (for words such as *man* or *child*), *the thing* (for words such as *chair* or *pencil*), *a person or thing with particular characteristics* (for words such as *young* or *long*), or *an activity or situation* (for phrases such as *stand up* or *is wearing*). You do not need to memorize these words; concentrate on recognizing their meaning when you see them and when your instructor uses them.

Classroom Activities

In the preliminary chapter, **Paso** (*Step*) **A,** you will be doing three types of class activities: (1) TPR; (2) descriptions of classmates; and (3) descriptions of pictures.

TPR (Total Physical Response): TPR is a technique developed by James Asher, Professor Emeritus, at San Jose State University in Northern California. In TPR activities your instructor gives a command that you act out. This type of activity may seem somewhat childish at first, but if you relax and let your body and mind work together to absorb Spanish, you will be surprised at how quickly and how much you can understand. You do not have to understand every word your instructor says, only enough to perform the action called for. If you don't understand a command, sneak a look at your fellow classmates to see what they are doing.

Descriptions of students: On various occasions, your instructor will describe students in your class. You should try to remember the name of each of your classmates and identify who is being described.

Descriptions of pictures: Your instructor will bring pictures to class and describe the people in them. Your goal is to identify the picture being described.

In addition, *you will learn to say a few common phrases of greeting and leave-taking* in Spanish. You will practice these in short dialogues with your classmates. Don't try to memorize the dialogues; just have fun with them. Your pronunciation will not be perfect, but if you are able to communicate with native speakers, then your accent is good enough. Your accent will continue to improve as you listen and interact in Spanish.

Lecturas

Reading is a valuable activity that will help you acquire Spanish and learn about the Spanish-speaking world. When you read in Spanish, *focus on the meaning;* that is, "get into" the context of the story or reading selection. You do not need to know every word to understand a text. There may be a word or two that you will have to look up occasionally, to aid comprehension. But if you find yourself looking up many words and translating into English, *you are not reading.* As your ability to comprehend spoken Spanish improves, so will your reading ability, and as reading becomes easier you will, in turn, comprehend more spoken Spanish.

You may want to keep the following techniques in mind as you approach all of the reading materials in *Dos mundos:*

1. Look at the title, pictures, and any other clues outside the main text for an introduction to what the reading is about.
2. Scan the text for cognates and other familiar words.
3. Skim over the text to get the gist of it without looking up words.
4. Use context to make intelligent guesses about unfamiliar words.
5. Read in Spanish, picturing the story or information instead of trying to translate it in your mind as you go.

Gramática y ejercicios

The final section of each chapter is a grammar study and reference manual. The grammar exercises are meant to be completed at your own pace, at home, in order to allow you time to check the forms of which you are unsure. Your reference tools are the grammar explanations, the Verb Charts, appendices, and the Answer Key to grammar exercises in Appendix 4. We advise you to use your knowledge of grammar when it does not interfere with communication; for example, when you edit your writing. If you do so, your writing will have a more polished feel.

Also, some students find that studying grammar helps them understand classroom activities better.

The beginning of most **Actividades de comunicación y lecturas** sections has a reference note (**Lea** [*Read*] **Gramática...**) that tells you which subsection of grammar in that chapter to read. Keep in mind that grammar explanations teach you *about* Spanish; they do not *teach* you Spanish. Only real comprehension and communicative experiences will do that. Grammar references are there to help you look up any information you may need or to help you clear any doubts you may have.

Remember that your instructor and the text materials can open the door to communicating in Spanish, but you must enter by yourself!

Tips for Success

Here are some suggestions for a successful experience acquiring Spanish.

Getting Started

■ Familiarize yourself with the *Dos mundos* text and the *Cuaderno de actividades*.
■ Do not expect to be able to communicate as clearly in Spanish as you do in your native language.
■ Remember that each individual will acquire Spanish at a different rate.
■ Be patient; it is not possible to fully acquire a new language in one or two semesters of study.
■ Celebrate your accomplishments; it is possible to communicate with native speakers even though your Spanish is not yet fluent.

Listening

■ Focus on understanding the general meaning.
■ Listen for key words.
■ Use contextual clues and body language to understand native speakers.
■ Listen to the **Actividades auditivas** four or five times each before checking the Answer Key.
■ Listen to the feedback you get from your instructor and native speakers.

Reading

■ Concentrate on the topic and the main ideas.
■ Use context to make logical guesses at meaning.
■ Read in Spanish as much as possible.

Speaking

■ Go over the **Actividades de comunicación** before going to class.
■ Don't rush through activities; use them to develop natural conversations in Spanish with your classmates.
■ Use gestures and act out ideas and messages.
■ Ask: **¿Cómo se dice _____ en español?**
■ Speak Spanish to your instructor and classmates whenever possible.
■ Don't be afraid to make mistakes; beginners are not expected to speak perfectly.
■ Don't be overly concerned about your pronunciation.
■ Use the Audio Program that accompanies the *Cuaderno* to listen for correct pronunciation of vocabulary and do the pronunciation exercises included in each chapter.

Writing

■ Keep your sentences simple and direct.
■ Refer back to the grammar points you have studied to edit and refine your writing.
■ Use the reference tools in the appendices: Verb Charts; Grammar Summary Tables; Syllabication, Stress, and Spelling.

Spanish Outside the Classroom

■ Watch Spanish-language movies, video, and television.
■ Listen to Spanish-language radio.
■ Read newspapers in Spanish (available on the Internet).
■ Talk with native speakers.
■ Use the *Dos mundos* website at **www.mhhe.com/dosmundos7** to review grammar and vocabulary, take practice quizzes, listen to audio components, and explore links to other Internet sites in Spanish.

The Cast of Characters and *Los amigos animados*

Many of the activities and exercises in *Dos mundos* are based on the lives of a Cast of Characters from different parts of the Spanish-speaking world. Additionally, these characters are brought to life through Flash™ animation technology in the **Los amigos animados** segments. The animations are found on the Video, within CENTRO, and on the Online Learning Center.

Los amigos estadounidenses (U.S. friends) are a group of students at the University of Texas at San Antonio. Although they are all majoring in different subjects, they know each other through Professor Adela Martínez's 8:00 A.M. Spanish class.

la profesora Martínez
Luis   Alberto
Mónica Carmen Esteban Nora Lan Pablo

Los amigos hispanos (Hispanic friends) live in various parts of the Spanish-speaking world. In **México** you will meet Silvia Bustamante and her boyfriend, Ignacio (Nacho) Padilla.

Silvia y Nacho

You will also get to know Raúl Saucedo and his family. Raúl lives with his parents in Mexico City but is currently studying at the University of Texas at San Antonio; he knows many of the students in Professor Martínez's class. You will meet Raúl's grandmother doña María Eulalia González de Saucedo, as well as other members of his extended family: his three older siblings, Ernesto, Andrea and Paula (who are twins), and their families.

doña María Eulalia y Raúl

Raúl's older brother Ernesto is married to Estela Ramírez. They have three children, Amanda, Guillermo, and Ernestito. Andrea is married to Pedro Ruiz, and they have two young daughters, Marisa and Clarisa. Paula is a single travel agent who lives and works in Mexico City.

la familia Saucedo
Ernesto
Estela
Ernestito   Amanda y Guillermo

la familia Ruiz
Pedro →
Clarisa   Paula
Marisa
Andrea

The Saucedo children have school friends. Amanda's best friend is Graciela Herrero, whose brother is Diego Herrero. Amanda has a boyfriend, Ramón Gómez, and Graciela's boyfriend is Rafael Quesada.

Graciela   Diego   Ramón   Rafael

There are also friends and neighbors of the Saucedo and Ruiz families: don Eduardo Alvar and don Anselmo Olivera; doña Lola Batini; and doña Rosita Silva and her husband, don Ramiro.

don Eduardo   don Anselmo   doña Lola   doña Rosita   don Ramiro

Carla   Rogelio   Marta

In **Puerto Rico** you will meet Carla Espinosa and her friend Rogelio Varela, students at the University of Puerto Rico in Río Piedras. You will also meet Marta Guerrero, a young Mexican woman living in Puerto Rico.

In **España** (Spain) you will accompany an American student, Clara Martin, on her travels. Her friends in Spain are Pilar Álvarez and Pilar's boyfriend, José Estrada.

Pilar   Clara   José

You will get to know Ricardo Sícora in Caracas, **Venezuela.** He is 19 years old and has recently graduated from high school.

Ricardo

In **Argentina** you will meet Adriana Bolini, a young woman who works for a computer company, and her friend, Víctor Ginarte.

On the radio you will listen to Mayín Durán, who is from **Panamá.** Mayín works as an interviewer and reporter for KSUN, Radio Sol de California, in Los Angeles.

Adriana y Víctor

You will meet the Yamasaki family in **Perú:** Susana Yamasaki González and her two sons, Armando and Andrés.

In **Miami** you will meet Professor Rubén Hernández Arenas and his wife, Doctora Virginia Béjar de Hernández.

Mayín

Susana

Armando y Andrés

Rubén y Virginia

La clase y los estudiantes

Sobre los artistas: The Cunas live on the San Blas Islands, on the north coast of Panama. The women make the **mola** fabrics for their own dresses by cutting and sewing various layers of cloth together.

Una mola, artesanía de los indígenas cuna de Panamá

METAS

In **Paso A** you will learn to understand a good deal of spoken Spanish and get to know your classmates. The listening skills you develop during these first days of class will enhance your ability to understand Spanish and will also make learning to speak Spanish easier.

ACTIVIDADES DE COMUNICACIÓN

- Los nombres de los compañeros de clase
- ¿Quién es?
- Los colores y la ropa
- Los números (0–39)
- Los mandatos en la clase
- Los saludos

GRAMÁTICA Y EJERCICIOS

A.1 Naming and Describing: The Verbs **llamarse** and **llevar**

A.2 Spelling: The Spanish Alphabet

A.3 Identifying People and Things: Subject Pronouns and the Verb **ser**

A.4 Identifying People and Things: Gender

A.5 Responding to Instructions: Commands

¡Conozca Panamá!

Nombre del país: Panamá

Ciudad capital: Panamá

Ciudades principales: Colón, El Porvenir, Bocas del Toro

Moneda: el balboa, dólar EU.

Idiomas: español (oficial), inglés, lenguas indígenas

Población: 3.250.000

Día de la Independencia: el 28 de noviembre

Fiestas típicas: el Carnaval (febrero o marzo)

Comidas típicas: el arroz con pollo, el arroz con leche, las empanadas

Música típica: el tamborito, el congo, la salsa, el merengue, el reggae, el vallenato

Gente famosa: Rubén Blades, Omar Torrijos

Código de país por Internet: .pa

Voces panameñas

un chuncho	car
fulo/a	**rubio/a**
ofí	**sí**
un(a) pelado/a	**un(a) niño/a**

MULTIMEDIA

 ONLINE LEARNING CENTER www.mhhe.com/dosmundos7

 C E N T R O Your media center for languages   QUIA ● DVD

Actividades de comunicación

Los nombres de los compañeros de clase

✳ **Lea Gramática A.1–A.2.**

Actividad 1   Diálogos: Los amigos

—¿Cómo se llama el amigo
  de _____?
—Se llama _____.
—Y, ¿cuál es el apellido
  de _____?
—Es _____.

—¿Cómo se llama la amiga
  de _____?
—Se llama _____.
—Y, ¿cuál es el apellido
  de _____?
—Es _____.

¿Quién es?

✱ **Lea Gramática A.3.**

Actividad 2 Identificaciones: ¿Cómo se escribe?

1. ¿Se escribe Quesada con ese o con zeta?
2. ¿Se escribe Galván con be grande o con ve chica?
3. ¿Se escribe Muñoz con ene o con eñe?
4. ¿Se escribe Herrero con hache o sin hache?
5. ¿Se escribe Reyes con i griega o con doble ele (elle)?
6. ¿Se escribe Rojas con ge o con jota?

Actividad 3 Asociaciones: Las descripciones de las personas famosas

¿Quién es _____?

1. rubio/a ~ moreno/a
2. alto/a ~ bajo/a
3. guapo/bonita ~ feo/a
4. joven ~ viejo/a
5. delgado/a (flaco/a) ~ gordo/a
6. rico ~ pobre

Salma Hayek	Antonio Banderas	Zac Efron	Justin Timberlake
Penélope Cruz	Matt Damon	Barbra Streisand	Danny DeVito
Dakota Fanning	Oprah Winfrey	Angelina Jolie	Tiger Woods

Los colores y la ropa

✳ **Lea Gramática A.3–A.4.**

Actividad 4 Asociaciones: Los colores

¿De qué color es _____? Es _____.

a. el automóvil   b. la casa   c. el lápiz

d. la planta   e. el gato   f. la rosa   g. el libro de español

h. el perro   i. el arco iris   j. la naranja   k. la puerta

1. rojo/a   **4.** color café   **6.** azul   **8.** anaranjado/a
2. amarillo/a   **5.** blanco/a   **7.** morado/a   **9.** ¿ ?
3. verde

Actividad 5 Identificaciones: Mis compañeros de clase

Mire a cuatro compañeros de clase. Diga el nombre de cada estudiante, la ropa y el color de la ropa que lleva.

NOMBRE		ROPA	COLOR
1. Carmen	lleva	una blusa	amarilla.
2. _____	lleva	_____	_____
3. _____	lleva	_____	_____
4. _____	lleva	_____	_____
5. _____	lleva	_____	_____

Los números (0–39)

0 cero	10 diez	20 veinte
1 uno	11 once	21 veintiuno
2 dos	12 doce	22 veintidós
3 tres	13 trece	23 veintitrés
4 cuatro	14 catorce	24 veinticuatro…
5 cinco	15 quince	30 treinta
6 seis	16 dieciséis	31 treinta y uno
7 siete	17 diecisiete	32 treinta y dos
8 ocho	18 dieciocho	33 treinta y tres…
9 nueve	19 diecinueve	39 treinta y nueve

Actividad 6 Identificaciones: ¿Cuántos hay?

Cuente los estudiantes en la clase que...

LLEVAN

_____ pantalones vaqueros
_____ lentes
_____ minifalda
_____ blusa
_____ chaqueta
_____ botas
_____ aretes

TIENEN

_____ barba
_____ bigote
_____ el pelo largo/corto
_____ el pelo castaño/rubio
_____ los ojos azules/castaños
_____ tatuajes
_____ iPod

Los mandatos en la clase

✳ **Lea Gramática A.5.**

Ian   Pablo   Nora   Esteban   Alberto   Carmen   Luis   Mónica

Actividad 7   Identificaciones: Los mandatos

a. Dé una vuelta.   **f.** Salte.
b. Abra el libro.   **g.** Corra.
c. Cierre el libro.   **h.** Mire hacia arriba.
d. Camine.   **i.** Muéstreme el reloj.
e. Saque un bolígrafo.

Los saludos

Actividad 8   Diálogos: Los saludos

1. Nacho Padilla saluda a Ernesto Saucedo.
   NACHO: Buenos días. ¿Cómo está usted?
   SR. SAUCEDO: Muy bien, gracias. ¿Y usted?
   NACHO: Muy bien.
2. La señora Silva habla por teléfono con el señor Alvar.
   SRA. SILVA: Señor Alvar, ¿cómo está usted?
   SR. ALVAR: Estoy un poco cansado. ¿Y usted?
   SRA. SILVA: Regular.
3. Amanda habla con doña Lola Batini.
   DOÑA LOLA: Buenas tardes, Amanda.
   AMANDA: Buenas tardes, doña Lola. ¿Cómo está la familia?
   DOÑA LOLA: Bien, gracias.
4. Rogelio Varela presenta a Carla.
   ROGELIO: Marta, ésta es mi amiga Carla.
   CARLA: Mucho gusto.
   MARTA: Igualmente.
5. Un nuevo amigo / Una nueva amiga en la clase de español.
   USTED: _____, éste/ésta es mi amigo/a _____.
   AMIGO/A 1: _____.
   AMIGO/A 2: _____.

Estudiantes en la Universidad Nacional de San Marcos en Lima, Perú

Vocabulario

Las preguntas y las respuestas

Questions and Answers

¿Cómo está usted?	How are you?
(Muy) Bien, gracias.	(Very) Well, thanks.
Estoy bien (regular).	I am fine/OK.
Estoy un poco cansado/a.	I am a little tired.
¿Cómo se escribe su apellido?	How do you spell (write) your last name?
Se escribe eme-o-o-ere-e.	It is spelled m-o-o-r-e.
¿Cómo se llama(n)?	What is his/her (their) name?
Se llama(n)...	His/Her (Their) name is . . .
¿Cómo se llama usted?	What is your name?
Me llamo...	My name is . . .
¿Cuál es su nombre?	What is your name?
Mi nombre es...	My name is . . .
¿Cuántos/as... (hay)?	How many . . . (are there)?
¿De qué color es... ?	What color is (it) . . . ?
¿Quién (es)? / ¿Quiénes (son)?	Who (is it) / Who (are they)?

La descripción

Description

Es...	He/She/It is . . .
alto/a	tall; high
bajo/a	short
bonito/a	pretty
de estatura mediana	of medium height
delgado/a	thin
famoso/a	famous
feo/a	ugly
gordo/a	fat
guapo/a	handsome
joven	young
moreno/a	brown(dark)-skinned
nuevo/a	new
pobre	poor
rico/a	rich
rubio/a	blonde
viejo/a	old
Tiene...	He/She has . . .
barba	(a) beard
bigote	(a) moustache
Tiene el pelo (cabello)...	His/Her hair is . . . (He/She has . . . hair.)
castaño	brown
corto	short
lacio	straight
largo	long
mediano	medium (length)
negro	black
rizado	curly
rubio	blond
Tiene los ojos...	His/Her eyes are . . . (He/She has . . . eyes.)
azules	blue
castaños	brown
negros	black (dark brown)
verdes	green

Los colores

Colors

amarillo/a	yellow
anaranjado/a	orange
azul	blue
blanco/a	white
color café	brown
gris	gray
morado/a	purple
negro/a	black
rojo/a	red
rosado/a	pink
verde	green

La ropa

Clothes

¿Quién lleva... ?	Who is wearing . . . ?
un abrigo	a coat
una blusa	a blouse
botas	boots
una camisa	a shirt
una camiseta	a T-shirt
una chaqueta	a jacket
una corbata	a tie
una (mini)falda	a (mini) skirt
los pantalones	pants
los pantalones cortos	shorts
los (pantalones) vaqueros	jeans
un saco	a sports coat
un sombrero	a hat
un suéter	a sweater
un traje	a suit
un vestido	a dress
los zapatos (de tenis)	(tennis) shoes

Las personas

People

el amigo / la amiga	friend
el compañero / la compañera de clase	classmate
don	*title of respect used with a man's first name*
doña	*title of respect used with a woman's first name*
el / la estudiante	student
la familia	family
el hombre	man
el muchacho / la muchacha	boy, young man / girl, young woman

la mujer	woman
el niño / la niña	boy / girl
el profesor / la profesora	professor
el/la recepcionista	receptionist
el señor / la señora	man; Mr. / woman; Mrs.
la señorita	young lady; Miss
yo, usted, él/ella	I, you (*pol.*), he/she
nosotros/as, ustedes, ellos/ellas	we, you (*pl.*), they

Los verbos
Verbs

es	is
habla (por teléfono)	speaks (on the telephone)
hay	there is / there are
lleva(n)	is (are) wearing
llevo	I am wearing
presenta	introduces
saluda	greets
somos	we are
son	are
soy	I am
tiene	he/she has / you have
tienen	they have

Las cosas
Things

el arco iris	rainbow
la casa	house
el gato	cat
el lápiz	pencil
los lentes	glasses
el libro (de español)	(Spanish) book
la naranja	orange
el perro	dog
la puerta	door
el reloj	clock; watch
el tatuaje	tattoo

PALABRAS SEMEJANTES (*Cognates*)**:** el automóvil, la foto(grafía), la planta, la rosa

Los saludos y las despedidas
Greetings and Good-byes

Buenos días.	Good morning.
Buenas tardes.	Good afternoon.
Buenas noches.	Good evening. / Good night.
Hasta luego.	See you later.
Hola.	Hi.
Adiós.	Good-bye.

Las presentaciones
Introductions

Ésta es mi amiga... / Éste es mi amigo...	This is my friend . . .

Mucho gusto.	Pleased to meet you.
Igualmente.	Same here.

Los mandatos
Commands

abra(n) (el libro)	open (the book)
baile(n)	dance
camine(n)	walk
cante(n)	sing
cierre(n)	close
corra(n)	run
cuente(n)	count
dé/den una vuelta	turn around
diga(n)	say
escriba(n)	write
escuche(n)	listen
estudie(n)	study
hable(n)	talk
lea(n)	read
levánte(n)se	stand (get) up
mire(n) (hacia arriba/abajo)	look (up/down)
muéstre(n)me	show me
pónga(n)se de pie	stand up
salte(n)	jump
saque(n) (un bolígrafo)	take out (a pen)
siénte(n)se	sit down

Palabras del texto
Words from the Text

¿Comprende(n)?	Do you (all) understand?
el español	Spanish
la gramática	grammar
no	no, not
¡Ojo!	Attention!
la página	page
el paso	step
por favor	please
¿Qué?	What?
¿Quién(es)?	Who?
sí	yes

PALABRAS SEMEJANTES: la actividad, las asociaciones, la comunicación, la descripción, el diálogo, la identificación

Los números
Numbers

cero	0
uno	1
dos	2
tres	3
cuatro	4
cinco	5
seis	6
siete	7
ocho	8
nueve	9

diez	10
once	11
doce	12
trece	13
catorce	14
quince	15
dieciséis	16
diecisiete	17
dieciocho	18
diecinueve	19
veinte	20
veintiuno	21
veintidós	22
veintitrés	23
veinticuatro	24
veinticinco	25
veintiséis	26
veintisiete	27
veintiocho	28
veintinueve	29
treinta	30
treinta y uno	31

treinta y dos	32
treinta y nueve	39

Palabras útiles

Useful Words

ahora	now
cada	each, every
con	with
de	of, from
el, la, los, las	the
en	in, on
este/esta	this
grande	big
mi(s)	my
pequeño/a	small
sin	without
su(s)	your
un (una)	a
¿Verdad?	(Is that) true? Really?
y	and

Gramática y ejercicios

Introduction

The **Gramática y ejercicios** sections of this book are written for your use outside of class. They contain grammar explanations and exercises that are presented in non-technical language, so it should not be necessary to go over all of them in class.

The **Lea Gramática...** notes that begin most new topics in the **Actividades de comunicación y lecturas** sections give the grammar point(s) you should read at that time. Study them carefully, then do the exercises in writing and check your answers in the back of the book. If you have little or no trouble with the exercises, you have probably understood the explanation. Remember: It is not necessary to memorize these grammar rules.

Keep in mind that successful completion of a grammar exercise means only that you have understood the explanation. It does not mean that you have *acquired* the rule. True acquisition comes not from study of grammar but from hearing and reading a great deal of meaningful Spanish. Learning the rules of grammar through study will allow you to use those rules when you have time to stop and think about correctness, as during careful writing.

If you have trouble with an exercise or do not understand the explanation, ask your instructor for assistance. In difficult cases, your instructor will go over the material in class to be sure everyone has understood but probably won't spend too much time on the explanations, in order to save class time for real communication experiences.

The grammar explanations in **Paso A** contain basic information about Spanish grammar.

Some Useful Grammatical Terms

You may recall from your study of grammar in your native language that sentences can be broken down into parts. All sentences have at least a subject (a noun or pronoun) and a verb.

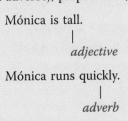

Mónica   runs.
  | |
noun, subject   *verb*

In addition, sentences may have objects (nouns and pronouns), modifiers (adjectives and adverbs), prepositions, conjunctions, and/or articles.

Mónica is tall.
        |
    adjective

Mónica runs quickly.
         |
      adverb

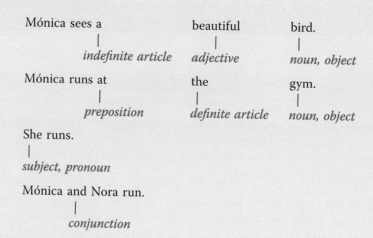

Mónica and Nora run.
|
conjunction

A.1 Naming and Describing: The Verbs *llamarse* and *llevar*

A. The most common way to ask someone's name is to use the verb **llamarse**.

—¿Cómo **se llama** usted?* —*What is your name?*
—Nora.   —*Nora.*

You may answer the question either briefly, by saying your name (as in the preceding example), or in a complete sentence with the pronoun **me** (*myself*) and the verb **llamo** (*I call*).

—**Me llamo** Nora.   —*My name is Nora.*

To ask what someone else's name is, use the following question-and-answer pattern.

—**¿Cómo se llama** el amigo —*What's Nora's friend's name?*
de Nora?
—**Se llama** Luis.   —*His name is Luis.*

Here is another way to ask someone's name.

—**¿Cuál es su nombre?**   —*What is your name?*
—**Mi nombre es** Esteban. —*My name is Esteban.*

> To ask someone's name:
> **¿Cuál es su nombre?**
> or
> **¿Cómo se llama usted?**
> To tell someone your name:
> **Mi nombre es...**
> or
> **Me llamo...**

B. The Spanish verb **llevar** corresponds to the English verb *to wear.*

Mónica **lleva** un suéter azul. *Mónica is wearing a blue sweater.*

Notice that Spanish verbs change their endings according to the subject of the sentence.

> Spanish verbs change endings. These endings tell you who is performing the action.

Yo **llevo** pantalones grises. Mis *I'm wearing gray pants. My*
amigos **llevan** pantalones   *friends are wearing black*
negros.   *pants.*

---

*Literally this means *How do you call yourself?* You will learn about **tú**, another way of addressing people, in **Gramática B.1.**

Here are some of the common endings for Spanish verbs.*

llevar = to wear

	llevar (to wear)	
(yo)	llev**o**	*I wear*
(usted, él/ella)	llev**a**	*you (sing.) wear; he/she wears*
(nosotros/as)	llev**amos**	*we wear*
(ustedes, ellos/as)	llev**an**	*you (pl.) wear; they wear*

The subject pronouns (**yo, usted, nosotros, ellas,** etc.) are in parentheses because it is not always necessary to use them in Spanish. The verb itself or the context usually tells you who the subject is.

—¿Qué ropa llev**a** (usted) hoy? —*What are you wearing today?*
—Llev**o** una falda verde y una —*I am wearing a green skirt*
   blusa blanca.   *and a white blouse.*
—¿Y ellos?   —*And what about them?*
—Llev**an** traje y corbata.   —*They are wearing a suit and tie.*

These endings are used on most Spanish verbs, and you will soon become accustomed to hearing and using them.

In **Paso C** you will see the forms of the verb **tener** (*to have*), which you have also heard in class.

tengo = I have
tiene = he/she has

La profesora Martínez **tiene** el *Professor Martínez has black*
   pelo negro.   *hair.*
Yo **tengo** los ojos azules.   *I have blue eyes.*

Ejercicio 1

Complete los diálogos con estos verbos: **me llamo, se llama, llevo, lleva, llevan.**

—¿Cómo _____¹ usted?
—_____² Esteban Brown.
—Esteban, ¿cómo _____³ la amiga de Mónica?
—_____⁴ Carmen.
—Y, ¿cómo se llama la profesora?
—¿La profesora de español? _____⁵ Adela Martínez.

—¿Qué ropa _____⁶ la profesora Martínez hoy?
—_____⁷ un vestido rojo muy bonito.
—Y Luis y Alberto, ¿qué ropa _____⁸ ellos?
—_____⁹ camiseta y pantalones vaqueros.
—Y yo _____¹⁰ pantalones vaqueros y un suéter.

---

*You will learn more about verb endings in **Gramática C.5, 1.2,** and **3.2.**

A.2 Spelling: The Spanish Alphabet

LETTER	NAME	EXAMPLE	LETTER	NAME	EXAMPLE
a	a	Ana	ñ	eñe	Íñigo
b	be, be grande	Bárbara	o	o	Olga
c	ce	Celia	p	pe	Pedro
d	de	David	q	cu	Quintín
e	e	Ernesto	r	ere	Mario
f	efe	Franco	s	ese	Sara
g	ge	Gerardo	t	te	Tomás
h	hache	Hortensia	u	u	Úrsula
i	i	Isabel	v	uve, ve chica	Vicente
j	jota	Juan	w	doble ve, uve doble	Walter
k	ca	Kati	x	equis	Ximena
l	ele	Laura	y	i griega	Yolanda
m	eme	Miguel	z	zeta	Zulema
n	ene	Nora			

Learn how to spell your first and last names in Spanish; that is what you will be expected to spell most frequently.

A. Letters are feminine: **la «ele», la «i», la «equis».** The letter combination **ll** (often referred to as **elle** or **doble ele**) is pronounced like a *y*. The letter combinations **ch**, **ll**, and **rr** cannot be divided when splitting a word into syllables. Until recently, the letter combinations **ch** and **ll** were considered single units, had separate names (**che** and **elle** or **doble ele**), and affected alphabetization (for example, **chico** after **cumpleaños, llamar** after **luna**). You will still see this pattern of alphabetization in many dictionaries and textbooks. The grouping **rr** is not considered a separate letter by the **Real Academia.**

B. **B** and **v** are pronounced identically, so speakers use different devices to differentiate them; the most common is to call one **la be grande** and the other **la ve chica** (or **la be larga** and **la ve corta**). Many people say **la be de burro, la ve de vaca** (**b** as in **burro**, **v** as in **vaca**). The letters **k** and **w** are used mostly in words of foreign origin: **kilo, whisky.**

C. Spanish speakers do not normally spell out entire words but rather tend to refer only to the letters that might cause confusion. For example, if the name is **Rodríguez**, one might ask: **¿Se escribe con *zeta* o con *ese*?** (*Is it written with a z or with an s?*) Common spelling questions asked by most Latin Americans are the following.

s, z ¿Con **ese** o con **zeta**? y, ll ¿Con **i griega** o con **doble ele**?
c, s ¿Con **ce** o con **ese**? g, j ¿Con **ge** o con **jota**?
c, z ¿Con **ce** o con **zeta**? v, b ¿Con **ve chica** o con **be grande**?

Because the letter **h** is never pronounced in Spanish, a common question is: **¿Con o sin *hache*?** (*With or without an* **h***?*)

Only with foreign words (or perhaps very unfamiliar Spanish words) do Spanish speakers spell out the entire word.

—¿Cómo se escribe *Dorwick,* por favor?
—Se escribe: **de-o-ere-doble ve-i-ce-ca.**
—Gracias.

Ejercicio 2

Escoja la respuesta correcta.

MODELO: ¿Cómo se escribe _____apato?
(a.) con zeta
b. con ese

1. ¿Cómo se escribe tre_____e?
a. con ce
b. con zeta
2. ¿Cómo se escribe mu_____er?
a. con ge
b. con jota
3. ¿Cómo se escribe nue_____o?
a. con ve chica
b. con be grande
4. ¿Cómo se escribe a_____ul?
a. con zeta
b. con ese
5. ¿Cómo se escribe pá_____ina?
a. con ge
b. con jota

6. ¿Cómo se escribe _____abla?
a. con hache
b. sin hache
7. ¿Cómo se escribe amari_____o?
a. con doble ele
b. con i griega
8. ¿Cómo se escribe _____ombre?
a. con hache
b. sin hache
9. ¿Cómo se escribe cie_____e?
a. con ere
b. con erre
10. ¿Cómo se escribe lle_____an?
a. con ve chica
b. con be grande

A.3 Identifying People and Things: Subject Pronouns and the Verb *ser*

A. Spanish uses the verb **ser** (*to be*) to identify things or people.

—¿Qué **es** eso?   —*What is that?*
—**Es** un bolígrafo.   —*It's a pen.*

—¿Quién **es**?   —*Who is it?*
—**Es** Luis.   —*It's Luis.*

> **ser** = *to be* (identification)
> **Soy estudiante.** (*I am a student.*)

B. Personal pronouns are used to refer to a person without mentioning the person's name. Here are some of the most common personal pronouns that can serve as the subject of a sentence, with the corresponding present-tense forms of **ser**. It is not necessary to memorize these pronouns. You will see and hear them again and again.

ser (*to be*)			
(yo)	**soy**	*I*	*am*
(tú)	**eres***	*you (inf. sing.)*	*are*
(usted)	**es**	*you (pol. sing.)*	*are*
(él†/ella)	**es**	*he/she*	*is*
(nosotros/nosotras)	**somos**	*we*	*are*
(vosotros/vosotras)‡	**sois**	*you (inf. pl.)*	*are*
(ustedes)	**son**	*you (pol. pl.)*	*are*
(ellos/ellas)	**son**	*they*	*are*

> Remember that most subject pronouns in Spanish are used only when there is a possibility of confusion:
> **(Yo) Soy estudiante.** (*I'm a student.*)
> **(Nosotros) Somos amigos.** (*We're friends.*)

yo = *I*
tú = *you* (informal singular)
usted = *you* (polite singular)
él = *he*
ella = *she*

nosotros = *we* (masculine)
nosotras = *we* (feminine)
vosotros = *you* (masculine informal plural)
vosotras = *you* (feminine informal plural)
ustedes = *you* (plural)
ellos = *they* (masculine)
ellas = *they* (feminine)

—¿Usted es profesor?
—Sí, soy profesor de historia.

—*Are you a professor?*
—*Yes, I'm a history professor.*

C. Spanish does not have a subject pronoun for *it* or for *they,* referring to things. When subject pronouns *are* used in Spanish, they often express emphasis.

¿Mi automóvil? Es pequeño.
¿Las faldas? Son caras.
Yo soy de Atlanta.

My car? It's small.
The skirts? They're expensive.
I am from Atlanta.

D. Subject pronouns may be used by themselves without verbs, either for emphasis or to point someone out.

¿Quién, **yo**? Yo no soy de Texas; soy de Nueva York.

Who, me? I'm not from Texas; I'm from New York.

—¿Cómo está usted?
—Estoy bien. ¿Y **usted**?

—*How are you?*
—*I'm fine. And you?*

E. The pronouns **ellos** (*they*), **nosotros** (*we*), and **vosotros** (*you, inf. pl.*) can refer to groups of people that consist of males only or of males and females. On the other hand, **ellas** (*they, fem.*), **nosotras** (*we, fem.*), and **vosotras** (*you, inf. pl. fem.*) can refer only to two or more females.

—¿Y **ellos**? ¿Quiénes son?
—¿Esteban y Mónica? Son amigos.

—*And those guys (they)? Who are they?*
—*Esteban and Mónica? They're friends.*

---

*Tú is an informal singular form of *you,* whereas **usted** is a polite singular form of *you.* See **Gramática B.1** for more information.
†The pronoun **él** (*he*) has an accent to distinguish it in writing from the definite article **el** (*the*).
‡The pronouns **vosotros/vosotras** are used only in Spain. Latin America uses **ustedes** for both polite and informal plural *you.*

—¿Y **ellas**? ¿Son amigas?

—Sí, Nora y Carmen son compañeras de mi clase de español.

—¿Y Esteban y Alicia? ¿Son amigos?

—Sí, son muy buenos amigos.

—*What about them? Are they friends?*

—*Yes, Nora and Carmen are classmates from my Spanish class.*

—*And what about Esteban and Alicia?*

—*Yes, they are very good friends.*

Ejercicio 3

Escoja el pronombre lógico.

MODELO: —Y *ella*, ¿lleva pantalones? →
—¿Quién, Mónica? Lleva una falda azul.

1. —¿_____ es profesor aquí?
   —¿Quién, Raúl? No, es estudiante.
2. —¿_____ son mexicanos?
   —Sí, Silvia y Nacho son mexicanos.
3. —¡Viejos, _____! No, doña María Eulalia y yo somos muy jóvenes.
4. —Señor Ruiz, _____ tiene bigote, ¿verdad?
5. —¿Y _____? ¿Son estudiantes aquí?
   —No, Pilar y Clara son estudiantes en Madrid.

a. ellos
b. usted
c. ellas
d. él
e. nosotros

Ejercicio 4

Complete los diálogos con la forma correcta del verbo **ser: soy, es, somos, son.**

—¿Cómo se llama usted?
—_____[1] Raúl Saucedo.

—¿Quién _____[2] ella?
—¿La chica de la blusa roja? Se llama Mónica. Ella y Carmen (ellas) _____[3] amigas.

—¿_____[4] estudiantes ustedes?
—¡No! El profesor López y yo (nosotros) _____[5] profesores de la universidad.

A.4 Identifying People and Things: Gender

A. Nouns (words that represent people or things) in Spanish are classified as either masculine or feminine. Masculine nouns often end in **-o** (**sombrero**); feminine nouns often end in **-a** (**falda**). In addition, words ending in **-ción, -sión,** or **-dad** are also feminine.

> Masculine nouns usually end in **-o.**
> Feminine nouns usually end in **-a.**

Madrid es una ciu**dad** bonit**a**.
La civiliza**ción** maya fue muy avanzad**a**.

Madrid is a pretty city.
Mayan civilization was very advanced.

You will acquire these endings later. For now, don't worry about them as you speak. You can refer to your text if you have any doubts when you are editing your writing.

El and **la** both mean *the*. **El** is used with masculine nouns, and **la** is used with feminine nouns.

Un and **una** both mean *a/an*. **Un** is used with masculine nouns, and **una** is used with feminine nouns.

Spanish nouns are classified grammatically as either masculine or feminine. The articles change according to grammatical gender and agree with the nouns they modify.
un abrigo = *a coat*
una blusa = *a blouse*
una universidad = *a university*
el libro = *the book*
la casa = *the house*

But the terms *masculine* and *feminine* are grammatical classifications only; Spanish speakers do not perceive things such as notebooks or doors as being "male" or "female." On the other hand, words that refer to males are usually masculine (**amigo**), and words that refer to females are usually feminine (**amiga**).

Esteban es mi **amigo** y Carmen es una **amiga** de él.	*Esteban is my friend, and Carmen is a friend of his.*

B. Because Spanish nouns have gender, adjectives (words that describe nouns) *agree* with nouns: They change their endings from **-o** to **-a** according to the gender of the nouns they modify. Notice the two words for *black* in the following examples.

Lan tiene el pelo **negro**.	*Lan has black hair.*
Luis lleva una chaqueta **negra**.	*Luis is wearing a black jacket.*

C. Like English, Spanish has definite articles (*the*) and indefinite articles (*a, an*). Articles in Spanish also change form according to the gender of the nouns they accompany.

	DEFINITE (*the*)	INDEFINITE (*a, an*)
Masculine	el suéter	un sombrero
Feminine	la blusa	una chaqueta

Hoy Mónica lleva **un** vestido nuevo.	*Today Mónica is wearing a new dress.*
La chaqueta de Alberto es azul.	*Alberto's jacket is blue.*

D. How can you determine the gender of a noun? The gender of the article and/or adjective that modifies the noun will tell you whether it is masculine or feminine. In addition, the following two simple rules will help you determine the gender of a noun most of the time.

Rule 1: A noun that refers to a male is masculine; a noun that refers to a female is feminine. Sometimes they are a pair distinguished by the endings **-o/-a;** other times they are completely different words.

un muchacho	una muchacha	*boy/girl*
un niño	una niña	*(male) child / (female) child*
un amigo	una amiga	*(male) friend / (female) friend*
un hombre	una mujer	*man/woman*

For some nouns referring to people, the masculine form ends in a consonant and the feminine form adds **-a** to the masculine noun.*

un profesor	una profesora	*(male) professor / (female) professor*
un señor	una señora	*a man (Mr.) / a woman (Mrs.)*

---

*This rule includes a few common animals. Some pairs end in **-o/-a;** others end in consonant / consonant + **-a.**

un gato	una gata	*(male) cat / (female) cat*
un perro	una perra	*(male) dog / (female) dog*
un león	una leona	*lion/lioness*

Other nouns do not change at all; only the accompanying article changes.

un elefante	(*male*) *elephant*
una elefante	(*female*) *elephant*
un estudiante	(*male*) *student*
una estudiante	(*female*) *student*
un joven	*young man*
una joven	*young woman*
un recepcionista	(*male*) *receptionist*
una recepcionista	(*female*) *receptionist*

Rule 2: For most nouns that refer to things (rather than to people or animals), the gender is reflected in the last letter of the word. Nouns that end in **-o** are usually grammatically masculine (**un/el vestido**), and nouns that end in **-a** are usually grammatically feminine (**una/la puerta**).*

Words that end in **-d** (**una/la universidad**) or in the letter combinations **-ción** or **-sión** (**una/la nación; una/la diversión**) are also usually feminine.

> Nouns that end in **-o** are usually masculine; nouns that end in **-a** are usually feminine.

MASCULINE: -o	FEMININE: -a, -ción, -sión, -d
un/el bolígraf**o**	una/la cas**a**
un/el sombrer**o**	una/la puert**a**
un/el libr**o**	una/la descrip**ción**
un/el vestid**o**	una/la universi**dad**

Words that refer to things may also end in **-e** or in consonants other than **-d** and **-ión.** Most of these words that you have heard so far are masculine, but some are feminine.

un/el borrador	*eraser*	una/la clase	*class*
un/el automóvil	*automobile*	una/la luz	*light*
un/el lápiz	*pencil*	una/la mujer	*woman*
un/el traje	*suit*		
un/el reloj	*clock*		

> Don't worry if you can't remember all these rules! Note where they are in this book so you can refer to them when you are editing your writing and when you are unsure of what gender a noun is.

Ejercicio 5

Conteste según el modelo.

MODELO: ¿Es un bolígrafo? (lápiz) →
No, no es un bolígrafo. Es *un* lápiz.

1. ¿Es una chaqueta? (camisa)
2. ¿Es una mujer? (hombre)
3. ¿Es una falda? (vestido)
4. ¿Es un sombrero? (blusa)
5. ¿Es una naranja? (reloj)

> You will develop a *feel* for gender as you listen and read more in Spanish.

---

*Three common exceptions are **la mano** (*hand*), **el día** (*day*), and **el mapa** (*map*).

Ejercicio 6

Complete las oraciones con **el** o **la.**

1. _____ estudiante es rubia.
2. _____ profesor de matemáticas es guapo.
3. _____ clase es buena.
4. _____ reloj es negro.
5. _____ lápiz es amarillo.
6. _____ puerta es blanca.
7. _____ motocicleta es negra.
8. _____ automóvil es nuevo.
9. _____ casa es grande.
10. _____ sombrero es rojo.

A.5 Responding to Instructions: Commands*

Singular commands (to one person) end in **-a** or **-e.** Plural commands (to more than one person) end in **-an** or **-en.**

In English the same form of the verb is used for giving commands, whether to one person (singular) or to more than one person (plural).

Steve, please stand up.
Mr. and Mrs. Martínez, please stand up.

In Spanish, however, singular commands end in **-a** or **-e,** and plural commands add an **-n.**

Alberto, **saque** el libro por favor.	*Alberto, please take out your book.*
Alberto y Nora, **saquen** el libro, por favor.	*Alberto and Nora, please take out your books.*
Mónica, **abra** la puerta.	*Mónica, open the door.*
Mónica y Luis, **abran** la puerta.	*Mónica and Luis, open the door.*

Ejercicio 7

Escriba la forma correcta del mandato con verbos de la lista.

abra(n) open   corra(n) run   escuche(n) listen   saque(n) take out
camine(n) walk   cuenta(n) count   estudie(n) study   siénte(n)se seat
cante(n) sing)   diga(n) say   lea(n) read
cierre(n) close   escriba(n) write salte(n) jump

1. —Lan y Mónica, _____ «Buenas tardes».
2. —Alberto, _____ su nombre con lápiz.
3. —Nora y Luis, _____ de cero a quince por favor.
4. —Pablo y Esteban, _____ el libro.
5. —Carmen, _____ la Actividad 2 en la página 6.
6. —Nora, _____ un bolígrafo.
7. —Lan y Esteban, _____ el diálogo.
8. —Luis, _____ la puerta, por favor.

---

*Your instructor will give you commands during the Total Physical Response activities. Other classroom instructions will also use command forms. You will learn more about how to give commands in **Gramática 11.1** and **14.3.**

Las descripciones

Sobre el artista: Sergio Velásquez (Managua, 1955) studied drawing and printing at the National School of Plastic Arts and the Workshop for Graphic and Monumental Art in Nicaragua. His work, characterized by monumental, voluptuous women with an earthy yet mysterious glow, clearly aims to represent poor working women of Nicaragua, with **mestizo** (European and Indian) features. His paintings have been shown in the Americas as well as in Europe and Africa.

Vendedora de ayotes, por Sergio Velásquez (Nicaragua)

METAS

In **Paso B** you will continue to develop your listening and speaking abilities in Spanish. You will learn more vocabulary with which to describe your immediate environment. You will also get to know your classmates better as you converse with them.

ACTIVIDADES DE COMUNICACIÓN

- Hablando con otros
- Las cosas en el salón de clase y los números (40–69)
- El cuerpo humano
- La descripción de las personas

EN RESUMEN

GRAMÁTICA Y EJERCICIOS

B.1 Addressing Others: Informal and Polite *you* (**tú/usted**)

B.2 Expressing Existence: **hay**

B.3 Describing People and Things: Negation

B.4 Describing People and Things: Plural Forms

B.5 Describing People and Things: Adjective-Noun Agreement and Placement of Adjectives

¡Conozca Nicaragua!

Nombre del país: República de Nicaragua

Ciudad capital: Managua

Ciudades principales: Granada, León, Matagalpa

Moneda: el córdoba

Idiomas: español (oficial), inglés, lenguas indígenas

Población: 5.700.000

Día de la Independencia: el 15 de septiembre

Fiestas típicas: el Día de la Inmaculada Concepción, el Día de la Liberación Nacional

Comidas típicas: el gallo pinto, el nacatamal, el vigorón, la sopa de mondongo, el quesillo

Música típica: Combination of indigenous, European, and African elements

Gente famosa: Rubén Darío, Daniel Ortega

Código de país por Internet: .ni

Voces nicaragüenses

un caite	un zapato
el merol	food
un pipe	un niño
tuanis	bueno, bonito, excelent
vos	The pronoun **vos** is used instead of **tú**

Actividades de comunicación

Hablando con otros

⁕ **Lea Gramática B.1.**

ustedes · usted · la profesora · los estudiantes

la madre · tú · la hija · tú o usted · tú · tú · los amigos · tú/usted · tú/usted · los profesores

Actividad 1 Identificaciones: ¿*Tú* o *usted*?

Usted habla con estas personas. ¿Usa **tú** o **usted**?

1. un amigo de la universidad
2. el profesor de matemáticas
3. una niña de diez años
4. un amigo de su papá
5. una señora de sesenta y cinco años
6. una recepcionista
7. su doctor
8. su hermano/a

Actividad 2 Diálogos abiertos: ¿Cómo estás tú? ¿Cómo está usted?

Palabras útiles

(muy) bien   regular
(un poco / muy)
 cansado/a

DOS ESTUDIANTES EN EL SALÓN DE CLASE

E1: Hola, *Mónica*. ¿Cómo estás?
E2: *Muy bien*. ¿Y tú?
E1: *Regular*.

DOS PROFESORES EN LA OFICINA

E1: Buenos días, *profesora Martínez*. ¿Cómo está usted?
E2: Estoy *muy bien*. ¿Y usted, *profesor López*?
E1: *Un poco cansado*. ¿Cómo está la familia?
E2: *Bien*, gracias. ¿Y su familia?
E1: Está *muy bien*.

Las cosas en el salón de clase y los números (40–69)

✳ Lea Gramática B.2–B.4.

Actividad 3   Identificaciones: ¿Qué hay en el salón de clase?

MODELOS: En mi clase hay... → *un lápiz amarillo.*
En mi clase hay... → *una pizarra grande.*

1. una computadora
2. una ventana
3. una pizarra
4. un reloj
5. un bolígrafo
6. una pantalla
7. un libro
8. una puerta
9. un mapa
10. un cartel

a. azul ~ color café
b. moderno/a ~ antiguo/a
c. interesante ~ aburrido/a
d. fácil ~ difícil
e. blanco/a ~ negro/a ~ gris
f. largo/a
g. viejo/a ~ nuevo/a
h. pequeño/a ~ grande
i. ¿ ?

Actividad 4   Intercambios: El salón de clase

MODELO: E1: ¿Cuántos/as _____ hay en el salón de clase?
E2: Hay _____.

1. estudiantes
2. mesas
3. borradores
4. pizarras

5. ventanas
6. paredes
7. puertas
8. luces

Actividad 5   Intercambios: ¿Cuánto cuesta?

MODELO: E1: ¿Cuánto cuesta *el diccionario?*
E2: Cuesta *$59.49 (cincuenta y nueve dólares y cuarenta y nueve centavos).*

el diccionario

40 cuarenta	50 cincuenta	60 sesenta
41 cuarenta y uno	52 cincuenta y dos	63 sesenta y tres
45 cuarenta y cinco	58 cincuenta y ocho	69 sesenta y nueve

el cuaderno   la calculadora   la mochila   la silla

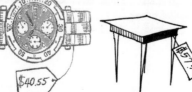

el reloj   la mesa   el cartel   la patineta

El cuerpo humano

✳ **Lea Gramática B.5.**

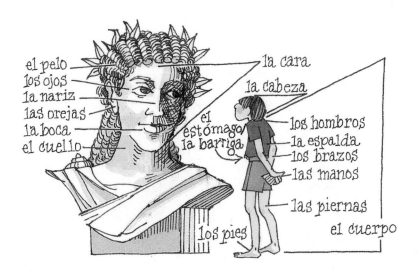

el pelo
los ojos
la nariz
las orejas
la boca
el cuello

la cara
la cabeza

el estómago/
la barriga

los hombros
la espalda
los brazos
las manos

las piernas

los pies

el cuerpo

Actividad 6   Descripción de dibujos: ¿Quién es?

Mire a estas personas. Escuche la descripción que da su profesor(a) y diga cómo se llama la persona.

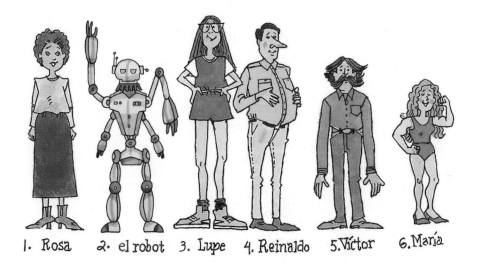

1. Rosa   2. el robot   3. Lupe   4. Reinaldo   5. Víctor   6. María

La descripción de las personas

✳ Lea Gramática B.5.

pelo rubio
ojos azules

joven y
talentosa

bonita
pelo negro
ojos negros

seria
y callada

de estatura
mediana
pelo castaño corto
ojos castaños

divertido
y generoso

alto
delgado
fuerte

idealista
y tímido

bajo
guapo
pelo negro rizado
ojos negros

simpático y
entusiasta

lentes   barba   bigote

Mónica   Lan   Esteban   Alberto   Luis

Actividad 7   Diálogo: La nueva amiga

ESTEBAN: ¿Cómo es tu nueva amiga, Luis?

LUIS: Es alta, delgada y de pelo castaño. ¡Y muy talentosa!

ESTEBAN: ¿Cómo se llama?

LUIS: Cecilia Teresa.

ESTEBAN: Es un nombre muy bonito.

LUIS: ¡Es una chica muy bonita también!

Actividad 8 Intercambios: Mis compañeros y yo

Diga cómo es usted. Dé tres descripciones afirmativas y dos negativas.

MODELO: E1: Soy *talentoso/a, idealista* y *trabajador(a).* No soy *agresivo/a* ni *tonto/a.* ¿Y tú?
   E2: Yo soy *cómico/a, atlético/a* y *generoso/a.* No soy *tímido/a* ni *tacaño/a.*

agresivo/a	entusiasta	mentiroso/a	sincero/a
antipático/a	estudioso/a	nervioso/a	tacaño/a
atlético/a	filosófico/a	optimista	talentoso/a
callado/a	generoso/a	perezoso/a	temperamental
cómico/a	idealista	pesimista	tímido/a
conservador(a)	impulsivo/a	práctico/a	tonto/a
considerado/a	inteligente	serio/a	trabajador(a)
egoísta	materialista	simpático/a	

Actividad 9 Diálogo abierto: Los nuevos amigos

E1: ¿Tienes nuevos amigos en esta clase?
E2: Sí, tengo dos.
E1: ¿Cómo se llaman?
E2: Se llaman *Cristina* y *Daniel* y son muy *talentosos.*
E1: ¿Y son *trabajadores* (*perezosos*) también?
E2: ¡Claro que sí! (¡Claro que no!)

Actividad 10 Entrevista: Mi mejor amigo/a

ESTUDIANTE 1

1. ¿Cómo se llama tu mejor amigo/a?
2. ¿De qué color tiene los ojos?
3. ¿Es alto/a, bajo/a o de estatura mediana?
4. ¿De qué color tiene el pelo?
5. ¿Tiene bigote/barba?
6. ¿Cómo es? ¿Es simpático/a? ¿tímido/a? ¿trabajador(a)? ¿Es _____?

ESTUDIANTE 2

Se llama _____.
Tiene los ojos _____.
Es _____.
Tiene el pelo _____.
(No) Tiene _____.
Es _____.

¡OJO!

Para expresar la palabra «tacaño/a», uno se puede tocar el codo con la mano.

En resumen

De todo un poco

A. Un mundo ideal

Use su imaginación y complete estas descripciones.

1. El salón de clase ideal es _____ y _____. En el salón de clase hay _____. No hay _____.
2. El amigo / La amiga ideal es _____ y _____. No es _____.
3. El/La estudiante ideal es _____ y _____. No es _____.
4. El profesor / La profesora ideal es _____ y _____. No es _____.
5. El novio (El esposo) / La novia (La esposa) ideal es _____ y _____. No es _____.

B. Su opinión

Exprese su opinión con su compañero/a.

MODELO: E1: El cartel es *bonito.*
             E2: Sí, es *bonito.* (No, es *feo.*)

1. La clase de español es (interesante ~ aburrida).
2. Hay muchos estudiantes (inteligentes ~ tontos) en esta clase.
3. El profesor / La profesora de español es (reservado/a ~ entusiasta).
4. El salón de clase es (moderno ~ tradicional).
5. El campus es (grande ~ pequeño).

¿Cómo es su campus, grande o pequeño?

Vocabulario

These words come from the *Actividades de comunicación*. You are not expected to memorize the entire list. Your instructor may tell you which sections he or she wants to emphasize. Be patient, you will be familiar with most of these words by the end of the chapter.

Las cosas en el salón de clase

Things in the Classroom

el borrador	eraser
el cartel	poster
el cuaderno	workbook; notebook
el diccionario	dictionary
el escritorio	desk
la luz (las luces)	light (lights)
la mesa	table
la pantalla	screen
el papel	paper
la pared	wall
el piso	floor
la pizarra	(chalk)board
la pluma	pen (*Mex.*)
el pupitre	desk (student)
la silla	chair
el techo	roof; ceiling
la tiza	chalk
la ventana	window

REPASO (*Review*): **el bolígrafo, el lápiz, el libro, la puerta, el reloj, el texto**

El cuerpo humano

The Human Body

la barriga	tummy; belly
la boca	mouth
el brazo	arm
la cabeza	head
la cara	face
el cuello	neck
la espalda	back
el estómago	stomach
el hombro	shoulder
la mano	hand
la nariz	nose
el ojo	eye
la oreja	ear
el pie (los pies)	foot
la pierna	leg

Las personas

People

el chico / la chica	young man / young woman
el esposo / la esposa	husband / wife
el hermano / la hermana	brother / sister
el novio / la novia	boyfriend / girlfriend
tú	you (*inf.*)
el vecino / la vecina	neighbor

PALABRAS SEMEJANTES: el doctor / la doctora, la mamá, el papá, el robot

Las descripciones

Descriptions

¿Cómo es él/ella?	What is he/she like?
¿Cómo es usted? / ¿Cómo eres tú?	What are you like?
abierto/a	open
aburrido/a	boring; bored
antiguo/a	antique; ancient
antipático/a	unpleasant
callado/a	quiet
de... años	. . . years old
derecho/a	right
difícil	difficult
divertido/a	fun
egoísta	selfish, self-centered
entusiasta	enthusiastic
fácil	easy
fuerte	strong
izquierdo/a	left
mejor	best; better
mentiroso/a	dishonest, liar
perezoso/a	lazy
serio/a	serious
simpático/a	nice, pleasant
tacaño/a	stingy
tímido/a	shy
tonto/a	silly, dumb
trabajador(a)	hard-working

PALABRAS SEMEJANTES: afirmativo/a, agresivo/a, atlético/a, cómico/a, conservador(a), considerado/a, estudioso/a, filosófico/a, generoso/a, ideal, idealista, impulsivo/a, inteligente, interesante, materialista, moderno/a, negativo/a, nervioso/a, optimista, pesimista, práctico/a, reservado/a, sincero/a, talentoso/a

Los verbos

Verbs

busque	look for
complete	complete
conteste(n)	answer
de(le)	give (to him/her)
eres	you (*inf. sing.*) are
exprese	express
mueva	move
señale	point to
¿Tienes... ?	Do you have . . . ?
Tengo...	I have . . .
usa	uses

Expresiones útiles

Useful Expressions

Claro que sí/no	Of course (not)
¿Cómo estás tú?	How are you?
¿Cuánto cuesta(n)?	How much is (are) . . . ?
Cuesta(n)...	It costs (They cost) . . .
de nada	You're welcome.
Gracias	Thank you.
¿Qué tal?	How's it going?

Palabras del texto

Words from the Text

de todo un poco	a bit of everything
el dibujo	drawing
en resumen	to sum up
la entrevista	interview
hablando	talking
intercambios	interactions
el modelo	model

Palabras útiles

Useful Words

la calculadora	calculator
el centavo	cent

la computadora	computer
esto	this (thing)
la mochila	backpack
mucho/a(s)	a lot, many
el mundo	world
muy	very
o	or
otro/a	other, another
la patineta	skateboard
también	also
tu(s)	your (*inf.*)

PALABRAS SEMEJANTES: el campus, el dólar / los dólares, la imaginación, la lista, el mapa, las matemáticas, la oficina, la opinión, la universidad

Los números

Numbers

cuarenta	forty
cuarenta y uno	forty-one
cuarenta y cinco	forty-five
cincuenta	fifty
cincuenta y uno	fifty-one
cincuenta y dos	fifty-two
cincuenta y ocho	fifty-eight
sesenta	sixty
sesenta y nueve	sixty-nine

Gramática y ejercicios

B.1 Addressing Others: Informal and Polite *you* (*tú/usted*)

A. English speakers use the pronoun *you* to address a person directly, whether or not they know that person well. In older forms of English, speakers used an informal pronoun—*thou*—among friends, but today *you* is used with everyone.

Spanish has two pronouns that mean *you,* singular: **usted** and **tú.** The polite (*pol.*) pronoun **usted** is appropriate for people you do not know well, such as salespeople, receptionists, other professionals, and especially for people older than you. The informal (*inf.*) pronoun **tú** is reserved for friends, peers, children, and other people you know well. In some places in Latin America, including Argentina and Central America, speakers use **vos** instead of **tú** as the informal pronoun for *you.* Everyone who uses **vos,** however, also understands **tú.**

In the activities and exercises, *Dos mundos* addresses you with **usted.** You should use **tú** when speaking to your classmates. Some instructors address their students with **tú;** others use **usted.**

Soy puertorriqueño. ¿Y **tú**? ¿De dónde eres?	*I'm Puerto Rican. And you? Where are you from?*
Soy profesora de español. ¿Y **usted**? ¿Es **usted** estudiante?	*I'm a professor of Spanish. And you? Are you a student?*

> Both **tú** and **usted** mean *you* (singular). **Tú** is used when speaking to family, friends, and children. **Usted** is used to speak to people you don't know well and people older than you.

B. Although both **tú** and **usted** correspond to *you,* the verb forms used with each are different. Present-tense verb forms for **tú** always end with the letter **-s.** Present-tense verb forms for **usted** end in **-a** or **-e** and are always the same as the forms for **él/ella.**

¿Tiene**s** (**tú**) una blusa gris?	*Do you have a gray blouse?*
¿Tiene **usted** un vestido blanco?	*Do you have a white dress?*

> Use **tú** when speaking to your classmates. Use **usted** when addressing your instructor (unless he/she asks you to use **tú**).

We introduced the forms of the verb **ser** (*to be*) in **Gramática A.3.** The **tú** form of **ser** is **eres;** the **usted** form of **ser** is **es** (the same as the form for **él/ella**).

(**Tú**) **Eres** un buen amigo.	*You are a good friend.*
Usted es muy amable, señora Saucedo.	*You are very nice, Mrs. Saucedo.*

> Present-tense verb forms for **tú** always end in **-s.**

C. Spanish distinguishes between singular *you* (**tú** or **usted**) and plural *you* (**ustedes**). Many American speakers of English make this distinction by saying "you guys" or "you all." The verb forms used with **ustedes** end in the letter **-n** and are the same as those used with the pronoun **ellos/as.**

—¿Cómo **están ustedes**?	*—How are you (all)?*
—Bien, gracias.	*—Fine, thanks.*

Most speakers of Spanish do not distinguish between informal and polite address in the plural. **Ustedes** is used with everyone. In Spain, however, most speakers prefer to use **vosotros/as** for the informal plural *you* and reserve **ustedes** for the polite plural *you.*

The regional pronouns **vos** and **vosotros/as** do not appear in the exercises and activities of *Dos mundos.* You will learn them quickly if you travel to areas where

> The plural of both **tú** and **usted** in Latin America is **ustedes.** In Spain, the plural of **tú** is **vosotros/as** and the plural of **usted** is **ustedes.**

they are frequently used. The verb forms corresponding to **vosotros/as** are listed with other verb forms and are given in Appendix 1. The verb forms corresponding to **vos** are footnoted in the grammar explanations. In the listening activities of the *Cuaderno de actividades,* the characters from countries where **vos** and **vosotros/as** are prevalent use those pronouns. Thus, the *Cuaderno de actividades* will give you an opportunity to hear **vos** and **vosotros/as** and their accompanying verb forms, even though you will not need to use them yourself.

Ejercicio 1

Usted habla con estas personas: ¿usa **tú** o **usted**?

1. una amiga de su clase de español
   a. ¿Tiene usted dos clases hoy?
   b. ¿Tienes dos clases hoy?
2. la recepcionista
   a. ¿Cómo estás?
   b. ¿Cómo está usted?
3. un niño
   a. Tú tienes una bicicleta nueva.
   b. Usted tiene una bicicleta nueva.
4. una persona de cuarenta y nueve años
   a. ¿Cómo se llama usted?
   b. ¿Cómo te llamas?
5. un vecino de setenta años
   a. Estoy bien. ¿Y tú?
   b. Estoy bien. ¿Y usted?

B.2 Expressing Existence: *hay*

hay = *there is / there are*
Hay is used with singular or plural nouns.

The verb form **hay** expresses the idea of existence. When used with singular nouns it means *there is;* with plural nouns it means *there are.*

—¿Qué **hay** en el salón de clase? —*What is there in the classroom?*
—**Hay** dos puertas y una ventana. —*There are two doors and a window.*

Whereas the verb **ser** (*to be*) identifies nouns (see **Gramática A.3**), **hay** simply states their existence.

—¿Qué **es**? —*What is that?*
—**Es** un bolígrafo. —*It's a pen.*

—¿Cuántos **hay**? —*How many are there?*
—**Hay** tres. —*There are three.*

Ejercicio 2

To make a sentence negative, place **no** before the verb.
Hay perros en el salón de clase.
No hay perros en el salón de clase.

Imagínese qué cosas o personas hay o no hay en el salón de clase de la profesora Martínez.

MODELOS: lápices → *Hay* lápices en el salón de clase.
perros → *No hay* perros en el salón de clase.

1. libros en la mesa
2. un reloj en la pared
3. una profesora
4. un automóvil
5. un profesor
6. papeles en los pupitres
7. un bolígrafo en el pupitre de Alberto
8. muchos cuadernos
9. una bicicleta
10. una ventana

B.3 Describing People and Things: Negation

In a negative sentence, the word **no** precedes the verb.

Amanda es una chica muy simpática. (Amanda) **No es** tímida.	*Amanda is a very nice girl. She is not shy.*
Ramón **no es** mi novio. Es el novio de Amanda.	*Ramón isn't my boyfriend. He's Amanda's boyfriend.*

There are no additional words in Spanish that correspond to the English negatives *don't* and *doesn't*.

Guillermo **no tiene** el pelo largo ahora.	*Guillermo doesn't have long hair now.*
Yo soy hombre; **no llevo** vestidos.	*I am a man; I don't wear dresses.*

Spanish, like many other languages in the world, often uses more than one negative in a sentence.*

No hay **nada** en este salón de clase.	*There is nothing in this classroom.*

Ejercicio 3

Cambie estas oraciones afirmativas a oraciones negativas.

MODELOS: Luis es un chico alto. → Luis **no** es un chico alto.
En el salón de clase hay 68 tizas. → En el salón de clase **no** hay 68 tizas.

1. En el salón de clase hay diez pizarras.
2. Mónica tiene el pelo negro.
3. Carmen lleva una blusa muy fea.
4. Mi carro es morado.
5. La profesora Martínez tiene barba.

B.4 Describing People and Things: Plural Forms

Spanish and English nouns may be singular (**camisa**, *shirt*) or plural (**camisas**, *shirts*). Almost all plural words in Spanish end in **-s** or **-es**: **blusas** (*blouses*), **pantalones** (*pants*), **suéteres** (*sweaters*), **zapatos** (*shoes*), and so on. In Spanish, unlike English, articles before plural nouns and adjectives that describe plural nouns must also be plural. Here are the basic rules for forming plurals in Spanish.

A. Words that end in a vowel (**a, e, i, o, u**) form their plural by adding **-s**.

SINGULAR	PLURAL
el brazo	los brazos
el ojo	los ojos
el pie	los pies
la pierna	las piernas

---

*You will learn more about negative words and their placement in **Gramática 8.3.** In **Gramática 3.4** you will learn how to answer questions in the negative.

Words that end in a consonant add **-es.**

SINGULAR	PLURAL
el borrador	los borrador**es**
la pare**d**	las pared**es**
el profesor	los profesor**es**

If the consonant at the end of a word is **-z,** it changes to **-c** and adds **-es.**

SINGULAR	PLURAL
el lápi**z**	los lápi**ces**
la lu**z**	las lu**ces**

> To form plurals: Words ending in vowels add **s;** words ending in consonants add **-es;** words ending in **-z** change to **-c** and add **-es.** In time, you will acquire a feel for the plural formations.

B. Adjectives that describe plural words must also be plural.

ojo**s** azul**es**	*blue eyes*	oreja**s** grande**s**	*big ears*
brazo**s** largo**s**	*long arms*	pie**s** pequeño**s**	*small feet*

En mi salón de clase hay dos ventana**s** grande**s**, varia**s** silla**s** vieja**s**, cinco pizarra**s** verde**s** y diez luc**es.**

In my classroom there are two large windows, several old chairs, five green chalkboards, and ten lights.

Ejercicio 4

Marisa y Clarisa tienen muchas cosas. ¡Pero Marisa siempre tiene una y Clarisa dos!

MODELO: Marisa tiene un suéter azul, pero Clarisa tiene dos... →
suéteres azules.

> **tienen** = *have*
> **tiene** = *has*

1. Marisa tiene un par de zapatos, pero Clarisa tiene dos...
2. Marisa tiene un perro nuevo, pero Clarisa tiene dos...
3. Marisa tiene una chaqueta roja, pero Clarisa tiene dos...
4. Marisa tiene un lápiz amarillo, pero Clarisa tiene dos...
5. Marisa tiene una amiga norteamericana, pero Clarisa tiene dos...

Ejercicio 5

¡Ahora Clarisa tiene una y Marisa tiene dos!

MODELO: Clarisa tiene un sombrero grande, pero Marisa tiene dos... →
sombreros grandes.

1. Clarisa tiene un cuaderno pequeño, pero Marisa tiene dos...
2. Clarisa tiene un gato negro, pero Marisa tiene dos...
3. Clarisa tiene una fotografía bonita, pero Marisa tiene dos...
4. Clarisa tiene un reloj bonito, pero Marisa tiene dos...
5. Clarisa tiene un libro difícil, pero Marisa tiene dos...
6. Clarisa tiene una amiga divertida, pero Marisa tiene dos...

B.5 Describing People and Things: Adjective-Noun Agreement and Placement of Adjectives

A. Adjectives must agree in gender and number with the nouns they describe; that is, if the noun is singular and masculine, the adjective must also be singular and masculine. Adjectives that end in **-o** in the masculine form and **-a** in the feminine form will appear in the vocabulary lists in *Dos mundos* like this: **bonito/a.** Such adjectives have four possible forms.

> A singular adjective is used to describe a singular noun. A plural adjective is used to describe a plural noun.

	SINGULAR	PLURAL
Masculine	viejo	viejos
Feminine	vieja	viejas

Carmen lleva un suéter **bonito** y una falda **nueva.**	*Carmen is wearing a pretty sweater and a new skirt.*
Mis zapatos de tenis son **viejos.**	*My tennis shoes are old.*

B. Adjectives that end in a consonant,* the vowel **-e,** or the ending **-ista** have only two forms because the masculine and feminine forms are the same.

	SINGULAR	PLURAL
Masculine/Feminine	joven	jóvenes
	interesante	interesantes
	pesimista	pesimistas
	azul	azules

Luis lleva una camisa **azul** y un sombrero **azul.**	*Luis is wearing a blue shirt and a blue hat.*
Mi amigo Nacho es **pesimista,** pero mi amiga Silvia es **optimista.**	*My friend Nacho is pessimistic, but my friend Silvia is optimistic.*

C. In Spanish adjectives generally follow the noun they modify: **zapatos nuevos, camisas blancas, faldas bonitas, sombreros negros.** Adjectives that express inherent characteristics may precede the noun: **la blanca nieve.**[†] You should not worry too much about placement. For now, you may place descriptive adjectives after the noun.

D. If an adjective modifies two nouns, one masculine and one feminine, the adjective will take the masculine form.

> Mónica es simpátic**a** y considerad**a.**
> Alberto y Mónica son simpátic**os** y considerad**os.**
> Mi blusa y mi falda son blanc**as.**
> Mi blusa y mi vestido son roj**os.**

---

*Adjectives of nationality that end in a consonant are an exception, since they (like adjectives that end in **-o/-a**) have four forms: **inglés, inglesa, ingleses, inglesas.** See **Gramática C.4** for more information.
†Limiting adjectives (numerals, possessives, demonstratives, and indefinite adjectives) also precede the noun: **dos amigos, mis zapatos, esta mesa, otro ejemplo.**

Ejercicio 6

Seleccione todas las descripciones posibles.

MODELO: Alberto → *chico, guapo, estudiante*

Nora   Alberto   Esteban   Carmen   la profesora Martínez   Luis   Pablo   Mónica

1. Nora	**a.** mujer	**i.** estudiante
2. Alberto	**b.** chico	**j.** profesor
3. Esteban y Carmen	**c.** secretaria	**k.** mexicana
4. la profesora Martínez	**d.** chica	**l.** altas
5. Luis	**e.** guapo	**m.** bajo
6. Pablo	**f.** niñas	**n.** morena
7. Mónica y Carmen	**g.** amigos	**o.** rubio
	h. estudiantes	

Ejercicio 7

Escriba frases completas con la información. Use las formas femeninas para las mujeres.

MODELOS: Arnold Schwarzenegger: alto, fuerte → Arnold Schwarzenegger
es alto y fuerte.
Oprah Winfrey: simpático, rico → Oprah Winfrey es simpática y rica.

1. Ashley y Mary Kate Olsen: rico, bonito
2. Will Smith: delgado, elegante
3. Hillary Clinton: inteligente, rubio
4. Jennifer López: materialista, talentoso
5. George Clooney: guapo, tímido

Ejercicio 8

Escriba frases completas con la información. Use la forma correcta: masculina o femenina, singular o plural.

MODELOS: casa: nuevo, pequeño → La casa es nue**va** y pequeñ**a**. / La casa nue**va**
es pequeñ**a**.
lápices: amarillo, viejo → Los lápices son amaril**los** y viej**os**. / Los
lápices amaril**los** son viej**os**.

1. libros: difícil, divertido
2. chica: bajo, tímido
3. mujeres: tacaño, trabajador
4. amigo: inteligente, perezoso
5. robots: fuerte, aburrido

Mi familia y mis amigos

Sobre el artista: Fernando Botero (1932–) was born in Medellín, Colombia. His work, characterized by the plump figures of his subjects, is shown in museums and galleries around the world.

Familia, por Fernando Botero (Colombia)

METAS

In **Paso C** you will discuss your family, things you own, and people's ages. You will also talk about languages and nationalities.

ACTIVIDADES DE COMUNICACIÓN

- La familia
- ¿Qué tenemos?
- Los números (10–110) y la edad
- Los idiomas y las nacionalidades

EN RESUMEN

GRAMÁTICA Y EJERCICIOS

C.1 Expressing Possession: The Verbs **tener** and **ser de(l)**

C.2 Expressing Possession: Possessive Adjectives

C.3 Expressing Age: The Verb **tener**

C.4 Describing People: Adjectives of Nationality

C.5 Talking about Habitual Actions: Present Tense of Regular **-ar** Verbs

¡Conozca Colombia!

Nombre del país: República de Colombia

Ciudad capital: Bogotá

Ciudades principales: Medellín, Cali, Barranquilla, Cartagena

Moneda: el peso

Idiomas: español

Población: 44.000.000

Día de la Independencia: el 20 de julio, el 7 de agosto

Fiestas típicas: el Carnaval de Bogotá, el Carnaval de Barranquilla, la Feria de Cali, la Feria de las Flores

Comidas típicas: el ajiaco, la bandeja paisa, el sancocho

Música típica: el vallenato, la cumbia

Gente famosa: Gabriel García Márquez, Shakira, Fernando Botero

Código del país por Internet: .co

Voces colombianas

un cucho / una cucha	a respected older person, such as a parent or professor
un chompo	**una chaqueta**
¡Añoni!	Great!
una barra	**un peso colombiano**
un(a) parcero/a	**un(a) amigo/a**
sisas / nocas	**sí / no**

La familia

✳ **Lea Gramática C.1.**

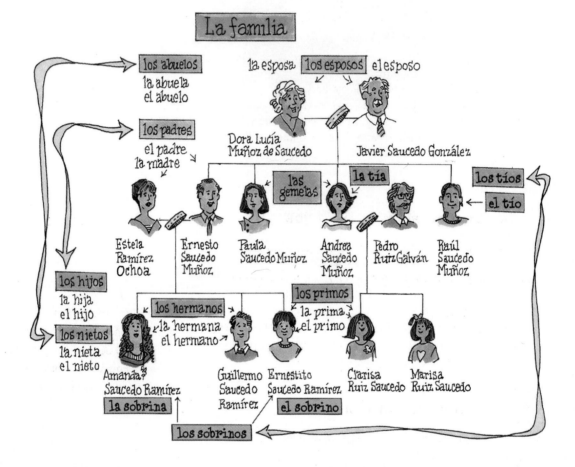

¡OJO!

En España y América Latina las personas solteras normalmente usan dos apellidos, el de su padre y el de su madre: Ernesto Saucedo Muñoz, Andrea Saucedo Muñoz. En América Latina, algunas (*some*) mujeres casadas usan «de» y el apellido de su esposo: Dora Lucía Muñoz de Saucedo.

Actividad 1 Identificaciones: La familia Saucedo (Parte 1)

¿Cierto o falso? Conteste según el dibujo.

1. La esposa de Pedro se llama Andrea.
2. Dora y Javier tienen cuatro hijos: tres hijas y un hijo.
3. Estela es la hermana de Ernesto.
4. Raúl es soltero.
5. Estela, Paula, Andrea y Raúl son hermanos.
6. Paula y Raúl tienen cinco sobrinos.
7. Amanda no tiene primos.
8. Dora tiene cinco nietos: tres nietas y dos nietos.
9. Pedro y Raúl son hermanos.
10. Andrea es la tía de Clarisa y Marisa.

Actividad 2   Intercambios: La familia Saucedo (Parte 2)

Conteste según el dibujo de la familia Saucedo.

MODELOS: E1: ¿Cómo se llama *el hermano* de *Ernesto, Paula y Andrea*?
E2: Se llama *Raúl.*

E1: ¿Cuántos *hermanos* tiene *Amanda*?
E2: Tiene *dos.*

Actividad 3   Diálogo: ¿Quién es?

Don Eduardo Alvar habla con Paula Saucedo.

DON EDUARDO: Perdone, señorita Saucedo. ¿Quién es ese joven (muchacho)?
PAULA SAUCEDO: Su nombre es Jorge Saucedo.
DON EDUARDO: ¿Saucedo? ¿Es su hermano?
PAULA SAUCEDO: No. Su apellido es Saucedo también, pero no es mi hermano. Mis hermanos se llaman Raúl y Ernesto.

Actividad 4   Diálogo abierto: Mis hijos

E1: ¿Cómo se llama usted, *señor (señora, señorita)*?
E2: Me llamo _____.
E1: ¿Es usted *casado/a (soltero/a, viudo/a, divorciado/a)*?
E2: Soy _____.
E1: ¿Tiene usted hijos?
E2: Sí, tengo _____ hijo(s) y _____ hija(s). (No, no tengo hijos.)

¡OJO!

En las familias hispanas, los niños reciben mucha atención de sus padres y abuelos. Frecuentemente, los abuelos viven con la familia.

Actividad 5   Entrevista: Mi familia

1. ¿Cómo se llama tu *padre (madre, hermano/a, abuelo/a)*?
Mi *padre* se llama _____.
2. ¿Cuántos *hermanos (primos, abuelos, nietos)* tienes?
Tengo *dos hermanos.* (Tengo *un primo.* Tengo *una nieta.*)
3. ¿Eres casado/a? ¿Tienes hijos? Soy _____.
Tengo *dos* hijos. (*No tengo hijos.*)

¿Qué tenemos?

✳ Lea Gramática C.1–C.2.

Doña Lola tiene un coche nuevo.

Los discos compactos son de Amanda.

Ernestito y su perro Lobo son amigos.

Actividad 6   Diálogo: El coche de don Eduardo

ERNESTITO: ¿Cómo es su coche, señor Alvar?
DON EDUARDO: Mi coche es azul; es un poco viejo.
ERNESTITO: Yo no tengo coche, pero tengo una bicicleta nueva.
DON EDUARDO: Sí, y tu bicicleta es muy bonita.

Actividad 7   Descripción de dibujos: ¿De quién... ?

1. ¿Quién tiene dos camisas nuevas?
2. ¿Quién tiene dos perros?
3. ¿De quién es el vestido nuevo?
4. ¿Quién tiene una computadora?
5. ¿De quién es el carro nuevo?
6. ¿Quiénes tienen helados?

Actividad 8 Entrevista: Mi mascota y mi carro

1. —¿Tienes *mascota?*
   —Sí, tengo _____. / No, no tengo *mascota.*
2. —¿Cómo es?
   —Mi _____ es _____.
3. —¿Tienes *carro (motocicleta, bicicleta)?*
   —Sí, tengo un _____ (Ford, Toyota, Volvo). / No, no tengo *carro.* Tengo *motocicleta (bicicleta).*
4. —¿Cómo es tu *carro (motocicleta, bicicleta)?*
   —Mi *carro (motocicleta, bicicleta)* es _____.

Los números (10–110) y la edad

✳ **Lea Gramática C.3.**

10 diez	76 setenta y seis
20 veinte	80 ochenta
30 treinta	82 ochenta y dos
40 cuarenta	90 noventa
50 cincuenta	94 noventa y cuatro
60 sesenta	100 cien
70 setenta	110 ciento diez

Actividad 9 Diálogos: ¿Cuántos años tienen?

GRACIELA: Amanda, ¿quién es esa niña?
AMANDA: Es mi prima, Clarisa.
GRACIELA: ¿Cuántos años tiene?
AMANDA: Tiene sólo seis años y es muy inteligente.

DON EDUARDO: Señor Ruiz, ¿cuántos hijos tiene usted?
PEDRO RUIZ: Tengo dos hijas.
DON EDUARDO: ¿Y cuántos años tienen?
PEDRO RUIZ: Bueno, Clarisa tiene seis años y Marisa tiene cuatro.
DON EDUARDO: ¡Sólo dos hijas! ¡Cómo cambia el mundo!

Actividad 10 Diálogo abierto: ¿Cuántos años tienes?

E1: ¿Cuántos años tienes?
E2: Tengo _____ años.
E1: ¿Tienes hermanos?
E2: Sí, tengo _____ hermanos: _____ hermano(s) y _____ hermana(s). (No, no tengo hermanos; soy hijo único / hija única.)
E1: ¿Cómo se llama tu hermano/a mayor (menor)?
E2: Se llama _____.
E1: ¿Cuántos años tiene?
E2: Tiene _____ años.

Los idiomas y las nacionalidades

Hans Schumann es alemán y habla alemán.

Gina Sfreddo es italiana y habla italiano.

Iara Gomes y Zidia Oliveira son brasileñas y hablan portugués.

Masato Hamazaki y Goro Nishimura son japoneses y hablan japonés.

Rehana Hezar y Neda Nikraz son iraníes y hablan persa.

✳ **Lea Gramática C.4–C.5.**

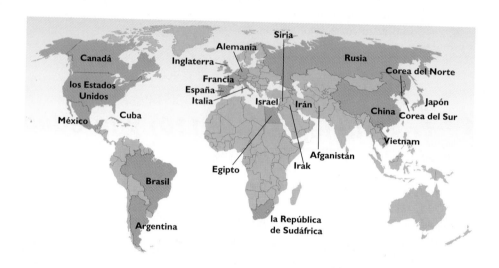

PAÍS	NACIONALIDAD	IDIOMA(S)
Afganistán	afgano/a	dari, pashto
Alemania	alemán, alemana	alemán
Argentina	argentino/a	español
Brasil	brasileño/a	portugués
Canadá	canadiense	inglés, francés
China	chino/a	chino
Corea (del Norte / del Sur)	coreano/a	coreano
Cuba	cubano/a	español
Egipto	egipcio/a	árabe
España	español(a)	español
Estados Unidos	estadounidense	inglés
Francia	francés, francesa	francés
Inglaterra	inglés, inglesa	inglés
Irán	iraní	persa
Irak	iraquí	árabe
Israel	israelí	hebreo
Italia	italiano/a	italiano
Japón	japonés, japonesa	japonés
México	mexicano/a	español
República de Sudáfrica	sudafricano/a	inglés, afrikaans, lenguas africanas
Rusia	ruso/a	ruso
Siria	sirio/a	árabe
Vietnam	vietnamita	vietnamita

Actividad 11 Asociaciones: ¿Qué nacionalidad? ¿Qué idioma?

Diga cuál es la nacionalidad de estas personas y qué idioma(s) hablan.

MODELO: Salma Hayek... México →
                Salma Hayek es mexicana y habla español.

PERSONA	PAÍS
1. Fidel Castro	Cuba
2. Ignacio Lula da Silva	Brasil
3. David Beckham	Inglaterra
4. Vladimir Putin	Rusia
5. Nicolas Sarkozy	Francia
6. Hosni Mubarak	Egipto
7. Celine Dion	Canadá
8. el rey Juan Carlos de Borbón	España
9. Alessandro del Piero	Italia
10. Gael García Bernal	México

Salma Hayek, actriz mexicana

Juan Carlos de Borbón, rey de España

Actividad 12 Diálogo abierto: Amigos internacionales

E1: ¿Tienes un amigo *mexicano* (una amiga *mexicana*)?
E2: Sí, se llama _____.
E1: ¿Hablas *español* o *inglés* con él (ella)?
E2: Hablo *inglés*. (Normalmente hablo *inglés,* pero a veces hablo *español* con él/ella.)

Actividad 13 Intercambios: Las vacaciones

MODELO: E1: Quiero viajar a *París* durante las vacaciones.
E2: ¿Hablas *francés*?
E1: Sí, hablo *un poco de francés.* (No, no hablo *nada de francés.* / Sí, hablo *francés muy bien.*)

CIUDADES

Roma	Madrid	Río de Janeiro
Londres	Buenos Aires	Montreal
Toronto	Moscú	Berlín
Los Ángeles	Pekín	Tokio

IDIOMAS

italiano	ruso	francés
inglés	chino	alemán
español	portugués	japonés

Frases útiles

un poco de   muy bien
nada de

De todo un poco

Entrevista: Su familia y sus amigos

Entreviste a su compañero/a.

—¿Son estadounidenses tus padres?
—Sí/No, mis padres son _____.
—¿Cuántos años tienen ellos?
—Mi padre tiene _____ años y mi madre tiene _____ años.
—¿Qué idiomas hablan?
—Mis padres hablan _____. (Mi padre habla _____ y mi madre habla _____.)
—¿Tienes muchos hermanos?
—Sí, tengo _____. (No, tengo sólo _____. / No, soy hijo único / hija única.)
—¿Cómo se llaman tus hermanos?
—Mis hermanos se llaman _____ y _____. (Mi hermano/a se llama _____.)
—¿Tienes un amigo / una amiga de *España*? (*México, Irán, Rusia, Italia, Francia,*
  etcétera)
—Sí, tengo un amigo / una amiga de _____.
—¿Cómo se llama tu amigo/a?
—Él/Ella se llama _____.
—¿Qué idiomas habla él/ella?
—Habla _____ y _____. (Habla sólo _____.)

Vea el **Resumen cultural** en este capítulo del *Cuaderno de actividades.*

Una familia hispana: la madre, el padre (los padres) y dos hijos (una hija y un hijo)

Vocabulario

La familia

The Family

el abuelo / la abuela	grandfather/grandmother
los abuelos	grandparents
el gemelo / la gemela	twin
el hijo / la hija	son / daughter
el hijo único / la hija única	only child (only son / only daughter)
los hijos	sons (sons and daughters; children)
la madre	mother
el nieto / la nieta	grandson / granddaughter
el padre	father
los padres	parents
el primo / la prima	cousin
el sobrino / la sobrina	nephew / niece
el tío / la tía	uncle / aunt

REPASO: el esposo, la esposa, el hermano, la hermana

Los países

Countries

Alemania	Germany
Corea del Norte / del Sur	North / South Korea
España	Spain
(los) Estados Unidos	United States
Inglaterra	England
(la) República de Sudáfrica	South Africa

PALABRAS SEMEJANTES: Afganistán, Argentina, Brasil, Canadá, China, Cuba, Egipto, Francia, Irak, Irán, Israel, Italia, Japón, México, Rusia, Siria, Vietnam

Las nacionalidades

Nationalities

alemán/alemana	German
brasileño/a	Brazilian
chino/a	Chinese
egipcio/a	Egyptian
español(a)	Spanish
estadounidense	American (United States citizen)
francés/francesa	French
inglés/inglesa	English
ruso/a	Russian
sudafricano/a	South African

PALABRAS SEMEJANTES: afgano/a, americano/a, árabe, argentino/a, canadiense, coreano/a, cubano/a, iraní, iraquí, israelí, italiano/a, japonés/japonesa, mexicano/a, portugués/portuguesa, sirio/a, vietnamita

Los idiomas

Languages

el alemán	German
el chino	Chinese
el español	Spanish
el francés	French
el hebreo	Hebrew
el inglés	English
las lenguas africanas	African languages
el ruso	Russian

PALABRAS SEMEJANTES: el afrikaans, el árabe, el coreano, el italiano, el japonés, el pashto, el portugués, el vietnamita

Las ciudades

Cities

Londres	London
Moscú	Moscow
Pekín	Beijing

PALABRAS SEMEJANTES: Berlín, Buenos Aires, Los Ángeles, Madrid, Montreal, Río de Janeiro, Roma, Tokio, Toronto

Los adjetivos

Adjectives

casado/a	married
divorciado/a	divorced
mayor (que)	older (than)
menor (que)	younger (than)
soltero/a	single, unmarried
viudo/a	widowed

Los verbos

Verbs

hablar	to speak
¿Hablas... ?	Do you speak . . . ?
Hablo...	I speak
quiero	I want
tener	to have
viajar	to travel

Expresiones útiles

Useful Expressions

¡Cómo cambia el mundo!	How the world changes!
¿Cuántos años tiene(s)?	How old are you?
Tengo... años.	I am . . . years old.

¿Cuántos... tiene(s)?	How many . . . do you have?
¿De quién es/son... ?	Whose is/are . . . ?
nada de	nothing, any (at all)
perdone	pardon me; excuse me
un poco de	a little
¿Qué tiene(n)... ?	What do/does . . . have?
¿Quién(es) tiene(n)... ?	Who has . . . ?

REPASO: mi(s), tu(s), su(s)

Palabras útiles
Useful Words

a veces	sometimes
la bicicleta	bicycle
bueno...	well . . .
el carro / el coche	car
de la	of the
del (de + el)	of the (*required contraction*)
durante	during
la edad	age
el helado	ice cream

el (la) joven	young person
la mascota	pet
pero	but
según	according to
sólo	only

PALABRAS SEMEJANTES: el disco compacto, la frase, internacional, la motocicleta, la parte, normalmente, las vacaciones

Los números
Numbers

setenta	seventy
ochenta	eighty
ochenta y cuatro	eighty-four
noventa	ninety
noventa y siete	ninety-seven
cien	one hundred
ciento uno	one-hundred one
ciento diez	one-hundred ten

Gramática y ejercicios

C.1 Expressing Possession: The Verbs *tener* and *ser de(l)*

Just like English, Spanish has several ways of expressing possession. Unlike English, however, Spanish does not use an apostrophe and *s*.

A. Perhaps the simplest way of expressing possession is to use the verb **tener*** (*to have*). Like the verb **ser, tener** is classified as an irregular verb because of changes in its stem.† The endings that attach to the stem, however, are regular.

tener = *to have*

tener (*to have*)		
(yo)	tengo	*I have*
(tú)	tienes	*you (inf. sing.) have*
(usted, él/ella)	tiene	*you (pol. sing.) have; he/she has*
(nosotros/as)	tenemos	*we have*
(vosotros/as)	tenéis	*you (inf. pl., Spain) have*
(ustedes, ellos/as)	tienen	*you (pl.) have; they have*

English: 's
    Mike**'s** new car
    Sarah**'s** friends
Spanish: **de** + person
    el carro nuevo **de Miguel**
    los amigos **de Sara**

—Profesora Martínez, ¿**tiene**
    usted un automóvil nuevo?
—Sí, **tengo** un Toyota verde.

—*Professor Martínez, do you*
    have a new automobile?
—*Yes, I have a green Toyota.*

B. The verb **ser** (*to be*) followed by the preposition **de** (*of*) can also be used to express possession. The equivalent of the English word *whose* is **¿de quién?** (literally, *of whom?* or *to whom?*).

—**¿De quién** es el cuaderno?
—**Es de** Carmen.

—*To whom does the notebook belong?*
—*It's Carmen's.*

C. The preposition **de** (*of*) followed by the masculine article **el** (*the*) contracts to **del** (*of the*).

de + **el** = **del**
de + **la** remains **de la**

—**¿De quién** es el bolígrafo?
—**Es del** profesor.

—*Whose pen is this?*
—*It's the professor's.*

The other combinations of **de** + article do not contract: **de la, de los, de las.**

Los zapatos **de la** niña son bonitos.
Los libros **de los** estudiantes.
    son nuevos.

The girl's shoes are pretty.
The students' books
    are new.

---

*Recognition: **vos tenés**
†See **Gramática C.5** for more information on verb stems.

Ejercicio 1

Diga qué tienen estas personas. Use las formas del verbo **tener.**

MODELO: Luis *tiene* una bicicleta negra.

1. Pablo _____ una chaqueta negra.
2. Esteban y yo _____ un coche viejo.
3. Mónica, tú no _____ el libro de español, ¿verdad?
4. (Yo) _____ dos lápices y un cuaderno sobre mi pupitre.
5. Nora y Alberto no _____ hijos, ¿verdad?

Ejercicio 2

Diga de quién son estas cosas.

MODELO: Mónica / bolígrafo → El bolígrafo *es de* Mónica.

1. la profesora Martínez / carro

2. Luis / camisa

3. Nora / perro

4. Esteban / lentes

5. Alberto / saco

6. Carmen / bicicleta

C.2 Expressing Possession: Possessive Adjectives

Possession can be indicated by the following possessive adjectives. The particular adjective you choose depends on the owner, but the adjective itself, like other Spanish adjectives, agrees in number and gender with the word it describes: that is, with the *object owned*, not with the owner.

su = *his, her, your, their*
(*one item*)
sus = *his, her, your, their*
(*multiple items*)

Remember that you will acquire much of this material in time as you listen to and read Spanish.

SINGULAR OWNER

mi	*my*
tu*	*your (inf. sing.)*
su	*your (pol. sing.), his/her*

PLURAL OWNER

nuestro/a	*our*
vuestro/a	*your (inf. pl., Spain)*
su	*your (pl.); their*

¿**Mi** hermano? Tiene el pelo negro.
Nuestro carro nuevo es rojo.
Nuestra profesora es Adela Martínez.

My brother? He has black hair.
Our new car is red.
Our professor is Adela Martínez.

SINGULAR POSSESSION (PLURAL POSSESSIONS)

mi(s)	*my*
tu(s)	*your (inf. sing.)*
su(s)	*your (pol. sing.), his/her*

SINGULAR POSSESSION (PLURAL POSSESSIONS)

nuestro(s)/a(s)	*our*
vuestro(s)/a(s)	*your (inf. pl., Spain)*
su(s)	*your (pl.); their*

Mi falda es vieja, pero **mis** zapatos son nuevos.
Clarisa y Marisa tienen una casa grande. **Su** casa es grande.
Raúl, ¿**tus** hermanas son gemelas?
Clarisa y Marisa tienen dos tías y un tío. **Su** tío se llama Raúl.

My skirt is old, but my shoes are new.

Clarisa and Marisa have a big house. Their house is big.
Raúl, are your sisters twins?
Clarisa and Marisa have two aunts and one uncle. Their uncle's name is Raúl.

Keep in mind that the pronoun **su(s)** can have various meanings: *your, his, her,* or *their.* The context normally clarifies to whom **su(s)** refers.

Luis no tiene **sus** libros.
El señor y la señora Ruiz tienen **su** coche aquí.

Luis doesn't have his books.
Mr. and Mrs. Ruiz have their car here.

Generally speaking, use **usted** and **su(s)** when addressing a person by his or her last name.

Señor Saucedo, ¿es **usted** mexicano? ¿Y **sus** padres?

Mr. Saucedo, are you Mexican? And your parents?

When using a first name to address someone, use **tú** and **tu(s).**

Raúl, **tu** amiga es inglesa, pero **tú** y **tus** padres son mexicanos, ¿no?

Raúl, your friend is English, but you and your parents are Mexican, aren't you?

*****Tú** (with an accent mark) corresponds to *you;* **tu** (without an accent mark) corresponds to *your.*

Ejercicio 3

Complete estas oraciones con la forma apropiada del adjetivo posesivo: **mi(s), tu(s), su(s)** o **nuestro(s)/a(s).**

MODELO: Estela, ¿dónde están *tus* hijos?

1. Mi novia no tiene _____ libro de matemáticas.
2. El profesor no tiene _____ botas.
3. No tienes _____ reloj, ¿verdad?
4. No tengo _____ zapatos de tenis.
5. No tenemos _____ cuadernos.
6. —Señores Ruiz, ¿dónde están _____ hijas?
   — _____ hijas, Clarisa y Marisa, están en casa.
7. Guillermo no tiene _____ chaqueta.
8. Estela y Ernesto no tienen _____ automóvil todavía.
9. Graciela, _____ ojos son muy bonitos.
10. No tengo _____ bicicleta aquí.

> **los señores Ruiz** = Mr. and Mrs. Ruiz

Ejercicio 4

Complete los diálogos con la forma apropiada del adjetivo posesivo.

MODELO: RAÚL: ¡Qué inteligente es *tu* amiga!
ALBERTO: Sí, y ella es idealista, también.

1. RAÚL: Silvia, _____ perro, Sultán, es muy inteligente.
   SILVIA: Gracias, Raúl, pero no es _____ perro. Es de Nacho.

2. CLARA: Pilar, ¿tienen carro _____ padres?
   PILAR: Sí, _____ padres tienen un Seat rojo.

3. JOSÉ: ¿Cómo se llama la novia de Andrés?
   PILAR: _____ novia se llama Ana.

4. ABUELA: Marisa y Clarisa, ¡qué bonitas son _____ faldas! ¿Son nuevas?
   MARISA: Sí, abuelita. Y _____ zapatos son nuevos también.

Possession may also be indicated by the use of possessive pronouns. These pronouns agree in gender and number with the noun they describe; that is, with the item possessed.

¿Es ésta tu blusa?	*Is this one your blouse?*
No, no es **mía;** es **tuya.**	*No, it's not mine; it's yours.*
¿Son de Alfredo estos zapatos?	*Are these shoes Alfredo's?*
Sí, son **suyos.**	*Yes, they are his.*
¿Es de Carmen este libro?	*Is this book Carmen's?*
No, no es **suyo;** es **mío.**	*No, it's not hers; it's mine.*
¿Son de ustedes estos cuadernos?	*Do these notebooks belong to you (all)?*
Sí, son **nuestros.**	*Yes, they are ours.*

For more practice with these pronouns see the **Expansión gramatical 1** in the *Cuaderno de actividades*.

SINGULAR OWNER (SINGULAR AND PLURAL POSSESSIONS)		PLURAL OWNER (SINGULAR AND PLURAL POSSESSIONS)	
mío(s)/mía(s)	*mine*	nuestro(s)/nuestra(s)	*ours*
tuyo(s)/tuya(s)	*yours (inf. sing.)*	vuestro(s)/vuestra(s)	*yours (inf. pl., Spain)*
suyo(s)/suya(s)	*his/hers/yours (pol. sing.)*	suyo(s)/suya(s)	*theirs/yours (pol. pl.)*

C.3 Expressing Age: The Verb *tener*

> English: **I am** 24 (years old).
> Spanish: **Tengo** 24 (años).

In English, the verb *to be* is used for telling age (*I am 21 years old*), but in Spanish the verb **tener** expresses age. To ask about age, use the question **¿Cuántos años... ?** (*How many years . . . ?*)

—Señora Saucedo, **¿cuántos años tiene** usted?	—*Mrs. Saucedo, how old are you?*
—**Tengo** treinta y cinco (años).	—*I'm 35 (years old).*

¿RECUERDA?

In **Gramática C.1** you learned the present-tense forms of the verb **tener.** Review them now, if necessary.

Ejercicio 5

Escriba la edad de estos amigos.

MODELO: Rogelio Varela / 21 → Rogelio Varela *tiene 21 años.*

1. Adriana Bolini / 35
2. Carla Espinosa / 22
3. Rubén Hernández Arenas / 38
4. Susana Yamasaki González / 33
5. doña María Eulalia González de Saucedo / 79

Ejercicio 6

Escriba la edad de estas personas.

¿RECUERDA?

In **Gramática B.5** you learned that adjectives that end in **-o/-a** have four forms:

rojo (*masc. sing.*)
roja (*fem. sing.*)
rojos (*masc. pl.*)
rojas (*fem. pl.*)

don Eduardo Alvar (n. 1930) Estela Saucedo (n. 1975) Ernestito Saucedo (n. 2002) Amanda Saucedo (n. 1996) doña Lola Batini (n. 1968)

C.4 Describing People: Adjectives of Nationality

A. Adjectives of nationality that end in **-o/-a,** just like other adjectives that end in **-o/-a,** have four forms.

	SINGULAR	**PLURAL**
Masculine	chin**o**	chin**os**
Feminine	chin**a**	chin**as**

Victoria no es **china,** pero habla chino muy bien.

Victoria is not Chinese, but she speaks Chinese very well.

B. Adjectives of nationality that end in a consonant have four forms also.

	SINGULAR	**PLURAL**
Masculine	inglés*	ingles**es**
Feminine	ingles**a**	ingles**as**

John es **inglés,** pero su madre es **española.**

John is English, but his mother is Spanish.

C. Adjectives of nationality that end in **-e** have only two forms.

	SINGULAR	**PLURAL**
Masculine/Feminine	canadiens**e**	canadiens**es**

D. Adjectives of nationality and the names of languages are not capitalized in Spanish. Names of countries, however, are capitalized.

> Do capitalize names of countries in Spanish:
> **Colombia**
> **Panamá**
> **España**
> **Inglaterra**
> Do not capitalize nationalities or languages in Spanish:
> **colombiano**
> **panameñas**
> **español**
> **inglés**

Ejercicio 7

¿De qué nacionalidad son estas personas?

MODELO: el señor Shaoyi He → *Es chino.*

1. _____C_____ la señorita Fernández
2. _____G_____ los señores Watanabe
3. _____H_____ el señor Hartenstein
4. _____I_____ las hermanas Lemieux
5. _____F_____ la señorita Cardinale y la señorita Lomeli
6. _____B_____ la señorita Tang
7. _____E_____ el señor Thatcher
8. _____A_____ la señorita Nikraz
9. _____D_____ los señores Hassan

a. iraní
b. chino/china
c. español/española
d. sirio/siria
e. inglés/inglesa
f. italiano/italiana
g. japonés/japonesa
h. alemán/alemana
i. francés/francesa

---

*See the *Cuaderno de actividades*—**Capítulos 2, 3, 5, 8,** and Appendix 3 of this text—for details on written accent marks.

infinitive = verb form ending in **-ar, -er,** or **-ir**

You will not find the conjugated forms of a verb—**hablo, hablas, habla,** and so forth—as main entries in a dictionary. You must know the infinitive in order to look up a verb.

C.5 Talking about Habitual Actions: Present Tense of Regular *-ar* Verbs

A. The verb form listed in the dictionary and in most vocabulary lists is the *infinitive.* In Spanish many infinitives end in **-ar** (**llamar, llevar**), but some end in **-er** (**tener**) or in **-ir** (**vivir**). The forms of the verb are called its *conjugation.* Below is the present-tense conjugation of the regular **-ar** verb **hablar.** * Regular verbs are classified as such because their *stem* (the infinitive minus the ending) remains the same in all forms; the only change is in the endings, which are added to the stem.

¿RECUERDA?

In Spanish the forms of a verb change to show who is performing the action. You have already seen the forms of **llevar (Gramática A.1), ser (Gramática A.3),** and **tener (Gramática C.1).** Now look at the drawings on this page and notice the forms of the verb **hablar** (*to speak*).

hablar (*to speak*)		
(yo)	hablo	*I speak*
(tú)	hablas	*you (inf. sing.) speak*
(usted, él/ella)	habla	*you (pol. sing.) speak; he/she speaks*
(nosotros/as)	hablamos	*we speak*
(vosotros/as)	habláis	*you (inf. pl., Spain) speak*
(ustedes, ellos/as)	hablan	*you (pl.) speak; they speak*

B. Remember that Spanish verb endings indicate, in many cases, who or what the subject is, so it is not always necessary to mention the subject explicitly. That is why the pronouns are in parentheses in the preceding table.

—¿**Hablas** español?   —*Do you speak Spanish?*
—Sí, y **hablo** inglés también.   —*Yes, and I speak English too.*

These endings take time to acquire. You can understand and communicate with an incomplete knowledge of them, but they are important; make sure you include them when you write.

---

*Recognition: **vos hablás**

Ejercicio 8

Estamos en una fiesta en casa de Esteban. Complete estas oraciones con la forma correcta del verbo **hablar.**

1. Esteban, las dos chicas rubias _____ alemán, ¿verdad?
2. Mónica, ¿_____ francés tu padre?
3. Alberto y Luis no _____ francés.
4. Nora, ¿_____ tú chino?
5. No, yo no _____ chino, pero _____ un poco de japonés.

Ejercicio 9

¿Qué idiomas hablan estas personas? Complete cada oración con la forma correcta del verbo **hablar** y el idioma apropiado.

1. Adriana Bolini es argentina y _____ italiano y _____.
2. Los señores Saucedo son mexicanos y _____ _____.
3. Li Yuan Tseng y Mei Chang son chinos y _____ _____.
4. Kevin Browne y Stephen Craig son ingleses. _____ _____.
5. Talia Meir y Behira Sefamí son israelíes. _____ _____.
6. ¿Eres rusa? Entonces, tú _____ _____.

Los datos personales y las actividades

METAS

In **Capítulo 1** you will learn to tell time and give personal information: your address, your phone number, and your birthday. You and your classmates will talk about sports and other leisure-time activities you enjoy.

LATIN JAZZ II, por Casimiro González (Cuba)

Sobre el artista: Casimiro González nació en La Habana, Cuba. Estudió arte en la Escuela Nacional de Bellas Artes y ahora vive en los Estados Unidos. Sus pinturas, de vivos colores, se exhiben en Francia, Italia, España, México, Colombia, Argentina, Puerto Rico, Alemania y el Canadá.

¡Conozca Cuba!

Nombre del país: la República de Cuba

Ciudad capital: La Habana

Ciudades principales: Santiago, Guantánamo, Holguín, Camagüey, Cienfuegos

Moneda: el peso cubano

Idiomas: el español

Población: 11.400.000

Día de la Independencia: el 10 de octubre

Fiestas típicas: el Carnaval, el Triunfo de la Revolución

Comidas típicas: el lechón asado, la yuca con mojo, «moros y cristianos», los tostones, el congrí oriental, el picadillo a la criolla

Música típica: el son, la rumba, el danzón, el mambo, la salsa

Gente famosa: José Martí, Nicolás Guillén, Reinaldo Arenas, Chucho Valdés, Omara Portuondo, Fidel Castro, Celia Cruz

Código del país por Internet: .cu

Voces cubanas

la fruta bomba	**la papaya**
¿Qué bola asere?	**¿Qué tal amigo?**
una saya	**una falda**
un socio	**un amigo**
un taco	**un zapato**

En este capítulo...

 **ACTIVIDADES DE COMUNICACIÓN**

- Las fechas y los cumpleaños
- Datos personales: El teléfono y la dirección
- La hora
- Las actividades favoritas y los deportes

 **EN RESUMEN**

 **LECTURAS Y CULTURA**

- **Ventanas culturales**
  Nuestra comunidad: La misión personal de Rigoberta Menchú
- **Enlace a la música:** Cuba
- **Ventanas al pasado**
  Frida y Diego
- **Lectura**
  La pasión por los deportes

GRAMÁTICA Y EJERCICIOS

1.1 Counting: Numbers 100–1000 and Dates

1.2 Talking about Habitual Actions: Present Tense of Regular **-er** and **-ir** Verbs

1.3 Asking Questions: Question Formation

1.4 Telling Time: Hours and Minutes

1.5 Expressing Likes and Dislikes: **gustar** + Infinitive

MULTIMEDIA   ONLINE LEARNING CENTER   www.mhhe.com/dosmundos7
CENTRO   Your media center for languages   QUIA   DVD

Actividades de comunicación y lecturas

Las fechas y los cumpleaños

✳ **Lea Gramática 1.1.**

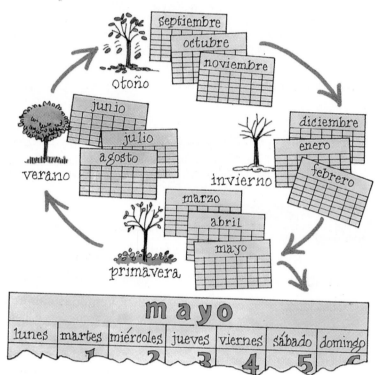

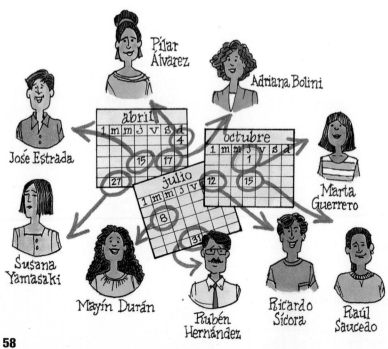

Actividad 1 Intercambios: El cumpleaños

Hágale preguntas a su compañero/a sobre los dibujos de la
página anterior.

MODELOS: E1: ¿Cuándo nació *José Estrada*?
E2: Nació el *15 de abril.*

E1: ¿Quién nació el *15 de octubre*?
E2: *Raúl Saucedo.*

Actividad 2 Intercambios: Los estudiantes de la profesora Martínez

MODELO: E1: ¿Cuándo nació *Mónica Clark*?
E2: Nació *el 19 de agosto de 1992.*
E1: ¿Dónde nació?
E2: Nació en *Ann Arbor, Michigan.*

NOMBRE	LUGAR DE NACIMIENTO	FECHA DE NACIMIENTO
Carmen Bradley	Corpus Christi, Texas	23 de junio de 1991
Mónica Clark	Ann Arbor, Michigan	19 de agosto de 1992
Albert Moore	Seattle, Washington	22 de diciembre de 1979
Nora Morales	San Antonio, Texas	4 de julio de 1985
Luis Ventura	Albuquerque, Nuevo México	1 de diciembre de 1989
Lan Vo	Long Beach, California	5 de noviembre de 1990

Actividad 3 Intercambios: ¿Qué quieres para tu cumpleaños?

MODELO: E1: ¿Quieres *un reloj* para tu cumpleaños?
E2: Sí, quiero *un reloj.* (No, no quiero *un reloj,* quiero *una mochila.*)

1. un reloj

2. una computadora

3. una bicicleta

4. un iPod

5. una patineta

6. un suéter

7. una tabla de snowboard

8. entradas para un concierto

(continúa)

9. un coche

10. una mochila

11. una cámara digital

12. un televisor

13. discos compactos

14. un equipo de música

Datos personales: El teléfono y la dirección

✳ **Lea Gramática 1.2–1.3.**

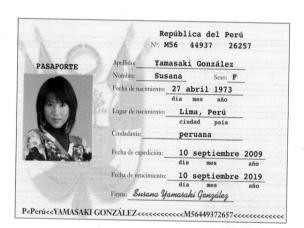

República del Perú
Nº M56 44937 26257

PASAPORTE

Apellido: **Yamasaki González**

Nombre: **Susana** Sexo: **F**

Fecha de nacimiento: **27 abril 1973**
  día   mes   año

Lugar de nacimiento: **Lima, Perú**
  ciudad país

Ciudadanía: **peruana**

Fecha de expedición: **10 septiembre 2009**
  día   mes   año

Fecha de vencimiento: **10 septiembre 2019**
  día   mes   año

Firma: *Susana Yamasaki González*

P<Perú<<YAMASAKI GONZÁLEZ<<<<<<<<<<<M56449372657<<<<<<<<<<<

Actividad 4   Entrevista: Sus datos personales

Usted es turista y su compañero/a es agente de inmigración. Conteste las preguntas que el agente le hace.

1. ¿Cómo se llama usted?
2. ¿Cuál es su ciudadanía? (estadounidense, mexicana, vietnamita, canadiense, iraní, china, inglesa, etcétera)
3. ¿Cuál es su fecha de nacimiento?
4. ¿Cuál es su lugar de nacimiento?
5. ¿Cuál es su dirección?
6. ¿Cuál es su número de teléfono?
7. ¿Cuál es su estado civil? ¿Es usted soltero/a? (casado/a, divorciado/a, viudo/a)

VENTANAS CULTURALES   Nuestra comunidad

La misión personal de Rigoberta Menchú

Rigoberta Menchú es de Guatemala, está casada y tiene un hijo. Rigoberta es una mujer **maya quiché** muy fuerte. Su misión personal es **ayudar** a la **gente indígena** de su país y de todo el mundo. Rigoberta viaja mucho. Visita escuelas y universidades para hablar de sus experiencias y para describir la mala situación de los indígenas guatemaltecos.

   Esta mujer excepcional recibe el **Premio Nóbel de la Paz** en 1992. En su libro autobiográfico *Me llamo Rigoberta Menchú y así me nació la conciencia* (1983), Rigoberta narra una historia muy humana que protesta la violencia militar. La famosa indígena Menchú tiene una **meta** importante: justicia social para Guatemala y toda la América Latina.

Comprensión

1. Describa a Rigoberta Menchú. ¿De dónde es? ¿Cómo es ella?
2. Rigoberta viaja a escuelas y universidades para hablar de...
   a. su familia   **b.** su Premio Nóbel
   c. la situación de los indígenas de Guatemala   **d.** sus amigos

VOCABULARIO ÚTIL

maya quiché	*indigenous people from western Guatemala*
ayudar	*to help*
la gente indígena	*indigenous people*
el Premio Nobel de la Paz	*the Nobel Peace Prize*
la meta	*goal*

Actividad 5   Diálogo abierto: Datos personales

E1: ¿Cómo te llamas?
E2: Me llamo _____. ¿Y tú?
E1: _____. ¿Dónde vives?
E2: Vivo en la calle _____, número _____. ¿Y tú?
E1: Vivo en la calle _____, número _____.
E2: Y, ¿cuál es tu dirección electrónica?
E1: Es _____ @ _____. (No tengo.) ¿Y tu dirección?
E2: Es _____ @ _____. (No tengo.) ¿Tienes (teléfono) celular?
E1: Sí, mi número es el _____. (No, no tengo.) ¿Y tú?
E2: Sí, mi número es el _____. (No, no tengo.)

Enlace a la música

Cuba

La música popular cubana es rítmica, apasionada, y nace de la unión de dos culturas: la española y la africana. En el siglo[1] XVI llegan a Cuba los esclavos[2] africanos para trabajar en las plantaciones de caña de azúcar.[3] La religión de estos esclavos se combina con la católica, y de manera similar surge la expresión musical afrocubana, en ceremonias religiosas que se celebran con mucha danza. El tambor,[4] que tiene varios tipos y nombres —bongó, tumbadora— es el instrumento principal en estas ceremonias. El tambor facilita el ritmo, y el ritmo es esencial en todas las formas musicales de Cuba.

Algunos de los estilos musicales cubanos más importantes son la rumba, el danzón, el son y el mambo. La rumba es música de fiesta que nace en los puertos[5] de La Habana y se hace popular en el siglo XIX. También de ese siglo data el danzón, pieza instrumental con influencia europea. El danzón es la música preferida por la clase alta. A comienzos[6] del siglo XX llega el son, con su estilo de ritmo sincopado y sus canciones poéticas. El son incorpora instrumentos de las tres culturas principales de Cuba: la indígena, la africana y la de los campesinos[7] blancos. Por eso se le considera la forma más representativa de la música popular cubana.

Hay otras formas musicales que datan del siglo XX. En la década de los 50 es muy popular el bolero, un tipo de canción romántica, y también el mambo, que transforma el danzón con ritmos africanos. Durante los años 60 surgen cantautores[8] de fama mundial, como Pablo Milanés y Silvio Rodríguez. En los años 70 se forman grupos muy populares; entre ellos Los Van Van, que combinan el son, el jazz y el rock en sus canciones. La rica tradición musical de Cuba también nos ofrece la salsa y el jazz cubano. Además, de este país caribeño son Ibrahim Ferrer y Omara Portuondo, cantantes admirados y estrellas[9] de la película *Buena Vista Social Club*.

Comprensión

1. ¿Cuáles de estas formas musicales *no* son típicas de Cuba?

    a. el mambo **b.** el danzón **c.** el rock **d.** el son **e.** el bolero **f.** el blues **g.** la rumba

2. ¿Cuál es la forma más representativa de la música popular cubana? ¿Por qué?

[1]*century* [2]*slaves* [3]*caña... sugarcane* [4]*drum* [5]*ports* [6]*A comienzos... At the beginning* [7]*peasants* [8]*singer-songwriters* [9]*stars*

La hora

★ **Lea Gramática 1.4.**

¿Qué hora es?

Es la una.

Son las tres.

Son las nueve menos diez.

Es la una y media.

Son las diez menos veinte.

Son las once y cuarto.

Es mediodía.

Son las siete y seis.

Son las tres menos veinticinco.

Es medianoche.

¡OJO!

En muchas partes del mundo hispano se usa el reloj de 24 horas. Después del mediodía, 1:00 = 13:00, 2:00 = 14:00, 3:00 = 15:00, etcétera. La medianoche (12:00) = 00:00.

Actividad 6   Diálogo: ¿Qué hora es?

SRA. SILVA: Perdón, don Anselmo, ¿qué hora tiene?
DON ANSELMO: *Son las siete y cuarto.*
SRA. SILVA: Muchas gracias.

PAULA SAUCEDO: Oye, Ernesto, ¿qué hora tienes?
ERNESTO SAUCEDO: *Es casi medianoche.*
PAULA SAUCEDO: *¡Ya es tarde!*

Expresiones útiles

Es mediodía.
Son las 5:00 de la mañana.

Es hora de comer.
¡Es (muy) temprano!

Actividad 7 Intercambios: ¿Qué hora es?

Escuche a su profesor(a). Diga el nombre de la ciudad que corresponde a la hora que él/ella dice. Luego, hágale preguntas a su compañero/a según el modelo.

MODELO: E1: ¿Qué hora es en _____?
E2: Es la _____. / Son las _____.

San Juan

Chicago

San Francisco

Nueva York

París

Berlín

La Habana

Madrid

Moscú

Caracas

Washington, D.C.

México, D.F.

Buenos Aires

Bogotá

El Paso

Actividad 8 Del mundo hispano: Programas de televisión

Hágale preguntas sobre la siguiente teleguía a un compañero / una compañera.

1. ¿A qué hora es el programa *Ruleta de la suerte*? ¿En qué canal se presenta?
2. ¿A qué hora es el programa *España directo*? ¿En qué canal se presenta?
3. ¿A qué hora es el programa *Informativos Telecinco*? ¿En qué canal se presenta?
4. ¿A qué hora es el programa *Destilando amor*? ¿En qué canal se presenta?
5. ¿En qué canal se presenta el programa *Los Simpson*? ¿A qué hora es?
6. ¿En qué canal se presenta el programa *¿Sabes más que un niño de primaria?* ¿A qué hora es?
7. ¿En qué canal se presenta el programa *Aquí hay tomate*? ¿A qué hora es?
8. ¿En qué canal se presenta el programa *Pasapalabra*? ¿A qué hora es?

Expresiones útiles

Es a la(s) _____.   Se presenta en el canal _____.

Miércoles, 2 de agosto

TVE

06:00 Noticias 24h Informativo

10:00 Saber vivir: *Consulta de nutrición y cocina de verano*

11:30 Por la mañana Magazine. Presentado por Silvia Jato e Iñaki del Moral

13:15 El negociador Concurso dinámico y cargado de premios

14:00 Informativo territorial Programa informativo

14:30 Corazón de verano Conozca la información de la vida de los famosos

15:00 Telediario I Informativo. Presentación: Ana Blanco y Julián Reyes (deportes)

15:55 El tiempo

16:00 Amar en tiempos revueltos Telenovela ambientada en la guerra civil española y los primeros años del franquismo

16:50 Destilando amor Telenovela

17:45 La viuda de blanco Telenovela

18:25 España directo Las noticias más importantes en las ciudades y pueblos de España

20:00 Gente Magazine. Presentado por Sonia Ferrer y María José Molina

21:00 Telediario 2 Informativo

21:55 El tiempo

22:00 El ojo público del ciudadano: *¡Jóvenes y consumo!* Presentado por Juan Ramón Lucas

00:30 La transición: *El Rey* Documental sobre el primer gobierno de la monarquía

01:45 Telediario 3 Informativo

02:15 Historia sobre ruedas Documental

03:30 Noticias 24h Informativo

Antena 3

06:00 Las noticias de la mañana Informativo

06:30 Megatrix Programía infantil que incluye *El Equipo A, Shin Chan, Heidi, Lizzie, El Príncipe de Bel Air*

12:30 Ruleta de la suerte Concurso ¡Gánese un coche nuevo!

14:00 Los Simpson Dibujos animados

15:00 Noticias I Informativo. Presentado por Pilar Galán y José Luque

15:55 El tiempo con Joan Escoda

16:00 Los Simpson Dibujos animados

16:30 Zorro Telenovela

18:00 En antena splash Magazine vespertino con Ximo Rovira

19:15 El diario de verano Talkshow con Yolanda Vásquez

20:15 Uno contra 100 Concurso. Presentado por Carlos Sobera

21:00 Antena 3 Noticias 2 Informativo. Presentado por Lourdes Maldonado y José Luque. Incluye El tiempo

22:00 ¿Sabes más que un niño de primaria? Concurso. Ramón García es el 'maestro' y presentador en este programa en el cual los adultos tienen que contestar preguntas de la Educación Primaria

23:15 Video por un tubo Humor. El programa ofrece una selección de los mejores instantes de los videos caseros

01:00 Boston legal: *Armados* Lori y Brad defienden a una mujer acusada de haber asesinado a su esposo y la amante de él

02:30 Supernova Concurso

Tele 5

06:30 Fusión sonora Música

07:00 Informativo Telecinco matinal Presentado por Yolanda Benítez

08:45 Día de suerte Concurso

09:45 Jake 2.0: *El último hombre* Serie

10:45 El programa de verano Magazine. Presentado por Maxim Huerta y Óscar Martínez

14:30 Informativo Telecinco Presentado por Agustín Hernández

15:30 Aquí hay tomate Magazine. Las andanzas de las estrellas con suculentas exclusivas

17:00 Yo soy Bea Telenovela Capítulo 263. Bea recibe una sorpresa cuando acude a la cita

17:45 Está pasando Magazine. Presentado por Emilio Pineda y Lucía Riaño

20:15 Pasapalabra Concurso. Presentado por Christián Gálvez

20:55 Informativos Telecinco Informativo. Presentado por Ángeles Blanco

21:20 Escenas de matrimonio Humor. Muestra las divertidas reacciones de tres parejas ante situaciones similares

22:00 Nadie es perfecto Reality Show dirigido por Jesús Vásquez. Hay dos equipos, uno que intenta mejorar su aspecto físico y el otro que intenta mejorar su conocimiento de la cultura

01:00 TNT Show presentado por Yolanda Flores

02:15 Noche de suerte Concurso

03:15 Infocomerciales Televenta

Las actividades favoritas y los deportes

✳ **Lea Gramática 1.5.**

Un fin de semana típico de los Saucedo

A Guillermo y a sus amigos les gusta jugar al fútbol.

A Estela le gusta ir de compras.

A Amanda y a Graciela les gusta jugar al tenis.

A Ernesto le gusta leer.

A Ernesto y a Guillermo les gusta ver un partido de béisbol en el estadio.

A Ernestito le gusta andar en bicicleta.

A Amanda le gusta ver su telenovela favorita.

A los Saucedo les gusta cenar en un restaurante italiano.

Actividad 9 Intercambios: El fin de semana

MODELOS: E1: ¿A quién le gusta *jugar al basquetbol*?
E2: A *Ricardo Sícora*.

E1: ¿Qué le gusta hacer a *Ricardo los sábados*?
E2: Le gusta *ir al cine*.

● **REFRÁN**

No puedes andar y quieres correr.

(*You're biting off more than you can chew. Literally, You can't walk and you want to run.*)

NOMBRE	LOS SÁBADOS LE GUSTA	LOS DOMINGOS LE GUSTA...
Ricardo Sícora, 18 años Caracas, Venezuela	ir al cine	jugar al basquetbol
Adriana Bolini, 35 años Buenos Aires, Argentina	explorar el Internet	jugar al tenis
Raúl Saucedo, 19 años México, D.F., México	salir a bailar	ver un partido de fútbol
Nacho Padilla, 21 años México, D.F., México	ver la televisión	andar en patineta
Carla Espinosa, 22 años San Juan, Puerto Rico	ir de compras	ir a la playa

Actividad 10 Preferencias: Los gustos

Exprese su opinión.

MODELO: E1: (A mí) No me gusta acampar.
         E2: A mí tampoco.

1. Por lo general (no) me gusta...
2. Durante las vacaciones (no) me gusta.....
3. Por la noche, a mis padres (no) les gusta....
4. A mi profesor(a) de español (no) le gusta....

Y tú, ¿qué dices?

¡Qué interesante!	¡No lo creo!	A mí no
¡Qué divertido!	¡No me digas!	A mí también
¡Qué aburrido!	A mí sí	A mí tampoco
No me gusta _____,		ni _____

Frases útiles

acampar
andar en bicicleta
bailar por la noche
cenar en restaurantes elegantes
cocinar
correr
dormir todo el día
hacer ejercicio
ir a fiestas
ir al cine
jugar en la nieve
leer el periódico
nadar en una piscina
patinar en el hielo
trotar
ver la televisión

Actividad 11 Entrevista: ¿Qué te gusta hacer?

MODELO: E1: ¿Te gusta *viajar*?
         E2: Sí, *me gusta mucho* viajar. (No, *no me gusta viajar*.)

1. ver la televisión
2. cenar en restaurantes
3. pescar
4. bailar en discotecas
5. cocinar
6. viajar en carro
7. escuchar música
8. escribir mensajes electrónicos
9. sacar fotos
10. trabajar en el jardín

VENTANAS AL PASADO

Frida y Diego

Diego Rivera (1886–1957) es fundador del muralismo
mexicano junto con David Alfaro Siqueiros y José Clemente
Orozco. Rivera estudia pintura en México y París, donde vive
doce años. Muchos de sus murales celebran la victoria sobre
los conquistadores españoles y también la Revolución
Mexicana. Otros **temas** frecuentes son las **costumbres**
mexicanas, el **obrero,** la educación y la historia. Influye en
Rivera la escultura de los mayas y los aztecas, pero Rivera
combina también el estilo y los colores brillantes del arte
popular en sus murales.

Frida Kahlo (1907–1954), esposa
de Diego Rivera, es una artista
extraordinaria por su persistencia en
situaciones difíciles. A la edad de
seis años sufre de poliomielitis; a los
18 años sufre un serio accidente en
un autobús. Mientras se recupera del
accidente, **aprende** a pintar. En su **obra**
predominan los **autorretratos,** por
razones obvias: las consecuencias de
su accidente afectan su movilidad. Los
símbolos de Frida son **sencillos** y
revelan sus sufrimientos y su relación
con Diego.

VOCABULARIO ÚTIL	
los temas	*themes*
las cos-	*customs,*
tumbres	*habits,*
	practices
el obrero	*worker*
aprende	*learns*
la obra	*work of art*
los auto-	*self-portraits*
rretratos	
sencillos	*simple*

Comprensión

1. ¿Cuáles son los temas frecuentes en
   la obra de Diego Rivera?
   a. las costumbres   **b.** la educación   **c.** los accidentes
   d. la historia   **e.** las relaciones personales
2. Frida Kahlo persiste en situaciones difíciles. ¿Cuáles son estas situaciones?
   a. la poliomielitis   **b.** un accidente en su casa
   c. la Revolución Mexicana   **d.** un accidente en un autobús

Actividad 12 Intercambios: Los Juegos Panamericanos

MODELOS:
> E1: ¿Qué días hay competición de *baloncesto* (*basquetbol*)?
> E2: *Del 15 al 19 de octubre y del 21 al 22 de octubre.*
>
> E1: ¿A qué hora del día son las competiciones de *gimnasia el 15 de octubre?*
> E2: *Por la mañana, por la tarde y por la noche.*

XV Juegos Deportivos Panamericanos
Octubre 2011
Calendario de competencia
Guadalajara, México

Evento	V 14	S 15	D 16	L 17	M 18	M 19	J 20	V 21	S 22	D 23	L 24	M 25	M 26	J 27	V 28	S 29	D 30
Acto de inauguración	●																
Acuáticos																	
Clavados						●	●	●	●								
Natación											●	●	●	●	●	●	●
Polo acuático			●	●	●	●	●	●	●	●							
Arquería		●	●	●	●	●	●										
Atletismo																	
Campo y pista					●	●	●	●	●								
Maratón					●	●											
Baloncesto		●	●	●	●	●	●	●									
Béisbol		●	●	●	●	●		●	●	●	●						
Boxeo								●	●	●	●	●	●		●	●	
Ciclismo											●	●	●	●	●		
Fútbol		●	●	●		●	●	●		●	●		●		●	●	●
Gimnasia		●	●	●	●												
Judo									●	●	●	●					
Levantamiento de pesas												●	●	●	●		
Lucha		●	●	●	●												
Patinaje												●	●				
Pelota vasca				●	●	●	●	●	●	●	●	●			●		
Tenis					●	●	●	●	●	●							
Tenis de mesa								●	●	●	●	●	●		●	●	
Triatlón										●	●						
Voleibol			●	●	●	●	●	●	●		●	●	●	●	●	●	●
Clausura																	●

Leyenda: ● Mañana ● Tarde ● Noche

Medallero de los países hispanos en los Juegos Olímpicos de verano

País	●	●	●	Total
Cuba	65	53	52	170
España	29	39	27	95
Argentina	15	23	22	60
México	10	19	23	52
Chile	2	6	4	12
Uruguay	2	2	6	10
Perú	1	3	0	4
Venezuela	1	1	7	10
Colombia	1	2	6	9
Costa Rica	1	1	2	4
República Dominicana	1	0	1	2
Ecuador	1	0	0	1
Puerto Rico	0	1	5	6
Paraguay	0	1	0	1
Panamá	0	0	2	2

Actividad 13 Del mundo hispano: Escríbanos

Lea la página de la revista *Eres* que aparece en la siguiente página. Hay un grupo de muchachos de México que quieren entablar (tener) correspondencia con otros muchachos. Hágale preguntas a su compañero/a acerca de la información que hay sobre ellos.

MODELO: E1: ¿Cuántos años tiene *Efraín Ayala*?

                    E2: Tiene *dieciocho*.

                    E1: ¿Cuál es su número de celular?

                    E2: Es el *559-8-13-03-85*.

                    E1: ¿Cuál es su dirección electrónica?

                    E2: Es *efar63@telmex.net.mx*.

                    E1: ¿Cuál es su deporte favorito?

                    E2: Su deporte favorito es *el fútbol*.

                    E1: ¿Qué le gusta hacer *a él*?

                    E2: Le gusta *andar en patineta e ir a los antros*.

Y TÚ, ¿QUIÉN ERES?

MIGUEL ÁNGEL OJEDA GALVÁN
(21 años)
cel: (228) 8-41-37-43
dirección electrónica: migan@metronet.mx
pasatiempos: ir a la playa, jugar al voleibol, tocar la guitarra y explorar el Internet

EFRAÍN AYALA RAMÍREZ
(18 años)
cel: (559) 8-13-03-85
dirección electrónica: efar63@telmex.net.mx
pasatiempos: andar en patineta, ir a los antros, jugar al fútbol y tener amigos por correspondencia

GEMA LETICIA VILLANUEVA G.
(24 años)
cel: (777) 3-19-68-43
dirección electrónica: gemavilla@gmail.com
pasatiempos: ir a la piscina, escuchar música, ver la tele y tener correspondencia con amigos en español o en inglés

MARÍA CRUZ RODRÍGUEZ R.
(17 años)
cel: (331) 4-28-65-88
dirección electrónica: marcruz7@cen.net.mx
pasatiempos: andar en bici, escuchar la música de Carlos Vives, jugar al tenis, leer *Eres*

ANTONIO MANUEL OLIVARES REYES
(20 años)
cel: (351) 5-15-92-78
dirección electrónica: amor@uam.edu.mx
pasatiempos: jugar al básquetbol, escuchar la música de Maná, ir al cine y salir con amigos

ANA JAZMÍN PRECIADO MENDOZA
(19 años)
cel: (228) 8-41-37-43
dirección electrónica: ajaz24@infoweb.mex
pasatiempos: bailar en los antros, escuchar música, en especial Shakira, nadar, pasear y leer novelas

En resumen

De todo un poco

La curiosidad

Trabaje con otros estudiantes. Escriban dos o tres preguntas para estas personas famosas o interesantes.

1. el presidente de los Estados Unidos
2. un actor de cine muy famoso
3. una actriz bonita
4. una mujer atractiva en una fiesta
5. un chico muy guapo en la clase de español
6. su profesor(a) de español

¡Dígalo por escrito!

Descripción de personas

De su revista favorita, seleccione una foto de una o más personas y tráigala a clase. Descríbales la foto a sus compañeros. ¡Use su imaginación!

- ¿Cómo se llama?
- ¿Dónde nació?
- ¿Dónde vive ahora? ¿Con quién(es) vive?
- ¿Cuántos años tiene?
- ¿Qué deportes le gustan?
- ¿Qué idioma(s) habla?
- ¿Cómo es?
- ¿Qué ropa lleva?
- ¿Qué le gusta hacer?
- ¿ ?

Ahora, escriba una descripción de la foto. Incluya la información básica (vea las preguntas de arriba) y otros detalles interesantes/descriptivos.

¡Cuéntenos usted!

Cuéntenos sobre su pariente favorito. ¿Qué relación tiene con usted? (¿es su tío/a, primo/a, abuelo/a... ?) ¿Cómo se llama? ¿Dónde vive? ¿Cuántos años tiene? ¿Cómo es? ¿Qué le gusta hacer en su tiempo libre? ¿Qué les gusta hacer a ustedes juntos?

MODELO: Mi prima es mi pariente favorito. Se llama Isabel y vive en Chicago. Isabel tiene 24 años y es estudiante en la universidad. Es muy inteligente, generosa y optimista. Le gusta mucho montar en bici. Nos gusta ir a museos de arte juntas.

Palabras útiles

¿Cuál... ?
¿Cuándo... ?
¿Cuántos... ?
¿Cómo... ?
¿Dónde... ?
¿Por qué... ?
¿Qué... ?
¿Quién... ?

PISTAS* PARA LEER
1. Scan title and vocabulary box. What is the main idea of this reading?
2. Now scan text for names of famous Hispanics in sports.
3. Skim the **Lectura** to get the gist of it.
4. As you read, keep these questions in mind: What are the most popular sports in the Hispanic world? Are those sports popular in the United States?

VOCABULARIO ÚTIL

la natación	swimming
la liga mayor	major league
se destaca	stands out
la Serie Mundial	World Series (baseball)
el lanzador	(baseball) pitcher
el ciclismo	cycling
el surfeo	surfing
la velocista	sprinter
la vida diaria	daily life

LECTURA

La pasión por los deportes

Rafael Nadal

Los hispanos sienten pasión por los deportes, ya sea el béisbol, el fútbol o deportes individuales como la **natación** y el esquí. Los deportes profesionales son la forma de entretenimiento más popular en España y América Latina, y los deportistas famosos tienen muchos admiradores.

El fútbol es el deporte favorito de muchos mexicanos y de muchos centro y sudamericanos. Pero los españoles también se apasionan con el fútbol; el Real Madrid es uno de los mejores equipos del mundo hispano. Otro equipo excelente es el del Club Deportivo Chivas USA, basado en Los Ángeles, que tiene jugadores de **liga mayor**. Entre los futbolistas famosos está el legendario Diego Maradona, de Argentina. Y en tiempos recientes **se destaca** Leandro Depetris, también argentino, a quien se le compara con Maradona. Depetris es el futbolista más joven de todos; ¡empieza a jugar profesionalmente a la edad de once años!

El béisbol es un deporte muy popular y se juega en los países del Caribe, que son Puerto Rico, Cuba, Venezuela y la República Dominicana. Muchos caribeños miran la **Serie Mundial** en la televisión o la escuchan en la radio. Es un público muy entusiasta. Hay beisbolistas hispanos de fama internacional, como el dominicano Vladimir Guerrero y el colombiano Orlando Cabrera. Dos de los **lanzadores** más admirados son Orlando Hernández y José Contreras, deportistas que forman parte de una larga y rica tradición de béisbol en Cuba.

Algunos hispanos también practican el esquí. En los Andes de Chile y Argentina hay sitios formidables para esquiar, y los españoles esquían en la Sierra Nevada. Hay además otros deportes individuales que apasionan a los hispanos, como el **ciclismo,** el baloncesto, el tenis, el golf y hasta el **surfeo.** ¿Sabía usted que la peruana Sofía Mulánovich es una de las surfistas más admiradas por los *fans* de ese deporte? Y dos mexicanas de talento admirable son la **velocista** Ana Guevara y la campeona de golf Lorena Ochoa. Entre los tenistas hispanos hay varios reconocidos: los argentinos David Nalbandian y Guillermo Cañas, y el español Rafael Nadal. A Nadal se le considera uno de los dos mejores tenistas del mundo.

Pistas means both "clues" and "tracks."

Como puede ver, la pasión por los deportes es un aspecto esencial de la cultura hispana y las actividades deportivas son parte de la **vida diaria** en España y todos los países de América Latina.

Comprensión

¿Cierto o falso?

1. El fútbol se practica mucho en México y Argentina.
2. El futbolista más joven es Diego Maradona.
3. Hay tres beisbolistas famosos en el Caribe.
4. Los hispanos practican deportes individuales y también en equipo.
5. Los peruanos no tienen interés en el surfeo.
6. La lectura habla de cuatro tenistas famosos de España.
7. En Chile, Argentina y España hay sitios formidables para esquiar.
8. La golfista Lorena Ochoa es de México.

Un paso más... ¡a escribir!

Imagínese que usted es un deportista famoso / una deportista famosa. ¿Qué deporte practica? ¡Descríbase! Puede incluir una descripción física y también de su personalidad.

MODELO: Me llamo _____ y juego al _____. Soy muy famoso/a. Tengo muchos admiradores. Practico este deporte _____ (frecuencia). Soy _____ (descripción física). ¿Mi personalidad? Soy _____ y _____ .

> Vea el **Resumen cultural** en este capítulo del *Cuaderno de actividades.*

Vocabulario

Los meses del año

Months of the Year

enero	January

PALABRAS SEMEJANTES: febrero, marzo, abril, mayo, junio, julio, agosto, septiembre, octubre, noviembre, diciembre

Las estaciones

Seasons

la primavera	spring
el verano	summer
el otoño	fall, autumn
el invierno	winter

Los días de la semana

Days of the Week

(el) lunes	Monday
(el) martes	Tuesday
(el) miércoles	Wednesday
(el) jueves	Thursday
(el) viernes	Friday
(el) sábado	Saturday
(el) domingo	Sunday

¿Cuándo?

When?

(ante)ayer	(day before) yesterday
hoy	today
luego	then, later
(pasado) mañana	(day after) tomorrow
por la mañana/ tarde/noche	in the morning / afternoon (evening) / at night
temprano	early
todo el día	all day (long)

Los datos personales

Personal Data

la calle	street
la ciudadanía	citizenship
¿Cómo te llamas (tú)?	What is your name?
el correo electrónico	e-mail
¿Cuál es su/tu dirección electrónica?	What is your e-mail (address)?
Es mgomez arroba micorreo punto com.	It's mgomez@micorreo.com.
¿Cuándo es el día de su/ tu cumpleaños?	When is your birthday?
¿Cuándo (Dónde) nació/ naciste?	When (Where) were you (was he/she) born?
Nací el (en)...	I was born on (in) . . .
la dirección	address
¿Dónde vive usted (vives tú)?	Where do you live?
Vivo en...	I live in/at . . .
el estado civil	marital status
la fecha (de nacimiento)	date (of birth)
el lugar (de nacimiento)	place (of birth)

PALABRAS SEMEJANTES: el pasaporte, el sexo
REPASO: el apellido, casado/a, divorciado/a, soltero/a, viudo/a

La hora

Time; Hour

la medianoche	midnight
el mediodía	noon
¿Qué hora es?	What time is it?
Es la una y media.	It is one-thirty.
Son las nueve menos diez (minutos).	It is ten (minutes) to nine.
¿A qué hora es la película?	What time is the movie?
Es a las 8:30.	It's at 8:30.
Oye, ¿qué hora tienes?	Hey, what time do you have?
Perdón, ¿qué hora tiene?	Excuse me, what time do you have?
y cuarto / menos cuarto	quarter after / quarter till
y media	half past

Los deportes

Sports

el basquetbol (baloncesto)	basketball
el equipo	team
el estadio	stadium
el fútbol (americano)	soccer (football)
jugar (al tenis)	to play (tennis)
nadar (en una piscina)	to swim (in a pool)
el partido	game (in sports), match
patinar (en el hielo)	to skate (on ice)
pescar	to fish
practicar un deporte	to play a sport

PALABRAS SEMEJANTES: el bate, el béisbol, la competición

Las actividades del tiempo libre

Leisure Time Activities

acampar	to camp (go camping)
andar en bicicleta/ patineta	to ride a bicycle / to skateboard
bailar	to dance
cenar	to dine, have dinner

cocinar	to cook
comer	to eat
correr	to run
dormir	to sleep
escribir mensajes electrónicos	to write e-mail
escuchar (música)	to listen (to music)
explorar el Internet	to surf the Internet
hacer	to do; to make
hacer ejercicio	to exercise
ir	to go
a fiestas	to parties
a la playa	to the beach
a los antros	to dance clubs
al cine	to the movies
de compras	shopping
jugar (en la nieve)	to play (in the snow)
leer el periódico (revistas)	to read the newspaper (magazines)
pasear	to go for a walk (ride)
sacar fotos	to take photos
salir (a bailar)	to go out (dancing)
tocar la guitarra	to play the guitar
trabajar en el jardín	to work (in the garden)
trotar	to jog
ver	to see; to watch
la televisión	television
un partido de...	a game of . . .
una telenovela	a soap opera

Palabras y expresiones del texto

Words and Expressions from the Text

cuéntenos	tell us (command)
describa(n)	describe (command)
¡Dígalo por escrito!	Say it in writing!
la firma	signature
los gustos	likes
Hágale preguntas a...	Ask . . . questions.
la lectura	reading (n.)
el refrán	saying
según	according to
seleccione(n)	choose (command)
se presenta	is shown
siguiente(s)	next; following
sobre	about
trabaje(n)	work (command)
traiga(n)	bring (command)
vea(n)	see (command)

PALABRAS SEMEJANTES: corresponde, en detalle, la frase, incluya(n), la preferencia, use

Los sustantivos

Nouns

las entradas (para un concierto)	tickets (for a concert)

el equipo de música	sound system
el fin de semana	weekend
la tabla de snowboard	snowboard
el (teléfono) celular/móvil	cell phone
la teleguía	television guide
el televisor	television set

PALABRAS SEMEJANTES: el actor / la actriz, el/la agente, la cámara digital, el canal, la correspondencia, la curiosidad, el grupo, la información, la inmigración, el presidente / la presidenta, el programa, la relación, el restaurante, el/la turista

Palabras útiles

Useful Words

a, al / a la	to, to the
acerca de	about
aquí	here
casi	almost
para	for
pero	but
querer	to want
quiero	I want
quieres	you want

PALABRAS SEMEJANTES: anterior, asociado/a, atractivo/a, básico/a, correcto/a, descriptivo/a, elegante, favorito/a, hispano/a, panamericano/a, típico/a

Expresiones útiles

Useful Expressions

A mí no	Not me.
A mí sí	Me too.
¿A quién le gusta... ?	Who likes to . . . ?
¡Felicidades!	Congratulations!
¡Feliz cumpleaños!	Happy birthday!
más o menos	more or less
No lo creo.	I don't believe it.
¡No me digas!	You don't say!
¡Qué aburrido/divertido!	How boring/fun!
¿Qué le/te/les gusta hacer?	What do you (pol. sing. / inf. / pl.) like to do?
Le gusta...	He/She likes (You [pol. sing.] like) (to) . . .
Les gusta...	They / You (pl.) like (to) . . .
Nos gusta...	We like (to) . . .
Te gusta...	You (inf.) like (to) . . .
(No) Me gusta...	I (don't) like (to) . . .
A mí también/tampoco.	I do too . . . / I don't either.
Por lo general	Generally; In general
¿Por qué?	Why?
Ya es tarde.	It's late already.
Y tú, ¿qué dices?	And you? What do you say?

Gramática y ejercicios

100 = **cien**	
101 = **ciento uno**	
161 = **ciento sesenta y uno**	
doscientos (200) hombres	
doscientas (200) mujeres	
quinientos (500) edificios	
quinientas (500) sillas	

1.1 Counting: Numbers 100–1000 and Dates

A. Here are the hundreds, from 100 to 1000. Note particularly the pronunciation and spelling of 500, 700, and 900. The word for *one hundred* is **cien,** but when combined with other numbers it is **ciento(s).** From 200 to 900, there is also a feminine form.

154	ciento cincuenta y cuatro		600	seiscientos/as
200	doscientos/as		700	setecientos/as
300	trescientos/as		800	ochocientos/as
400	cuatrocientos/as		900	novecientos/as
500	quinientos/as		1000	mil

—¿Cuántos estudiantes de
  España hay en el grupo?
  ¿Hay **cien**?
—No, hay **ciento cincuenta
  y cuatro.**

—*How many students from
  Spain are in the group?
  Are there a hundred?*
—*No, there are one hundred
  and fifty-four.*

—¿Cuántas sillas hay?
—Hay **doscientas diez**.

—*How many chairs are there?*
—*There are two hundred and ten.*

B. To state a year in Spanish, use **mil** (1000) followed by hundreds in the masculine form (if necessary).

1832	mil ochocientos treinta y dos
1993	mil novecientos noventa y tres
2009	dos mil nueve

5 = **cinco**	
15 = **quince**	
50 = **cincuenta**	
500 = **quinientos**	
7 = **siete**	
70 = **setenta**	
700 = **setecientos**	
9 = **nueve**	
90 = **noventa**	
900 = **novecientos**	

Ejercicio 1

Escriba las siguientes fechas.

MODELO: 2009 → Dos mil nueve

1. 1876
2. 1588
3. 1775
4. 1991
5. 2006
6. 1945
7. 1011
8. 1929
9. 1615
10. 2025

1.2 Talking about Habitual Actions: Present Tense of Regular -er and -ir Verbs

Following are the present-tense conjugations of the regular -er and -ir verbs **leer** and **vivir.***

leer (*to read*)

(yo)	leo	*I read*
(tú)	lees	*you (inf. sing.) read*
(usted, él/ella)	lee	*you (pol. sing.) read; he/she reads*
(nosotros/as)	leemos	*we read*
(vosotros/as)	leéis	*you (inf. pl., Spain) read*
(ustedes, ellos/as)	leen	*you (pl.) read; they read*

vivir (*to live*)

(yo)	vivo	*I live*
(tú)	vives	*you (inf. sing.) live*
(usted, él/ella)	vive	*you (pol. sing.) live; he/she lives*
(nosotros/as)	vivimos	*we live*
(vosotros/as)	vivís	*you (inf. pl., Spain) live*
(ustedes, ellos/as)	viven	*you (pl.) live; they live*

It takes time to acquire these endings. As you read, listen, and interact more in Spanish, you will be able to use them with greater accuracy.

Remember that, because Spanish verb endings indicate in many cases who or what the subject is, it is not necessary to use subject pronouns in every sentence.

—¿Dónde vives? —*Where do you live?*
—Vivo en San Juan. —*I live in San Juan.*

Ejercicio 2

Complete estas oraciones con la forma correcta del verbo **leer.**

leer = *to read*

1. Muchos españoles _____ el periódico *El País.*
2. ¿_____ (tú) muchas novelas?
3. Mi amigo _____ la Biblia todos los días.
4. (Yo) _____ libros en español.
5. Profesora, ¿_____ (usted) muchas composiciones?

*For recognition: **vos leés, vivís**

vivir = *to live*

As you saw in **Gramática C.5** and **1.2,** Spanish verb endings usually indicate who the subject is, so it is generally not necessary to use subject pronouns (**tú, usted, él/ella, nosotros/as, vosotros/as, ustedes, ellos/as**) in questions.

¿Tienes (tú) teléfono?
¿Dónde vive (ella)?
¿Cómo se llaman (ustedes)?

Ejercicio 3

Complete estas oraciones con la forma correcta del verbo **vivir.**

1. Pablo _____ en Texas.
2. (Nosotros) No _____ en México.
3. Susana y sus hijos _____ en Perú.
4. ¿_____ (vosotros) en España?
5. (Yo) _____ en los Estados Unidos.
6. ¿_____ (ustedes) en Panamá?

1.3 Asking Questions: Question Formation

You have already seen and heard many questions in Spanish.

¿Cómo se llama usted?	¿Es alto Guillermo?
¿Qué hora es?	¿Habla usted español?
¿Cuándo nació José?	¿Tienen (ustedes) hijos?
¿Qué tiene Amanda?	¿Eres (tú) sincera?

A. Statements in Spanish are normally formed by using a subject, then the verb, and then an object and/or description.

Ernestito   tiene   un perro   grande.
| | | | |
subject   verb   object   adjective

Amanda   es   delgada.
| | | |
subject   verb   adjective

Negative statements are formed by using a negative immediately before the verb.

Ernestito no tiene un perro grande.
Amanda no es delgada.

Note that in Spanish no additional words, such as *does* or *do*, are needed to turn a statement into a question.

B. Questions are usually formed by placing the subject after the verb, with the object and/or any description either following or preceding the subject.*

¿Es joven Esteban?	*Is Esteban young?*
¿Eres trabajadora, Nora?	*Are you (Nora) (a) hard-working (person)?*
¿Tiene hermanos Amanda?	*Does Amanda have brothers and sisters?*
¿Quieres un reloj para el día de tu cumpleaños?	*Do you want a watch for your birthday?*
¿Nació en abril Pilar?	*Was Pilar born in April?*

---

*Questions with the verb **gustar** are slightly different. The question starts with the verb **gustar** and places the **a** phrase at the end: **¿Le gusta cantar a la profesora Martínez? ¿Les gusta hablar español a los estudiantes? ¿Te gusta bailar a ti?** See **Gramática 8.2** for more information on using these phrases.

To answer a question negatively use **No, no** + verb.

¿Hay gatos en el salón de clase?
No, no hay gatos en el salón de clase.
¿Viven tus padres en Guadalajara?
No, no viven en Guadalajara; viven en Morelia.

C. Another way to ask questions is using interrogative words: **¿Qué?, ¿Cuándo?, ¿(De) Quién?, ¿Dónde?, ¿Cuántos?, ¿Cómo?, ¿Cuál?,** or **¿Por qué?** These words are placed before the verb to create questions.

¿Cuántos hermanos tienes, Guillermo?	*How many brothers (and sisters) do you have, Guillermo?*
¿Dónde vive Susana?	*Where does Susana live?*
¿Cómo está usted hoy?	*How are you today?*
¿Quién es el joven alto?	*Who is the tall young man?*
¿Cuándo nació usted?	*When were you born?*
¿Por qué no hablamos inglés en clase?	*Why don't we speak English in class?*
¿Qué te gusta hacer en tu tiempo libre?	*What do you like to do in your free time?*
¿Cuál es más bonito?	*Which one is prettier?*
¿De quién es este libro?	*Whose book is this?*

Question words always have a written accent:

¿Qué? = *What?*
¿Cuándo? = *When?*
¿Quién(es)? = *Who?*
¿De quién? = *Whose?*
¿Dónde? = *Where?*
¿Cuánto/a/os/as? = *How much? / How many?*
¿Cómo? = *How?; What?*
¿Cuál(es)? = *Which?; What?*
¿Por qué? = *Why?*

Ejercicio 4

Convierta las siguientes oraciones en preguntas.

MODELO: Amanda y Graciela son amigas. →
¿Son amigas Amanda y Graciela?

1. Ernesto y Estela están casados.
2. Clarisa y Marisa son inteligentes.
3. Don Eduardo tiene un carro nuevo.
4. Nosotros vivimos en Puerto Rico.
5. Pedro lee el periódico.

Ejercicio 5

Cambie las siguientes oraciones por preguntas. Use **¿Cómo?, ¿Dónde?, ¿Qué?, ¿Cuándo?, ¿Cuántos/as?**

MODELO: Amanda tiene 14 años. →
¿Cuántos años tiene Amanda?

1. Rubén Hernández vive en Florida.
2. Susana habla japonés.
3. La clase de español es los lunes y los miércoles.
4. Ernesto y Estela tienen tres hijos.
5. El primer ministro de España se llama José Luis Rodríguez Zapatero.

Ejercicio 6

Complete las preguntas según los dibujos.

MODELO: → ¿Cómo *estás*?

1. ¿Cuál _____?   **2.** ¿Cómo _____?   **3.** ¿Cuándo _____?

4. ¿Cuántos _____?   **5.** ¿Dónde _____?

1.4 Telling Time: Hours and Minutes

¿Qué hora es? =
What time is it?

1.15: Es la una y cuarto.
2.30: Son las dos y media.
3.25: Son las tres y
veinticinco.
5.45: Son las seis menos
cuarto.

The phrase **¿Qué hora es?** is often used in Spanish to ask what time it is. Another common question is **¿Qué hora tiene usted?** (*What time do you have?*) In both cases, the answer usually begins with **son.**

—¿Qué hora es?   —*What time is it?*
—**Son** las tres.   —*It's three o'clock.*

Es (not **son**) is used to tell the time with one o'clock and between one o'clock and two o'clock.

—¿**Es** la una?	—*Is it one o'clock?*
—No, **es** la una y veinte.	—*No, it's one twenty.*

Use **y** (*and*) to express minutes after the hour.

—¿Son las seis **y** diez?	—*Is it ten after six?*
—No, son las seis **y** veinte.	—*No, it's twenty after six.*

Use **menos** (*less*) or **para** (*to, till*) to express minutes before the hour.

Son las siete **menos** veinte.	*It's twenty to seven.* (Literally: *It's seven less twenty.*)
Son veinte **para** las siete.	*It's twenty to (till) seven.*

Use **cuarto** (*quarter*) and **media** (*half*) for fifteen and thirty minutes, respectively.

—¿Qué hora tiene usted?	—*What time do you have?*
—Son las tres y **cuarto** (**media**).	—*It's a quarter after (half past) three.*

Use **a** to express *when* (*at what time*) an event occurs.

a la una	*at one o'clock*
a las cuatro y media	*at four thirty*
Tengo clase **a** las nueve.	*I have class at nine.*
El concierto es **a** las ocho.	*The concert is at eight.*

> ***a** la una = **at** one o'clock*
> ***a** las siete menos cuarto = **at** six forty-five / quarter to seven*

Ejercicio 7

¿Qué hora es?

MODELOS: 2:20 → *Son las dos y veinte.*
2:40 → *Son las tres menos veinte.*

1. 4:20	**5.** 7:07	**9.** 12:30
2. 6:15	**6.** 5:30	**10.** 5:15
3. 8:13	**7.** 3:35	
4. 1:10	**8.** 1:49	

Ejercicio 8

¿A qué hora es... ?

MODELO: ¿A qué hora es el concierto? (8:30) →
El concierto es a las ocho y media.

1. ¿A qué hora es la clase de español? (11:00)
2. ¿A qué hora es el baile? (9:30)
3. ¿A qué hora es la conferencia? (10:00)
4. ¿A qué hora es la clase de álgebra? (1:00)
5. ¿A qué hora es la fiesta del Club Internacional? (7:30)

Gustar is used to express likes and dislikes.

Me gusta bailar.
(*I like to dance.*)

¿*Te* gusta patinar?
(*Do you like to skate?*)
A **Ernestito** *le* **gusta jugar al fútbol.**
(*Ernestito likes to play soccer.*)
A **Estela y** *a* **Ernesto** *les* **gusta ir al cine.**
(*Estela and Ernesto like to go to the movies.*)
***Nos* gusta cocinar.**
(*We like to cook.*)

1.5 Expressing Likes and Dislikes: *gustar* + Infinitive

A. The Spanish verb **gustar** expresses the meaning of English *to like*. From a grammatical point of view, however, it is similar to the English expression *to be pleasing to someone.**

> **Me gusta** leer. *I like to read. (Reading is pleasing to me.)*

Gustar is usually used with pronouns that tell *to whom* something is pleasing. Here are the pronoun forms.[†]

SINGULAR		PLURAL	
me	*to me*	nos	*to us*
te	*to you (inf. sing.)*	os	*to you (inf. pl., Spain)*
le	*to you (pol. sing.); to him/her*	les	*to you (pl.); to them*

> —¿Qué **te** gusta hacer? —*What do you like to do?*
> —**Me** gusta aprender cosas nuevas. —*I like to learn new things.*

> —¿Qué **les** gusta hacer? —*What do you like to do?*
> —**Nos** gusta cocinar. —*We like to cook.*

B. Since **le gusta** can refer to *you (pol. sing.)*, *him*, or *her*, and **les gusta** can refer to *you (pl.)* or *them*, Spanish speakers often expand the sentence to be more specific. They use phrases with **a** (*to*), such as **a mi papá** (*to my father*), **a Juan** (*to Juan*), or **a los estudiantes** (*to the students*), in addition to using the pronoun **le** or **les**.[‡]

> **A Carmen le** gusta cantar. *Carmen likes to sing.*

> —¿**A usted le** gusta lavar su carro? —*Do you like to wash your car?*
> —No, no **me** gusta. —*No, I don't like to.*

> —¿**Les** gusta acampar **a Guillermo y a Ernestito**? —*Do Guillermo and Ernestito like to go camping?*
> —Sí, **les** gusta mucho. —*Yes, they like it very much.*

---

*You will learn more about the verb **gustar** and similar verbs in **Gramática 8.2**.
†Recognition: (**A vos**) Te gusta
‡You will learn more about phrases with **a**, **le**, and **les** in **Gramática 7.4, 8.2, 10.5, 13.4**, and **13.5**.

C. The verb form that follows **gustar** is an infinitive, such as **hablar** (*to speak*), **leer** (*to read*), or **vivir** (*to live*).

PRONOUN	+	*gusta*	+	INFINITIVE
me				estudiar (*to study*)
te				jugar (*to play*)
le				comer (*to eat*)
nos	+	gusta	+	correr (*to run*)
os				competir (*to compete*)
les				escribir (*to write*)

Ejercicio 9

¿Qué les gusta hacer a Ernestito y a Guillermo? Complete los diálogos con **me, te, les** o **nos**.

MODELO: AMANDA: Graciela, ¿*te* gusta bailar?
                GRACIELA: Sí, *me* gusta mucho bailar.

1.   MAESTRA: Ernestito, ¿_____ gusta andar en bicicleta?
         ERNESTITO: Sí, _____ gusta mucho. Tengo una bici nueva.

2.   ERNESTITO: Guillermo, ¿_____ gusta jugar al béisbol?
         GUILLERMO: No, pero _____ gusta jugar al fútbol.

3.   PEDRO: Ernestito y Guillermo, ¿_____ gusta escuchar la música rock?
         LOS CHICOS: ¡Claro que sí! _____ gusta mucho.

Ejercicio 10

¿Qué le(s) gusta hacer a las siguientes personas?

1. A Ernestito _____ gusta _____.
2. A Estela (la madre de Ernestito) no _____ gusta _____.
3. A Clarisa y a Marisa (las primas de Ernestito) _____ gusta _____.
4. A Ernestito _____ gusta _____.
5. Al perro _____ gusta _____.

Mis planes y preferencias

METAS

In **Capítulo 2** you will discuss your plans for the future and your preferences. You will also talk about your classes and the weather.

Green Bananas, por Miguel Suárez-Pierra (Ecuador)

Sobre el artista: Miguel Suárez-Pierra nació en Ecuador. Este premiado artista se graduó de arquitecto en la Universidad Católica de Guayaquil. También tiene experiencia como profesor de arte para jóvenes. Su arte se expone en muchas galerías en Ecuador y los Estados Unidos.

¡Conozca Ecuador!

Nombre del país: la República del Ecuador

Ciudad capital: Quito

Ciudades principales: Guayaquil, Riobamba, Cuenca

Moneda: el dólar estadounidense

Idiomas: el español, (oficial), el quechua, otras lenguas indígenas

Población: 13.800.000

Día de la Independencia: el 24 de mayo

Fiestas típicas: el Carnaval, fiestas religiosas y regionales

Comidas típicas: la guatita con mondongo, el maní y papas, el encebollado, el seco de chivo, los llapingachos, los patacones

Música típica: el pasillo, el pasacalle, el yarabí

Gente famosa: Juan Montalvo, Jorge Icaza, Rafael Correa

Código del país por Internet: .ec

Voces ecuatorianas

una caleta	una casa
un(a) gato/a	una persona de ojos verdes o azules
un(a) guambra	un(a) joven
el/la ñaño/a	el/la hermano/a
el taita	el padre

En este capítulo...

ACTIVIDADES DE COMUNICACIÓN

- Los planes
- Las clases
- Las preferencias y los deseos
- El tiempo

EN RESUMEN

LECTURAS Y CULTURA

- **Ventanas al pasado**
  La primera universidad
- **Ventanas culturales**
  Nuestra comunidad: Edward James Olmos, actor y activista
- **Enlace a la música**
  La música andina
- **Lectura** De paseo

GRAMÁTICA Y EJERCICIOS

2.1 Expressing Future Plans: **ir** + **a** + Infinitive

2.2 Sequencing: Ordinal Adjectives

2.3 Stating Preferences and Desires: **preferir** and **querer** + Infinitive

2.4 Pointing Out People and Objects: Demonstrative Adjectives

2.5 Describing the Weather: Common Expressions

Los planes

✳ **Lea Gramática 2.1.**

Andrea Ruiz habla de los planes de su familia para el fin de semana

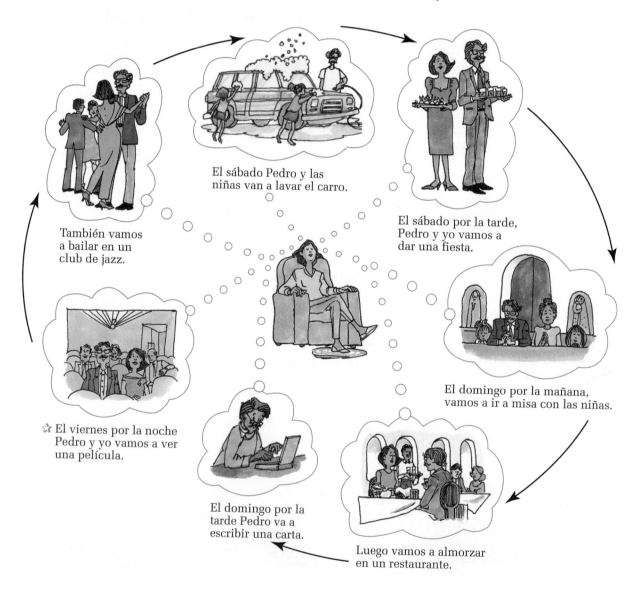

El sábado Pedro y las niñas van a lavar el carro.

El sábado por la tarde, Pedro y yo vamos a dar una fiesta.

También vamos a bailar en un club de jazz.

☆ El viernes por la noche Pedro y yo vamos a ver una película.

El domingo por la mañana, vamos a ir a misa con las niñas.

El domingo por la tarde Pedro va a escribir una carta.

Luego vamos a almorzar en un restaurante.

Actividad 1 Preferencias: Los planes

Hable de sus planes.

MODELO: E1: El domingo por la tarde voy a *limpiar mi cuarto.*
E2: ¡Qué aburrido!

1. Mañana por la mañana voy a...
2. El viernes por la noche mis amigos van a...
3. El domingo por la tarde voy a...
4. Durante las vacaciones mis amigos y yo vamos a...
5. Este invierno voy a...

Y tú, ¿qué dices?

¡Qué aburrido!	¿Dónde?	¿A qué hora?
¡Qué divertido!	¿Con quién?	Yo también.
¡Qué buena idea!	¿Cuándo?	Yo no.

Actividad 2 Narración: ¿Qué va a hacer Carmen el sábado?

Palabras útiles

bailar en un club
dar una fiesta
descansar
dormir
esquiar
estudiar mucho
ir al cine
jugar al boliche
jugar al tenis
levantar pesas
limpiar mi cuarto
pasar tiempo con...
pasear por el centro
patinar en el hielo
practicar un deporte
reparar mi carro
salir a cenar
trabajar en el jardín
viajar
¿_____?

Palabras útiles

primero	por la
luego	mañana
después	por la tarde
más tarde	por la noche
	por último

Actividad 3 Intercambios: Tus planes

Pregúntele a su compañero/a qué va a hacer en las siguientes ocasiones.

MODELO: E1: ¿Qué vas a hacer *en tu próximo cumpleaños*?
E2: Voy a *salir a cenar con mi familia. ¿Y tú*?
E1: ¿Yo? Voy a...

OCASIONES

durante las próximas
  vacaciones
el próximo fin de
  semana
el próximo verano
el viernes por la noche
en tu próximo cumpleaños
esta noche
hoy, después de clases

ACTIVIDADES

acampar
descansar
escribir cartas
estudiar
ir a la playa
ir al cine
ir a muchas
  fiestas

ir de compras
leer un libro
  interesante
nadar en un lago/río
salir a cenar
trabajar
ver la televisión
viajar

Actividad 4 Del mundo hispano: Madrid en el verano

Imagínese que usted está en Madrid en el mes de julio. Mire la lista de actividades de verano en la siguiente página y decida qué va a hacer. Mire también las **Actividades posibles** y las **Preguntas y respuestas útiles.**

Actividades posibles: jugar al boliche, levantar pesas, nadar, pasear en barca, salir a bailar, salir a cenar, tomar el sol, ver los animales, viajar a Ávila/Toledo en tren

Preguntas y respuestas útiles

¿Cuánto cuesta la entrada?	Cuesta *6,5 euros.*
¿Dónde está?	Está en *la calle Alcalá.*
¿A qué hora abren/cierran?	Abren/Cierran a *las 9:00.*
¿A qué hora sale/llega el tren?	Sale/Llega a *las 10:30.*
¿En qué restaurante (piscina,...)?	En *el Café de Oriente.*

MODELO: E1: Voy a *nadar en la piscina.*
E2: ¿Dónde?
E1: En *el Polideportivo de San Blas.*
E2: ¿Cuánto cuesta *la entrada*?
E1: Cuesta *cuatro euros para los adultos.*

Estanque del Parque del Retiro, Madrid, España

Madrid en el verano

Barcas

En los lagos del Retiro y la casa de Campo y en el río Manzanares. Desde las 10 de la mañana hasta la puesta del sol. Paseos de una hora. Precios: 3 euros por dos personas o 2 euros por persona.

Trenes turísticos

Ciudad de Toledo (viernes y domingos). Salida de la estación de Chamartín a las 9,05 h.; regreso de Toledo a las 19,45 h. Precios: adultos, 12 euros; niños de cuatro a doce años, 9 euros.

Murallas de Ávila (sábados). Salida de la estación de Chamartín a las 9,15 h.; regreso de Ávila a las 19,40 h. Precios: adultos, 10 euros; niños de cuatro a doce años, 9 euros.

Parques acuáticos

Acuópolis. Toboganes, rompeolas, Lago de Aventura, restaurantes, terrazas, parking gratuito. Abierto todos los días de la 1 a las 20 h. Precios: adultos, 14 euros; menores de catorce años, 10 euros.

Lagosur. Km 9 carretera de Toledo a Leganés. Abierto de las 11 a las 19 h. Precios: adultos, 12 euros; menores de 10 años, 9 euros.

Viernes y sábados abierto también desde las 23 h. hasta las 3 h. Precios: hombres, 10 euros; mujeres, 8 euros. No se admite a menores de 18 años.

Gimnasios

Gimnasio Ángel López. Squash (nueva instalación), karate, gimnasia, pesas, aerobic, ballet infantil y adulto, baile español y rítmica. Amparo Usera, 14, Tel. 91 457 83 98.

Gimnasio Argüelles. Karate, squash, aerobic, gimnasia, jazz, musculación, piscina. Andrés Mellado, 21, Tel. 91 267 56 71 22.

Piscinas

Los precios de estas piscinas son de 4 euros para los adultos y 2 euros para los niños. El horario de las piscinas es de las 10 a las 20 h.

Centro. Polideportivo de la Latina. Plaza de la Cebada 1, una piscina climatizada.

San Blas. Polideportivo de San Blas. Avenida de Hellín, 79; una piscina climatizada, una olímpica, una para nadadores no expertos, una infantil.

Boleras

Bolera Club Stella. Arlabán, 7. Tel. 91 231 01 92.

Bowling Chamartín. Estación de Chamartín. Tel. 91 315 71 19.

Discotecas al aire libre

La Fiesta. Paseo Virgen del Puerto (puente Segovia) abierto de las 22 hasta las 4 h.

El Jardín del Sur. Disco-piscina. Carretera Toledo km 8. Tel. 91 688 13 35.

Restaurantes con terraza

Café Oriente. Plaza de Oriente, 2. Abierto 20 a 2 h. Tel. 91 241 39 24.

Casa Domingo. Alcalá, 39. Abierto 18 a 1 h. Tel. 91 276 01 37.

Casa Rafa. Narváez, 68. Especialidad: pescado. Tel. 91 358 47 39.

Zoo

Casa de Campo. Metro Batán. Abre a las 10 h., cierra a las 21,30 h. Delfinario abierto todas las tardes. Menores de ocho años, 5 euros; mayores, 7 euros. Tel. 91 711 98 54.

Las clases

✳ **Lea Gramática 2.2.**

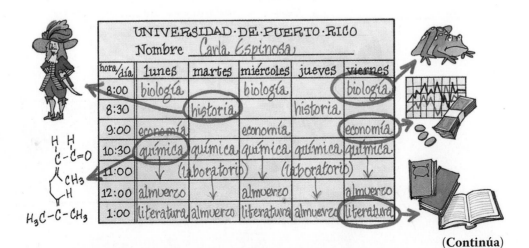

hora/día	lunes	martes	miércoles	jueves	viernes
8:00	biología		biología		biología
8:30		historia		historia	
9:00	economía		economía		economía
10:30	química	química	química	química	química
11:00		(laboratorio)		(laboratorio)	
12:00	almuerzo		almuerzo		almuerzo
1:00	literatura	almuerzo	literatura	almuerzo	literatura

UNIVERSIDAD DE PUERTO RICO
Nombre Carla Espinosa

(Continúa)

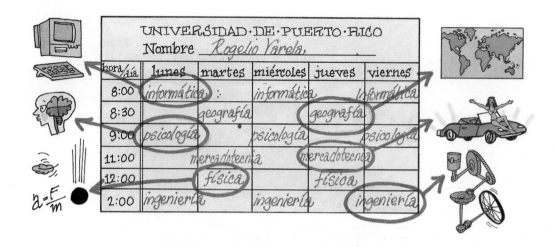

Actividad 5 Entrevista: Las clases

1. E1: ¿Qué clases tienes este semestre/trimestre?
   E2: Tengo _____, _____ y _____.
2. E1: ¿Cuál es tu clase *favorita / más difícil / más interesante*?
   E2: Mi clase *favorita / más difícil / más interesante* es _____.
3. E1: ¿A qué hora es esa clase?
   E2: Es a la(s) (*hora*) los (*días de la semana*).
4. E1: ¿Cómo se llama el profesor / la profesora de esa clase?
   E2: Se llama _____ y es *cómico*.
5. E1: ¿Cuál es tu especialidad en la universidad?
   E2: Mi especialidad es *la economía*. (No sé todavía.)

¡OJO!

En México, los estudiantes asisten primero a la escuela primaria por seis años. Luego, pasan a la escuela secundaria donde cursan primer, segundo y tercer año de secundaria. Después, van a la preparatoria, que ofrece las materias necesarias para entrar a la universidad. Al terminar, entran a la universidad para seguir los cursos profesionales.

Actividad 6 Intercambios: Las clases

Ramón tiene muchas clases en su primer año de preparatoria. Mire el horario de la siguiente página y pregúntele a su compañero/a cuál es la primera (segunda, tercera, cuarta, etcétera) clase de Ramón, a qué hora es y quién es el profesor / la profesora.

MODELO: E1: ¿Cuál es la *primera* clase de Ramón?
          E2: Su primera clase es la clase de *inglés*.
          E1: ¿A qué hora es?
          E2: Es a *las 7:45*. / Es de *las 7:45* a *las 8:30*.
          E1: ¿Quién es el profesor o la profesora?
          E2: Es *el señor García*.

SAGRADO CORAZÓN

Nombre: *Ramón Gómez*   Año: *Primero de preparatoria*

hora	materia	salón de clase	profesor(a)
7:45→8:30	inglés	403	Manuel García
8:40→9:25	matemáticas	207	Eugenia Ibarra
9:35→10:20	geografía	201	Daniel Contino
10:30→11:05	alemán	402	Alma Morales de Braun
11:05→11:20	descanso		
11:30→12:15	literatura española	405	Consuelo Acuña de Ramos
12:25→1:10	historia de México	408	Héctor Magaña M.
1:20→3:20	almuerzo		
3:30→4:15	biología	214	Isabel Santizo de Barragán
4:25→5:10	música	311	Víctor Álvarez

Palabras útiles

Es a la(s) _____
Es de la(s) _____ a
la(s) _____

Actividad 7   Del mundo hispano: La Universidad del Valle de México

Las especialidades en la siguiente página son las más importantes en el México de hoy. Trabaje con un compañero / una compañera para contestar las preguntas.

1. ¿Qué campus ofrece todas las especialidades? ¿Cuál ofrece menos especialidades? ¿Cuál ofrece más?
2. ¿Cuántos campus ofrecen la especialidad en ingeniería mecánica industrial? ¿en mercadotecnia? ¿en diseño de la moda?
3. Nombren las especialidades más atractivas (en su opinión).
4. ¿Se ofrecen esas especialidades en su universidad? ¿Estudian ustedes alguna de esas especialidades?
5. ¿Cuáles son las especialidades en el área de ciencias sociales? ¿Y en ciencias de la salud?
6. En su opinión, ¿cuáles son las especialidades más importantes hoy en día? ¿Por qué?

Folleto (*brochure*) para la licenciatura (*degree*) en ingeniería biomédica de la Universidad Iberoamericana en México, D.F.

UNIVERSIDAD DEL VALLE DE MÉXICO

ESPECIALIDADES - LICENCIATURA

	CENTRO		SUR		EDO. MEX.	QRO.
	SAN RAFAEL	TEXCOCO	SAN ÁNGEL	TLALPAN	LOMAS VERDES	QUERÉTARO
CIENCIAS SOCIALES						
CIENCIAS DE LA COMUNICACIÓN	•	•		•	•	•
PEDAGOGÍA		•				
DERECHO	•		•	•	•	•
PSICOLOGÍA	•	•		•	•	
RELACIONES INTERNACIONALES	•		•	•	•	•
TECNOCIENCIAS						
INGENIERÍA INDUSTRIAL Y DE SISTEMAS				•	•	•
INGENIERÍA EN TELECOMUNICACIONES	•			•	•	
INGENIERÍA EN SISTEMAS COMPUTACIONALES	•	•	•	•	•	•
INGENIERÍA MECÁNICA INDUSTRIAL				•		
INGENIERÍA EN TECNOLOGÍA INTERACTIVA					•	
INGENIERÍA MECATRÓNICA				•	•	•
ARTE Y HUMANIDADES						
ARQUITECTURA	•	•		•	•	•
DISEÑO GRÁFICO	•	•	•	•	•	•
DISEÑO DE LA MODA					•	•
ECONOMÍA - ADMINISTRACIÓN						
ADMINISTRACIÓN DE EMPRESAS		•	•	•	•	•
ADMINISTRACIÓN DEL DEPORTE Y RECREACIÓN				•	•	
ADMINISTRACIÓN DE CAPITAL HUMANO				•		
MERCADOTECNIA	•	•	•	•	•	•
RELACIONES PÚBLICAS					•	
ECONOMÍA	•					
CIENCIAS DE LA SALUD						
MEDICINA						•
ODONTOLOGÍA						•
FISIOTERAPIA				•	•	•

VENTANAS AL PASADO

La primera universidad

Tanto España como América Latina tienen universidades **antiguas** muy respetadas. La más antigua de España, la Universidad de Salamanca, se funda en 1218 por orden del rey Alfonso IX de León. El campus de esta universidad es considerado **Patrimonio de la Humanidad** por la **ONU. A pesar de** sus edificios antiguos, **actualmente** ofrece una educación amplia y moderna a 40.000 estudiantes universitarios.

En la República Dominicana está la primera universidad de América Latina: la Universidad Autónoma de Santo Domingo, establecida por orden del Papa Paulo III en 1538. Esta universidad ofrece acceso a la educación universitaria a muchos ciudadanos, pues **cuenta con** once campus en distintas regiones del país. La Universidad de Santo Domingo tiene una población de 143.000 estudiantes, entre los cuales hay un 65% (por ciento) de mujeres.

VOCABULARIO ÚTIL

antiguas/ antiguos	*old*
el Patrimonio de la Humanidad	*World Heritage Site*
la ONU (Organización de Naciones Unidas)	*UN (United Nations)*
a pesar de	*in spite of*
actualmente	*currently*
cuenta con	*tiene*
sin embargo	*however*

Hoy en día hay universidades importantes en todas las ciudades de España y América Latina: la Universidad Autónoma de Barcelona, la Universidad Nacional Autónoma de México y la Universidad de Santiago de Chile, entre otras. **Sin embargo,** las Universidades de Salamanca y de Santo Domingo tienen el honor de ser las primeras.

Universidad de Salamanca

Comprensión

¿Cierto o falso?

1. La Universidad de Salamanca es antigua pero ofrece una educación moderna.
2. La primera universidad latinoamericana está en México.

Las preferencias y los deseos

✳ **Lea Gramática 2.3.**

Los planes para el sábado

Pedro y Andrea quieren quedarse en casa hoy.

Las niñas prefieren merendar en el parque.

(Continúa)

Doña Lola quiere coser.

Guillermo y sus amigos prefieren andar en patineta.

Don Anselmo y don Eduardo quieren pescar.

Doña Rosita prefiere ir al parque.

Ramón prefiere andar en motocicleta.

El señor Saucedo prefiere nadar.

Actividad 8 Entrevista: Mis actividades favoritas

MODELO: E1: ¿Prefieres *nadar en la piscina o en el mar?* →
E2: Prefiero *nadar en el mar.* /
Me gustan *las dos actividades.* /
No me gusta *ninguna de las dos.*

1. ¿ ...hacer ejercicio en un gimnasio o correr?
2. ¿ ...andar en patineta o en bicicleta?
3. ¿ ...hablar por teléfono o usar el correo electrónico?
4. ¿ ...leer el periódico o ver la televisión?
5. ¿ ...merendar en un parque o comer en casa?
6. ¿ ...leer una novela o una revista?
7. ¿ ...chatear o textear?

Actividad 9 Diálogo abierto: Una invitación

E1: ¿Te gusta *jugar al tenis*?
E2: Sí, me gusta mucho.
E1: ¿Quieres *jugar al tenis* en *el parque* el *domingo*?
E2: ¿A qué hora?
E1: A *las once.*
E2: Perfecto. Nos vemos el *domingo* a *las once.*

Palabras útiles

Actividades	¿Dónde?	¿Cuándo?
acampar	la casa de un amigo	el domingo a las 9:00 de la mañana
correr	el centro	el jueves a las 7:30 de la tarde
ir a conciertos (ir a un concierto)	el cine Buñuel	el miércoles a las 8:30 de la noche
ir a fiestas (ir a una fiesta)	la discoteca ¡Latino!	el sábado a las 2:00 de la tarde
ir al cine (ver una película)	la montaña	el sábado a las 8:00 de la noche
ir de compras	el parque Marín	el sábado a las 10:00 de la mañana
nadar	la piscina de San Blas	el viernes a las 4:00 de la tarde
salir a bailar	el restaurante El Criollo	el viernes a las 8:00 de la noche
salir a cenar	el teatro Lorca	el viernes a las 10:00 de la noche

Actividad 10 Intercambios: ¿Cuáles son sus actividades favoritas?

Converse con su compañero/a sobre sus preferencias.

MODELO: E1: ¿Qué prefieres hacer *los lunes a las cuatro de la tarde*?
E2: Prefiero *escribir mensajes electrónicos*. ¿Y tú?

HORA Y DÍA

1. ¿ ...los sábados, a las siete de la mañana?
2. ¿ ...los viernes, a las ocho de la noche?
3. ¿ ...los lunes, a las cuatro de la tarde?
4. ¿ ...los domingos, a las diez de la mañana?
5. ¿ ...los sábados, a las tres de la tarde?

ACTIVIDADES

a. jugar al tenis
b. cocinar
c. descansar
d. correr
e. escribir mensajes electrónicos
f. montar a caballo
g. bailar
h. ver la televisión
i. dormir
j. leer el periódico
k. ¿ ?

Actividad 11 Intercambios: ¿Qué quieres hacer?

Mire los dibujos y complete las oraciones.

MODELO: RAÚL: ¿Quieres comer algo?
LUIS: No, prefiero estudiar un poco más.

1.
ESTEBAN: ¿Quieres tomar un chocolate caliente?
NORA: No, prefiero _____

4.
CARMEN: ¿Quieren estudiar una hora más?
LAN Y LUIS: No, preferimos

_____

2.
CARMEN: ¿Quieres ir de compras?
LAN: No, prefiero _____

5.
JOSÉ: ¿Quieres dar un paseo?
PILAR: No, prefiero _____

3.
PEDRO: ¿Quieres ver una película en la televisión?
ANDREA: No, prefiero _____

Actividad 12 **Del mundo hispano: ¿Qué prefieren hacer los españoles en su tiempo libre?**

Converse con un compañero / una compañera sobre los pasatiempos de los españoles y los europeos.

MODELOS: E1: ¿Cuál es la *quinta* preferencia de los españoles?
E2: *Recibir visitas.*

E1: ¿Y de los europeos?
E2: Los europeos *prefieren tomar te o café.*

Actividad 13 **Conversación: El hombre perfecto**

A. Trabajando en grupos, organicen estas descripciones en dos columnas: (1) el macho y (2) el hombre liberado.

- Le gusta ver películas violentas.
- Prefiere jugar al fútbol americano.
- Sale a bailar con frecuencia.
- Le gusta jugar al tenis.
- Prefiere montar en motocicleta.
- Le gusta escuchar rock metálico.
- Prefiere la música clásica.

- Prefiere manejar un Hummer.
- Prefiere salir con sus amigos.
- Prefiere cocinar.
- Le gusta mucho salir por la noche.
- Prefiere tomar cerveza.
- Siempre quiere llevar vaqueros, botas y chaqueta negra.

(Continúa)

B. Ahora, escriban una lista para describir uno de los siguientes estereotipos de la mujer.

1. la mujer tradicional **2.** la mujer liberada **3.** la supermujer

---

REFRÁN

Querer es poder.

(*Where there's a will, there's a way.* Literally, *To want is to be able to.*)

VENTANAS CULTURALES Nuestra comunidad

Edward James Olmos, actor y activista

Edward James Olmos nació en un barrio de Los Ángeles, California. Hijo de inmigrantes mexicanos, Olmos es un hombre de múltiples talentos. Empieza su carrera en la música, luego trabaja de actor en el teatro, el cine y la televisión. Ganador de un Emmy y un Golden Globe, lo conocemos como el maestro Jaime Escalante en la película *Stand and Deliver* y el padre y **representante** de Selena Quintanilla-Pérez en la película sobre la famosa cantante mexicoamericana. El famoso actor también hace el **papel** del **teniente** Castillo en la serie de televisión *Miami Vice* y del capitán de una **nave espacial** en el programa de ciencia ficción *Battlestar Galactica*.

Además de ser un actor muy versátil, Olmos es productor y director de cine. Pero también tiene otros intereses que ocupan su tiempo, como por ejemplo su trabajo social en la comunidad hispana y en su fundación, Latino Public Broadcasting, y su participación en **ferias** del libro. Olmos visita muchas escuelas al año para llevar su mensaje a los jóvenes: es importante estudiar. Además, él opina que debemos transformar la imagen negativa de los latinos en la televisión, el cine y las noticias. Porque entre los hispanos de este país hay doctores, maestros, escritores, políticos, deportistas, astronautas y muchos más que contribuyen de manera positiva a nuestra sociedad.

VOCABULARIO ÚTIL

el representante	*manager*
el papel	*part (in a play or movie)*
el teniente	*lieutenant*
la nave espacial	*spaceship*
las ferias	*fairs*

Comprensión

1. Edward James Olmos es un actor muy versátil. ¿Qué papeles hace?
   a. deportista **b.** maestro **c.** doctor **d.** capitán **e.** político **f.** teniente

2. ¿Cuál es el mensaje que Olmos lleva a los jóvenes?

El tiempo

✳ **Lea Gramática 2.4–2.5.**

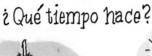

¿Qué tiempo hace?

Hace sol.

Hace mucho calor.

Hace buen tiempo.

Hace fresco.

Hace mucho frío.

Hace viento.

Está nublado.

Llueve.

Nieva.

Hoy es un día de primavera y hace buen tiempo.

Aquellos jóvenes prefieren andar en motocicleta.

Esos chicos prefieren jugar al fútbol.

Esa chica prefiere jugar al tenis.

Estos niños prefieren andar en bici.

Esta señora prefiere leer una novela en el parque.

Este señor prefiere tomar una siesta.

Estas mujeres prefieren pasear.

Usted está aquí.

Actividad 14 Intercambios: El clima

Mire el gráfico y hágale preguntas a su compañero/a sobre la temperatura en estas ciudades del mundo hispano.

Ciudad	enero	julio
Guanajuato, México		
temperatura mínima	7°C	14°C
temperatura máxima	22°C	26°C
Tegucigalpa, Honduras		
temperatura mínima	15°C	18°C
temperatura máxima	25°C	27°C
Bogotá, Colombia		
temperatura mínima	5°C	7°C
temperatura máxima	19°C	18°C
Quito, Ecuador		
temperatura mínima	10°C	9°C
temperatura máxima	19°C	19°C
Lima, Perú		
temperatura mínima	20°C	16°C
temperatura máxima	26°C	19°C
Santiago, Chile		
temperatura mínima	12°C	3°C
temperatura máxima	29°C	14°C
Bariloche, Argentina		
temperatura mínima	6°C	-2°C
temperatura máxima	21°C	6°C
La Habana, Cuba		
temperatura mínima	18°C	23°C
temperatura máxima	26°C	31°C
Potosí, Bolivia		
temperatura mínima	3°C	-7°C
temperatura máxima	18°C	14°C
Sevilla, España		
temperatura mínima	6°C	19°C
temperatura máxima	16°C	35°C

E1: ¿Cuál es la temperatura *máxima* en *Sevilla* en *julio*?
E2: La temperatura *máxima* en *Sevilla* en *julio* es de 35 grados centígrados.

E1: Entonces, ¿qué tiempo hace en *Sevilla* en *julio*?
E2: Hace *mucho calor.*

Actividad 15 Definiciones: Las estaciones y el clima

Lea estas descripciones y diga qué estación representa cada una: la primavera, el verano, el otoño o el invierno.

1. Hace mucho frío y a veces nieva.
2. Llueve mucho, a veces hace viento, nacen muchos animales y hay muchas flores y plantas nuevas.

3. Las clases empiezan y hay árboles de hojas amarillas, anaranjadas y de color café. Es la temporada del fútbol americano.

4. Es la estación de las vacaciones. Hace mucho calor y muchas personas van a nadar al lago o a la piscina.

Ahora, diga qué estación tiene cada país en estos meses.

1. España: diciembre, enero, febrero. Es _____.
2. Chile: diciembre, enero, febrero. Es _____.
3. México: septiembre, octubre, noviembre. Es _____.
4. Perú: septiembre, octubre, noviembre. Es _____.
5. Uruguay: marzo, abril, mayo. Es _____.
6. Argentina: junio, julio, agosto. Es _____.

Actividad 16 Descripción de dibujos: ¿Qué quieren comprar?

A. Mire el dibujo de la tienda El Gran Deportista y diga qué quieren Ernestito, Guillermo y Amanda.

MODELO: E1: ¿Qué quiere *Amanda*?
E2: *Amanda* quiere *esa raqueta y esas pelotas*.

B. Ahora charle con su compañero/a sobre los objetos que quieren comprar ustedes en El Gran Deportista.

MODELO: E1: ¿Qué quieres comprar tú?
E2: Yo quiero *aquella tabla de snowboard*. ¿Y tú?
E1: Yo prefiero *este casco para andar en bicicleta*.

Enlace a la música

La música andina

Los Andes se extienden desde Venezuela en el norte de Sudamérica, hasta Chile en el sur. En esta región andina hay varias culturas indígenas, entre ellas la *chibcha* de Colombia, la *quechua* de Ecuador, Perú y Bolivia y la *aimara* de Chile. La antigua civilización de los incas incluía[1] las culturas de los quechua y los aimara.

Estas culturas producen una música hermosa, notable por sus instrumentos de viento: *la quena* y *la zampoña*. La quena es un tipo de flauta fabricada de una caña hueca[2] o de un hueso[3] de cóndor, que produce un sonido triste y dulce.[4] La zampoña o *seku* tiene dos líneas de tubos de bambú y produce un sonido misterioso.

La música andina se toca también con otros instrumentos indígenas como *el bombo, el charango* y *las charchas* o las cascabeles.[5] El bombo es un tambor[6] de madera y piel[7] de animal que se toca con un palo. El charango, hecho del caparazón del armadillo,[8] es una pequeña guitarra de diez cuerdas.[9] Las charchas son instrumentos de percusión y se fabrican de las pezuñas[10] de varios animales.

La música andina contemporánea utiliza también la guitarra, el violín y las maracas. Si a usted le interesa esta música melódica, puede escuchar la de los grupos Inti-Illimani de Chile, los Kjarkas de Bolivia o Takisuyo del este de los Estados Unidos.

Comprensión

1. ¿Cuáles son los países de la región de Los Andes?
2. La música andina se toca con varios instrumentos indígenas como el charango y los cascabeles. ¿Qué otros instrumentos se utilizan en la música andina contemporánea?
  a. la guitarra **b.** el piano **c.** el violín **d.** la flauta **e.** las maracas

[1]*included* [2]*caña... hollow cane* [3]*bone* [4]*sweet* [5]*small bells* [6]*drum* [7]*skin* [8]*caparazón... armadillo shell*
[9]*strings* [10]*hooves*

En resumen

De todo un poco

A. El clima, la ropa y las actividades

MODELO:
> E1: ¿Qué ropa llevas cuando *hace frío*?
> E2: Cuando hace frío llevo *chaqueta, bufanda y botas*.
> E1: ¿Y qué te gusta hacer?
> E2: Me gusta *caminar y jugar en la nieve*. También me gusta *hacer snowboard*.

Frases útiles

hace fresco	hace viento	llueve	hace mucho frío
hace mucho calor	nieva	hace mucho sol	está nublado

B. Mire los dibujos y hable del tiempo y de los deseos y preferencias de las personas.

1.   **2.**   **3.**   **4.**

5.   **6.**   **7.**   **8.**

MODELO:
> E1: ¿Qué tiempo hace en el *primer* dibujo?
> E2: *Nieva y hace frío.*
> E1: ¿Qué quiere hacer *el joven*?
> E2: *El joven* quiere *esquiar*.

103

¡Dígalo por escrito!

Las preferencias

Mire la Actividad 12 en este capítulo y haga una lista de las preferencias de los estadounidenses o de la gente de su país. Compare su lista con la lista de las preferencias de los españoles. Si quiere, ilustre su lista con dibujos, como en la actividad.

¡Cuéntenos usted!

Cuéntenos sobre un fin de semana perfecto. ¿Qué va a hacer el viernes por la noche? ¿Con quién va a hacerlo? El sábado por la mañana, ¿qué prefiere hacer? ¿Qué va a hacer el sábado por la noche? ¿Qué prefiere hacer el domingo por la mañana? El domingo por la tarde, ¿qué prefiere hacer?

MODELO: Durante mi fin de semana perfecto, voy a hacer muchas cosas. El viernes por la noche voy a salir con mis amigos a una discoteca. Vamos a bailar y hablar con muchos chicos. Voy a regresar a casa a las 2:00 de la mañana. El sábado voy a dormir hasta muy tarde y...

PISTAS PARA LEER
1. Scan title, photo, and vocabulary box. Can you tell what places are described in this reading?
2. Scan text for cognates (words that are similar in English and Spanish).
3. Now skim the reading with these questions in mind: What leisure activities are described? Where do these activities take place?

VOCABULARIO ÚTIL

planear	to plan
disfrutar	to enjoy
de paseo	for a stroll
el banco	bench
la fuente	fountain
las cartas	cards
fundan	found
construyen	build
encontrar	to find

LECTURA

De paseo

En general, a los hispanos no les gusta **planear** demasiado su tiempo libre. Muchos prefieren **disfrutar** del momento presente y hacer las cosas de un modo espontáneo. La gente sale con el pretexto de visitar a los amigos, comprar algo o pasear por las calles y la plaza.

En las calles siempre hay mucha actividad de todo tipo, especialmente en las calles del centro, como la Gran Vía en Madrid, y en las zonas comerciales, como la Calle Florida en Buenos Aires. Pero la plaza es el lugar que muchos hispanos prefieren para ir **de paseo**. En casi todas las plazas hay **bancos** y árboles, y algunas tienen una **fuente**. La gente va a la plaza para sentarse, conversar o simplemente para mirar a las personas que pasan. En algunos pueblos, la gente juega allí a diferentes juegos como el dominó o las **cartas**.

El lugar que hoy llamamos *plaza* se origina en España. Cuando los españoles **fundan** sus ciudades, **construyen** la plaza como centro urbano. En Madrid, capital española, hay numerosas plazas; dos de las más populares son la Plaza Mayor y la Plaza de España. La Plaza Mayor es muy grande y tiene cafés y restaurantes. Pero también hay plazas pequeñas en los barrios de Madrid y otras ciudades hispanas, como en Sevilla, ciudad pintoresca al sur de España.

Las plazas son lugares ideales para descubrir y explorar la cultura de la gente. En la plaza uno puede tener conversaciones interesantes, dar un paseo agradable y, posiblemente, **encontrar** nuevos amigos.

Comprensión

Complete las oraciones lógicamente, según la lectura. Puede haber más de una respuesta correcta.

1. Generalmente, los hispanos prefieren...
   a. planear actividades.
   b. ser espontáneos durante su tiempo libre.
   c. pensar en el presente.
2. A los hispanos les gusta pasear por...
   a. las calles.
   b. la plaza.
   c. el patio de su casa.
3. Normalmente, en la plaza, las personas...
   a. juegan y conversan.
   b. hacen su tarea o trabajan.
   c. miran a otras personas.
4. Los españoles crean las plazas...
   a. en el siglo XX.
   b. como centro de la ciudad.
   c. para descansar.

Un paso más... ¡a conversar!

Describa su lugar favorito. ¿Dónde está? ¿Por qué le gusta pasar tiempo allí? ¿Prefiere estar solo/a en ese lugar o con otras personas? ¿Con quiénes?

Vea el **Resumen cultural** en este capítulo del *Cuaderno de actividades.*

Vocabulario

Las actividades

Activities

almorzar	to have lunch
andar en motocicleta	to ride a motorcycle
andar en velero	to go sailing
caminar	to walk
charlar	to chat
coser	to sew
dar una fiesta	to give a party
dar un paseo	to go for a walk
desayunar	to have breakfast
descansar	to rest
escribir (cartas)	to write (letters)
esquiar	to ski
estudiar	to study
ir a (+ *infin.*)	to be going to (plan)
voy a...	I am going to . . .
va a...	He/She is going to . . .
jugar al boliche	to bowl
lavar (el carro)	to wash (the car)
levantar pesas	to lift weights
limpiar	to clean
merendar	to have a picnic
montar a caballo	to ride a horse
pasar tiempo	to spend time
pasear en barca	to go for a boat ride
preferir	to prefer
prefiero	I prefer
prefiere	you prefer; he/she prefers
recibir (visitas)	to receive; to have company
reparar	to fix
tomar (una siesta)	to take (a nap)
tomar café/té	to drink coffee/tea
tomar el sol	to sunbathe
volar una cometa	to fly a kite

PALABRAS SEMEJANTES: chatear, invitar, surfear, textear, visitar

Las materias

School Subjects

el diseño de la moda	fashion design
la especialidad	major
la informática	data processing
la ingeniería (mecánica)	(mechanical) engineering
el mercadotecnia	marketing
la química	chemistry

PALABRAS SEMEJANTES: la antropología, el arte, la biología, las ciencias sociales, la economía, la física, la geografía, la historia, la literatura, la psicología, la sociología

El tiempo

The Weather

bajo cero	minus, below zero
el clima	weather; climate
Está nublado.	It is overcast (cloudy).
los grados (centígrados)	degrees (centigrade)
Hace (muy) buen/mal tiempo.	The weather is (very) fine/bad.
Hace (mucho) calor/frío.	It's (very) hot/cold.
Hace fresco.	It's cool.
Hace sol.	It's sunny.
Hace (mucho) viento.	It's (very) windy.
llover	to rain
Llueve (mucho).	It rains (a lot).
la lluvia	rain
nevar	to snow
Nieva (mucho).	It snows (a lot).
la nieve	snow
el pronóstico del tiempo	weather forecast
¿Qué tiempo hace?	What is the weather like?

PALABRAS SEMEJANTES: la temperatura máxima/mínima

¿Cuándo?

When?

con frecuencia	frequently
después	after
esta noche	tonight
hasta	until
más tarde	later
por último	lastly
tarde	late
todavía	still, yet

REPASO: ahora, anteayer, a veces, ayer, hoy, mañana, pasado mañana, por la mañana/tarde/noche, temprano

Los lugares

Places

el centro	downtown
la ciudad	city
la discoteca	dance club
el lago	lake
el mar	sea
la montaña	mountain
la preparatoria	prep school; high school
el río	river

PALABRAS SEMEJANTES: el campus, el club de jazz, el laboratorio, el parque, el teatro

Los números ordinales

Ordinal Numbers

primer, primero/a	first
segundo/a	second
tercer, tercero/a	third
cuarto/a	fourth
quinto/a	fifth
sexto/a	sixth
séptimo/a	seventh
octavo/a	eighth
noveno/a	ninth
décimo/a	tenth

Las descripciones

Descriptions

algún / alguna	some
buen(o) / buena	good
deportivo/a	sports-related
ese, esa / esos, esas	that / those
este, esta / estos, estas	this / these
europeo/a	European
ningún / ninguna	none; not any
próximo/a	next
todo/a	all
último/a	last

PALABRAS SEMEJANTES: atractivo/a, clásico/a, importante, industrial, liberado/a, macho/a, metálico/a, norteamericano/a, romántico/a, tradicional, violento/a

Otros verbos útiles

Other Useful Verbs

abrir	to open
cerrar (ie)	to close
cierra	he/she/it closes
comprar	to buy
contestar	to answer
empezar (ie)	to start, begin
empieza	he/she/it starts
llegar	to arrive
manejar	to drive
nacer	to be born
ofrecer	to offer
quedarse en casa	to stay at home

PALABRAS SEMEJANTES: comparar, usar

Los sustantivos

Nouns

el almuerzo	lunch
el árbol	tree
el balón	(large sports) ball
el casco	helmet
la cerveza	beer
el chocolate caliente	hot chocolate
el descanso	break; rest
el deseo	want, desire
la entrada	entrance
la(s) flor(es)	flower(s)
la gente	people
la gorra	cap
el horario	schedule
la misa	Mass
el pasatiempo	hobby
los patines	skates
la pelota	ball
la respuesta	answer
la temporada	season (of practice)

PALABRAS SEMEJANTES: el animal, el área, el cereal, el estereotipo, el gráfico, la invitación, la novela, el plan, el presente, la radio, el semestre, el trimestre
REPASO: el bate, la bicicleta, la patineta

Palabras del texto

Words from the Text

converse	converse (command)
decidir	to decide
imagínese	imagine (command)
la oración	sentence
Pregúntele...	Ask him/her . . .

PALABRAS SEMEJANTES: asociar, la columna, la conversación, la definición, describir, mencionar, la narración, la ocasión, organizar, representar

Palabras y expresiones útiles

Useful Words and Expressions

algo	something
como	like, as
en general	in general
entonces	so, then
los dos / las dos	both
Nos vemos.	See you.
si	if

PALABRAS SEMEJANTES: el club, la idea, posible, el tren

Gramática y ejercicios

ir = to go
¿Qué vas a hacer esta noche? (*What are you going to do tonight?*)
Voy a estudiar. (*I'm going to study.*)

2.1 Expressing Future Plans: *ir* + *a* + Infinitive

The most common way of expressing future plans is to use the verb **ir** (*to go*) plus the preposition **a** (*to*) followed by an infinitive. This construction is commonly referred to as the *informal future*, because Spanish has another future tense, generally reserved for talking about longer term future plans.*

—¿Qué **vas a hacer** mañana?   —*What are you going to do tomorrow?*
—**Voy a esquiar.**   —*I am going to ski.*

—¿Qué **van a hacer** ustedes este fin de semana?   —*What are you going to do this weekend?*
—**Vamos a ir** al cine.   —*We're going to go to the movies.*

—¿Qué **van a hacer** Esteban y Alberto después de la clase?   —*What are Esteban and Alberto going to do after class?*
—**Van a jugar** al basquetbol.   —*They're going to play basketball.*

Here are the forms of the irregular verb **ir**.[†]

¡Vamos a salir a cenar!
(*Let's go out to eat!*)

The expression **Vamos a** + infinitive is frequently used to express *Let's . . .*

ir (*to go*)		
(yo)	**voy**	*I am going; go*
(tú)	**vas**	*you (inf. sing.) are going; go*
(usted, él/ella)	**va**	*you (pol. sing.) are going; he/she is going; go; goes*
(nosotros/as)	**vamos**	*we are going; go*
(vosotros/as)	**vais**	*you (inf. pl., Spain) are going; go*
(ustedes, ellos/as)	**van**	*you (pl.) are going; they are going; go*

Ejercicio 1

Lea esta conversación sobre los planes de algunos compañeros de clase. Complete las oraciones con las formas correctas del verbo **ir**.

MODELO: Luis *va* a hacer ejercicio en el parque.

1. —¿Qué _____ a hacer tú después de la clase?
   —(Yo) _____ a ir de compras con una amiga.

---

*You will learn how to form the future tense in **Gramática 15.1.**
[†]Recognition: **vos vas**

2. —¿Y qué _____ a hacer Esteban y Carmen?
   —Esteban _____ a estudiar y Carmen _____ a trabajar.
3. —¿Y la profesora Martínez? ¿Qué _____ a hacer ella?
   —Creo que _____ a leer la tarea de sus estudiantes, pero nosotros
   _____ a ir al cine.
4. —Pablo, ¿cuándo _____ a estudiar tú?
   —(Yo) _____ a estudiar más tarde, probablemente esta noche.
5. —¿Y tú, Alberto? ¿Cuándo _____ a hacer la tarea para la clase de español?
   —(Yo) _____ a hacer mi tarea mañana por la mañana.

2.2 Sequencing: Ordinal Adjectives

Ordinal adjectives are used to put things and people into a sequence or order. The ordinals in English are *first, second, third, fourth,* and so on. Here are the ordinals from *first* to *tenth* in Spanish.

primero/a	sexto/a
segundo/a	séptimo/a
tercero/a	octavo/a
cuarto/a	noveno/a
quinto/a	décimo/a

Mi **segunda** clase es difícil.　　*My second class is difficult.*

As with **uno** (*one*), the words **primero** and **tercero** drop the final **-o** when used before a masculine singular noun.

Estoy en el **primer** (**tercer**) año.　　*I am in the first (third) grade.*

> **primer, primero/a** = *first*
> **segundo/a** = *second*
> **tercer, tercero/a** = *third*
> **cuarto/a** = *fourth*
> **quinto/a** = *fifth*
> **sexto/a** = *sixth*
> **séptimo/a** = *seventh*
> **octavo/a** = *eighth*
> **noveno/a** = *ninth*
> **décimo/a** = *tenth*

> **¡OJO!**
>
> The feminine form of the ordinal is used if the referent is *la persona: Guillermo es el cuarto,* but *Es la cuarta persona.*

Ejercicio 2

Conteste las preguntas según el dibujo.

1. ¿Quién es la primera persona*?
2. ¿Quién es la segunda persona?
3. ¿Es Guillermo la quinta?
4. ¿Es Amanda la primera?
5. ¿Es doña Lola la tercera?
6. ¿Quién es la sexta persona?
7. Don Anselmo es la quinta persona, ¿verdad?
8. ¿Quién es el primer hombre?
9. ¿Quién es la segunda mujer?
10. ¿Es don Anselmo el tercer hombre?

Ernesto　doña Lola　Amanda　don Anselmo
Estela　　Guillermo　Ramón

---

*Persona is a feminine word, even when it refers to a man.

2.3 Stating Preferences and Desires: *preferir* and *querer* + Infinitive

preferir = *to prefer, would rather*

querer = *to want*

¿Qué quieres hacer ahora? (*What do you want to do now?*)

Quiero descansar. (*I want to rest.*)

¿Qué prefieres hacer? (*What do you prefer to do? [What would you rather do?]*)

Prefiero comer ahora. (*I prefer to eat now.*)

The verbs **preferir*** (*to prefer, would rather*) and **querer*** (*to want*) are used to express preferences and desires. They are often followed by an infinitive. (Remember that infinitives are the nonconjugated verb forms that end in -**ar, -er,** or -**ir.**)

—¿Qué **quieres** hacer este invierno?
—**Quiero** esquiar.
—¿Qué **prefiere** hacer Pablo?
—**Prefiere** viajar.

—*What do you want to do this winter?*
—*I want to ski.*
—*What does Pablo prefer to do?*
—*He would rather travel.*

Note that the **e** of the stem of these verbs changes to **ie,** except in the **nosotros/as** and **vosotros/as** forms.[†]

		querer (*to want*)	preferir (*to prefer*)	
(yo)		quiero	prefiero	*I want/prefer*
(tú)		quieres	prefieres	*you (inf. sing.) want/prefer*
(usted, él/ella)		quiere	prefiere	*you (pol. sing.) want/prefer; he/she wants/prefers*
(nosotros/as)		queremos	preferimos	*we want/prefer*
(vosotros/as)		queréis	preferís	*you (inf. pl., Spain) want/prefer*
(ustedes, ellos/as)		quieren	prefieren	*you (pl.) want/prefer; they want/prefer*

Ej. 3. All answers are verb forms with stem vowel *ie.*

Ejercicio 3

Complete estas oraciones según el modelo.

MODELO: Nora *quiere* patinar, pero Luis *prefiere* jugar al tenis.

1. Yo _____ ir al cine, pero Esteban _____ salir a bailar.
2. Nora _____ ver la televisión, pero Alberto _____ ir de compras.
3. Lan _____ pasear por el parque, pero yo _____ dormir todo el día.
4. Nora _____ comer comida china, pero Carmen y Pablo _____ cocinar en casa.
5. Mónica _____ dar una fiesta, pero Alberto _____ bailar en la discoteca.

*Recognition: **vos preferís, querés**
[†]Verbs like **preferir** and **querer** that use more than one stem in their conjugation are known as *irregular verbs.* You will learn more about this type of verb beginning in **Gramática 3.3.**

6. El padre de Esteban _____ acampar, pero yo _____ ir a la playa.

7. Carmen _____ sacar fotos, pero Lan _____ escribir una carta.

8. Luis _____ dibujar, pero yo _____ tocar la guitarra.

9. Mónica y Pablo _____ ir a pasear por el centro, pero yo _____ dormir toda la tarde.

10. Luis y Alberto _____ descansar, pero Esteban _____ leer el periódico.

Ejercicio 4

¿Qué quieren hacer estas personas? Conteste según el modelo.

MODELO: ¿Qué quiere hacer Guillermo? → *Quiere jugar al basquetbol.*

1. ¿Qué quiere hacer Ernestito?

2. ¿Qué prefiere hacer usted, señor Saucedo?

3. ¿Qué quieren hacer Estela y Andrea?

4. Luis y Nora, ¿qué prefieren hacer ustedes?

5. ¿Qué prefieren hacer Diego y Rafael?

6. ¿Qué quiere hacer Amanda?

¡OJO!

Ejercicio 4. In items 2 and 4 the questions are addressed to the characters in the drawings. For item 2, answer using the first-person singular (**yo**) and for item 4, answer using the first-person plural (**nosotros**).

Ejercicio 5

Escriba los planes y las preferencias de estas personas.

	PLANES		PREFERENCIAS/DESEOS
MODELO:	Nora *va a leer*	pero	*prefiere (quiere) dormir.*

1. Lan

2. Carmen

3. Esteban

4. Alberto

5. Pablo

6. Mi compañera

7. Yo

2.4 Pointing Out People and Objects: Demonstrative Adjectives

A. Demonstrative adjectives are normally used to point out nouns.

Quiero terminar **esta lección** primero.	*I want to finish this lesson first.*
Esos tres **muchachos** quieren andar en moto.	*Those three boys want to ride motorcycles.*

Demonstrative adjectives are placed before the noun that they modify and must agree in gender and number with that noun.

aquí/acá (*here*) (*close to the person speaking*)

SINGULAR		PLURAL	
este libro	*this book*	estos pantalones	*these pants*
esta señora	*this lady*	estas casas	*these houses*

allí/allá (*there*) (*at some distance from the person speaking*)

ese libro	*that book*	esos pantalones	*those pants*
esa señora	*that lady*	esas casas	*those houses*

> este/esta = *this*
> este libro = *this book*
> esta fotografía = *this photo*

> estos/estas = *these*
> estos cuadernos = *these notebooks*
> estas tareas = *these homework assignments*

—Amanda, ¿no te gusta **esta blusa**?	*—Amanda, don't you like this blouse?*
—No, prefiero **esa blusa** roja.	*—No, I prefer that red blouse.*
—**Estos pantalones** son nuevos. ¿Te gustan?	*—These pants are new. Do you like them?*

> ese/esa = *that*
> ese cartel = *that poster*
> esa silla = *that chair*

> esos/esas = *those*
> esos papeles = *those papers*
> esas chicas = *those girls*

Use the demonstrative pronouns **esto** or **eso** when the object has not been identified.

—Estela, ¿sabes qué es **esto**?	*—Estela, do you know what this is?*
—No, no sé.	*—No, I don't know.*

> esto/eso = *this/that* (*unidentified object*)

The demonstratives **aquel, aquellos, aquella,** and **aquellas** indicate that the person or thing pointed out is more distant (generally far away in space or in time from both speakers).

—¿Ves **aquella casa**?	*—Do you see that house (over there)?*
—¿**Aquella casa** de los árboles grandes?	*—That house with the big trees?*
Estudio biología en **este edificio** y estudio química en **aquel edificio**.	*I study biology in this building, and I study chemistry in that building (over there).*

> aquel/aquella = *that*
> aquel edificio = *that building*
> aquella plaza = *that plaza*

> aquellos/aquellas = *those*
> aquellos árboles = *those trees*
> aquellas puertas = *those doors*

B. Although most adjectives in Spanish are placed after the noun they modify (**una casa moderna, unos zapatos negros**), the ordinal adjectives (**Gramática 2.2**) and the demonstrative adjectives are both placed before the noun: **La *tercera casa* es la de mi prima.** ***Esos jóvenes*** **son mis amigos.** A few adjectives may be placed before or after the noun, with differences in meaning.

Es un gran* hombre.	*He is a great man.*
Es un hombre grande.	*He is a big man.*
La señora Rivera es una vieja amiga de la familia.	*Mrs. Rivera is an old (long-time) family friend.*
Es una señora vieja.	*She is an old woman.*
Ahora tengo un nuevo coche.	*Now I have a new (different) car.*
Mi vecino tiene un coche nuevo.	*My neighbor has a new (new model) car.*
¡El pobre niño no comprende la tarea!	*The poor child doesn't understand the assignment!*
Ese niño es de una familia muy pobre.	*That boy comes from a very poor family.*

Ejercicio 6

Amanda está hablando con Graciela de su ropa. Complete las oraciones con **este, esta, estos** o **estas.**

MODELO: Me gusta *esta* blusa azul.

1. _____ blusa es mi favorita.
2. _____ zapatos son muy viejos.
3. _____ pantalones son nuevos.
4. _____ faldas son bonitas, pero un poco viejas.
5. _____ suéter es de mi mamá.

Ejercicio 7

Doña Lola y doña Rosita están en la plaza hablando de sus vecinos. Complete las oraciones con **ese, esa, esos** o **esas.**

MODELO: *Esa* señora es una cocinera magnífica.

1. _____ señoritas trabajan en la oficina con Paula Saucedo.
2. _____ chico es Guillermo, el hijo de Ernesto y Estela Saucedo.
3. _____ muchacha se llama Amanda. Tiene 14 años.
4. _____ señores juegan a las cartas con don Anselmo.
5. _____ muchachos son compañeros de escuela de Ernestito.

Ejercicio 8

este/estos; esta/estas
ese/esos; esa/esas

Imagínese que usted está en una fiesta con Esteban. Él no conoce a muchas personas y por eso le hace a usted las siguientes preguntas. Complete las preguntas de Esteban con las formas correctas de **este** o **ese.**

1. ¿Cómo se llama _____ señora que está hablando con Nora allí cerca de la puerta?

---

*The words **bueno, malo, primero,** and **tercero** shorten to **buen, mal, primer,** and **tercer** when placed before a masculine singular noun. **Es un buen chico. Es una buena profesora.** The word **grande** shortens to **gran** before any singular noun. **Isabel Allende es una gran escritora. Camilo José Cela y Gabriel García Márquez son grandes escritores.**

2. Creo que _____ señor que está aquí a la derecha es amigo de tu padre, ¿verdad?

3. ¿Son actores _____ dos jóvenes que están allí en la cocina?

4. ¿Se llama Jesús _____ muchacho que está aquí detrás de nosotros?

5. ¿Cómo se llaman _____ muchachas que están sentadas aquí justamente enfrente de nosotros?

Ejercicio 9

Usted vende zapatos. ¿Cuáles recomienda? Use formas de **este, ese** y **aquel,** según la distancia entre usted y los dibujos.

Usted está aquí

1. _____ zapatos son mejores para jugar al tenis.

2. _____ zapatos son para un señor que trabaja en una oficina.

3. _____ zapatos son bonitos y muy elegantes.

4. _____ zapatos son para una mujer que trabaja en una oficina.

5. _____ botas son para la lluvia.

6. _____ sandalias me gustan mucho.

EL CLUB DE TITO

Restaurante y salón de baile
Avenida Jalapa 1475, México, D.F.
Teléfono: 2-46-98-71

SÁBADOS: B a i l e

Desde las 8:00 de la noche hasta las 5:00 de la mañana
Especialidad de la casa: *PIÑA COLADA*
¡ORQUESTA DE BETO RODRÍGUEZ!

el domingo, 5 de octubre
Escuche la música de JORGE MANRICO
¡directamente de Guadalajara!
¡Baile hasta las dos de la mañana!

VIERNES: B a i l e

Desde las 6:00 de la tarde
con la música de PEPE FUENTES

2.5 Describing the Weather: Common Expressions

Spanish speakers use several verbs to describe weather conditions.

> Most Spanish weather expressions use either **hacer** or **haber:**
>
> **Hace frío.** (*It's cold.*)
> **Hace calor.** (*It's hot.*)
> **Hace buen/mal tiempo.** (*The weather is good/bad.*)
> **Hay neblina.** (*It's foggy.*)
>
> But to talk about resultant states, use **estar** + adjective:
> **Está nublado.** (*It's cloudy.*)
>
> **Nevar** and **llover** use just the verb:
> **Nieva.** (*It's snowing.* [*It snows.*])
> **Llueve.** (*It's raining.* [*It rains.*])

A. If a weather expression refers to a phenomenon that can be felt (good weather, heat, cold, wind), use **hacer.**

—¿Qué tiempo **hace** hoy?   —*What's the weather like today?*
—**Hace frío.**   —*It's cold.*

Other weather expressions with **hacer** are **hace calor** (*it's hot*), **hace buen/mal tiempo** (*the weather is good/bad*), **hace viento** (*it's windy*), **hace sol** (*it's sunny*), and **hace fresco** (*it's cool*).

B. If a weather expression refers to a phenomenon that can be seen, use **haber.**

—**Hay neblina** por la costa.   —*It's foggy (There is fog) along the coast.*

—**Hay nubes** hoy.   —*It's cloudy (There are clouds) today.*

C. For resultant states (that is, conditions that result from a specific phenomenon, such as **Hay nubes** or **Hace sol**), use **estar** with the appropriate adjective.

—**Está nublado** hoy.   —*It's cloudy today.*
—**Está soleado** en las montañas.   —*It's sunny in the mountains.*

D. To talk about rain and snow, use only the corresponding verb (**llover** or **nevar**).

—Siempre **llueve** aquí por la tarde.   —*It always rains here in the afternoon.*
—**Nieva** mucho en Montana.   —*It snows a lot in Montana.*

Note in all of these weather expressions that Spanish does not use a pronoun corresponding to English *it.*

Ejercicio 10

Diga qué tiempo hace.

1.

2.

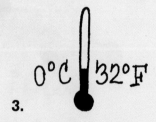

3.

4.

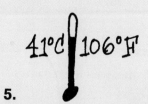

5.

6.

Ejercicio 11

Diga si son posibles o imposibles estas combinaciones.

1. —¿Hace sol?
   —Sí, y también hace calor.
2. —¿Hace mal tiempo?
   —Sí, y llueve mucho.
3. —¿Hace buen tiempo?
   —Sí, y hace mucho frío.
4. —¿Hace calor?
   —Sí, y también nieva.
5. —¿Hace frío?
   —Sí, y también hace mucho calor.

Las actividades y los lugares

METAS

In **Capítulo 3** you will discuss daily activities and learn useful vocabulary related to the three daily meals: breakfast, lunch, and dinner. You will also talk about places in the city and on your campus as well as about where you and others are from.

Sobre la artista: Soraida Martínez —artista, diseñadora y autora de herencia puertorriqueña— nació en Harlem, Nueva York. Desde 1992, Soraida es la creadora del reconocido «Verdadismo»: estilo de arte abstracto y contemporáneo que contiene un comentario social sobre el racismo, el sexismo y los estereotipos. Soraida se graduó de la universidad con concentración en bellas artes y especialización en el diseño.

Little Girl from Harlem, por Soraida Martínez (Estados Unidos)

«Cuando era niña y vivía en Harlem, siempre supe que Harlem era un tipo de exilio; lo que no sabía era por qué tenía que estar yo allí. Hubo tiempos felices así como tiempos tristes pero, para escapar, yo siempre soñaba despierta. Soñaba con un patio, con crecer e ir a la escuela de arte, con alejarme de allí.»

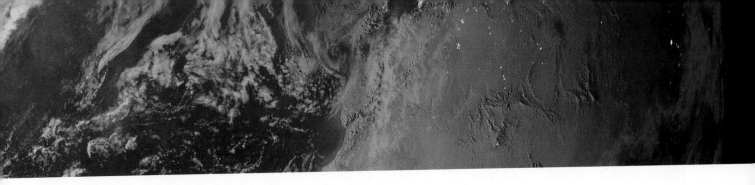

¡Conozca los Estados Unidos!

Nombre del país: los Estados Unidos de América

Ciudad capital: Washington, D.C.

Ciudades principales: Nueva York, Los Ángeles, Chicago, Miami, San Francisco

Moneda: el dólar estadounidense

Idiomas: el inglés (oficial), el español, el chino, el francés, el tagalo y otros

Población hispana: 45.000.000

Día de la Independencia: el 4 de julio

Fiestas hispanas típicas: el Cinco de Mayo y las Fiestas Patrias en Los Ángeles, el Desfile Nacional Puertorriqueño en Nueva York, el Festival de la Calle Ocho en Miami

Comidas típicas: los tacos, los burritos, las enchiladas, el plátano frito, el arroz con frijoles, el sándwich cubano, las pupusas, las tapas

Música típica: el jazz latino, el rock en español, la salsa, el merengue, la bachata, la cumbia, el reggaetón, el mariachi, la norteña, la ranchera, el *Tex-Mex*

Gente famosa: César Chavez, Sandra Cisneros, Dolores Huerta, Edward James Olmos, Cristina García, Bill Richardson, Julia Álvarez, Gloria Estefan

Código de país por Internet: .us

Voces hispanas

la chanza	chance
guachar	to watch
el lonche	lunch
la marketa	market
el pana	buddy
la troca	truck
el vacunclín	vacuum cleaner

En este capítulo...

 ACTIVIDADES DE COMUNICACIÓN

- Las actividades diarias
- Las tres comidas
- Los lugares
- ¿De dónde es usted?

 EN RESUMEN

 LECTURAS Y CULTURA

- **Ventanas al pasado**
  Antoni Gaudí, gran arquitecto
- **Enlace al cine**
  El cine en México y en España
- **Lectura**
  La presencia vital de los hispanos

 GRAMÁTICA Y EJERCICIOS

3.1 Talking about Habitual Actions: Present Tense of Regular Verbs

3.2 Using Irregular Verbs: **hacer, salir, jugar**

3.3 Referring to Objects already Mentioned: Direct Object Pronouns **lo, la, los,** and **las**

3.4 Asking and Answering Questions

3.5 Talking about Location and Origin: **estar en, ir a,** and **ser de**

  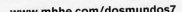

Las actividades diarias

⭐ **Lea Gramática 3.1–3.2.**

Un día típico en la vida de la familia Saucedo

Ernesto lee el periódico todas las mañanas.

Los Saucedo y sus hijos desayunan juntos.

Ernesto sale de la casa a las 8:30.

Ernesto espera el autobús.

Amanda y sus hermanos caminan al parque.

Guillermo juega al fútbol con sus amigos.

Berta limpia la casa.

Estela prepara la cena.

La familia Saucedo cena a las 8:00.

Actividad 1 Intercambios: Las actividades diarias

MODELOS: E1: ¿Quién *va a misa*?
           E2: *Silvia.*

           E1: ¿Cuándo *hace ejercicio Mayín*?
           E2: *Los jueves por la noche.*

REFRÁN

Al que madruga, Dios lo ayuda.

(*The early bird gets the worm.* Literally, *God helps those who get up early.*)

	SILVIA BUSTAMANTE MÉXICO, D.F.	ADRIANA BOLINI BUENOS AIRES	MAYÍN DURÁN LOS ÁNGELES
los lunes por la mañana	va en metro al trabajo	maneja y habla por celular	va en coche a la estación de radio
los miércoles por la tarde	trabaja en la estación de autobuses	diseña sitios Web	escribe un reportaje
los jueves por la noche	estudia	asiste a una reunión	hace ejercicio en el gimnasio
los sábados por la tarde	lleva su ropa a la lavandería	pasea por el parque	lee el periódico
los domingos por la mañana	va a misa	juega al tenis	ve la televisión

Actividad 2 Asociaciones: Las actividades típicas

¿Cuáles son las actividades típicas de estas personas?

1. un profesor / una profesora
2. un ama de casa
3. un hombre / una mujer de negocios
4. un(a) estudiante
5. un(a) recepcionista

Actividades posibles: almuerza en un restaurante, asiste a clases, charla con un amigo en la cafetería, cocina, estudia, habla por teléfono, hace la compra, hace la tarea, lee las tareas de los estudiantes, lee una revista o el periódico, limpia la casa, prepara las lecciones, trabaja en su oficina, va a la biblioteca, va al correo

Actividad 3   Narración: Un día en la vida de Carla Espinosa

Palabras útiles

primero	después	finalmente
luego	más tarde	por último
¿A qué hora?	A la(s)...	

Actividad 4   Preferencias: ¿Con qué frecuencia?

Diga con qué frecuencia usted hace estas actividades durante la semana. Use **siempre, con frecuencia, a veces, de vez en cuando** y **casi nunca.**

MODELO: De vez en cuando hago la tarea en la biblioteca. ¿Y tú?

1. Veo la televisión por la noche.
2. Salgo a cenar con amigos.
3. Juego al basquetbol.
4. Voy al cine.
5. Lavo el carro.
6. Hago ejercicio aeróbico.
7. Preparo la cena.
8. Como en el carro.
9. Escucho música mientras estudio.
10. Visito sitios Web en el Internet.

Actividad 5 Asociaciones: Las actividades de mi familia

En su familia, ¿quién hace las siguientes actividades?

MODELOS: estudia(n) en la universidad →
Mis hermanos estudian en la universidad.

trabaja(n) los sábados →
Nadie en mi familia trabaja los sábados.

Mi esposo/a	Mi(s) hermano(s)/a(s)	Mi(s) hijo(s)/a(s)
Mis padres	Mi(s) primo(s)/a(s)	Nadie

1. sale(n) mucho con sus amigos
2. hace(n) *snowboard* en el invierno
3. ve(n) la televisión
4. va(n) al cine los fines de semana
5. lee(n) el periódico por la mañana
6. escucha(n) música clásica
7. trabaja(n) los sábados
8. nada(n) en el verano
9. anda(n) en patineta
10. juega(n) a los videojuegos

Actividad 6 Entrevista: El fin de semana

GENERALMENTE LOS VIERNES POR LA NOCHE...

1. ¿Sales con tus amigos? ¿Vas al cine? ¿Vas a una discoteca o a un club?
2. ¿Trabajas? ¿Hasta qué hora?
3. ¿Cenas en un restaurante?
4. ¿Lees un libro? ¿Exploras el Internet? ¿Juegas a las cartas?
5. ¿Vas a (Das) una fiesta? ¿Dónde? ¿Con quién(es)?

GENERALMENTE LOS SÁBADOS...

1. ¿Practicas algún deporte? ¿Cuál prefieres?
2. ¿Ves la televisión? ¿Qué programas te gustan?
3. ¿Vas de compras? ¿Adónde?
4. ¿Trabajas? ¿Dónde? ¿Cuántas horas?
5. ¿Estudias? ¿Dónde? ¿Con quién(es)?

Las tres comidas

✴ **Lea Gramática 3.3.**

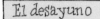
El desayuno

los huevos

el cereal

el yogur

el pan tostado con mantequilla

la fruta

el jugo de naranja

la leche

el café el té

¿La leche? La bebemos todas las mañanas.

El almuerzo

la sopa

las galletas

los tacos

el sándwich de jamón y queso

la hamburguesa

las papas fritas

los refrescos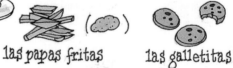

las galletitas

¿Las papas fritas? Siempre las como para el almuerzo.

La cena

la ensalada de lechuga y tomate

el bistec la papa al horno

las legumbres

el pan

la cerveza

¿El pan? Lo como todos los días.

el pollo frito

los espaguetis

el helado el pastel

el postre

Actividad 7 Conversación

Diga si son saludables o no estas comidas y bebidas. Luego diga si le gustan o no.

MODELOS: E1: ¿Es saludable el pastel de chocolate?
E2: No, no es saludable, pero es delicioso.
E1: ¿Te gusta el pastel de chocolate?
E2: Sí, me gusta mucho con leche.

E1: ¿Son saludables los huevos revueltos?
E2: Sí, son muy saludables.
E1: ¿Te gustan los huevos revueltos para el desayuno?
E2: No, no me gustan; prefiero el cereal.

EL DESAYUNO	EL ALMUERZO	LA CENA
los huevos revueltos	la sopa	las legumbres
la fruta	la hamburguesa	el pollo frito
el pan tostado	un sándwich de jamón y queso	el arroz
la leche	los tacos	el bistec
el café / el té	las papas fritas	el pescado
el yogur	la ensalada	el pastel de chocolate
el cereal	los burritos	el helado

Actividad 8 Conversación

Vea las listas de comidas y bebidas de la **Actividad 7** y diga con qué frecuencia las come o las bebe. Use los pronombres **lo, la, los, las.**

MODELO: E1: ¿Las papas fritas? ¿Las comes con frecuencia?
E2: No, no las como casi nunca, porque no son saludables.
(Sí, las como todos los días porque me gustan mucho.)

Actividad 9 Entrevista: ¿Qué comes… ?

1. ¿Qué desayunas todos los días? ¿Desayunas algo diferente los sábados? ¿Y los domingos?
2. ¿Dónde almuerzas de lunes a viernes? ¿A qué hora almuerzas? ¿Qué te gusta almorzar?
3. ¿Qué prefieres para la cena: bistec o pescado? ¿Cuál es el más saludable? ¿Y sales a cenar los fines de semana?
4. ¿Prefieres desayunar pan tostado o cereal? ¿Prefieres almorzar en casa o en la cafetería de la universidad?
5. ¿Te gusta cocinar o prefieres salir a cenar? ¿Cuál es tu restaurante favorito?
6. ¿A qué hora desayunas/almuerzas/cenas? ¿Sabes que en España y algunos países latinoamericanos el almuerzo es a las 2:00 ó 3:00 de la tarde y la cena a las 9:00 ó 10:00 de la noche? ¿Te gusta ese horario? ¿Por qué?

Los lugares

✳ **Lea Gramática 3.5**

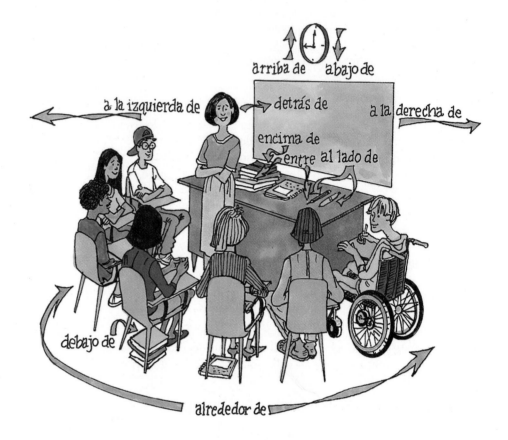

Actividad 10   Intercambios: La Universidad Estatal del Oriente

Mire el plano de la página siguiente. Escuche mientras su profesor(a) describe dónde están algunos edificios. Escriba el nombre del edificio en el lugar apropiado.

Edificios: la biblioteca, la cafetería, la Facultad de Ciencias Sociales, la Facultad de Medicina, el gimnasio, el teatro

Ahora, pregúntele a su compañero/a dónde están los edificios en el plano.

MODELOS: E1: ¿Dónde está *el teatro*?
E2: Está *enfrente de la Facultad de Bellas Artes.*

E1: ¿En qué calle está *la cafetería*?
E2: Está en la *avenida de las Rosas,* al lado de la librería.

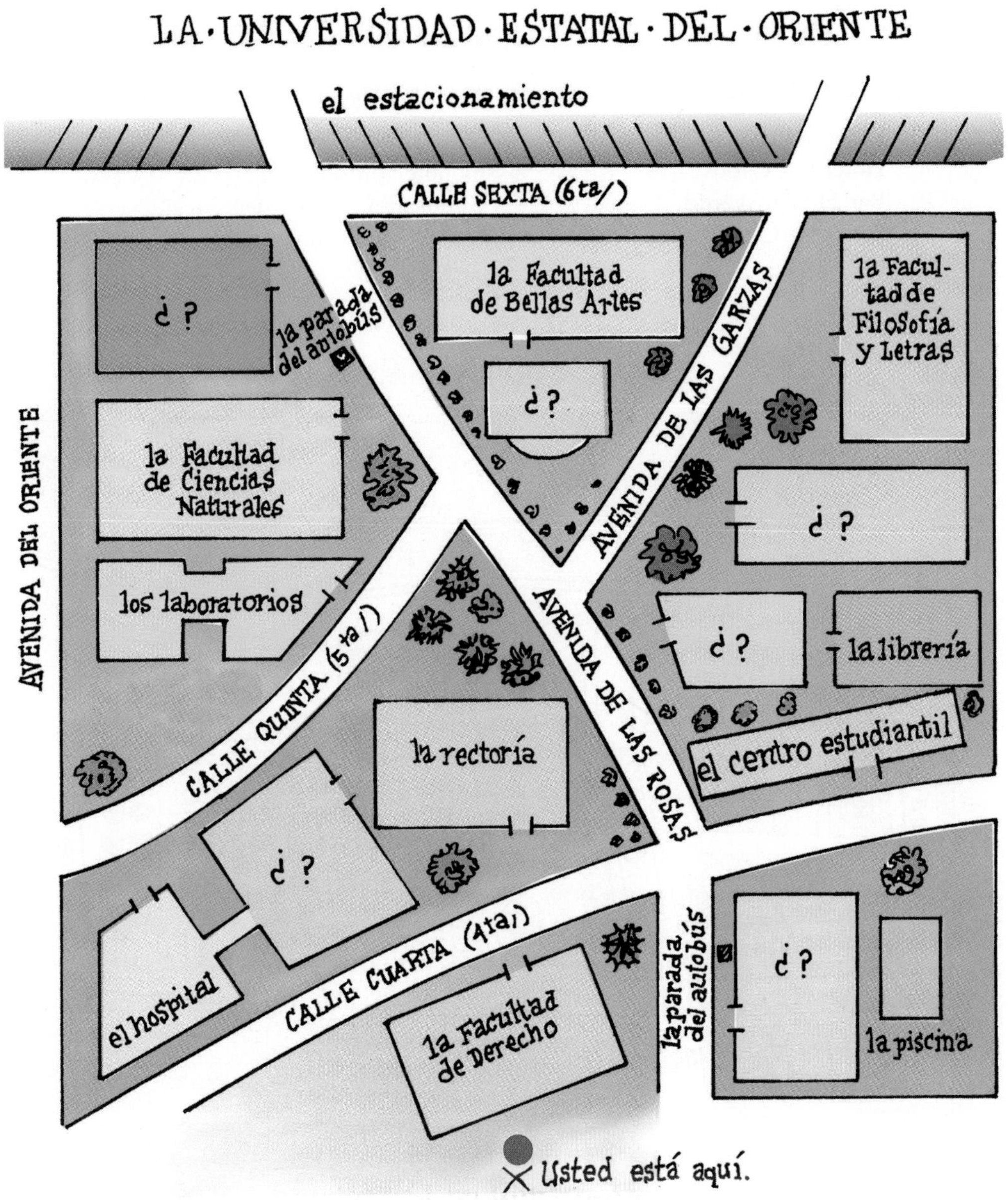

LA·UNIVERSIDAD·ESTATAL·DEL·ORIENTE

el estacionamiento

CALLE SEXTA (6ta/)

¿?

la Facultad de Bellas Artes

la parada del autobús

¿?

AVENIDA DE LAS GARZAS

la Facultad de Filosofía y Letras

AVENIDA DEL ORIENTE

la Facultad de Ciencias Naturales

¿?

los laboratorios

AVENIDA DE LAS ROSAS

¿?

la librería

CALLE QUINTA (5ta/)

la rectoría

el centro estudiantil

¿?

el hospital

CALLE CUARTA (4ta/)

la Facultad de Derecho

la parada del autobús

¿?

la piscina

X Usted está aquí.

Palabras útiles

al lado de
a la derecha de
a la izquierda de
detrás de
enfrente de
entre

Actividad 11   Intercambios: En nuestra universidad

Pregúntele a su compañero/a dónde están los siguientes lugares en su universidad.

MODELO: E1: ¿Dónde está *la cafetería*?
              E2: Está *detrás de...*

1. la biblioteca
2. el gimnasio
3. la librería
4. el teatro
5. la Facultad de _____
6. ¿ ?

Actividad 12 Descripción de dibujos: ¿Dónde está?

Escuche a su profesor(a) y escriba el numero que corresponde a estos lugares.

Videocentro
Hotel Los Cabos
Bar El Gato Verde
Farmacia Cruz Blanca

Café Cibernético
Biblioteca Municipal
Gimnasio Cabo Verde
Museo Nacional

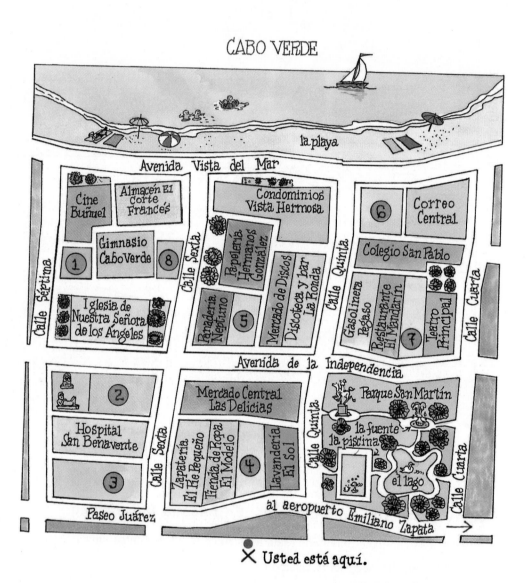

Actividad 13 Asociaciones: ¿Para qué vamos a estos lugares?

Empareje estas actividades con los lugares.

MODELOS: el parque →
Vamos al parque *para merendar con nuestros amigos.*

la papelería →
Vamos a la papelería *para comprar papel, lápices y cuadernos.*

LUGAR	ACTIVIDAD
1. el cine e	**a.** para comprar zapatos
2. la playa g	**b.** para ver las exhibiciones
3. el mercado h	**c.** para comprar estampillas y para mandar cartas
4. una panadería f	**d.** para rezar
5. un museo b	**e.** para ver una película
6. la iglesia d	**f.** para comprar pan o pasteles
7. el correo c	**g.** para tomar el sol y nadar
8. un hospital j	**h.** para comprar comida
9. una zapatería a	**i.** para leer y estudiar
10. la biblioteca i	**j.** para recibir atención médica

VENTANAS AL PASADO

Antoni Gaudí, gran arquitecto

Antoni Gaudí i Cornet es uno de los arquitectos más famosos de Europa. Nace en 1852 en la provincia de Tarragona, en la costa mediterránea de España. A los 26 años recibe en Barcelona su título de arquitecto y **conoce** a Eusebi Güell, político y miembro de una prestigiosa familia **catalana.** Con el **apoyo** económico de Güell, el joven arquitecto Gaudí puede **realizar** varias obras impresionantes, entre ellas el Parque Güell. Este lugar, originalmente una **urbanización de lujo,** es hoy en día un parque público en la ciudad de Barcelona.

Gaudí crea una arquitectura impresionante basada en líneas curvas y formas geometrizadas, en líneas modernas y también medievales, que **al mismo tiempo** se incorpora a la **naturaleza.** También se ven en sus obras elementos árabes, sobre todo en su uso de **torres, ladrillos, piedras** y mosaicos. Entre sus muchas obras arquitectónicas están la villa *El Capricho* en Cantabria, el Palacio Güell, el Parque Güell, la Casa Milà y el Colegio Teresiano en Barcelona. En esta ciudad también está la Iglesia de la Sagrada Familia, obra que Gaudí nunca termina.

Antoni Gaudí muere trágicamente en 1926 a la edad de 74 años, **atropellado** por un **tranvía** en Barcelona. La construcción continúa en la Iglesia

VOCABULARIO ÚTIL	
conoce	*meets*
catalán (catalana)	*from the region of Cataluña in Spain*
el apoyo	*support*
realizar	*to accomplish*
la urbanización de lujo	*upscale neighborhood*
al mismo tiempo	*at the same time*
la naturaleza	*nature*
la torre	*tower*
el ladrillo	*brick*
la piedra	*stone*
atropellado	*run over*
el tranvía	*streetcar*

(Continúa)

Iglesia de La Sagrada Familia

de la Sagrada Familia y se estima que va a finalizarse para el año 2052: ¡200 años después del nacimiento de este creativo y prodigioso arquitecto!

Comprensión

1. ¿Cuál de estas oraciones describe la arquitectura de Gaudí?
   a. tiene influencia francesa   **b.** es ultramoderna
   c. tiene formas geometrizadas
2. ¿Quién ayuda al joven arquitecto Gaudí a realizar sus obras impresionantes?

Frases y palabras útiles

después de clase
el próximo fin de semana
el próximo mes
el próximo sábado
esta noche
este fin de semana
este viernes
hoy
el *lunes* por la tarde
mañana por la mañana
mañana por la tarde
mañana por la noche
pasado mañana

Actividad 14   Preferencias: ¿Cuándo?

Exprese los planes. Complete cada oración con una de las palabras o frases de la lista.

MODELO: E1: Voy a estudiar en la biblioteca a las 5:00 de la mañana.
           E2: *¡No lo creo!*

1. Voy a estudiar en la biblioteca...
2. Mis amigos van a ir a un antro...
3. Mi profesor(a) de español va a explorar el Internet...
4. Mi novio/a (amigo/a, esposo/a) va a ir conmigo al cine...
5. Voy a salir de vacaciones...

Y tú, ¿qué dices?

¡Qué interesante!	¡Buena idea!	¿De veras?
¡Qué divertido!	Yo también.	¿De verdad?
¡Qué aburrido!		¡No lo creo!

Actividad 15   Intercambios: El cine en Sevilla

Lea esta guía del cine en Sevilla. Luego, use el modelo para hablar con su compañero/a sobre varias películas.

MODELO: E1: ¿Quieres ir al cine?
           E2: Tal vez... ¿Qué película quieres ver?
           E1: En *los cines Alameda* exhiben *Café solo o con ellas*.
           E2: ¿A qué hora?
           E1: A las *17:30, 19:15, 20:00* y *21:45* horas.
           E2: Perfecto, ¿por qué no vamos el viernes a las *19:15* (*a las 7:15 de la tarde*)?

Guía del ocio – el cine en Sevilla

Cines Alameda
Tel 954. 91.57.62
Alameda de Hércules 9
5 salas
lunes a jueves 3,5€
viernes, sábado y domingo 5€.

Las vidas posibles. Argentina, drama, de Sandra Gugliotta con Germán Palacios y Ana Celetano. Ganadora del Primer Premio del World Cinema Fund. La esposa de Luciano viaja a la Patagonia en busca de él. Ahí conoce a un hombre igual a Luciano, pero quien lleva otra vida y está casado con otra mujer. No recomendable para menores de 14 años. 18:45, 20:00, 22:15.

La leyenda de la Nahuala. México, animación, de Ricardo Arnaiz. Uno de los cuentos de terror de Nando se vuelve realidad y es secuestrado por la bruja Nahuala. Para todos los públicos. 16:45, 18:45, 21:00.

Café solo o con ellas. España, comedia, de Álvaro Díaz Lorenzo. Javi, Hugo, Dani y Pedro son cuatro amigos preocupados por sus relaciones con el sexo opuesto. Sólo adultos. 17:30, 19:15, 20:00 y 21:45.

Cinesa
Tel 954. 91.54.32
Plaza de Armas
8 salas
antes de las 16:00 3€
viernes, sábado y domingo 5,5€.

Sultanes del sur. México, acción, de Alejandro Lozano. Cuatro delincuentes roban un banco y escapan a Buenos Aires donde se encuentran con un mafioso malvado. Sólo adultos. 18:00, 20:00, 22:00 y 0:00.

Luz silenciosa. México, Francia y Holanda, drama, de Carlos Reygadas. Johan y su familia son menonitas del norte de México. Contra la ley de Dios y del hombre, Johan se enamora de otra mujer. No recomendable para menores de 14 años. 17:30, 19:15, 20:00 y 21:45.

Volver. España, aclamado drama, de Pedro Almodóvar, ganador del Premio Goya 2007. Raimunda (Penélope Cruz) y su hermana Sole (Lola Dueñas) viven con la presencia de su madre muerta (Carmen Maura). No recomendable para menores de 14 años. 17:30, 19:15, 20:00 y 21:45.

Arcos Multicines
Tel 954. 25.44.88
Avenida Andalucía
15 salas
lunes – viernes 4€
sábado y domingo 5€
parejas 3€ por persona

La carta esférica. España, drama, de Imanol Uribe con Carmelo Gómez y Aitana Sánchez-Gijón. Un marinero conoce a una bonita mujer y otros dos hombres; todos buscan el tesoro de un barco hundido cerca de las costas de Cartagena. No recomendable para menores de 14 años. 16:30, 18:30, 20:45.

Harry Potter y la Orden del Fénix. EU, drama, de David Yates. Harry regresa a la escuela Hogwarts para empezar su quinto año de estudios. Todos los públicos. 16:45, 18:45, 21:00 y 23:00.

Un buen día lo tiene cualquiera. España, comedia de Santiago Lorenzo. Tras perder su trabajo y su casa, Arturo decide participar en un programa para estudiantes que viven en una casa de ancianos solitarios por un alquiler módico. Entra a vivir con Onofre, un encantador abuelito de doble personalidad. Todos los públicos. 17:30, 19:15, 20:30 y 21:45.

Enlace al cine

El cine en México y en España

¿Hay películas buenas, con temas universales y de directores mexicanos? Definitivamente y son excelentes; ¡algunas reciben premios en Cannes y Hollywood! Lo mismo decimos de muchas películas españolas. Piense por ejemplo en estas historias: una niña crea un complicado mundo de fantasía para escapar de una realidad brutal (*El laberinto del fauno*); un regalo de agradecimiento tiene repercusiones serias en varios países del mundo (*Babel*); una madre muerta vuelve, pero... ¡está viva! (*Volver*).

El cine llega a México en 1896, ocho meses después de aparecer[1] en Francia. La primera «película» mexicana presenta al presidente Porfirio Díaz a caballo por el parque de Chapultepec (1896). Otros filmes de ese tiempo reflejan la cultura mexicana. Luego, entre 1910 y 1920, se filma la Revolución mexicana (una terrible guerra[2] civil). Por eso se dice que desde su principio, el cine mexicano documenta la historia del país. Hay períodos de mucha creatividad durante «La Edad de Oro»[3] entre 1930 y 1950 con películas como *Doña Bárbara* y *María Candelaria*. Entre los directores importantes de esa época están Fernando de Fuentes (*Vámonos con Pancho Villa*) y Emilio «El Indio» Fernández (*María Candelaria, La perla*). Los actores más reconocidos de la «Edad de Oro» son Cantinflas, «el Charlie Chaplin de México»; Pedro Infante; María Félix y Dolores del Río. En el siglo[4] XXI hay mucha creatividad pero poco apoyo.[5] Los tres directores mexicanos más famosos ahora trabajan fuera de México y crean películas que resultan populares y también artísticas. Ellos son Guillermo del Toro (*El laberinto del fauno*), Alfonso Cuarón (*Children of Men, Y tu mamá también*) y Alejandro González Iñárritu (*Amores perros, Babel*).

Las primeras películas españolas aparecen también en 1896 y documentan las costumbres[6] populares. Por eso, como en México, el cine es parte íntegra de la historia y la cultura de la España del siglo XX. En este país hay también grandes directores. Los más famosos incluyen a Luis Buñuel (*El perro andaluz, Viridiana*) y los ganadores del Oscar a la mejor película extranjera Pedro Almodóvar (*Todo sobre mi madre, Volver*), y el chileno-español Alejandro Amenábar (*Mar adentro, The Others*). También hay otros muy conocidos,[7] como Fernando Trueba, Carlos Saura y dos mujeres: Icíar Bollaín y Pilar Miró.

Hoy en día en ambos[8] países trabajan actores de gran talento y fama internacional como Penélope Cruz, Antonio Banderas, Carmen Maura y Javier Bardem en España. Ahora los más famosos de México son Gael García Bernal y Salma Hayek, actriz y productora (*Ugly Betty*). Todos, como los directores, son admirados en el mundo entero.

Comprensión

1. ¿Qué características tienen en común el cine de México y el de España?
2. Diga el nombre del director de cada una de las siguientes películas: *Volver, Mar adentro, El laberinto del fauno, Y tu mamá también, Babel.*

[1]*appearing*   [2]*war*   [3]*La... The Golden Age*   [4]*century*   [5]*support*   [6]*customs*   [7]*muy... well-known*   [8]*both*

¿De dónde es usted?

✳ **Lea Gramática 3.5.**

ESPAÑA
español
española

PORTUGAL
portugués
portuguesa

Pilar Álvarez
Madrid, España

MÉXICO, AMÉRICA CENTRAL y EL CARIBE

Rubén Hernández
Miami, Florida
La Habana, Cuba

Silvia Bustamante
México, D.F.

CUBA
cubano/a

PUERTO RICO
puertorriqueño/a

Carla Espinosa
San Juan, P.R.

MÉXICO
mexicano/a

LA REPÚBLICA DOMINICANA
dominicano/a

GUATEMALA
guatemalteco/a

PANAMÁ
panameño/a

EL SALVADOR
salvadoreño/a

NICARAGUA
nicaragüense

COSTA RICA
costarricense

Mayín Durán
Los Ángeles, California
Panamá, Panamá

HONDURAS
hondureño/a

COLOMBIA
colombiano/a

Ricardo Sícora
Caracas, Venezuela

Susana Yamasaki
Lima, Perú

VENEZUELA
venezolano/a

ECUADOR
ecuatoriano/a

BRASIL
brasileño/a

PERÚ
peruano/a

PARAGUAY
paraguayo/a

BOLIVIA
boliviano/a

CHILE
chileno/a

URUGUAY
uruguayo/a

ARGENTINA
argentino/a

SUDAMÉRICA

Adriana Bolini
Buenos Aires, Argentina

La presencia hispana en los Estados Unidos es fuerte y se expresa de muchas formas. En la foto, un mural en el distrito de La Misión (*Mission District*) de la ciudad de San Francisco, California.

Actividad 16 Identificaciones: Las capitales

Consulte los mapas que aparecen al principio y al final del texto para completar las siguientes oraciones.

1. La capital de Venezuela es _____.
   - **a.** Bogotá
   - **b.** Tegucigalpa
   - **c.** Caracas
   - **d.** La Paz
2. _____ es la capital de Ecuador.
   - **a.** Quito
   - **b.** La Habana
   - **c.** Montevideo
   - **d.** Lima
3. La capital de Nicaragua es _____.
   - **a.** Asunción
   - **b.** Bogotá
   - **c.** San José
   - **d.** Managua
4. _____ es la capital de Argentina.
   - **a.** San Juan
   - **b.** Buenos Aires
   - **c.** Santiago
   - **d.** Madrid
5. La capital de Guatemala es _____.
   - **a.** San Salvador
   - **b.** Santo Domingo
   - **c.** Guatemala
   - **d.** Panamá

Actividad 17 Entrevista: ¿De dónde... ?

1. E1: ¿De dónde eres?
   E2: Soy de _____.
2. E1: ¿De dónde es tu padre?
   E2: Es de _____.
3. E1: ¿De dónde es tu madre?
   E2: Es de _____.
4. E1: ¿Tienes un amigo de algún país hispano?
   E2: Sí, tengo un amigo / una amiga de _____.
5. E1: ¿Cómo se llama tu amigo/a?
   E2: Se llama _____.

En resumen

De todo un poco

A. Entrevista: Las actividades favoritas y los lugares

Charle con un compañero / una compañera.

1. ¿Qué te gusta hacer cuando vas a la playa? ¿Te gusta nadar o prefieres tomar el sol? ¿Te gusta andar en velero o prefieres jugar al voleibol?
2. ¿Qué haces cuando estás en una biblioteca? ¿Lees periódicos? ¿Estudias? ¿Usas una computadora?
3. ¿Cómo se llama tu parque favorito? ¿Qué haces allí? ¿Practicas un deporte? ¿Cuál? ¿Caminas? ¿Corres? ¿Cuándo vas al parque?
4. ¿Vas mucho al cine? ¿Con quiénes? ¿Qué tipo de películas te gusta? (*románticas, cómicas, musicales, de acción, de misterio, de horror, de ciencia ficción*)
5. ¿Qué tipo de música prefieres (*folclórica, alternativa, rock, popular, clásica, reggaetón*)? ¿Cuáles son tus artistas favoritos? ¿Prefieres escuchar la radio, poner discos compactos o escuchar música en tu iPod?

B. El mapa de Sudamérica: ¿Dónde están estos países?

Trabajen en grupos de cuatro. Una persona debe leer las siguientes instrucciones; las otras tres personas deben seguir las instrucciones y escribir los nombres de los países en el mapa que el profesor / la profesora va a darles.

INSTRUCCIONES

1. Brasil es el país más grande de Sudamérica. Está *al lado derecho* del mapa. Venezuela está al norte de Brasil, *al lado izquierdo* de Guyana. Escriba Venezuela en el lugar apropiado.
2. Ahora vamos a Colombia. Está *al lado izquierdo* de Venezuela.
3. Ahora escriban «Ecuador» en el país pequeño que está al sur, *debajo de* Colombia y *al lado del* Océano Pacífico.
4. *Al lado izquierdo de* Brasil, *en medio del* mapa, está Bolivia. Está *lejos del* mar.
5. *Al lado izquierdo de* Brasil y *debajo de* Ecuador y Colombia, escriban «Perú». Este país está *entre* Brasil, Bolivia y el Océano Pacífico.
6. *Debajo de* Perú, al sur, está Chile. Éste es un país largo y angosto (delgado). Está *al lado del* Océano Pacífico.
7. *Al lado derecho de* Chile está otro país muy grande, Argentina.
8. *Al lado derecho de* Argentina, y *al lado izquierdo del* Océano Atlántico, está Uruguay. Éste es un país muy pequeño.
9. *Arriba de* Argentina, al norte, y *debajo de* Bolivia y Brasil está otro país pequeño, Paraguay. No está *cerca del* mar.

Ahora, comparen su trabajo con el mapa que aparece al final del texto.

¡Dígalo por escrito!

Los pasatiempos y las actividades

Imagínese que usted recibe una carta de su amiga Silvia Bustamante, una estudiante de México. Ella le pregunta: «¿Cómo pasas el tiempo libre?» ¿Qué le va a contestar usted? Escríbale una carta, contestando su pregunta y también incluyendo algunas preguntas para ella. Empiece su carta así: Querida Silvia:... Termine su carta con: Un abrazo de... [el nombre de usted].

¡Cuéntenos usted!

Cuéntenos sobre su lugar favorito en su ciudad o estado. ¿Es una playa, un museo, un restaurante, una librería u otro lugar? ¿Dónde está? ¿Cuánto tiempo tarda para ir a ese lugar? ¿Hay mucha gente allí o es un lugar muy tranquilo? ¿Qué hace allí? ¿Prefiere ir solo/a o acompañado/a?

PISTAS PARA LEER

1. Skim the **Lectura.** Can you tell what its topic is?
2. Scan the last paragraph: What words of nationality are used to describe Hispanics in the United States? Which words do you find useful?
3. When you read, use context to figure out words you don't know and try to guess their meaning. But remember: guessing the exact meaning is not crucial to overall comprehension!

VOCABULARIO ÚTIL

la comunidad	*community*
los ciudadanos	*citizens*
Estado Libre Asociado	*Common-wealth*
los neoyorriqueños	*Nuyoricans (New York Puerto Ricans)*
ganador	*winner*
se destaca	*stands out*
se encuentran	*are found*
rebasa	*surpasses*
sea cual sea	*whatever might be*

LECTURA

La presencia vital de los hispanos

La palabra *Hispanic* se usa en los Estados Unidos con frecuencia para describir a todos los latinos. Pero en la **comunidad** hispana hay personas de varios países que forman grupos diferentes; cada uno de estos grupos tiene una historia interesante y muy particular. Hay hispanos en casi todas las ciudades estadounidenses. Algunos son emigrantes de España, otros de la América Latina. En su totalidad, los hispanos contribuyen de manera importante a la vida cultural y económica de los Estados Unidos.

El primer grupo grande es el de los mexicoamericanos o chicanos, que viven principalmente en el oeste y suroeste: en los estados de California, Nuevo México, Arizona, Texas y Colorado. Entre los hispanos de este grupo hay muchos escritores, actores, músicos, artistas y políticos. Usted seguramente reconoce el nombre de Edward James Olmos, actor de cine y televisión, y el del famoso guitarrista Carlos Santana. Una de las escritoras más estimadas de los Estados Unidos es Sandra Cisneros, autora chicana de la novela *The House on Mango Street.* Entre los políticos y activistas también hay gente de gran impacto, como César Chávez y Dolores Huerta.

El segundo grupo lo forman los puertorriqueños. Oficialmente, los puertorriqueños son **ciudadanos** estadounidenses, pues desde 1952 Puerto Rico es un **Estado Libre Asociado** de los Estados Unidos. El primer congresista hispano de Illinois, Luis V. Gutiérrez, es de padres puertorriqueños. Y de Puerto Rico son el cantante Marc Anthony y la escritora Esmeralda Santiago. Muchos puertorriqueños viven en Nueva York y se les llama **neoyorriqueños**. Entre ellos hay gente reconocida, como el poeta Tato Laviera y la estrella de cine Jennifer López.

Los cubanos forman el tercer grupo, que reside especialmente en Florida, Nueva Jersey y California. Los cubanoamerianos cuentan con novelistas de mucho éxito, como Oscar Hijuelos, **ganador** del Premio Pulitzer en 1990, y

Cristina García, autora de *Dreaming in Cuban*. En la televisión **se destaca** Daisy Fuentes, en el cine Andy García y Cameron Díaz. ¿Le gusta a usted la música de Gloria Estefan? Gloria es una cubanoamericana muy famosa.

Tenemos un cuarto grupo, el de los centroamericanos que **se encuentran** en California y los estados del este. Las comunidades más grandes de salvadoreños están en el área de Washington, D.C. y en Los Ángeles. Además de estos cuatro grupos, hay españoles, peruanos, dominicanos, bolivianos, venezolanos, paraguayos y colombianos. ¿Conoce usted la música de Shakira o de Juanes? ¿Le gustan las películas de John Leguizamo? Los tres son colombianos.

La población hispana en los Estados Unidos **rebasa** los 40 millones e incluye una enorme variedad de culturas e historias nacionales. Algunas personas de esta comunidad prefieren llamarse *Hispanic* o *Hispanic American;* otras usan las palabras *Latino* y *U.S. Latino;* también hay quienes son más específicos y mencionan su nacionalidad: peruano, cubano, salvadoreño. Pero **sea cual sea** la palabra preferida o el término oficial, la presencia hispana es cada día más visible y vital en los Estados Unidos.

Comprensión

A. Diga qué grupo(s) de hispanos predomina(n) en cada ciudad.

CIUDAD	GRUPO(S)
Houston	_____
Miami	_____
Nueva York	_____
Albuquerque	_____
Los Ángeles	_____

B. ¿Quién habla en cada caso? Indique si es una persona mexicoamericana (**M**), puertorriqueña (**P**), cubanoamericana (**C**) o de otro grupo de hispanos (**O**).

1. _____ Vivo en Los Ángeles; una de mis escritoras favoritas es Sandra Cisneros.

2. _____ Soy de una isla que es un Estado Libre Asociado. Me consideran ciudadano de los Estados Unidos.

3. _____ Soy bilingüe y vivo en Texas. Mis padres nacieron en Guadalajara.

4. _____ Vivo en Washington, D.C.; me gusta vivir aquí porque hay mucha gente de mi país.

5. _____ Nací en una isla del Caribe. Ahora vivo con muchos de mis compatriotas en Miami.

Un paso más... ¡a conversar!

1. ¿Cuántos hispanos famosos puede mencionar? ¿De qué países son?

2. ¿Conoce a alguna persona hispana? ¿Tiene amigos españoles o latinoamericanos? Describa a una de estas personas y diga si pertenece a alguno de los grupos mencionados en la **Lectura**.

Vea el **Resumen cultural** en este capítulo del *Cuaderno de actividades.*

Vocabulario

¿Dónde está... ?

Where is . . . ?

abajo de	below
adentro de	inside
afuera de	outside
a la derecha/izquierda de	to the right/left of
al lado de	to the side of
allí	there
al norte/sur/este/oeste	to the north/south/east/west
alrededor de	around
aquí	here
arriba de	above
cerca de	close to
debajo de	under
detrás de	behind
encima de	on top of
enfrente de	in front of
en medio de	in the middle of
entre	between
lejos de	far from
sobre	above, on top of

Los lugares de la universidad

Places in the University

la biblioteca	library
el edificio	building
el estacionamiento	parking lot
la Facultad de Bellas Artes	School of Fine Arts
la Facultad de Ciencias Naturales	School of Natural Sciences
la Facultad de Ciencias Sociales	School of Social Sciences
la Facultad de Derecho	School of Law
la Facultad de Filosofía y Letras	School of Humanities
la Facultad de Medicina	School of Medicine
la librería	bookstore
la parada del autobús	bus stop
la rectoría	office of the president

PALABRAS SEMEJANTES: la cafetería, el centro estudiantil, el gimnasio, el laboratorio, la oficina

Los lugares de la ciudad

Places in the City

el almacén	department store
la avenida	avenue
el colegio	private school
el correo	post office
la escuela	school
la fuente	fountain

la gasolinera	gas station
la iglesia	church
la lavandería	laundromat
el (super)mercado	(super)market
el metro	subway
la panadería	bakery
la papelería	stationery store
la tienda	store
la tienda de regalos	gift shop
la zapatería	shoe store

PALABRAS SEMEJANTES: el aeropuerto, el bar, el café, el condominio, la farmacia, el hospital, el hotel, el museo, el videocentro
REPASO: el cine, la discoteca, el restaurante, el teatro

Otros lugares

Other Places

Vea la página 133 para una lista de países hispanos y nacionalidades.

el Caribe	the Caribbean
Sudamérica	South America

PALABRAS SEMEJANTES: América Central, el Océano Atlántico, el Océano Pacífico

El origen

Origins

¿De dónde es usted (eres tú)?	Where are you from?
Soy de...	I am from . . .
¿De dónde es... ?	Where is . . . from?
Es de...	He/She is from . . .

Las actividades diarias

Daily Activities

almorzar (ue)	to eat lunch
asistir (a)	to attend
beber	to drink
diseñar	to design
esperar (el autobús)	to wait for (the bus)
hacer la compra	to do the (grocery) shopping
ir al trabajo	to go to work
jugar a las cartas	to play cards
jugar a los videojuegos	to play video games
llevar	to take, carry
mandar	to send
mirar	to look
poner	to put
discos compactos	to play CDs
una película	to show a movie

recoger	to pick up, gather
regresar	to return
rezar	to pray

PALABRAS SEMEJANTES: completar, conversar, corresponder, exhibir, preparar, recibir

Las comidas y las bebidas

Foods and Beverages

el agua (*f.*)	water
el arroz	rice
la cena	dinner
el desayuno	breakfast
las galletitas	cookies
las galletas	crackers, cookies
los huevos (revueltos)	(scrambled) eggs
el jamón	ham
el jugo (de naranja)	(orange) juice
la leche	milk
la lechuga	lettuce
las legumbres	vegetables
la mantequilla	butter
el pan	bread
el pan tostado	toast
la papa (al horno)	(baked) potato
las papas fritas	French fries
el pastel	pastry, cake
el pescado	fish
el pollo (frito)	(fried) chicken
el postre	dessert
el queso	cheese
el refresco	(soft) drink

PALABRAS SEMEJANTES: el bistec, el burrito, la ensalada, la fruta, la hamburguesa, el sándwich, la sopa, el taco, el tomate, el yogur

REPASO: el almuerzo, el café, el cereal, la cerveza, el chocolate, el helado, el té

Los sustantivos

Nouns

el abrazo	hug
el ama de casa	housewife
la atención médica	healthcare
la estampilla	(postage) stamp
el euro	euro
el hombre / la mujer de negocios	businessman/ businesswoman
nadie	no one / nobody
el reportaje	newspaper report, article
la reunión	meeting
la tarea	homework
la vida	life

PALABRAS SEMEJANTES: la acción, el/la artista, la capital, la ciencia ficción, la estación, la exhibición, la gasolina, el horror, el misterio, el programa, el reggaetón, el sitio Web, el tipo, el voleibol

¿Cuándo?

When?

¿Con qué frecuencia?	How often?
de las... a las...	from (time) . . . to (time)
de vez en cuando	from time to time
finalmente	finally
generalmente	usually, generally
mañana por la mañana (la tarde) (la noche)	tomorrow morning (afternoon) (evening)
mientras	meanwhile
(casi) nunca	(almost) never
siempre	always
todos los días	every day

REPASO: con frecuencia, por lo general, próximo

Los adjetivos

Adjectives

apropiado	appropriate
enfermo/a	sick
juntos/as	together
saludable	healthy

PALABRAS SEMEJANTES: alternativo/a, central, cibernético/a, delicioso/a, diferente, folclórico/a, latinoamericano/a, municipal, musical, popular, varios/as

Palabras del texto

Words from the Text

el cuadro	graph
Empareje(n)...	Pair up, Match . . . (*command*)
Empiece(n)...	Begin . . . (*command*)
el pronombre	pronoun
seguir las instrucciones	to follow directions
Termine(n)...	Finish . . . (*command*)

PALABRAS SEMEJANTES: el espacio en blanco, la lección

Palabras y expresiones útiles

Useful Words and Expressions

¿Adónde... ?	To where . . . ?
al principio	at the beginning
conmigo	with me
¿De veras? / ¿De verdad?	Really?
el plano	map (of a room or city)
Querido/a...	Dear . . .

Gramática y ejercicios

As you have seen in **Gramática A.1, C.5,** and **1.2,** Spanish verb endings tell us who is performing the action. The subject pronouns (**yo, tú, usted, ella, nosotros,** etc.) are often omitted.

3.1 Talking about Habitual Actions: Present Tense of Regular Verbs

A. You already know that the endings of Spanish verbs must correspond to the subject of the sentence: that is, to the person or thing that does the action.

—Nora, ¿cuándo estudi**as**?　　　　—Nora, when do you study?
—Estudi**o** por la mañana.　　　　—I study in the morning.

—¿Qué hac**en** ustedes los domingos?　　—What do you do on Sundays?
—Visit**amos** a nuestros abuelos.　　　—We visit our grandparents.

B. Most Spanish verbs end in **-ar.** Here are the endings for **-ar** verbs.*

llegar = to arrive

	llegar (*to arrive*)	
(yo)	lleg**o**	*I arrive*
(tú)	lleg**as**	*you (inf. sing.) arrive*
(usted, él/ella)	lleg**a**	*you (pol. sing.) arrive; he/she arrives*
(nosotros/as)	lleg**amos**	*we arrive*
(vosotros/as)	lleg**áis**	*you (inf. pl., Spain) arrive*
(ustedes, ellos/as)	lleg**an**	*you (pl.) arrive; they arrive*

—¿A qué hora lleg**as** a la escuela?　　—What time do you arrive at school?
—Generalmente lleg**o** a las 9:00.　　　—Generally I arrive at 9:00.

C. Verbs that end in **-er** and **-ir** use identical endings, except for the **nosotros/as** and **vosotros/as** forms.†

comer = to eat

	comer (*to eat*)	
(yo)	com**o**	*I eat*
(tú)	com**es**	*you (inf. sing.) eat*
(usted, él/ella)	com**e**	*you (pol. sing.) eat; he/she eats*
(nosotros/as)	com**emos**	*we eat*
(vosotros/as)	com**éis**	*you (inf. pl., Spain) eat*
(ustedes, ellos/as)	com**en**	*you (pl.) eat; they eat*

---

*Recognition: **vos llegás**
†Recognition: **vos comés, escribís**

escribir (to write)

escribir = to write

(yo)	escrib**o**	I write
(tú)	escrib**es**	you (inf. sing.) write
(usted, él/ella)	escrib**e**	you (pol. sing.) write; he/she writes
(nosotros/as)	escrib**imos**	we write
(vosotros/as)	escrib**ís**	you (inf. pl., Spain) write
(ustedes, ellos/as)	escrib**en**	you (pl.) write; they write

—¿Dónde com**en** al mediodía? —Where do you eat at noon?
—Com**emos** en casa. —We eat at home.

—¿Escrib**es** la tarea a máquina? —Do you type the homework?
—No, escrib**o** los ejercicios a mano. —No, I write the exercises by hand.

D. The verb form must agree with the subject even when the subject is not explicitly stated. When the subject is expressed, it may be a pronoun, as in the preceding table, or a noun.

La profesora Martínez no **habla** francés. Professor Martínez does not speak French.

The subject may also consist of a noun + pronoun. A subject combining a noun or pronoun with **yo** takes the **nosotros/as** form.

Nora y yo no **hablamos** italiano. Nora and I don't speak Italian.

A subject combining a noun or pronoun with **tú** or **usted** takes the plural form.

Alberto y tú hablan español con Raúl. You and Alberto speak Spanish with Raúl.

E. Central America, Argentina, and Uruguay use a different subject pronoun—**vos**—and verb form for informal singular address.*

—¿Qué hora ten**és vos**? —What time do you have?
—Tengo las 6:30. —I have 6:30.

—¿Cuándo lleg**ás vos**? —When do you arrive?
—Llego a las 9:00 de la noche. —I arrive at 9:00 P.M.

> These agreement rules take some time to acquire. Think about them when you are editing your writing; don't be overly concerned about them in speech.
>
> Note that the principal differences between **-ar** verbs and **-er** and **-ir** verbs are the vowels **a** and **e**.

> In Central America, Argentina, and Uruguay, **vos** = **tú**.

Ejercicio 1

Combine las personas de la lista A con las actividades de la lista B.

MODELO: Mi hermano y yo jugamos al tenis.

LISTA A
1. la profesora Martínez
2. yo
3. tú
4. mi hermano y yo
5. mis compañeros de clase
6. vosotros

LISTA B
a. hacen la tarea para mañana
b. maneja un carro nuevo
c. jugamos al tenis
d. como demasiado
e. habláis español
f. lees el periódico

---

*You may learn more about **vos** forms in the **Expansión gramatical** section of the *Cuaderno de actividades*.

Ejercicio 2

Éstas son las actividades de Amanda, su familia y sus amigos. Escriba la forma correcta del verbo entre paréntesis.

MODELO: Amanda *llama* a Graciela muy temprano en la mañana. (llamar)

1. Graciela y yo _____ las composiciones juntas. (escribir)
2. Mi novio Ramón _____ ropa muy elegante. (llevar)
3. Mi mamá y yo _____ la casa los sábados. (limpiar)
4. Mis padres _____ juntos por la mañana. (desayunar)
5. Mi hermano Guillermo _____ las tiras cómicas los domingos. (leer)
6. Andrea y Pedro Ruiz _____ juntos al mediodía. (comer)
7. Ernestito _____ mucho en su bicicleta. (andar)
8. (Yo) _____ por teléfono con mi amiga Graciela. (hablar)
9. Amanda, Guillermo y Ernestito _____ a la escuela de lunes a viernes. (asistir)
10. Ramón, Graciela y yo siempre _____ música rock en la radio. (escuchar)

3.2 Using Irregular Verbs: *hacer, salir, jugar*

A verb that uses more than one stem in its conjugation is considered irregular. Here are the forms of three common irregular verbs.

A. The present tense of **hacer*** (*to do; to make*) uses two stems: **hag-** for the **yo** form and **hac-** for all others.

hacer (*to do; to make*)

(yo)	hago	*I do*
(tú)	haces	*you (inf. sing.) do*
(usted, él/ella)	hace	*you (pol. sing.) do; he/she does*
(nosotros/as)	hacemos	*we do*
(vosotros/as)	hacéis	*you (inf. pl., Spain) do*
(ustedes, ellos/as)	hacen	*you (pl.) do; they do*

—¿Qué **haces** después de clases?   —*What do you do after school?*
—**Hago** mi tarea.   —*I do my homework.*

B. The present tense of **salir**† (*to leave; to go out*) uses the stems **salg-** for the **yo** form and **sal-** for all others.

¿RECUERDA?

In **Gramática C.5** and **1.2** you learned that verbs that use only one stem in their conjugations—such as **hablar, comer, vivir**—are regular verbs. Irregular verbs, on the other hand, use more than one stem in their conjugations. You saw the forms of two such irregular verbs, **preferir** and **querer,** in **Gramática 2.3.** Review those forms now, if necessary.

hacer = *to do; to make*
(Yo) Hago. = *I do; I make.*
(Tú) Haces. = *You (inf. sing.) do; you make.*
(Nosotros) Hacemos. = *We do; we make.*

*Recognition: **vos hacés**
†Recognition: **vos salís**

salir (*to leave; to go out*)

(yo)	sal**go**	*I leave*
(tú)	sal**es**	*you (inf. sing.) leave*
(usted, él/ella)	sal**e**	*you (pol. sing.) leave; he/she leaves*
(nosotros/as)	sal**imos**	*we leave*
(vosotros/as)	sal**ís**	*you (inf. pl., Spain) leave*
(ustedes, ellos/as)	sal**en**	*you (pl.) leave; they leave*

salir = *to leave; to go out.*
(Yo) Salgo. = *I leave; I go out.*
(Tú) Sales. = *You (inf. sing.) leave; you go out.*
(Nosotros) Salimos. = *We leave; we go out.*

To express a point of departure with **salir,** use the preposition **de,** even if the preposition *from* is not used in English.

—¿A qué hora **sales de** tu casa por la mañana?
—**Salgo** a las 7:30.

—*What time do you leave home in the morning?*
—*I leave at 7:30.*

C. The present tense of the verb **jugar*** (*to play*) uses the stem **jug-** from the infinitive for the **nosotros/as** and **vosotros/as** forms and **jueg-** for all other forms. This verb follows the same pattern as **preferir** and **querer** in **Gramática 2.3.**†

jugar (*to play*)

(yo)	j**ue**go	*I play*
(tú)	j**ue**gas	*you (inf. sing.) play*
(usted, él/ella)	j**ue**ga	*you (pol. sing.) play; he/she plays*
(nosotros/as)	jugamos	*we play*
(vosotros/as)	jugáis	*you (inf. pl., Spain) play*
(ustedes, ellos/as)	j**ue**gan	*you (pl.) play; they play*

jugar = *to play*
(Yo) Juego. = *I play.*
(Tú) Juegas. = *You (inf. sing.) play.*
(Nosotros) Jugamos. = *We play.*

Remember that there are two words spelled **juego: el juego** (*the game*) and **(yo) juego** (*I play*).

Los sábados **juego** al fútbol con mis amigos.
¡Me gusta mucho ese **juego**!

Saturdays I play soccer with my friends.
I like that game a lot!

---

*Recognition: **vos jugás**
†The verb **almorzar** (to eat lunch) follows the same pattern: **almuerzo, almuerzas, almuerza, almorzamos, almorzáis, almuerzan.**

Ejercicio 3

Complete las conversaciones con la forma correcta de **hacer, salir** o **jugar.**

MODELO: —Luis, ¿cuándo *haces* las tareas?
—*Hago* las tareas por la tarde.

1. —Señor Saucedo, ¿a qué hora _____ usted de casa para su trabajo?
—_____ a las 8:30.
2. —Guillermo, ¿_____ al fútbol por la tarde?
—Sí, _____ después de clases.
3. —Señor Padilla, ¿_____ usted ejercicio todos los días?
—No, _____ ejercicio en el gimnasio solamente los lunes y los miércoles.
4. —Ernesto y Estela, ¿_____ ustedes al tenis?
—Sí, _____ al tenis los sábados.

3.3 Referring to Objects already Mentioned: Impersonal Direct Object Pronouns *lo, la, los,* and *las*

When referring to things already mentioned, Spanish speakers use the direct object pronouns **lo** and **la,** which correspond to the English object pronoun *it:* **lo** refers to masculine words and **la** refers to feminine words. The pronouns **los** and **las** correspond to the English *them:* **los** refers to masculine words and **las** to feminine words.

lo = it (*m.*)
la = it (*f.*)
los = them (*m. pl.*)
las = them (*f. pl.*)
¿Quién va a preparar los sándwiches?
(*Who is going to fix the sandwiches?*)
Pedro y Andrea siempre los preparan.
(*Pedro and Andrea always fix them.*)

—Ernesto, ¿toma usted **café?**
—Sí, **lo** tomo todas las mañanas.

—Amanda, ¿quién prepara **la cena** en tu casa?
—Por lo general mi mamá **la** prepara.

—Guillermo, ¿te gustan **los huevos revueltos?**
—Sí, me gustan mucho; **los** como los domingos para el desayuno.

—¿Quién quiere estas **galletitas?**
—Yo **las** quiero.

—*Ernesto, do you drink coffee?*
—*Yes, I drink it every morning.*

—*Amanda, who fixes dinner at your house?*
—*Generally my mom fixes it.*

—*Guilllermo, do you like scrambled eggs?*
—*Yes, I like them a lot; I have them for breakfast on Sundays.*

—*Who wants these cookies?*
—*I want them.*

It takes time to acquire these pronouns. You will find that you understand them easily when you see them in written Spanish. You will gradually come to recognize them in speech as you hear more spoken Spanish.

DIRECT OBJECT PRONOUNS

lo	*it (m.)*
la	*it (f.)*
los	*them (m.)*
las	*them (f.)*

Like other pronouns, direct object pronouns are usually placed before the verb.*

¿La ensalada? Ernestito no **la** come nunca.

Salad? Ernestito never eats it.

*You will learn more about the placement of pronouns in **Gramática 8.1** and **13.5.**

Ejercicio 4

Complete los diálogos con **lo, la, los** o **las.**

1. —¿Comes mucho yogur?
   No, no _____ como nunca porque no me gusta.
2. —¿Beben ustedes mucha leche?
   —Sí, _____ bebemos con las tres comidas.
3. —¿Prepara tu mamá muchos postres?
   —No, ella sólo _____ prepara de vez en cuando.
4. —Te gustan las hamburguesas?
   —Sí, _____ como siempre para el almuerzo.
5. —¿Toman cerveza Amanda y Guillermo?
   —Claro que no _____ toman; ¡son muy jóvenes!
6. — Doña Lola, ¿dónde compra usted las legumbres?
   —_____ compro en el Mercado Central.
7. —¿Te gustan los tacos de pollo?
   —Sí, me gustan mucho; _____ como con frecuencia.
8. —¿Comen mucho helado Amanda y Graciela?
   —Sí, _____ comen después de las clases todos los días.

3.4 Asking and Answering Questions

A. As you learned in **Capítulo 1,** questions in Spanish are formed by placing the verb before the subject, with any object or description following or preceding the verb. Answers are regular statements preceded by the word **sí** or the word **no.** A negative answer can have one or two negative words, depending on whether you are simply answering the question or offering the correct information as well. Here are some examples.

QUESTION: ¿Vive Pilar en España?	*Does Pilar live in Spain?*
ANSWER: Sí, Pilar vive en España.	*Yes, Pilar lives in Spain. / Yes, she does.*
QUESTION: ¿Tiene un perro pequeño Ernestito?	*Does Ernestito have a Small dog?*
ANSWER: No, (Ernestito) no tiene un perro pequeño.	*No, he doesn't have a Small dog.*
No, tiene un perro grande.	*No, he has a large dog.*
QUESTION: ¿Es delgada Andrea?	*Is Andrea slim?*
ANSWER: Sí, Andrea es delgada.	*Yes, Andrea is slim. / Yes, she is.*
QUESTION: ¿Hablan español ellos?	*Do they speak Spanish?*
ANSWER: No, (ellos) no hablan español.	*No, they do not speak Spanish.*
No, hablan alemán.	*No, they speak German.*

¿RECUERDA?

In **Gramática 1.3** you learned that statements in Spanish are formed by using the subject, then the verb, and then the object and/or description. You also learned that negative statements are made by using a negative immediately before the verb. You also read that questions are generally formed by placing the subject after the verb:

¿Vive Susana en Perú?
¿Es gordo Ramón?
¿Lees (tú) muchas novelas?

Remember that additional words, such as *does* or *do,* are unnecessary to turn a statement into a question in Spanish.

B. Interrogative (question) words like **¿Qué?, ¿Cuándo?, ¿(De) Quién(es)?, ¿Dónde?, ¿Cómo?, ¿Cuánto(s)?, ¿Cuánta(s)?, ¿Cuál?,** or **¿Por qué?** are placed before the verb to create questions.

¿Cuánto cuesta el libro?	*How much is the book?*
¿Dónde está la biblioteca?	*Where is the library?*
¿Cuál es tu número de teléfono?	*What is your phone number?*
¿Quién tiene A en el examen?	*Who has an A on the exam?*
¿Cuándo quieres desayunar?	*When do you want to have breakfast?*
¿Por qué no comemos enchiladas hoy?	*Why don't we have (eat) enchiladas today?*
¿Qué vas a hacer esta noche?	*What are you going to do tonight?*

Ejercicio 5

Imagínese que usted es Amanda. Escriba preguntas según los modelos. Use la forma correcta de **tú, usted** o **ustedes.**

MODELOS: Pregúntele a doña Lola si va en metro al trabajo. →
Doña Lola, ¿va usted en metro al trabajo?

Pregúntele a Rafael si lee el periódico por la mañana. →
Rafael, ¿lees el periódico por la mañana?

1. Pregúntele a su papá si toma mucho café en el trabajo.
2. Pregúntele a Diego si él y sus amigos juegan al béisbol.
3. Pregúnteles a Graciela y a Diego si tienen una computadora.
4. Pregúntele a Raúl si hace ejercicio en un gimnasio.
5. Pregúntele a Pedro Ruiz si trabaja por la noche.
6. Pregúntele a don Eduardo si prepara café por la mañana.
7. Pregúntele a su mamá si cocina por la mañana o por la tarde.
8. Pregúntele a Clarisa si ve la televisión por la noche.
9. Pregúntele a doña Rosita Silva si asiste a misa los domingos.
10. Pregúntele a doña Lola si lava su ropa en casa o en una lavandería.

¡OJO!

Note that the items require **tú, usted,** and **ustedes.** Keep in mind that the person asking the questions is Amanda, a teenager. Remember that the pronoun **tú** is usually dropped but that the pronoun **usted** is normally included.

Ejercicio 6

Haga preguntas con estas oraciones. Use palabras interrogativas como: **cuál, cuándo, cuánto, dónde, quién, qué, por qué.**

MODELO: La profesora está en la biblioteca. → ¿Dónde está la profesora?

1. Mi esposo está en la casa.
2. Mi cumpleaños es el 22 de julio.
3. Tengo una novela muy buena en mi mochila.
4. La dirección de mis hermanos es Calle Bolívar número 513.
5. No voy a jugar al tenis hoy porque estoy cansado/a.
6. El libro de química cuesta $120.00.

3.5 Talking about Location and Origin: *estar en, ir a,* and *ser de*

Estar is used for location:
¿Dónde está Susana?
(*Where is Susan?*)
Está en la escuela.
(*She's at school.*)

A. *Estar + en*

Use the verb **estar*** (*to be*) to locate people and objects.

—¿Dónde **está** la profesora Martínez? —*Where is Professor Martínez?*
—**Está** en clase. —*She's in class.*

—Esteban, ¿dónde **está** su libro? —*Esteban, where is your book?*
—**Está** en casa. —*It's at home.*

Here are the present-tense forms of the irregular verb **estar.**

estar (*to be*)		
(yo)	est**oy**	*I am*
(tú)	est**ás**	*you (inf. sing.) are*
(usted, él/ella)	est**á**	*you (pol. sing.) are; he/she is*[†]
(nosotros/as)	est**amos**	*we are*
(vosotros/as)	est**áis**	*you (inf. pl., Spain) are*
(ustedes, ellos/as)	est**án**	*you (pl.) are; they are*

estar = *to be*

B. *Ir + al / a la*

Gramática ilustrada

Raúl y Mónica **van al** cine.

Raúl y Mónica **están en** el cine.

¿RECUERDA?

Remember from **Gramática 2.1** that the present-tense forms of **ir** are **voy, vas, va, vamos, vais,** and **van.**[‡] These verb forms can mean *going* or simply *go(es)*.

---

*Recognition: **vos estás**
[†]Remember that there is no Spanish equivalent for the English subject pronoun *it*. The third-person verb form conveys the meaning of *it* as well as of *he* or *she*.
[‡]Recognition: **vos vas**

adónde = *where (to)*
ir a = *to go to*
   Voy al cine. (*I'm going to the movies.*)

Ir a + infinitive is used to express the future:
   Mañana voy a trabajar. (*Tomorrow I'm going to work.*)
este viernes = *this Friday*
el próximo viernes = *next Friday*
   El próximo mes vamos a empezar las clases. (*Next month we're going to start classes.*)

In **Gramática A.3** you saw how the verb **ser** is used to identify people and things, whereas the verb **estar** is used to locate people and objects (**Gramática 3.5A**). Review those verbs and their conjugations now, if necessary.

The distinction between **ser** and **estar** takes a while to acquire. Keep listening to and reading Spanish and you will develop a feel for it.

ser = origin
estar = location
   ¿De dónde es usted? (*Where are you from?*)
   Soy de Perú. (*I'm from Peru.*)
   ¿Dónde está usted? (*Where are you?*)
   Estoy aquí, en el patio. (*I'm here, on the patio.*)

¿Adónde? (*[To] Where?*) is used to ask where someone is going. The verb **ir** (*to go*) followed by the preposition **a** (*to*) is used to express the idea of movement toward a location. Note that **a** + **el** contracts to **al** (*to the*).

—**¿Adónde vas?**
—**Voy al** parque.
—*Where are you going?*
—*I'm going to the park.*

—**¿Adónde van** ustedes los sábados?
—**Vamos al** trabajo y luego **vamos a la** biblioteca para estudiar.
—*Where do you go on Saturdays?*
—*We go to work and then we go to the library to study.*

—**¿Adónde va** la profesora Martínez?
—**Va a la** universidad.
—*Where's Professor Martínez going?*
—*She's going to the university.*

The expression **ir** + **a** + *location,* used with the following expressions of time, indicates when you are going.

este viernes	*this Friday*	el próximo sábado	*next Saturday*
este fin de semana	*this weekend*	la próxima semana	*next week*
esta primavera	*this spring*	el próximo mes	*next month*

Vamos a ir al restaurante El Tecolote **la próxima semana.**   *We're going to go to the El Tecolote restaurant next week.*

C. *Ser de*

1. A form of the verb **ser** (*to be*) followed by **de** (*from, of*) can specify origin. The following questions show you how to ask where someone is from.

—**¿De dónde es** Adriana Bolini?
—**Es de** Buenos Aires.
—*Where is Adriana Bolini from?*
—*She's from Buenos Aires.*

—Raúl, **¿de dónde eres?**
—**Soy de** México.
—*Raúl, where are you from?*
—*I'm from Mexico.*

As you know, **ser** can be followed directly by an adjective of nationality (see **Gramática C.4**).

—Sr. Saucedo, **¿es** usted argentino?
—No, **soy** mexicano.
—*Mr. Saucedo, are you Argentinean?*
—*No, I'm Mexican.*

2. Two verbs in Spanish correspond to the English verb *to be.* **Estar** is used to express location; **ser** is used to tell where someone is from.

Clara **es de** los Estados Unidos, pero este año **está en** España.
Ernesto y Estela **son de** México, pero ahora **están** en Italia.
Clara is from the United States, but this year she's in Spain.
Ernesto and Estela are from Mexico, but they're in Italy.

Ejercicio 7

Diga dónde están estas personas.

MODELO: Mi hijo *está en* la escuela.

1. Yo _____ la biblioteca.
2. Luis y Nora _____ su clase de biología.
3. Tú _____ la rectoría.
4. Esteban y yo _____ el edificio de Ciencias Naturales.
5. La profesora Martínez _____ su oficina.
6. Nora y yo _____ enfrente del hospital.
7. Esteban, ¿_____ detrás del teatro?
8. Profesora Martínez, ¿_____ usted en la librería ahora?
9. Alberto y Pablo _____ la universidad.
10. Nosotros _____ aquí en la Facultad de Derecho.

Ejercicio 8

¿Adónde van estas personas? Complete las oraciones con la forma apropiada del verbo **ir** y **al** o **a la**.

MODELO: Usted *va al* parque los domingos.

1. Mis compañeros y yo _____ tienda nueva enfrente de la universidad.
2. Mis hermanos siempre _____ cine los sábados.
3. (Nosotros) _____ supermercado a comprar fruta.
4. La profesora Martínez _____ oficina a trabajar.
5. (Yo) _____ playa a tomar el sol y nadar.
6. (Yo) Siempre _____ biblioteca a leer y estudiar.
7. Esteban y Carmen _____ restaurante chino que está cerca de aquí para cenar.
8. Luis _____ plaza a pasear con una amiga.
9. (Nosotros) _____ librería a comprar el libro de español.
10. (Tú) _____ trabajo después de las clases.

a + **el** = **al** (obligatory contraction)
Voy al mercado.

a + **la** (no contraction)
Voy a la escuela.

Ejercicio 9

Diga de dónde son las siguientes personas y dónde están ahora.

MODELO: Adriana: Argentina (Washington, D.C.) →
Adriana es de Argentina, pero ahora está en Washington, D.C.

1. Ernesto y Estela: México (Roma)
2. Mayín: Panamá (Los Ángeles)
3. Rogelio y Carla: Puerto Rico (Nueva York)
4. Pilar: España (Guatemala)
5. Ricardo: Venezuela (España)

La vida diaria y los días feriados

METAS

In **Capítulo 4** you will discuss daily activities and how you feel. You will share your family's holiday customs with your classmates, and you will also learn about holidays and celebrations in the Hispanic world.

Mercadito, por Rafael González y González (Guatemala)

Sobre el artista: Rafael González y González (1908–1996) nació en Guatemala. Es el padre de la pintura maya Tz'utujil en ese país. Pinta las costumbres y tradiciones de su pueblo maya, principalmente la gente en la vida diaria y en sus celebraciones.

¡Conozca Guatemala!

Nombre del país: la República de Guatemala

Ciudad capital: Guatemala

Ciudades principales: Antigua, Quetzaltenango, Huehuetenango, Chichicastenango, Puerto Barrios

Moneda: el quetzal

Idiomas: español (oficial), veintitrés lenguas amerindias

Población: 13.000.000

Día de la Independencia: el 15 de septiembre

Fiestas típicas: la Fiesta de la Virgen del Tránsito, la Quema del Diablo

Comidas típicas: el tapado, el pepián, el jocón

Música típica: la música maya, fusión de música maya, española y afrocaribeña

Gente famosa: Rigoberta Menchú, Jacobo Arbenz, Miguel Ángel Asturias

Código del país por Internet: .gl

Voces guatemaltecas

alunado/a	enojado/a
bolo	borracho
un chapín / una chapina	un(a) guatemalteco/a
un(a) patojo/a	un(a) muchacho/a
un traste	un plato/utensilio de cocina

En este capítulo...

ACTIVIDADES DE COMUNICACIÓN

- Los días feriados y las celebraciones
- La rutina diaria
- Los estados físicos y anímicos

 **EN RESUMEN**

LECTURAS Y CULTURA

- **Ventanas culturales**
  Las costumbres: El carnaval de Barranquilla
- **Ventanas al pasado**
  Las calaveras de Posada
- **Enlace a la literatura**
  «Versos sencillos», por José Martí
- **Lectura**
  ¡Grandes fiestas!

GRAMÁTICA Y EJERCICIOS

4.1 Discussing Habitual Actions: Verbs with Stem-Vowel Changes (**ie, ue**) in the Present Tense

4.2 Discussing Habitual Actions: Irregular Verbs

4.3 Describing Daily Routine: Reflexives

4.4 Ordering Events: Infinitives after Prepositions

4.5 Describing States

MULTIMEDIA ONLINE LEARNING CENTER www.mhhe.com/dosmundos7

 CENTRO QUIA DVD

Actividades de comunicación y lecturas

Los días feriados y las celebraciones

✳ **Lea Gramática 4.1–4.2.**

Actividad 1 Definiciones: ¿Qué día es?

Trabaje con un compañero / una compañera. Lean la descripción y escojan el día feriado que se describe.

DESCRIPCIÓN	DÍAS FERIADOS		
1. Una persona celebra el día en que nació con globos, un pastel y regalos.	**a.** el cumpleaños	**b.** el Año Nuevo	**c.** el Día de los Enamorados
2. Tres personas en camellos les traen regalos a los niños el 6 de enero.	**a.** la Navidad	**b.** el Día de Reyes (los Reyes Magos)	**c.** Jánuca

3. La gente celebra el fin de un año y el principio de otro.	**a.** la Nochevieja	**b.** la Independencia	**c.** el Día de los Muertos
4. Los niños se visten de Drácula, de Frankenstein, etcétera y piden dulces.	**a.** el Día de la Madre	**b.** el día de su santo	**c.** el Día de las Brujas
5. Se celebra durante ocho días en diciembre. Cada día se enciende una vela más y a veces los niños reciben pequeños regalos.	**a.** el Día (de Acción) de Gracias	**b.** Jánuca	**c.** la Semana Santa

Actividad 2 Preferencias: Las fiestas

MODELO: E1: ¿Qué prefieres hacer para celebrar *tu cumpleaños*?
            E2: Durante el día, prefiero *quedarme en casa y ver la televisión.* Por la noche, me gusta *salir a cenar* con mis amigos.

¿Qué prefieres hacer para celebrar...

  1. tu cumpleaños?
  2. el Día de la Independencia?
  3. la Navidad u otro día feriado? (Jánuca, la Pascua, la Pascua Judía, el Ramadán)
  4. tu aniversario de boda u otro aniversario importante?
  5. el Día de la Madre o el Día del Padre?
  6. la Nochevieja o el Año Nuevo?

Actividades posibles: celebrar con mis parientes, cenar en casa, comer pastel, dar una fiesta, ir a la playa, ir al cine, ir a un café, ir de compras, merendar en el parque, quedarme en casa, recibir regalos, salir a bailar, salir a cenar en un restaurante, ver la televisión

Actividad 3   Definiciones: ¿Qué día es?

  1. El _____ es un día de fiesta en los Estados Unidos. Las familias se reúnen y preparan una comida abundante.
  2. Los hispanos celebran este día más que los norteamericanos. Es el día antes de la Navidad, la _____.
  3. Es la semana antes del Domingo de Pascua. Las personas religiosas, especialmente en España y en Latinoamérica, asisten a varias ceremonias en las iglesias. Es la _____.
  4. El _____ es una fiesta de 30 días. Cada día la gente no come desde temprano en la mañana hasta la noche. Cada noche hay una gran cena familiar.
  5. Mucha gente espera el primer día de enero con bailes y fiestas muy alegres. Esperan la medianoche con impaciencia. Es la _____.
  6. En muchos países hispanos, los niños no reciben regalos el 25 de diciembre. Los reciben el 6 de _____, el Día de _____.
  7. El _____ es una fiesta de ocho noches. Cada noche se enciende una vela más, hasta nueve. A veces los niños reciben un regalo.
  8. En México se celebra el 16 de septiembre; en Argentina es el 9 de julio; en los Estados Unidos es el 4 de julio. Es el _____.

¡OJO!

En algunos países hispanos las personas celebran su cumpleaños y también celebran el día de su santo. Si un hombre se llama José, entonces celebra el día de San José, el 19 de marzo. Si una mujer se llama Natalia, entonces celebra su santo el día de Santa Natalia, el 27 de julio.

el día de su santo

Actividad 4   Entrevista: Los días feriados

1. ¿Cómo te gusta celebrar tu cumpleaños?
2. ¿Qué haces el Día de Acción de Gracias? ¿Celebras esta fiesta en casa con tu familia o vas a la casa de otros parientes o amigos? ¿Qué comen?
3. ¿Qué aspecto de la Navidad te gusta más? ¿Qué aspecto te gusta menos?
4. ¿Celebras el Año Nuevo con tu familia o con tus amigos? ¿Qué hacen para celebrarlo?
5. ¿Con quién celebras el Día de la Independencia: con tu familia o con tus amigos? ¿Van a un parque o se quedan en casa? ¿Ven los fuegos artificiales?
6. ¿Qué otras fiestas celebras con tu familia o tus amigos? ¿Qué hacen para celebrar esas fiestas? ¿Dan muchos regalos? ¿Ponen decoraciones en casa?

© Joaquín Salvador Lavado, QUINO, Toda Mafalda, Ediciones de La Flor, 1993

VENTANAS CULTURALES   Las costumbres

El carnaval de Barranquilla

Imagine una fiesta en la que participan **miles** de personas. El lugar de esta fiesta es una ciudad entera, sus calles, casas, parques y plazas. Hay música y baile, **desfiles** y **carrozas.** Así es el carnaval, la festividad más popular en los países del Caribe y América Central.

El carnaval se origina en España y tiene muchos elementos de la cultura africana. Se celebra durante cuatro días en febrero o marzo; cuatro días de total diversión antes de la celebración religiosa de la **cuaresma.** Hay varios países que celebran el carnaval; entre otros, Venezuela, Puerto Rico, Cuba, Panamá y Colombia. Algunos carnavales son muy famosos, como el panameño, el de Oruro en Bolivia y el de Barranquilla.

La ciudad de Barranquilla es un centro urbano en Colombia adonde van muchas personas de todo el Caribe para participar en el carnaval. Como otros carnavales, la fiesta colombiana tiene una **reina,** grupos de bailes folclóricos, **disfraces** impresionantes y comida deliciosa. La cumbia, música típica de Colombia, se escucha en todas partes. Los colombianos celebran así una de sus más grandes fiestas: bailan, cantan y se divierten.

VOCABULARIO ÚTIL	
miles	*thousands*
los desfiles	*parades*
las carrozas	*floats*
la cuaresma	*Lent*
la reina	*queen*
los disfraces	*costumes*
(*sing.* disfraz)	

Comprensión

1. Mencione algunos países donde se celebra el carnaval.

2. ¿Cuál de estas descripciones *no* caracteriza el carnaval de Barranquilla?

    a. la gente lleva disfraces

    b. hay muchos fuegos artificiales

    c. todo el mundo baila

    d. hay comida deliciosa

    e. tiene una reina

La rutina diaria

✳ **Lea Gramática 4.3–4.4.**

Una mañana en la casa de los Saucedo

Ernesto se afeita.

Estela se maquilla.

Ernestito se lava los dientes.

Amanda se pone la ropa.

Guillermo se levanta.

Actividad 5 Orden lógico: Primero… luego…

Ponga en orden estas actividades. Use las palabras **primero, luego** y **después.**

1. **a.** Me seco.   **b.** Me lavo los dientes.   **c.** Me baño.
2. **a.** Me maquillo.   **b.** Me levanto.   **c.** Me pongo la ropa.
3. **a.** Me peino.   **b.** Me afeito.   **c.** Me ducho.
4. **a.** Me baño.   **b.** Me levanto.   **c.** Me despierto.
5. **a.** Me lavo el pelo.   **b.** Me quito la ropa.   **c.** Me seco el pelo.
6. **a.** Me lavo los dientes.   **b.** Desayuno.   **c.** Preparo el desayuno.
7. **a.** Me pongo el pijama.   **b.** Me acuesto.   **c.** Me quito la ropa.

¡OJO!

En la cultura hispana existe la costumbre de comer con la familia. Al mediodía todos regresan a casa a almorzar. Después de la comida, los adultos regresan al trabajo y los niños a la escuela. Porque la vida urbana hace difícil el regreso a casa, ahora en muchas casas no hay almuerzos en familia, solamente desayunos y cenas.

Actividad 6 Conversación: Las actividades diarias

Busque las actividades que no están en orden lógico o que son imposibles y diga por qué.

1. Todas las mañanas (yo) me despierto, me levanto, me acuesto, me ducho y me visto.
2. Por la tarde, mis hermanitos regresan de la escuela, juegan con el perro, hacen su tarea y salen para el trabajo.
3. Lobo, el perro de Ernestito, duerme, fuma un cigarrillo, come, se lava los dientes y juega con Ernestito.
4. Todos los domingos mis amigos y yo almorzamos en un restaurante, vamos al cine, nos despertamos, cenamos y nos acostamos temprano.
5. De lunes a viernes, mi profesor(a) de español desayuna, sale para la universidad, lava su ropa y lee en la biblioteca.
6. Después de las diez de la noche, los estudiantes hacen su tarea, ven televisión, asisten a clase, escuchan al profesor / a la profesora, se lavan los dientes y se acuestan.
7. Por la mañana, tú te duchas, te afeitas, te secas, te lavas los dientes, sales para el trabajo y luego te vistes, ¿verdad?

Actividad 7 Descripción de dibujos: La rutina

A. Escuche mientras su profesor(a) describe cada uno de los siguientes dibujos. Diga el número que corresponde al dibujo.
B. Trabaje con un compañero / una compañera para describir las diferencias entre los dibujos 1 y 2 y entre los dibujos 3 y 4.

1. Un lunes a las 6:30 con la familia Saucedo

2. Un jueves a las 6:30 con la familia Saucedo

Guillermo Ernestito Amanda y Estela Ernesto

3. Un sábado a las 9:00 de la mañana con los estudiantes

Alberto Mónica y Lan Raúl Esteban

4. Un domingo a las 9:00 de la mañana con los estudiantes

Alberto Lan Raúl Esteban y Mónica

Actividad 8 Intercambios: Las actividades diarias

A. Escuche a su profesor(a) mientras él/ella describe los dibujos. Diga el nombre de la persona en cada dibujo.

B. Ahora pregúntele a su compañero/a qué hace cada persona antes o después. Use *antes de / después de.*

MODELO: E1: ¿Qué hace Amanda *después de* jugar al tenis?
E2: *Después de* jugar al tenis, Amanda toma un refresco.

1. Paula   **2.** Guillermo   **3.** Pedro   **4.** Raúl

5. doña Lola   **6.** don Eduardo   **7.** doña Rosita   **8.** Ernesto

Palabras útiles

primero	por último
luego	a la(s)...
después	desde la(s)...
más tarde	hasta la(s)...
finalmente	

Actividad 9   Narración: La rutina de Adriana

Actividad 10   Entrevista: Preguntas personales

1. ¿A qué hora te despiertas? ¿Te despiertas a esa hora los fines de semana también?
2. ¿Te gusta levantarte temprano o tarde? ¿Quién se levanta primero donde tú vives?
3. ¿Te duchas (te bañas) por la mañana o por la noche? ¿Qué marca de jabón usas?
4. ¿Te lavas el pelo todos los días? ¿Qué marca de champú prefieres? ¿Usas un acondicionador? ¿De qué marca es?
5. ¿Te afeitas con navaja o con afeitadora (eléctrica)?
6. ¿Te maquillas todos los días o prefieres maquillarte sólo cuando sales de noche?
7. ¿Te pones perfume/colonia todos los días? ¿Qué marca prefieres?
8. ¿A qué hora te acuestas? ¿Te gusta leer antes de acostarte o prefieres ver la televisión? ¿Cuántas horas duermes?

VENTANAS AL PASADO

Las calaveras de Posada

¡Sólo en México una persona se hace famosa jugando con la muerte! José Guadalupe Posada (1852–1913) trabaja en **imprentas** donde hacen **tarjetas de felicitación,** anuncios, carteles para eventos públicos, **etiquetas** para cigarrillos y otras cosas. Pero también trabaja para un periódico de oposición, *El Jicote*. Son los tiempos del dictador Porfirio Díaz (1876–1911): tiempos difíciles de represión política. En 1884, en la ciudad de México, Posada trabaja en una imprenta donde publican almanaques y poesía. En este tiempo empieza a crear los dibujos que desde fines del siglo XIX se asocian con el Día de los Muertos en México.

VOCABULARIO ÚTIL	
las imprentas	*printing houses*
las tarjetas de felicitación	*birthday cards*
las etiquetas	*labels*
las calaveras	*skulls*
los esqueletos	*skeletons*
vivo/a	*alive*
la riqueza	*wealth*

Son interesantes obras de crítica social, parte de las populares **«calaveras»:** versos humorísticos y sarcásticos ilustrados con calaveras o **esqueletos** de gente **viva,** que baila, que se pasea, que pelea. Con sus dibujos, Posada nos presenta la **riqueza,** la miseria, la injusticia, la alegría: la esencia del pueblo mexicano.

Comprensión

1. En México, los dibujos de Posada se asocian con...
  a. el Día de la Independencia
  b. el Día de las Brujas
  c. el Día de los Muertos
  d. la Pascua

2. ¿Qué palabras describen la obra de Posada?
  a. almanaque
  b. tarjeta
  c. novela
  d. anuncio
  e. arquitectura

Los estados físicos y anímicos

✶ **Lea Gramática 4.5.**

Ernesto

está contento

Estela

están tristes

está enojado

está enferma

está aburrido

está ocupada

está preocupado

Ramón   Amanda

tienen hambre

tienen prisa

tiene sueño

tiene sed

tiene calor

Guillermo

tiene frío

tiene miedo

Actividad 11 Conversación: Las emociones

Diga si usted está de acuerdo o no con las siguientes afirmaciones.

Frases útiles

(No) Estoy de acuerdo.
Depende.

1. Es bueno gritar si uno está enojado.
2. Si uno está deprimido, es mejor consultar a un psicólogo.
3. Si uno tiene frío, es mejor tomar una limonada.
4. Si uno está de mal humor, es buena idea hablar con un buen amigo o un pariente.
5. Si uno está aburrido, es preferible ver la televisión.
6. Si uno tiene prisa y va a llegar tarde a clase, es mejor manejar muy rápido.
7. Es recomendable quedarse en casa cuando uno está muy enfermo.
8. Si uno tiene miedo, es buena idea comerse las uñas.

Actividad 12 Preferencias: ¿Qué hace usted en estas situaciones?

Exprese su opinión.

MODELO: E1: Cuando tengo calor *bebo café caliente.*
E2: *¡Ni pensarlo!*

1. Cuando estoy triste...
2. Cuando estoy contento/a...
3. Cuando estoy cansado/a...
4. Cuando estoy aburrido/a...
5. Cuando tengo hambre...
6. Cuando tengo frío...
7. Cuando tengo calor...
8. Cuando tengo prisa...

Actividad 13 Asociaciones: Los estados anímicos

¿Qué estado de ánimo asocia usted con las siguientes ocasiones?

1. Es medianoche y usted ve un ladrón en el patio.
2. Tiene un examen de español en diez minutos.
3. Es un sábado de verano. Hace sol y mucho calor. Usted trabaja en el jardín.
4. Es la Nochevieja y usted está en una fiesta con sus amigos.
5. Usted tiene una entrevista para un trabajo en 10 minutos y de pronto recibe una llamada de su abuela.
6. Usted recibe una mala nota en su examen de biología.
7. Encuentra a su perro comiendo su mejor camisa.
8. Es la una y usted está en una reunión de trabajo.

Comunicación en el Internet

:-)	alegre
:-o	sorprendido/a
:-<	enojado/a
:-@	a gritos
:-(	triste
:-e	desilusionado/a
:-I	indiferente
:-D	me da risa

Palabras útiles

camino rápidamente
como hamburguesas
compro ropa nueva
doy un paseo
duermo
escucho música
exploro el Internet
leo un libro
llamo a un(a) amigo/a
me baño (con agua caliente)
me ducho
me lavo los dientes
me pongo un suéter
me quedo en casa
me quito la chaqueta
prefiero estar solo/a
salgo en el carro
tomo café caliente
tomo el autobús
tomo un refresco
tomo un vaso de leche
voy de compras

Y tú, ¿qué dices?

Sí, yo también
Yo tampoco.
Yo sí. / Yo no.
¡Qué buena idea!
¡Ni pensarlo!
¡Qué ocurrencia!

Actividad 14   Intercambios: Los estados físicos y anímicos

Lea las situaciones y mire los dibujos. Luego diga cómo está o qué tiene Guillermo.

1. Son las 7:55. Guillermo va a llegar tarde a su clase de las 8:00 de la mañana.
2. Guillermo tiene un examen difícil hoy.
3. Guillermo tiene una mala nota en matemáticas. Su padre va a estar muy enojado.
4. Guillermo recibe una invitación para el Baile de los Enamorados.
5. Su padre le dice: —¡NO vas a ir al Baile de los Enamorados porque tienes un 6 en el examen de matemáticas!
6. Su abuela está en el hospital pero está mejor.
7. Después de correr, Guillermo... Y también...

Actividad 15   Entrevista: ¿Qué haces?

A. ¿Qué haces cuando estás *triste*? (*nervioso/a, de buen/mal humor, enamorado/a*)
B. ¿Qué haces cuando tienes *frío*? (*calor, sueño, sed, miedo*)

Palabras útiles

beber: bebo	gritar: grito
bostezar: bostezo	llorar: lloro
comerse las uñas: me como las uñas	ponerse: me pongo...
dormir: duermo	sonreír: sonrío
esconderse: me escondo	soñar con: sueño con

Enlace a la literatura

«Versos sencillos», por José Martí

Selección de su libro *Versos sencillos* (1891)

La poesía del escritor cubano José Martí (1853–1895) se considera una de las mejores obras en lengua española. Entre los libros de poemas de Martí están *Ismaelillo* (1882), dedicado a su hijo, *Versos libres* (1882) y *Versos sencillos*. La poesía de *Versos sencillos* parece simple —por eso el poeta la considera «sencilla»[1]—, pero es muy rica en imágenes y símbolos, y expresa además el gran humanismo de este escritor. En la siguiente selección, el poeta habla de su hijo y sus poemas y describe su personalidad: es un hombre sincero a quien le gusta la naturaleza.[2]

Versos sencillos

Yo soy un hombre sincero
De donde crece la palma,[3]
Y antes de morirme[4] quiero
Echar[5] mis versos del alma.[6]

Yo vengo de todas partes,
Y hacia[7] todas partes voy:
Arte soy entre[8] las artes.
En los montes,[9] monte soy.

Oigo un suspiro,[10] a través
De[11] las tierras y la mar,
Y no es un suspiro, —es
Que mi hijo va a despertar.

Con los pobres de la tierra
Quiero yo mi suerte[12] echar:
El arroyo[13] de la sierra
Me complace[14] más que el mar.

Todo es hermoso y constante,
Todo es música y razón,
Y todo, como el diamante,
Antes de luz es carbón.[15]

Mi verso es de un verde claro
Y de un carmín encendido:[16]
Mi verso es un ciervo herido[17]
Que busca en el monte amparo.[18]

Actividad creativa: Usted es poeta

Use los versos de José Martí como guía y escriba un poema para expresar sus sentimientos.

Yo soy _____
De donde _____,
Y antes de morirme quiero _____.
Yo vengo de _____
Y hacia _____ voy:
_____ soy entre _____
En _____, _____ soy.

[1]*unaffected* [2]*nature* [3]*crece... the palm tree grows* [4]*antes... before I die* [5]*To cast; To express* [6]*soul* [7]*toward* [8]*among* [9]*mountains* [10]*sigh* [11]*a... through* [12]*luck* [13]*brook* [14]*Me... Pleases me* [15]*coal* [16]*carmín... bright crimson* [17]*ciervo... wounded deer* [18]*shelter*

En resumen

De todo un poco

A. ¡Los Reyes Magos vienen mañana!

Mire los dibujos y ponga en orden las siguientes oraciones, para que coincidan con los dibujos.

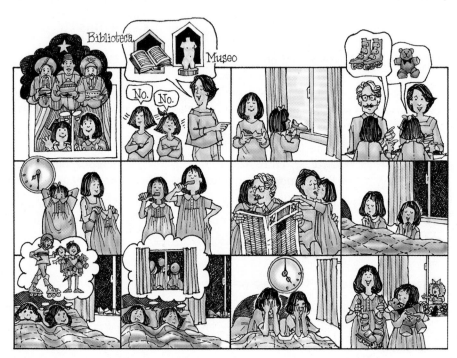

a. __6__ Se lavan los dientes.

b. __5__ Finalmente son las siete y media. Se ponen el pijama.

c. __11__ Se despiertan a las cinco de la mañana. Tienen miedo de mirar hacia la ventana.

d. __9__ Se acuestan pero no se duermen. Hablan de los juguetes que esperan recibir.

e. __2__ Su madre quiere llevarlas al museo y a la biblioteca, pero ellas prefieren quedarse en casa.

f. __1__ Es el cinco de enero. Son las 5:00 de la tarde. Clarisa y Marisa están nerviosas e impacientes.

g. __8__ Rezan antes de acostarse.

h. __12__ Corren a la ventana. Ahí están los juguetes que quieren. ¡Qué contentas están!

i. __7__ Les dicen «Buenas noches» a sus padres con un beso.

j. __3__ Ponen los zapatos en la ventana y esperan... ¡Los Reyes Magos van a venir mañana muy temprano!

k. __10__ Por fin se duermen. Sueñan que los Reyes Magos no les traen nada.

l. __4__ Cenan con sus padres y charlan sobre los juguetes que quieren.

B. Entrevista con su profesor(a)

Trabaje con dos o tres estudiantes. Escriban preguntas para entrevistar a su profesor(a). Cada grupo va a escribir ocho buenas preguntas para saber más sobre él/ella: sobre su vida en casa, su rutina diaria, sus estados de ánimo, sus actividades favoritas, sus preferencias, cómo celebra los días feriados, etcétera.

MODELOS: ¿A qué hora se levanta usted durante la semana?
¿Qué le gusta hacer después del trabajo?
¿Qué hace usted cuando está aburrido/a?
¿Cómo celebra el Año Nuevo?
¿Qué le gusta hacer los viernes por la noche?

Después, cada grupo debe hacerle sus preguntas al profesor / a la profesora. Tomen apuntes sobre la información para luego escribir una composición sobre él/ella.

¡Dígalo por escrito!

Los días feriados

Describa su día feriado favorito y diga cómo lo celebra, dónde, con quién(es) y cómo se prepara (qué hace) para esa celebración.

¡Cuéntenos usted!

Cuéntenos sobre su día feriado favorito. ¿Cómo se llama esta celebración? ¿Es un día feriado religioso para usted? ¿Lo celebra usted con amigos o familiares? ¿Se celebra de día, de noche o durante varios días? ¿Comen ustedes comida típica o tradicional? ¿Hay algún símbolo asociado con esa fiesta?

LECTURA

¡Grandes fiestas!

Las grandes fiestas del mundo hispano representan diferentes culturas y tradiciones: algunas tienen su origen en la religión católica, otras en tradiciones indígenas y otras más celebran eventos históricos. Pero todas estas fiestas tienen varios elementos en común: la participación de mucha gente, la alegría y la música.

Vamos primero a España. Estamos en Valencia, hermosa ciudad al este de la península ibérica y en la costa del Mar Mediterráneo. Queremos participar en la celebración de las Fallas de Valencia, una fiesta que dura varios días. Estamos aquí el 19 de marzo para ver el final de la fiesta con un evento espectacular: la **quema** de numerosas esculturas de **cartón** y **madera,** todas impresionantes. Los artistas que participan en las Fallas fabrican estos monumentos durante todo el año. Las esculturas pueden ser bellas, satíricas o cómicas, y siempre son muy elaboradas. Algunas representan personas; otras, eventos sociales. Las mejores reciben un **premio** y se guardan en el Museo de las Fallas. ¡Pero todas las otras se queman!

Visitemos ahora otra hermosa ciudad española. Nos vamos a Sevilla, en el sur de España. Hoy es un lunes de abril, por la noche, y estamos en el barrio de Los

(Continúa)

La feria de Sevilla

VOCABULARIO ÚTIL

la quema	*burning*
el cartón	*cardboard*
la madera	*wood*
el premio	*prize, award*
los farolillos	*lantern*
la portada de luces	*lit-up façade*
la estrella	*ferris wheel*
los fuegos artificiales	*fireworks*
la bendición	*blessing*
la fortaleza	*fortress*
la colina	*hill*
el santo patrono	*patron saint*
el desfile	*parade*
la efigie	*effigy*

Remedios. Hay **farolillos** en las calles. Escuchamos guitarras y gente que canta sevillanas, la alegre música de esta región. ¡Hoy comienza la Feria de Sevilla! Pasamos por la hermosa **portada de luces** y vemos mujeres con hermosos trajes flamencos. Tenemos todas las diversiones típicas de una feria, hasta una enorme **estrella**. Esta gran festividad termina en una semana, con **fuegos artificiales**.

Ahora queremos saltar a Perú. Es el 24 de junio y estamos en Cuzco para la Fiesta del Sol, Inti Raymi. Este evento de la cultura inca celebra el comienzo de un nuevo año. Inti Raymi es uno de los festivales más grandes de América del Sur, con la participación de miles de personas de Perú y de todo el mundo. Hoy es el día más importante del festival, cuando un actor representa a Sapa Inca, Hijo del Sol, y pide la **bendición** del sol en la Plaza Qorikancha. Luego hay una procesión del Sapa Inca con muchas personas hasta la **fortaleza** de Sacsayhuamán, en las **colinas** de Cuzco. Después de esta procesión, comienza el nuevo año.

Estamos ahora en el sur de México. Participamos en la Guelaguetza, fiesta popular de Oaxaca que se realiza todos los años en julio. Hay un público enorme que ve con nosotros este espectáculo colorido de bailes regionales. En la Guelaguetza participan músicos y danzantes de las ocho regiones del estado de Oaxaca. Cada grupo lleva la ropa típica de su pueblo y presenta sus danzas. Luego le ofrece al público su «guelaguetza», que es un regalo de su región, como frutas, pan o chocolate. Después de la Guelaguetza vamos con la gente a pasear por la ciudad, donde hay muchas actividades culturales.

Bueno, terminemos el verano en América Central. Vamos a El Salvador. Muchas de las fiestas salvadoreñas son religiosas. La más popular es la del **santo patrono** del país, Salvador del Mundo. Esta festividad se celebra en la capital, con actividades religiosas y recreativas. Hoy es el 5 de agosto y estamos aquí para ver el **desfile** con que comienza la festividad. En este desfile los salvadoreños cargan una **efigie** de su santo patrón para expresar su devoción y

El festival de Inti Raymi

En resumen :: **167**

La Guelaguetza

su espíritu festivo. Nuestro viaje termina, pero sólo por ahora. Porque este paseo fantástico va a continuar para usted.

Comprensión

Busque la definición correcta.

1. _____ La Guelaguetza
2. _____ Inti Raymi
3. _____ El Museo de las Fallas
4. _____ El Salvador del Mundo
5. _____ La Feria de Sevilla

a. Esta fiesta comienza con un desfile.
b. El día más importante de esta fiesta es el 24 de junio.
c. Aquí están las esculturas que ganan premios.
d. Se escucha música alegre, las sevillanas.
e. Hay bailes regionales y regalos.
f. Un actor representa al Hijo del Sol.
g. Esta fiesta termina con fuegos artificiales.
h. El público recibe regalos de los danzantes.
i. Es parte de un evento espectacular de España.
j. Se celebra con actos religiosos y actividades de diversión.

Un paso más... ¡a escribir!

Usted tiene un amigo o una amiga de otro país. Esta persona quiere saber cuáles son las grandes fiestas nacionales que usted celebra. Escríbale una breve descripción de sus dos fiestas favoritas. ¿Por qué le gustan? ¿Qué hace usted en estas festividades? ¿Las celebra con la familia o con amigos?

MODELO: Estimado /a _____:

Mis dos fiestas favoritas son _____ y _____. Me gustan porque _____. Estas fiestas se celebran con varias actividades. Por ejemplo, yo _____, _____ y _____. Normalmente, celebro estas fiestas con _____.

Vea el **Resumen cultural** en este capítulo del *Cuaderno de actividades.*

Vocabulario

These words come from the *Actividades de communicación*. You are not expected to memorize the entire list. You instructor may tell you which sections he or she wants to emphasize. Be patient; you will be familiar with most of these words by the end of the chapter.

Los días feriados y las celebraciones

Holidays and Celebrations

el aniversario de boda	wedding anniversary
el Año Nuevo	New Year
el Día de Acción de Gracias	Thanksgiving
el Día de las Brujas	Halloween
el Día de los Enamorados	Valentine's Day
el Día de la Independencia	Independence Day
el Día de la Madre	Mother's Day
el Día de los Muertos	All Souls' Day (November 2nd)
el Día del Padre	Father's Day
el Día de los Reyes Magos	Epiphany, Day of the Magi (January 6th)
el día del santo	saint's day
el Día de Todos los Santos	All Saints' Day (November 1st)
el Domingo de Pascua	Easter Sunday
la fiesta	holiday; party
el Jánuca	Hanukkah
la(s) Navidad(es)	Christmas
la Nochebuena	Christmas Eve
la Nochevieja	New Year's Eve (December 31st)
la Pascua Judía	Passover
el Ramadán	Ramadan
la Semana Santa	Holy Week

La rutina diaria

Daily Routine

acostarse	to go to bed
me acuesto / se acuesta	
afeitarse	to shave
arreglarse	to get ready
bañarse	to bathe
despertarse (ie)	to wake up
me despierto / se despierta	
dormir (ue)	to sleep
duermo / duerme	
ducharse	to take a shower
lavarse los dientes	to brush one's teeth
lavarse el pelo	to wash one's hair
levantarse	to get up
maquillarse	to put on makeup
peinarse	to comb one's hair
ponerse (perfume / la ropa)	to put on (perfume/clothes)
quitarse (la ropa)	to take off (one's clothes)
secarse (el pelo)	to dry (one's hair)
venir	to come
vengo / viene	
vestirse (i)	to get dressed
me visto / se viste	
volver (ue)	to return, go back
(vuelvo / vuelve)	

Los estados físicos y anímicos

Physical and Mental States

el estado de ánimo	mental state
estar...	to be . . .
alegre	happy
contento/a	happy
de buen/mal humor	in a good/bad mood
deprimido/a	depressed
enamorado/a	in love
enojado/a	angry
mejor	better (health-wise)
ocupado/a	busy
preocupado/a	worried
solo/a	alone, lonely
triste	sad
tener...	to be . . .
calor	hot
frío	cold
hambre	hungry
miedo	afraid
prisa	in a hurry
sed	thirsty
sueño	sleepy

PALABRA SEMEJANTE: nervioso/a
REPASO: aburrido/a, enfermo/a

¿Cuándo?

When?

antes de	before
de lunes a viernes	Monday through Friday
de pronto	suddenly
desde la(s)... hasta la(s)	from . . . until . . .
después de	after

REPASO: ayer, después, hoy, luego, mañana, pasado mañana el próximo... (día, mes)

Los verbos

Verbs

bostezar	to yawn
comerse las uñas	to bite one's nails
dar	to give
doy / da	
encender (ie)	to light; to turn on
enciendo / enciende	
encontrar (ue)	to find
encuentro / encuentra	
entrevistar	to interview

escoger	to choose
escojo / escoge	
esconder(se)	to hide (oneself)
estar de acuerdo	to agree
gritar	to yell, scream
llamar	to call (on the phone)
llorar	to cry
pedir (i)	to ask for;
pido / pide	to request
ponerse (*irreg.*) + *adj.*	to become, get + *adj.*
me pongo / se pone	
quedarse (en casa)	to stay (at home)
recibir regalos	to get gifts
reunirse	to get together
me reúno / se reúne	
saber	to know
sé / sabe	
sonreír	to smile
soñar (ue) (con)	to dream (about)
tomar apuntes / un examen	to take notes / a test
traer	to bring
traigo / trae	

PALABRAS SEMEJANTES: celebrar, coincidir, consultar

Los sustantivos

Nouns

el acondicionador	conditioner
la afeitadora (eléctrica)	(electric) razor
el baile	dance
el beso	kiss
el camello	camel
la colonia	cologne
los dulces	candy
el fin	end
los fuegos artificiales	fireworks
el globo	balloon
el hermanito	little brother
el jabón	soap
el juguete	toy
el ladrón / la ladrona	thief
la llamada	(telephone) call

la marca	brand
la navaja	razor; razor blade
la nota	note, grade
el pariente / la parienta	relative
el regalo	gift
la toalla	towel
el vaso	glass
la vela	candle

PALABRAS SEMEJANTES: la afirmación, el aspecto, la ceremonia, el champú, la composición, la decoración, la diferencia, la emoción, etcétera, la (im)paciencia, la invitación, Latinoamérica, la limonada, el patio, el pijama, el psicólogo / la psicóloga, la situación

Los adjetivos

Adjectives

caliente	hot
malo/a	bad

PALABRAS SEMEJANTES: abundante, eléctrico/a, familiar, (im)paciente, (im)posible, preferible, recomendable, religioso

Palabras y expresiones útiles

Useful Words and Expressions

ahí	there, over there
depende	(it) depends
en orden lógico	in logical order
es mejor/peor	it is better/worse
especialmente	especially
estar de acuerdo	to agree
nada	nothing
¡Ni pensarlo!	Don't even think of it!
por fin	at last
¡Qué bueno!	That's great!
¡Qué ocurrencia!	What a silly idea!
rápidamente	quickly, rapidly
rápido	quick, fast
¡Yo no!	I don't!
¡Yo sí!	I do!

Gramática y ejercicios

4.1 Discussing Habitual Actions: Verbs with Stem-Vowel Changes (*ie, ue*) in the Present Tense

A. Here is the present tense of several commonly used verbs that follow the same pattern of stem-vowel changes as **querer** and **preferir**: **cerrar** (*to close*), **pensar** (*to think*), **empezar** (*to begin*), **perder** (*to lose*), and **encender** (*to light; to turn on*).*

	cerrar	**pensar**	**empezar**	**perder**	**encender**
(yo)	cierro	pienso	empiezo	pierdo	enciendo
(tú)	cierras	piensas	empiezas	pierdes	enciendes
(usted, él/ella)	cierra	piensa	empieza	pierde	enciende
(nosotros/as)	cerramos	pensamos	empezamos	perdemos	encendemos
(vosotros/as)	cerráis	pensáis	empezáis	perdéis	encendéis
(ustedes, ellos/as)	cierran	piensan	empiezan	pierden	encienden

¿RECUERDA?

Recall from **Gramática 2.3** that the verbs **querer** (**quiero, quieres, quiere, queremos, queréis, quieren**) and **preferir** (**prefiero, prefieres, prefiere, preferimos, preferís, prefieren**) use two stems in their present-tense conjugations. The stem containing the vowel **e** appears only in the infinitive and in the **nosotros/as** and **vosotros/as** forms. The stem containing **ie** occurs in the rest of the forms.

—¿A qué hora **cierran** ustedes la Nochevieja?
—**Cerramos** a las 5:00 de la tarde.

—¿**Encienden** ustedes las velas de Jánuca cada año?
—Sí, las **encendemos** por ocho noches seguidas.

—*What time do you close on New Year's Eve?*
—*We close at 5:00 P.M.*

—*Do you light Hanukkah candles every year?*
—*Yes, we light them for eight nights in a row.*

B. Three other verbs follow the same pattern as **jugar**: **dormir** (*to sleep*), **volver** (*to return, go back*), and **almorzar** (*to have lunch*).†

	jugar	**dormir**	**volver**	**almorzar**
(yo)	juego	duermo	vuelvo	almuerzo
(tú)	juegas	duermes	vuelves	almuerzas
(usted, él/ella)	juega	duerme	vuelve	almuerza
(nosotros/as)	jugamos	dormimos	volvemos	almorzamos
(vosotros/as)	jugáis	dormís	volvéis	almorzáis
(ustedes, ellos/as)	juegan	duermen	vuelven	almuerzan

---

*Recognition: **vos querés, preferís, cerrás, pensás, empezás, perdés, encendés**
†Recognition: **vos jugás, dormís, volvés, almorzás**

—¿A qué hora **vuelven** a casa después de una fiesta?
—A veces no **volvemos** hasta las 3:00 ó 4:00 de la madrugada.

—*What time do you return home after a party?*
—*Sometimes we don't return until 3:00 or 4:00 in the morning.*

> **cierro** = *I close*
> **cerramos** = *we close*
> **empiezo** = *I begin*
> **empezamos** = *we begin*

> **juego** = *I play*
> **jugamos** = *we play*
> **vuelvo** = *I return*
> **volvemos** = *we return*

Ejercicio 1

¿Qué hacen usted y sus amigos? Complete estas oraciones con la forma correcta del verbo entre paréntesis.

MODELO: —¿*Cierran* ustedes los ojos en clase? (cerrar) →
—No, no *cerramos* los ojos en clase.

1. —¿_____ ustedes en su clase de español? (dormir)
   —¡Claro que no! Nunca _____ en clase, porque nos divertimos.
2. —¿_____ ustedes en casa o en el trabajo? (almorzar)
   —Generalmente _____ en casa con la familia.
3. —¿_____ ustedes al trabajo después de almorzar? (volver)
   —Sí, _____ a las 2:00.
4. —¿_____ ustedes al tenis los fines de semana? (jugar)
   —A veces _____, a veces no.
5. —¿_____ ustedes mucho al tenis en el invierno? (jugar)
   —No, _____ poco porque hace demasiado frío.
6. —¿_____ ustedes frecuentemente cuando _____ al basquetbol?
   (perder, jugar)
   —No, casi nunca _____ cuando _____ al basquetbol.
7. —¿_____ ustedes ir al cine por la tarde? (preferir)
   —No, _____ ir por la mañana con los niños.
8. —¿_____ ustedes las vacaciones en mayo o en junio? (empezar)
   —Normalmente _____ las vacaciones en junio.

> These forms may be difficult to remember, but they will feel more natural as you hear and read more Spanish. Therefore, don't try to memorize all of this, but do refer to the rules when you edit your writing.

4.2 Discussing Habitual Actions: Irregular Verbs

A. As you know, an irregular verb is one that uses more than one stem to form its conjugation. (In many cases the irregularity is only in the **yo** form.) Here are some common verbs that add a **g** in the **yo** form: **tener** (*to have*), **venir** (*to come*), **salir** (*to leave; to go out*), and **poner** (*to put*).*

> **vengo** = *I come*
> **viene** = *he/she comes; you come*
> **venimos** = *we come*

	tener	**venir**	**salir**	**poner**
(yo)	tengo	vengo	salgo	pongo
(tú)	tienes	vienes	sales	pones
(usted, él/ella)	tiene	viene	sale	pone
(nosotros/as)	tenemos	venimos	salimos	ponemos
(vosotros/as)	tenéis	venís	salís	ponéis
(ustedes, ellos/as)	tienen	vienen	salen	ponen

*Recognition: **vos tenés, venís, salís, ponés**

—¿Siempre **viene** usted temprano?   —*Do you always come early?*
—Sí, casi siempre **vengo** a las 8:00.   —*Yes, I almost always come at 8:00.*

—¿Dónde **pongo** mi ropa?   —*Where do I put my clothes?*
—Aquí mismo, encima de esta silla.   —*Right here, on this chair.*

> **digo** = *I say*
> **dice** = *he/she says; you say*
> **decimos** = *we say*

B. The verbs **traer** (*to bring*) and **oír** (*to hear*) insert **ig** in the **yo** form.* In addition, **oír** adds a **y** in all but the **yo, nosotros/as,** and **vosotros/as** forms. The verbs **hacer** and **decir** change the **c** to **g** in the **yo** form. **Decir** (*to say, tell*) also changes the stem vowel **e** to **i** in all but the **nosotros/as** and **vosotros/as** forms.†

	traer	oír	hacer	decir
(yo)	traigo	oigo	hago	digo
(tú)	traes	oyes	haces	dices
(usted, él/ella)	trae	oye	hace	dice
(nosotros/as)	traemos	oímos	hacemos	decimos
(vosotros/as)	traéis	oís	hacéis	decís
(ustedes, ellos/as)	traen	oyen	hacen	dicen

—¿Qué **traes** a las fiestas?   —*What do you bring to parties?*
—**Traigo** mis discos compactos y algo de comer.   —*I bring my CDs and something to eat.*

—¿No **oyes** un ruido extraño?   — *Don't you hear a strange noise?*
—No, no **oigo** nada.   —*No, I don't hear anything.*

Ejercicio 2

Un amigo le hace preguntas sobre su clase de español. Contéstele según el modelo.

MODELO: —Generalmente, ¿vienes temprano a la clase de español?
—Sí, *vengo* temprano todos los días.

1. —¿Traes tu perro a la clase de español?
   —¡Claro que no! _____ solamente el libro y el cuaderno.
2. —¿Pones tu libro de español debajo de la mesa?
   —No, _____ el libro encima de la mesa.
3. —¿Le dices «Buenos días» en español al profesor / a la profesora?
   —¡Qué va! A las 2:00 de la tarde le _____ «Buenas tardes».

---

*Recognition: **vos traés, oís**
†Recognition: **vos hacés, decís**

4. —¿Oyes música en tu clase?

—Sí, _____ canciones en español, naturalmente.

5. —¿Sales de tu clase a las 3:00?

—No, _____ a las 2:50.

6. —¿Siempre vienes a la clase preparado/a?

—Sí, casi siempre _____ preparado/a.

7. —¿Tienes mucha tarea?

—Sí, _____ tarea todos los días, excepto el domingo.

8. —¿Qué haces en tu clase?

—_____ un poco de todo: converso, leo, escribo.

4.3 Describing Daily Routine: Reflexives

A. In English, pronouns that indicate that the subject of a sentence does something to himself or herself are called *reflexive;* they end in *-self* (*-selves*).

He cut himself.	Babies often talk to themselves.
She looked at herself in the mirror.	We didn't blame ourselves.

Some actions that the subject does to himself or herself are not expressed with reflexive pronouns in English. For example, *I get up at 7:00. I take a bath and then get dressed.* In such sentences, Spanish always uses a reflexive pronoun: **Yo me levanto a las 7:00. Me baño y luego me pongo la ropa.**

B. Here is the present tense of the verb **levantarse** (*to get up*) with reflexive pronouns.*

> Actions done to oneself are expressed using reflexive words:
> **Me afeito.**
>   (*I shave* [*myself*].)
> **Nos ponemos la ropa.**
>   (*We put on our clothes.*)

	levantarse	
(yo)	me levanto	*I get up*
(tú)	te levantas	*you (inf. sing.) get up*
(usted, él/ella)	se levanta	*you (pol. sing.) get up; he/she gets up*
(nosotros/as)	nos levantamos	*we get up*
(vosotros/as)	os levantáis	*you (inf. pl., Spain) get up*
(ustedes, ellos/as)	se levantan	*you (pl.) get up; they get up*

C. Following is a list of verbs with the reflexive pronouns **me** (*myself*) and **se** (*himself, herself, yourself* [*pol. sing.*]) that you can use to describe your daily routine or that of someone else. Notice that the infinitives with the reflexive pronoun end in **se.**

---

*Recognition: **vos te levantás**

INFINITIVE

Me acuesto. / Se acuesta.*	acostarse	*I go to bed. / He/She goes to bed; You (pol. sing.) go to bed.*
Me despierto. / Se despierta.†	despertarse	*I wake up. / He/She wakes up; You (pol. sing.) wake up.*
Me levanto. / Se levanta.	levantarse	*I get up (out of bed). / He/She gets up; You (pol. sing.) get up.*
Me baño. / Se baña.	bañarse	*I take a bath. / He/She takes a bath; You (pol. sing.) take a bath.*
Me ducho. / Se ducha.	ducharse	*I take a shower. / He/She takes a shower; You (pol. sing.) take a shower.*
Me lavo el pelo. / Se lava el pelo.	lavarse el pelo	*I wash my hair. / He/She washes his/her hair; You (pol. sing.) wash your hair.*
Me seco. / Se seca.	secarse	*I dry off. / He/She dries off; You (pol. sing.) dry off.*
Me afeito. / Se afeita.	afeitarse	*I shave. / He/She shaves; You (pol. sing.) shave.*
Me lavo los dientes. / Se lava los dientes.	lavarse los dientes	*I brush my teeth. / He/She brushes his/her teeth; You (pol. sing.) brush your teeth.*
Me peino. / Se peina.	peinarse	*I comb my hair. / He/She combs his/her hair; You (pol. sing.) comb your hair.*
Me maquillo. / Se maquilla.	maquillarse	*I put on makeup. / He/She puts on makeup; You (pol. sing.) put on makeup.*
Me pongo la ropa. / Se pone la ropa.	ponerse la ropa	*I put on my clothes. / He/She puts on his/her clothes; You (pol. sing.) put on your clothes.*
Me quito la ropa. / Se quita la ropa.	quitarse la ropa	*I take off my clothes. / He/She takes off his/her clothes; You (pol. sing.) take off your clothes.*
Me (des)visto. / Se (des)viste.	(des)vestirse	*I (un)dress. / He/She (un)dresses; You (pol. sing.) (un)dress.*

Me levanto temprano y **me ducho** en seguida. Generalmente **me lavo** el pelo. Luego **me seco** y **me peino.**

I get up early, and I take a shower right away. Generally I wash my hair. Afterward I dry off and comb my hair.

---

*Acostarse is a stem-changing verb: the stem vowel **o** changes to **ue** in all but the **nosotros/as** and **vosotros/as** forms.

†**Despertarse** is also a stem-changing verb: the stem vowel **e** changes to **ie** in all but the **nosotros/as** and **vosotros/as** forms.

Alberto **se levanta** tarde. **Se ducha** rápidamente, pero no **se afeita. Se pone la ropa** y **se peina.**

Alberto gets up late. He showers quickly, but he doesn't shave. He dresses and combs his hair.

D. Reflexive pronouns are normally placed directly before the verb (**me seco**), but they may be attached to infinitives (**secarme**) and present participles (**secándome**).

Me gusta **afeitarme** primero y luego **bañarme.**

I like to shave first and then take a bath.

Ernesto va a **levantarse** y **bañarse** inmediatamente.

Ernesto is going to get up and take a bath immediately.

—Amanda, ¿qué estás haciendo?
—Estoy **lavándome** los dientes.

—Amanda, what are you doing?
—I'm brushing my teeth.

Ejercicio 3

¿Qué oración de la página siguiente describe mejor los siguientes dibujos?

1. _____ d

2. _____ b

3. _____ f

4. _____ e

5. _____ c

6. _____ g

7. _____ a

a. Él se quita la camisa, pero ella se pone los zapatos.
b. Él sale para el trabajo a las 8:00, pero su hijo sale para la escuela a las 8:30.
c. Ella lee novelas después de trabajar, pero él prefiere ver la televisión.
d. Este joven se ducha por la mañana, pero las niñas prefieren bañarse por la noche.
e. Él se afeita la cara, pero su esposa se afeita las piernas.
f. A él no le gusta bañarse, pero le gusta bañar al perro.
g. Se acuesta a las 11:30 y se levanta a las 6:00.

Ejercicio 4

Imagínese que su hermanito de tres años le hace estas preguntas. Contéstele correctamente.

MODELO: ¿Te lavas los dientes con jabón? →
No, me lavo los dientes con pasta de dientes.

1. ¿Te bañas antes de las 5:00 de la mañana?
2. ¿Te lavas el pelo con detergente?
3. ¿Te afeitas en la lavandería?
4. ¿Te levantas temprano los domingos?
5. ¿Te quitas la ropa en la universidad?
6. ¿Te peinas en la biblioteca?
7. ¿Te maquillas en la clase de español?
8. ¿Te duchas en el patio?

4.4 Ordering Events: Infinitives after Prepositions

A. When telling a story or relating a sequence of events, speakers use "sequencing" words to let listeners know the order in which the events occur. You have already used many of these sequencing words in the **Narración** activities, for example:

primero	*first*		antes	*before*
luego	*then*		finalmente	*finally*
después	*afterward*		por último	*at last*
más tarde	*later (on)*			

Primero me baño y **luego** me cepillo los dientes. **Después,** preparo el desayuno. **Luego** voy al trabajo y trabajo hasta las 6:00 de la tarde. **Finalmente** vuelvo a casa a eso de las 8:00.

First I take a bath, and then I brush my teeth. Afterward, I fix breakfast. Then I go to work and work until 6:00 P.M. Finally I return home about 8:00.

B. The words **después** and **antes** by themselves express the meanings *after(ward)* and *before.*

Después, vamos a cenar con Pedro y Andrea Ruiz.

Afterward, we're going to have dinner with Pedro and Andrea Ruiz.

C. The preposition **de** follows **antes** and **después** before a noun or an infinitive. (English uses the *-ing* form instead of the infinitive.) Don't forget to attach any object pronouns to the end of the infinitive.

Antes de acostarme, quiero terminar la tarea.	*Before going to bed, I want to finish my homework.*
Vamos a terminar la tarea **antes de (después de) la comida.**	*We are going to finish our home work before (after) the meal.*
Después de jugar al béisbol, voy a ir a la playa.	*After playing baseball, I'm going to go to the beach.*

> **antes de** + infinitive
> **Antes de ducharse, Ramón se afeita.**
> (*Before showering, Ramón shaves.*)
> **después de** + infinitive
> **Después de estudiar, vamos a salir a bailar.**
> (*After studying, we are going out dancing.*)

Ejercicio 5

¿Qué oración describe mejor cada dibujo?

1. _C_   2. _E_   3. _D_

4. _A_   5. _B_

a. Prepara la cena después de trabajar.
b. Limpian la casa antes de salir a jugar.
c. Siempre se lava los dientes después de comer.
d. Después de hacer ejercicio se ducha.
e. Antes de acostarse, apaga la luz.

Ejercicio 6

Complete las oraciones lógicamente.

1. Nos gusta lavar el coche después de...
2. El señor Saucedo lee el periódico antes de...
3. Pedro Ruiz dice: «Después de levantarme por la mañana, me gusta... »
4. Antes de acostarse, es necesario...
5. Guillermo siempre hace la tarea antes de...

a. desayunar.
b. apagar las luces.
c. almorzar.
d. salir a jugar con sus amigos.
e. salir a pasear.

Ejercicio 7

Haga una oración lógica con **antes de** o **después de.**

MODELO: hacer la tarea / ver la televisión (nosotros) →
Después de hacer la tarea, vamos a ver la televisión.
(Antes de ver la televisión, vamos a hacer la tarea.)

1. preparar la comida / hacer la compra (Estela)
2. limpiar la casa / invitar a unos amigos (Pedro y Andrea Ruiz)
3. dormir una siesta / ir al videocentro (Guillermo)
4. correr / bañarse (tú)
5. salir a bailar / ponerse la ropa (nosotros)

4.5 Describing States

A. *Estar* + Adjective

Use **estar** (**estoy, estás, está, estamos, estáis, están**) to describe how someone is, or is feeling, at a particular time.

—¿Cómo **estás**?   —*How are you?*
—**Estoy** un poco deprimido.   —*I'm a bit depressed.*

—¿Cómo **está** José Luis hoy?   —*How is José Luis today?*
—**Está** enfermo.   —*He's sick.*

—¿Cómo **están** ustedes?   —*How are you?*
—**Estamos** muy bien, gracias.   —*We are fine, thank you.*

Remember that **ser** is used to identify or describe the inherent characteristics of someone or something, *not* to tell how that person or thing is (feeling) at a particular moment.

Alberto **es alto, delgado, joven**   *Alberto is tall, thin, young,*
  y muy guapo.   *and very handsome.*
Hoy **está confundido y cansado.**   *Today he's confused and tired.*

> **Estar** (*To be*) describes a state (how someone is at a particular time):
> —**¿Cómo estás?**
> (*How are you?*)
> —**Estoy cansada.**
> (*I'm tired.*)

Ejercicio 8

Describa el estado físico o anímico de estas personas.

MODELOS: Carmen → Carmen *está nerviosa.*
yo → Yo *estoy cansado.*

1. yo
2. mi primo
3. Luis y yo
4. Nora
5. tú (*f.*)
6. Pablo y Mónica

a. está nervioso
b. están ocupados
c. estoy enojado/a
d. estamos preocupados
e. estás contenta
f. está deprimida

Ejercicio 9

Graciela

Mire los dibujos y haga preguntas. Use la forma correcta de **estar** y adjetivos como (**un poco**) **triste, ocupado/a, cansado/a, enojado/a, deprimido/a, alegre, irritado/a, contento/a, enamorado/a**, etcétera.

MODELO: ¿Está cansada Graciela?

Clarisa y Marisa   Ernesto   Ramón ♥ ♥ Amanda

1.   2.   3.

Guillermo

AGENCIA DE VIAJES   Silvia   Nacho

4.   5.

B. *Tener* + Noun

Some states of being are described in Spanish with the verb **tener** (*to have*), although they correspond to the verb *to be* in English. Common states expressed with **tener** are **tener hambre** (*to be hungry*), **tener sueño** (*to be sleepy*), **tener sed** (*to be thirsty*), **tener prisa** (*to be in a hurry*), **tener frío** (*to be cold*), **tener calor** (*to be hot*), and **tener miedo** (*to be afraid*).

—Ernesto, ¿cuándo quieres comer? **Tengo** mucha **hambre.**

—Estela, ¿quieren ir al cine tú y Ernesto esta noche?
—No, gracias. **Tenemos** mucho **sueño** y queremos acostarnos.

—Guillermo, ¿**tienes sed**?
—Sí, **tengo** mucha **sed.** Vamos a tomar algo.

—¿Por qué **tiene prisa** Amanda?
—Porque su clase empieza a las 8:00.

—Ernesto, *when do you want to eat? I'm very hungry.*

—Estela, *do you and Ernesto want to go to the movies tonight?*
—No, thanks. *We're very sleepy and want to go to bed.*

—Guillermo, *are you thirsty?*
—Yes, *I'm very thirsty. Let's get something to drink (drink something).*

—*Why is Amanda in a hurry?*
—*Because her class begins at 8:00.*

¡OJO!

Other useful expressions that use this structure:

estar de acuerdo	*to agree*
estar mejor	*to be (feel) better*
tener éxito	*to be successful*
tener razón	*to be right*
tener suerte	*to be lucky*

With the words **calor/frío** (*heat/cold*) and **caliente** (*hot*), several combinations are possible.

To describe people, use **tener** + **calor/frío.**

—Nora, ¿tú no **tienes calor**?　　　　—Nora, aren't you hot?
—No, no **tengo calor.** Me　　　　　　—No, I'm not hot. I love the sun.
　gusta mucho el sol.

To describe things, use **estar** + **caliente/frío.**

Lan, cuidado. No toques la　　　　　*Lan, be careful. Don't touch*
estufa. **Está** muy **caliente.**　　　　*the stove. It's very hot.*

To describe the weather, use **hacer** + **calor/frío.**

Ay, Pablo, **hace mucho frío** hoy.　　　*Pablo, it's really cold today.*
Voy a ponerme un abrigo.　　　　　　*I'm going to put on a coat.*

Ejercicio 10

Mire los dibujos. ¿Cuál es la oración que mejor identifica cada dibujo?

MODELO:　　Tiene sed.

a. Tienen miedo.　　　　　　　**f.** Está enojado.
b. Tiene prisa.　　　　　　　　**g.** Está preocupado.
c. Tienen calor.　　　　　　　**h.** Está deprimido.
d. Hace mucho calor.　　　　　**i.** Tiene hambre.
e. Nieva hoy.

1. _____　　　　2. _____　　　　3. _____

4. _____　　　　5. _____

Ejercicio 11

Describa el estado de estas personas. Estados posibles: **tener + calor, frío, hambre, prisa, sed, sueño, miedo.**

MODELO: (Yo) *Tengo prisa* porque la clase empieza a las 4:00.

1. A mediodía, Mayín _____.
2. Si (tú) _____, ¿por qué no te pones un suéter?
3. (Nosotros) _____ porque la temperatura está a 45°C hoy.
4. A medianoche (yo) _____.
5. Estoy en casa. Son las 8:55 y tengo una clase a las 9:00. (Yo) _____.
6. Hace mucho sol hoy. Guillermo y Ernestito quieren tomar agua fría porque _____.
7. Cuando estoy solo/a de noche, a veces _____.
8. ¿Tienes algo para tomar? (Yo) _____.

El Día de los Muertos

¿**U**na fiesta que celebra la muerte[1]? ¡Así es! En México, el primero y el segundo día de noviembre son días dedicados al recuerdo de los familiares y amigos fallecidos.[2] El primero de noviembre es el Día de Todos los Santos y se dedica a los niños muertos. El 2 de noviembre es el

Día de los Muertos y en ese día la gente honra a sus familiares: un tío, una esposa, una prima o un padre muerto. La tradición de honrar a los difuntos[3] es una mezcla de tradiciones católicas europeas con tradiciones de las culturas indígenas[4] de América.

Los preparativos para estos días empiezan a fines de[5] octubre y en algunas regiones las celebraciones duran hasta mediados de[6] noviembre. En los mercados se vende papel picado,[7] flores de cempasúchil,[8] calaveras y ataúdes de azúcar[9] decorados de colores vivos, juguetes[10] de papel maché en forma de esqueletos y un pan[11] especial: el pan de muerto. En las casas y en edificios públicos se construyen ofrendas[12] que recuerdan a los amigos o familiares fallecidos.

Las ofrendas se adornan con velas,[13] papel picado, flores y pan de muerto. Es costumbre poner objetos queridos[14] del difunto: por ejemplo, una comida o bebida favorita, o un recuerdo de sus gustos: un collar,[15] un libro, un instrumento musical y, si es posible, una foto.

También es costumbre dejar un vaso de agua en el altar. ¿Sabe por qué? Porque los espíritus tienen sed después de su largo viaje al mundo de los vivos.[16] Se forma una senda[17] de pétalos de cempasúchil que guía al espíritu del muerto de la puerta hasta la ofrenda.

En muchos pueblos, por la mañana las familias van al panteón o cementerio y limpian las tumbas de sus seres queridos[18] en preparación para la celebración de esa noche. De noche encienden[19] velas, ofrecen flores y comen comidas tradicionales en honor a los difuntos. Esa misma noche por las calles del pueblo hay desfiles de gente enmascarada[20] que pasa por las calles tocando música. El Día de los Muertos les permite a los mexicanos recordar y honrar a aquellas personas que siempre viven en el corazón de sus amigos y familiares. ■

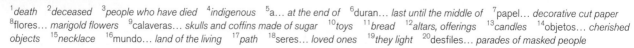

[1]*death* [2]*deceased* [3]*people who have died* [4]*indigenous* [5]*a… at the end of* [6]*duran… last until the middle of* [7]*papel… decorative cut paper* [8]*flores… marigold flowers* [9]*calaveras… skulls and coffins made of sugar* [10]*toys* [11]*bread* [12]*altars, offerings* [13]*candles* [14]*objetos… cherished objects* [15]*necklace* [16]*mundo… land of the living* [17]*path* [18]*seres… loved ones* [19]*they light* [20]*desfiles… parades of masked people*

Shakira,
volcán de sonido

La joven colombiana Shakira Mebarak es una artista famosa. Shakira es cantautora, lo cual quiere decir que compone[1] las canciones que interpreta en sus discos. Y muchas de esas canciones son hermosos poemas al ritmo de rock. Para ser tan joven, Shakira escribe como una poeta de gran experiencia. Explora temas tradicionales —el amor, las relaciones humanas— desde una perspectiva fresca y nueva. Las melodías de esta talentosa compositora[2] son contagiosas. Predomina la instrumentación eléctrica, pero también las suaves guitarras y el piano.

Shakira es bilingüe y bicultural, de madre colombiana y padre libanés.[3] Su estilo y varias de sus canciones reflejan la influencia libanesa. De hecho, en su segundo disco Shakira canta parte de la canción «Ojos así» en árabe. Después del gran éxito[4] de sus discos en español, Shakira se hace famosa en todo el mundo con su primer compacto en inglés, *Laundry Service* (2002). Luego llegan dos discos en 2005, *Fijación Oral, Vol. 1*, que tiene canciones populares como «La pared» y «La tortura»; y *Oral Fixation, Vol. 2* con el triunfo de su canción «Hips Don't Lie». Ganadora de numerosos Grammys, Shakira parece tímida al conversar, pero cuando canta se transforma en un volcán de sonido, en pura energía.

[1] *she composes* [2] *composer* [3] *Lebanese* [4] *success*

El arpa[1] se considera uno de los instrumentos musicales más antiguos; es el instrumento que toca el rey David en la Biblia. Los españoles traen el arpa a las Américas durante la colonización y hoy día forma

El arpa, instru- mento nacional de Paraguay

parte del repertorio musical de muchos países: México, Venezuela, Ecuador y Perú, entre otros. Pero en Paraguay el arpa llega a ser el instrumento nacional.

El arpa paraguaya es más pequeña que la clásica; tiene entre 32 y 36 cuerdas[2] y tiene una caja de resonancia[3] más grande que produce una música sonora[4] y clara. Su menor tamaño[5] hace posible ponerla sobre el hombro para tocarla caminando en procesiones o desfiles. En varios países hispanoamericanos, el arpa se toca como acompañamiento,[6] pero en Paraguay el arpa es el instrumento principal de un conjunto,[7] como solista o en dúo.

El arpista paraguayo por excelencia es Félix Pérez Cardoso, pero también se destacan[8] Rito Pedersen, Ismael Ledesma y Clelia Carolina Sanabria. Además hay intérpretes de la música del arpa de otros países como Lucia Shiomitsu y Toshiko Nezu Sandoval de Japón o Arami de Francia. ¿Quiere escuchar las lindas melodías del arpa paraguaya? Pues, le recomendamos buscar uno de los muchos videos en Internet para apreciar el instrumento nacional de Paraguay.

[1] *harp* [2] *strings* [3] *caja de… sound box* [4] *sonorous, resonant finger* [5] *Su… Its smaller size* [6] *accompaniment* [7] *band, musical group* [8] *Se… stand out*

CAPÍTULO 5

Las clases y el trabajo

METAS

In **Capítulo 5,** you will discuss classroom activities and your classmates' talents and abilities. You will also talk about careers, obligations, activities in progress, and recreational plans for the future.

Campesinos, por Héctor Poleo (Venezuela)

Sobre el artista: Héctor Poleo (1918–1989) nace en Venezuela. Este premiado artista estudia arte en Caracas y a los 19 años tiene su primera exhibición. También estudia en México donde le influye el arte del muralista Diego Rivera. En 1948 se traslada a París y empieza a experimentar con la abstracción geométrica inspirada en temas folklóricos e indígenas. Sus obras se exponen en Venezuela, Francia, Cuba, Los Estados Unidos y Francia.

¡Conozca Venezuela!

Nombre del país: la República Bolivariana de Venezuela

Ciudad capital: Caracas

Ciudades principales: Valencia, Maracaibo, Ciudad Bolívar, Mérida

Moneda: el bolívar

Idiomas: el español (oficial), lenguas indígenas

Población: 26.000.000

Día de la Independencia: el 5 de julio

Fiestas típicas: el Día de la Candelaria, el Carnaval, el Velorio de la Cruz de Mayo, el Natalicio de Simón Bolívar

Comidas típicas: la arepa, el pabellón criollo, el mondongo, las hallacas

Música típica: el joropo, la gaita de Zulia, la salsa, el merengue

Gente famosa: Simón Bolívar, Hugo Chávez, Oscar D'Leon, Carlos Raúl Villanueva, Carolina Herrera, Rómulo Gallegos

Voces venezolanas

una bala fría	comida rápida
un bolo	un bolívar
un(a) catire	un(a) rubio/a
una llave	un amigo
los pisos	los zapatos
una rumba	una fiesta

En este capítulo...

ACTIVIDADES DE COMUNICACIÓN

- Las actividades de los estudiantes
- Las habilidades
- Las carreras y las actividades del trabajo
- Las actividades futuras

EN RESUMEN

LECTURAS Y CULTURA

- **Ventanas culturales**
  La lengua: Las palabras extranjeras
- **Enlace a la música**
  El rock en español
- **Ventanas culturales**
  La vida diaria: La diversidad profesional
- **Lectura**
  El lenguaje del cuerpo

GRAMÁTICA Y EJERCICIOS

5.1 Indicating to Whom Something Is Said: Indirect Object Pronouns with Verbs of Informing

5.2 Expressing Abilities: **saber** and **poder** + Infinitive

5.3 Referring to Actions in Progress: Present Progressive

5.4 Expressing Obligation and Duty: **tener que, deber, necesitar, hay que, es necesario**

5.5 Expressing Plans and Desires: **pensar, quisiera, me gustaría, tener ganas de**

Actividades de comunicación y lecturas

Las actividades de los estudiantes

✳ **Lea Gramática 5.1.**

Alberto les habla a sus compañeros.

Mónica no le pone atención a la profesora.

La profesora nos dice «Buenos días».

La profesora nos hace preguntas.

Le contestamos a la profesora.

Nora le lee las Ventanas culturales a Esteban.

Carmen le hace una pregunta a la profesora Martínez.

La profesora le explica la gramática a Carmen.

Palabras útiles

(casi) nunca
raras veces
de vez en cuando
a veces
muchas veces
con frecuencia
(casi) siempre
todos los días

Actividad 1 Conversación: ¿Con qué frecuencia?

¿Con qué frecuencia hacen ustedes las siguientes actividades en la clase de español?

MODELOS: Escribimos las palabras nuevas en el cuaderno *todos los días.*
La profesora *siempre* nos hace preguntas y nosotros *casi siempre* le contestamos en español.

1. Les hablamos a los compañeros de clase.
2. Tomamos apuntes.
3. Entendemos casi todo cuando la profesora / el profesor nos habla en español.
4. Contestamos las preguntas del profesor / de la profesora.
5. Le ponemos atención al profesor / a la profesora.
6. Usamos el celular.
7. Aprendemos palabras nuevas.
8. Le hacemos preguntas al profesor / a la profesora.
9. Hacemos la tarea en clase.
10. Dormimos una siesta.
11. Le decimos «Buenas noches» al profesor / a la profesora.
12. Terminamos la clase temprano.

Actividad 2 Preferencias: La clase de español

Aquí hay varias actividades relacionadas con la clase de español. Póngalas en orden, del número 1 (¡Me gusta mucho!) al número 7 (¡No me gusta nada!). Después, compare sus respuestas con las de sus compañeros de clase.

1. En el salón de clase:
   a. _____ tomar exámenes
   b. _____ trabajar en grupos
   c. _____ escuchar al profesor / a la profesora cuando nos habla
   d. _____ hablarles a mis compañeros en español
   e. _____ ver videos
   f. _____ participar en conversaciones
   g. _____ escuchar canciones hispanas o cantar en español

2. Fuera del salón de clase:
   a. _____ estudiar para los exámenes
   b. _____ escribir composiciones
   c. _____ hacer la tarea de gramática
   d. _____ escuchar las actividades auditivas
   e. _____ hablarles a mis amigos hispanos en español
   f. _____ visitar sitios Web en español
   g. _____ escuchar una emisora de radio hispana

Actividad 3 Descripción de dibujos: En la universidad

A. Escuche a su profesor(a) mientras él/ella describe las actividades de los estudiantes norteamericanos. Diga el número del dibujo que corresponde a cada descripción.

1.

2.

3.

4.

B. Diga qué diferencias hay entre los dibujos 1 y 2 y entre los dibujos 3 y 4.

Actividad 4 Entrevista: La clase de español

1. ¿Te asigna mucha tarea el profesor / la profesora? ¿Lees todas las lecturas?
2. ¿Dónde escuchas las actividades auditivas: en tu coche, por Internet, en casa, en el laboratorio de lenguas o en la biblioteca?
3. ¿Quién te explica la gramática cuando no la comprendes, el profesor / la profesora o un compañero / una compañera de clase?
4. ¿A qué hora empieza esta clase? ¿Llegas tarde a clase? Cuando llegas tarde, ¿qué le dices al profesor / a la profesora?
5. ¿Te hace muchas preguntas el profesor / la profesora? ¿Te gusta? ¿Siempre le contestas en español? ¿Piensas en español cuando hablas español?
6. ¿Te gusta la clase de español? ¿Qué cosas *no* te gusta hacer en la clase? ¿Qué cosas te gusta hacer en la clase?

Actividad 5 Del mundo hispano: La Escuela de Idiomas Nerja

ESCUELA DE IDIOMAS NERJA
CURSOS DE ESPAÑOL DURANTE TODO EL AÑO

estancias de 1 a 36 semanas
clases de 4 ó 6 horas diarias

Nuestros programas incluyen:
• cursos intensivos individuales o en grupo
• cursos de español comercial • cursos para profesores
• diploma de español como lengua extranjera (D.E.L.E.)

Actividades culturales y sociales
• excursiones • cocina española
• baile flamenco • cine español • fiestas
NIVELES: ELEMENTAL, INTERMEDIO I Y II,
AVANZADO I Y II, Y SUPERIOR.

OFERTA PARA EL VERANO

• **12 semanas curso intensivo**
• **12 semanas de alojamiento**
• **20 horas por semana**
• **2.903 €**

precios sujetos a cambio

ALOJAMIENTO:
• en residencia con baño privado y
televisor, terraza y piscina
• con familia a corta distancia de la escuela
• en un piso con otros estudiantes

**PROFESORES ESPECIALIZADOS
EN METODOLOGÍA INNOVADORA**

NUESTRA ESCUELA DISPONE DE:
• librería • biblioteca • cafetería
• centro multimedia

PIDA INFORMACIÓN DETALLADA A:

Escuela de Idiomas Nerja
C/Almirante Ferrándiz, No 73, Apartado 46
E-29780 Nerja, Málaga, España
Tfno: 34 95 252 1687 • Fax: 34 95 252 2119
correo e: idnerja@idnerja.es

*Escuela de Idiomas Nerja en la Costa del Sol, en un pueblo andaluz de
20.000 habitantes. Nerja está en la orilla del mar y está rodeado de
montañas, a cincuenta minutos del aeropuerto de Málaga. La escuela
está situada en el centro en una casa típica con jardín tropical.
Está cerca de las tiendas y las playas.*

Lea este anuncio de la Escuela de Idiomas Nerja y conteste las preguntas de su profesor(a). Luego, trabaje con su compañero/a para contestar las siguientes preguntas.

1. ¿Cuántas horas de clase tienen los estudiantes al día?
2. ¿Son cursos individuales o para grupos?
3. ¿De cuántas semanas es el curso intensivo? ¿Cuánto cuesta?
4. ¿Qué instalaciones hay en esta escuela? ¿Hay cafetería? ¿Qué más hay?
5. ¿Cuál es la dirección de la Escuela de Idiomas Nerja?
6. Describa la ciudad de Nerja. ¿Le gustaría estudiar allí? ¿Por qué?

VENTANAS CULTURALES La lengua

Las palabras extranjeras

Algunos hispanos **lamentan** el exceso de uso del inglés en la lengua española. Porque hoy para viajar sacamos *tickets*, para divertirnos escuchamos el *iPod*, cuando acampamos hacemos *camping*. Y si usted se mantiene en **buena forma** es porque sabe hacer *footing* y toma clases de *body-fitness*. En la televisión ya no hay anuncios, sino *spots*, y la gente de negocios trabaja en el *business*. Al usar la computadora, podemos *chatear*, escribir en el *blog* y hacer *mailings*. Y en las películas del director español Pedro Almodóvar, las personas **se flipean**.

Entendemos esta preocupación de algunos hispanos, pero el uso de palabras **extranjeras** ocurre con frecuencia en todos los idiomas. ¡Es un proceso natural! Es verdad que en español comemos bistec (que viene de *beef steak*) y también sándwiches. Llevamos suéter y jeans. Sufrimos estrés. Y cuando se habla de deportes, los hispanos juegan al fútbol, al voleibol, y hacen un **jonrón** o meten un gol. Pero el inglés también tiene muchas palabras de otras lenguas y especialmente del español. ¿Puede pensar en algunas?

Aquí tiene varias; para empezar: *vista, plaza, sierra, rodeo, patio* y *siesta*. Otras palabras de origen español, un poco modificadas, son *cigar* (cigarro) y *lasso* (lazo). Muchos **préstamos** vienen del árabe, como *alcove* (alcoba), *spinach* (espinaca) y adobe. El inglés usa también palabras de origen indígena que ya forman parte del español moderno: *tamale* (tamal), de la lengua náhuatl en México; *alpaca* y *condor* del idioma quechua en Perú, *jaguar* del guaraní en Paraguay; además *hurricane* (huracán), *barbecue* (barbacoa) y *cayman* (caimán), de la lengua de los indígenas del Caribe. Y una gran cantidad de nombres de ciudades y estados norteamericanos son españoles; por ejemplo, Colorado, California, Nevada, San Francisco y Santa Fe.

El realidad no debemos preocuparnos porque hacemos *camping*, compramos *tickets* y nos flipeamos. Las palabras extranjeras son parte natural de muchos idiomas.

Una agencia de viajes en Guatemala

VOCABULARIO ÚTIL

lamentan	*regret*
la buena forma	*good shape (health)*
se flipean	*flip*
extranjeras	*foreign*
el jonrón	*home run*
los préstamos	*borrowings*

Comprensión

1. ¿Cuáles de estas palabras son de origen indígena?
   a. alpaca **b.** alcoba **c.** condor **d.** jaguar **e.** hurricane **f.** espinaca
2. Mencione otros cinco lugares en los Estados Unidos que tienen nombres españoles.

Las habilidades

⭐ **Lea Gramática 5.2.**

Estela conversa con su amiga Lola.

doña Lola   Estela

LOLA: Estela, ¿sabes montar a caballo?

ESTELA: Sí, y también sé jugar al polo.

LOLA: Y tus hijos, ¿saben ellos montar a caballo también?

ESTELA: No, pero saben patinar.

ESTELA: Ahora mi hijo Guillermo no puede patinar; tiene una pierna fracturada. Sólo puede leer y ver la televisión.

LOLA: ¡Pobre chico!

Actividad 6 **Descripción de dibujos: ¿Qué saben hacer estas personas?**

Escuche a su profesor(a) mientras él/ella describe los talentos de las siguientes personas. Diga quién es cada persona que describe.

Me gusta mucho mi país, Perú.

はじめまして。

A lot of North American tourists come to Cuzco.

Susana

Estela

Doña María Eulalia

Pilar

Raúl

Nacho

Ricardo

Adriana

Actividad 7 Orden lógico: Ernestito quiere bañar al perro

Busque el orden correcto de estas oraciones.

_____ ERNESTITO: Mamá, tengo ocho años. ¡Sé bañar a un perro!

_____ ESTELA: Perfecto, pero también vas a...

_____ ESTELA: Bueno, hijo, después de bañarlo, vas a secarlo muy bien.

_____ ERNESTITO: Ya sé, mamá.

_____ ESTELA: Sí, hijo, pero antes de traer al perro, prepara el agua y el jabón.

_____ ERNESTITO: Mamá, mamá, ¿puedo bañar a Lobo?

_____ ERNESTITO: Ya está todo listo, mamá.

Palabras útiles

No, no sé *esquiar*.

Sí, sé *esquiar* un poco (muy bien).

No, no sé *esquiar*, pero quiero aprender.

Actividad 8 Entrevistas: ¿Qué sabes hacer? ¿Qué puedes hacer?

LAS HABILIDADES

MODELO: E1: ¿Sabes *esquiar*?
E2: Sí, sé *esquiar* muy bien.

1. patinar en el hielo
2. jugar al basquetbol
3. nadar
4. diseñar sitios Web
5. reparar carros
6. montar en motocicleta
7. bucear
8. hablar otro idioma (¿cuál?)
9. tocar algún instrumento musical
10. pintar
11. andar en patineta
12. bailar música salsa

EN TU CASA O EN LA RESIDENCIA ESTUDIANTIL

MODELO: E1: ¿Puedes *hacer la tarea en casa (en la residencia estudiantil)*?
E2: No, no puedo *hacer la tarea en casa porque hay muchas distracciones.*

1. cenar a la hora que quieras
2. tener animales domésticos donde vives
3. ver la televisión a cualquier hora
4. dormir hasta las 10:00 de la mañana
5. escuchar música y hacer la tarea a la vez

Enlace a la música

El rock en español

Carlos Santana
(guitarrista)

La frase «rock en español» se refiere a grupos de gran diversidad, pero todos con una característica en común: cantan en español. Muchos críticos y *fans* opinan que los rockeros hispanos tocan la música más innovadora[1] hoy en día. Esto se debe[2] en parte a los estilos tan diversos que estos grupos incorporan. El grupo argentino Los Fabulosos Cadillacs, por ejemplo, combina salsa, reggae y rock. Y el grupo mexicano Maldita Vecindad ofrece una fusión de ska y rock. Pero también se escucha en algunos la influencia de los estilos rap, punk, soul, y de la música tradicional hispana, como el mariachi de México, el tango de Argentina y el bolero de Cuba.

Además de su fusión musical, varios de estos grupos tienen un mensaje social importante, pues sus canciones exploran cuestiones urgentes: la pobreza,[3] la inmigración y la represión política. En efecto, varios grupos se forman durante los años 80 en Chile, Argentina y México con el impulso de denunciar los abusos del gobierno.[4] Hay muchos, como Serú Girán y Maná, que ya tienen dos décadas de triunfos; otros, como el grupo cubanoamericano Tango 36 y el español El Canto del Loco triunfan en tiempos recientes. Y entre los más populares están La Ley, Soda Stereo, Molotov, Café Tacuba, El Tri, Plastilina Mosh, Los Enanitos Verdes, Los Skarnales y Cadena Perpetua. A todos los une su pasión por el rock y su deseo de cantar en español.

Comprensión

1. ¿De qué manera son innovadores los grupos de rock en español?
  a. cantan en inglés   **b.** se forman recientemente   **c.** incorporan estilos diversos
2. ¿Qué estilos musicales incorporan estos grupos?

[1]la... *the most innovative music*   [2]Esto... *This is because*   [3]*poverty*   [4]*government*

Las carreras y las actividades del trabajo

⭐ **Lea Gramática 5.3–5.4.**

El ama de casa está planchando.

La cajera está contando el dinero.

El trabajador social está escribiendo un informe.

El peluquero está cortando el pelo.

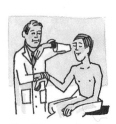

El médico está examinando al enfermo.

El dependiente debe arreglar la ropa.

El cocinero está preparando la comida y el mesero les está sirviendo a los clientes.

Los bomberos tienen que apagar el incendio.

El plomero necesita reparar la tubería.

El empleado debe entrar al trabajo a las 9:00.

El mecánico tiene que reparar el automóvil en el taller.

La abogada defiende a los acusados y la juez decide casos criminales.

La enfermera debe cuidar a los enfermos.

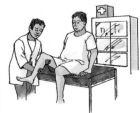

El terapeuta está trabajando con un paciente.

Los obreros están trabajando en la fábrica.

Actividad 9 Asociaciones: ¿Dónde trabaja?

MODELO: Un mecánico trabaja en un taller de reparaciones.

1. ___f___ un(a) electricista
2. ___d___ un mesero / una mesera
3. ___j___ un peluquero / una peluquera
4. ___b___ un médico / una doctora
5. ___k___ un(a) piloto
6. ___h___ un cajero / una cajera
7. ___n___ un secretario ejecutivo / una secretaria ejecutiva
8. ___i___ un dependiente / una dependienta

a. en un cuarto con muchas computadoras
b. en su consultorio y en un hospital
c. en un autobús
d. en un restaurante
e. en la cocina de un restaurante
f. en la calle o en una casa, con cables eléctricos
g. en una fábrica

(Continúa)

9. ___O___ un(a) cantante
10. ___l___ un profesor / una profesora
11. ___g___ un obrero industrial / una obrera industrial
12. ___m___ un(a) mecánico
13. ___e___ un cocinero / una cocinera
14. ___c___ un(a) chofer
15. ___a___ un programador / una programadora

h. en un banco
i. en una tienda
j. en una peluquería
k. en un avión
l. en una universidad
m. en un taller de reparaciones
n. en una oficina
o. en un club nocturno

Actividad 10 Identificaciones: Encuentre las diferencias

Mire los dibujos y encuentre las diferencias entre el dibujo de la derecha y el de la izquierda. ¿Qué están haciendo estas personas?

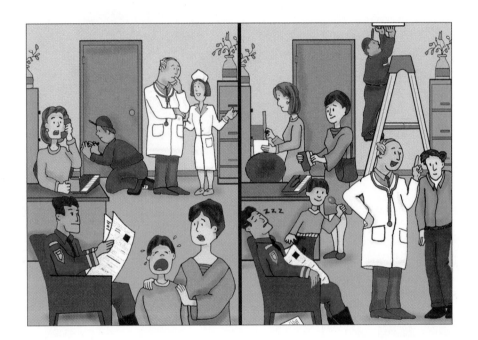

Palabras y frases útiles

archivar
consolar
el documento
la escalera
Está _____ ndo.
llorar
el/la paciente
pagar
la paletita

Actividad 11 Encuesta: Su opinión, por favor

Lea esta lista de profesiones y oficios y marque el más interesante (=1), el más aburrido (=2), el más peligroso (=3), el más necesario (=4) y el más prestigioso (=5).

_____ abogado/a
_____ agente de seguros
_____ ama de casa
_____ (mujer) bombero
_____ contador(a)
_____ electricista
_____ gerente

_____ hombre/mujer de negocios
_____ médico
_____ plomero/a
_____ (mujer) policía
_____ programador(a)
_____ terapeuta
_____ trabajador(a) social

Ahora, compare su opinión con las de sus compañeros y diga por qué usted piensa así.

Actividad 12 Narración: ¡Cuántas obligaciones!

Éstas son las actividades del trabajo de la profesora Martínez y de Luis y Carmen. ¿Qué tienen que hacer?

Palabras útiles

Tiene que	Necesita	Debe
calificar	jaula	servir

Adela Martínez (profesora)

Luis (mesero)

Carmen (asistente de veterinario)

Actividad 13 Del mundo hispano: ¿Busca empleo?

Conteste las preguntas según la información en estos avisos clasificados.

1. ¿Qué tienen que hacer las personas que trabajan en el bar Noche de Ronda?
2. ¿Qué aptitudes necesita tener el/la chofer?
3. Si usted quiere el trabajo de secretario/a, ¿qué experiencia necesita tener?
4. Si usted quiere trabajar de tres a cuatro horas al día, ¿a qué número debe llamar?
5. ¿Qué tiene que saber hacer el cocinero / la cocinera?
6. ¿Es necesario ser hombre para obtener el trabajo de terapeuta?
7. ¿Qué compañía necesita personas que hablen inglés y español?
8. Si usted sabe reparar coches, ¿a qué número tiene que llamar?

SE NECESITA cocinero/a con experiencia en comida mexicana. Venga personalmente a la Calle Obregón 838.

BAR «Noche de Ronda» necesita meseras/os para atender mesas. Sueldo y comisión. Si le interesa, favor de llamar al 56-45-67-94.

SECRETARIA/O con tres años de experiencia. Algo de inglés y que escriba a máquina mínimo 50 ppm, para trabajo estable de oficina cerca del centro. Llame sólo de 5 a 7 P.M. 55-58-03-49.

DEPENDIENTE/A h/m para trabajo de media jornada. Llame al 55-49-05-34.

CHOFER h/m. Con experiencia. Debe hablar inglés. Compañía «Transportes El Blanco» en Coyoacán. 55-17-42-58.

TERAPEUTA h/m con experiencia. Para trabajo en clínica. Llame de 9 a 11 A.M. al Dr. Tamayo al 56-89-30-78.

ATENCIÓN: Compañía Hnos. Menéndez necesita varias personas bilingües para sus oficinas en Laredo y Ciudad Juárez. Llame al 56-94-93-21o al 93-57-06-43 desde las 10 hasta las 14.

TALLER DE REPARACIONES busca mecánico con experiencia. Cinco días por semana. Buen sueldo. 56-44-91-83

Actividad 14 Entrevista: El trabajo

1. ¿Tienes trabajo de jornada completa o de media jornada ahora? ¿Es bueno el sueldo?
2. ¿Dónde trabajas? ¿Vives cerca o lejos de tu trabajo?
3. ¿A qué hora entras y a qué hora sales? ¿Te gustan tus horas de trabajo? ¿Es simpático/a tu jefe/jefa?
4. ¿Qué tienes que hacer? ¿Hay actividades diferentes o siempre la misma cosa? De todas las actividades de tu trabajo, ¿cuál te gusta más? ¿Por qué?
5. ¿Cuáles son los aspectos más desagradables de tu trabajo? ¿Por qué son desagradables?

Diccionario cibernético

at (@)	**la arroba**
attachment	**el archivo adjunto**
blog	**la bitá cora**
click	**hacer *clic*, pulsar**
dot (.)	**el punto**
download	**bajar**
electronic mail	**el correo electrónico**
e-mail	**el *e-mail*, el *mail*, el mensaje electrónico**
Internet (web)	**el Internet (la red)**
keyboard	**el teclado**
link	**el enlace**
mouse	**el ratón, la rata**
printer	**la impresora**
search engine	**el buscador**
slash (/)	**raya**
Web page	**la página Web**
wireless	**inalámbrico/a**
www	**doble u (v), doble u (v), doble u (v)**

VENTANAS CULTURALES   La vida diaria

La diversidad profesional

La diversidad profesional caracteriza al mundo hispano. Hay profesionales de todo tipo: artistas, maestros, músicos, escritores, arquitectos, ingenieros, astronautas y científicos. Pablo Picasso y Frida Kahlo son dos de los artistas más famosos, aunque muchos otros **se destacan** hoy en día, como Fernando Botero. Entre los científicos de renombre está el biólogo español Francisco José Ayala, ganador de numerosos **premios,** y el doctor venezolano Baruj Benacerraf, quien gana el Premio Nobel de medicina de 1980. También hay escritores que reciben el Premio Nobel, entre ellos la poeta chilena Gabriela Mistral y el novelista colombiano Gabriel García Márquez.

La agencia NASA cuenta con varios astronautas latinos: el peruano Carlos Noriega, el español Michael López Alegría y los mexicoamericanos Ellen Ochoa y José M. Hernández. Y de Venezuela es el músico Gustavo Dudamel, quien con **apenas** 28 años ya es director de la Orquesta Filarmónica de Los Ángeles. Además, el mundo de la política tiene un gran número de mujeres, entre ellas cuatro presidentas: Violeta Chamorro en Nicaragua, Mireya Moscoso en Panamá, Michelle Bachelet en Chile y Cristina Fernández de Kirchner en Argentina.

Pero hay muchos otros trabajadores que hacen una labor importante, como los obreros y los **campesinos.** La economía de Honduras, Colombia, Ecuador, Guatemala y Nicaragua depende de la agricultura y de sus campesinos. Y las industrias del petróleo en Venezuela y la del vino en Chile dependen de sus obreros. La diversidad **laboral** también caracteriza al mundo hispano.

El joven director Gustavo Dudamel

VOCABULARIO ÚTIL

se destacan	stand out
los premios	awards
apenas	barely
los campesinos	peasants
laboral	labor (adj.)

Comprensión

1. ¿Cuál es la profesión de los siguientes hispanos?
   a. Michael López Alegría   **b.** Fernando Botero
   c. Gustavo Dudamel   **d.** Michelle Bachelet
2. ¿Quiénes son los ganadores del Premio Nobel que se mencionan y cuál es su profesión?

Las actividades futuras

✳ **Lea Gramática 5.5.**

Éstos son los planes y los deseos de Pilar Álvarez, José Estrada y Clara Martin.

Estudio informática porque quisiera ganar mucho dinero.

Después de graduarse, José va a ir de vacaciones a Guatemala.

Nos gustaría ir a bailar este viernes por la noche.

Clara piensa quedarse en casa el viernes por la noche. Tiene ganas de descansar.

Actividad 15 **Narración: El fin de semana de Esteban**

Narre los planes de Esteban para el fin de semana.

el viernes por la tarde
①

el viernes por la noche
②

el sábado por la mañana
③

el sábado por la tarde
④

el sábado por la noche
⑤

el domingo por la mañana
⑥

el domingo por la tarde
⑦

el domingo por la noche
⑧

Palabras útiles

acampar en las montañas
andar en patineta
asistir a la universidad
diseñar una página Web
divertirme mucho /
 divertirnos mucho
dormir
estudiar
ir al cine
levantarme temprano /
 levantarse temprano
limpiar la casa
merendar con la familia
quedarme en casa
 quedarse en casa
salir a bailar
salir con los amigos

¡OJO!

Con frecuencia, los hispanos incluyen a toda la familia en sus planes. Por lo general, los domingos se reúnen padres, abuelos, hijos y nietos para comer juntos.

● REFRÁN

No dejes para mañana lo que puedes hacer hoy.

(*Don't leave for tomorrow what you can do today.*)

Actividad 16 Preferencias: Los planes

Complete cada oración con una o dos de las actividades de la lista.

MODELO: E1: El próximo verano a mi mejor amigo/a le gustaría *viajar.*
          E2: *¿Adónde? (¿A qué país?)*

1. El sábado por la noche pienso...
2. Este fin de semana voy a ...
3. Esta noche tengo ganas de...
4. Durante las vacaciones mis amigos y yo quisiéramos...
5. El próximo verano a mi mejor amigo/a le gustaría...

Y tú, ¿qué dices?

¿Dónde?	¿Adónde?	¿Con quién(es)?
¡Qué divertido!	Yo también	¿Por qué?
¡Qué aburrido!		¿Otra vez?

Actividad 17 Encuesta: ¿Cuáles son sus planes?

1. Mañana, antes de venir a clases,...
2. Hoy, después de clases,...
3. Esta noche, antes de acostarme,...
4. Antes de salir para el trabajo,...
5. Este fin de semana,...
6. Durante las vacaciones de invierno (verano, primavera),...
7. Después de graduarme,...

Frases útiles

voy a _____.
pienso _____.
quisiera _____.
me gustaría _____.
tengo ganas de _____.

Estudiantes de Derecho en la Universidad de La Habana, Cuba

En resumen

De todo un poco

A. ¿Qué oficio o carrera deben escoger?

Trabajen en grupos de tres para adivinar qué carreras son más apropiadas para las siguientes personas.

1. Juan Limón: Es una persona activa; nunca descansa. Nunca tiene miedo y le gustaría ser héroe. Sabe manejar muy bien.
2. Guadalupe Morales: Siempre contesta todas las preguntas que le hace la profesora de biología. Sabe mucho del cuerpo humano. No necesita dormir muchas horas. Le gusta ayudar a la gente enferma.
3. Ángela López: Les hace muchas preguntas a los profesores. No es tímida. Nunca está nerviosa cuando habla en público. Cree que la justicia es muy importante y le gustaría defender a las personas inocentes.
4. Lilián Torreón: Piensa trabajar en un hospital o en una clínica. Sabe bastante sobre el cuerpo humano y sabe usar las manos para tratar a los deportistas que tienen accidentes.

B. Un juego

Trate de adivinar la profesión de estas seis personas: los Hurtado (Jaime y Ana), los Pérez (Hugo y Cecilia) y los Salinas (Alejandro y Olivia). Las posibilidades son **doctor(a), dentista, ingeniero/a, maestro/a, secretario/a** y **abogado/a.** Use la siguiente información para encontrar la solución.

1. Ana trabaja en un hospital, pero no es doctora.
2. El esposo de la abogada es ingeniero.
3. La secretaria está casada con un doctor.
4. El esposo de la dentista trabaja en una escuela.
5. Jaime trabaja con enfermeras.
6. Alejandro enseña matemáticas.

¡Dígalo por escrito!

Descripciones de dos amigos

Escriba descripciones completas de dos amigos o miembros de su familia. Después de dar el nombre y el apellido de cada persona, dé una breve descripción física. Luego hable de los planes y deseos para el futuro que tienen estas personas. Hable también de sus habilidades y de su personalidad. Para estas últimas partes, use las descripciones de la actividad anterior (**De todo un poco A**) como modelos.

¡Cuéntenos usted!

Cuéntenos sobre su trabajo ideal. ¿Dónde trabaja usted? ¿Cuál es su sueldo? ¿Cuáles son sus horas de trabajo? ¿Qué hace usted?

LECTURA

El lenguaje del cuerpo

PISTAS PARA LEER
Focus on the main idea in each paragraph. The following questions can guide you. Paragraph 1: Do we use only words when we communicate? P2: Are most gestures universal? P3: What cultural difference is mentioned? P4: How do gestures help us succeed in speaking a foreign language?

VOCABULARIO ÚTIL

el lenguaje por señas	sign language
gesticulan	gesture
avivar	to liven up
el pulgar	thumb
el índice	index finger
la sonrisa	smile
anglosajona	Anglo-Saxon

Cuando hablamos necesitamos las palabras, ¿no es cierto? Pero las palabras no son siempre necesarias para la comunicación: el **lenguaje por señas** utiliza exclusivamente las manos y los dedos. Todos combinamos las palabras con gestos, expresiones de la cara y un lenguaje corporal que nos ayuda a expresar nuestras ideas y nuestras emociones. En la cultura hispana, las manos generalmente «hablan» mucho; las personas **gesticulan** con las manos para poner énfasis y **avivar** la comunicación.

Hay gestos universales; otros varían de cultura a cultura. En algunos casos, un gesto que se usa en un país puede crear problemas en otro, porque significa algo diferente. Piense, por ejemplo, en la seña tan popular en los Estados Unidos para decir «OK»: el **pulgar** y el **índice** unidos en forma de círculo. Este gesto expresa optimismo, pero no en todos los países. En España y Francia significa «cero» y en Japón es «dinero». Otro ejemplo interesante es la **sonrisa,** que para muchos de nosotros quiere decir alegría y felicidad. Pues en algunos países de África, la sonrisa puede ser interpretada como preocupación. ¡Qué diferencia!

Hay varias diferencias entre la cultura hispana y la cultura **anglosajona** de los Estados Unidos. La distancia entre dos personas que se saludan, por ejemplo: un norteamericano extiende todo el brazo para darle la mano a su amigo y mantener así una distancia física apropiada. Dos amigos hispanos, sin embargo, extienden menos el brazo y a veces hasta se abrazan. En general, el contacto físico no es tan necesario para el norteamericano.

Es importante aprender las palabras para comunicarnos, pero si aprendemos también el lenguaje del cuerpo, nuestra comunicación se hace más rica y expresiva. ¿Cuáles son algunos de los gestos que caracterizan a las personas de Estados Unidos o a las de su país de origen? ¿Qué significan? Aquí tiene algunos de los gestos que caracterizan a los hispanos. Éstos son los más usados en España y en América Latina. ¡Aprenda el lenguaje del cuerpo!

1. No.

2. Quiero comer.

3. ¡Excelente!

4. furioso/a (enojado/a)

5. tacaño/a

6. muy amigos

7. Un momentito...

8. dinero (cuesta mucho)

9. ¡Ojo! ¡Tenga cuidado!

Comprensión

Mire los dibujos y después indique qué gesto se puede usar en las siguientes situaciones.

1. Un chico tiene mucha hambre.
2. El profesor está muy contento con la clase.
3. El/La recepcionista de una oficina le dice que usted tiene que esperar.
4. Una muchacha ve a su novio con otra chica.
5. El hombre no quiere comprarle un helado a su hijo.

Un paso más... ¡a escribir!

Escoja una de las situaciones de la actividad de **Comprensión** y escriba un diálogo corto entre las dos personas, haciendo referencia a los gestos que hacen cuando hablan. Aquí tiene un ejemplo para la primera situación.

MODELO: HIJO: Papá, tengo mucha hambre.
                   (*El hijo pone la mano cerca de la boca y mueve la mano.*)
               PAPÁ: Bueno, estoy preparando sándwiches. Un momentito.
                   (*El papá hace un gesto con los dedos.*)
               HIJO: ¿Sándwiches? ¡Súper! ¡Excelente!
                   (*El hijo se besa los dedos y luego los extiende.*)

Vea el **Resumen cultural** en este capítulo del *Cuaderno de actividades.*

Vocabulario

Las actividades de los estudiantes

Student Activities

aprender	to learn
comprender	to comprehend
decir (i)	to say
digo / dice	
empezar (ie)	to begin
enseñar	to teach
entender (ie)	to understand
explicar	to explain
pensar (ie)	to think
pensar en	to think about
poner atención	to pay attention
terminar	to finish

REPASO: hacer preguntas, tomar apuntes

Las habilidades

Abilities

poder (ue)	to be able to
saber (+ *infin.*)	to know how to (*do something*)

Las profesiones y el empleo

Professions and Employment

el abogado / la abogada	lawyer
el/la agente de seguros	insurance agent
el bombero / la mujer bombero	firefighter
el cajero / la cajera	cashier
el/la cantante	singer
el/la chofer	driver
el cocinero / la cocinera	cook
el contador / la contadora	accountant
el dependiente / la dependienta	clerk, salesperson
el/la deportista	athlete
el/la electricista	electrician
el enfermero / la enfermera	nurse
el/la gerente	manager
el ingeniero / la ingeniera	engineer
el jefe / la jefa	boss
el/la juez	judge
el maestro / la maestra	teacher
el médico	doctor
el mesero / la mesera	waiter / waitress
el obrero / la obrera (industrial)	(industrial) worker
el peluquero / la peluquera	hairdresser
el plomero / la plomera	plumber
el policía / la mujer policía	policeman / policewoman
el/la terapeuta	therapist
el trabajador / la trabajadora social	social worker

PALABRAS SEMEJANTES: el/la asistente, el/la dentista, el/la mecánico, el/la piloto, el programador / la programadora, el secretario (ejecutivo) / la secretaria (ejecutiva)
REPASO: el ama de casa, el doctor / la doctora

Los lugares del trabajo

Workplaces

el avión	plane
el club nocturno	nightclub
la cocina	kitchen
el consultorio	doctor's office
el empleo	job
la fábrica	factory
la peluquería	beauty parlor
el taller de reparación	garage; repair shop

PALABRAS SEMEJANTES: el banco, la clínica, la compañía

Las actividades del trabajo

Work Activities

apagar (incendios)	to turn off (to put out fires)
arreglar	to fix
atender (ie) mesas	to wait on tables
ayudar	to help
calificar	to grade
contar (el dinero)	to count (money)
cortar (el pelo)	to cut (hair)
cuidar (de)	to take care of
entrar al trabajo	to start work
escribir a máquina	to type
ganar dinero	to earn money
pintar	to paint
servir (i)	to serve
sirvo / sirve	
tratar	to treat
vender	to sell

PALABRAS SEMEJANTES: archivar, asignar, defender, examinar, programar

Los verbos

Verbs

adivinar	to guess
bucear	to skin dive or scuba dive
buscar	to look for
cantar	to sing
creer	to believe
dibujar	to draw
divertirse (ie)	to have fun
me diverto	I have fun
se divierte	you (*pol. sing.*) have fun; he/she has fun
escalar montañas	to go mountain climbing

hornear	to bake
ir de vacaciones	to go on vacation
necesitar	to need
obtener	to obtain
pagar	to pay
tratar de (+ *infin.*)	to try to (*do something*)

PALABRAS SEMEJANTES: consolar, graduarse, marcar, participar

Los sustantivos

Nouns

el anuncio	announcement, ad
el aviso clasificado	classified ad
la canción	song
la carrera	course of study
el cliente / la cliente	customer
el curso	course
el empleado / la empleada	employee
el informe	report
la jaula	cage
la jornada completa	full time (work)
la media jornada	part-time (work)
el oficio	job, position
la residencia estudiantil	college dormitory
el sueldo	salary
la tubería	plumbing; pipes

PALABRAS SEMEJANTES: el accidente, el acusado / la acusada, el animal doméstico, la aptitud, el caso criminal, la comisión, la distracción, el documento, la experiencia, el héroe, la instalación, la justicia, el/la paciente, la posibilidad, el público, la solución, el talento, el violín

Los adjetivos

Adjectives

desagradable	unpleasant
listo/a	ready
el mismo / la misma	the same
peligroso/a	dangerous

PALABRAS SEMEJANTES: activo/a, bilingüe, fracturado/a, individual, inocente, intensivo/a, necesario/a, prestigioso/a, relacionado/a
REPASO: pobre

¿Con qué frecuencia?

How Often?

a cualquier hora	at any time
a la vez	at the same time
al día	per day
muchas veces	many times
otra vez	again
raras veces	rarely

REPASO: a veces, de vez en cuando, nunca, siempre, todos los días

Las obligaciones

Obligations

deber (+ *infin.*)	ought to, should (*do something*)
Es necesario (+ *infin.*)	It's necessary to (+ *verb*)
hay que (+ *infin.*)	one has to (*do something*)
necesitar (+ *infin.*)	need to (+ *verb*)
tener que (+ *infin.*)	to have to (*do something*)

El futuro

The Future

me (te, le, nos, os, les) gustaría (+ *infin.*)	I (you [*inf. sing.*], you [*pol. sing.*] /he/she, we, you [*inf. pl., Spain*], you [*pl.*] / they) would like to (*do something*)
pensar (ie) (+ *infin.*)	to plan to (*do something*)
quisiera (+ *infin.*)	I (you [*pol. sing.*], he/she would like to (*do something*)
tener ganas de (+ *infin.*)	to feel like (*doing something*)

REPASO: ir a (+ *infin.*), preferir (ie) (+ *infin.*), querer (ie) (+ *infin.*)

Palabras y frases del texto

Words and Phrases from the Text

las actividades auditivas	listening activities
la encuesta	poll

Palabras y frases útiles

Useful Words and Phrases

así	this way
bastante	enough
bastante (+ *adj.*)	quite (+ *adj.*)
favor de (+ *infin.*)	please (+ *action*)
Venga(n)	Come (*command*)

Gramática y ejercicios

¿RECUERDA?

In **Gramática 1.5** you learned to use indirect object pronouns with the verb **gustar** to say to whom something is pleasing. Review that construction now, if necessary.

5.1 Indicating to Whom Something Is Said: Indirect Object Pronouns with Verbs of Informing

Gramática ilustrada

A. Indirect object pronouns (**los pronombres de complemento indirecto**) are used with verbs of informing, which tell to whom something is said, told, explained, reported, asked, answered, and so on.*

> Indirect object pronouns:
> **me, te, le, nos, os, les**

> It takes a good deal of time to acquire these forms. Begin by understanding them and focus more on usage as you start to acquire them.

me	*to me*	nos	*to us*
te	*to you (inf. sing.)*	os	*to you (inf. pl., Spain)*
le	*to you (pol. sing.); to him/her*	les	*to you (pl.); to them*

—¿Qué **les explica** la profesora Martínez?
—**Nos explica** el significado de las palabras nuevas.

—*What does Professor Martínez explain to you?*
—*She explains the meaning of new words to us.*

Amanda ya no **me habla.**

Amanda doesn't speak to me anymore.

¡Pobre Ernestito! Su mamá siempre **le dice** que no.

Poor Ernestito! His mother always says no to him.

---

*Recognition: The indirect object pronoun for **vos** is **te.**

206

B. Just like reflexive pronouns, indirect object pronouns are placed before the main verb or attached to infinitives (the **-ar**, **-er**, or **-ir** form of the verb) and present participles (the **-ndo** form of the verb).

—¿Qué **te va** a decir tu papá?

—No sé qué va a **decirme**.

—*What is your father going to say to you?*

—*I don't know what he is going to say to me.*

Esteban **nos está** leyendo la respuesta.

Esteban está **leyéndonos** la respuesta.

Esteban is reading the answer to us.

C. When using **le** or **les**, it is very common to use a phrase with **a** to specify the person (or thing) involved. Spanish requires the pronoun even when the phrase with **a** is used.

—**¿A quién le** escribe Clara la carta?

—**Le** escribe la carta **a su amiga Norma.**

—*To whom is Clara writing the letter?*

—*She's writing the letter to her friend Norma.*

Yo siempre **le** aviso **a mi jefe** con tiempo si no voy a ir al trabajo.

I always tell my boss ahead of time if I'm not going to go to work.

> Indirect object pronouns are placed before the verb or attached to the infinitive:
> **Mi novia ya no me habla.** (*My girlfriend doesn't talk to me anymore.*)
> **Mi novia ya no quiere hablarme.** (*My girlfriend doesn't want to talk to me anymore.*)

> As you read and listen to more Spanish, you will get a feel for these pronouns and how to use them.

Ejercicio 1

Complete las siguientes oraciones basándose en los dibujos. Use **me, te, le, nos** o **les**.

MODELO: Carmen **les** dice «Buenos días» **a sus amigas.**

1. Esteban dice:
— _____ contesto **a mis compañeros.**

2. La profesora Martínez _____ explica la lección **a los estudiantes.**

3. Nosotros _____ hacemos muchas preguntas **a la profesora.**

4. Nora _____ lee la Ventana cultural **a nosotros.**

5. —Lan, ¿_____ dices qué tenemos de tarea?
—Sí, Luis, ahora _____ digo cuál es la tarea para mañana.

6. Carmen _____ escribe una carta **a sus padres.**

7. _____ decimos «Adiós» **a la profesora** y ella _____ dice «Hasta luego».

8. —Nora, ¿_____ dices la respuesta número 5, por favor?
—Sí, Lan, en un momento _____ digo todas las respuestas.

Ejercicio 2

Complete estos diálogos con **me, te, le, nos** o **les**.

In **Gramática 3.2** you learned that a verb that uses more than one stem in its conjugation is considered irregular. Some verbs, like **hacer** (*to do; to make*), use a different stem only in the **yo** form; other verbs, like **jugar** (*to play*), use the different stem in all but the infinitive and the **nosotros/as** and **vosotros/as** forms. Review those conjugations now, if necessary.

5.2 Expressing Abilities: *saber* and *poder* + Infinitive

A. In the present tense, the verb saber (*to know facts, information*)* is irregular only in the **yo** form: **sé, sabes, sabe, sabemos, sabéis, saben.**

—**¿Sabes** cuándo va a llegar Alberto?
—No, no **sé.**

—*Do you know when Alberto is going to arrive?*
—*No, I don't know.*

Saber followed by an infinitive means *to know how to do something.* Note that there is no need to include a separate word to convey the English *how to.*

—**¿Sabes hablar** francés?
—No, pero **sé hablar** un poco de árabe.

—*Do you know how to speak French?*
—*No, but I know how to speak a little Arabic.*

—¿Quién **sabe jugar** al ajedrez?
—Yo **sé jugar** al dominó, pero no al ajedrez.

—*Who knows how to play chess?*
—*I know how to play dominoes, but not chess.*

---

*Recognition: **vos sabés**

B. The verb **poder*** followed by an infinitive usually indicates potential (*can, to be able to do something*) or permission (*may*). **Poder** is a stem-changing verb and so uses two stems: **pod-** for the infinitive and the **nosotros/as** and **vosotros/as** forms and **pued-** for all other present-tense forms: **puedo, puedes, puede, podemos, podéis, pueden.**

—¿Van a correr una vuelta más Carmen y Nora?
—No **pueden.** Ya están cansadas.

—Guillermo, ¿vas a jugar al fútbol el domingo?
—No **puedo.** Tengo un examen el lunes.

—*Are Carmen and Nora going to run another lap?*
—*They can't. They're already tired.*

—*Guillermo, are you going to play soccer on Sunday?*
—*I can't. I have an exam on Monday.*

> **saber** = *to know facts, information*
> **saber** + infinitive = *to know how to do something*
> **¿Sabes bucear?** (*Do you know how to scuba dive?*)
> **No, no sé bucear, pero sé nadar.** (*No, I don't know how to scuba dive, but I know how to swim.*)

Ejercicio 3

¿Qué (no) saben hacer estos vecinos hispanos? Complete las oraciones con la forma apropiada de **saber.**

MODELO: Ernestito dice: «Yo no *sé* mucho de matemáticas.»

1. Doña Lola dice: «Yo _____ montar a caballo.»
2. Don Eduardo, ¿_____ usted hablar italiano?
3. Clarisa y Marisa no _____ andar en bicicleta todavía, porque son muy pequeñas.
4. Ernestito le pregunta a Guillermo: «¿_____ esquiar?»
5. Amanda le dice a Ramón: «Graciela y yo todavía no _____ manejar.»

> **poder** = *can, to be able to*
> **¿Puedes salir esta noche?** (*Can you go out tonight?*)
> **No, no puedo; mañana tengo un examen de biología.** (*No, I can't; I have a biology test tomorrow.*)

Ejercicio 4

¿Qué (no) pueden hacer estos vecinos hispanos? Complete las oraciones con la forma apropiada de **poder.**

MODELO: Nosotros no *podemos* esperarte hoy después de clase porque tenemos mucha prisa.

1. Ernestito le pregunta a Guillermo: «¿_____ salir a jugar conmigo?»
2. Andrea les pregunta a Estela y a Ernesto: «¿_____ venir a cenar con nosotros mañana?»
3. Silvia no _____ salir con Nacho mañana porque va a trabajar.
4. Doña Lola y doña Rosita no _____ ver su programa favorito de televisión mañana porque van a ir de compras.
5. Amanda le pregunta a su mamá: «¿_____ Graciela y yo ir a la plaza a pasear después de comer?»

5.3 Referring to Actions in Progress: Present Progressive

To describe an action that is taking place at the moment, Spanish uses a form of **estar** (*to be*) and an **-ndo** (*-ing*) form called a present participle.[†] This combination is called the *present progressive.*

> The present progressive (**estar** + verb ending in **-ndo**) is used to express actions in progress:
> **Estoy leyendo un libro.** (*I am reading a book.*)

---

*Recognition: **vos podés**
†Recognition: **vos estás jugando**

estar + -ndo

estoy		jugando (*playing*)
estás		caminando (*walking*)
está	+	fumando (*smoking*)
estamos		escuchando (*listening*)
estáis		escribiendo (*writing*)
están		comiendo (*eating*)

—¿Qué **está haciendo** el médico?
—**Está examinando** a un paciente.

—*What is the doctor doing?*
—*He is examining a patient.*

—Guillermo, ¿qué **estás haciendo**?
—**Estoy escribiendo** una composición.

—*Guillermo, what are you doing?*
—*I'm writing a composition.*

The present participle (**-ando, -iendo**) is formed from the infinitive.

jugar → jug**ando**   comer → com**iendo**

hablar → habl**ando**   vivir → viv**iendo**

> In present participles of **-ar** verbs: replace **-ar** of the infinitive with **-ando.**
> In **-er** and **-ir** verbs: replace **-er/-ir** of the infinitive with **-iendo/-yendo.**

When a present participle is irregular, it will be noted as follows: **dormir (durmiendo), leer (leyendo).**

—¿**Está durmiendo** el juez ahora?
—No, **está hablando** con un abogado.

—*Is the judge sleeping now?*
—*No, he is speaking with a lawyer.*

—Estela, ¿qué **estás leyendo**?
—**Estoy leyendo** una novela.

—*Estela, what are you reading?*
—*I'm reading a novel.*

Ejercicio 5

1. ¿Qué está haciendo Guillermo?

2. ¿Qué están haciendo estos señores?

3. ¿Qué está haciendo el mecánico?

4. ¿Qué está haciendo la señora Saucedo?

5. ¿Qué están haciendo Pedro y Andrea?

6. ¿Qué está haciendo la enfermera?

Ejercicio 6

Lea las situaciones y luego complete las frases correctamente diciendo qué están haciendo las personas mencionadas. Use estos verbos: **atender, calificar, dar, reparar, servir, vender.**

MODELO: —Mira qué incendio tan grande. ¿Dónde están los bomberos?
—Ya *están apagando* el incendio.

1. —¿Dónde está la profesora Martínez?
   —Está en el salón, _____ _____ los exámenes.
2. —Por favor, señorita, quiero hablar con el gerente.
   —Lo siento, en este momento _____ _____ a otro cliente.
3. —Voy a llamar al mesero. Quiero un poco de agua.
   —Pues está ocupado. Les _____ _____ la comida a los clientes de la mesa de al lado.
4. —¿Qué está haciendo el terapeuta en este momento?
   —Le _____ _____ un masaje en el brazo al famoso jugador de béisbol, Vladimir Guerrero.
5. —Necesito hablar con el Sr. Pérez, el plomero, pero no contesta el teléfono.
   —Pues está en mi casa. _____ _____ la tubería de la cocina.
6. —¿Quién es ese hombre que está con tu padre?
   —Es un agente de seguros. Le _____ _____ un seguro de vida a papá.

5.4 Expressing Obligation and Duty: *tener que, deber, necesitar, hay que, es necesario*

The verbs **tener que** (*to have to*), **deber** (*should, ought to*), and **necesitar** (*to need to*) and the impersonal expressions **hay que** (*one must*) and **es necesario** (*it is necessary to*) are always followed by infinitives.

—¿A qué hora **tenemos que estar** en el teatro?
—A las nueve. **Hay que llegar** un poco antes para recoger los boletos.
—¡Pero **necesito estudiar** más!
—Está bien, pero **debemos salir** pronto.

—*What time do we have to be at the theater?*
—*At 9:00. We have to (One must) get there a little early to pick up the tickets.*
—*But I need to study more!*
—*OK, but we should leave soon.*

¿RECUERDA?

You have already seen and used many times the combination of conjugated verb + infinitive: for example, in **Gramática 2.3** (**preferir** and **querer** + infinitive) and **Gramática 5.2** (**saber** and **poder** + infinitive).

Hay que llegar a tiempo al trabajo.
One must (We have to) arrive on time to work.

¿Qué tienes que hacer este fin de semana?
What do you have to do this weekend?

Ejercicio 7

Esteban cuenta lo que él y sus compañeros de clase tienen que hacer hoy. Complete las oraciones con una forma de **tener que**.

1. Luis _____ trabajar hasta las doce.
2. Carmen y Nora _____ prepararse para un examen de sociología.
3. Yo _____ terminar la tarea para mi clase de matemáticas.
4. Alberto y yo _____ lavar el carro.
5. Mónica, ¿qué _____ hacer tú esta noche?

> **Debo estudiar y también necesito lavar el carro y limpiar la casa.**
> *I ought to study, and I also need to wash the car and clean the house.*

Ejercicio 8

Estela Saucedo está hablando de lo que ella y su familia deben hacer mañana. Complete estas oraciones con la forma apropiada de **deber.**

1. Ernesto _____ ir en autobús al trabajo.
2. Yo _____ limpiar la cocina.
3. Ernestito, tú _____ hacer la tarea para la escuela.
4. Guillermo y Amanda _____ recoger sus libros.
5. Ernesto, tú y yo _____ llevar a los niños al parque a jugar.

¿RECUERDA?

You already know that the verbs **ir** + **a** (see **Gramática 2.1**) and **querer** (see **Gramática 2.3**) followed by infinitives are commonly used to talk about future actions in Spanish.

5.5 Expressing Plans and Desires: *pensar, quisiera, me gustaría, tener ganas de*

A. The verb **pensar*** (*to think*) followed by an infinitive expresses the idea of *to think about* or *to plan on doing* something. Here are the forms of **pensar (ie): pienso, piensas, piensa, pensamos, pensáis, piensan.**

> —¿Qué **piensan hacer** ustedes durante las vacaciones?
> —**Pensamos viajar** a Europa.

> —*What are you thinking about doing for vacation?*
> —*We're planning on traveling to Europe.*

When not followed by an infinitive, **pensar (ie)** usually expresses *to think:* **pensar que** (*to think that*), **pensar de** (*to think about, have an opinion of*), **pensar en** (*to think about someone or something, have one's thoughts on*).

> —¿Qué **piensas del** nuevo plan?
> —**Pienso que** es muy bueno.

> —*What do you think about the new plan?*
> —*I think that it's very good.*

> —Ramón, ¿**piensas** mucho **en** Amanda?
> —No, **pienso en** ella solamente de vez en cuando.

> —*Ramón, do you often think about Amanda?*
> —*No, I think about her only from time to time.*

---

pensar = *to think*
pensar + infinitive = *to think about, plan on doing (something)*

> **¿Qué piensas hacer después de clases?**
> (*What are you planning to do after school?*)
> **Pienso ir a la biblioteca y luego voy a trabajar.** (*I'm planning to go to the library, and then I'm going to work.*)

B. **Quisiera** and **me (le) gustaría**† are also frequently used to indicate future desires, especially those that are speculative. Both forms are equivalent to English *would like.* Neither has a **yo** form ending in **-o.** You will learn more about these forms in **Gramática 15.5** and **15.6.**

---

quisiera = *I would like*
me gustaría = *I would like*

> **Quisiera salir a cenar esta noche.** (*I'd like to eat out tonight.*)
> **Me gustaría ver una película.** (*I'd like to see a movie.*)

(yo)	quisiera	me gustaría	*I would like*
(tú)	quisieras	te gustaría	*you (inf. sing.) would like*
(usted, él/ella)	quisiera	le gustaría	*you (pol. sing.) would like; he/she would like*
(nosotros/as)	quisiéramos	nos gustaría	*we would like*
(vosotros/as)	quisierais	os gustaría	*you (inf. pl., Spain) would like*
(ustedes, ellos/as)	quisieran	les gustaría	*you (pl.) would like; they would like*

---

*Recognition: **vos pensás**
†Recognition: **vos quisieras, a vos te gustaría**

Quisiéramos viajar este verano si tenemos tiempo.	*We would like to travel this summer if we have time.*
A mi esposa **le gustaría viajar** a España.	*My wife would like to travel to Spain.*
Estoy cansado; **quisiera descansar** un poco.	*I'm tired; I would like to rest a while.*

C. Tener ganas de (*to feel like* [*doing something*]) is also followed by an infinitive.

Tenemos ganas de quedarnos en casa esta noche.	*We feel like staying home tonight.*
Tengo ganas de salir a bailar.	*I feel like going out dancing.*

> **tener ganas de** +
> infinitive = *to feel like*
> (*doing something*)

Ejercicio 9

¿Qué quisieran hacer estos estudiantes el próximo sábado? Escoja la forma correcta: **quisiera, quisieras, quisiéramos** o **quisieran.**

1. Luis _____ ir al campo a montar a caballo.
2. Carmen y yo _____ ir de compras.
3. Alberto y Pablo _____ merendar con unas amigas.
4. Mónica, ¿ _____ quedarte en casa a descansar?
5. Esteban dice: «Yo _____ jugar al tenis.»

Ejercicio 10

¿Qué les gustaría hacer a Estela Saucedo y a su familia? Escoja la forma correcta del pronombre: **me, te, nos, le** o **les.**

1. A Guillermo _____ gustaría jugar al fútbol con sus amigos.
2. A mis hijos, Amanda y Guillermo, _____ gustaría ir al campo a merendar.
3. A mi esposo, Ernesto, _____ gustaría ir al cine.
4. A mí _____ gustaría salir a comer en un buen restaurante.
5. A Andrea y a mí _____ gustaría jugar a las cartas el sábado en la noche.

Ejercicio 11

¿Qué piensan hacer Pilar y sus amigos? Use las formas apropiadas de **pensar.**

1. El hermano de Pilar _____ quedarse en casa esta noche para estudiar.
2. Clara, ¿_____ tú ir de compras mañana?
3. José y yo _____ visitar a mis abuelos el sábado.
4. José y Clara _____ ir al Museo del Prado por la tarde.
5. Pilar dice: «Yo _____ hacer mi tarea el domingo por la noche.»

CAPÍTULO 6

La residencia

METAS

In **Capítulo 6,** you will talk about where you live and what you do there. You and your classmates will discuss what you have done recently. You will also learn how to introduce people to each other.

Casita con dos entradas, por Ana Griselda Hine (Costa Rica)

Sobre la artista: Ana Griselda Hine nace en Costa Rica en 1949 y estudia artes plásticas en la Universidad de Costa Rica. En 1983, con una beca Fulbright-Laspau, obtiene una maestría en la Universidad de Cincinnati. Enseña en la Universidad de Costa Rica (1976–1990) y en la Universidad Nacional (1979–1981). Hoy se dedica a la pintura e imparte talleres de pintura en su estudio. Su arte es muy conocido en Costa Rica y Puerto Rico donde recibe muchos reconocimientos. Es excelente ilustradora de libros y también se destaca como acuarelista.

¡Conozca Costa Rica!

Nombre del país: la República de Costa Rica

Ciudad capital: San José

Ciudades principales: Limón, Puntarenas, Alajuela

Moneda: el colón

Idiomas: el español

Población: 4.200.000

Día de la Independencia: el 15 de septiembre

Fiestas típicas: el Día de Juan Santamaría, el Día de la Virgen de Los Ángeles, el Día de los Parques Nacionales, el Día del Boyero, las Fiestas de la Virgen del Mar

Comidas típicas: el gallo pinto, el casado, los patacones, el agua dulce, el guaro

Música típica: el punto guanacastero, bailes indígenas y provinciales, la soca, la salsa, el merengue, la cumbia

Gente famosa: Ana Istarú, Óscar Arias Sánchez, José Figueres Ferrer

Código del país por Internet: .cr

Voces costarricenses

Chepe	San José
mae	guy/dude
un pelón	una fiesta
¡Pura vida!	Life is good!
¡Qué chiva!	How cool!
un(a) tico/a	un(a) costarricense
Ticolandia/Tiquicia	Costa Rica
el yodo	el café

En este capítulo...

ACTIVIDADES DE COMUNICACIÓN

- El vecindario y la casa
- Las actividades en casa
- Las actividades con los amigos
- Las presentaciones

EN RESUMEN

LECTURAS Y CULTURA

- **Enlace a la literatura**
  «Cuadrados y ángulos», por Alfonsina Storni
- **Ventanas al pasado**
  La historia de las mascotas
- **Ventanas culturales**
  Las costumbres: De casa en casa: La tradición de las posadas
- **Lectura**
  Las hermosas ciudades hispanas

GRAMÁTICA Y EJERCICIOS

6.1 Making Comparisons of Inequality: **más/menos**

6.2 Making Comparisons of Equality: **tan/tanto**

6.3 Talking about Past Actions: The Preterite of Regular Verbs (Part 1)

6.4 Knowing People, Places, and Facts: **conocer** and **saber**

6.5 Referring to People already Mentioned: Personal Direct Object Pronouns

El vecindario y la casa

✳ Lea Gramática 6.1–6.2.

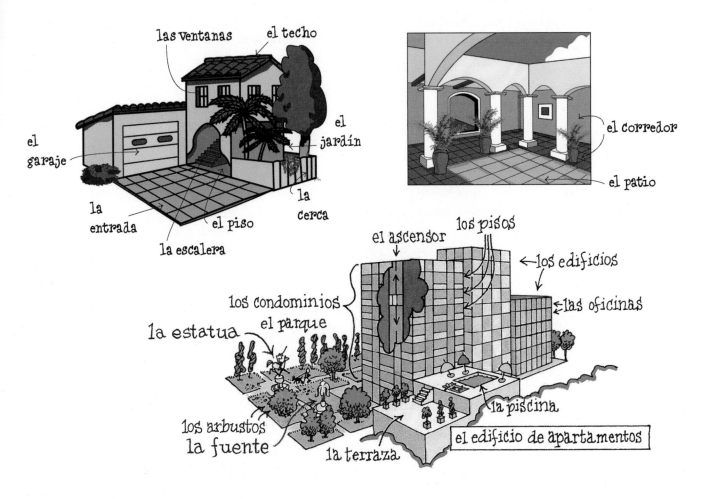

Actividad 1 Encuesta: ¿Qué hay en su casa?

Diga sí o no. Si la respuesta es **no,** explique por qué no.

MODELO: En mi casa hay tres dormitorios. En mi casa no hay cancha de tenis porque no soy rico/a.

1. En mi vecindario hay...
   a. una cancha de tenis.
   b. una biblioteca.
   c. muchos árboles.
   d. muchos edificios altos.
   e. un parque.
   f. ¿ ?

2. En la sala de mi casa hay...
   a. una cama.
   b. un lavabo.
   c. varias lámparas.
   d. muchas plantas.
   e. una alfombra.
   f. ¿ ?

3. En la cocina de mi casa hay...
   a. una estufa.
   b. un lavaplatos.
   c. un pasillo.
   d. un estante con libros.
   e. un horno de microondas.
   f. ¿ ?

4. En mi dormitorio hay...
   a. una cama matrimonial.
   b. un arbusto.
   c. un armario.
   d. muchas almohadas.
   e. una cómoda.
   f. ¿ ?

Actividad 2 Identificaciones: ¿Para qué sirve?

Mire los siguientes objetos y aparatos y diga para qué sirven.

MODELO: Una lámpara sirve para ver y leer de noche.

Frases útiles

para apoyar la cabeza cuando uno duerme	para lavarse los dientes
	para lavarse las manos
para barrer	para preparar el té o calentar agua
para calentar la comida rápidamente	para secarse
	para verse la cara
para guardar la ropa	para ver y leer de noche

5. una cómoda 1. una lámpara 2. un horno de microondas 3. una almohada 4. una escoba 6. un cepillo de dientes 7. una tetera 8. un lavabo 9. un espejo 10. una toalla

Actividad 3 Intercambios: Los aparatos domésticos

MODELO: E1: ¿Cuál cuesta más, *el calentador* o *la cafetera*?
E2: *El calentador* cuesta más. (*El calentador* cuesta más que *la cafetera.*)

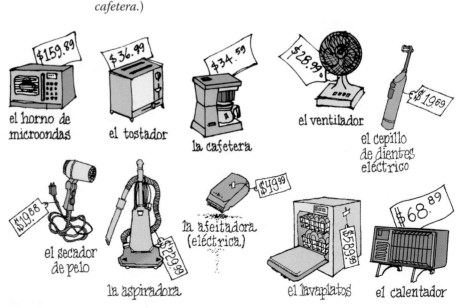

el horno de microondas $159.89
el tostador $36.99
la cafetera $34.59
el ventilador $28.99
el cepillo de dientes eléctrico $19.69
el secador de pelo $19.88
la aspiradora $29.99
la afeitadora (eléctrica) $49.99
el lavaplatos $58.99
el calentador $68.89

1. ¿Cuál cuesta más, el horno de microondas o la cafetera? ¿el ventilador o el secador de pelo?
2. ¿Cuál cuesta menos, la cafetera o el cepillo de dientes eléctrico? ¿la aspiradora o el tostador?
3. ¿Cuál de estos tres objetos es el más caro: el tostador, la afeitadora o la cafetera?
4. ¿Cuál de estas tres cosas es la más cara: el lavaplatos, la afeitadora o la aspiradora?
5. ¿Cuál de estas tres cosas cuesta menos: el secador de pelo, el calentador o el cepillo de dientes eléctrico?
6. ¿Cuál cuesta más, el ventilador o el tostador?
7. ¿Cuál cuesta menos, la afeitadora o el cepillo de dientes eléctrico?

Actividad 4 Descripción de dibujos: Comparación de casas

Escuche las preguntas que le hace su profesor(a) y contéstelas según los dibujos.

la casa de los Ruiz:
3 dormitorios
2 baños
2 balcones

la casa de los Silva:
2 dormitorios
1 baño

la casa de los Saucedo:
5 dormitorios
3 baños
1 biblioteca
3 balcones

Ahora, hágale preguntas sobre las casas a su compañero/a. (Se puede comparar **baños, dormitorios, puertas, ventanas, balcones, pisos** y **árboles.**)

MODELOS: E1: ¿Cuántas *ventanas* tiene la casa de los *Saucedo*?
E2: Tiene *ocho*. Tiene *más que* la casa de los *Ruiz*.

E1: ¿Cuántos *árboles* tiene la casa de los *Silva*?
E2: Tiene *tres*. Tiene *tantos como* la casa de los *Ruiz*. Tiene *menos que* la casa de los *Saucedo*.

Actividad 5 Del mundo hispano: Apartamentos en México

Nora va a pasar un semestre estudiando en la ciudad de México. Quiere alquilar un departamento o un cuarto. Éstas son sus preferencias. ¿Cuál de estos departamentos o habitaciones le gustaría a usted? ¿Por qué?

¡OJO!

En general, las casas y los apartamentos en los países hispanos son más pequeños que los de los Estados Unidos. Por eso, en algunos casos, la gente sale a pasear a los parques y en las plazas.

(Continúa)

Se ALQUILA departamento. Dos recámaras. Sala, comedor, cocina, baño. Lugar céntrico. Alquiler módico. Llamar a Luz María Galván. Tel. 6-59-50-69. Calle 12 no. 420, México, D.F.

Se ALQUILA habitación amueblada. Preferible: joven estudiante, callado y serio. Alquiler bajo. Derecho a cocina. Favor de enviar datos personales. Isabel la Católica 96 (centro), México, D.F. Tel. 5-85-72-44

Se ALQUILA departamento amueblado. Dos recámaras. Dos baños. Cocina amplia: estufa, refrigerador, alacenas grandes y todos los utensilios. Ascensor. Avenida Juárez no. 420, México, D.F.

Departamento una recámara, bien decorado. Ventanas grandes. Vista agradable. Cerca de todo transporte. Llamar al 7-79-09-22 o escribir a Sres. Gallegos, Luis Kuhne no. 755, México 20, D.F.

Actividad 6 Entrevista: El lugar donde vives

TU VECINDARIO

1. ¿Vives en un vecindario viejo o nuevo? ¿Te gusta vivir allí? ¿Por qué?
2. ¿Hay edificios de apartamentos en tu vecindario? ¿condominios?
3. ¿Hay una gasolinera cerca de tu casa (apartamento)?
4. ¿Cuál es el centro comercial más cercano a tu casa (apartamento)? ¿Te gusta ir de compras allí? ¿Por qué?
5. ¿Llevas tu ropa a la lavandería o tienes lavadora y secadora en tu casa (apartamento)?
6. ¿Hay algún parque en el vecindario? ¿Tiene piscina? ¿Vas a menudo? ¿Qué haces allí?

TU CASA

1. ¿Vives en una residencia estudiantil, en un apartamento o en una casa? ¿Es de uno o dos pisos?
2. ¿Tienes tu propio dormitorio o compartes un dormitorio con alguien? ¿Con quién? ¿Qué muebles y aparatos eléctricos hay en tu dormitorio?
3. ¿Tiene patio o terraza tu casa (apartamento)? ¿Cómo es?
4. ¿Tiene garaje para dos coches tu casa (apartamento)? ¿Qué hay en el garaje?
5. De todas las cosas que tienes, ¿cuál te gusta más? ¿Cuál es el aparato más útil que tienes en tu casa (apartamento)?

Enlace a la literatura

«Cuadrados y ángulos», por Alfonsina Storni

Selección de su libro *El dulce daño* (1918)

Alfonsina Storni (1892–1938), argentina, es una de las poetas más estimadas de América Latina. En su corta vida, Storni trabaja de maestra y periodista[1] y publica varios libros de poesía. Entre todos sus libros, *El dulce daño* (1918) es uno de los más íntimos y personales. Sus últimas publicaciones son *Mundo de siete pozos* (1936) y *Mascarilla y trébol* (1938). Muchos de los poemas de Storni describen la gran ciudad: sus edificios, el tráfico, los parques. En «Cuadrados y ángulos» la poeta critica un lugar donde todo —las casas, la gente— tiene la misma forma.

Cuadrados y ángulos[2]

Casas enfiladas,[3] casas enfiladas,
casas enfiladas.
Cuadrados, cuadrados, cuadrados.
Casas enfiladas.
Las gentes ya tienen el alma cuadrada,[4]
Ideas en fila[5]
y ángulos en la espalda.
Yo misma he vertido ayer una lágrima,[6]
Dios mío, cuadrada.[7]

Actividad creativa: Las casas de su barrio

¿Le gusta su barrio? ¿Cómo son sus casas? Use «Cuadrados y ángulos» como modelo para escribir un breve poema sobre las casas de su barrio. Por ejemplo, puede describir casas grandes, pequeñas, feas, bonitas, nuevas, viejas. Puede también escribir sobre el color de las casas o mencionar otros lugares en su barrio.

[1]*journalist*   [2]Cuadrados... *Squares and angles*   [3]*in a row*   [4]el... *square souls*   [5]en... *in a row, in line*
[6]Yo... *Just yesterday I shed a tear myself*   [7]Dios... *Oh, God, it (my tear) was square*

© Joaquín Salvador Lavado (QUINO) Toda Mafalda—Ediciones de La Flor, 1993.

Las actividades en casa

En la casa de los Ruiz

De noche es necesario prender (encender) la luz.

Marisa debe apagar la luz.

La empleada doméstica tiene que limpiar el piso.

Andrea necesita preparar la cena.

Hay que barrer aquí.

Pedro tiene que cortar el césped.

Clarisa debe regar las plantas.

En la casa de los Saucedo

La empleada doméstica tiene qué desempolvar...

...y pasar la aspiradora.

Hay que tender las camas.

Hay que lavar los platos.

Ernestito tiene que darles de comer al gato y al perro.

Amanda tiene que secar la ropa y planchar.

Actividad 7 Descripción de dibujos: ¿Qué tiene que hacer?

A. Escuche a su profesor(a). ¿A cuál de los siguientes dibujos corresponde su descripción?

1. Luis
2. Pablo
3. Mónica / Lan
4. Nora
5. Carmen
6. Esteban

B. Ahora, describa usted los dibujos. Su compañero/a debe identificarlos.

¡OJO!

En los hogares hispanos donde hay una empleada doméstica, normalmente ella hace casi todos los quehaceres.

REFRÁN

Escoba nueva siempre barre bien.

(*A new broom sweeps clean.*)

Actividad 8 Descripción de dibujos: ¡El cuarto de Esteban es un desastre!

Con su compañero/a, decidan qué debe hacer Esteban para arreglar su cuarto.

MODELO: Esteban debe recoger la ropa y necesita apagar el televisor. También tiene que...

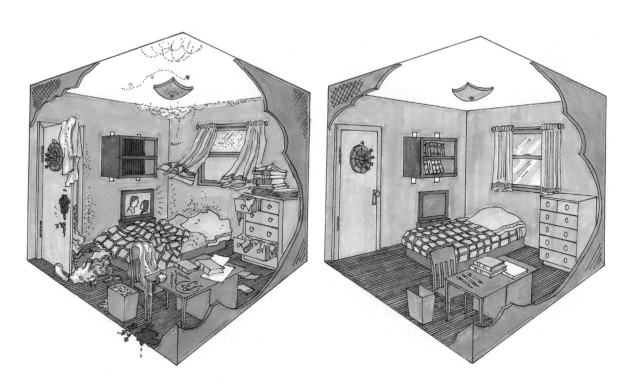

Actividad 9 Entrevista: Los quehaceres y las diversiones en casa

1. En tu casa (apartamento), ¿quién tiene que limpiar el refrigerador, desempolvar, pasar la aspiradora, limpiar el microondas, limpiar los baños, darles de comer a las mascotas, lavar la ropa, cortar el césped?
2. De todos los quehaceres, ¿cuál te gusta más/menos?
3. ¿Qué aspecto de tu casa (apartamento) te gusta más? ¿Por qué?
4. ¿Qué te gusta hacer en casa (en tu apartamento)?
5. ¿Pasas mucho tiempo en casa (en tu apartamento) los fines de semana o prefieres salir? ¿Te visitan mucho tus amigos los fines de semana?

Las actividades con los amigos

✳ **Lea Gramática 6.3.**

1. —¿Vio usted la
televisión?
—Sí, vi las
noticias.

2. —¿Ya escribió los
exámenes?
—Sí, escribí dos
anoche.

3. —¿Visitó a sus amigos
este fin de semana?
—Sí, visité al profesor
López y conocí a su
esposa.

1. —¿Limpiaste la casa
el sábado?
—Pues limpié la sala.

2. —¿Estudiaste mucho?
—Estudié para la
clase de química.

3. —¿Saliste a comer en
algún restaurante?
—Sí, almorcé en un
restaurante cerca
de mi casa.

Actividad 10 **Encuesta: ¿Qué hice?**

Ponga las siguientes actividades en orden cronológico.

Palabras útiles

primero	después	por último
luego	más tarde	

(Continúa)

1. Esta mañana (yo)...
   a. me lavé el pelo.
   b. desayuné.
   c. me desperté.
   d. corrí dos millas.
2. Ayer por la tarde (yo)...
   a. volví a casa.
   b. asistí a una clase.
   c. preparé el almuerzo.
   d. salí para el trabajo.
3. Anoche, antes de acostarme, (yo)...
   a. vi la televisión.
   b. planché una blusa / una camisa.
   c. lavé los platos.
   d. preparé la comida.
4. El sábado pasado (yo)...
   a. invité a unos amigos a cenar.
   b. cené con mis amigos.
   c. limpié la casa.
   d. barrí el patio.

Actividad 11 Intercambios: El fin de semana

Aquí tiene usted algunas de las actividades del fin de semana pasado de Guillermo, Estela y el señor Alvar. Coméntelas con su compañero/a.

MODELOS: E1: ¿Quién *preparó la comida (el viernes)*?
E2: *Estela.*

E1: ¿Cuándo *sacó fotos el señor Alvar*?
E2: *El domingo.*

NOMBRE	EL VIERNES	EL SÁBADO	EL DOMINGO
Guillermo Saucedo Ramírez	Bailó en una fiesta. Se acostó tarde.	Se levantó tarde. Limpió su cuarto.	Ayudó a su padre. Salió a pasear.
Estela Ramírez de Saucedo	Preparó la comida. Habló por teléfono.	Charló con la vecina. Almorzó con una amiga.	Visitó a su madre. Descansó toda la tarde.
el señor Alvar	Escribió una carta. Tocó el piano.	Jugó con sus nietos. Barrió el patio.	Asistió a misa. Sacó unas fotos.

Actividad 12 Narración: Un fin de semana de Nora Morales

Palabras útiles

primero	después	finalmente
luego	más tarde	

El viernes

El sábado

El domingo

Actividad 13   Entrevistas: ¿Qué hiciste?

EL FIN DE SEMANA PASADO

1. ¿Limpiaste tu cuarto (tu casa)?
2. ¿Saliste con amigos? ¿Adónde?
3. ¿Comiste en un restaurante? ¿Cuál? ¿Con quién(es)?
4. ¿Practicaste algún deporte? ¿Con quién(es)? ¿Dónde?
5. ¿Fuiste al cine? ¿Qué película viste? ¿Te gustó? ¿Por qué?

ANOCHE

6. ¿Trabajaste? ¿A qué hora volviste a casa?
7. ¿Estudiaste? ¿Qué?
8. ¿Hablaste por teléfono con tus amigos? ¿Escuchaste música?
9. ¿Viste la televisión? ¿Exploraste el Internet?
10. ¿A qué hora te acostaste?

ESTA MAÑANA

11. ¿A qué hora te levantaste? ¿Te bañaste?
12. ¿Desayunaste? ¿Qué tomaste?
13. ¿A qué hora saliste para la universidad? ¿A qué hora llegaste?
14. ¿A qué clase asististe primero?
15. ¿Leíste el periódico?

VENTANAS AL PASADO

La historia de las mascotas

Los españoles **trajeron** perros de **guerra,** llamados *dogos,* a las Américas para **someter** a los indígenas. Los indígenas ya tenían perros, pero eran más pequeños, animales de compañía o de **caza.** El perro de los aztecas, que no tenía pelo, se llamaba *xoloitzcuintle* que significa «perro asistente del **dios** Xolotl», el dios de la vida y la muerte.

Durante la colonia muchos de estos dogos **se mezclaron** con los perros nativos, lo que resultó en una raza mixta de perros **callejeros.** Mucha gente veía a esos animales como **portadores** de la **rabia** y los mataba.

Pero hoy en día la situación de las mascotas es diferente: ahora hay grupos de voluntarios dedicados a la protección de animales. En Puerto Rico trabaja el grupo Save-a-Sato (*sato* significa «perro callejero» en esta isla); en Argentina trabaja el grupo No lo Abandones. Y en España hay mucha gente dedicada al **rescate** de mascotas abandonadas, como la Asociación Amor a los Animales en Madrid. En México, la Asociación Pro-Defensa Animal (APRODEA), trabaja con veterinarios voluntarios para vacunar y esterilizar perros y gatos. Además, la Universidad Autónoma de México provee una clínica móvil en México, D.F., que esteriliza a más de 800 animales cada mes.

La historia de las mascotas es larga e interesante, y el momento presente es muy **alentador.** Mucha gente ahora entiende que los animales son también habitantes de nuestro planeta y que necesitan cuidado y protección.

La organización Save-a-Sato, Puerto Rico

VOCABULARIO ÚTIL

trajeron	*brought*
la guerra	*war*
someter	*to subdue*
la caza	*hunting*
el dios	*god*
se mezclaron	*mixed*
callejero	*of the street*
los portadores	*carriers*
la rabia	*rabies*
el rescate	*rescue*
alentador	*encouraging*

Comprensión

1. ¿Cómo resultó la raza mixta de los perros callejeros?
2. Describe la situación de las mascotas hoy en día.

Las presentaciones

⚹ **Lea Gramática 6.4–6.5.**

ESTEBAN: Mónica, quiero presentarte a mi
amigo, Jorge.
MÓNICA: Hola, Jorge. ¿Qué tal?
JORGE: ¿Qué tal, Mónica?

ESTELA SAUCEDO: Señor Luján, quisiera
presentarle a mi amiga, la
señora Medrano.
SR. LUJÁN: Mucho gusto en conocerla,
señora.
SRA. MEDRANO: Igualmente, señor Luján.

DOÑA ROSITA: Señorita Batini, me
gustaría presentarle a mi
nuevo vecino, el señor
Marcos.
LOLA BATINI: Mucho gusto en
conocerlo, señor.
SR. MARCOS: Encantado, señorita
Batini.

Actividad 14 Diálogos abiertos: Las presentaciones

Su amigo quiere conocer a su profesor(a) de español.

E1: Profesor/Profesora _____, quiero presentarle a mi amigo/a
_____. Es _____.
E2: Mucho gusto en conocerlo/a.
E3: _____.

Ahora presente a dos de sus compañeros que no se conocen.

E1: Oye, _____, ¿conoces a mi amigo/a _____?
E2: No, no _____ conozco.
E1: _____, te presento a _____. Él/Ella estudia _____ aquí en
la universidad.
E2: Mucho gusto, _____.
E3: Igualmente.

Actividad 15 **Entrevista: ¿Conoces tu vecindario?**

1. ¿Conoces a los vecinos de la casa (del apartamento) de la izquierda? ¿de la derecha? ¿de enfrente?
2. ¿Sabes el nombre de la escuela más cercana a tu casa (apartamento)? ¿Conoces al director / a la directora de esa escuela?
3. ¿Sabes dónde hay un buen restaurante cerca de tu casa (apartamento)? ¿Conoces a los dueños? ¿a los meseros?
4. ¿Sabes cuánto cuesta un apartamento pequeño en la ciudad o pueblo donde vives?
5. ¿Conoces a alguien con piscina en su casa?
6. ¿Sabes cuánto cuesta una casa en tu vecindario?
7. ¿Sabes dónde está el parque _____?
8. ¿Sabes dónde está la biblioteca pública más cercana?

VENTANAS CULTURALES   Las costumbres

De casa en casa: La tradición de las posadas

La tradición de las **posadas** tiene su origen en una historia de la Biblia: la virgen María y su esposo José **buscan alojamiento** en Belén, porque el niño Jesús va a nacer. Así, con este episodio del Nuevo Testamento, empezó esta popular celebración del pueblo mexicano. En sus comienzos las posadas se celebraban sólo en la iglesia. Pero con el tiempo se transformaron en un evento de la comunidad, celebrado también en casa, con la familia y los amigos.

Todos los años, entre el 16 y el 24 de diciembre, los mexicanos conmemoran este pasaje de la Biblia de una manera muy especial, organizando procesiones por los barrios de su ciudad. En muchas vecindades, niños y adultos van de casa en casa buscando alojamiento. Los niños llevan **velas** o **faroles,** tocan a las puertas y siguen su camino hasta la iglesia o su casa. Si hay un **nacimiento,** los pequeños se acercan al niño Jesús y le ofrecen flores. Algunas personas se visten de María y José, y representan así la **búsqueda** de alojamiento. La fiesta continúa después con tamales, chocolate caliente y otras sabrosas comidas. Los chicos también reciben regalos, por supuesto: ricos **buñuelos,** refrescos, dulces. A veces rompen una piñata.

Hoy en día, esta celebración es una de las más populares de México. Pero en los Estados Unidos también podemos apreciar las posadas. En muchas ciudades —San Diego, San Antonio y Chicago, entre otras—, la comunidad mexicana mantiene viva la festiva tradición de diciembre.

VOCABULARIO ÚTIL

la posada	*inn, hotel*
buscan alojamiento	*are looking for lodging*
la vela	*candle*
el farol	*paper lantern*
el nacimiento	*nativity scene*
la búsqueda	*search*
el buñuelo	*fritter*

Comprensión

1. ¿Cuál es el origen de la tradición de las posadas?
2. ¿Qué hacen los mexicanos para celebrar las posadas? Mencione un mínimo de dos actividades.

De todo un poco

A. ¿Cómo es tu casa/apartamento?

Trabajando en parejas, hablen de su casa (apartamento), su vecindario y sus obligaciones. Pueden usar la siguiente guía.

- descripción de la casa (del apartamento): los cuartos, los muebles, el patio, etcétera
- descripción del vecindario: las escuelas, la biblioteca, las tiendas, la lavandería, la gasolinera, etcétera
- las obligaciones que tiene cada miembro de la familia: lavar, planchar, cocinar, cortar el césped, etcétera

B. En grupos de 3 ó 4 describan la casa ideal. Si quieren, una persona puede hacer un dibujo. ¿Dónde está la casa ideal? ¿Cómo es la cocina? ¿Qué hay en ella? ¿Cómo es la sala? ¿y los otros cuartos? ¿Cómo es el patio/jardín? ¿Qué otras cosas especiales hay en la casa ideal?

¡Dígalo por escrito!

Casa a la venta

Imagínese que usted es agente de bienes raíces (*real estate*). Busque una foto o haga un dibujo de una casa. Luego, escriba un anuncio para una revista de bienes raíces describiendo esa casa. Debe incluir en su anuncio una descripción detallada de la casa, los cuartos, los aparatos domésticos que tiene, la vecindad, el precio y, claro, la foto o el dibujo.

¡Cuéntenos usted!

Cuéntenos sobre el cuarto o el lugar favorito de su casa. ¿Cómo es? ¿Es un lugar tranquilo o de mucha actividad? ¿Prefiere estar en ese lugar solo/a o acompañado/a? ¿Qué hace usted cuando está allí? ¿Duerme? ¿Escucha música? ¿Lee?

PISTAS PARA LEER
1. Look at the photographs. Describe what you see. Do you know of any cities in your country that look similar?
2. Scan the first two paragraphs for characteristics of Hispanic cities.
3. As you read, locate on a map the cities and countries mentioned.

VOCABULARIO ÚTIL

antiguas	*ancient*
la mezcla	*mixture*
reconstruida	*reconstructed*
los siglos	*centuries*
el cerro	*hill*
parecido	*like*
el ambiente	*ambience, atmosphere*

LECTURA

Las hermosas ciudades hispanas

Muchas ciudades hispanas son **antiguas** y grandes. Algunas tienen entre trescientos y cuatrocientos años, y en España varias datan del Imperio Romano. Hay ciudades de América Latina, como Arequipa, al sur de Perú, donde se nota en sus edificios la **mezcla** de la cultura indígena y la cultura española. En algunas ciudades, la parte más vieja está **reconstruida** y hoy en día es una zona de interés turístico, como el Viejo San Juan en Puerto Rico, la ciudad colonial de Santo Domingo en la República Dominicana y el Quito colonial en Ecuador.

Las ciudades hispanas están generalmente divididas en zonas con nombres variados, por ejemplo: Argüelles, La Loma y La Villa. Algunas zonas son residenciales; otras son industriales o comerciales. Más que nada, en la típica ciudad hispana hay zonas mixtas: calles con casas particulares, apartamentos, tiendas y oficinas. En muchos casos, los adultos trabajan lejos de casa, pero hacen sus compras en las tiendas de su vecindario, en donde sus niños juegan.

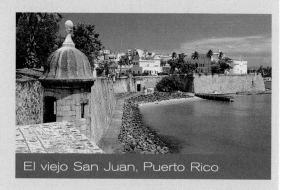

El viejo San Juan, Puerto Rico

Cartagena, en Colombia, es un ejemplo de ciudad con áreas mixtas, con su arquitectura colonial impresionante, su centro lleno de casas particulares y también de actividad comercial, y sus bellas playas. A propósito, si a usted le interesa la arquitectura, debe ir a la ciudad de San Miguel de Allende, en México, donde va a encontrar hermosos edificios que datan de los **siglos**

La Plaza Mayor en Madrid, España

dieciocho y diecinueve. Varias casas de San Miguel de Allende son ahora monumentos históricos.

En muchas ciudades la plaza es un lugar central de gran vitalidad. Las plazas en México se llaman a veces «zócalo». El Zócalo de la ciudad de México es particularmente grande. La Plaza Mayor de Madrid, España, tiene cafés y restaurantes de comida española típica. En la ciudad de Cuzco, que está en las montañas de Perú (parte de los Andes), hay una bella plaza, la Plaza de Armas. También son populares las plazas de Valparaíso, en Chile. Valparaíso está situada en la costa y sobre **cerros**. Esta ciudad chilena tiene, además de plazas hermosas, panoramas espectaculares.

Hay ciudades hispanas con calles y barrios famosos; por ejemplo, el Paseo de la Reforma en la ciudad de México, que es un amplio bulevar **parecido** al de Champs Elysées de París. En Madrid, la Gran Vía es la calle de más tránsito y público en toda la ciudad. Otra calle muy conocida, especialmente por sus tiendas, es la Calle Florida en Buenos Aires. Si a usted le gusta el **ambiente** de una ciudad cosmopolita y elegante, debe ir a Buenos Aires, capital de Argentina. Allí va a encontrar grandes avenidas, numerosos parques, teatros y museos.

Como puede ver, muchas ciudades hispanas son antiguas, grandes y verdaderamente hermosas.

Comprensión

Indique si las siguientes descripciones corresponden a las ciudades hispanas (H), a las ciudades norteamericanas (N) o a las dos (D).

1. _____ Son muy viejas.
2. _____ Hay ciudades que datan del Imperio Romano.
3. _____ En algunas ciudades el centro es una zona turística.
4. _____ Hay mucha actividad comercial en el centro.
5. _____ Hay gran cantidad de restaurantes.
6. _____ Muchas personas viven en el centro.
7. _____ Cada zona tiene su propio nombre.
8. _____ Se hacen las compras lejos de la casa.
9. _____ Los edificios de algunas ciudades son monumentos históricos.
10. _____ Tienen calles famosas.

Un paso más... ¡a conversar!

1. Describa la ciudad donde usted nació o la ciudad donde vive ahora. ¿Qué aspectos de esta ciudad le gustan más? ¿Cuáles no le gustan y por qué?
2. Considere las diez características de la actividad de **Comprensión.** ¿Cuáles describen la ciudad donde usted vive? Por ejemplo, ¿hay calles famosas en su ciudad?

Vea el **Resumen cultural** en este capítulo del *Cuaderno de actividades.*

Vocabulario

Los cuartos y otras dependencias

Rooms and Other Parts of the House

el ascensor	elevator
el baño (el cuarto de baño)	bathroom
la cerca	fence
la chimenea	fireplace
el comedor	dining room
el corredor	corridor, hallway
el dormitorio	bedroom
la escalera	stairway, stairs
la habitación	room
el pasillo	hall
el piso	story, floor; apartment (*Spain*)
la recámara	bedroom (*Mex.*)
la sala	living room

PALABRAS SEMEJANTES: el balcón, el garaje, el patio, la terraza
REPASO: la cocina, el jardín

Los muebles y los aparatos eléctricos

Furniture and Electrical Appliances

la alacena	kitchen cupboard
la alfombra	carpet, rug
la almohada	pillow
el aparato (doméstico)	(household) appliance
el armario	closet
la aspiradora	vacuum cleaner
la bañera	bathtub
la cafetera	coffeepot
el calentador	heater
la cama (matrimonial)	(double) bed
el cepillo (de dientes)	(tooth) brush
la cómoda	chest of drawers
la cortina	curtain; drapes
el cuadro	picture (*on a wall*)
la ducha	shower
la escoba	broom
el espejo	mirror
el estante	shelf
la estufa	stove, range
el fregadero	kitchen sink
el gabinete	cabinet
el horno (de microondas)	(microwave) oven
el inodoro	toilet
el lavabo	bathroom sink
la lavadora	washing machine
el lavaplatos	dishwasher
la mesita	coffee table
el secador (de pelo)	hair dryer
la secadora	(clothes) dryer
el sillón	easy chair

la taza	cup, mug; toilet bowl
la tetera	teapot
el tocador	dresser
el ventilador	fan

PALABRAS SEMEJANTES: la lámpara, el piano, el plato, el refrigerador, el sofá, el tostador, el utensilio
REPASO: la afeitadora, la silla, el televisor, la toalla, el vaso

La casa y el vecindario

House and Neighborhood

el arbusto	bush
la cancha de tenis	tennis court
la casa particular	private home
el centro comercial	shopping center
el departamento	apartment (*Mex.*)
el dueño / la dueña	owner
la estatua	statue
el pueblo	town

PALABRAS SEMEJANTES: el apartamento, la residencia, la vista
REPASO: el árbol, la ciudad, el colegio, el condominio, el edificio, la escuela, la fuente, la gasolinera, la iglesia, el lugar, el parque, la piscina, la plaza, el supermercado, el techo, la tienda

Los quehaceres domésticos

Household Chores

barrer	to sweep
calentar (ie)	to warm up
caliento / calienta	
cortar el césped	to cut (mow) the grass
dar de comer	to feed
desempolvar	to dust
guardar (ropa)	to put away (clothes)
pasar la aspiradora	to vacuum
regar (ie)	to water
riego / riega	
sacar la basura	to take out the trash
tender (ie) la cama	to make the bed
tiendo / tiende	

REPASO: ayudar, cocinar, lavar, limpiar, planchar, secar

Los verbos

Verbs

alquilar(se)	to rent; to be rented
se alquila	for rent
apoyar	to support
cerrar (ie)	to close
cierro / cierra	

compartir	to share
conocer	to know; to meet
conozco / conoce	
enviar	to send
prender (la luz)	to turn on (the light)

PALABRAS SEMEJANTES: comentar, identificar, incluir, ordenar
REPASO: apagar, deber (+ *infin.*), **encender (ie), hay que** (+ *infin.*), **necesitar, pasar tiempo, tener que** (+ *infin.*)

Los sustantivos

Nouns

alguien	someone
el alquiler	rent
los bienes raíces	real estate
el director / la directora	(school) principal
la diversión	entertainment
el empleado doméstico / la empleada doméstica	servant
la entrada	entrance, driveway
las noticias	news
la pareja	pair, couple
el precio	price
la venta	sale

PALABRAS SEMEJANTES: el desastre, la milla, el objeto, el transporte
REPASO: la mascota

Los adjetivos

Adjectives

agradable	pleasant, nice
amplio/a	roomy
amueblado/a	furnished
barato/a	inexpensive
caro/a	expensive
módico/a	moderate (in price)
propio/a	own
serio/a	serious
útil	useful

PALABRAS SEMEJANTES: cronológico/a, decorado/a

¿Cuándo? ¿Con qué frecuencia?

When? How Often?

a menudo	often
anoche	last night
(el mes/año) pasado	last (month/year)

REPASO: ahora, antes de / después de, ayer, esta noche, hoy, mañana, por la mañana/tarde/noche

Las comparaciones

Comparisons

bueno, mejor, el/la mejor	good, better, (the) best
malo, peor, el/la peor	bad, worse, (the) worst
el/la más (+ *adj.*)	the most (+ *adj.*)
más/menos que (de)	more/less than
tan... como	as . . . as
tanto(s)/tanta(s)... como	as much / as many . . . as

Las presentaciones

Introductions

Encantado/a.	Delighted (Pleased) to meet you.
Gusto en conocerlo/a.	Nice to meet you.
Quiero presentarle a...	I want to introduce you (*sing. pol.*) to . . .
Quiero presentarte a...	I want to introduce you (*inf.*) to . . .

REPASO: igualmente, mucho gusto, ¿Qué tal?

Palabras y expresiones útiles

Useful Words and Phrases

¿Para qué sirve... ?	What is . . . used for?
pues	well, then

6.1 Making Comparisons of Inequality: *más/menos*

Gramática ilustrada

Guillermo es **más alto que** Ramón.
Ramón es **menos alto que** Guillermo.

Amanda es **más seria que** Graciela.
Graciela es **menos seria que** Amanda.

Amanda recibe **mejores notas que** Graciela.

Graciela recibe **peores notas que** Amanda.

Ramón es **mejor atleta que** Guillermo.
Guillermo es **mejor estudiante que** Ramón.

Ernestito es **el más grande de** los tres.

Marisa es **la más pequeña de** los tres.

---

más que = *more than*
menos que = *less than*

A. Use the words **más... que** (*more . . . than*) and **menos... que** (*less . . . than*) to make unequal comparisons in Spanish. English often uses the ending *-er* (e.g., *taller*) in such comparisons, but Spanish uses **más/menos** + adjective.

Guillermo es **más** alto **que** Ramón.	*Guillermo is taller than Ramón.*
Graciela es **menos** seria **que** Amanda.	*Graciela is less serious than Amanda.*
Yo tengo **más** experiencia **que** Pilar.	*I have more experience than Pilar.*
José tiene **menos** tiempo **que** Clara.	*José has less time than Clara.*

236

B. To single out a member of a group as "the most" or "the least," add an article (**el, la, los, las**) to this construction. Note that English often uses the ending -*est*: **el más gordo** (*the fattest*), **las más grandes** (*the biggest ones*), **la más cara** (*the most expensive one*), **el menos útil** (*the least useful*). (Also note that Spanish uses **de** where English uses *of* or *in*.)

Adriana es **la más** simpática (**de** las tres que conozco).	Adriana is the nicest (*of the three I know*).
Éstas son **las** casas **más** modernas **del** vecindario.	These are the most modern houses in the neighborhood.
Aquí tiene usted **el** cuarto **más** grande **de** la casa.	Here you have the largest room in the house.

el más alto = *the tallest* (*m. sing.*)
los más altos = *the tallest* (*m. pl.*)
la más alta = *the tallest* (*f. sing.*)
las más altas = *the tallest* (*f. pl.*)

C. There are special comparative and superlative forms for **bueno** and **malo.**

bueno	mejor	el/la mejor	*good/better/best*
malo	peor	el/la peor	*bad/worse/worst*

el/la mejor = *the best* (*sing.*)
los/las mejores = *the best* (*pl.*)
el/la peor = *the worst* (*sing.*)
los/las peores = *the worst* (*pl.*)

En mi opinión, la cocina es **el mejor** cuarto de la casa.	In my opinion, the kitchen is the best room in the house.
No hay nada **peor** que el ruido de los coches cuando uno quiere dormir.	There is nothing worse than traffic noise when you want to sleep.

D. The special forms **mayor / el/la mayor** (*older/oldest*) and **menor / el/la menor** (*younger/youngest*) are used to compare ages.

Mi hermano **mayor** se llama Jaime y mi hermana **menor** se llama Leticia.	My older brother is named Jaime, and my younger sister is named Leticia.

mi hermana mayor = *my older sister*
mi hermano menor = *my younger brother*

Ejercicio 1

Haga comparaciones. Use **más/menos que.**

MODELO: El sofá cuesta $150. El sofá-cama cuesta $500. (cuesta) →
El sofá-cama cuesta *más que* el sofá. (El sofá cuesta *menos que* el sofá-cama.)

1. La mesa pesa 25 kilos. El sillón pesa 48. (pesa)
2. En mi casa viven ocho personas. En la casa de los vecinos viven cinco. (viven)
3. La casa de los López tiene cuatro dormitorios. La casa de los vecinos tiene dos. (tiene)
4. En el patio de mis abuelos hay tres árboles. En nuestro patio hay cinco. (hay)
5. En la casa de los Ruiz hay tres dormitorios. En la casa de los Saucedo hay cinco. (hay)

pesa = *weighs*

Ejercicio 2

Exprese su opinión. Use **mejor, peor, mayor, menor** o **el/la más... de...**

> MODELO: el Mercedes Benz; el Jaguar (mejor) →
> En mi opinión, el Jaguar es *mejor que* el Mercedes.

desierto = *desert*

1. vivir en el desierto; vivir en el centro de la ciudad (peor)
2. vivir en una casa; vivir en un apartamento (mejor)
3. un ventilador; un horno de microondas; un refrigerador (útil)
4. mi hermano Armando tiene 12 años; mi hermana Irma tiene 10 (mayor)
5. mi hijo tiene 6 meses; tu hija tiene 1 año (menor)
6. un Ferrari que cuesta $300.000; un Rolls-Royce que cuesta $460.000; un BMW que cuesta $65.000 (caro)

6.2 Making Comparisons of Equality: *tan/tanto*

Gramática ilustrada

Ramón no es **tan alto como** Guillermo.

Marisa y Clarisa son **tan inteligentes como** Ernestito.

Andrea no tiene **tanto tiempo libre como** su hermana, Paula.

Graciela tiene **tantos amigos como** Amanda.

tan + adjective + **como** = *as* + adjective + *as*

A. When stating that qualities are (or are not) equal or identical (*as pretty as / not as pretty as*), use **(no) tan... como. Tan** never changes form in comparisons or contrasts of qualities.

Marisa es **tan** inteligente **como** Clarisa.	*Marisa is as intelligent as Clarisa.*
Ramón **no** es **tan** alto **como** Guillermo.	*Ramón is not as tall as Guillermo.*

tanto/a/os/as + noun + **como** = *as much/ many* + noun + *as*

B. When equating quantities (*as much/many as*), use **tanto... como. Tanto** agrees with the noun that follows: **tanto, tanta, tantos, tantas.**

Andrea no tiene **tanto dinero como** Paula.	*Andrea doesn't have as much money as Paula.*
Ustedes tienen **tantas clases como** nosotros.	*You have as many classes as we do.*

Ejercicio 3

Haga comparaciones. Use **tan... como.**

MODELO: El Parque de Chapultepec es muy grande. El Parque Juárez es pequeño. (grande) →
El Parque Juárez no es *tan grande como* el Parque de Chapultepec.

1. La piscina de los señores Montes es muy bonita. La piscina de los señores Lugo es muy bonita también. (bonita)
2. El edificio de la avenida Oriente tiene seis pisos. El edificio nuevo de la avenida del Libertador tiene diez. (alto)
3. La lavandería nueva de la calle Ebro es muy limpia. La lavandería vieja de la avenida Almendros no es muy limpia. (limpia)
4. Los condominios «Princesa» son muy modernos. Los condominios «San Juan» tienen ya veinte años. (modernos)

Ejercicio 4

Haga comparaciones. Use **tantos/as... como.**

MODELO: Mi casa tiene dos dormitorios. Su casa tiene cuatro. →
Mi casa no tiene *tantos* dormitorios *como* su casa.

1. La sala de nuestra casa tiene cuatro lámparas. La sala de su casa tiene sólo dos lámparas.
2. La casa de los señores Saucedo tiene ocho cuartos. La casa de los señores Ruiz tiene seis cuartos.
3. La casa de mis padres tiene dos baños. La casa de los vecinos también tiene dos baños.
4. El patio de doña Lola tiene muchas flores y plantas. El patio de don Anselmo tiene pocas flores y plantas.

6.3 Talking about Past Actions: The Preterite of Regular Verbs (Part 1)

Gramática ilustrada

hablé = *I spoke*
comí = *I ate*
viví = *I lived*
hablaste = *you (inf. sing.) spoke*
comiste = *you (inf. sing.) ate*
viviste = *you (inf. sing.) lived*
habló = *you (pol. sing.) spoke; he/she spoke*
comió = *you (pol. sing.) ate; he/she ate*
vivió = *you (pol. sing.) lived; he/she lived*

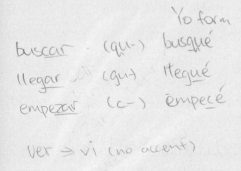

The Spanish past tense (preterite), like the English present tense, is formed by adding a set of endings to the stem. Here are the singular preterite endings of the regular verbs **hablar** (*to speak*), **comer** (*to eat*), and **vivir** (*to live*).*

	-ar verbs	**-er verbs**	**-ir verbs**
(yo)	hablé	comí	viví
(tú)	hablaste	comiste	viviste
(usted, él/ella)	habló	comió	vivió

Note the written accent marks. They tell you where to put the stress. Also note that the singular endings for **-er** and **-ir** verbs are the same.

The following are some time expressions that often act as clues to help you recognize the preterite. You can use them to talk about the past.

> **anoche, ayer, ayer por la mañana (tarde, noche), anteayer, el lunes (martes, miércoles, etc.) pasado, el mes (año) pasado, esta mañana, la semana pasada, ya**

Hablé con la vecina nueva **ayer.**   *I spoke with the new neighbor yesterday.*

—¿**Ya comiste?**   —*Did you already eat?*
—Sí, **comí** en casa.   —*Yes, I ate at home.*

Ejercicio 5

¿Hizo usted estas actividades ayer? Conteste sí o no.

MODELO: trabajar → Sí, *trabajé* siete horas. (No, *no trabajé.*)

1. comprar un espejo
2. comer en un restaurante
3. hablar por teléfono
4. escribir una carta
5. estudiar cuatro horas
6. abrir la ventana
7. visitar a un amigo / una amiga
8. correr por la mañana
9. tomar un refresco
10. lavar los platos

Ejercicio 6

Diga si cada una de las siguientes personas hizo las actividades indicadas.

MODELO: Christina Aguilera / cantar en la ducha esta mañana →
Christina Aguilera *cantó* en la ducha esta mañana.

1. mi madre / charlar con el presidente la semana pasada
2. el presidente de México / comer tacos en la calle ayer
3. la profesora de español / salir con Antonio Banderas anoche
4. yo / jugar al tenis con Rafael Nadal ayer a medianoche
5. Hugo Chávez / visitar los Estados Unidos el mes pasado

---

*The plural endings and many common verbs that are irregular in the preterite are introduced in **Gramática 7.1, 7.2,** and **7.3.**

6.4 Knowing People, Places, and Facts: *conocer* and *saber*

A. Conocer (*to know*) is used in the sense of *to be acquainted* or *familiar with*; it is normally used with people and places. **Saber** (*to know*) is used in the sense of *to know facts, information*, or, when followed by an infinitive, *to know how to* (*do something*). Here are the present-tense forms of conocer* and **saber.**

	conocer (*to know people, places*)	saber (*to know facts, information*)	
(yo)	conozco	sé	*I know*
(tú)	conoces	sabes	*you (inf. sing.) know*
(usted, él/ella)	conoce	sabe	*you (pol. sing.) know; he/she knows*
(nosotros/as)	conocemos	sabemos	*we know*
(vosotros/as)	conocéis	sabéis	*you (inf. pl., Spain) know*
(ustedes, ellos/as)	conocen	saben	*you (pl.) know; they know*

Note that the preposition **a** precedes a direct object noun when that noun is a person. This use of **a** is called the *personal a*.

—**¿Conoces a** Carla Espinosa?
—Sí, y **conozco** también **a** su hermano.
—¿Y **conoces** también **a** su amigo Rogelio?
—No, **a** él no lo **conozco.**

—*Do you know Carla Espinosa?*
—*Yes, and I also know her brother.*
—*And do you also know her friend Rogelio?*
—*No, I don't know him.*

—**¿Conoces** muy bien la ciudad de México?
—Todavía no.

—*Do you know Mexico City well?*
—*Not yet.*

—**¿Sabes** nadar?
—No, no **sé** nadar.

—*Do you know how to swim?*
—*No, I don't know how to swim.*

—**¿Sabes** dónde está el restaurante?
—No, no **sé.**

—*Do you know where the restaurant is?*
—*No, I don't know.*

—**¿Sabes** si hay una biblioteca cerca?
—No, no **sé.**

—*Do you know if there is a library nearby?*
—*No, I don't know.*

B. The preterite of **conocer** (**conocí, conociste, conoció**) expresses the meaning *met* (*for the first time*) in English.

Conocí a Raúl la semana pasada.   *I met Raúl last week.*

¿RECUERDA?

Spanish uses two different verbs to express the English verb *to know.* You have already seen and practiced the forms of one of these verbs, **saber,** which means *to know facts, information.* When followed by an infinitive, **saber** expresses the idea *to know how to* (*do something*). Return to **Gramática 5.2** to review the verb **saber** in more detail.

conocer = *to know people, places*
saber = *to know facts, information*
saber + inf. = *to know how to* (*do something*)
Conozco a Adriana. (*I know Adriana.*)
Sé que Adriana vive en Buenos Aires. (*I know that Adriana lives in Buenos Aires.*)

conocer in the preterite = *met* (*for the first time*)

*Recognition: **vos conocés**

Ejercicio 7

—¿Conoce usted a los vecinos que viven enfrente?
—Sí, los conozco muy bien. Su apellido es Saucedo.

El señor Valdés lleva sólo una semana viviendo en el vecindario de San Vicente. Está hablando con su vecino, don Eduardo. Complete con las frases apropiadas las preguntas del señor Valdés.

¿Conoce usted...
¿Sabe usted...

1. a los dueños de la casa de la esquina (*corner*)?
2. a doña Rosita?
3. si hay una farmacia cerca?
4. si hay una alberca (*piscina*) pública cerca?
5. al director del colegio que está en la esquina?
6. un buen restaurante chino?
7. dónde está el Parque de Colón?
8. si hay una lavandería en el centro comercial El Toro?
9. cuánto cuesta ponerle un techo nuevo a la casa?
10. a la vecina de la casa amarilla?

6.5 Referring to People already Mentioned: Personal Direct Object Pronouns

A. Personal direct object pronouns (**los pronombres de complemento directo**) are used with verbs such as *to see* (*someone*), *to remember* (*someone*), *to know* (*someone*), *to love* (*someone*), *to take* (*someone somewhere*), *to invite* (*someone*), and so forth. Here are some examples of direct object pronouns in English.

Raúl Saucedo? I don't remember *him.*
Ernestito and his brother and sister? We saw *them* yesterday.
I'm José Estrada. You remember *me,* don't you?

B. You already know four of the personal direct object pronouns, because they are the same as the reflexive pronouns and the indirect object pronouns: **me** (*me*), **te** (*you*), **nos** (*us*), and **os** (*you; inf. pl., Spain*).

Usted no **me** conoce todavía. Soy Raúl Saucedo.	*You don't know me yet. I'm Raúl Saucedo.*
Te quiero mucho.	*I love you a lot.*
Tú no **nos** recuerdas, ¿verdad?	*You don't remember us, do you?*

C. Four other direct object pronouns are used, according to the gender and number of the person(s) referred.*

lo	*him, you (pol. m. sing.)*		los	*them, you (pl.)*
la	*her, you (pol. f. sing.)*		las	*them, you (females only)*

---

*Some Spanish speakers from Spain use **le/les** instead of **lo/los** as the direct object pronoun to refer to males.

—¿Conoces a **José Estrada**, el novio de Pilar?
—Sí, **lo** conozco.

—¿Mi hija Margarita? **La** llevo todos los días a la escuela.

—¿No **lo** vi a usted ayer, señor Torres?
—Sí, **me** vio en la biblioteca.

—¿Y tus **parientes**? ¿**Los** ves con frecuencia?
—Sí, durante las fiestas **los** invitamos a casa a cenar con nosotros.

—¿Vas a visitar a tus **hermanas** mañana?
—Sí, **las** voy a ver al mediodía.

—Mamá, ¿cuándo vas a recoger**nos**?
—Paso a recoger**las** a las 2:45.

—Do you know José Estrada, Pilar's boyfriend?
—Yes, I know him.

—My daughter Margaret? I take her to school every day.

—Didn't I see you yesterday, Mr. Torres?
—Yes, you saw me in the library.

—And your relatives? Do you see them frequently?
—Yes, during the holidays we invite them to our house to have dinner with us.

—Are you going to visit your sisters tomorrow?
—Yes, I'm going to see them at noon.

—Mom, when are you going to pick us up?
—I'll pick you up at 2:45.

> In the sentence *John saw her*, the word *her* is a direct object pronoun. Direct object pronouns answer the questions *Whom?* or *What?*

> In the sentence **Juan la conoce** (*John knows her*), **la** is a direct object pronoun.

> —¿**Dónde está Lan?**
> —**No sé. No *la* veo.**
> [*la* = **Lan**]
> —*Where is **Lan**?*
> —*I don't know. I don't see **her**.* [*her* = *Lan*]

> —¿**Conoces a *los Silva*?**
> —**Sí, *los* conocí ayer.**
> [**los** = **los Silva**]
> —*Do you know **the Silvas**?*
> —*Yes, I met **them** yesterday.* [**them** = *the Silvas*]

Ejercicio 8

Complete estos diálogos con pronombres de complemento directo.

MODELO: —¿Conoces a Marta Guerrero?
—Sí, *la* conozco.

1. —¿Conocen ustedes a los señores Saucedo?
   —Sí, _____ conocemos muy bien.
2. —¿Conoces tú a doña Rosita?
   —Sí, _____ conozco un poco.
3. —¿Y a Pedro Ruiz?
   —Sí, _____ conozco también.
4. —¿Conoce Estela Saucedo a Silvia y a Nacho?
   —Sí, ella _____ conoce un poco.
5. —Señor, yo no _____ conozco.
   —¿No me conoce? ¡Soy Ernesto Saucedo, su vecino!
6. —¿Conoce usted al esposo de Andrea Ruiz?
   —No, no _____ conozco.
7. —¿Conocen ustedes a la señorita Batini?
   —Sí, _____ conocemos muy bien; es amiga de mi madre.
8. —¿Conocen los señores Saucedo a los señores Silva?
   —Sí, los señores Saucedo _____ conocen muy bien; son vecinos.
9. —¿Conoces tú a Guillermo?
   —Sí, _____ conozco muy bien; es mi mejor amigo.
10. —¿Conoce Amanda a Graciela?
    —Sí, _____ conoce muy bien; son muy buenas amigas.

Hablando del pasado

METAS

In **Capítulo 7** you will continue to talk about things that happened in the past: your own experiences and those of others.

Pintura de la serie *Tango argentino*, por Guillermo Alio (Argentina)

Sobre el artista: Guillermo Alio nació en Tucumán, Argentina, en 1950. Estudió en la Escuela de Bellas Artes en Buenos Aires. Sus obras se exhiben en varios países de América del Sur y Europa, los Estados Unidos, México e Israel. Actualmente da conferencias sobre arte en Argentina y otros países.

¡Conozca Argentina!

Nombre del país: la República Argentina

Ciudad capital: Buenos Aires

Ciudades principales: Córdoba, Mar del Plata, Mendoza, Salta, San Miguel de Tucumán

Moneda: el peso argentino

Idiomas: el español

Población: 40.300.000

Día de la Independencia: el 9 de julio

Fiestas típicas: el Día del Veterano y de los Caídos en la Guerra de las Malvinas, el Día del Trabajador, el Día del Libertador José de San Martín, el Día de la Inmaculada Concepción

Comidas típicas: las empanadas, la parrillada, la humita, el locro, la pasta, la pizza, el dulce de leche, el alfajor, el mate

Música típica: la milonga, el tango, la nueva canción, el rock argentino, la música gauchesca

Gente famosa: José de San Martín, Diego Maradona, Eva Perón, Atahualpa Yupanqui, Mercedes Sosa, Carlos Gardel, Jorge Luis Borges, Julio Cortázar

Voces argentinas

amarrete	tacaño/a
che	hey; buddy
el bife	el bistec
la campera	la chaqueta
un despelote	un lío
ni a ganchos	no (enfático)

En este capítulo...

ACTIVIDADES DE COMUNICACIÓN

- Mis experiencias
- Las experiencias con los demás
- Hablando del pasado

EN RESUMEN

LECTURAS Y CULTURA

- **Enlace a la literatura**
  «Cuando salimos de El Salvador», por Jorge Argueta
- **Ventanas culturales**
  Las costumbres: La Diablada de Oruro
- **Ventanas al pasado**
  La independencia de Sudamérica
- **Lectura**
  Machu Picchu: Un viaje por el tiempo

GRAMÁTICA Y EJERCICIOS

7.1 Talking about Past Actions: The Preterite of Regular Verbs (Part 2)

7.2 Relating Past Events (Part 1): Verbs with Irregular Preterite Forms

7.3 More about Relating Past Events (Part 2): Stem-Changing Verbs in the Preterite

7.4 Reporting the Past: Indirect Object Pronouns with **decir**

7.5 Expressing *ago:* **hacer** + Time

MULTIMEDIA

 ONLINE LEARNING CENTER   www.mhhe.com/dosmundos7

 C E N T R O   Your media center for languages   QUIA   DVD

Actividades de comunicación y lecturas

Mis experiencias

★ Lea Gramática 7.1–7.2.

Por la mañana...

Me lavé el pelo.

Desayuné rápidamente.

Salí de casa.

Asistí a la clase de biología.

Tomé café con algunos amigos.

Escribí un informe para la clase de química.

Por la tarde...

Volví a casa a las dos.

Almorcé con mi mamá.

Trabajé por cuatro horas en una tienda de ropa.

Anoche...

Cené con mi familia.

Leí un poco antes de acostarme.

Me acosté temprano.

Actividad 1 Orden lógico: Mis actividades

Ordene lógicamente las siguientes actividades.

_____ Leí una novela.
_____ Me duché.
_____ Me puse el pijama.
_____ Trabajé. / Asistí a clases.
_____ Me acosté.
_____ Hice la tarea.
_____ Cené.
_____ Desayuné.
_____ Salí para el trabajo / la universidad.
_____ Lavé los platos.
_____ Volví a casa.
_____ Me vestí.

Actividad 2 Narración: La rutina

Complete lógicamente cada secuencia con la actividad que falta. Los puntos rojos indican la actividad que falta.

MODELO: Anoche cené, luego me quité la ropa, •, me lavé los dientes y me acosté. (me duché)

1. Hoy me desperté, me levanté inmediatamente, me duché, me lavé el pelo y •. Después me puse ropa limpia y salí para la universidad.
2. Anoche llegué del trabajo, me quité la ropa, me puse el pijama, cené, • y me acosté.
3. Esta mañana me desperté tarde. Me quité rápidamente el pijama, me duché, me sequé y •. Luego tomé un vaso de leche (no desayuné porque no tuve tiempo) y salí para el trabajo.
4. El sábado pasado mi novio/a me invitó al cine. Primero •, me duché y •. Luego • y me puse ropa limpia. Un poco más tarde me peiné. Finalmente salí para el cine con mi novio/a.
5. El domingo pasado me desperté, desayuné, me quité el pijama, me duché, me sequé, me vestí y •. Llegué a la cancha de tenis y jugué un partido con mi amigo.

Actividad 3 Encuesta: La última vez

¿Cuándo fue la última vez que usted hizo las siguientes actividades?

MODELO: ¿Cuándo habló con su mamá por teléfono? →
Hablé con ella *la semana pasada.*

Posibilidades

esta mañana	la semana pasada	hace _____ días,
ayer	ayer por la mañana (tarde, noche)	(semanas,
anteayer	el lunes (martes,...) pasado	meses, años)
anoche	el año pasado	

(Continúa)

1. ¿Cuándo lavó su carro?
2. ¿Cuándo se bañó?
3. ¿Cuándo se cortó el pelo?
4. ¿Cuándo navegó por el Internet?
5. ¿Cuándo asistió a clase? ¿a un concierto?
6. ¿Cuándo estudió más de una hora?
7. ¿Cuándo vio la televisión? ¿una película?
8. ¿Cuándo fue a la playa? ¿al lago? ¿al río?
9. ¿Cuándo fue de compras?
10. ¿Cuándo leyó el periódico? ¿una revista?

Actividad 4 Narración: El fin de semana de Ricardo Sícora

Palabras útiles

primero	luego	más tarde
poco después	también	finalmente

Enlace a la literatura

«Cuando salimos de El Salvador», por Jorge Argueta

Selección de su libro *Una película en mi almohada* (2001)

Jorge Argueta es un poeta salvadoreño que llegó a los Estados Unidos en 1980 y desde entonces vive en San Francisco, California. Además de ser autor de poemas y cuentos, Argueta es maestro. Una de sus muchas publicaciones es *Xóchitl, la niña de las flores* (2003), una hermosa historia para niños. En el conmovedor[1] poema aquí incluido, Argueta describe su experiencia al tener que abandonar su país.

Cuando salimos de El Salvador

Cuando salimos de El Salvador
para venir a los Estados Unidos
mi papá y yo salimos huyendo[2]
una madrugada[3] de diciembre

Salimos sin decirles adiós
a parientes, amigos o vecinos
No me despedí de[4] Neto
mi mejor amigo

No me despedí de Koki
mi periquito parlanchín[5]
ni de la señorita
Sha-Sha-She-Sha
mi perrita favorita

Cuando salimos de El Salvador
en el autobús yo no dejaba de llorar[6]
porque allá se habían
quedado[7] mi mamá
mis hermanitos y mi abuela

Actividad creativa: Una experiencia memorable

Imagínese que usted está escribiendo su autobiografía y quiere contar una experiencia memorable que tuvo durante un viaje. ¿Qué recuerdos importantes o interesantes tiene de esta experiencia? ¿Qué pasó? Narre su historia en una página, en prosa o en forma poética.

[1]*moving* [2]*fleeing* [3]*dawn* [4]*No... I didn't say good-bye to* [5]*talkative* [6]*no... couldn't stop crying* [7]*allá... had remained behind*

Las experiencias con los demás

✳ Lea Gramática 7.3–7.4.

Dos chicos vinieron a la fiesta de mi hijo. Bebieron demasiado.

Se afeitaron y se vistieron con cuidado.

Llegaron un poco tarde y les dijeron «¡Disculpen!» a sus amigos.

Bailaron y se divirtieron, pero bebieron mucha cerveza y...

¡Se sintieron mal! Tuvieron que regresar a casa a pie.

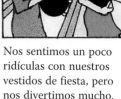

¡No quisimos beber en la fiesta!

Nos pusimos unos vestidos lindos.

Llegamos a la fiesta y nos sirvieron cerveza; no la aceptamos.

No nos quedamos en la fiesta. Preferimos ir a jugar al boliche.

Nos sentimos un poco ridículas con nuestros vestidos de fiesta, pero nos divertimos mucho.

Actividad 5   Intercambios: El fin de semana de los vecinos

A continuación ustedes tienen una lista de lo que hicieron algunos de los vecinos de Ernesto y Estela durante el fin de semana.

MODELOS: E1: ¿Qué hicieron *los Olivera* el viernes?
E2: Limpiaron la casa.

E1: ¿Quiénes *salieron a cenar el sábado*?
E2: *Los Silva.*

	LOS OLIVERA	LOS SILVA	LOS RUIZ
el viernes	Limpiaron la casa.	Fueron al cine y vieron una película romántica.	Viajaron a Acapulco con sus hijas.
el sábado	Dieron una fiesta y se divirtieron mucho.	Salieron a cenar.	Pasaron el día en la playa.
el domingo	Durmieron hasta las once; no hicieron nada.	Asistieron a un espectáculo de baile.	Almorzaron en un restaurante elegante.

Actividad 6 **Narración: Las vacaciones de Rubén y Virginia Hernández**

los Hernández
(Rubén y Virginia)

Actividad 7 **Encuesta: ¿Cuándo?**

Diga con quién y cuándo hizo usted las siguientes actividades. Luego comente sus respuestas con un compañero / una compañera.

MODELO: Fuimos al cine. → *Mi amigo Jorge y yo* fuimos al cine *anoche.*

Posibilidades

Mis amigos y yo	Mi novio/a y yo	Mi familia y yo	Mi esposo/a y yo

1. Practicamos un deporte.
2. Esquiamos en las montañas.
3. Dormimos en el campo, al aire libre.
4. Dimos una fiesta.
5. Vimos una película.
6. Bailamos.
7. Nos divertimos muchísimo.
8. Montamos a caballo.
9. Corrimos varios kilómetros.
10. Estudiamos en la biblioteca.

Y tú, ¿qué dices?

¿Dónde?
¿Cuál?
¡Qué divertido!
¡Qué aburrido!
¡Qué envidia!
¿De veras?

Actividad 8 Intercambios: Las vacaciones recientes

Pregúntele a su compañero/a qué hicieron las personas en las fotos en esta página.

MODELO: E1: ¿Qué hicieron las personas en la playa?
E2: *Tomaron el sol y nadaron.*

Una playa en Puerto Rico

Las montañas en Chile

El cine en Barcelona, España

Un restaurante en Sevilla, España

De compras en Guatemala

Un club nocturno en *la República Dominicana*

Actividad 9 Narración: Los héroes y el ladrón

Los dibujos de la página anterior representan una aventura de Guillermo y su hermano Ernestito. Las siguientes oraciones describen cada dibujo. Póngalas en orden según los dibujos.

_____ Guillermo le ató las manos al ladrón y Ernestito llamó a la policía.

_____ Los chicos se pusieron rojos. Pero se sintieron muy bien porque hicieron algo heroico.

_____ Guillermo y Ernestito oyeron unos gritos desesperados.

_____ Corrieron detrás del ladrón.

_____ Miraron por la ventana y vieron a dos hermosas chicas asustadas.

_____ Lo atraparon y le quitaron las bolsas de las chicas.

_____ Ellas les dijeron: «¡Ayúdennos, por favor! ¡Aquel hombre nos robó las bolsas!»

_____ Las chicas les dijeron: «¡Muchísimas gracias!» y les dieron un beso.

_____ El policía arrestó al ladrón.

_____ Salieron y les preguntaron: «¿Qué les pasa?»

> **REFRÁN**
>
> **Más vale solo que mal acompañado.**
>
> (*Better to be alone than in bad company.*)

Actividad 10 Conversación: Los recuerdos

¿Le pasó algo semejante (similar) a usted? ¿Qué hizo?

1. Una vez en un restaurante encontré una mosca en la ensalada. (Yo)...
2. Un día alguien chocó mi carro por detrás. (Yo)...
3. Un día vi a mi novio/a almorzando con mi mejor amigo/a.
4. Un día bebí mucho en una fiesta.
5. Un día mi perro arruinó mis zapatos.
6. Una vez invité a varios amigos a una fiesta. Todos aceptaron la invitación pero nadie asistió.
7. Un día que estaba solo/a en casa escuché ruidos y pasos en el piso de abajo.

VOCABULARIO ÚTIL

Lo castigué.	Lloré.	Pedí otra ensalada.	Salí sin pagar.	Llamé a la policía.
Me enojé.	Me puse furioso/a.	Me quejé.	Me enfermé.	Tuve miedo.

Actividad 11 Entrevista: El sábado pasado

Imagínese que su compañero/a es una persona famosa: un actor / una actriz, el presidente de los Estados Unidos, una estrella de televisión o un jugador / una jugadora de fútbol, de basquetbol o de tenis. Hágale preguntas sobre las actividades del sábado pasado.

1. ¿Se levantó tarde? ¿A qué hora se levantó?
2. ¿Leyó el periódico? ¿Tomó café, té o no tomó nada?
3. ¿Hizo ejercicio? ¿Practicó algún deporte?
4. ¿Dónde almorzó? ¿Con quién?
5. ¿Salió con algún amigo / alguna amiga? ¿Adónde fueron? ¿Se divirtieron?
6. ¿Dio una fiesta en casa? ¿A quiénes invitó?
7. ¿Vio la televisión? ¿Leyó una novela? ¿A qué hora se acostó?
8. ¿... ?

La Diablada de Oruro

La ciudad de Oruro se encuentra al oeste de Bolivia. Esta ciudad tiene tan sólo 150.000 habitantes, pero cada febrero llegan casi medio millón de personas para celebrar el Carnaval de Oruro. En este Carnaval distintos grupos de bailadores presentan muchos tipos de baile. El baile más famoso es el de los **diablos,** la Diablada, en el cual los danzantes, **disfrazados** de diablos, bailan por las calles de Oruro durante más de 15 horas.

La Diablada nace de la mitología de los indígenas y de la interpretación indígena del cristianismo. Los indígenas andinos **creían** en el Supay, el **dios** de los muertos y del mundo subterráneo. Para recibir su protección, los mineros indígenas **le ofrecían coca** y alcohol al Supay. Por ser Supay el dios de los muertos, los españoles lo asociaron con el diablo cristiano. En 1789 al pie de una montaña, **apareció** una imagen de la Virgen de la Candelaria. Los mineros adoptaron esta Virgen como su santa patrona y la nombraron La Virgen del **Socavón** o Mamita del Socavón. En honor a ella y para calmar al Supay, empezaron a celebrar la Diablada durante el carnaval. Los **disfraces** de diablo que llevan los bailadores representan una mezcla de las dos religiones: incluyen **lagartos, serpientes y ranas,** símbolos importantes de la mitología indígena y los **cuernos,** símbolo cristiano del diablo. Además de los diablos, también figura en la Diablada el arcángel San Miguel, símbolo cristiano del bien. Las máscaras y los disfraces son verdaderamente impresionantes y los artesanos trabajan todo el año para hacerlos.

En el carnaval de Oruro participan varios conjuntos con diferentes nombres: Gran Tradicional Diablada Auténtica de Oruro, Conjunto Tradicional Folklórico Diablada Oruro, Diablada Ferroviaria, Diablada Artística Urus. El sábado es el primer día del festival, Día de la Entrada, y empieza con un **desfile** a las nueve de la mañana con **sacerdotes** y políticos **encabezando** la procesión. Les sigue una estatua de la Virgen del Socavón y luego vienen los conjuntos de bailadores. Como en febrero puede hacer mucho calor, los jóvenes se divierten **tirando** globos de agua a los espectadores. Los bailadores y los músicos llegan a las puertas de la iglesia del Socavón y allí se quitan la máscara para entrar y recibir la **bendición** del sacerdote.

El carnaval de Oruro continúa durante diez días con música, bailes y alegría en las calles. Esta celebración de carnaval es la más grande de Hispanoamérica. La Organización de Naciones Unidas (ONU) nombró esta celebración **Patrimonio Oral e Inmaterial de la Humanidad,** siendo esto motivo de gran **orgullo** para todos los bolivianos.

Comprensión

1. ¿Cómo se llama el dios de la muerte de los indígenas andinos? ¿Cómo se llama la santa patrona de los mineros de Oruro?
2. ¿Cuáles son las actividades de celebración de la Diablada de Oruro? Mencione tres.

VOCABULARIO ÚTIL

los diablos	*devils*
disfrazados	*disguised, costumed*
creían	*believed*
el dios	*god*
le ofrecían coca	*offered him coca leaves*
apareció	*appeared*
el socavón	*mineshaft*
los disfraces (*sing.* el disfraz)	*disguises*
lagartos, serpientes y ranas	*lizards, snakes and frogs*
los cuernos	*horns*
el desfile	*parade*
los sacerdotes	*priests*
encabezando	*heading*
tirando	*throwing*
la bendición	*blessing*
Patrimonio Oral e Inmaterial de la Humanidad	*Oral and Intangible Human Heritage*
el orgullo	*pride*

Hablando del pasado

✳ **Lea Gramática 7.5.**

20.000 a.C.

Los indígenas americanos llegaron al continente desde Asia hace más de 20.000 años.

12 de octubre de 1492

Cristóbal Colón llegó a América hace más de cinco siglos.

17 de octubre de 1813

Hace más de 197 años que Bernardo O'Higgins, el libertador de Chile, dijo: «O vivir con honor o morir con gloria».

24 de julio de 1783

Hace más de 227 años que nació Simón Bolívar, el caudillo de la emancipación americana.

17 de agosto de 1850

Hace más de 160 años que murió José de San Martín, el libertador de Argentina, Chile y Perú.

5 de mayo de 1862

Los mexicanos ganaron la batalla de Puebla hace aproximadamente 148 años.

Actividad 12 Asociaciones: Hablando del pasado

Busque las actividades que *no* son lógicas y explique por qué no lo son.

1. Soy Ernesto. Esta mañana me levanté muy tarde.
   a. El despertador no sonó.
   b. Llegué temprano al trabajo.
   c. Desayuné tranquilamente en casa.
   d. Manejé el carro muy rápido, en vez de tomar el autobús, para llegar pronto a la oficina.

2. Hace una semana Ramón fue a acampar en las montañas con su familia.
   a. Su hermano se bañó en el río.
   b. Su hermana bailó toda la noche en una discoteca.
   c. Su papá escaló una montaña.
   d. Su mamá preparó el desayuno.

3. Soy Amanda. Hace dos días fui con algunas amigas a comprar el nuevo disco compacto de Julieta Venegas.
   a. Tomamos el metro.
   b. No pagamos mucho por el disco compacto.
   c. Compramos un taco en la tienda de música.
   d. Encontramos otro disco compacto de Juanes que nos gustó.

4. Hace un año Estela y Ernesto fueron a Europa.
   a. Visitaron el Museo del Prado en Madrid.
   b. Comieron en restaurantes franceses muy buenos.
   c. Subieron a las pirámides de Teotihuacán.
   d. Cruzaron el canal entre Inglaterra y Francia.

Actividad 13 Entrevista: Hechos memorables... una entrevista algo indiscreta

MODELO: E1: ¿Cuánto tiempo hace que empezaste a estudiar español? →
         E2: Hace *seis meses* que empecé a estudiar español.

1. ¿Cuánto tiempo hace que saliste solo/a con un amigo / una amiga por primera vez?
2. ¿Cuánto tiempo hace que te dieron tu primer beso?
3. ¿Cuánto tiempo hace que te graduaste en la escuela secundaria? ¿que te matriculaste en la universidad?
4. ¿Cuánto tiempo hace que nació tu primer hijo / primera hija (primer sobrino / primera sobrina)?
5. ¿Cuánto hace que cumpliste años? ¿Cuántos (años) cumpliste?
6. ¿Cuánto hace que un policía te puso una multa por manejar a exceso de velocidad?

La independencia de Sudamérica

Desde los tiempos de la independencia de los Estados Unidos y de la Revolución Francesa, los jóvenes **criollos** no estaban contentos **a causa de** la preferencia que mostraba España por los **peninsulares.** Cansados de los abusos de poder de los españoles, los criollos **soñaban con** la independencia de sus países.

Simón Bolívar

En el norte de Sudamérica, el criollo Simón Bolívar liberó de los españoles el territorio que ahora ocupan Venezuela, Colombia, Ecuador y Panamá. Formó un solo país en 1819 y lo llamó la Gran Colombia. Su objetivo final era hacer del continente un solo país, fuerte y unido. Pero en vez de incluir más territorios libres, la Gran Colombia se disolvió en 1830. Triste por este evento, Bolívar comentó: «He **arado** en el mar.» Bolívar, gran patriota, murió solo y pobre.

José de San Martín

Después de contribuir a la independencia de su país, el argentino José de San Martín cruzó los Andes en 1817 para liberar a Chile. Victorioso, con la ayuda de Bernardo O'Higgins, siguió hasta Perú, en donde **logró** la liberación del país, abolió la **esclavitud** y estableció la libertad de **imprenta.**

Otro gran patriota, Antonio José de Sucre, contribuyó a la independencia de Ecuador, Perú y Bolivia, y fue el primer presidente de Bolivia. Era muy joven y Bolívar lo consideraba su sucesor natural, pero fue asesinado en 1830, a la edad de 35 años.

Todos los países tienen grandes fiestas para el Día de la Independencia, aunque la independencia sólo benefició a la clase alta. Las masas continuaron viviendo en la miseria, al igual que hoy en día. Ahora, sin embargo, hay movimientos indígenas, como el de los Zapatistas en el sur de México y el de los indígenas de Colombia, Bolivia y Ecuador, que **luchan** contra la explotación.

VOCABULARIO ÚTIL

los criollos	children of Spaniards born in the Americas
a causa de	due to
los peninsulares	Spaniards living in the Americas
soñaban con	would (used to) dream about
arado	plowed
logró	achieved
la esclavitud	slavery
la imprenta	printing press
luchan	fight

Comprensión

1. ¿Qué países liberaron los tres héroes criollos mencionados en la lectura?
2. ¿Qué resultado tuvieron los movimientos de independencia en Sudamérica?

En resumen

De todo un poco

¿Quién lo hizo?

Diga a cuál de las siguientes personas corresponda con cada descripción.

a. Penélope Cruz
b. Pablo Picasso
c. Evo Morales
d. Hernán Cortés
e. Rafael Nadal

f. Michelle Bachelet
g. la reina Isabel la Católica
h. Frida Kahlo
i. Gabriel García Márquez
j. Alfonso Cuarón

1. _____ Escritor colombiano que recibió un Premio Nobel de Literatura en 1982 por sus novelas y cuentos. Hace más de 40 años que se publicó su obra más famosa, *Cien años de soledad*.

2. _____ Se graduó de la Universidad de Chile con título en medicina pediatra hace casi treinta años. Fue elegida presidenta de Chile en 2006. Fue la primera mujer elegida para ese cargo en América del Sur.

3. _____ Tenista español quien ganó el Torneo Abierto de Francia en 2005, 2006 y 2007. Fue finalista en Wimbledon en 2006 y 2007 y ganó el torneo en 2008.

4. _____ Director de cine nacido en México D.F. hace casi 50 años. Dirigió las películas *Y tu mamá también* y *Harry Potter y el prisionero de Azkaban*, entre otras.

5. _____ Conquistó a los aztecas hace aproximadamente 500 años. Quemó sus barcos para no regresar a España.

6. _____ Este famoso artista español murió hace casi 40 años. Pintó más de 1.500 obras, entre las cuales *Guernica*[1] es quizás la más famosa. Vivió y trabajó muchos años en Francia.

7. _____ Esta artista mexicana murió hace más de 50 años, pero hoy en día su arte es todaví a muy popular. Sufrió un accidente muy grave a los 18 años.

8. _____ Se casó con Fernando II de Aragón y gobernó Castilla de 1474 a 1504. Apoyó a Cristóbal Colón.

9. _____ Este activista indígena aymara fue elegido presidente de Bolivia en 2005. Fue el primer presidente indígena de América del Sur.

10. _____ Actriz famosa quien nació en Madrid hace más de 35 años. Actuó en *Volver* del director español Almodóvar. En 2006 fue nominada para los premios Óscar.

Ahora, trabajando en grupos, preparen dos o tres descripciones de personas famosas para toda la clase.

¡Dígalo por escrito!

¡Soy inocente!

Debido a un error de identidad, la policía sospecha que usted participó en un robo que ocurrió el sábado pasado. La policía lo/la interroga a usted. Escriba un diálogo explicando exactamente lo que hizo usted el sábado pasado.

---

[1]Para leer más sobre esta obra, vea la revista en la *Vida y cultura* al fin del **Capítulo 15.**

¡OJO!

En muchos países hispanos se usa la palabra *castellano* para referirse al idioma español. Se oye especialmente en Chile, Argentina y España. Esto se debe a que la reina Isabel la Católica, que era de Castilla, unificó las provincias de España e impuso su idoma: el castellano.

MODELO: POLICÍA: ¿Qué hizo usted el sábado pasado?
                     USTED: Pues, primero...

              POLICÍA: ¿A qué hora? ¿Solo/a o acompañado/a? ¿Fue usted a
                       trabajar? ¿Cuántas horas y dónde?

¡Cuéntenos usted!

Imagínese la noche de un fin de semana perfecto. ¿Qué hizo usted? ¿Salió con amigos
o se quedó en casa? ¿Adónde fue?

LECTURA

Machu Picchu: Un viaje por el tiempo

El año pasado mi maestra de historia organizó una excursión a
Machu Picchu y mis compañeros y yo fuimos **a pie** con ella por
una parte del **Camino Inca.** La excursión fue como un viaje fantástico por el
tiempo.

Primero tomamos un tren a la estación de Chachabamba, donde empezó
nuestra **caminata** a Machu Picchu. La caminata que mucha gente hace por el
Camino Inca es de 43 kilómetros y dura varios días, pero nosotros caminamos
8 kilómetros, nada más.

En el tren me senté al lado de la ventanilla para ver el **paisaje.** Pasamos por
montañas muy verdes, **a lo largo** del Río Urubamba. Me gustó mucho ver ese
paisaje tan bonito desde el tren, pero lo que más me gustó de la excursión fue la
caminata. ¡Algún día quiero caminar los 43 kilómetros del Camino Inca!

PISTAS PARA LEER
Armando González Yamasaki,
autor/narrador de esta
Lectura, es un niño
peruanojaponés de 13 años
que vive en Cuzco, Perú, con
su familia. Armando describe
aquí su excursión a las ruinas
de Machu Picchu, que fue una
experiencia fantástica. Al leer,
visualice el viaje de Armando;
por ejemplo: *montañas verdes,
paisaje bonito, ciudad mágica.*

VOCABULARIO ÚTIL

a pie	*on foot*
el Camino Inca	*the Inca Trail*
la caminata	*walk, hike*
el paisaje	*landscape*
a lo largo	*along*
los precipicios	*cliffs*
incaica	*Incan*
la cordillera	*mountain range*
los antepasados	*ancestors*
las cumbres	*peaks*

(Continúa)

Mi maestra nos dijo que ese camino era como un viaje espiritual para muchas personas indígenas. «Ese camino» dijo, «nos da la oportunidad de admirar el esplendor de Machu Picchu.»

Durante la excursión vimos varios valles, túneles y **precipicios**. Cuando paramos a comer y descansar, la maestra nos habló de la cultura **incaica**. «Esta cultura se mantiene muy viva en los países andinos» explicó la maestra, «los que están en la **cordillera** de los Andes: Colombia, Ecuador, Perú, Bolivia, Chile y Argentina. La civilización incaica se desintegró cuando llegaron los españoles. Pero los quechuas, indígenas del Imperio Incaico, resistieron la asimilación a la cultura hispana. Por eso los quechuas de hoy tienen tanto en común con sus **antepasados** y celebran sus tradiciones diariamente.»

Cuando llegamos al final de la ruta, un sitio llamado Intipunku, todos los estudiantes nos quedamos callados, admirando la vista de Machu Picchu. Mi maestra describió así esa vista: «Es una ciudad mágica entre dos grandes y eternas **cumbres.**»

Me alegré mucho de estar en esa ciudad mágica y pensé en el gran misterio de Machu Picchu. ¿Cómo pudieron los incas construir su ciudad en un lugar tan remoto? ¿Cómo llevaron las piedras hasta allí arriba? ¿Para qué construyeron Machu Picchu? ¿Por qué la abandonaron? Los expertos también se hacen esas preguntas, pero nadie tiene las respuestas. Qué importa eso, ¿verdad? Lo importante es que Machu Picchu existe. Al estar allí, sentí que estaba viajando por el tiempo, visitando un pasado fantástico.

Comprensión

¿Qué hicieron Armando, sus compañeros y la maestra de historia? Busque el orden correcto.

_____ En el tren, Armando se sentó al lado de la ventanilla.
_____ Llegaron a una estación donde empezó la caminata.
_____ El tren pasó por montañas y a lo largo de un río.
_____ Armando pensó en el misterio de Machu Picchu.
_____ Armando se alegró de estar allí.
_____ Vieron túneles y precipicios.
_____ Descansaron y comieron.
_____ Los estudiantes vieron una ciudad mágica.
_____ La maestra les habló de la cultura incaica.

Un paso más... ¡a conversar!

¿Hizo usted una excursión a pie alguna vez, como la caminata de Armando? ¿Caminó mucho? ¿Cuántas millas o kilómetros? ¿Con quién hizo la excursión? ¿Fue una buena experiencia? Describa alguna anécdota interesante de su caminata.

Vea el **Resumen cultural** en este capítulo del *Cuaderno de actividades.*

Vocabulario

La naturaleza

Nature

la arena	sand
la mosca	fly
la ola	wave
el oso (panda)	(panda) bear
la palmera	palm tree

REPASO: el árbol, el lago, el mar, la montaña, el río, el sol

Los lugares

Places

el aire libre	outdoors
la alberca	swimming pool (*Mex.*)
el campo	country(side)
la escuela primaria/secundaria	elementary/high school
el (jardín) zoológico	zoo

PALABRAS SEMEJANTES: América Latina, Asia, el continente, la pirámide

Los verbos en el pasado (irregulares)

Verbs in the Past (Irregular)

almorzar (ue)	to have lunch
almorcé / almorzó	
buscar	to look for
busqué / buscó	
cruzar	to cross
crucé / cruzó	
dar	to give
di / dio	
decir	to say; to tell
dije / dijo	
divertirse (ie, i)	to have a good time
me divertí / se divirtió	
dormir (ue, u)	to sleep
dormí / durmió	
empezar	to start
empecé / empezó	
estar	to be
estuve / estuvo	
hacer	to do; to make
hice / hizo	
ir	to go
fui / fue	
jugar (ue)	to play
jugué / jugó	
leer	to read
leí / leyó	
llegar	to arrive
llegué / llegó	

oír	to hear
oí / oyó	
ponerse (+ *adj.*)	to get; to become (+ *adj.*)
me puse / se puso	
preferir (ie, i)	to prefer
preferí / prefirió	
querer (ie)	to want
quise / quiso	
sentirse (ie, i) (bien / mal)	to feel (good / bad, ill)
me sentí / se sintió	
ser	to be
fui / fue	
servir (i)	to serve
serví / sirvió	
tener	to have
tuve / tuvo	
traer	to bring
traje / trajo	
venir	to come
vine / vino	
ver	to see
vi / vio	
vestirse	to get dressed
me vestí / se vistió	

Más verbos

More Verbs

atar	to tie
atrapar	to catch; to trap
casarse	to get married
castigar	to punish
chocar	to crash (into)
conquistar	to conquer
cumplir años	to have a birthday
dirigir	to direct
enfermarse	to get sick
enojarse	to get angry
estacionar	to park
faltar	to miss; to be lacking
ganar	to win; to earn
gobernar	to govern
hospedarse	to stay (*at a hotel*)
matricularse en	to enroll in
morir (ue) (u)	to die
preguntar	to ask
publicar	to publish
quejarse	to complain
quemar	to burn
quitar	to take away
robar	to steal
salir para (*un lugar*)	to leave for (*a place*)
saludar	to greet
sonar (ue)	to ring; to go off (*alarm*)
subir	to go up

PALABRAS SEMEJANTES: aceptar, arrestar, arruinar, sufrir

Otros sustantivos

Other Nouns

el barco	boat
la batalla	battle
la bolsa	purse
el cargo	position, responsibility
el caudillo	leader
el (reloj) despertador	alarm (clock)
el escritor / la escritora	writer
el espectáculo	show
la estrella de cine / de televisión	movie / television star
el exceso de velocidad	speeding
el grito	shout, scream
el hecho	event
el jugador / la jugadora	player
la multa	traffic ticket; penalty
la obra (de arte)	work (of art)
el premio	prize, award
un rato	a while
el recuerdo	memory
el ruido	noise
el siglo	century
el título	title; degree
el torneo	tournament
el traje de baño	bathing suit

PALABRAS SEMEJANTES: la aventura, la confesión, la emancipación, la gloria, el honor, el kilómetro, el libertador, la medicina, el Premio Nobel, la posibilidad, el/la tenista
REPASO: el ladrón / la ladrona, el metro

Los adjetivos

Adjectives

asustado/a	frightened
demasiado/a(s)	too much (many)
elegido/a	elected
hermoso/a	beautiful
lindo/a	pretty
muchísimo/a	very much
nacido/a	born

PALABRAS SEMEJANTES: azteca, desesperado/a, furioso/a, heroico/a, histórico/a, indígena, indiscreto/a, memorable, reciente, ridículo/a

Los adverbios

Adverbs

algo	somewhat
con cuidado	carefully
en vez de	instead of
poco después	a little later
pronto	soon

PALABRAS SEMEJANTES: aproximadamente, inmediatamente, lógicamente, tranquilamente

Palabras y expresiones útiles

Useful Words and Expressions

¡Auxilio!	Help!
¿Cuánto tiempo hace que... ?	How long ago . . . ?
disculpe(n)	excuse me
Hace... (+ time) (que)	(Time) ago . . .
Hace más de...	It has been more than (+ time)
Hoy en día	Nowadays
lo que	that which, what
los demás	the rest, others
por	through
¡Qué envidia!	Lucky you! (I envy you!)
¿Qué pasa?	What's wrong?
¿Qué pasó?	What happened?
quizás	perhaps
la (última) vez	(last) time

Gramática y ejercicios

¿RECUERDA?

In **Gramática 6.3** you learned that the past tense (preterite) is formed by adding a set of endings to the verb stem. There are only two sets of endings for regular verbs: one for **-ar** verbs and one for **-er/-ir** verbs. Review that section briefly, if necessary.

7.1 Talking about Past Actions: The Preterite of Regular Verbs (Part 2)

Gramática ilustrada

A. You have already seen and used the singular preterite forms of regular verbs many times. Here is the complete set of preterite forms, singular and plural.*

	hablar	**comer**	**escribir**
(yo)	hablé	comí	escribí
(tú)	hablaste	comiste	escribiste
(usted, él/ella)	habló	comió	escribió
(nosotros/as)	hablamos	comimos	escribimos
(vosotros/as)	hablasteis	comisteis	escribisteis
(ustedes, ellos/as)	hablaron	comieron	escribieron

Singular preterite forms:

-ar	**-er/-ir**
-é	-í
-aste	-iste
-ó	-ió

Plural preterite forms:

-ar	**-er/-ir**
-amos	-imos
-asteis	-isteis
-aron	-ieron

Note the following details about the difference between present and preterite forms.

- In regular preterite forms, the stress is always on the final syllable of the **yo** and **usted, él/ella** forms.

Generalmente me levanto a las ocho, pero ayer **me levanté** a las siete.
Usually I get up at 8:00, but yesterday I got up at 7:00.

- **Tú** forms in the preterite do not end in **-s.**

Normalmente me llamas por la noche, pero anoche no me **llamaste.**
Normally you call me at night, but last night you didn't call me.

- Though both present and preterite third-person plural forms end in **-n,** it is always **-ron** in the preterite.

Por lo general mis padres **salen** poco, pero la semana pasada **salieron** cinco veces.
Usually my parents go out very little, but last week they went out five times.

- Notice that the present and preterite **nosotros/as** forms are different in **-er** verbs.

Por lo general **comemos** un poco de carne, pero ayer no **comimos** ninguna.
Usually we eat a little meat, but yesterday we didn't eat any.

In **-ar** and **-ir** verbs, however, the **nosotros/as** form is the same in the preterite and the present tense (**hablamos, escribimos**). The context clarifies whether the speaker intends the present tense or the preterite.

Siempre **salimos** temprano para la universidad, pero ayer **salimos** un poco tarde.
We always leave early for the university, but yesterday we left a little late.

---
*Recognition: **vos hablaste, comiste, escribiste**

buscar: busqué/buscó

llegar: llegué/llegó
jugar: jugué/jugó

empezar: empecé/
    empezó
almorzar: almorcé/
    almorzó

Don't try to remember all of this. Refer to this information when you are writing. In time, you will acquire much of it through listening and reading.

B. If the stem of an **-er/-ir** verb ends in a vowel (**le-er**), the **i** of the **-ió** and **-ieron** endings changes to **y** in the preterite.

> **leer:** leí, leíste, leyó, leímos, leísteis, leyeron
> **oír:** oí, oíste, oyó, oímos, oísteis, oyeron

> Yo **leí** el libro, pero Esteban no lo **leyó**.
> *I read the book, but Esteban didn't read it.*

C. Regular verbs that end in **-car, -gar,** and **-zar** change the spelling of the preterite **yo** form in order to preserve the same sound as the infinitive.*

> **buscar:** bus**qué**, buscaste, buscó, buscamos, buscasteis, buscaron
> **llegar:** lle**gué**, llegaste, llegó, llegamos, llegasteis, llegaron
> **almorzar:** almor**cé**, almorzaste, almorzó, almorzamos, almorzasteis, almorzaron

> **Llegué** al centro a las 4:00.
> *I arrived downtown at 4:00.*

Ejercicio 1

¿Qué hizo Adriana ayer por la mañana? Busque el orden más lógico.

_____ Leyó el periódico.
_____ Llegó al trabajo a las 8:30.
_____ Desayunó cereal con leche y fruta.
_____ Se bañó.
_____ Comió una hamburguesa.
_____ Se levantó a las 7:00.
_____ Almorzó con un amigo.
_____ Manejó el coche al trabajo.
_____ Se puso la ropa (Se vistió).

¿Y qué hizo usted ayer por la mañana? Escriba una lista de cinco a siete actividades.

¡OJO!

In **Ejercicio 1,** your answers to the second part should be original.

Ejercicio 2

Complete los diálogos con formas de **llegar** y **leer.**

> JOSÉ: ¿A qué hora _____¹ (tú) a la universidad?
> CLARA: _____² a las ocho y media. ¿Y tú?
> JOSÉ: Pilar y yo no _____³ hasta las nueve y media porque el metro _____⁴ tarde.
> CLARA: ¿_____⁵ el artículo sobre el viaje a la luna la semana pasada?
> JOSÉ: Sí, lo _____.⁶ (**Lo** *refers back to* **el artículo.**)
> CLARA: ¿Lo _____⁷ Pilar y Andrés?
> JOSÉ: No sé si Andrés lo _____,⁸ pero lo _____⁹ Pilar y yo.

---

*For more information on spelling changes in the preterite, see **Capítulo 7** in the *Cuaderno de actividades.*

Ejercicio 3

Éstas son las actividades de Pilar y su hermana Gloria un domingo del verano pasado en Madrid. ¿Qué oración corresponde a qué dibujo?

a. _____ Leyeron (por) un rato antes de apagar las luces.
b. _____ Caminaron desde la estación del metro hasta su apartamento.
c. _____ Almorzaron hamburguesas en el Burger King de la Gran Vía.
d. _____ Salieron a pasear por el centro de Madrid.
e. _____ Vieron una película francesa.
f. _____ Llegaron a su apartamento a las 12:00 de la noche.
g. _____ Regresaron en el metro.

Ahora, piense en un domingo del verano pasado. ¿Qué actividades hicieron usted y sus amigos (o parientes)? Haga una lista de cinco a siete actividades.

MODELO: Mis amigos y yo *escuchamos música y bailamos en una discoteca.*

7.2 Relating Past Events (Part 1): Verbs with Irregular Preterite Forms

Some verbs have a different stem in the preterite and a slightly different set of endings.*

	tener	**estar**	**poder**	**poner**	**saber**	**hacer**
(yo)	tuve	estuve	pude	puse	supe	hice
(tú)	tuviste	estuviste	pudiste	pusiste	supiste	hiciste
(usted, él/ella)	tuvo	estuvo	pudo	puso	supo	hizo
(nosotros/as)	tuvimos	estuvimos	pudimos	pusimos	supimos	hicimos
(vosotros/as)	tuvisteis	estuvisteis	pudisteis	pusisteis	supisteis	hicisteis
(ustedes, ellos/as)	tuvieron	estuvieron	pudieron	pusieron	supieron	hicieron

---

*Recognition: The **vos** forms in the preterite (regular and irregular) are identical to the **tú** forms: **vos quisiste, fuiste, hiciste.**

	venir	querer	decir	traer	conducir	traducir
(yo)	vine	quise	dije	traje	conduje	traduje
(tú)	viniste	quisiste	dijiste	trajiste	condujiste	tradujiste
(usted, él/ella)	vino	quiso	dijo	trajo	condujo	tradujo
(nosotros/as)	vinimos	quisimos	dijimos	trajimos	condujimos	tradujimos
(vosotros/as)	vinisteis	quisisteis	dijisteis	trajisteis	condujisteis	tradujisteis
(ustedes, ellos/as)	vinieron	quisieron	dijeron	trajeron	condujeron	tradujeron

Many of the most common verbs in Spanish are irregular. Do not try to memorize each form, but refer to the chart when you write. In time, you will acquire these forms through listening and reading.

The preceding tables provide the preterite forms of most common irregular verbs. Look at the tables and you will notice the most important differences!

- Unlike regular preterite verb endings, the endings of the **yo** and **usted, él/ella** forms are not stressed in the last syllable.

—¿Dónde **pusiste** mi chaqueta?
—La **puse** encima de la cama.

—Where did you put my jacket?
—I put it on the bed.

—¿Quién **vino** contigo?
—Nadie; **vine** solo.

—Who came with you?
—Nobody; I came alone.

- The verb **hacer** has a spelling change from **c** to **z** in the **usted, él/ella** form.

Ayer en el gimnasio Alberto **hizo** su tarea y yo **hice** ejercicio.

Yesterday at the gym Alberto did his homework and I exercised.

- The verbs **conducir, decir, traducir,** and **traer** drop the **i** in the **ustedes, ellos/as** form.

—¿Qué te **dijeron** de mí?
—Me **dijeron** que estás locamente enamorado de Carmen.

—What did they tell you about me?
—They told me that you are madly in love with Carmen.

—¿Qué **trajeron** ustedes de comer?
—Trajimos refrescos y sandwiches.

—What did you bring to eat?
—We brought sodas and sandwiches.

- The verbs **dar** and **ver** take the **-er/-ir** endings, but with no written accents. The verbs **ser** and **ir** share the same stem in the past tense. Their forms are thus identical, so the meaning must be inferred from the context.

fui = *I went/was*
fue = *you (pol. sing.) went/were; he/she went/was*

ser/ir (*to be / to go*)

(yo)	**fui**	*I was/went*
(tú)	**fuiste**	*you (inf. sing.) were/went*
(usted, él/ella)	**fue**	*you (pol. sing.) were/went; he/she was/went*
(nosotros/as)	**fuimos**	*we were/went*
(vosotros/as)	**fuisteis**	*you (inf. pl., Spain) were/went*
(ustedes, ellos/as)	**fueron**	*you (pl.) were/went; they were/went*

—¿Qué te **dieron**?
—Mi tío me **dio** dinero.

—*What did they give you?*
—*My uncle gave me money.*

—¿Adónde **fue** Luis anoche?
—**Fue** al cine.

—*Where did Luis go last night?*
—*He went to the movies.*

—¿Qué **fue** ese ruido?
—No **fue** nada. ¡Estás imaginando cosas!

—*What was that noise?*
—*It wasn't anything. You are imagining things!*

Ejercicio 4

Éstas son las actividades de ayer de algunos de los vecinos hispanos. Complete las oraciones con la forma correcta del pretérito de **ver, ir, dar, hacer, decir, traer, poner** o **venir.**

1. Ernesto Saucedo _____ una fiesta para sus amigos.
2. Dice Ernesto: «_____ más de treinta personas a mi fiesta.»
3. Dice Andrea: «Yo _____ una botella de tequila.»
4. Todos _____ que la fiesta fue fantástica.
5. Amanda _____ a Graciela hablando con su novio, Rafael.
6. Ernestito le _____ una cadena de identificación a su perro.
7. Guillermo _____ la tarea para su clase de biología.
8. Dora y Javier _____ al teatro.

Ejercicio 5

Cuente lo que hicieron estas personas.

MODELO: (Soy Pilar.) Anoche fui al cine con mi hermana. Después cenamos en un restaurante y dimos un paseo por el centro. Me acosté muy tarde. →
Pilar *fue* al cine con su hermana. Después *cenaron* en un restaurante y *dieron* un paseo por el centro. Pilar *se acostó* muy tarde.

1. (Soy Ricardo Sícora.) Un sábado por la mañana fui con mis hermanos Pablo y Enrique y unos amigos a una playa cerca de Caracas a bucear. Llegamos temprano a la playa, así que descansé un rato antes de nadar. Buceamos una hora y vimos muchísimos peces y animales marinos. Por la noche hicimos una fogata en la playa y cocinamos pescado en ella. Luego toqué la guitarra y todos cantamos y bailamos hasta muy tarde.
2. (Soy Silvia Bustamante.) Anoche fui con mi novio Nacho Padilla a una fiesta. Llegamos a las 9:00 y cuando entré, vi a Luisa Hernández, una amiga del Instituto de Inglés, donde estudié el año pasado. La saludé y salimos al patio a charlar de los viejos amigos del Instituto. Más tarde bailé mucho con Nacho y tomé una copa de champaña. ¡Regresé a casa un poco mareada!

Ejercicio 6

Diga qué hacen las siguientes personas generalmente, qué hicieron ayer por la tarde y qué van a hacer mañana.

MODELO: Generalmente *Adriana juega al tenis por la tarde,* pero ayer *tradujo un documento del italiano al español* y mañana *va a aprender un nuevo programa de informática.*

	GENERALMENTE	AYER	MAÑANA
Pilar	asistir a clase	dormir toda la tarde	visitar a una amiga
Andrea y Pedro	almorzar con sus hijas	estar en casa todo el día	ir de compras
Adriana	jugar al tenis después de salir del trabajo	traducir un documento del italiano al español	aprender a usar un nuevo programa de informática
doña Lola	quedarse en casa	tomar café con sus amigas	cocinar toda la tarde
Carla y Rogelio	estudiar en la biblioteca	ir a la playa	lavar el carro

7.3 More about Relating Past Events (Part 2): Stem-Changing Verbs in the Preterite

¿RECUERDA?

You'll recall from **Gramática 4.1** that a small number of verbs have stem-vowel changes in the present-tense forms in which the spoken stress is on the stem vowel: **pienso** versus **pensar**, **duermo** versus **dormir**. (See also **Gramática 2.3, 3.2,** and **5.2** to review other familiar verbs with this type of stem change.)

Present:
  cierro/cierra
  pienso/piensa
Past:
  cerré/cerró
  pensé/pensó

A. In most cases, the vowels of stem-changing verbs do *not* change in the preterite forms. Here is a comparison of present-tense and preterite forms of the verbs **cerrar** (*to close*) and **contar** (*to tell, relate*).

		cerrar		contar	
		PRESENT	PAST	PRESENT	PAST
(yo)		cierro	cerré	cuento	conté
(tú)		cierras	cerraste	cuentas	contaste
(usted, él/ella)		cierra	cerró	cuenta	contó
(nosotros/as)		cerramos	cerramos	contamos	contamos
(vosotros/as)		cerráis	cerrasteis	contáis	contasteis
(ustedes, ellos/as)		cierran	cerraron	cuentan	contaron

B. A few verbs, however, all in the **-ir** group, do change their stem vowel in the **usted, él/ella** and the **ustedes, ellos/as** forms of the preterite. There are two possible changes: **e → i** and **o → u.** The present-tense and preterite forms of the verbs **divertirse**

(*to have a good time*) and **dormir** (*to sleep*) are given below.* Other common verbs with this change are **sentir** (*to feel*), **sugerir** (*to suggest*), **preferir** (*to prefer*), **mentir** (*to lie*), and **morir** (*to die*).

	divertirse		**dormir**	
	PRESENT	*PAST*	*PRESENT*	*PAST*
(yo)	me divierto	me divertí	duermo	dormí
(tú)	te diviertes	te divertiste	duermes	dormiste
(usted, él/ella)	se divierte	se divirtió	duerme	durmió
(nosotros/as)	nos divertimos	nos divertimos	dormimos	dormimos
(vosotros/as)	os divertís	os divertisteis	dormís	dormisteis
(ustedes, ellos/as)	se divierten	se divirtieron	duermen	durmieron

Yo **dormí** bien. Estela **durmió** mal.

—¿**Se divirtió** usted anoche?
—Sí, **me divertí** mucho.

I slept well. Estela slept poorly.

—*Did you have fun last night?*
—*Yes, I had a great time.*

> Present:
>   me div**ie**rto /
>   se div**ie**rte
>   d**ue**rmo/d**ue**rme
> Past:
>   me div**e**rtí / se div**i**rtió
>   d**o**rmí/d**u**rmió

Ejercicio 7

Complete los siguientes diálogos con la forma correcta de los verbos.

DORMIR
—¿Cuántas horas _____¹ tú anoche?
— _____² solamente cinco.
—¿Generalmente _____³ tan pocas horas?
—No, generalmente _____⁴ por lo menos siete, a veces ocho.

SENTIR(SE)
—¿Tú te _____⁵ mal ahora?
—No, me _____⁶ bastante bien.
—Pero anoche te _____⁷ muy mal, ¿verdad?
—Sí, anoche me _____⁸ mal por un dolor de cabeza.

DIVERTIR(SE)
—¿Te _____⁹ anoche en la fiesta?
—Sí, me _____¹⁰ muchísimo. ¿Se _____¹¹ tu esposa?
—No, no se _____¹² porque no le gustó la música.

MENTIR
—Tú me _____,¹³ ¿verdad?
—No, no te _____.¹⁴ Te dije la verdad.
—Pues, alguien me _____.¹⁵
—No fui yo.

> Do not try to memorize all these forms, but refer to the chart when you write. In time, you will acquire the forms through listening and reading.

---

*This same stem-vowel change also occurs in the present participle: **durmiendo** (*sleeping*), **divirtiéndose** (*having fun*).

¿RECUERDA?

In **Gramática 5.1** you learned that the indirect object pronouns (**me, te, le, nos, os, les**) are frequently used with verbs of informing such as **hablar, preguntar,** and **contestar.** Review that section briefly.

7.4 Reporting the Past: Indirect Object Pronouns with *decir*

In the preterite, the verb **decir** (*to say; to tell*) is commonly used with indirect object pronouns to report speech.

decir		
(yo)	dije	I said
(tú)	dijiste	you (inf. sing.) said
(usted, él/ella)	dijo	you (pol. sing.) said; he/she said
(nosotros/as)	dijimos	we said
(vosotros/as)	dijisteis	you (inf. pl., Spain) said
(ustedes, ellos/as)	dijeron	you (pl.) said; they said

Le dije que... = *I told you (pol. sing.)/him/her that . . .*
Me dijo que... = *You (pol. sing.)/He/She told me that . . .*
Le dijimos que... = *We told you (pol. sing.)/him/her that . . .*

Remember that **dijo** is a *preterite* form, not a present-tense form.

Le dije que... — *I told (said to) you/him/her that . . .*
Te dijimos que... — *We told (said to) you that . . .*
Me dijo que... — *You/He/She told (said to) me that . . .*
Me dijeron que... — *You/They told (said to) me that . . .*

Note that the phrase **Le dijo que...** has several possible meanings; interpretation depends on the context.

Le dijo que... —
He/She told him that . . .
He/She told her that . . .
He/She told you that . . .
You told him/her that . . .

Don Anselmo fue a la casa de doña Rosita y **le dijo que** sus hijos van a llegar pasado mañana.

Don Anselmo went to doña Rosita's house and told her that his children are going to arrive the day after tomorrow.

Ejercicio 8

Complete esta conversación telefónica usando pronombres de complemento indirecto (**me, te, le, nos, les**) y las formas correctas del pretérito del verbo **decir** (**dije, dijiste, dijo, dijimos, dijeron**).

GRACIELA: No oigo bien, Amanda. ¿Qué _____¹ _____²?
AMANDA: _____³ _____⁴ que no voy a estar en casa esta noche.
GRACIELA: ¡Ay, lo mismo _____⁵ _____⁶ tu hermano Guillermo! ¿Adónde vas?
AMANDA: Es que mi madre _____⁷ _____⁸ que hay una venta especial con precios muy rebajados hoy en El Palacio de Hierro.
GRACIELA: ¿Y qué _____⁹ _____¹⁰ tú a ella? ¿No _____¹¹ _____¹² que hoy tenemos mucha tarea?
AMANDA: Hmmm... no, pero _____¹³ _____¹⁴ que tú quieres ir con nosotras. Es verdad, ¿no?

GRACIELA: Ay, sí, Amanda, sí quisiera acompañarlas, pero... ¡_____¹⁵
_____¹⁶ a mi papá que no voy a comprar más ropa este mes!

AMANDA: Pues, ven con nosotras pero... ¡deja tu dinero en casa!

GRACIELA: ¡Imposible!

7.5 Expressing *ago:* hacer + Time

The verb **hace** followed by an amount of time is equivalent to English expressions of time with *ago.*

hace cinco minutos — *five minutes ago*
hace una hora — *an hour ago*
hace dos años — *two years ago*

—¿Cuándo salió Ricardo? — *—When did Ricardo leave?*
—**Hace una hora.** — *—An hour ago.*

There are two ways to formulate the question *How long ago did . . . ?*

¿Cuánto (tiempo) hace que + preterite?
¿Hace cuánto (tiempo) que + preterite?

—Srta. Durán, ¿**cuánto (tiempo) hace que** usted **fue** a México? — *—Ms. Durán, how long ago did you go to Mexico?*
—**Fui hace tres años.** — *—I went three years ago.*

> **¿Cuánto hace que llegaste?**
> *How long ago did you arrive?*
> **Hace una hora.**
> *An hour ago.*
>
> **¿Hace cuánto tiempo que usted se graduó?**
> *How long ago did you graduate?*
> **Hace 10 años.**
> *Ten years ago.*

Ejercicio 9

Estela está de mal humor hoy y acusa a Ernesto de no hacer nada para ayudarla. ¿Cómo puede defenderse Ernesto?

MODELO: ESTELA: ¡Tú nunca lavas los platos en esta casa!
ERNESTO: Pero, Estela, *lavé* los platos *hace una hora.* (Pero, Estela, *los lavé hace una hora.*)

1. ¡Tú nunca limpias el baño!
2. ¡Tú nunca barres el patio!
3. ¡La alfombra está sucia porque tú nunca pasas la aspiradora!
4. ¡Nunca bañas al pobre perro!
5. Estoy cansada de comer las mismas cosas. ¡Tú nunca me llevas a ningún restaurante elegante!

> **¡OJO!**
> In **Ejercicio 9,** use first-person preterite forms and any appropriate time expression after **hace: dos días, unas horas, una semana,** etc.

Ejercicio 10

¿Sabe usted mucho de historia? ¿Cuánto hace que... ?

MODELO: ¿Cuánto (tiempo) hace que terminó la Segunda Guerra Mundial? (1945) →
Terminó hace más de sesenta años.

1. ¿Cuánto tiempo hace que Alejandro G. Bell inventó el teléfono? (1876)
2. ¿Cuánto tiempo hace que Gustavo Eiffel construyó la Torre Eiffel? (1889)
3. ¿Cuánto hace que murió Pancho Villa? (1923)
4. ¿Cuánto tiempo hace que Colón llegó a América? (1492)
5. ¿Cuánto hace que murió Francisco Franco, el dictador de España? (1975)
6. ¿Cuánto hace que Alemania se unificó? (1990)
7. ¿Cuánto hace que los países de la antigua Unión Soviética se independizaron? (1991)

> **¡OJO!**
> In **Ejercicio 10,** use short answers with **hace** + time only. Answers will vary according to the year in which the text is used.

La comida

METAS

In **Capítulo 8** you will learn to talk about food, nutrition, shopping for and preparing food, and ordering meals in restaurants.

Bodegón con chiles, por Antonio Vinciguerra (Honduras)

Sobre el artista: Antonio Vinciguerra nació en San Pedro Sula, Honduras, en 1954. Estudió humanidades y ciencias antes de iniciar su carrera de artista. Sus obras se exhiben en exposiciones públicas y también en colecciones privadas. En *Bodegón con chiles* utiliza la técnica de pastel óleo. Vinciguerra reside en Honduras.

¡Conozca Honduras!

Nombre del país: la República de Honduras

Ciudad capital: Tegucigalpa

Ciudades principales: San Pedro Sula, La Ceiba, El Progreso

Moneda: el lempira

Idiomas: el español (oficial), las lenguas amerindias

Población: 7.500.000

Día de la Independencia: el 15 de septiembre

Fiestas típicas: el Día de la Virgen de Suyapa, el Nacimiento del General Francisco Morazán

Comidas típicas: las baleadas, la sopa de caracol, el atol, los pasteles de picadillo, el ayote en miel

Música típica: la punta, los bailes folclóricos regionales

Gente famosa: José Antonio Velásquez, Ramón Amaya Amador, Ramón Villeda Morales

Código del país por Internet: **.hn**

Voces hondureñas

a todo mecate	muy rápido
andar hule	tener poco dinero
un cipote	un niño/muchacho
un pingüino	un helado

¡Conozca El Salvador!

Nombre del país: la República de El Salvador

Ciudad capital: San Salvador

Ciudades principales: Santa Ana, San Miguel

Moneda: el dólar

Idiomas: el español (oficial), el nahuatl

Población: 7.000.000

Día de la Independencia: el 15 de septiembre

Fiestas típicas: las Fiestas de Agosto al Divino Salvador del Mundo, el Día de los Indios, el Día de la Reina de la Paz

Comidas típicas: la pupusa, la yuca frita, el pan con pavo, el atol de elote, los tamales de elote, el chilate con nuegados

Música típica: Instrumentos: los raspadores, los timbales.

Gente famosa: Farabundo Martí, Alberto Masferrer, Roque Dalton, el arzobispo Óscar Arnulfo Romero, Pancho Lara

Código del país por Internet: **.sv**

Voces salvadoreñas

un(a) bicho/a	un bebé
un(a) chero/a	una persona
el chuzón	el autobús
un(a) guanaco/a	un(a) salvadoreño/a
el pisto	el dinero

En este capítulo...

ACTIVIDADES DE COMUNICACIÓN

- Las comidas, las bebidas y la nutrición
- La compra y la preparación de la comida
- Los restaurantes

EN RESUMEN

LECTURAS Y CULTURA

- **Ventanas culturales**
  La lengua: Comidas y palabras
- **Enlace a la literatura**
  «Jitomates risueños», por Francisco X. Alarcón
- **Ventanas culturales**
  Las costumbres: ¡Estoy como agua para chocolate!
- **Lectura**
  Los deliciosos platos andinos

GRAMÁTICA Y EJERCICIOS

8.1 More about Referring to People and Objects already Mentioned: Personal and Impersonal Direct Object Pronouns **lo, la, los,** and **las**

8.2 More about Expressing Likes: The Verbs **gustar** and **encantar**

8.3 Making Negative Statements and Questions: *No, never*

8.4 Expressing *one* or *you:* The Impersonal **se**

8.5 Using Stem-Changing Verbs Like **pedir** and **servir:** Present-Tense and Preterite Forms

Actividades de comunicación y lecturas

Las comidas, las bebidas y la nutrición

✳ **Lea Gramática 8.1–8.2.**

Los platos típicos

la paella
(España)

el tamal
(México y
Centroamérica)

el casado de pollo
(Costa Rica)

¿La paella?
La hice ayer.

el plátano frito
(El Caribe, México y
Centroamérica)

las empanadas
(Argentina y Sudamérica)

el chile relleno
(México)

el flan
(México y España)

la parrillada
(Argentina)

las enchiladas ← el arroz

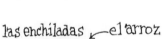

las tortillas de maíz

los frijoles

El arroz, los frijoles y las tortillas
contienen muchos carbohidratos.

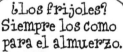
¿Los frijoles?
Siempre los como
para el almuerzo.

Las bebidas

las aguas frescas

la   la
jamaica   horchata

el batido de leche

el café con leche

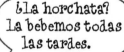
¿La horchata?
La bebemos todas
las tardes.

La leche contiene calcio y proteína.

la cerveza

el vino rosado

el vino tinto

el vino blanco

276

Las carnes, las aves, el pescado y los mariscos

la carne de res
el cangrejo
la langosta
los camarones
las almejas
el hígado
el pescado
las ostras
la chuleta de cerdo

El pollo frito contiene mucha grasa.
La carne, el pollo y los mariscos tienen mucha proteína.

Las legumbres

las mazorcas de maíz
el apio
las zanahorias
el ajo
los guisantes
las habichuelas
los tomates
la cebolla
el pepino
los rábanos
las calabacitas

Las legumbres son muy nutritivas. Muchas contienen vitamina A.

Las frutas

la piña
la naranja
el durazno
la sandía
las uvas
las fresas
el mango
los albaricoques
la papaya
la toronja
la manzana
el plátano (la banana)

La naranja y la toronja contienen mucha vitamina C.
La sandía y la papaya tienen mucho azúcar.
El albaricoque contiene mucho calcio.

Actividad 1 Conversación: Las comidas del día

A. Diga si comemos estas comidas para el desayuno, para el almuerzo o para la cena.

MODELOS: ¿Los huevos revueltos? *Los comemos para el desayuno.*
¿La sopa? *La comemos para el almuerzo o la cena.*

los huevos revueltos	el pollo frito	la ensalada de lechuga
los guisantes	las enchiladas	el tocino
las legumbres	la coliflor	el yogur
la sopa	los tacos	las chuletas de cerdo
el pan tostado con jalea	los panqueques	las papas fritas
las hamburguesas	el cereal	el arroz
un sándwich	los espárragos	el maíz

B. Ahora mire la lista de comidas otra vez y diga con qué frecuencia las come y si le gustan o no.

MODELOS: E1: ¿El yogur? Nunca lo como; no me gusta.
E2: A mí tampoco me gusta.

E1: ¿Las papas fritas? Siempre las como. ¡Me encantan!
E2: A mí no. Prefiero la ensalada.

Y tú, ¿qué dices?

(No) Me gusta(n)...	A mí, sí.	(Casi) Nunca
Me encanta(n)	A mí, no.	Siempre
A mí también.		A veces
A mí tampoco.		De vez en cuando

Actividad 2 Intercambios: La nutrición

¿Qué comidas son más ricas en proteína, en carbohidratos y en vitaminas? ¿Cuáles contienen más grasa? Mire los dibujos de las comidas al comienzo del capítulo. Trabajando con su compañero/a, pónganlas en uno (o más) de los cinco grupos de la siguiente tabla.

MODELO: E1: El arroz tiene muchos carbohidratos.
E2: Sí, y la carne de res contiene proteína y mucha grasa.

LA PROTEÍNA	LOS CARBOHIDRATOS	EL CALCIO	LA VITAMINA A Ó C	LA GRASA
	el arroz			las papas fritas

Actividad 3 Intercambios: ¿Qué vamos a comer hoy?

Primero, mire la lista de comidas. Luego prepare dos menús completos para el día (desayuno, almuerzo y cena): un menú con comida saludable solamente y otro con sus comidas y bebidas favoritas. Luego, converse con su(s) compañero(s) sobre los dos menús.

DESAYUNO	ALMUERZO	CENA
◆ fruta: toronja, naranja, piña, durazno, uvas, etc. ◆ cereal frío ◆ panqueques ◆ huevos rancheros, fritos, revueltos, etc. ◆ pan tostado (mantequilla) ◆ pan tostado a la francesa ◆ salchichas/ tocino ◆ café/té caliente ◆ leche (descremada) ◆ batido de leche ◆ donas ◆ avena ◆ yogur ◆ ¿ ?	◆ sopa: de legumbres, de frijoles, de cebolla, etc. ◆ ensalada de tomate ◆ ensalada de fruta fresca ◆ un sándwich: de atún, de jamón y queso, de pollo ◆ hamburguesa ◆ papas fritas ◆ tacos ◆ burritos ◆ limonada ◆ jugos naturales ◆ agua mineral ◆ refresco ◆ té caliente/helado ◆ ¿ ?	◆ pescado: a la parrilla, frito, al horno, etc. ◆ bistec ◆ ensalada verde ◆ legumbres: bróculi, coliflor, habichuelas, etc. ◆ camarones ◆ langosta ◆ enchiladas ◆ tamales ◆ chiles rellenos ◆ helado ◆ pastel o flan ◆ galletas de chocolate ◆ cerveza, vino, etc. ◆ ¿ ?

MODELO:
E1: ¿Qué comidas saludables escogiste?
E2: Escogí *media toronja y yogur* para el desayuno. Para el almuerzo, escogí *ensalada de frutas y agua mineral*. Para la cena, escogí *ensalada verde y pescado a la parrilla*.
E1: ¿Y qué prefieres *desayunar/almorzar/cenar*?
E2: Prefiero...

Actividad 4 Definiciones: Los alimentos

Combine cada definición de la izquierda con un alimento de la derecha.

1. Es una legumbre anaranjada que contiene vitamina A.
2. Esta fruta de cáscara amarilla crece en las zonas tropicales.
3. Es un postre hecho de huevos, leche y azúcar. Es muy popular en los países hispanos.
4. Es una legumbre larga y verde que se usa con frecuencia en las ensaladas.
5. Son muy populares en la cocina mexicana. Se sirven con tortillas.
6. Éstas son uvas secas.
7. Es una bebida preparada con leche y helado o leche y fruta.
8. Es un plato de arroz, carne y mariscos, típico de España.

a. el batido de leche
b. la paella
c. la zanahoria
d. los frijoles
e. el plátano
f. el flan
g. el durazno
h. el pepino
i. las pasas
j. la manzana

VENTANAS CULTURALES La lengua

Comidas y palabras

Usted come sándwiches a veces, ¿no es cierto? Pues si pide un sándwich en un restaurante de España, debe llamarlo «bocadillo». ¿Le gusta el pastel? Entonces aprenda sus otros nombres: «bizcocho» en Puerto Rico, «queque» en Costa Rica y «torta» en España. Los cubanos lo llaman «cake», que se pronuncia «quey». Para decir «helado» en México, se usa una palabra del clima: algo frío y blanco que cae del cielo. ¿Puede **adivinar** lo que es? Sí, el helado es «la nieve».

Las legumbres son verduras en algunos países y hortalizas en otros. En todos los sitios, los vegetales son plantas de cualquier tipo. La palabra que se usa en Uruguay y Argentina para la fresa es «frutilla» y en Argentina las habichuelas se llaman «chauchas». En España, México y otros países la banana es «plátano». Los españoles llaman «patata» a la papa y **«zumo»** al jugo de fruta. La palabra para **«batata»** es «camote» en México y en los países andinos, «ñame» en Colombia y Venezuela y «boniato» en Cuba.

En muchos casos, los nombres de las frutas y legumbres se originan en el idioma indígena de cada país. Por ejemplo, las habichuelas son «ejotes» en México. La palabra «ejote» (*éjotl*) es náhuatl, idioma que **hablaban** los aztecas, habitantes de México al llegar los españoles en 1519. En todo el mundo hispano hay muchos alimentos que **heredamos** de los antiguos mexicanos: entre otros, *aguácatl* (aguacate), *élotl* (elote), *xocólatl* (chocolate), *jitómatl* (**jitomate**) y *guajólotl* (guajolote, pavo). También de origen náhuatl son *cóyotl*, *tómatl* y *chilli*. Es fácil adivinar lo que significan esas **palabras prestadas,** ¿verdad?

VOCABULARIO ÚTIL

adivinar	*to guess*
el zumo	*fruit juice*
la batata	*sweet potato*
hablaban	*spoke (used to speak)*
heredamos	*we inherited*
jitomate	*red tomato (Mex.)*
las palabras prestadas	*borrowed words*

Comprensión

1. ¿Cómo se le llama al pastel en los siguientes países?
    a. Puerto Rico **b.** Costa Rica **c.** España **d.** Cuba
2. ¿Cómo se dicen en español estas palabras del náhuatl?
    a. cóyotl **b.** aguácatl **c.** tómatl **d.** xocólatl **e.** jitómatl

Actividad 5   Conversación: La mesa

el cuenco
la fuente de sopa
el cucharón
el salero y el pimentero
la jarra
la copa
la cuchara
el vaso
la taza
el platillo
el tenedor
el cuchillo
la cucharita
la servilleta
el plato
el plato hondo
el mantel

Parte 1. Diga para qué sirven estos objetos de la mesa. Use las siguientes palabras y frases útiles.

MODELO: *El salero* sirve para *guardar la sal.*

Parte 2. ¿Sabe poner la mesa? Pregúntele a un compañero / una compañera dónde va cada objeto en la mesa. Miren el dibujo y usen **al lado de, entre, a la derecha de, a la izquierda de, enfrente de** o **encima de.**

MODELO: E1: ¿Dónde va *el tenedor*?
              E2: Va *a la izquierda del* plato.

Una familia a la mesa

Actividad 6 Entrevista: La comida en casa

1. ¿Qué desayunas por lo general? ¿Qué comiste esta mañana antes de salir de casa? ¿Qué almuerzas normalmente? ¿Qué almorzaste hoy? (¿Qué vas a almorzar hoy?)

2. ¿Qué bebidas prefieres para el desayuno / el almuerzo / la cena? ¿Tomas café o té durante el día? ¿Lo tomas con o sin azúcar? ¿con o sin leche?

3. ¿Prefieres comer más al mediodía o por la noche? ¿Por qué? ¿Comes entre comidas? ¿Qué comes?

4. ¿Cenas en tu casa generalmente o sales a cenar? ¿Con quién? ¿Qué cenas? ¿Qué prefieres comer de postre?

5. Generalmente, ¿comes mientras ves la televisión? ¿Te gustan las palomitas de maíz? ¿Les pones mantequilla o sal? ¿Qué otra cosa te gusta comer en casa?

Enlace a la literatura

«Jitomates risueños», por Francisco X. Alarcón

Selección de su libro *Jitomates risueños* (1997)

Francisco X. Alarcón (1954) es un famoso poeta chicano que vive y trabaja de profesor en Davis, California. Alarcón ha publicado varios libros: *Cuerpo en llamas* (1990) y *Del otro lado de la noche* (2002), entre otros. Sus poemas para niños aparecen en *Jitomates risueños* (1997) y *Los ángeles andan en bicicleta* (1999). El poema aquí incluido presenta una hermosa imagen de los tomates.

Jitomates[1] risueños

en el jardín   risueños[3]
plantamos   se ponen
jitomates   colorados[4]

los vegetales   convirtiendo
más felices   sus arbustos
de todos   alambrados[5]

alegres   en árboles
se redondean[2]   de Navidad
de sabor   en primavera

Actividad creativa: En el jardín

¿Le gustan los jitomates? ¿Qué otras frutas o legumbres le gustan? Escriba un breve poema sobre su legumbre o fruta favorita. Empiece con los versos de Alarcón:

En el jardín
plantamos...

[1]*Tomatoes (Mex.)*   [2]*se... they grow round*   [3]*laughing, giddy*   [4]*se... they turn red*   [5]*sus... their wire-framed bushes*

La compra y la preparación de la comida

✴ **Lea Gramática 8.3–8.4.**

una taza de harina

una media taza de azúcar

una cucharada de mantequilla

una cucharadita de sal

media cucharadita de bicarbonato de soda

un tarro de mayonesa

el aderezo para la ensalada

una lata de atún

un paquete de fideos

la carne molida

A mí no me gusta el atún.

¡A mí tampoco!

la sopa enlatada

la comida preelaborada

los guisantes congelados

Muchas comidas preelaboradas contienen conservantes y colorantes.

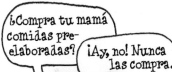
¿Compra tu mamá comidas pre- elaboradas?

¡Ay, no! Nunca las compra.

Se cortan varias rebanadas de tomate.

Se ralla el queso.

Se corta una papaya en trozos pequeños.

Se pica la cebolla.

¿Hay papayas?

Sí, pero ninguna está madura.

Actividad 7 Definiciones: La preparación de la comida

Combine cada descripción de la izquierda con una palabra de la derecha.

1. Se pone en la ensalada.
2. Para preparar un sándwich de queso, se corta el queso en _____.
3. Se usa mucho en la preparación de pasteles y galletas.
4. Si no se encuentran frutas o legumbres frescas, se pueden comprar _____.
5. Es un líquido dorado, muy espeso y dulce que se usa mucho en el té.
6. La receta pide ¼ de _____ de sal.

a. congeladas
b. la harina
c. la papaya
d. la miel
e. cucharadita
f. el aderezo
g. vainilla
h. rebanadas

TASCA MEDITERRANEA

purísima
165

especialidad
TAPAS
calientes
y frías

• sandwichs con sabor mediterráneo
• desagunos
• onces
• almuerzos ejecutivos (plato de fondo + ensalada y postre) €8.50

abierto desde las 9.30 A.M.

Actividad 8 Del mundo hispano: Supermercado El Diamante

Imagínese que usted va a ir al supermercado El Diamante en Puerto Rico para hacer la compra. Estudie las dos listas y use la ilustración de la página siguiente para calcular el precio total de cada una.

LISTA 1

1 paquete de tocino
2 latas de sopa de legumbres
2 aguacates
3 libras de carne molida
2 libras de limones
14 onzas de avena

LISTA 2

1 libra de carne molida
1 tarro de 16 onzas de mayonesa
3 libras de cebollas amarillas
1 paquete de zanahorias
2 libras de manzanas
1 sandía de ocho libras

Actividad 9 Asociaciones: Las comidas y la cocina

A. Busquen la palabra que no pertenece a cada grupo y expliquen por qué.

MODELO: la salchicha, la hamburguesa, la chuleta de cerdo, la pera
La pera no pertenece a esta lista porque *no es carne.*

1. el apio, el pepino, las nueces, los guisantes
2. el flan, el helado, las aceitunas, el pastel
3. la miel, el panecillo, la mermelada, la jalea
4. la sal, el azúcar, la harina, la mostaza
5. la horchata, las almejas, los camarones, la langosta

B. ¿Cual es su opinión?

MODELO: E1: ¿Te gusta(n) el/la/los/las _____?
E2: Sí, me encanta(n). / No, no me gusta(n) para nada.

Actividad 10 Orden lógico: ¿Cómo se prepara(n)... ?

Ponga en orden los pasos para la preparación de estas comidas.

UNA QUESADILLA

_____ Se saca la quesadilla de la sartén.

_____ Se dobla la tortilla.

_____ Se saca una lata de chiles y una tortilla de harina.

_____ Se pone en una sartén con un poco de aceite.

_____ Se pone el queso y un chile sobre un lado de la tortilla.

_____ Se tapa la sartén y se fríe la quesadilla tres minutos de cada lado.

_____ Se ralla el queso.

_____ Se sirve con salsa y se come.

LOS CHILES RELLENOS

_____ Se baten los huevos.

_____ Se pelan los chiles.

_____ Se mojan los chiles en el huevo batido.

_____ Se asan los chiles.

_____ Se cortan varias rebanadas de queso.

_____ Se les quitan las semillas.

_____ Se pone una rebanada de queso en cada chile.

_____ Se fríen.

Actividad 11 Narración: Vamos a preparar pupusas

Ponga en orden los pasos en la página siguiente para la preparación de las pupusas, una comida típica de El Salvador.

Palabras útiles

primero   después

luego   finalmente

LOS PASOS

_____ Se amasa bien y se hace una tortilla.

_____ Se sirve con el curtido (una ensalada de repollo [*cabbage*], vinagre y chile).

_____ Se palmea para formar de nuevo una tortilla.

_____ Se sacan los ingredientes: la harina de maíz, el queso fresco y los frijoles.

_____ Dentro de la tortilla se pone una cucharada de queso y otra de frijoles.

_____ Se calienta la sartén y se fríe las pupusas de cada lado por dos o tres minutos.

_____ Se le agrega agua a la harina de maíz y se mezcla.

_____ Se cierra la masa y se forma una bolita.

> **«Las pupusas», por Jorge Argueta**
>
> Las pupusas
> son redondas
> como la letra «O»
>
> Las pupusas
> son la más sabrosa
> memoria de casa
>
> Las pupusas
> las encontraba
> en la mesa
>
> cuando mi mamá
> me llamaba por las tardes
> «Jorgito, vente a comer»

Actividad 12 Entrevista: Hacer la compra

1. ¿Quién hace la compra en tu casa?
2. ¿Se compran todos los comestibles en un supermercado o en varias tiendas pequeñas?
3. ¿Compras muchas legumbres y frutas?
4. ¿Compras muchas comidas preelaboradas? ¿Lees las etiquetas de las comidas para determinar si contienen colorantes o conservantes?
5. ¿Quién prepara las comidas en tu casa? ¿Te gusta cocinar? ¿Qué platos sabes preparar?
6. ¿Compras mucha comida chatarra (*junk food*)? ¿Qué compras?

VENTANAS CULTURALES   Las costumbres

¡Estoy como agua para chocolate!

Si una persona mexicana exclama «¡Estoy como agua para chocolate!», eso quiere decir que está muy enojada, a punto de **hervir** como el agua. Esta expresión tiene su origen en la preparación del chocolate caliente en México. Para hacerlo, se pone agua a calentar y, cuando empieza a hervir, se le echan **trozos** de chocolate en barra. Luego **se bate** todo a mano con un **molinillo** y muy pronto **queda lista** la rica y tradicional bebida.

La famosa escritora mexicana Laura Esquivel usó esta expresión coloquial para dar título a su novela *Como agua para chocolate* (1990); cada capítulo del libro empieza con una **receta** de la cocina de México. Si usted quiere descubrir aspectos interesantes de la cultura mexicana, le recomendamos esta novela, en la cual se combinan los temas de la comida, el **enojo** y el amor apasionado. También puede ver la película, que resultó ser muy popular.

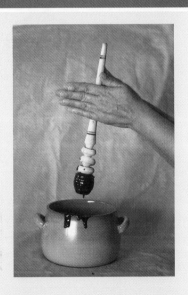

Comprensión

1. Describa la preparación del chocolate caliente en México.
2. ¿Cuáles son los temas de la novela *Como agua para chocolate*?

VOCABULARIO ÚTIL	
hervir	*boil*
los trozos	*pieces, chunks*
se bate	*is whipped*
el molinillo	*beater, whip*
queda lista	*is ready*
la receta	*recipe*
el enojo	*anger*

Los restaurantes

✳ **Lea Gramática 8.5.**

Pedro y Andrea pidieron una ensalada, bistec al punto, papas fritas y bróculi.

El cocinero les preparó un plato especial.

El mesero les sirvió la comida.

Andrea tomó una copa de vino tinto, pero Pedro prefirió tomar agua mineral.

Comieron con gusto.

Pagaron la cuenta con su tarjeta de crédito.

Dejaron una buena propina.

la carne cruda   el bistec   poco asado/ poco cocido   al punto/ cocido   bien asado/ bien cocido

Actividad 13 Narración: Mayín Durán sale a cenar

Lea las siguientes oraciones y póngalas en orden, según los dibujos. Luego, trabaje con un compañero / una compañera para narrar la historia.

_____ Comieron y conversaron.

_____ Pidieron la cuenta.

_____ Mayín pidió agua mineral y su amigo pidió un refresco.

_____ Mayín y su amigo pidieron la comida.

_____ Los dos pidieron postre.

_____ Pagaron la cuenta y dejaron una propina.

_____ Salieron a cenar.

_____ El mesero les sirvió la comida.

_____ Tomaron sus bebidas y conversaron, y luego el mesero les preguntó si estaban listos para pedir la comida.

_____ Salieron a pasear.

_____ El mesero les preguntó si querían tomar algo.

_____ Leyeron el menú.

Actividad 14 Intercambios: Restaurante Mi Casita

A. Lea el menú del Restaurante Mi Casita. Luego hágale preguntas a un compañero / un compañera sobre los precios. Siga el modelo.

MODELO: E1: ¿Cuánto cuestan *los tamales de puerco*?
E2: Cuestan *$80.00* pesos.

Restaurante Mi Casita

Rica comida mexicana e internacional a precios módicos

Plato del día:
Lasaña, pan de ajo, ensalada mixta, sopa minestrone $100.00

Antojitos mexicanos

Se sirven para el almuerzo y la cena. (Con cada uno se incluye pan o tortillas, ensalada, arroz y frijoles o sopa del día.)

Enchiladas (3)	verdes o rojas	$73.50
Tostadas (2)	de res o de pollo	62.00
Tacos (4)	de res o de pollo	63.50
Burritos (2)	de res y/o frijoles	55.00
Chiles rellenos (2) de carne o queso		77.50
Tamales de puerco con chile verde (3)		80.00
Tamales dulces con almendras y pasas (3)		50.00

Rincón internacional

De España:	Rica paella valenciana (mínimo tres personas)	$300.00
De Perú:	Sabrosísimo cebiche	60.00
De los Estados Unidos:	Las mejores hamburguesas al sur de la frontera	65.50
De Italia:	Exquisita pizza de la casa (tamaño grande)	180.00
De China:	Delicioso y ligero chop suey de pollo	98.50

Desayuno
(Incluye pan o tortillas.)

Huevos rancheros	$70.00
Cereal frío	30.00
Avena	35.50
Leche (vaso)	20.00
Jugos frescos (vasito)	28.50
Fruta fresca (3 piezas)	57.40

Sopas

Caldo de res con legumbres	$52.00
Crema de espárragos	40.00
Crema de hongos	38.50
Minestrone	45.50
Sopa del día	22.00

Bebidas

Cerveza Carta Blanca	$40.00
Cerveza Tecate	35.00
Cerveza Superior	32.00
Cerveza Bohemia	36.00
Refrescos	15.00
Limonada (vaso)	25.00
Té helado con limón	20.50
Tehuacán (agua mineral)	25.00
Tehuacán de sabores	33.50
Café	22.50
Té caliente	19.00
Vino tinto (copa)	65.50
Vino blanco (copa)	70.00

Postres

Arroz con leche	$25.00
Flan	35.50
Helado de fresa o vainilla	30.00
Melocotón en almíbar	32.00
Mango en almíbar	34.50
Pastel (rebanada)	40.00

Expresiones útiles

Me encanta(n).
(No) Tengo mucha hambre.
Estoy a dieta.
(No) Tengo mucha sed.
No traigo mucho dinero.
Es/Son saludable(s).

B. Escoja la(s) comida(s) que va a pedir. Siga el modelo.

MODELO: E1: ¿Qué vas a pedir?
E2: Creo que voy a pedir *los chiles rellenos* porque *me encantan*. ¿Y tú, qué vas a pedir?

 **ctividad 15   Del mundo hispano: Dónde comer en San José, Costa Rica**

RECOMENDAMOS

 **Le Monastère**
27 San Rafael de Escazú
puntos Reservaciones al 289-4404. Comida internacional al estilo francés. Hermosa vista de 270° desde San José hasta el Golfo de Nicoya. De 10,200 a 28,440 (en colones) por persona.

 **Machu Picchu**
19 125 metros al norte
puntos del Kentucky Fried Chicken, por el Paseo Colón. Reservaciones al 222-7384. Comida peruana, especialmente mariscos, con el sabor auténtico del Perú. De 7,725 a 12,185 (en colones) por persona.

La Masía de Triquell
21 Sabana Norte, de la
puntos Agencia Datsun 175 metros al oeste y 175 metros al norte. Reservaciones al 296-3528. Comida española e internacional. La mejor paella de Costa Rica. De 8,175 a 30,475 (en colones) por persona.

 **El Balcón de Europa**
11 Calle 9, entre
puntos Avenidas Central y Primera. Reservaciones 220-4821. Platillos italianos y costarricenses. De 4,900 a 14,220 (en colones) por persona.

 **Ram Luna**
25 En Aserrí. Reserva-
puntos ciones al 230-3060. Ambiente elegante y familiar. Vista de San José. Comida internacional y costarricense. Buffet y bailes folclóricos los miércoles desde las 17:00. De 10,200 a 24,375 (en colones) por persona. Buffet de los miércoles: 14,220 (en colones) por persona.

A. Primero, lea las recomendaciones de una revista turística de San José. Luego, conteste estas preguntas con un compañero / una compañera.

1. De los cinco restaurantes que se recomiendan, ¿cuál es el mejor? ¿Cuántos puntos recibió? ¿Cuál es el peor? ¿Cuántos puntos recibió?
2. De los restaurantes que se recomiendan en la revista, ¿cuáles son «buenos»? ¿Cuáles son «normales»? ¿Cuáles son «muy buenos»? ¿Hay alguno «excelente»?
3. ¿Qué elementos se deben considerar para calificar un restaurante? ¿Cuál es el más importante, en su opinión? ¿Por qué?
4. ¿En cuál de los restaurantes es más barata la comida?
5. ¿En cuál de todos le gustaría cenar? ¿Por qué?

B. Ahora use las calificaciones de la revista para hablar con su compañero/a de algunos restaurantes de su ciudad.

 30–26 puntos
Excelente

 25–21 puntos
Muy bueno

 20–16 puntos
Bueno

 15–11 puntos
Normal

 10–6 puntos
Regular

 5–0 puntos
Malo

ctividad 16   Entrevista: Los restaurantes

1. ¿Qué clase de restaurante te gusta más?
2. ¿Te gusta la comida japonesa? ¿la comida china? ¿Qué otro tipo de comida (árabe, coreana, vegetariana...) te gusta?
3. ¿Cuál es el restaurante más elegante cerca de tu casa? ¿Comes allí con frecuencia? ¿Te gusta la comida? ¿el ambiente? ¿Te gustan los precios? ¿Es necesario hacer una reservación?
4. ¿Cuánto consideras que se debe pagar por una comida excelente en un buen restaurante?
5. ¿Cuántas veces por semana comes fuera de casa? ¿Comes frecuentemente en algún lugar en especial? ¿Dónde? ¿Cuánto dejas de propina? ¿El 15 por ciento (15%)?
6. ¿Vas mucho a los restaurantes de «servicio rápido»? ¿Cuál de ellos es tu favorito? ¿Por qué?

De todo un poco

Cuadros de preferencias

Complete los siguientes cuadros según sus propias preferencias.

EN MI CASA SERVIMOS LAS SIGUIENTES COMIDAS
CON FRECUENCIA

COMIDAS	RAZÓN
1.	
2.	
3.	
4.	
5.	

ALGUNAS POSIBILIDADES

No tiene mucha grasa.

Es saludable.

Tiene poco colesterol.

Nos encanta a todos.

Los ingredientes son baratos.

EN MI CASA NUNCA SERVIMOS ESTAS COMIDAS

COMIDAS	RAZÓN
1.	
2.	
3.	
4.	
5.	

ALGUNAS POSIBILIDADES

Tiene mucha grasa.

Es muy picante.

Tiene mucho colesterol.

No nos gusta.

Los ingredientes cuestan mucho.

Ahora, charle con un compañero / una compañera sobre el contenido de los cuadros.

¡Dígalo por escrito!

Usted es el dueño.

Imagínese que usted tiene un restaurante. Invente el menú usando el vocabulario de las comidas de los **Capítulos 3** y **8.** En el menú, además de las comidas, las bebidas y los precios, incluya el nombre del restaurante, la dirección y el horario (*Abierto de la(s) _____ a la(s) _____*).

¡Cuéntenos usted!

Descríbanos una cena ideal. ¿Es una cena en casa o en un restaurante? ¿Qué comidas se sirven? ¿Hay sopa o ensalada? ¿Qué hay de beber? ¿Cuáles son los platos principales? ¿Quién prepara la comida? ¿Con quién cena usted? ¿Qué prefiere de postre?

LECTURA

Los deliciosos platos andinos

Venezuela
(la arepa, las hallacas)

Colombia
(la arepa, las hallacas)

Ecuador
(el locro)

Perú (papas a
la huancaina,
el cebiche)

Bolivia
(los anticuchos)

Chile
(el caldillo
de congrio,
el vino)

PISTAS PARA LEER

Recuerde que «andino» quiere decir que viene de la región de los Andes. Al leer, considere estas preguntas: ¿Cuál es el ingrediente básico de la comida andina? ¿Qué platos de los países en la región de los Andes se mencionan? ¿Le gustaría probar estas especialidades? **Sugerencia:** Lea también la **Nota cultural** sobre otros platos hispanos en el *Cuaderno de actividades.*

VOCABULARIO ÚTIL

netamente	*distinctly*
los puestos	*food stands*
el relleno	*filling, stuffing*
cubierto	*covered, wrapped*
la mazorca	*ear of corn*
rociadas	*sprinkled*
el ají	*chili*
humilde	*humble*
la brocheta	*kabob*
el maní	*peanut*

La región andina de la América del Sur tiene una rica tradición indígena. Hablamos de los países que se encuentran en la cordillera de los Andes: Venezuela, Colombia, Ecuador, Perú, Bolivia y Chile. La cultura de los incas predomina en gran parte de ese territorio, especialmente en Perú, Ecuador y Bolivia. El 55 por ciento de la población boliviana, por ejemplo, es de origen indígena y habla quechua, el idioma de los incas. La presencia incaica es también muy visible en la sociedad ecuatoriana. El 30 por ciento de la población de Ecuador es monolingüe —habla solamente la lengua quechua— y una tercera parte es bilingüe —habla quechua y español.

Se entiende, entonces, el origen **netamente** indígena de muchos platos andinos. Considere el maíz, que se ha cultivado en la región de los Andes por 4.000 años. El maíz —*choclo* en quechua— es un ingrediente básico de varias comidas típicas de esta región. Los colombianos y los venezolanos lo comen en forma de arepa, una masa de maíz tostada o frita rellena de queso. El alimento rápido que más se consume en la zona andina es el choclo tostado, que se vende en **puestos** por todas partes.

Una comida muy popular en la región andina es el tamal, el cual uno encuentra con diferentes nombres en varios países. Lo llaman «humitas» en Ecuador, Bolivia y Chile; «hallacas» en Venezuela y Colombia. El tamal es una masa de maíz que puede ser dulce o salada; puede llevar un **relleno** de carne de res o pollo, y siempre se cocina **cubierto** con hojas de **mazorca** o de plátano.

Hay especialidades en cada país. En Ecuador las especialidades son sus deliciosas sopas, como el locro, una sopa espesa hecha con papas, pescado y queso. El alimento principal en Perú es la papa, ¡que allí tiene más de 1.000

(Continúa)

variedades! La papa es otra legumbre que los indígenas andinos han cultivado por miles de años. Se prepara de muchas maneras, como las ricas papas a la huancaína (de la ciudad de Huancayo), que son papas hervidas y **rociadas** con una salsa cremosa de queso y **ají**. Pero el plato peruano más conocido es sin duda el cebiche: pescado crudo que «se cocina» en jugo de limón, al cual se le pone también cilantro, ajo, cebolla, choclo, ají y camote.

El cebiche, plato típico de Perú

Una de las comidas rápidas más populares en Bolivia es el anticucho. En las esquinas de cualquier ciudad boliviana —La Paz, Cochabamba— encuentra usted anticucheras: una **humilde** parrilla, humo, intenso olor a carne. Los anticuchos se hacen con carne de corazón de res a la parrilla, servida al estilo **brocheta.** A veces se les pone una salsa de **maní** picante. Muchos bolivianos de todas las edades comen anticuchos.

Mencionemos por último una de las especialidades chilenas, que es el caldillo de congrio. Este plato se hace con pescado fresco, papas, tomate y hierbas. El pescado, a propósito, se come mucho en Chile, país que también produce vinos

Pequeño restaurante en Lima, Perú

excelentes conocidos en todo el mundo. Hay otros deliciosos platos de la cocina andina que deberíamos mencionar, como la chicha morada, el saltado de pollo y el tallarín de legumbres. Pero... mejor descubra usted estas ricas comidas.

Comprensión

Indique qué ingredientes de la siguiente lista se usan en cada plato.

Ingredientes: ajo, carne de res, cebolla, cilantro, corazón de res, hierbas, jugo de limón, maíz, papas, papas hervidas, pescado crudo, pescado fresco, pollo, queso, tomate

MODELO: el tamal → *El tamal se hace con masa de maíz, a veces con un relleno de carne y siempre con hojas de mazorca o plátano.*

1. el locro
2. el caldillo de congrio
3. las papas a la huancaína
4. el cebiche
5. la arepa
6. el anticucho
7. las hallacas

Un paso más... ¡a escribir!

Escoja tres de los platos andinos que se mencionan en la **Lectura** y compárelos con un plato que usted conoce; por ejemplo, la pizza, el sushi, los espaguetis, alguna sopa. Luego explique si son similares o no, y por qué le gusta o no le gusta ese plato.

Plato andino   *Plato que yo conozco.*   *Me gusta / No me gusta porque...*

Vea el **Resumen cultural** en este capítulo del *Cuaderno de actividades.*

Caldillo de congrio

Vocabulario

El desayuno

Breakfast

la avena	oatmeal
los huevos (fritos, cocidos)	eggs (fried, hard-boiled)
el panecillo	roll, bun
el pan tostado (a la francesa)	(French) toast
el tocino	bacon
la tostada	toast (*Spain*); crispy tortilla with toppings (*Mex.*)

PALABRAS SEMEJANTES: la dona, los panqueques
REPASO: el cereal, los huevos revueltos, el pan, el pan tostado

El almuerzo y la cena

Lunch and Dinner

el caldo	clear soup
los fideos	noodles
las galletas	crackers
el plato	prepared dish
la salchicha	sausage, frankfurter

PALABRAS SEMEJANTES: el perro caliente, la pizza, la tortilla
REPASO: el arroz, la ensalada, la hamburguesa, la papa (patata) al horno, las papas fritas, el queso, el sándwich, la sopa

El restaurante

The Restaurant

el ambiente	atmosphere
comer fuera	to eat out
la comida	meal; food
la cuenta	bill, check
dejar (una) propina	to leave a tip
la tarjeta de crédito	credit card

PALABRAS SEMEJANTES: el menú (la carta), por ciento, el precio, la reservación
REPASO: atender (ie) la mesa, el mesero / la mesera, pagar, servir (i)
PLATILLOS DEL MUNDO HISPANO: el burrito, el casado de pollo, el cebiche, el chile relleno, las empanadas, la enchilada, los huevos rancheros, la paella valenciana, la parrillada, la pupusa, la quesadilla, el taco, el tamal, las tapas, la tortilla española

La carne

Meat

el ave (*f.*)	poultry
la carne de cerdo/puerco	pork
la carne molida	ground beef
la carne de res	beef
las chuletas (de cerdo/puerco)	(pork) chops
el hígado	liver
el pavo (el guajolote)	turkey

REPASO: el bistec, el jamón, el pollo (frito)

El pescado y los mariscos

Fish and Seafood

las almejas	clams
el atún	tuna
los camarones	shrimp
el cangrejo	crab
la langosta	lobster
las ostras	oysters

Las legumbres

Vegetables

el apio	celery
la calabacita	zucchini
la calabaza	pumpkin
la cebolla	onion
los frijoles	beans
los guisantes / los chícharos	green peas
las habichuelas / los ejotes	green beans
los hongos	mushrooms
el maíz	corn
la mazorca de maíz / el elote	ear of corn
el pepino	cucumber
el rábano	radish
la zanahoria	carrot

PALABRAS SEMEJANTES: el bróculi, la coliflor, los espárragos
REPASO: la lechuga, el tomate (el jitomate)

Las frutas y las nueces
Fruits and Nuts

el aguacate	avocado
el albaricoque (el chabacano)	apricot
los cacahuates	peanuts
el durazno (el melocotón)	peach
la fresa (la frutilla)	strawberry
la manzana	apple
la nuez (las nueces)	walnut(s); nut(s)
las pasas	raisins
la piña (el ananá)	pineapple
el plátano	banana
la sandía	watermelon
la toronja (el pomelo)	grapefruit
las uvas	grapes

PALABRAS SEMEJANTES: la banana, el limón, el mango, el melón, la papaya, la pera
REPASO: la naranja (la china)

Los postres
Desserts

el arroz con leche	rice pudding
el flan	sweet custard

REPASO: el chocolate, las galletitas, el helado, el pastel, el yogur

Las bebidas
Drinks

el batido (de leche, de frutas)	(milk, fruit) shake
la horchata	sweet rice drink
la jamaica	sweet drink made with hibiscus flowers
el té caliente/frío (helado)	(hot, iced) tea
el vino (blanco, rosado, tinto)	(white, rosé, red) wine

PALABRAS SEMEJANTES: el agua mineral, la limonada
REPASO: el agua, el café, la cerveza, el jugo (el zumo), la leche, el refresco

Los condimentos, las especias y otros ingredientes
Condiments, Spices and Other Ingredients

el aceite	oil
la aceituna	olive
el aderezo	(salad) dressing
el ají	(bell/chili) pepper
el ajo	garlic

el almíbar	syrup
el azúcar	sugar
el conservante	preservative
la harina	flour
la jalea	jelly
la miel	honey
la mostaza	mustard
la pimienta	pepper
la sal	salt

PALABRAS SEMEJANTES: el bicarbonato de soda, el colorante, la crema, la grasa, la mayonesa, la mermelada, la salsa, la vainilla, el vinagre
REPASO: la mantequilla

La mesa y los cubiertos
Table Setting and Utensils

la cuchara	spoon
la cucharita	teaspoon
el cucharón	ladle
el cuchillo	knife
el cuenco	large serving bowl
la fuente de sopa	soup tureen
la jarra	pitcher
el mantel	tablecloth
el pimentero	pepper shaker
el platillo	saucer
el plato hondo	bowl
el salero	salt shaker
la servilleta	napkin
el tenedor	fork

REPASO: el plato, la taza, el vaso

Las medidas y los recipientes
Measurements and Containers

la botella	bottle
la copa	wineglass
la cucharada	tablespoon (measurement)
la cucharadita	teaspoon (measurement)
la lata	can
la libra	pound
la onza	ounce
el paquete	package
la rebanada	slice
la sartén	(frying) pan
el tarro	jar

Los verbos
Verbs

agregar	to add
amasar	to knead
asar	to roast
batir	to beat
contener	to contain

crecer	to grow
cubrir	to cover
desear	to want, desire
doblar	to fold
estar a dieta	to be on a diet
freír (i)	to fry
mezclar	to mix
mojar	to dip; to wet
pedir (i)	to ask for; to order food
pelar	to peel
picar	to chop, mince
rallar	to grate
tapar	to cover

PALABRAS SEMEJANTES: calcular, combinar, considerar, determinar, formar, recomendar
REPASO: hacer la compra, hornear

La descripción de la comida

Describing Food

a la parrilla	grilled, charbroiled
al horno	baked
al punto, cocido/a	medium rare
bien asado/a, bien cocido/a	well-done
congelado/a	frozen
crudo/a	raw
descafeinado/a	decaffeinated
descremado/a	skimmed
dorado/a	golden brown
dulce	sweet
espeso/a	thick
enlatado/a	canned
fresco/a	fresh
maduro/a	ripe
medio/a	half
picante	hot (spicy)
poco asado/a, poco cocido/a	rare
rico/a	delicious
sabroso/a	flavorful, tasty
seco/a	dry

PALABRAS SEMEJANTES: concentrado/a, excelente, normal, tropical, turístico/a, vegetariano/a

Los sustantivos

Nouns

el alimento	food, meal
el antojito	snack (*Mex.*)
la bolita (de masa)	little ball (of dough)
la cáscara	peel
los comestibles	food; groceries
la comida chatarra	junk food (*Mex.*)
la comida preelaborada	convenience food
la etiqueta	label
las palomitas de maíz	popcorn
la receta	recipe
el restaurante de servicio rápido	fast-food restaurant
el sabor	taste, flavor
la semilla	seed
el trozo	piece

PALABRAS SEMEJANTES: el calcio, el carbohidrato, el colesterol, el líquido, la nutrición, la preparación, la proteína, el total, la vitamina, la zona

Palabras y expresiones del texto

Words and Expressions from the Text

pertenecer	to belong
la razón	reason
la tabla	table; graph

PALABRAS SEMEJANTES: el elemento, el punto, la recomendación

Palabras y expresiones útiles

Useful Words and Expressions

con gusto	with pleasure
dentro	inside; within
de nuevo	again
frecuentemente	frequently
Me encanta(n) el/la/los/las...	I really like . . .
poner la mesa	to set the table
¿Qué clase de... ?	What type of . . . ?

Gramática y ejercicios

8.1 More about Referring to People and Objects already Mentioned: Personal and Impersonal Direct Object Pronouns *lo, la, los,* and *las*

> **lo** = *you, him, it* (m.)
> **la** = *you, her, it* (f.)
> **los** = *you, them* (m. pl.)
> **las** = *you, them* (f. pl.)
>
> **¿Quién preparó los frijoles?** (*Who made the beans?*)
> **Papá los preparó.** (*Dad made them.*)

¿RECUERDA?

As you saw in **Gramática 3.3,** the object pronouns **lo, la, los,** and **las** serve as impersonal direct object pronouns. In other words, they can be used to replace the name of an object; thus **lo** and **la** are the equivalent of the English pronoun *it* and **los** and **las** are equivalent to *them:*

—¿Quién compró **el pastel**?	—*Who bought the cake?*
—**Lo** compró Raúl.	—*Raúl bought it.*
—¿Quién trajo **la fruta**?	—*Who brought the fruit?*
—**La** trajo Nora.	—*Nora brought it.*
—Carmen, ¿dónde pusiste **las servilletas**?	—*Carmen, where did you put the napkins?*
—**Las** puse en la mesa.	—*I put them on the table.*

In **Gramática 6.5,** you learned that the object pronouns **lo, la, los,** and **las** also serve as personal direct object pronouns:

—¿Viste a Alberto ayer?	—*Did you see Alberto yesterday?*
—No, no **lo** vi.	—*No, I didn't see him.*
¿La profesora Martínez? **La** vi ayer en el mercado, pero ella no me vio.	*Professor Martínez? I saw her yesterday at the market, but she didn't see me.*

Review these sections now, if necessary.

The Spanish direct object pronouns **lo, la, los,** and **las** may substitute for words referring to people *or* to things. For example, **la** in the first exchange below refers to **Mónica** (*her*); in the second one it refers to **la salsa** (*it*).

—¿Llamaste a **Mónica**?	—*Did you call Mónica?*
—Sí, **la** llamé ayer.	—*Yes, I called her yesterday.*
—Luis, ¿encontraste **la salsa**?	—*Luis, did you find the sauce?*
—Sí, **la** encontré en el refrigerador.	—*Yes, I found it in the refrigerator.*

These pronouns take time to acquire. You will find that you will gradually come to use them in your speech as you hear and read more Spanish.

Like other pronouns, direct object pronouns are usually placed before the verb. However, in the case of verb phrases, such as forms used to express the future (**voy a comprar**), or in forms expressing the present progressive (**estamos preparando**), there are two options:

- Pronouns may precede the first verb:
  —¿**Los fideos? Los** voy a comprar esta tarde.
  —¿**La paella? La** estamos preparando ahora.

- Or they may be attached to the end of the infinitive or the present participle (-**ndo** form):
  —¿**Los fideos?** Voy a comprar**los** esta tarde.
  —¿**La paella?** Estamos preparándo**la** ahora.

You will learn more about the placement of pronouns in **Gramática 13.5** and **Expansión gramatical.**

Ejercicio 1 utilizes open-ended questions. First use the correct direct object pronoun and then select a logical end to the sentence or create your own.

el congelador = *freezer*

Ejercicio 1

Conteste con **lo, la, los** o **las** y una terminación lógica.

MODELO: —¿Cuándo bebiste el jugo de naranja?
          —*Lo* bebí...

          a. hace diez años.
          (b.) anoche.
          c. antes de levantarme.

1. —¿Dónde pusiste la carne?
   — _____ puse en...
   a. el jardín.
   b. el supermercado.
   c. el congelador.
2. —¿Dónde compraste las legumbres?
   — _____ compré...
   a. en una tienda de ropa.
   b. en el supermercado.
   c. en la cafetería de la escuela.
3. —¿Cuándo trajiste el hielo?
   — _____ traje...
   a. el año pasado.
   b. hace diez minutos.
   c. hace dos semanas.
4. —¿Dónde pusiste la mayonesa?
   — _____ puse en...
   a. la mesa.
   b. el sofá.
   c. el dormitorio.
5. —¿Dónde pusiste los vasos?
   — _____ puse en...
   a. el armario.
   b. la cómoda.
   c. la alacena.
6. —¿Viste a Nora ayer?
   —Sí, _____ vi en...
   a. el tocino.
   b. el restaurante.
   c. la paella.
7. —¿Cuándo conociste a Luis?
   — _____ conocí...
   a. ayer.
   b. en el año 1810.
   c. pasado mañana.
8. —¿Llamaste a las chicas ya?
   —Sí, _____ llamé...
   a. en el año 2020.
   b. anoche.
   c. la semana próxima.
9. —¿Saludaste a la profesora?
   —Sí, _____ saludé...
   a. hace cinco minutos.
   b. el siglo pasado.
   c. el mes próximo.
10. —¿Oíste llegar a Lan y a Luis?
    —Sí, _____ oí llegar...
    a. a las 10:00 de la noche.
    b. mañana en la tarde.
    c. en el año 1521.

Ejercicio 2

La familia Saucedo se está preparando para la cena de Nochebuena. Usted es Estela. Conteste las preguntas de su familia: Use **lo, la, los** o **las** antes o después de la frase verbal.

MODELO: —Mamá, ¿a qué hora vas a servir la comida?
   —**La** voy a servir a medianoche. / Voy a servir**la** a medianoche.

1. —Mamá, ¿vamos a poner la mesa ahora?
   —No, hijo, _____ a las 11:00 de la noche.
2. —Mamá, ¿vas a preparar el aderezo ahora o más tarde?
   —Hija, _____ a las 10:00 de la noche.
3. —Mamá, ¿ya estás horneando los pasteles?
   —Sí, hijito, _____ ahora mismo.
4. —Mamá, ¿quién está rallando el queso?
   —Amanda _____ en este momento.
5. —Mamá, ¿vas a abrir las latas de aceitunas ahora?
   —No, Guillermo, no _____ todavía. Prefiero esperar un poco.

8.2 More about Expressing Likes: The Verbs *gustar* and *encantar*

A. Gustar can also be followed by a noun. If the noun is singular, use the singular form, **gusta;** if it is plural, use the plural form, **gustan.**

—¿Te gusta **la sandía?**	—*Do you like watermelon?*
—Sí, pero me gust**an** más **las uvas.**	—*Yes, but I like grapes better.*

The preterite forms are **gustó** (*sing.*) and **gustaron** (*pl.*).

—¿Te **gustó** el helado?	—*Did you like the ice cream?*
—Sí, me **gustó** mucho.	—*Yes, I liked it a lot.*
—Nos **gustaron** mucho esas galletitas.	—*We really liked those cookies.*

B. To ask who likes something, begin with **¿A quién... ?**

—**¿A quién** le gusta la pizza?	—*Who likes pizza?*
—¡A todos nos gusta!	—*We all do!*

To identify a specific person or persons who like(s) something, use the following pattern.

A + *name* + **le(s)** + **gusta(n)...**

A Lan le gusta leer novelas.	*Lan likes to read novels.*
A Graciela no **le gusta** la comida italiana.	*Graciela doesn't like Italian food.*
A Guillermo y **a Ernestito les gusta** mucho montar en bicicleta.	*Guillermo and Ernestito like to ride their bikes a lot.*

¿RECUERDA?

In **Gramática 1.5** you learned that the verb **gustar,** followed by an infinitive, is the most common Spanish equivalent for the English verb *to like* (*to do something*) and that **gustar** resembles the English verb phrase *to be pleasing* (*to someone*). You also learned that an indirect object pronoun (**me, te, nos, os, le,** or **les**) is used with **gustar** to identify the person to whom something is pleasing.

A Nora le gusta cocinar. (*Nora likes to cook.*)

Me gusta desayunar temprano. (*I like to eat breakfast early.*)

Use **gusta** if one item is being referred to; use **gustan** if more than one item is referred to:
Me gusta el café.
   (*I like coffee.*)
Me gustan las tortillas de maíz.
   (*I like corn tortillas.*)

C. To state more emphatically that someone likes something, use the preposition **a** followed by the person (noun or pronoun) and then the corresponding indirect object pronoun (**me, te, le, nos, os, les**) + **gusta(n).**

—¿**A Paula le gustan** las hamburguesas?	—*Does Paula like hamburgers?*
—¡¿**A Paula?!** No, **a ella** no **le gustan** las hamburguesas.	—*Paula?! No, she doesn't like hamburgers.*

The following emphatic phrases are made up of the preposition **a** followed by pronouns. Notice that these pronouns are the same as the subject pronouns, except for **mí** and **ti.***

> For emphasis, add:
> **a mí**
> **a ti**
> **a él / a ellos**
> **a ella(s)**
> **a usted(es)**
> **a nosotros/as**
> > **A mí me gusta el chocolate.** (*I like chocolate*).
> > **A ellas les gustan las papas fritas.** (*They like French fries.*)

a mí me gusta(n)	a nosotros/as nos gusta(n)
a ti te gusta(n)	a vosotros/as os gusta(n)
a usted le gusta(n)	a ustedes les gusta(n)
a él le gusta(n)	a ellos les gusta(n)
a ella le gusta(n)	a ellas les gusta(n)

Pues, **a mí me gustan** mucho todas las frutas, especialmente la papaya.	*Well, I really like all fruit, especially papaya.*
¿Y de veras **a ti no te gustan** las papas fritas?	*And do you really not like French fries?*

D. Emphatic short answers to questions with **gustar** are very common. Use the preposition **a** plus a pronoun or noun and the words **sí** or **no.**

—¿Le gustan las sardinas?	—*Do you like sardines?*
—¡**A mí, no!**	—*No, I don't!*
—¿Les gustan los postres de chocolate?	—*Do you like chocolate desserts?*
—**A mí, sí,** pero **a Nora, no.**	—*I do, but Nora doesn't.*

You can use the words **también** (*also*) and **tampoco** (*neither*) instead of **sí** and **no** in short answers.

> With **gustar:**
> **a mí también** = *me too*
> **a mí tampoco** = *me neither*

—A Pablo le gustan las fajitas.	—*Pablo likes fajitas.*
—Pues, **a mí también.**	—*Well, so do I.*
—Luis, a mí no me gustan mucho estos tacos.	—*Luis, I don't like these tacos very much.*
—**A mí tampoco.**	—*I don't either.*

E. There are other Spanish verbs that function like **gustar.** One common one used to express likes and dislikes is **encantar.** (You will learn more about this kind of verb in **Gramática 10.5.**)

> Remember to use **encanta** if referring to one item or **encantan** if more than one:
> **Les encanta la comida japonesa.** (*They really like Japanese food.*)
> **Nos encantan las papas fritas.** (*We adore French fries.*)

—A mí **me encanta** el flan.	—*I adore flan.*
—A mí también.	—*Me too.*
—**Nos encantan** los mariscos que sirven en este restaurante.	—*We love the seafood they serve in this restaurant.*
—A nosotros también.	—*So do we.*
A Ernesto y a Estela **les encanta** salir a cenar.	*Ernesto and Estela love to eat dinner out.*

The preterite forms of **encantar** are **encantó** and **encantaron.**

A ella **le encantó** la cena.	*She loved the dinner.*
Me encantaron esas enchiladas.	*I really liked those enchiladas.*

---

*Recognition: **a vos te gusta**

Ejercicio 3

Complete los siguientes diálogos.

Use **me/mí** y **te/ti.**

—¿_____¹ gustan las zanahorias?
—A mí no _____² gustan mucho. ¿Y a _____³?
—A _____,⁴ sí. Son muy buenas para la vista (los ojos).

Use **él/le, me/mí** y **te/ti.**

—¿A tu hermano _____⁵ gusta el pollo frito?
—A _____⁶ sí le gusta, pero a _____,⁷ no.
—¡A _____⁸ no te gusta el pollo! ¿Por qué no _____⁹ gusta?
—A _____¹⁰ sí me gusta el pollo, pero no _____¹¹ gusta el pollo frito.

Ejercicio 4

Haga oraciones que describan los gustos de las siguientes personas. Use (1) una forma del verbo **encantar** (**encanta** o **encantan**); (2) el pronombre apropiado (**me, te, le, les** o **nos**); y (3) el nombre de una comida.

MODELO: A mi hermana *le encantan las fresas.*

Sugerencias

el café	los dulces	el guacamole
los chiles rellenos	las fresas	las hamburguesas
el chocolate	los frijoles	las palomitas con mantequilla
la comida mexicana	la fruta	el pan

1. A mi mejor amigo/a _____.
2. A mis padres _____.
3. A mi profesor(a) de español _____.
4. A mi novio/a (esposo/a) _____.
5. A mí _____.
6. A mi mejor amigo/a y a mí _____.

8.3 Making Negative Statements and Questions: *No, never*

algo	*something*	nada	*nothing*
alguien	*somebody*	nadie	*nobody*
algún	*some*	ningún	*none, no one*
alguno/a/os/as		ninguno/a (de)	
siempre	*always*	nunca (jamás)	*never*
también	*also*	tampoco	*neither*

Whereas in standard English it is generally incorrect to have more than one negative in a sentence, in Spanish multiple negatives are frequently required.

A. Spanish often requires the use of multiple negatives in the same sentence when one responds negatively to a question.

—¿Tienes algo en el horno?

—**No, no** tengo **nada.**

—¿Hay alguien en la puerta?
—**No, no** hay **nadie.**

—Señora Silva, ¿va usted siempre al mercado los martes?
—**No, no** voy **nunca** los martes.

—*Do you have something in the oven?*
—*No, I don't have anything.*

—*Is there someone at the door?*
—*No, there is no one.*

—*Mrs. Silva, do you always go to the market on Tuesdays?*
—*No, I don't ever (I never) go on Tuesdays.*

algún (alguno/a/os/as) = *some, any*

ningún (ninguno/a) = *none, not any, neither one*

B. Alguno/a corresponds to English *some* or *any*, and **ninguno/a** corresponds to English *none, not any,* or *neither one.*

—¿Hay **algunos** postres sin azúcar?
—No, señor, no tenemos **ningún** postre sin azúcar.

—¿Hay **alguna** sopa sin carne?

—No, no hay **ninguna;** todas tienen carne.

—*Are there any desserts without sugar?*
—*No, sir, we don't have any desserts without sugar.*

—*Are there any soups without meat?*
—*No, there aren't any; they all have meat.*

Note that Spanish uses **ninguno/a** in the singular form.

C. Alguno and **ninguno** shorten to **algún** and **ningún** before masculine singular nouns.

—¿Hay **algún** restaurante en esta calle?
—No, no hay **ningún** restaurante por aquí.

—*Is there a restaurant on this street?*
—*No, there aren't any restaurants around here.*

Uno/Un, bueno/buen, primero/primer, and **tercero/tercer** follow the same rule.

¿Quieres pedir **una** copa de vino?

Sólo hay **un** plato mexicano en el menú.
¡Aquí sirven **unos** mariscos exquisitos!

Esteban es un **buen** cocinero.
Nora y Carmen también son **buenas** cocineras.

Vamos a sentarnos en la **tercera** mesa.
El **primer** plato es la sopa.

Do you want to order a glass of wine?

There is only one Mexican dish on the menu.
They serve excellent seafood here!

Esteban is a good cook.
Nora and Carmen are also good cooks.

Let's sit down at the third table.

The first course is the soup.

D. No is not used when the negative word precedes the verb.

Nunca como entre comidas.
Nadie fue al mercado.

I never eat between meals.
Nobody went to the market.

E. Express *I (you, we . . .) don't either* with a subject pronoun + **tampoco.**

—Yo no quiero comer helado. —*I don't want to eat ice cream.*
—**Yo tampoco.** —*I don't either. (Me neither.)*

Yo no quiero más arroz. **Tú** *I don't want more rice.*
tampoco, ¿verdad? *You don't either, do you?*

Ejercicio 5

Conteste las siguientes preguntas de forma negativa. Use **nada, nadie, nunca** o
ninguno/a.

MODELO: —¿Hay algo de comer en el refrigerador?
—No, no hay *nada.*

1. —¿Fue alguien al supermercado ayer?
   —No, no fue _____.
2. —¿Desayunaste algo esta mañana?
   —No, no comí _____.
3. —¿Siempre comes en restaurantes chinos?
   —No, _____ como en ellos.
4. —¿Invitaste a alguien a cenar esta noche?
   —No, no invité a _____.
5. —¿Compraste una sandía?
   —No, no encontré _____ madura.
6. —¿Quieres algo de tomar?
   —No gracias, no quiero _____.
7. —¿Te sirvo espinacas?
   —No, gracias. ¡_____ las como!
8. —¿Por qué no invitaste a Diego y a Ramón a la fiesta?
   —Los invité, pero _____ de los dos quiso venir.

La paella valenciana es la comida
más típica de la región mediterránea
de España, pero se come con gusto
en todos los países hispanas.

Ejercicio 6

Usted y Pedro Ruiz tienen gustos muy diferentes. En cada caso exprese una opinión
opuesta a la de Pedro.

MODELO: PEDRO: Me encantan las USTED: A mí, no. (A mí no me
almejas. gustan.)

1. PEDRO: No me gustan las hamburguesas. USTED: _____
2. PEDRO: Me encanta la horchata. USTED: _____
3. PEDRO: No me gustan los guisantes. USTED: _____

Usted y Ernesto Saucedo tienen los mismos gustos. En cada caso diga que usted está
de acuerdo con la opinión de Ernesto.

MODELO: ERNESTO: No me gustan las comidas USTED: A mí tampoco
preelaboradas. (A mí tampoco
me gustan).

4. ERNESTO: No me gusta el atún. USTED: _____
5. ERNESTO: No me gustan los huevos revueltos. USTED: _____
6. ERNESTO: Me gustan las pupusas. USTED: _____

Se + third-person singular verb is used to express *one, you,* or impersonal *they:*
Se come mucho ajo en España. (*One eats [They eat] lots of garlic in Spain.*) (*Lots of garlic is eaten in Spain.*)

Se + third-person verb form is often used for instructions:
Primero se hierve el agua, después se le agrega la sal y luego se ponen los fideos y se cuecen por ocho minutos. (*First you boil the water, then you add the salt, and then you put in the noodles and cook them for eight minutes.*)

In **Ejercicio 7,** the verb **necesitar** can be used twice. All others will be used once.

8.4 Expressing *one* or *you:* The Impersonal *se*

In addition to being a reflexive pronoun (see **Gramática 4.3**), **se** is also used in "impersonal" constructions.

In English this structure is expressed with the impersonal *you* (*You need good fruit to make a good fruit salad*), the pronoun *one* (*One should always think before acting*), the pronoun *they* (*They sell beer by the glass*), or the simple passive (*Beer is sold only by the glass here*).

—¿Cómo **se dice** *tablecloth* en español?
—**Se dice** «mantel».

—How do you say *tablecloth* in Spanish?
—You say **mantel**.

Aquí **se habla** español.

Spanish is spoken here. (*They speak Spanish here.*)

Primero **se agrega** la sal y después **se mezcla** todo.
No **se debe** dormir inmediatamente después de comer.

First you add the salt and then you mix everything.
One shouldn't (go to) sleep immediately after eating.

If the topic in question is plural, the verb is usually also plural.

—¿**Se sirven mariscos** frescos aquí?
—Sí, **se preparan camarones** deliciosos y el precio es muy módico.

—Are fresh shellfish served here?
—Yes, they prepare delicious shrimp, and the price is very moderate.

Ejercicio 7

Complete estas oraciones con la forma **se** impersonal de los siguientes verbos:
preparar, poner, cortar, lavar, agregar, necesitar, hablar y **batir.**

1. Para preparar un sándwich de jamón y queso, _____ el jamón y el queso en rebanadas.
2. Para alimentarse bien, _____ comer de los cuatro grupos esenciales de alimentos.
3. Primero _____ el bróculi y luego _____ en el agua a hervir.
4. En este restaurante _____ mariscos frescos y deliciosos.
5. Para hacer un buen guacamole, _____ cebolla y otros ingredientes.
6. Para hacer una tortilla española, _____ huevos y patatas.
7. ¿_____ francés en ese restaurante?
8. ¿_____ los huevos para la tortilla española?

8.5 Using Stem-Changing Verbs Like *pedir* and *servir*: Present-Tense and Preterite Forms

In a few verbs like **pedir** (*to order; to ask for*) and **servir** (*to serve*), the -e- of the infinitive changes to -i- in the present tense and the preterite. In the present, all forms of **pedir** and **servir** use the stems **pid-** and **sirv-** except for the **nosotros/as** and **vosotros/as** forms and the infinitive.*

	pedir	servir
(yo)	pido	sirvo
(tú)	pides	sirves
(usted, él/ella)	pide	sirve
(nosotros/as)	pedimos	servimos
(vosotros/as)	pedís	servís
(ustedes, ellos/as)	piden	sirven

In the preterite, only the **usted, él/ella,** and **ustedes, ellos/as** forms use the stem with **i**.

	pedir	servir
(yo)	pedí	serví
(tú)	pediste	serviste
(usted, él/ella)	pidió	sirvió
(nosotros/as)	pedimos	servimos
(vosotros/as)	pedisteis	servisteis
(ustedes, ellos/as)	pidieron	sirvieron

En este restaurante **sirven** excelente comida. La semana pasada me **sirvieron** una paella sabrosísima.

They serve excellent food in this restaurant. Last week they served me a delicious paella.

---

pedir = *to ask for*
present: **(yo) pido, (él) pide**
past: **(yo) pedí, (él) pidió**
servir = *to serve*
present: **(yo) sirvo, (él) sirve**
past: **(yo) serví, (él) sirvió**

Pedí camarones y fideos.
I ordered shrimp and pasta.
El mesero me sirvió almejas y arroz.
The waiter served me clams and rice.

*The **e → i** change also occurs in the present participles: **pidiendo** (*ordering*) and **sirviendo** (*serving*).
Recognition: **vos pedís, servís; vos pediste, serviste**

—Silvia, ¿qué platillo **pediste**
en el Restaurante Mi Casita?
—**Pedí** unas enchiladas de pollo.
Siempre **pido** lo mismo.

—*Silvia, what dish did you
order at Mi Casita Restaurant?*
—*I ordered chicken enchiladas.
I always order the same thing.*

The verbs **vestirse** (*to dress*) and **seguir** (*to follow*) conform to this same **e → i** pattern.*

vestirse		seguir	
PRESENT	**PAST**	**PRESENT**	**PAST**
me visto	me vestí	sigo	seguí
te vistes	te vestiste	sigues	seguiste
se viste	se vistió	sigue	siguió
nos vestimos	nos vestimos	seguimos	seguimos
os vestís	os vestisteis	seguís	seguisteis
se visten	se vistieron	siguen	siguieron

Raúl se **vistió** rápido anoche.
Estela no **siguió** la receta.

Raúl dressed quickly last night.
Estela didn't follow the recipe.

Reír (*to laugh*), **sonreír** (*to smile*), and **freír** (*to fry*) also follow this pattern, except that in the third-person preterite forms one **i** is dropped: **fri- + -ió → frió; fri- + -ieron → frieron.**[†]

freír	
PRESENT	**PAST**
frío	freí
fríes	freíste
fríe	frió
freímos	freímos
freís	freísteis
fríen	frieron

Doña Rosita **frió** las tortillas.
Don Eduardo **sonrió** cuando
le sirvieron su platillo favorito.

Doña Rosita fried the tortillas.
*Don Eduardo smiled when they
served him his favorite dish.*

---

*The **e → i** change also occurs in the present participles: **vistiendo/vistiéndose** and **siguiendo**.
[†]The present participles are: **friendo, sonriendo,** and **riendo**.

Recognition: Present: **vos te vestís, seguís, freís, sonreís, reís**
Preterite: **vos te vestiste, seguiste, freíste, sonreíste, reíste**

Ejercicio 8

Complete estos diálogos con las formas apropiadas de **servir** o **pedir**.

PILAR: ¿Qué vas a _____[1] ahora?

CLARA: Creo que voy a _____[2] pollo asado.

PILAR: En este restaurante _____[3] muy buenos mariscos.

CLARA: Entonces voy a _____[4] camarones fritos.

JOSÉ: ¿Qué _____[5] tú en un restaurante mexicano?

PILAR: Eso depende. Si _____[6] mariscos _____[7] un cóctel de mariscos.

JOSÉ: ¿Y si no hay mariscos?

PILAR: Entonces prefiero _____[8] un chile relleno.

PILAR: Ayer mi novio y yo fuimos a un restaurante francés muy elegante.

CLARA: ¿Qué _____[9] ustedes?

PILAR: _____[10] cóctel de mariscos, ensalada y carne de res en salsa de vino.

CLARA: Mmm. ¿Y les _____[11] postre también?

PILAR: Sí, yo _____[12] flan y mi novio _____[13] pastel de chocolate.

JOSÉ: Pilar, ¿_____[14] leche otra vez?

PILAR: No, ayer yo _____[15] una Coca-Cola y Clara _____[16] un vaso de leche.

JOSÉ: Ah sí, ya entiendo. Después ustedes _____[17] un sándwich de pollo.

PILAR: No, José. Después _____[18] un sándwich de jamón, pero el mesero nos _____[19] sándwiches de pollo.

JOSÉ: ¿Y a mí también me _____[20] un sándwich de pollo?

PILAR: No, hombre. ¡Tú no fuiste con nosotros!

La comida mexicana es muy variada. Entre los platillos más populares se encuentran los tacos.

© Joaquín Salvador Lavado (QUINO) Toda Mafalda—Ediciones de La Flor, 1993.

La niñez y la juventud

METAS

In **Capítulo 9** you will expand your ability to talk about your family. You will learn to express different kinds of memories: your habitual activities and those of others, as well as how you felt about things in the past.

Fragmento de *Salud para todos*, por Walter Solón (Bolivia)

Sobre el artista: Walter Solón nació en 1924 en Uyuni, una pequeña ciudad al suroeste de Bolivia. En sus murales Solón trata los temas de la opresión y la resistencia política, y muchas de sus obras muestran la injusticia de las dictaduras. Víctimas de una dictadura militar en Bolivia, Solón y su esposa escaparon a Perú después de ser torturados. Solón murió en 1999.

¡Conozca Bolivia!

Nombre del país: la República de Bolivia

Ciudad capital: Sucre es la capital y La Paz es la sede del gobierno

Ciudades principales: Cochabamba, Santa Cruz, Potosí

Moneda: el boliviano

Idiomas: el español, el quechua, el aimara, el guaraní (oficiales)

Población: 9.100.000

Día de la Independencia: el 6 de agosto

Fiestas típicas: la Fiesta de la Virgen de Candelaria, el Carnaval de Oruro

Comidas típicas: las salteñas, la sajta de pollo, el pacumutu, el silpancho, el thimpu, el pique macho, el mate de coca

Música típica: el carnavalito, el taquirari, la chovena, la chacarera, el kaluyo, el huayno. Entre los instrumentos folklóricos se incluyen el siku y la quena.

Gente famosa: Evo Morales, Gabriel René Moreno, Pedro Domingo Murillo

Código del país por Internet: .bo

Voces bolivianas

un cuero	una persona atractiva
echar un fonazo	llamar por teléfono
estar largado/a	no tener dinero
un jacho	un agente de policía
un k'anka	una persona estadounidense
raca	tacaño/a
la yeta	la mala suerte

En este capítulo...

ACTIVIDADES DE COMUNICACIÓN

- La familia y los parientes
- La niñez
- La juventud

EN RESUMEN

LECTURAS Y CULTURA

- **Ventanas culturales**
  Nuestra comunidad: Famosos y humanitarios
- **Enlace a la música**
  Canciones y rimas infantiles
- **Ventanas culturales**
  La vida diaria: Los chicos de la calle
- **Lectura**
  ¡Así piensan los niños!

GRAMÁTICA Y EJERCICIOS

9.1 Describing Family Relationships: The Reciprocal Reflexive Verbs **parecerse** and **llevarse bien**

9.2 Expressing *for, from,* and *to whom:* Prepositions + Pronouns

9.3 Saying What You Used to Do: The Imperfect Tense

9.4 Describing the Past: The Imperfect and Preterite of "State" Verbs

9.5 Saying What You Were Going to Do: The Imperfect of **ir** + **a** + Infinitive

La familia y los parientes

✳ **Lea Gramática 9.1–9.2.**

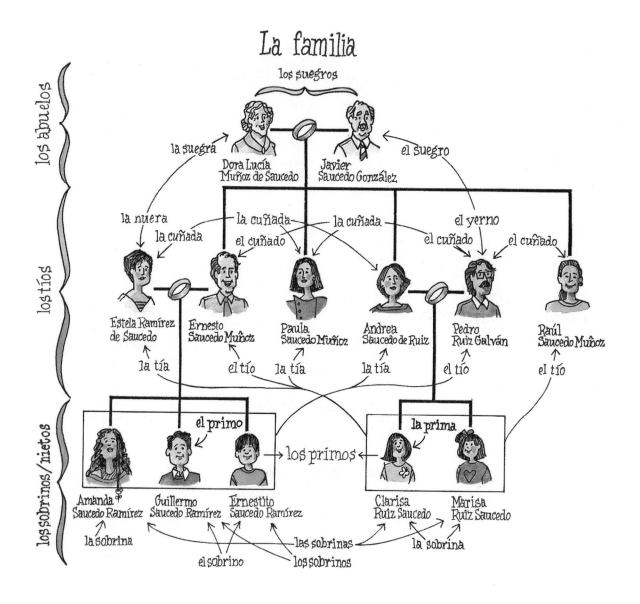

La familia

Actividad 1 Definiciones: La familia de Raúl

Mire el dibujo de arriba y escuche las oraciones que le va a leer su profesor(a). Diga si son ciertas o falsas.

MODELO: PROF.: «La tía de Clarisa y Marisa se llama Andrea.» →
E.: Falso. Andrea es *la madre* de Clarisa y Marisa.

Actividad 2 Intercambios: La familia de Raúl

Hágale estas preguntas a su compañero/a.

1. ¿Cómo se llaman las hermanas de Raúl? ¿Y el hermano?
2. ¿Cuántos sobrinos tiene Raúl? ¿Cómo se llaman?
3. ¿Tienen nueras Dora y Javier?
4. ¿Cómo se llaman los cuñados de Raúl?
5. ¿Cómo se llama el suegro de Pedro y Estela?
6. ¿Cómo se llaman las cuñadas de Estela?
7. ¿Cuántos nietos tienen Dora y Javier?
8. ¿Cómo se llaman los tíos de Clarisa y Marisa?
9. ¿Cómo se llaman los primos de Clarisa y Marisa?
10. ¿Cómo se llama el yerno de Dora y Javier?

Actividad 3 Descripción de dibujos: La familia de Mónica

Lea la siguiente descripción de la familia de Mónica. Basándose en el árbol genealógico, llene los espacios en blanco con los nombres o palabras apropiados.

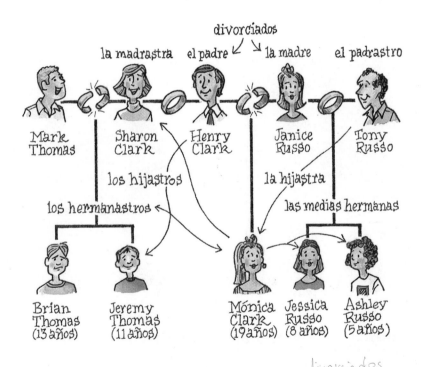

¡OJO!

En el mundo hispano, las relaciones entre los mayores y los jóvenes son íntimas y especiales. Conversan, comparten ideas, salen a pasear y juegan juntos. Los abuelos participan en las experiencias de sus nietos, y los nietos escuchan las historias y los recuerdos de sus abuelos. Así se mantiene viva la historia familiar.

Los padres de Mónica se llaman _____ y _____ y están _____. Mónica vive con su madre y su padrastro, Tony. Su madre y Tony tienen dos hijas, Jessica y Ashley. Ellas son las medias hermanas de Mónica. Jessica se parece a _____, pero Ashley se parece más a _____.

La nueva esposa de Henry Clark se llama _____. Sharon tiene dos hijos de su primer esposo; se llaman _____ y _____ y son los _____ de Mónica. Mónica no visita a sus hermanastros con frecuencia, pero se lleva bien con ellos. A Mónica le gusta hablar con Sharon, su _____, pero dice que su padrastro, Tony, no la comprende.

Actividad 4 **Diálogo abierto: La familia**

Diga a quién se parecen usted y otras personas de su familia. ¿Se llevan bien usted y estas personas?

> E1: ¿A quién te pareces?
>
> E2: Me parezco a _____.
>
> E1: ¿A quién se parece tu _____? (*hermano/a, hijo/a, primo/a, sobrino/a*)
>
> E2: Se parece a _____.
>
> E1: ¿Te llevas bien con tu _____? (*padre, madre, padrastro, madrastra, hermano/a, hermanastro/a, primo/a, tío/a, cuñado/a*)
>
> E2: Sí, me llevo bien (No, no me llevo bien) con él/ella porque _____.

Estas hermanas se parecen mucho porque son gemelas.

El hijo se parece a su padre.

Actividad 5 **Entrevista: Mi familia y mis parientes**

1. ¿Vives con tus padres o con otros parientes? ¿Están divorciados tus padres? ¿Tienes padrastro o madrastra? ¿Te llevas bien con él/ella?

2. ¿Están vivos o muertos tus abuelos? ¿Dónde viven? ¿Los ves con frecuencia? Si están muertos, ¿cuánto tiempo hace que murieron?

3. ¿Cuántos hermanos tienes? ¿Tienes medios hermanos o medias hermanas? ¿Te pareces a ellos/as? ¿Tienes hermanastros o hermanastras? ¿Te llevas bien con ellos/as?

4. ¿Cuántos tíos tienes? ¿Dónde viven? ¿Tienes muchos primos o pocos? ¿Celebras los días feriados con tus tíos y tus primos?

5. ¿Están casados tus hermanos? ¿Te llevas bien con tus cuñados? ¿Tienes sobrinos? ¿Cuántos años tienen? ¿Cómo se llaman?

6. ¿Estás casado/a tú? ¿Tienes hijos? ¿Cómo se llaman? ¿Están casados tus hijos? ¿Cómo se llama tu nuera/yerno? ¿Tienes nietos? ¿Cuántos años tienen?

La niñez

⭐ **Lea Gramática 9.3.**

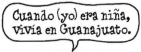

Mis amigas y yo jugábamos al escondite en el parque.

Leía las tiras cómicas los domingos.

Saltaba la cuerda.

Mis amigas y yo jugábamos con nuestras muñequitas en el jardín de la casa.

Mi abuela y yo preparábamos la cena.

Jugaba al bebeleche en el patio de recreo de la escuela.

Actividad 6 **Asociaciones: La niñez de algunas personas famosas**

Empareje a estas personas con las oraciones en la página siguiente que las describen.

a. Cristóbal Colón, navegante y explorador
b. Rigoberta Menchú, activista indígena guatemalteca
c. Carlos Santana, guitarrista mexicoamericano
d. Penélope Cruz, actriz española
e. Gael García Bernal, actor mexicano
f. Sandra Cisneros, escritora mexicoamericana

1. Actuaba en el teatro.
2. Soñaba con cambiar la sociedad.
3. Tocaba mucho la guitarra.
4. Quería descubrir «nuevos mundos».
5. Viajaba con frecuencia a México con sus padres.
6. Vivía en México.
7. Quería mejorar la vida de los indígenas de su país.
8. Asistía al Conservatorio Nacional de Madrid.
9. Vivía en Guatemala.
10. Navegaba.
11. Estudiaba ballet.
12. Vivía en España.
13. Soñaba con viajar.
14. Era bilingüe.
15. Hablaba maya quiché.
16. Vivía en Chicago.

Actividad 7   Conversación: ¡Viva el verano!

Mire el dibujo y piense en su niñez.

1. ¿Hacía usted las mismas cosas que los niños de los dibujos?
2. ¿Iba al cine? ¿Con quién(es)?
3. ¿Jugaba a la pelota? ¿Dónde?
4. ¿Volaba un papalote? ¿Dónde?
5. ¿Iba al zoológico? ¿Dónde? ¿Con quién(es)?
6. ¿Paseaba en bicicleta? ¿Dónde, en el parque o en su barrio?
7. ¿Tomaba helados? ¿Qué sabor prefería?
8. ¿Qué otras cosas hacía durante el verano?

Actividad 8 Descripción de dibujos: La niñez de los amigos norteamericanos

Mire la siguiente tabla y escuche las oraciones que le lee su profesor(a). Diga si son ciertas o falsas.

Ahora, hágale preguntas a un compañero / una compañera según la tabla.

MODELO: E1: ¿Qué hacía Lan siempre de niña?
              E2: *Sacaba buenas notas.*

Finalmente, hágale preguntas a su compañero/a sobre lo que él/ella hacía de niño/a.

MODELO: E1: De niño/a, ¿qué hacías tú después de las clases?
              E2: *Jugaba con mis amiguitos.*

Famosos y humanitarios

El **cantautor** dominicano Juan Luis Guerra opina que todo artista debe contribuir de alguna manera a su comunidad. Él representa y proyecta la cultura de su país con sus canciones, «Burbujas de amor» y «La llave de tu corazón» entre muchas otras. Pero también tiene una fundación, la Fundación Juan Luis Guerra, que ofrece cuidado médico a mucha gente pobre de la República Dominicana. En 2007, el cantautor abrió un **ala** de un hospital en su país para curar a niños **hidrocéfalos.** Para él, su trabajo humanitario es tan importante como su música. Y por suerte, ésta es la opinión de muchos otros hispanos célebres.

El famoso guitarrista mexicano Carlos Santana tiene la Fundación Milagro, que se enfoca especialmente en la educación de los niños pobres en Estados Unidos y México. Ganador de numerosos premios Grammy, Santana piensa que uno debe **dejar su huella** en el mundo. Ésta es la misma filosofía que motiva a Edward James Olmos. El talentoso actor mexicoamericano hace un trabajo social importante, al visitar con frecuencia escuelas y centros de detención juvenil para **alentar** a los jóvenes. Además, Olmos es fundador de Latino Public Broadcasting, una organización que produce programas para la comunidad hispana de Estados Unidos.

La cantante colombiana Shakira, artista de fama internacional por sus canciones y conciertos, es también conocida por su labor humanitaria. En 1997, Shakira creó la Fundación **Pies Descalzos** para ayudar a los niños pobres de Colombia, ofreciéndoles escuelas especiales. Como estos cuatro hispanos célebres, hay muchos otros que se dedican a ayudar a **los demás,** y que así dejan una huella significativa en el mundo.

Juan Luis Guerra, cantautor dominicano

VOCABULARIO ÚTIL

el cantautor	*singer-songwriter*
el ala	*wing*
hidrocéfalos	*hydrocephalic*
dejar su huella	*to leave a mark*
alentar	*to encourage*
Pies Descalzos	*Bare Feet*
los demás	*others*

Comprensión

1. ¿Qué tienen en común los cuatro hispanos mencionados?

2. ¿A quiénes benefician sus fundaciones?

Actividad 9 Entrevista: La niñez

1. De niño/a, ¿vivías en una ciudad o en un pueblo? ¿Te mudabas con frecuencia? ¿Por qué? ¿Te gustaba mudarte? ¿Por qué?
2. ¿Qué te gustaba hacer? ¿Jugabas con muñecas? ¿con carritos?
3. ¿Tenías perro o gato? ¿Cómo se llamaba?
4. ¿A qué escuela asistías? ¿Cómo era?
5. ¿Qué te gustaba hacer en la escuela? ¿Qué no te gustaba hacer?
6. ¿Tenías muchos amiguitos? ¿A qué jugaban en el recreo? ¿al gato? ¿a la pelota? ¿al escondite? ¿a la rayuela (al bebeleche)?
7. ¿Ibas al cine con frecuencia? ¿Qué películas te gustaba ver?
8. ¿Competías en algún deporte? ¿Cúal? ¿Te gustaba competir?

Enlace a la música

Canciones y rimas infantiles

El mundo hispano tiene una larga tradición de rimas y canciones infantiles que son una parte íntegra de la crianza[1] de los niños. La letra y la melodía de esta música ayudan a formar un enlace[2] profundo entre el niño y su cultura. Muchas de estas canciones tienen su origen hace 300 años en España, pero con el tiempo se desarrollaron[3] versiones distintas en América Latina. Hay canciones para arrullar[4] al niño, canciones y rimas que le enseñan al niño algo sobre el mundo en que vive y canciones que acompañan los juegos infantiles.

Las canciones de cuna[5] o nanas tienen una melodía dulce con el propósito[6] de ayudar al niño a dormir. Una de las más conocidas es «A la nanita nana», que es canción de cuna y villancico.[7] Otras nanas conocidas por todo el mundo hispano son «Señora Santa Ana» y «Este niño lindo». En el Caribe se canta «Duerme negrito», una canción que data de la época[8] de la esclavitud[9] y habla de la pobre mamá del negrito que trabaja sin pago. «Drume negrita»[10] es una nana moderna, escrita por el compositor cubano Eliseo Grenet en 1938. En Venezuela la canción de cuna más conocida es «Duérmete mi niño»; ¡la melodía es la misma del himno nacional[11] de ese país!

Además de cantar para adormecer a sus hijos, los padres y abuelos usan las canciones y las rimas para jugar con los niños y para enseñarles sobre el mundo. «Los elefantes» es una canción que le enseña al niño a contar y la canción «Pimpón» le enseña sobre la importancia del aseo.[12] Cuando un niño se lastima,[13] su madre le dice, «Sana,[14] sana, colita de rana,[15] si no sanas hoy, sanarás

Duérmete mi niño,

Duérmete mi niño
Que tengo que hacer,
Lavar los pañales[1]
Y hacer de comer.
Este niño quiere
Que lo duerma yo,
Duérmalo su madre
Que ella lo parió[2].

[1]diapers [2]lo...gave birth to him

mañana». Con la canción «Aserrín, aserrán, los maderos[16] de San Juan» el adulto le mueve los brazos al niño imitando el movimiento de una sierra[17] aserrando[18] el madero.

Los niños también cantan cuando juegan. La canción «La víbora de la mar» acompaña un juego similar al de *London Bridge Is Falling Down*. Para escoger a un niño para un juego, los niños dicen «De tin marín de dos pingüé, cúcara, mácara, títere fue».[19] «Arroz con leche» es otra canción muy conocida que acompaña un juego de niños. También hay canciones para saltar la cuerda como «Uva, pera, manzana y arroz, ¿a cuántos años me casaré yo? Uno, dos, tres, cuatro, cinco... » y así continúa hasta que el niño que salta se cae.[20]

Si quiere escuchar estas canciones infantiles y muchas otras le recomendamos la música de los cantantes mexicanos Cri-Cri y José-Luis Orozco o la de las argentinas Suni Paz y María Elena Walsh. La escritora cubana Alma Flor Ada y la española F. Isabel Campoy también se dedican a escribir colecciones de rimas y canciones infantiles. Aunque las canciones parezcan muy sencillas,[21] son una fuente rica de vocabulario y cultura. ¡Es posible cantar como los niños y aprender el español a la vez!

Los elefantes

Un elefante se balanceaba
Sobre la tela de una araña[1]
Como veía que resistía
Fue a llamar a otro elefante.
Dos elefantes se balanceaban...

[1]tela...spider web

[1]childrearing [2]link, connection [3]se... developed [4]sing to sleep [5]canciones... lullabies (cradle songs) [6]purpose [7]Christmas carol [8]era, time [9]slavery [10]Drume... Duerme negrita (en el español afro caribeño) [11]himno... national anthem [12]cleanliness, neatness [13]se... gets hurt [14]Get better, Heal [15]colita... frog's little tail [16]lumber, timber [17]saw [18]sawing [19]«De... «Eeny meeny miney moe . . . » [20]se... falls [21]simple

(Continúa)

Comprensión

1. ¿Qué propósito tienen las canciones que los padres y los abuelos les cantan a los niños? Y ¿cuándo usan las canciones y rimas los niños?

2. Diga si las siguientes canciones son canciones de cuna **C** o canciones que acompañan un juego **J**: «Este niño lindo», «Aserrín, aserrán», «Duerme negrito», «Señora Santa Ana», «víbora de la mar», «Arroz con leche».

La juventud

✳ Lea Gramática 9.4–9.5.

Pedro

Pedro Ruiz Galván era un joven muy guapo.

Bailaba con su novia Andrea en las fiestas.

Escribía cuentos para su clase de lengua.

En la escuela siempre se metía en líos.

Tenía muchos amigos. Iba al cine con ellos.

Conoció a su mejor amigo, Ernesto Saucedo Muñoz, cuando los dos tenían 13 años.

Quería casarse a los 15 años, pero su papá no quiso darle permiso.

Actividad 10   Intercambios: La juventud de los amigos hispanos

Hágale preguntas a su compañero/a sobre lo que hacían los amigos hispanos cuando eran más jóvenes.

MODELOS: E1: ¿Qué hacía *Ricardo después de las clases*?
E2: *Veía la televisión.*

E1: ¿Quién *esquiaba durante las vacaciones*?
E2: *Adriana.*

Actividad 11 Intercambios: La escuela secundaria

Diga qué hacía usted en estas situaciones cuando era estudiante.

MODELO: E1: Cuando mi madre no me permitía ver la televisión antes de hacer
la tarea *decía: «¡Pero si hoy no tengo tarea!»*.
E2: *¡Qué mentiroso/a!*

1. Cuando no quería ir a la escuela...
2. Cuando mi madre no me permitía ver la televisión antes de hacer la tarea...
3. Cuando quería comprar ropa nueva y no tenía dinero...
4. Cuando mi padre/madre no me daba permiso de salir...
5. Cuando tenía que entregar la tarea y no la tenía...

Y tú, ¿qué dices?

Yo también	¡Qué pícaro!
Yo no, yo...	¡Qué mentiroso!
¿De veras?	¡No lo creo!
¡Qué buena idea!	¿Y nunca tuviste problemas?

Frases y palabras útiles

- decía:
  «¡Ay, estoy enfermo/a.»
  «¡Pero si hoy no hay
  clases!»
  «¡Pero si hoy no tengo
  tarea!»
  «Anoche estaba enfermo/a.»
- le preguntaba al profesor /
  a la profesora, «¿Teníamos
  tarea?»
- la hacía rápidamente
  (durante la clase)
- me escapaba cuando
  todos estaban dormidos
- discutía con mi padre/
  madre
- lloraba
- gritaba
- trabajaba
- ahorraba dinero
- le pedía dinero a mi padre
  (madre, abuelo, tío...)
- iba al cine (a la playa...)

Este joven cubano va al trabajo en bicicleta.

Actividad 12   Intercambios: Mi familia y yo

Piense en las actividades que usted y su familia (su padre, su madre, sus hermanos, sus tíos, sus primos) hacían juntos cuando usted era niño/a. Escriba cinco de esas actividades y luego diga si le gustaba hacerlas o no y por qué. Comparta estas actividades con un compañero / una compañera de clase.

MODELOS: De niña, mi padre y yo surfeábamos. No me gustaba porque tenía miedo de las olas grandes.

De niño, mis hermanos y yo veíamos muchas películas. Me gustaba porque siempre comíamos dulces y palomitas.

Actividad 13   Entrevistas: La juventud

LA ESCUELA SECUNDARIA

1. ¿Cómo se llamaba tu escuela secundaria?
2. ¿Vivías lejos o cerca de la escuela? ¿Llegabas a la escuela a tiempo o tarde?
3. ¿Qué materia preferías? ¿Sacabas buenas notas?
4. ¿En qué actividades participabas? ¿En actividades deportivas? ¿En teatro? ¿Eras socio/a de algún club?
5. ¿Qué hacías después de las clases todos los días? ¿Estudiabas mucho? ¿Salías con tus amigos? ¿Adónde iban?

LOS VERANOS

1. Cuando eras más joven, ¿dónde pasabas los veranos?

2. ¿Visitabas a tus parientes? ¿Qué hacías con ellos?

3. ¿Trabajabas? ¿dónde? ¿Qué hacías? ¿Ganabas mucho dinero?

4. ¿Qué hacías por las tardes? ¿por las noches?

5. ¿Salías de vacaciones con tus padres? ¿Adónde iban? ¿Te gustaba?

Actividad 14 Entrevista: La juventud de una persona famosa

Imagínese que usted es una persona famosa: actor o actriz de cine, atleta, científico o político. Su compañero es periodista y le va a hacer preguntas sobre su juventud. Si no sabe qué hacía su personaje, puede inventar sus actividades.

E1: Buenas tardes Sr./Sra./Srta. _____. ¿Le puedo hacer algunas
preguntas sobre su vida?

E2: ¡Por supuesto!

E1: ¿_____?

Preguntas posibles

¿Dónde vivía?

¿Viajaba con frecuencia?

¿Le gustaba la escuela?

¿Veía mucho la televisión?

¿Practicaba algún deporte?

¿Leía mucho?

¿Cuál era su comida favorita?

¿Qué le gustaba hacer en su tiempo libre?

Los chicos de la calle

Los números son alarmantes: hay 40 millones de niños **desamparados** en las ciudades de América Latina. Son niños sin familia que viven en la calle y duermen en edificios abandonados y parques públicos. Muchos de ellos sufren abuso físico, usan drogas y están enfermos. Una de las razones de este problema es el rápido **crecimiento de la población** en las ciudades grandes. Otra razón es económica: la injusta distribución de **recursos.**

En 1992, la Organización de Naciones Unidas (ONU) publicó una resolución sobre la situación de los niños desamparados en todo el mundo. Desde ese año las condiciones de los niños sin hogar han mejorado un poco, aunque todavía es grave la situación. Por suerte, en América Latina hay varias organizaciones que están ayudando a los niños desamparados. Entre otras está Casa Alianza, que ofrece cuidado y refugio a 9.000 niños de la calle anualmente. La oficina central de esta organización está en San José, Costa Rica, aunque extiende sus servicios a Honduras, México y Nicaragua. Casa Alianza también tiene un sitio Web donde los niños hablan de su vida. En Buenos Aires, Argentina, hay un lugar llamado CAINA (Centro de Atención Integral a la Niñez y Adolescencia) que **socorre** a niños y adolescentes. Este centro provee comida, ducha y deportes a más de 2.000 chicos cada año. Además, el CAINA mantiene un sitio Web titulado *Chicos de la calle.* En este sitio, los jóvenes cuentan su historia en dibujos y narraciones. Sus historias nos revelan que los chicos de la calle son como todos los niños, a pesar de llevar una vida tan difícil.

El sitio Web *Chicos de la calle* de Casa Alianza contribuyen a cambiar la imagen negativa que hay de tantos jóvenes desamparados. Detrás de su imagen agresiva, aparecen estos niños con ilusiones de vivir una vida normal. Ellos desean lo mismo que mucha gente: un hogar, una familia y un futuro.

VOCABULARIO ÚTIL

desamparados	*homeless*
el crecimiento de la población	*population growth*
los recursos	*resources*
socorre	*helps*
a pesar de	*in spite of*

Comprensión

1. ¿Qué tipo de ayuda ofrece Casa Alianza a los niños desamparados?
2. Describa el sitio Web *Chicos de la calle.*

De todo un poco

Los recuerdos

¿Qué recuerdos tiene usted relacionados con su familia y con su niñez o juventud? Complete las siguientes oraciones.

MODELO: Recuerdo que para Pascua siempre *íbamos al parque a buscar huevitos.*

1. Recuerdo que en Navidad (Jánuca, Ramadán, el Año Nuevo,...) mi abuela (madre, tío,...) siempre...
2. Cuando era niño/a, para el Día de la Independencia (el 4 de julio) mi familia siempre...
3. Para mi cumpleaños, mis padres (tíos, primos, abuelos, hermanos,...) siempre...
4. Todavía recuerdo que para el Día de Acción de Gracias...

Ahora, comparta sus recuerdos con un compañero / una compañera.

¡Dígalo por escrito!

La niñez/juventud ideal

Piense en su niñez o juventud. ¿Fue ideal su niñez/juventud o hay cosas que quisiera cambiar? Escriba una composición sobre las actividades en la vida ideal de un niño / una niña o un joven / una joven.

MODELO: De niña mi familia y yo vivíamos en una isla en el Mar Caribe. Yo iba a la escuela en bicicleta y nadaba en el mar a la hora del almuerzo. Por la tarde...

Algunas actividades posibles

dormir en casa de amigos	nadar
asistir a conciertos	pasar tiempo con (*persona*)
comer muchos dulces	ver la televisión (videos)
no hacer la tarea	en mi cuarto
andar en patineta	ir de compras
jugar videojuegos	acampar en la montaña
ir a fiestas	salir con amigos
ir al cine	practicar deportes

¡Cuéntenos usted!

Cuéntenos sobre uno de sus primeros recuerdos. ¿Cuántos años tenía? ¿Dónde estaba? ¿Con quién estaba? ¿Qué hacía?

VOCABULARIO ÚTIL

díver	divertido
la propuesta	*proposal*
te escondes	*you hide*
precavida	*cautious*
la cuesta empinada	*steep hill*
¡te vas a caer!	*you'll fall!*
agarrada a los tirantes	*hanging on to suspenders*
hacerse grande	*become a big girl*
pensativa	*thoughtful*
un rato	*a while*
hubiese entendido	*she had understood*
prosiguió	*she continued*

LECTURA

¡Así piensan los niños!

¡QUÉ DÍVER!

María (3 años) y su amiga Patricia (5 años) estaban jugando en el jardín de nuestra casa. De pronto, María hizo una propuesta sugerente: «¿Por qué no jugamos a que tú te escondes detrás de ese árbol y yo te busco?»

(Ana Isabel Fernández, Palma)

NIÑA PRECAVIDA

Mi hija Ana (3 años) bajó corriendo por una cuesta muy empinada. «¡Ten cuidado, que te vas a caer!» exclamé al verla correr tan alocada. «No te preocupes, mamá», respondió ella. «¡Voy agarrada a los tirantes!»

(Lourdes Mejido, Badajoz)

LÓGICA INFANTIL

Le dije a mi hija Conchita (4 años) que tenía que comer todo el arroz para hacerse grande como papá y mamá. La pequeña se quedó pensativa y después de un rato me dijo: «Mami, yo tengo que comer para hacerme grande como papá y como tú, ¿verdad?»

«¡Sí, mi niña!» exclamé, contenta de que por fin lo hubiese entendido. «Oye —prosiguió ella— ¿y vosotros para qué coméis?»

(Conchita Palazón, Sardañola)

Comprensión

1. ¿Qué hacían María y Patricia?
2. ¿Por qué está preocupada la mamá de Ana? Según Ana, ¿por qué no necesita preocuparse su mamá?
3. Según la madre de Conchita, ¿para qué tienen que comer los niños todo lo que sus padres les sirven?
4. ¿Por qué pregunta Conchita para qué comen sus padres?

Un paso más... ¡a escribir!

¿Recuerda algo chistoso que usted o su hijo/a dijo cuando tenía cuatro, cinco, seis o siete años? Prepare con un compañero / una compañera una breve comedia sobre una experiencia cómica o interesante de la infancia. Escriban su diálogo para luego actuarlo en clase.

Vocabulario

La familia y los parientes

Family and Relatives

el cuñado / la cuñada	brother-in-law/sister-in-law
el hermanastro / la hermanastra	stepbrother/stepsister
el hijastro / la hijastra	stepson/stepdaughter
la madrastra	stepmother
el medio hermano / la media hermana	half brother / half sister
la nuera	daughter-in-law
el padrastro	stepfather
el suegro / la suegra	father-in-law/mother-in-law
los suegros	in-laws
el yerno	son-in-law

REPASO: el abuelo (abuelito) / la abuela (abuelita), el hermano (hermanito) / la hermana (hermanita), el hijo (hijito) / la hija (hijita), el hijo único / la hija única, la madre, el nieto / la nieta, el padre, los padres, el primo / la prima, el sobrino / la sobrina, el tío / la tía

Los verbos

Verbs

actuar	to act
ahorrar	to save
basarse en	to be based upon
cambiar	to change
competir (i)	to compete
dar permiso	to give permission
descubrir	to discover
discutir	to discuss; to argue
entregar	to hand in, turn in
jugar (ue)	to play
a la pelota	ball
a la rayuela (bebeleche: *Mex.*)	hopscotch
al escondite	hide-and-seek
al gato	tag
con carritos, muñecas	with little cars, dolls
llenar (el espacio en blanco)	to fill (in the blank)
llevarse bien	to get along well
mejorar(se)	to improve; to get better
meterse en líos	to get into trouble
mudarse	to move (residence)
parecerse	to look like
pelear	to fight
permitir(se)	to allow
recordar (ue)	to remember
sacar buenas/malas notas	to get good/bad grades
saltar la cuerda	to jump rope
soñar (con)	to dream (about)
subirse a los árboles	to climb trees
volar un papalote (*Mex.*)	to fly a kite

PALABRAS SEMEJANTES: escaparse, inventar
REPASO: casarse, preguntar, volar una cometa

Los sustantivos

Nouns

el árbol genealógico	family tree
el barrio	neighborhood
el científico / la científica	scientist
el cuento	story
la escuela	school
primaria	elementary school
secundaria	junior high / high school
el/la joven	young person
la juventud	youth
la niñez	childhood
el/la periodista	reporter
el personaje	character (in a story)
el/la político	politician
el pueblito	little town
el recreo	recess, break
el patio de recreo	playground
los recuerdos	memories
el socio / la socia	member
las tiras cómicas	comic strips

PALABRAS SEMEJANTES: el (la) activista, el animal doméstico, el (la) atleta, el explorador / la exploradora, el / la guitarrista, el navegante, la sociedad, la terminal de autobuses
REPASO: la mascota, la materia, la preparatoria, la vida

Los adjetivos

Adjectives

cierto/a	true
dormido/a	asleep
estar muerto/a (vivo/a)	to be dead (alive)
pocos/as	few

PALABRAS SEMEJANTES: falso/a

Palabras y expresiones útiles

a tiempo	on time
¿Cómo era... ?	What was/were . . . like?
de niño/a	as a child
había	there was/were
¡Qué mentiroso/a!	What a liar!
¡Qué pícaro/a!	What a rascal!
todavía	still
¡Viva... !	Hooray (for) . . . !; Long live . . . !

Gramática y ejercicios

¿RECUERDA?

You have already studied some reflexive verbs (see **Gramática 4.3**) that are used to express daily routine: **levantarse, ducharse, despertarse, vestirse, afeitarse, maquillarse,** and so on. Remember that reflexive verbs use a reflexive pronoun (**me, te, se, nos, os, se**) placed in front of the conjugated verb.

---

me levanto = *I get up*
te bañas = *you (inf. sing.) take a bath*
se afeita = *you (pol. sing.) shave; he/she shaves*
nos vestimos = *we get dressed*
se acuestan = *you (pl.) / they go to bed*

---

parecerse = *to look like*
—**¿A quién te pareces?**
(*Who do you look like?*)
—**Me parezco a mi hermana.**
(*I look like my sister.*)

9.1 Describing Family Relationships: The Reciprocal Reflexive Verbs *parecerse* and *llevarse bien*

Gramática ilustrada

Andrea y Paula son gemelas. Se parecen mucho.

Mónica y su padrastro no siempre se llevan bien.

Susana se lleva muy bien con sus hijos.

Some reflexive verbs have a special meaning. One such verb is **parecerse*** (*to look like*).

parecerse		
(yo)	me parezco	*I look like*
(tú)	te pareces	*you (inf. sing.) look like*
(usted, él/ella)	se parece	*you (pol. sing.) look like; he/she looks like*
(nosotros/as)	nos parecemos	*we look like*
(vosotros/as)	os parecéis	*you (inf. pl., Spain) look like*
(ustedes, ellos/as)	se parecen	*you (pl.) look like; they look like*

---

*Don't forget to use the personal **a** with this verb. See **Gramática 6.4.**
Recognition: **vos te parecés**

—¿A quién **te pareces**?

—**Me parezco a** mi tía Lila.
Nuestros hijos **se parecen**
a mi suegro.

—*Who do you look like?*

—*I look like my Aunt Lila.*
Our children look like my
father-in-law.

Another reflexive verb with special meaning is **llevarse... con** (*to get along . . .*
with).

—**Con** quién **te llevas** mejor,
con tu mamá o con tu papá?

—**Me llevo** mejor **con** mi papá.

—*With whom do you get along better,*
your mother or your father?

—*I get along better with my father.*

When used in plural form, some reflexive verbs can express reciprocal action (*to each*
other). Both **parecerse** and **llevarse** can be used in this way. (You will learn more
about other reciprocal reflexives in **Gramática 14.1.**)

Clarisa y Marisa no son gemelas,
pero **se parecen** mucho.

Mi abuela y yo **nos parecemos.**

Mi cuñada y yo **no nos llevamos
bien.**

Graciela y Amanda **se llevan** muy
bien; son muy buenas amigas.

Clarisa and Marisa are not twins,
but they look a lot alike.

My grandmother and I look alike.

My sister-in-law and I don't get
along well.

Graciela y Amanda get along
very well; they are very good friends.

> **llevarse bien con** = *to get*
> *along well with*
> —**¿Te llevas bien con tus**
> **hermanos?**
> (*Do you get along well with*
> *your siblings?*)
> —**Sí, me llevo bien con**
> **todos en mi familia.**
> (*Yes, I get along well with*
> *everyone in my family.*)

> Reflexive verbs are also used
> to express reciprocal actions
> (*each other*).

> **nos parecemos** = *we look*
> *alike (like each other)*
> **se parecen** = *they look*
> *alike (like each other)*
> **se llevan bien** = *they get*
> *along well (with each other)*

Ejercicio 1

Use las formas apropiadas del verbo **parecerse**
para completar las siguientes oraciones.

1. Ernestito _____ mucho a su padre.

2. Amanda y Guillermo son hermanos
   pero no _____.

   Amanda dice: «Yo _____ a papá;
   ¿a quién _____ tú, Guillermo?»

3. Andrea dice: «Yo _____ mucho a
   Paula, pero _____ menos a Raúl.»

4. Paula dice: «Sí, Andrea, tú y
   yo _____ mucho porque somos
   gemelas. Raúl _____ más a mamá.»

5. ¿A quién _____ más usted, a su
   padre o a su madre?

Ejercicio 2

Use las formas apropiadas del verbo **(no) llevarse** para terminar correctamente estas oraciones.

1. MÓNICA: Mis padres se divorciaron, pero ahora _____ bien.
2. SR. VO: Lan, ¿_____ bien con tus compañeros de clase?

   LAN: Sí, papá. En la clase de la profesora Martínez todos _____ muy bien; somos buenos amigos.
3. MÓNICA: Mis hermanastros y yo _____ bien, pero yo no _____ bien con mi padrastro.
4. NORA: Mis primos _____ muy bien; siempre les gusta estar juntos.
5. ESTEBAN: Raúl, ¿ahora _____ (tú) bien con las chicas?

   RAÚL: ¡Por supuesto, Esteban! Las chicas bonitas y yo _____ muy bien.

9.2 Expressing *for, from,* and *to whom:* Prepositions + Pronouns

A. As you saw in **Gramática 8.2,** pronouns often follow prepositions in Spanish.

a mí	*to, at me*	sin nosotros/as	*without us*
de ti, usted(es)	*of, from you*	con ellos/as	*with them*
en él	*in, on him/it*	para vosotros/as	*for you*
para ella	*for her*		

—¿Para quién es el regalo?
¿Es **para mí**?
—No, es **para él**.

—*Who is the present for?*
Is it for me?
—*No, it's for him.*

—¿**Sin** Rogelio? No podemos
ir **sin él**.

—*Without Rogelio? We can't go*
without him.

Adriana es una magnífica empleada.
Tengo mucha confianza **en ella**.

Adriana is a great employee.
I have a lot of confidence in her.

B. Con and **mí** combine to form **conmigo** (*with me*). **Con** and **ti** form **contigo** (*with you*).

---

conmigo = *with me*
contigo = *with you (inf. sing.)*

—Nora, ¿quieres ir **conmigo** al
cine esta tarde?
—No, Esteban. No puedo ir
contigo esta tarde. Tengo que
llevar a mi abuelita al aeropuerto.

—*Nora, do you want to go to the*
movies with me this afternoon?
—*No, Esteban. I can't go with*
you this afternoon. I have to
take my grandma to the airport.

Ejercicio 3

Graciela le dice a Amanda para quién(es) son algunas cosas y Amanda reacciona con sorpresa. ¿Qué dice Amanda en cada caso?

MODELO: Esta calculadora es para mi hermanito. →
¿Para *él*? ¡No lo creo! *¡Es muy pequeño!*

Posibilidades

¿Para _____?   ¡No me/te/le/nos/les gusta(n)!
¡No lo creo!   ¡Es muy pequeño/a!
¿Te/Le/Les gusta(n)?

1. Esta corbata es para mi tía.
2. Este abrigo es para ti.
3. Este disco compacto de música clásica es para Clarisa y Marisa.
4. Estos periódicos son para ti y para tus amigos.
5. Esta patineta es para mi abuelito.
6. Esta cerveza es para mí.
7. Estas muñecas son para la profesora de español.
8. Esta ensalada es para Lobo, el perro de Ernestito.

Ejercicio 4

Complete estos diálogos con **mí, ti, él, conmigo** o **contigo.**

1. DIEGO: Amanda, ¿quieres ir _____ᵃ al Baile de los Enamorados?
   AMANDA: No, Diego. Lo siento, pero no puedo ir _____ᵇ porque voy a ir con Ramón, mi novio.

2. RAFAEL: Graciela, estas rosas son para _____ᵃ ¿Te gustan?
   GRACIELA: ¿Para _____ᵇ? ¡Ay, Rafael, muchas gracias! Me encantan.

3. AMANDA: Graciela, ¿qué piensas tú de Luc, el nuevo estudiante francés?
   GRACIELA: ¿Qué pienso de _____ᵃ? Pues, no lo conozco, pero creo que es *muy* atractivo.
   AMANDA: Ajá... y yo voy a estudiar con _____ᵇ esta tarde... en mi casa.
   GRACIELA: ¡No lo creo, Amanda! ¡Vas a estudiar con _____ᶜ? ¿Sola? ¿Sin _____ᵈ? ¡Qué envidia!

9.3 Saying What You Used to Do: The Imperfect Tense

A. The Spanish imperfect tense is used to describe actions that occurred repeatedly or habitually in the past. To express the same idea, English often uses the phrases *used to* or *would,* or just the simple past.

¿A qué hora **te levantabas** en el verano?	*What time*	did you did you used to would you	get up in the summer?
Siempre **me levantaba** a las 9:00.	*I always*	got up used to get up would get up	at 9:00.

> The imperfect often means *used to* or *would:*
>
> **De niña, nadaba todos los días en el verano.** (*As a child, I used to [would] swim every day in the summer.*)
>
> **Cuando éramos jóvenes, íbamos al cine todos los sábados.** (*When we were young, we would go to the movies every Saturday.*)

Imperfect endings:
-ar verbs = **-aba**
-er/-ir verbs = **-ía**

(handwritten notes in margin)
1) charactor in the past
   Era alta
2) Decir la hora en el pasado
   ¿Qué hora era?
3) La edad

B. There are two patterns of endings for the imperfect: for **-ar** verbs, the **-aba** endings; for **-er/-ir** verbs, the **-ía** endings.*

	manejar	**comer**	**vivir**
(yo)	manejaba	comía	vivía
(tú)	manejabas	comías	vivías
(usted, él/ella)	manejaba	comía	vivía
(nosotros/as)	manejábamos	comíamos	vivíamos
(vosotros/as)	manejabais	comíais	vivíais
(ustedes, ellos/as)	manejaban	comían	vivían

Mis hermanos **comían** mucho cuando **visitábamos** a nuestros abuelos.

My brothers used to eat a lot when we visited (would visit) our grandparents.

—¿Qué **hacía** Raúl los domingos cuando **estaba** en la secundaria?
—**Jugaba** al tenis con sus amigos.

—What did Raúl used to do on Sundays when he was in high school?
—He used to play tennis with his friends.

C. Only three verbs are irregular in the imperfect.

Only **ir, ser,** and **ver** are irregular in the imperfect.

	ir	**ser**	**ver**
(yo)	iba	era	veía
(tú)	ibas	eras	veías
(usted, él/ella)	iba	era	veía
(nosotros/as)	íbamos	éramos	veíamos
(vosotros/as)	ibais	erais	veíais
(ustedes, ellos/as)	iban	eran	veían

Te **veía** más cuando trabajabas en esta oficina.
Cuando **era** muy joven, **íbamos** a la finca y mi padre me llevaba en su caballo.

I used to see you more when you worked in this office.
When I was very young, we used to go to the farm and my father would let me ride with him on his horse.

---

*Recognition: In the imperfect, the **vos** form is identical to the **tú** form: **manejabas, comías, vivías,** and so on.

Ejercicio 5

¿Qué hacían estas personas de niños?

MODELO: jugar mucho al tenis / Paula → Paula *jugaba* mucho al tenis.

1. andar en bicicleta / Guillermo
2. jugar con muñecas / Amanda y yo
3. leer las tiras cómicas del periódico los domingos / Andrea
4. bañarse en el mar en Acapulco / doña Lola y doña Rosita
5. comer muchos dulces / don Eduardo
6. limpiar su recámara / Estela
7. pasar las vacaciones en Acapulco / la familia Saucedo
8. escuchar música rock / Pedro Ruiz
9. ver dibujos animados en la televisión / Ernesto
10. cuidar el jardín / el abuelo de Ernestito

¡OJO!

Some Spanish speakers use **muñequitos** for cartoons instead of **dibujos animados.**

Ejercicio 6

Complete cada oración con el nombre de la(s) persona(s) y la forma apropiada del imperfecto.

MODELO: Ya no monta a caballo mucho, pero antes *montaba* a caballo todos los fines de semana.

1. _____ : Ya no juegan a las cartas, pero antes _____ todas las tardes.
2. _____ : Antes _____ a misa todos los domingos, pero ya no van mucho.
3. _____ : De niña _____ la cuerda, pero ya nunca salta la cuerda.
4. _____ : Ya no se pelea con sus hermanas, pero antes _____ mucho con ellas.
5. _____ : Ya no llora tanto cuando ve películas tristes, pero de adolescente _____ mucho.
6. _____ : Cuando tenía ocho años, no _____ bien con las niñas.
7. _____ : De niñas, _____ mucho.

9.4 Describing the Past: The Imperfect and Preterite of "State" Verbs

Gramática ilustrada

A. Some verbs express actions (*run, jump, eat*); others express states (*want, have, be, can*). In the narration of a past event, verbs describing states or ongoing conditions are usually conjugated in the imperfect tense.

> Verbs of state—for example, *to want, to have*—do not express action. When used in talking about the past, they are usually conjugated in the imperfect.

—Guillermo, ¿**sabías** la respuesta de la cuarta pregunta?
—**Sabía** una parte, pero no toda.

—Guillermo, did you know the answer to the fourth question?
—I knew part of it, but not all.

—¿Qué **querías** hacer?
—**Quería** ir al cine.
—¿Por qué no **podías** ir?
—Porque no **tenía** dinero.

—What did you want to do?
—I wanted to go to the movies.
—Why couldn't you go?
—Because I didn't have any money.

B. When Spanish speakers use state verbs in the preterite, they usually do so to convey that the state came to an end. English speakers often use completely different verbs to express that meaning. Compare the English equivalents of the following state verbs in the imperfect and in the preterite.

IMPERFECT		PRETERITE	
sabía	*I knew*	supe	*I found out*
no sabía	*I didn't know*	no supe	*I never knew*
conocía	*I was acquainted with*	conocí	*I met*
tenía	*I had*	tuve	*I had; I received*
quería	*I wanted*	quise	*I wanted (and tried)*
no quería	*I didn't want*	no quise	*I refused*
podía	*I was able, could*	pude	*I could (and did)*
no podía	*I wasn't able, couldn't*	no pude	*I (tried and) couldn't*

> **(yo) sabía** = *I knew*
> **(yo) supe** = *I found out*
>
> **usted conocía** = *you (pol. sing.) knew*
> **usted conoció** = *you (pol. sing.) met*

—¿**Supiste** lo que les pasó a Graciela y a Amanda? — *Did you find out what happened to Graciela and Amanda?*

—No, no **supe** nada. ¿Qué les pasó? — *No, I didn't find out (never heard) anything. What happened to them?*

—¿Por qué no **pudiste** terminar? — *Why weren't you able to finish?*
—**No quise** terminar porque me cansé mucho. — *I didn't try to finish because I got very tired.*

C. The verbs **ser** and **estar** are usually used in the imperfect; they are used in the preterite only when the state has explicitly come to an end within a specified amount of time.

> When used to express *was/were*, **ser** and **estar** are usually in the imperfect:
> **Estaba muy cansado.** (*I was very tired.*)
> **Éramos amigas íntimas en la escuela secundaria.** (*We were very close friends in high school.*)

INFINITIVE	IMPERFECT		PRETERITE	
ser	era	*I was*	fui	*I was*
estar	estaba	*I was*	estuve	*I was*

—¿Cómo **eras** de niño? — *What were you like as a child?*
—**Era** muy tímido. — *I was very shy.*

—¿Cuánto tiempo **fuiste** presidente del club? — *How long were you president of the club?*
—**Fui** presidente seis años. — *I was president for six years.*

—¿Dónde **estaban** tus padres anoche? — *Where were your parents last night?*
—**Estaban** con los abuelos. — *They were with my grandparents.*

—¿Cuánto tiempo **estuvieron** en España? — *How long were you in Spain?*
—**Estuvimos** allí de mayo a julio. — *We were there from May to July.*

> Within a limited or specified time frame, **ser** and **estar** may be used in the preterite to express *was/were*:
> **Estuvimos cinco días en Acapulco.** (*We were in Acapulco for five days.*)
> **Mi hijo fue presidente del Club de Español por dos años.** (*My son was president of the Spanish Club for two years.*)

Ejercicio 7

Complete las oraciones según el modelo. Use el imperfecto de los verbos en letra cursiva (*italics*).

MODELO: Ahora no *soy* tímido, pero de niño *era* muy tímido.

1. Ahora Guillermo *tiene* 12 años, pero cuando tú lo conociste _____ sólo 8 años.
2. Ahora *sé* muy bien las respuestas, pero esta mañana, cuando tomé el examen, no las _____.
3. Ahora *conocemos* muy bien a doña Rosita, pero hace un año no la _____.
4. Ahora Paula *es* agente de viajes, pero yo recuerdo cuando _____ secretaria.
5. Ahora Paula *está* aquí en México, pero hace una semana _____ en España.

Ejercicio 8

Complete las siguientes oraciones con la forma apropiada del imperfecto de estos «verbos de estado»: **conocer, estar, poder, querer, saber, ser** y **tener.**

1. Luis _____ sólo 10 años cuando viajó a Colombia.
2. Einstein _____ un joven muy inteligente, pero sacaba malas notas.
3. Yo no _____ a tu hermano. ¡Qué guapo es!
4. (Nosotros) _____ comprar un carro nuevo, pero no _____ dinero. Ahora, por fin tenemos suficiente dinero.
5. ¿Dónde _____ (tú) esta mañana?
6. Ayer almorcé a las 11:00 porque _____ mucha hambre.

Ahora, use la forma apropiada del pretérito de estos «verbos de estado»: **conocer, poder, querer, saber** y **tener.**

7. Ayer _____ que el hijo mayor de mi vecino es actor de cine.
8. Hoy no fui a trabajar porque no dormí anoche. Toda la noche _____ un dolor de cabeza horrible.
9. ¡Qué simpático es el esposo de Andrea Ruiz! Lo _____ anoche en la fiesta.
10. Ah, sí, la fiesta de fin de año... Los Ruiz me invitaron, pero yo no _____ ir. ¡A mí no me gustan las fiestas!
11. Ayer fui al parque con mis hijos; traté de patinar con ellos, pero no _____. ¡Me estoy poniendo viejo!

9.5 Saying What You Were Going to Do: The Imperfect of *ir + a +* Infinitive

The imperfect of **ir** (**iba, ibas, iba, íbamos, ibais, iban**) can be used in this construction to express past intentions (*was/were going to do something*).

Íbamos a esquiar el jueves, pero ahora dicen que va a llover.
Rubén y Virginia **iban a pasar** el día en el parque, pero decidieron visitar las pirámides.

We were going to ski on Thursday, but now they say it's going to rain.
Rubén and Virginia were going to spend the day at the park, but they decided to visit the pyramids.

The imperfect of **querer** and **pensar** + infinitive is similar in meaning.

Quería acampar en las montañas este verano, pero resulta que tengo que trabajar.

I wanted (was hoping) to go camping in the mountains this summer, but it turns out I have to work.

Carmen **pensaba pasar** el verano en España, pero no ahorró suficiente dinero.

Carmen was thinking about (was planning on) spending the summer in Spain, but she didn't save enough money.

> **iba a** + infinitive = *I/he/she/you (pol. sing.) was/were going to:*
> **Iba a viajar por Europa, pero tuve que trabajar.** (*I was going to travel through Europe, but I had to work.*)

Ejercicio 9

Invente una excusa. Use **iba** + **a** + infinitivo, seguido de su excusa.

> In **Ejercicio 9,** note that for the excuses themselves, you should use the preterite.

MODELO: ¿Por qué no me llamaste anoche? (llegar muy tarde)
Iba a llamarte, pero llegué muy tarde.

1. ¿Por qué no viniste en tu carro anoche? (quedarse sin gasolina)
2. ¿Por qué no trajiste flores? (la tienda cerrar temprano)
3. ¿Por qué no me compraste un regalo? (no tener tiempo)
4. ¿Por qué no cenaste con nosotros? (cenar antes en casa)
5. ¿Por qué no fuiste al Baile de los Enamorados? (asistir a un concierto)
6. ¿Por qué no me dijiste que no sabías bailar? (no poder)
7. ¿Por qué no llegaste a tiempo? (perder mi reloj)
8. ¿Por qué no asististe a clase ayer? (ir a ver a mi abuela enferma)

Círculo de Amigas

¿**Q**ué sabe usted de Nicaragua? ¿Que hubo una revolución en 1979? ¿Que hubo una sangrienta[1] contrarrevolución apoyada[2] por los Estados Unidos? ¿Que el huracán Mitch causó gran destrucción en 1998? ¿Que el país tiene una altísima tasa de desempleo[3] y que en

las zonas rurales predomina la pobreza[4]? Sí, lamentablemente, todo esto es cierto; pero también hay buenas noticias. En Jinotega, un pequeño pueblo nicaragüense, existe ahora un Círculo de Amigas que ayuda a los pobres de este país.

El Círculo de Amigas fue fundado por una profesora de español en California, Pat McCully. Ella visitó Nicaragua varias veces en los años ochenta, pero no visitó los sitios turísticos, sino las zonas rurales más remotas. Mientras charlaba con la gente, observaba su ropa harapienta[5] y sus viviendas[6] pobres y decidió hacer algo para ayudar.

McCully comenzó[7] por enseñar a las mujeres a coser. Así empezó el Círculo de Amigas: como un pequeño espacio en el que las mujeres podían aprender a coser la ropa de su familia. Con la ayuda de varias personas y las contribuciones de muchas otras, el Círculo de Amigas ha crecido.[8] Ahora tiene una pequeña

clínica médica y un centro de computación (con computadoras usadas).

Lo que es más importante, la organización ahora intenta ayudar a la gente a vivir mejor: construye viviendas modestas, compra estufas de propano y consigue barriles para que la gente pueda tener agua limpia en su casa. Y no sólo eso, sino que tiene un programa de apoyo para las niñas. El Círculo consigue patrocinadores[9] que contribuyen $50.00 por mes. Ese dinero asegura que la niña más pequeña* de una familia pueda asistir a la escuela y que toda la familia coma mejor.

Como podemos ver, esta organización crece[10] cada día más y provee una ayuda valiosa para el pueblo de Jinotega. ¿Quiere usted saber cómo puede participar? Pues hay muchas maneras: usted puede ser patrocinador(a) de una niña, puede regalar máquinas de coser, computadoras, lentes y otras cosas parecidas. Puede también contribuir con su talento. ■

[1]*bloody* [2]*backed* [3]*tasa… unemployment rate* [4]*poverty* [5]*ragged* [6]*homes* [7]*began* [8]*ha… has grown* [9]*sponsors* [10]*grows*

*Círculo de Amigas decided on the youngest female for two reasons: Whenever there are funds for school, it is often the boys who get this privilege. And why the youngest? Because the sooner a child starts her education, the more likely she is to continue with it.

Celia Cruz,
reina de la salsa

Celia Cruz es la cantante cubana más famosa y admirada. Murió el 16 de julio de 2003, pero sus canciones vivirán para siempre. Celia creó un estilo único con canciones alegres y movidas[1] de salsa. Ha pasado a la historia de la música internacional con diez nominaciones para el Grammy, muchos premios y varios doctorados honorarios. ¡Hasta hay una calle en Miami que lleva su nombre! Por todo esto, a Celia se le conoce como la «reina de la salsa». Nadie puede hacernos bailar como ella.

Celia nació en la Habana en un hogar de catorce hijos y pronto mostró interés por la música. Desde muy joven empezó a cantar en espectáculos escolares y fiestas de la comunidad. Celia encontró su inspiración en la tradición afrocubana de su país. En 1950 se incorporó como vocalista a La Sonora Matancera, la orquesta más popular del Caribe. Cantó con este grupo durante quince años, haciendo giras[2] por todo el mundo.

Después de la Revolución Cubana de 1959, Celia decidió exilarse en Nueva York. Lo demás, como dice el dicho, «es historia»; una historia de esfuerzo y grandes éxitos:[3] el aclamado disco *Duets* (1988) y un papel importante en la película *The Mambo Kings* (1992), entre otros.

Con la música, Celia le enseñó al mundo a apreciar su cultura y su rica tradición musical. En una de sus grabaciones[4] finales, la cantante expresó vivamente su mensaje personal: para Celia Cruz, como dice esta canción, «la vida es un carnaval».

[1]*upbeat*   [2]*tours*   [3]*accomplishments*   [4]*recordings*

Antes del almuerzo, antes de la cena... ¡unas deliciosas tapas con vino tinto! Las tapas son pequeñas porciones de comida que los españoles comen con una copa de vino o de licor.* Existe una gran

Las tapas

variedad de estos pequeños aperitivos.[1] Una tapa puede ser algo tan sencillo como trozos de queso, aceitunas, cacahuetes,[2] chorizo[3] asado o canapés. Pero también puede ser un platillo más elaborado, como por ejemplo, trocitos de la típica tortilla española de patatas. Otros tipos de tapas son los camarones a la parrilla, los camarones u hongos preparados con ajo, los calamares[4] fritos, las ancas de rana[5] o las anguilas.[6]

En España, las tapas se sirven en lugares que se llaman tascas. En las tascas los españoles se reúnen para beber y comer tapas antes del almuerzo o la cena. Ésta es la oportunidad para hablar de política, filosofía, literatura, cine, teatro... Con frecuencia, la gente va de una tasca a otra, especialmente si es antes de la cena. Pero, las tapas son más que una deliciosa costumbre española: son un estilo de vida. Y, además de formar parte íntegra de la cultura de España, resultan muy prácticas. ¡Cuando se come a la vez que se bebe, los efectos del alcohol no son tan fuertes!

[1]*appetizers*   [2]*cacahuates; also called* maní *(see* **Capítulo 7, Lectura***)*
[3]*sausage*   [4]*squid*   [5]*ancas... frog legs*   [6]*eels*

Originally only a free small plate of salted almonds or a slice of jamón serrano *(a very salty ham) were served. The slice of ham or the plate of almonds was placed on top of the wine glass as a cover, hence the name* tapas *(covers). People would eat the* tapa, *feel thirsty, and order another glass of wine.*

Nuestro planeta

METAS

In **Capítulo 10** you will talk about places to which you have traveled, including their geography and climate. You will also discuss transportation and automobile travel. Finally, you will learn about and discuss environmental issues and concerns.

Fuga a la tierra de la fertilidad, por Paul Leonor Chevalier (República Dominicana)

Sobre el artista: El artista dominicano Paul Leonor Chevalier estudió pintura en la Escuela Nacional de Bellas Artes en Santo Domingo. En 1995, se graduó magna cum laude en arquitectura en la Universidad Nacional Pedro Henríquez Ureña. Es miembro del Colegio Dominicano de Artistas Plásticos. Ha participado en numerosas exposiciones y ha recibido varios premios.

¡Conozca Puerto Rico!

Nombre del país: el Estado Libre Asociado de Puerto Rico

Ciudad capital: San Juan

Ciudades principales: Bayamón, Carolina, Ponce

Moneda: el dólar estadounidense

Idiomas: el español, el inglés (oficiales)

Población: 4.000.000

Día de la Independencia: No es independiente. Fue una dependencia de Estados Unidos desde 1898 hasta 1952, año en que se convirtió en estado libre asociado de Estados Unidos.

Fiestas típicas: el Día de los Inocentes/Festival de las Máscaras las fiestas nacionales de los Estados Unidos

Comidas típicas: el mofongo, los moros y cristianos, los tostones, la pasta de guayaba con queso blanco

Música típica: la bomba, la plena, la salsa, el reggaetón

Gente famosa: Luis Muñoz Marín, Rosario Ferré, Tito Puente, Raúl Juliá

Código del país por Internet: .pr

Voces puertorriqueñas

¡Ay bendito!	¡Qué lástima!
boricua	puertorriqueño/a
chévere	estupendo
estar pelao/a	no tener dinero
los mahones	jeans
el/la pana	un(a) buen(a) amigo/a
el temporal	el huracán

¡Conozca la República Dominicana!

Nombre del país: la República Dominicana

Ciudad capital: Santo Domingo

Ciudades principales: Santiago de los Caballeros, San Pedro de Macorís, San Francisco de Macorís, Barahona

Moneda: el peso dominicano

Idiomas: el español

Población: 9.400.000

Día de la Independencia: el 27 de febrero

Fiestas típicas: el Carnaval, el Día de la Virgen de la Altagracia, el Día de la Virgen de las Mercedes

Comidas típicas: la bandera, los pasteles en hoja, las habichuelas con dulce, el cocido de patas de vaca

Música típica: el merengue, la bachata

Gente famosa: Rafael Leónidas Trujillo, Juan Bosch, Juan Marichal, Juan Luis Guerra

Código del país por Internet: .do

Voces dominicanas

un chin de	un poco de
dar una bola	to give someone a ride
darse un jumo	emborracharse
(es)tá aperísimo	está de lo mejor
(es)tá nítido	that's cool
estar en olla	no tener dinero

En este capítulo...

ACTIVIDADES DE COMUNICACIÓN

- La geografía y el clima
- Los medios de transporte
- La ecología y el medio ambiente

EN RESUMEN

LECTURAS Y CULTURA

- **Enlace a la literatura**
  «Dos cuerpos», por Octavio Paz
- **Ventanas al pasado**
  Los caminos incas
- **Ventanas culturales**
  La lengua: Nuestro pequeño mundo azul
- **Lectura**
  Costa Rica, un país excepcional

GRAMÁTICA Y EJERCICIOS

10.1 Saying What You Have Done: The Present Perfect

10.2 Exclamations with **¡Qué... !, ¡Cuánto/a/os/as... !**

10.3 Expressing *by, through*, Destination, and Time: **por** and **para** (Part 1)

10.4 Describing Actions: Adverbs

10.5 Expressing Reactions: More Verbs Like **gustar**

Actividades de comunicación y lecturas

La geografía y el clima

¡Qué bosque tropical más húmedo!

¡Qué desastrosa fue esa inundación!

¡Cuántas islas hay en la costa de Chile!

¡Qué luna más hermosa!

✳ **Lea Gramática 10.1–10.2.**

Actividad 1   Definiciones: La geografía

1. __h__ la selva
2. __j__ el río
3. _____ la inundación
4. _____ el lago
5. __c__ la playa
6. _____ el desierto
7. __e__ la península
8. __a__ la isla
9. __b__ el valle
10. __f__ la bahía

a. porción de tierra rodeada completamente de agua
b. espacio entre dos montañas
c. parte de arena a la orilla del mar
d. lugar árido, a veces con mucha arena
e. porción de tierra rodeada de agua, pero unida a tierra firme por un lado
f. entrada del mar en la costa, más pequeña que un golfo
g. extensión de agua rodeada de tierra
h. lugar donde llueve mucho y hay mucha vegetación
i. desbordamiento de los ríos, los lagos o el mar, que cubre la tierra de agua
j. corriente de agua que generalmente corre hacia el mar

342

Actividad 2 Descripción de fotos: ¡Qué impresionantes son esas montañas!

A. Escuche la descripción que le da su profesor(a) y señale la foto correspondiente.

1. El nudo de Huascarán, Perú

2. Un arrecife de corales en la Isla Cocos, Costa Rica

3. La Cordillera Vilcabamba, Perú

4. La playa en Cancún, México

5. El lago Titicaca, Bolivia

6. San Felipe, México

7. Bariloche, Argentina

8. Salto del Laja, Chile

Palabras útiles

cataratas
cielo
estrellas
flores
luna
peces coloridos
profundo/a
olas
vegetación

B. Ahora, mire las demás fotos y exprese los pensamientos que se le ocurran. Use **¡Cuánto/a/os/as...** ! o **¡Qué...** !

Actividad 3 Del mundo hispano: El pronóstico del tiempo

Conteste las preguntas según la información de un periódico de Santo Domingo, República Dominicana.

Febrero

La temperatura de la semana: Santo Domingo, República Dominicana

VIERNES. Nubes dispersas y probabilidad de lluvia, 30% por la mañana, 40% por la noche. Temperatura máxima: 29° C (grados centígrados). Viento este-nordeste 10 km/h. Temperatura mínima 20° C.

SÁBADO. Probabilidad de lluvia 30% y nubes dispersas. Temperature máxima 30° C. Viento ligero todo el día. Temperatura mínima 21° C.

DOMINGO. Probabilidad de lluvia 60%. Lloviznas frecuentes. Neblina temprano, luego parcialmente nublado y mucha humedad. Temperatura máxima 27° C. Por la noche viento norte-nordeste 10 km/h. Temperatura mínima 20° C.

LUNES. Soleado, humedad muy baja. Temperatura máxima 28° C. Viento norte-nordeste 14 km/h. Noche: Parcialmente nublado. Temperatura mínima 20° C y viento ligero.

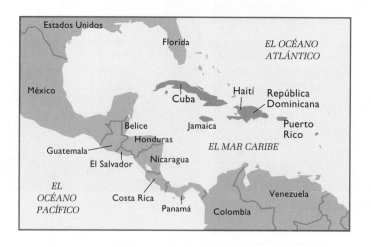

1. ¿Cuál va a ser el día más caluroso de esta semana?
2. ¿Qué noche va a hacer más fresco?
3. ¿Va a llover esta semana? ¿Qué día?
4. ¿Qué día va a estar nublado?
5. ¿Va a haber neblina? ¿Qué día?

Actividad 4 Descripción de dibujos: El tiempo

la escarcha   la humedad   la llovizna   la neblina   los relámpagos y los truenos   una tormenta   el rocío

Use estas palabras para completar las oraciones a continuación: **escarcha, fresco, humedad, llovizna, neblina, nubes, rocío, tormenta, truenos** y **viento.**

1. Después de los relámpagos, casi siempre vienen los _____.
2. Si por la noche baja la temperatura puede aparecer _____ en las ventanas y en los techos.
3. Antes de una _____, las _____ cubren el sol.
4. Una lluvia ligera también se llama _____.
5. Cuando hace mucho _____, la gente pierde el sombrero.
6. En las zonas tropicales hay mucha _____.
7. Hay que manejar lentamente cuando hay mucha _____.
8. Cuando la temperatura está a 15° C, hace _____.
9. Las gotas de agua que aparecen en las plantas por la mañana son _____.

A causa de las torrenciales lluvias de octubre y noviembre (2007) hubo terribles inundaciones en el estado mexicano de Tabasco. El 80% de su capital, Villahermosa, quedó bajo el agua.

Actividad 5 Del mundo hispano: Los recursos naturales

Lea el siguiente artículo y luego trabaje con un compañero / una compañera para decir si las afirmaciones de la página siguiente son ciertas o falsas. Corrijan las afirmaciones falsas con información del artículo.

Catalogado como uno de los ecosistemas más ricos del mundo por su abundante flora y fauna, el Mar de Cortés es todo un reto para buzos profesionales y aficionados.

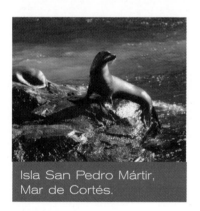

Isla San Pedro Mártir, Mar de Cortés.

EXPEDICIONES al Mar de Cortés

Por su gran concentración y diversidad de animales y aves marinos, los especialistas afirman que el Mar de Cortés y las lagunas de Baja California —a donde llega a aparearse la ballena gris después de recorrer 10.000 kilómetros— son la versión mexicana de las islas Galápagos. En este lugar se conocen bien muchos sitios de buceo por la belleza de sus cañones y montañas submarinas; las islas rocosas y áridas contrastan con la colorida variedad de plantas y animales debajo de la superficie: estrellas marinas, esponjas, anémonas y moluscos en abundancia, peces multicolores, delfines, leones marinos...

Quienes desean sumergirse en estas aguas y descubrir su extraordinaria vida marina, lo pueden hacer de junio a noviembre en expediciones organizadas que parten desde la amistosa ciudad de La Paz. Los paquetes incluyen tres inmersiones al día con tanques y pesas, experimentados maestros de buceo y tripulación, duchas de agua fresca, fácil acceso a la rampa de buceo, cubierta con área de sombra, un cocinero a bordo que prepara desayunos, comidas, refrigerios y bebidas, sistemas de video VHS y DVD, hotel y transporte al aeropuerto.

Salidas de junio a noviembre

Precio de los paquetes	Cabañas Los Arcos	Hotel Los Arcos
3 noches, 2 días de buceo	$3.745	$4.065
4 noches, 3 días de buceo	$4.875	$5.750
5 noches, 4 días de buceo	$6.300	$7.445
6 noches, 5 días de buceo	$7.490	$9.125
7 noches, 6 días de buceo	$8.745	$10.825

Todos los precios son por persona con base en ocupación doble, en pesos. Reservaciones en Expediciones Mar de Cortés al teléfono 1-612-483-6796.

● REFRÁN

Quien siembra vientos, recoge tempestades.

(*You reap what you sow*. Literally, *Those who plant winds, harvest storms*.)

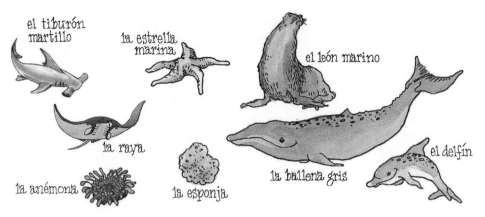

1. El Mar de Cortés se compara con las islas de Hawai.
2. Tanto en las Islas Galápagos como en el Mar de Cortés hay gran concentración y diversidad de animales y aves marinos.
3. En las lagunas de Baja California se pueden observar ballenas grises.
4. En este lugar hay abundancia de sitios de buceo muy bellos.
5. En el Mar de Cortés hay islas verdes y húmedas y arrecifes coloridos llenos de animales y plantas marinos.
6. Los paquetes turísticos incluyen tanques y pesas, lecciones de buceo, hotel y transporte aéreo.
7. Hay paquetes durante las cuatro estaciones del año: la primavera, el verano, el otoño y el invierno.

Ahora, hágale preguntas a su compañero/a acerca de los precios de los varios paquetes turísticos.

MODELO: E1: ¿Cuánto cuesta el paquete de seis noches con cinco días de buceo en Cabañas Los Arcos?
E2: Cuesta *$7.490.*

Actividad 6 Entrevistas: Los viajes, las actividades y el tiempo

¿ADÓNDE HAS VIAJADO?

1. ¿Has pasado tiempo en las montañas? ¿Dónde? ¿Qué hiciste? ¿Te gustó? ¿Por qué?
2. ¿Vives cerca del mar? Si no, ¿cuál es el mar más cercano a donde vives? ¿Cuántas veces has ido al mar / a la playa durante los últimos seis meses? ¿Cómo estaba el agua? ¿muy fría? ¿tibia?
3. ¿Hay un lago o río cerca de donde vives? ¿Cómo se llama? ¿Vas con frecuencia? ¿Qué haces allí?
4. ¿Has ido al desierto? ¿Dónde? ¿Cuándo? ¿Qué hiciste allí?
5. ¿Has visto una selva? ¿Dónde? ¿Te gustó? ¿Por qué? Explica.

LAS ACTIVIDADES Y EL TIEMPO

1. ¿Qué te gusta hacer cuando hace calor (frío, viento, mal tiempo)?
2. ¿Qué haces cuando llueve (nieva, hace buen tiempo, hay relámpagos y truenos)?
3. ¿Has vivido en un lugar muy húmedo? ¿en un lugar muy seco? ¿Dónde? ¿Te gustó? ¿Por qué?
4. ¿Has visto un huracán alguna vez? ¿Qué pasó? ¿Has visto un tornado alguna vez? ¿Dónde? ¿Causó daño?
5. ¿Has manejado alguna vez por la carretera en la neblina? ¿Tenías miedo? ¿Has pasado por una tormenta en avión? ¿Dónde? ¿Tuviste mucho miedo?

Enlace a la literatura

«Dos cuerpos», por Octavio Paz

Selección de su libro *Libertad bajo palabra: Obra poética* (*1935–1957*)

Poeta y ensayista de fama internacional, Octavio Paz (1914–1998) recibió el premio Nobel de Literatura en 1990. La obra poética de Octavio Paz es impresionante. Entre sus libros más famosos se encuentra *Piedra de sol* (1957), basado en el símbolo del Calendario Azteca. Se destacan también *Libertad bajo palabra* (1949), *Topoemas* (1971) y *El laberinto de la soledad* (1950).

Dos cuerpos

Dos cuerpos frente a frente
son a veces dos olas
y la noche es océano.

Dos cuerpos frente a frente
son a veces dos piedras[1]
y la noche desierto.

Dos cuerpos frente a frente
son a veces raíces[2]
en la noche enlazadas.[3]

Dos cuerpos frente a frente
son a veces navajas[4]
y la noche relámpago.

Dos cuerpos frente a frente
son dos astros[5] que caen
en un cielo vacío.[6]

Actividad creativa: El cuerpo humano y la naturaleza

En este hermoso poema de Octavio Paz, el poeta compara dos cuerpos humanos con olas, piedras, raíces y astros. ¿Con qué otros elementos de la naturaleza podríamos comparar el cuerpo humano? Escriba un poema haciendo esta comparación. Puede seguir el modelo de Paz.

Dos cuerpos frente a frente
son a veces...

[1]*rocks* [2]*roots* [3]*interlaced* [4]*blades* [5]*estrellas* [6]*empty*

Los medios de transporte

✳ **Lea Gramática 10.3–10.4.**

Se puede viajar
cómodamente por avión.

el avión

Salimos ahora para
España.

el tren

Los trenes en España salen
y llegan puntualmente.

Hicimos una gira en bicicleta por dos
semanas.

Hoy regresamos. Tenemos que estar en
Madrid para el lunes.

el letrero
Alto
el semáforo
(la señal)
la multa
la autopista
el tranvía
el transbordador
el metro

Actividad 7 Definiciones: El Transporte

LOS MEDIOS DE TRANSPORTE

1. _____ el avión
2. _____ el tren
3. _____ el barco
4. _____ el tranvía
5. _____ la bicicleta
6. _____ el autobús
7. _____ el transbordador
8. _____ el metro

a. medio de transporte que flota en el agua
b. medio de transporte subterráneo; se usa en las grandes ciudades del mundo
c. vehículo de dos ruedas que no usa gasolina
d. vehículo que puede transportar de 30 a 80 pasajeros
e. vehículo aéreo
f. medio de transporte que tiene vagones y una locomotora
g. tipo de tren que, empleado en las ciudades, usa electricidad
h. flota en el agua; sirve para transportar personas y vehículos

Actividad 8 Intercambios: Reservaciones por Internet

MODELO: E1: ¿Cuánto cuesta el pasaje a *Costa Rica* desde México?
E2: Cuesta *8.900 pesos.*

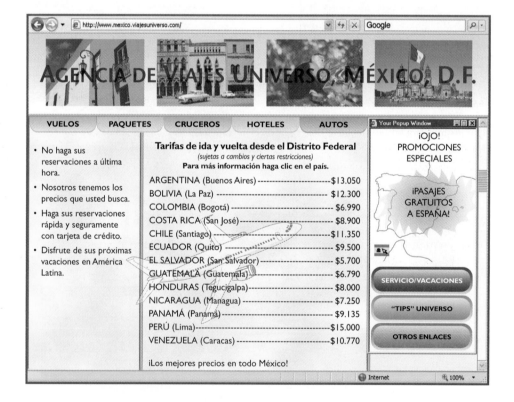

Actividad 9 **Conversación: Los medios de transporte: ventajas y desventajas**

Piense en las ventajas y las desventajas de cada uno de los siguientes medios de transporte: la bicicleta, el tren, el coche (el carro), el autobús, el metro, el taxi, el crucero, el avión y la motocicleta. Comparta sus ideas con el resto de la clase.

MEDIO DE TRANSPORTE	VENTAJA	DESVENTAJA
la bicicleta	no contamina el medio ambiente	es lenta
el tren		
el coche (el carro)		
el autobús		
el metro		
el taxi		
el crucero		
el avión		
la motocicleta		

Actividad 10 **Entrevistas: El transporte**

EL TRANSPORTE

1. ¿Usas mucho el autobús? ¿Por qué? ¿Andas mucho en bicicleta? ¿Andabas mucho en bicicleta de niño/a? ¿Cuál es tu forma de transporte preferida?
2. De niño/a, ¿viajabas mucho en auto con tu familia? ¿Adónde iban? ¿Te gustaba hacer viajes con tu familia?
3. ¿Has viajado por tren? ¿Adónde fuiste? ¿Te gusta viajar por tren? ¿Por qué? ¿Has viajado por avión? ¿Adónde has ido? ¿Te gusta viajar por avión? ¿Crees que es peligroso viajar por avión? Explica.
4. ¿Has andado alguna vez en motocicleta? ¿Te gustó? ¿Llevas casco cuando andas en moto? ¿Crees que es peligroso montar en moto? ¿Por qué?
5. ¿Has viajado en barco? ¿Adónde fuiste? ¿Te gustó el viaje? ¿Era grande o pequeño el barco? ¿Te mareas cuando viajas por barco?

¡OJO!

Las grandes capitales latinoamericanas como México, D.F. o Bogotá tienen serios problemas de contaminación ambiental debido al tránsito excesivo. Para solucionarlos han creado programas similares. El de México se llama «Hoy no circula» y el de Bogotá «Pico y Placa». Ambos restringen el tránsito de lunes a viernes. En Bogotá depende del último número de la placa. Cada día hay autos que no pueden salir en horarios pico (de 6:00 a 9:00 y de 16:00 a 19:00). En el D.F. se aplica a los autos que tienen más de diez años y se determina por medio de una calcomanía (*sticker*) y el último número de la placa; los autos no circulan de 5:00 a 22:00.

Los caminos incas

Muchos sabemos que la cultura inca es una de las más importantes de las Américas. Hemos oído hablar de esa hermosa fortaleza en los Andes, Machu Picchu. Sabemos también que los incas tenían grandes conocimientos de arquitectura, medicina y agricultura. Algo que no es tan conocido es su gran **dominio** de la ingeniería. Una de las mejores **pruebas:** la vasta red de caminos que incluía puentes, **depósitos** y *tambos* (lugares para descansar).

El imperio de los incas se extendió en pocos años por la zona de los Andes, donde el transporte y la comunicación parecen casi imposibles, sobre todo en ese tiempo primitivo en que no tenían **conocimiento** de la rueda ni usaban metales. La red de caminos impulsó la expansión del imperio y luego **fomentó** su organización. Por esos caminos transitaban los *chasquis,* mensajeros que aseguraban la comunicación entre todas las partes del imperio y el gobierno central en Cuzco. Un *chasqui* corría por los caminos hasta **encontrarse** con otro *chasqui* y darle la información que debía transmitir. El otro *chasqui* entonces empezaba a correr hasta encontrarse con el próximo *chasqui* y así hasta que la información llegaba a su destino. A los *chasquis* los entrenaban desde niños. Se alimentaban con una dieta especial para poder ir de un lugar a otro sin cansarse ni sufrir por la gran altitud de los Andes.

Los *chasquis* con frecuencia transportaban documentos importantes de una parte del imperio a otra por medio de *quipus* (**hilos** de colores **anudados**). Los *quipus* formaban un sistema **mnemotécnico** para registrar información, por ejemplo noticias sobre el censo, cantidades de productos conservados en los depósitos o noticias sobre los enemigos del **emperador.** En estos tiempos de tecnología avanzada, los poblados indígenas siguen usando los *quipus* para registrar los productos de las **cosechas** y el número de animales de las comunidades.

El camino Inca

VOCABULARIO ÚTIL

el dominio	*mastery*
la prueba	*proof*
el depósito	*storage*
el conocimiento	*knowledge*
fomentó	*promoted*
encontrarse	*to meet (each other)*
el hilo	*thread*
anudados	*knotted*
mnemotécnico	*mnemonic (memory aid)*
el emperador	*emperor*
la cosecha	*harvest*

Comprensión

1. ¿Qué conocimientos tenían los incas?

2. Describa a los *chasquis*. ¿Quiénes eran? ¿Qué hacían?

La ecología y el medio ambiente

✳ **Lea Gramática 10.5.**

Me parece que debemos tratar de eliminar la contaminación de los ríos.

Hay que eliminar la lluvia ácida porque nos urge salvar los árboles.

Sí, debemos encontrar otros medios de transporte.

Me preocupa mucho el sistema ecológico del desierto.

Nos molesta la contaminación del aire (el esmog).

A los científicos les interesa resolver el problema de la destrucción de las selvas tropicales.

A todos nos preocupa mucho el agujero en la capa de ozono.

A Nora y a Luis les parece que la energía solar es mucho más limpia y eficiente que la energía nuclear.

A Esteban y a Raúl les llama mucho la atención el número de especies que están en peligro de extinción.

¡OJO!

- En los EU (Estados Unidos) se usan 16.000.000 de barriles de petróleo cada año en la fabricación de botellas plásticas para agua.
- Se requieren dos litros de agua para producir una botella de plástico de un litro que se usa sólo una vez.

Ⓐctividad 11 Intercambios: Los amigos hispanos protegen el ambiente

A. Mire los dibujos en la siguiente página. Hágale preguntas a su compañero/a sobre lo que hacen estos amigos hispanos para proteger el medio ambiente.

MODELO:　　E1: ¿Qué hace *Ernesto* para proteger el medio ambiente?
　　　　　　E2: *Va a su trabajo en autobús en vez de manejar. También...*

Palabras útiles

la energía renovable
la energía verde

Ernesto

Palabras útiles

la bolsa de lona
sembrar legumbres
el reciclaje

Andrea

Palabras útiles

la botella de plástico / de
　aluminio
usar ambos lados
la impresora
pájaros cubiertos de petróleo

Paula

Palabras útiles

el carro híbrido
el combustible

Raúl

B. ¿Cuáles de estas actividades haces tú?

MODELOS:　　Yo reciclo el vidrio y el plástico.
　　　　　　Manejo un coche híbrido.

Actividad 12 **Intercambios: Especies en peligro de extinción, problemas y soluciones**

MODELOS:
E1: ¿Cuál es el hábitat del *quetzal*?
E2: El quetzal vive en *las selvas de Centroamérica*.

E1: ¿Cuál es la solución al problema *del quetzal*?
E2: No debemos *permitir su exportación*.

Reptiles

la serpiente

la tortuga

Insectos

la mariposa monarca

la abeja

la mariquita

ESPECIES EN PELIGRO DE EXTINCIÓN

el tucán

el quetzal

el guacamayo

la lapa roja

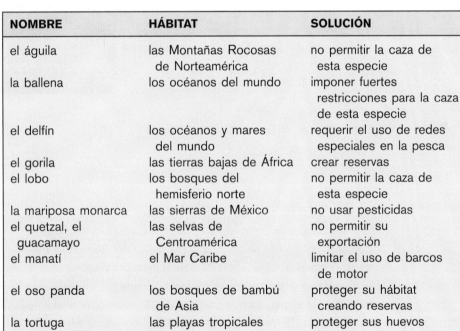

NOMBRE	HÁBITAT	SOLUCIÓN
el águila	las Montañas Rocosas de Norteamérica	no permitir la caza de esta especie
la ballena	los océanos del mundo	imponer fuertes restricciones para la caza de esta especie
el delfín	los océanos y mares del mundo	requerir el uso de redes especiales en la pesca
el gorila	las tierras bajas de África	crear reservas
el lobo	los bosques del hemisferio norte	no permitir la caza de esta especie
la mariposa monarca	las sierras de México	no usar pesticidas
el quetzal, el guacamayo	las selvas de Centroamérica	no permitir su exportación
el manatí	el Mar Caribe	limitar el uso de barcos de motor
el oso panda	los bosques de bambú de Asia	proteger su hábitat creando reservas
la tortuga	las playas tropicales	proteger sus huevos

Mamíferos

el leopardo cazador

el lobo

el oso

el manatí

¡OJO!

El 98% de todos los animales y plantas que han habitado la tierra ya se ha extinguido.

VENTANAS CULTURALES La lengua

Nuestro pequeño mundo azul

¿Sabe usted ya muchas palabras para hablar del medio ambiente? Sigamos hablando de este tema importante. ¿Con qué palabras podemos describir nuestro planeta? Podemos decir que la Tierra es fuerte y saludable y que es el único planeta donde sabemos que hay vida. Debemos tratar de conservarla, ¿no cree usted? Lo más crucial es la capa de ozono que cubre la Tierra. Esa capa nos protege de la radiación solar y debemos preocuparnos por no destruirla.

Nuestras acciones afectan el planeta. Hay productos químicos, como los aerosoles, que **dañan** el aire y el agua. Debemos **dejar de** usarlos. ¿Cree que reciclamos lo suficiente? Ciertos productos —el plástico, por ejemplo— se quedan con nosotros por miles de años. Todos los días **derrochamos** recursos naturales como el agua y producimos **toneladas** de basura. También creamos lluvia ácida. La lluvia ácida es **provocada** por gases tóxicos de las fábricas que se mezclan con la precipitación atmosférica, contaminando el suelo y la vegetación.

Pero el enemigo más grande de la Tierra es sin duda la energía nuclear, especialmente el uranio, metal radiactivo que se usó para crear la bomba atómica. Lo ideal es poner fin a la producción de armas nucleares. ¿Qué más podemos hacer para conservar la vida en la Tierra? Algo muy urgente es cuidar las selvas tropicales: desde el sudeste de México hasta la zona amazónica, los bosques de Petén en Guatemala, Darién en Panamá y Chocó en Colombia. Esas selvas son un ingrediente vital de la Tierra, pues proveen el oxígeno que necesitamos para vivir en nuestro pequeño y hermoso mundo azul.

Comprensión

1. ¿Por qué es importante conservar la capa de ozono de nuestro planeta?
2. ¿Qué nos ofrecen las selvas tropicales?

VOCABULARIO ÚTIL	
dañan	*harm*
dejar de	*stop*
derrochamos	*we waste*
las toneladas	*tons*
provocada	*triggered, produced*

Coquí es el nombre onomatopéyico de esta diminuta rana de Puerto Rico. Da un toque especial a la noche puertorriqueña con su melódico canto: «co-quí, co-quí».

¡OJO!

Puerto Rico también se conoce como la Isla del Encanto o por su nombre indígena: Borinquen. Es una isla de flora y fauna muy especiales. Abundan árboles tropicales como el flamboyán, la ceiba y el guayacán. En las playas llega a desovar (*lay eggs*) la tortuga marina más grande del mundo, el tinglar; ¡pesa hasta 800 libras! La Isla de Mona al oeste de Puerto Rico es el hábitat de las iguanas mona y unos cangrejos ermitaños, llamados *cobos,* que cada agosto descienden del monte a las playas para desovar. La pequeña rana de árbol llamada *coquí* es quizás el símbolo más conocido de Puerto Rico y su canto llena las noches tropicales.

Actividad 13 Asociaciones: El medio ambiente, problemas y soluciones

¿Les preocupan los siguientes problemas ecológicos? Digan qué podemos hacer para resolverlos y salvar el planeta.

MODELO: Nos preocupa *la sequía*. Creemos que no debemos *desperdiciar el agua*.

PROBLEMAS ECOLÓGICOS

1. el consumo excesivo de petróleo
2. el calentamiento global
3. el uso excesivo de productos plásticos
4. la destrucción del hábitat de algunas especies de animales y plantas
5. la contaminación de los ríos y los océanos
6. el agujero en la capa de ozono
7. los desperdicios de las plantas nucleares
8. la contaminación del aire en las grandes ciudades
9. la sequía; la escasez de agua
10. el uso excesivo de poliestireno

SOLUCIONES

a. usar pesticidas no tóxicos
b. imponerles fuertes restricciones a las industrias
c. usar menos energía
d. fomentar la agricultura orgánica
e. restringir el uso de los autos
f. criar animales en los zoológicos
g. controlar la natalidad
h. crear nuevas reservas naturales
i. desarrollar otros medios de transporte
j. reducir drásticamente o eliminar la producción de carburos fluorados
k. comprar productos en envases de vidrio y participar en programas de reciclaje
l. no desperdiciar el agua
m. pedir envases biodegradables o de cartón

¡OJO!

- La recolección, el transporte y la eliminación de la basura gasta energía y contamina el aire y la tierra; además, ocupa espacio vital en las ciudades.
- Sólo el 5% de la población mundial reside en los Estados Unidos, pero en este país se produce 25% de los gases de efecto invernadero.
- En los basureros, debido a la falta de oxígeno, los desperdicios no se descomponen, incluso si son biodegradables.

Biosfera de Sian Ka'an, México

Actividad 14 Del mundo hispano: El abecedario ecológico

Lea este artículo sobre varios temas ecológicos. Luego conecte las frases para tener una lista de las ideas principales del artículo.

ABECEDARIO ECOLÓGICO

Amazonia Es una zona selvática que comprende toda la zona norte de Brasil y una parte del oriente peruano, y que llega al sur de Colombia y Venezuela. Está conformada por densas selvas y grandes ríos. Tiene 7 millones de kilómetros cuadrados de vegetación. Muchos medicamentos tienen su origen en esta región. La Amazonia también alberga[1] 30 millones de especies animales. Pero la explotación de los recursos naturales de esta área está produciendo una tasa[2] de extinción animal de 100 especies animales por día.

Biosfera de Sian Ka'an En 1989 el gobierno de México estableció La Biosfera de Sian Ka'an: una reserva de 650.000 hectáreas (1.6 millones de acres) situada en la costa caribeña de la península de Yucatán. Esta biosfera alberga más de 100 especies de mamíferos y 336 especies de aves. Dos especies de tortugas marinas en peligro de extinción se anidan[3] en las playas de Sian Ka'an. Tiene una población de sólo 2.000 personas, en su su mayoría[4] indígenas mayas. El propósito de la biosfera es la protección de especies en peligro de extinción y la educación de la gente sobre la importancia de la biodiversidad.

Capa de ozono Los científicos nos dicen que el uso de los carburos fluorados y de otras sustancias químicas está causando la desaparición de la capa de ozono que nos protege de los rayos dañinos[5] del sol. El agujero más grande en la capa de ozono está en el hemisferio sur, por la Antártida, pero también hay otro agujero en el Ártico. Ya ha desaparecido más del 4% de esta capa protectora y en países como Chile y Australia ya se ha notado un aumento[6] en la incidencia del cáncer de la piel.

Desperdicios nucleares Mucha gente ve la energía nuclear como fuente de energía limpia, pero los desperdicios de los reactores nucleares, como el uranio y el plutonio, son sustancias químicas muy dañinas para el ser humano y otros animales. Además, son muy difíciles de almacenar.[7] Las armas[8] nucleares, como los misiles tan usados por los ejércitos modernos, dejan residuos de uranio en la tierra por años, con consecuencias graves para la fauna y la flora.

[1]gives shelter to [2]rate [3]se... nest [4]majority [5]damaging [6]increase [7]to store [8]weapons

1. La Amazonia cubre una área inmensa y...
2. La explotación de los recursos de la Amazonia causa...
3. En 1989 el gobierno de México estableció la Biosfera de Sian Ka'an, que...
4. El uso de los carburos fluorados y otras sustancias dañinas...
5. La capa de ozono está desapareciendo...
6. Los misiles usados por el ejército...

a. es una reserva inmensa situada en la costa caribeña de la península de Yucatán.
b. dejan residuos tóxicos en la tierra con consecuencias graves para la fauna y la flora.
c. y ya se ha notado un aumento en la incidencia del cáncer de la piel en el hemisferio del sur.
d. la extinción animal de 100 especies por día.
e. es el hábitat para 30 millones de especies animales.
f. ha causado la desaparición de 4% de la capa de ozono.

En resumen

De todo un poco

A. La geografía y el clima de América Latina

Trabaje con varios compañeros para poner los nombres de los siguientes mares y océanos, las cordilleras y los ríos más importantes de América Latina en el mapa que su profesor(a) le va a dar.

1. el Río Bravo
2. cuatro cordilleras:
   a. Sierra Madre Occidental
   b. Sierra Madre Oriental
   c. Sierra Madre del Sur
   d. cordillera de los Andes
3. el canal de Panamá
4. el lago Titicaca
5. el río Orinoco
6. el río Amazonas
7. el río Paraná
8. el río de la Plata
9. las cataratas del Iguazú
10. el Océano Atlántico
11. el Océano Pacífico
12. el Mar Caribe
13. el golfo de California
14. el golfo de México

B. ¡Salvemos el medio ambiente!

Haga una lista de medidas que cualquier ciudadano puede tomar para reducir la cantidad de basura que produce diariamente. Comparta sus ideas con la clase.

MODELO: Uno puede llevar sus propias bolsas de lona al supermercado.

¡Dígalo por escrito!

El medio ambiente y usted

Piense en algo que le preocupa a usted: un problema climático o ambiental o alguna especie de animal en peligro de extinción. Escriba una breve composición sobre el tema. Explique el problema, luego diga dónde ocurre, cuáles son sus causas principales y cuáles son las consecuencias. Para terminar, sugiera qué se puede hacer para mitigar o resolver este problema.

¡Cuéntenos usted!

Cuéntenos sobre un lugar geográfico que le impresionó. ¿Dónde fue? ¿Pasó usted mucho tiempo allí o estuvo sólo uno o dos días? ¿Le gustó o no? ¿Por qué?

VOCABULARIO ÚTIL

De entrada	To begin with
rechazan	reject
el oro	gold
A pesar de	In spite of
la reforestación	reforesting
el Movimiento Ambiental	Environmental Movement

LECTURA

Costa Rica, un país excepcional

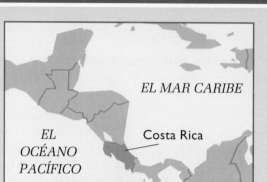

EL MAR CARIBE

Costa Rica

EL OCÉANO PACÍFICO

Parque Nacional Manuel Antonio

Costa Rica es un país único, no sólo en el mundo hispano sino en el mundo entero. Hay varios aspectos de la sociedad costarricense que contribuyen a formar esta imagen especial. **De entrada,** el país no tiene ejército, pues los ciudadanos de Costa Rica **rechazan** la guerra. Pero eso no es todo. Los costarricenses también están muy conscientes de la importancia de la naturaleza. El gobierno tiene reglas estrictas para la construcción de viviendas y hoteles en zonas selváticas. El 40 por ciento del territorio del país está poblado de bosques, y hay en Costa Rica uno de los sistemas más extensos de parques nacionales en todo el planeta.

La población de Costa Rica es de tres millones de habitantes. El país tiene una industria estable de turismo y exporta café, plátanos, carne, azúcar y cacao. El clima es de dos estaciones: la seca (diciembre a abril) y la húmeda (mayo a noviembre). El nombre del país es muy apropiado, pues la *costa* que da al Océano Atlántico es *rica* en selvas tropicales. Pero, en realidad, los exploradores españoles le dieron el nombre de Costa Rica a este país porque pensaban que iban a encontrar allí mucho **oro.**

Se nota que los costarricenses quieren conservar sus recursos naturales: las especies de animales, los bosques y las selvas. De hecho, el «ecoturismo» comenzó en Costa Rica. Entre otras ideas, el ecoturismo propone un tipo de turismo que no destruya el medio ambiente y pone énfasis en el daño que podemos causar al planeta. El ecoturismo también trata de educar a los turistas

Parque Nacional Braulio Carrillo

en cuestiones ambientales. Costa Rica está a la cabeza de este movimiento, ofreciendo periódicamente conferencias donde participan personas de todo el mundo.

Si a usted le interesa visitar hermosos sitios ecoturísticos, le esperan varios en Costa Rica. En el Lago Arenal puede pescar, navegar y andar en bicicleta a lo largo de la orilla. Puede visitar el fantástico Volcán Arenal, activo desde su erupción en 1968. Si pescar o surfear es su pasión, vaya a la Playa Tamarindo. En el bosque tropical de Monteverde le espera una experiencia inolvidable. Monteverde es una de las zonas de conservación más famosas en Centroamérica; tiene más de 100 especies de mamíferos, más de 400 especies de aves y 2.500 especies de plantas. Hay que dar una caminata por Monteverde para apreciar su belleza.

El volcán Arenal, activo desde 1968

(Continúa)

A **pesar de** su visión ecoturística, Costa Rica ha tenido que hacer algunos sacrificios debido a presiones económicas. Entre 1981 y 1990 el país perdió un dos por ciento de sus bosques, pues estaba exportando mucha madera. Como no había un plan oficial de **reforestación,** los bosques empezaron a desaparecer. Por suerte, miembros del **Movimiento Ambiental** convencieron al gobierno costarricense de la necesidad de sembrar más árboles, y ahora hay varias iniciativas de reforestación en Costa Rica.

Hay pocos países como Costa Rica, con una conciencia nacional del medio ambiente y donde la gente toma en serio las cuestiones ambientales. En nuestro planeta —devastado por las guerras y por la destrucción de la naturaleza— Costa Rica es un país excepcional.

Comprensión

Complete las oraciones con frases de la columna de la derecha.

1. En los años ochenta...
2. El Movimiento Ambiental le hizo ver al gobierno costarricense...
3. Costa Rica es un país pacífico, pues...
4. El gobierno costarricense no permite...
5. El nombre de Costa Rica se relaciona con...
6. Monteverde es un bosque tropical...
7. El ecoturismo...

a. nos informa sobre los daños que causamos al planeta.
b. Costa Rica estaba perdiendo una gran cantidad de bosques.
c. la importancia de plantar más árboles.
d. la construcción de muchos hoteles en zonas selváticas.
e. no cree en la guerra y no tiene ejército.
f. la búsqueda de oro de los exploradores españoles.
g. de una gran riqueza en su fauna y su flora.

Un paso más... ¡a escribir!

Vea el **Resumen cultural** en este capítulo del *Cuaderno de actividades.*

Imagínese que, por un momento fantástico, un árbol en el bosque tropical de Monteverde puede hablar. ¿Qué va a decir este árbol con respecto a su vida, a su medio ambiente y a sus vecinos? ¿Qué va a decir del ser humano? Escriba una composición titulada «El monólogo del árbol».

Vocabulario

La geografía

Geography

la Amazonia	Amazon Basin
el arrecife	reef
la bahía	bay
el bosque	forest
la catarata	waterfall
la colina	hill
la cordillera	(mountain) range
la isla	island
el llano	plain
la luna	moon
la orilla	shore, (river) bank
la selva (tropical)	(tropical) jungle
la sierra	mountains
el terremoto	earthquake
la tierra	land; earth

PALABRAS SEMEJANTES: el cañón, Centroamérica, la corriente, la costa, el desierto, el golfo, el hemisferio, la laguna, la península, el valle, la vegetación, el volcán, Yucatán

El clima

Weather

caluroso	warm, hot
el cielo	sky
el desbordamiento	overflow
la escarcha	frost
la humedad	humidity
la inundación	flood
la llovizna	drizzle
lloviznar	to drizzle
la lluvia (ácida)	(acid) rain
la neblina	fog
la nube	cloud
pronosticar	to forecast (*weather*)
el relámpago	lightning
el rocío	dew
soleado/a	sunny
la tormenta	storm
el trueno	thunder

PALABRAS SEMEJANTES: el aire, el ciclón, húmedo/a, el huracán, el tornado
REPASO: el centígrado, el grado, llover (ue), nevar (ie), nublado/a, el pronóstico, la temperatura mínima/máxima

Los medios de transporte

Means of Transportation

¡Alto!	Stop! (*Mex.*)
el asiento	seat
la autopista	freeway, expressway
la carretera	highway
el crucero	cruise ship
el letrero	sign
el pasaje	fare, ticket price
el pasajero / la pasajera	passenger
por avión (tren)	by plane (train)
la rueda	wheel
el semáforo	signal (light)
la señal	signal (light)
el transbordador	ferry
el tranvía	cable car, streetcar

PALABRAS SEMEJANTES: el taxi, transportar, el vagón (del tren), el vehículo
REPASO: el barco, la bici(cleta), el carro, el coche, la moto(cicleta)

La ecología y el medio ambiente

Ecology and the Environment

el agujero en la capa de ozono	hole in the ozone layer
la bolsa de lona	canvas bag
el calentamiento global	global warming
la caza	hunt; hunting
los desperdicios (nucleares)	(nuclear) waste
en peligro de extinción	in danger of extinction
la energía renovable	renewable energy
el envase	packing, packaging, bottle
la escasez	scarcity, shortage
la natalidad	birthrate
el reciclaje	recycling
el recurso (natural)	(natural) resource
la red (de pesca)	(fishing) net
la sequía	drought
el vidrio	glass (*material*)

PALABRAS SEMEJANTES: la biosfera, el carburo fluorado, la contaminación, la destrucción, el esmog, las especies, el hábitat, el pesticida, el petróleo, el planeta, la planta nuclear, la reserva, el residuo químico, el uso

Los animales

Animals

la abeja	bee
el águila	eagle
la ballena	whale
el delfín	dolphin
la esponja	sponge
la estrella (marina)	(sea) star; starfish
el guacamayo	parrot
el león (marino)	(sea) lion
el lobo	wolf
el mamífero	mammal
la mariposa	butterfly
el pájaro	bird

el pez (los peces)	fish
el tiburón	shark
la tortuga (marina)	tortoise; (sea) turtle

PALABRAS SEMEJANTES: el gorila, el insecto, el leopardo, el reptil, la serpiente

Los verbos

Verbs

bajar	to lower; to come down
corregir	to correct
crear	to create
criar	to raise (animals, children)
desarrollar	to develop
desperdiciar	to waste
hacer una gira	to take a tour
imponer	to impose
llamar la atención	to call attention
marearse	to get seasick
molestar	to bother
parecer	to seem
preocupar	to worry
proteger	to protect
requerir	to require
resolver	to solve
salvar	to save
sembrar	to plant
urgir	to be urgent

PALABRAS SEMEJANTES: anticipar, causar, compararse, conectar, contaminar, controlar, eliminar, establecer, flotar, fomentar, generar, interesar, limitar, observar, ocurrir, pasar, producir, reciclar, reducir, restringir

Los sustantivos

Nouns

el aumento	increase
el buceo	diving (underwater swimming)
el cáncer (de la piel)	(skin) cancer
la cantidad	quantity
el cartón	cardboard
el casco	helmet
el ciudadano / la ciudadana	citizen
los daños	damages
la desaparición	disappearance
la (des)ventaja	(dis)advantage
el ejército	army, military
la gira	tour
el gobierno	government
la gota	drop
la hoja (de papel)	leaf; sheet (of paper)
la impresora	printer
el pensamiento	thought
el poliestireno	styrofoam
el tema	theme
el viaje	trip

PALABRAS SEMEJANTES: la abundancia, la agricultura, el artículo, el bambú, la concentración, la consecuencia, el consumo, la diversidad, la electricidad, el espacio, la explotación, la exportación, la extensión, la fauna, la flora, la forma, la incidencia, la industria, la letra, la locomotora, el millón, el misil, el organismo, el plutonio, la porción, el problema, la producción, el producto, la restricción, el sistema, la sustancia, el tanque, el uranio

Los adjetivos

Adjectives

aéreo/a	pertaining to air (travel)
ambiental	environmental
ambos/as	both
bello/a	beautiful
cómodo/a	comfortable
cubierto/a	covered
dañino/a	harmful
lento/a	slow
ligero/a	light
lleno/a	full
profundo/a	deep
rocoso/a	rocky
rodeado/a	surrounded
tibio/a	warm
unido/a	connected; unified

PALABRAS SEMEJANTES: árido/a, biodegradable, caribeño/a, colorido/a, desastroso/a, ecológico/a, eficiente, excesivo/a, firme, grave, híbrido, húmedo/a, impresionante, inmenso/a, orgánico/a, plástico/a, positivo/a, preferido/a, principal, situado/a, subterráneo/a, tóxico/a, usado/a

Los adverbios

Adverbs

cómodamente	comfortably
diariamente	daily
lentamente	slowly

PALABRAS SEMEJANTES: completamente, drásticamente, puntualmente

Palabras y expresiones útiles

Useful Words and Expressions

acerca de	about
¡Cuánto/a/os/as… !	How many . . . !
hacia	toward
mil(es)	thousand(s)
para	to (in the direction of)
¡Qué + *noun* + tan/más + *adjective*!	What a + *adjective* + *noun*!

Gramática y ejercicios

10.1 Saying What You Have Done: The Present Perfect

A. The present perfect is formed with the present tense of the verb **haber*** (*to have*) followed by a form of the verb called the past participle.

—¿**Han visitado** ustedes Europa?
—Sí, **hemos visitado** España dos veces.

—*Have you visited Europe?*
—*Yes, we've visited Spain twice.*

This tense is used very similarly in English.

B. The present-tense forms of **haber** are irregular.

haber

(yo)	he	*I have*
(tú)	has	*you (inf. sing.) have*
(usted, él/ella)	ha	*you (pol. sing.) have; he/she has*
(nosotros/as)	hemos	*we have*
(vosotros/as)	habéis	*you (inf. pl., Spain) have*
(ustedes, ellos/as)	han	*you (pl.) have; they have*

—Ernesto, ¿**has recogido** el coche?

—No, todavía no **han llamado** del taller.

—*Ernesto, have you picked up the car?*
—*No, they haven't called yet from the garage.*

C. The past participle is formed by adding **-ado** to the stem of **-ar** verbs and **-ido** to the stem of **-er** and **-ir** verbs.

-ar

INFINITIVE	PAST PARTICIPLE
hablar	hablado
jugar	jugado
preparar	preparado

*Recognition: **vos habés**

-er / -ir

INFINITIVE	PAST PARTICIPLE
comer	com**ido**
vivir	viv**ido**
dormir	dorm**ido**

—¿Ya **han comprado** los señores Ruiz los boletos?
—No, no **han tenido** tiempo todavía.

—*Have the Ruizes already bought the tickets?*
—*No, they haven't had time yet.*

—Andrea, **¿has terminado?**
—No, el agente de viajes no **ha conseguido** las reservaciones todavía.

—*Andrea, have you finished?*
—*No, the travel agent hasn't gotten the reservations yet.*

D. A few verbs have irregular participles.

abrir: **abierto**	*to open / opened*
cubrir: **cubierto**	*to cover / covered*
decir: **dicho**	*to say / said; to tell / told*
escribir: **escrito**	*to write / written*
hacer: **hecho**	*to do / done; to make / made*
morir: **muerto**	*to die / died; dead*
poner: **puesto**	*to put / put*
resolver: **resuelto**	*to solve / solved*
romper: **roto**	*to break / broken*
ver: **visto**	*to see / seen*
volver: **vuelto**	*to return / returned*

The participles of verbs derived from these verbs are also irregular. For example, **describir** is derived from **escribir.**

describir: **descrito**	*to describe / described*
devolver: **devuelto**	*to return / returned*
inscribir: **inscrito**	*to enroll / enrolled*
reponer: **repuesto**	*to put back / put back*
suponer: **supuesto**	*to suppose / supposed*

—Estela, ¿dónde **has puesto** mis pantalones nuevos?
—Ya te **he dicho** que están encima de la cama.

—*Estela, where have you put my new pants?*
—*I've already told you that they're on top of the bed.*

Ernesto fue a la agencia de viajes hace dos horas y todavía no **ha vuelto.**

Ernesto went to the travel agency two hours ago and hasn't come back yet.

Note that **ya** (*already*) and **todavía no** (*not yet*) are adverbs commonly used with the present perfect tense.

Ejercicio 1

Éstas son algunas de las cosas que han hecho los amigos y parientes de Estela. Complete las oraciones con **comer, comprar, escribir, hablar, ir, limpiar, oír, pasar, ver** y **viajar.**

> When you see a comma after a proper name, it means you are addressing that person directly. Use **tú** or **usted.**

MODELO: Mis cuñados *han ido* mucho a Puerto Vallarta porque les gustan las playas y el sol.

1. Ernesto y yo _____ la nueva película de Almodóvar cuatro veces.
2. Ramón le _____ varias cartas a Amanda.
3. Yo _____ tres veces este mes a Cuernavaca.
4. La señorita Batini _____ una casa nueva.
5. Pedro, ¿_____ en un restaurante chino últimamente?
6. Guillermo no _____ con Ernesto hoy.
7. Graciela, tú nunca _____ a España, ¿verdad?
8. Marisa y Clarisa _____ su cuarto muy bien.
9. Ernestito, ¿_____? ¡Papá dice que vamos a ir de vacaciones en Florida!
10. Pedro y Andrea _____ sus vacaciones en Acapulco muchas veces.

Ejercicio 2

¿Cuántas veces ha hecho usted estas cosas? Haga preguntas y respuestas.

> Negative answers are expected for many items in Ejercicio 2.

MODELO: bucear en el mar Caribe →
—¿Cuántas veces *has buceado* en el mar Caribe?
—Nunca *he buceado* allí. (Mi hermana y yo *hemos buceado* en el mar Caribe dos o tres veces.)

1. viajar a México
2. esquiar en un lago
3. subir a una pirámide
4. acampar en la montaña
5. alquilar un coche
6. cocinar para diez personas
7. leer tres novelas en un día
8. correr cinco kilómetros sin parar
9. decirles una mentira a sus padres
10. romper un vaso en un restaurante

10.2 Exclamations with *¡Qué... !, ¡Cuánto/a/os/as... !*

A. Form exclamations with **qué** using **¡Qué** + *adjective* . . . !*

¡Qué bonita es la playa!	*How pretty the beach is!*
¡Qué interesante fue ese viaje!	*What an interesting trip that was!*

B. Use the pattern **¡Qué** + *noun* + **tan/más** + *adjective*! to express *What a(n) . . . !*

¡Qué país tan grande!	*What a large country!*
¡Qué viaje más divertido!	*What an enjoyable trip!*

> **¡Qué montañas tan altas!**
> *What tall mountains!*
> **¡Qué azul es el agua aquí!**
> *How blue the water is here!*

---

*Note that **qué** and **cuánto** take an accent mark in exclamations as well as in questions.

¡Cuántas personas hay en esta playa!

There sure are a lot of people on this beach! (What a lot of people there are on this beach!)

C. Use **cuánto/a/os/as** to express surprise about quantity.

¡**Cuánto** dinero tiene ese hombre!   *What a lot of money that man has!*

¡No te imaginas **cuántas** horas tuvimos que esperar!   *You can't imagine how many hours we had to wait!*

Ejercicio 3

Imagínese que usted está mirando las fotos de Susana Yamasaki y sus hijos, quienes acaban de regresar de un viaje por América Latina. Exprese su sorpresa al ver estas fotos.

MODELO: las pirámides de Teotihuacán: pirámides / altas →
Las pirámides de Teotihuacán... ¡Qué pirámides tan (más) altas!

1. Bolivia: país / interesante
2. un vuelo de Buenos Aires a México, D.F.: vuelo / largo
3. los Andes: montañas / altas
4. una selva tropical en Venezuela: selva / verde
5. una playa en el Caribe: arena / blanca

Ejercicio 4

Ahora imagínese que usted también ha hecho un viaje por España y por América Latina. Haga comentarios sobre los lugares interesantes que ha visto.

MODELO: azul / el agua del Caribe → ¡Qué azul es el agua del Caribe!

1. impresionantes / las ruinas de Machu Picchu
2. grande / el lago Titicaca
3. cosmopolita / la ciudad de Buenos Aires
4. húmeda / la selva de Ecuador
5. seco / el desierto de Atacama en Chile
6. alta / la torre de la Giralda en Sevilla
7. hermoso / el edificio del Alcázar de Segovia
8. inmenso / el parque del Retiro en Madrid
9. interesante / el Museo del Prado
10. antiguo / el acueducto de Segovia

por = movement *through* or *by,* or *means of transportation*
para = movement *toward a destination*

   Caminamos por la playa. (*We walked along the beach.*)
   Fuimos por tren. (*We went by train.*)
   Salen mañana para Cuzco. (*They leave tomorrow for Cuzco.*)

10.3 Expressing *by, through,* Destination, and Time: *por* and *para* (Part 1)

The prepositions **por** and **para** have distinct meanings.

A. Para indicates movement *toward* a destination.

Cuando era niño, salía **para** la escuela a las 7:30.   *When I was a kid, I used to leave for school at 7:30.*
Perdón, señor, ¿cuál es el tren que sale **para** Madrid?   *Excuse me, sir, which is the train that is leaving for Madrid?*

Por, on the other hand, indicates motion *through* or *by* (*along*) a place.

Pasamos **por** varios pueblos antes de llegar a Salamanca.	*We went through various villages before arriving in Salamanca.*
Por las noches caminábamos **por** la orilla del lago de Chapala.	*In the evenings we would take walks along the shore of Lake Chapala.*

Por is also used to indicate means of transportation.

Mis hermanos quieren viajar **por** barco, pero yo quiero ir **por** avión.	*My brothers want to travel by boat, but I want to go by plane.*

Note the contrast in usage in the following example.

Mañana salgo **para** París. Voy a viajar **por** tren.	*Tomorrow I'm leaving for Paris. I'll travel by train.*

B. Por and **para** can also be followed by expressions of time.

1. Use **por** to indicate length of time (although you may often omit **por** in these cases). Some examples of time expressions are **por una semana, por tres meses, por un año,** and **por mucho tiempo.**

Hoy tengo que trabajar en el taller (**por**) **diez horas.**	*Today I have to work in the shop for ten hours.*

You can also use **por** to express *during, in,* or *at* with parts of the day: **por la mañana, por la tarde, por la noche.**

Aquí **por la noche** todo el mundo sale a pasear.	*Here in (during) the evening everybody goes out for a walk.*

2. Use **para** to indicate a deadline by which something is expected to happen.

Hay que entregar el informe **para** las 10:00.	*We have to turn in the report by 10:00.*
La tarea es **para** el viernes.	*The homework is for (due) Friday.*

> **por** = *length of time, during*
> **para** = *deadline*
> **Estuvimos en España por tres semanas.** (*We were in Spain for three weeks.*)
> **Paula necesita terminar el trabajo para el lunes.** (*Paula needs to finish the job by Monday.*)

Ejercicio 5

Aquí tiene usted parte de una conversación entre Silvia Bustamante y su novio, Nacho Padilla. Escoja **por** o **para.**

SILVIA: Ayer trabajé _____[1] ocho horas en la terminal de autobuses.

NACHO: Yo manejé mi taxi _____[2] solamente cinco horas.

SILVIA: ¿Cuándo sales _____[3] Morelia?

NACHO: En dos días. Salgo _____[4] la mañana y voy a viajar _____[5] tres horas.

SILVIA: ¿No vas _____[6] avión?

NACHO: ¡Claro que no! Voy _____[7] tren. Es mucho más barato.

SILVIA: ¿Cuánto tiempo piensas quedarte allí?

NACHO: ¡Una semana! Necesito recoger unos documentos importantes. Van a estar listos _____[8] el próximo viernes.

-mente = *-ly*
cómodamente =
  comfortably
calmadamente = *calmly*

10.4 Describing Actions: Adverbs

Words that describe actions are called *adverbs*. Many adverbs are formed in Spanish by adding **-mente** to the feminine or neuter form of the adjective: **rápida** (*fast*) → **rápidamente** (*quickly*); **libre** (*free*) → **libremente** (*freely*).

—Amanda, ¿vas al cine **frecuentemente**?
—Sí, voy casi todos los fines de semana.

—Amanda, do you go to the movies frequently?
—Yes, I go almost every weekend.

En este país puedes hablar **abiertamente.**

In this country you can talk openly.

Ejercicio 6

Primero escoja el adjetivo más lógico entre **cómoda, constante, inmediata, puntual** y **rápida**. Luego forme un adverbio.

MODELO: (general) → *Generalmente* tomo el autobús número 73 para ir a la universidad.

1. ¡Los trenes en Japón transitan a 250 kilómetros por hora! Los pasajeros llegan _____ a su destino.
2. Me gusta viajar por tren. Me siento _____ y miro el paisaje por la ventanilla.
3. En España los trenes y los autobuses llegan y salen _____.
4. ¡Nunca he visto tantos autobuses! En la estación de autobuses de Guadalajara, los autobuses llegan y salen _____.
5. Tenemos que correr; el próximo autobús sale _____.

¿RECUERDA?

Recall from **Gramática 1.5** and **8.2** that **gustar** and **encantar** are used with indirect object pronouns.

me	*to me*
te	*to you (inf. sing.)*
le	*to you (pol. sing.); to him/her*
nos	*to us*
os	*to you (inf. pl., Spain)*
les	*to you (pl.); to them*

Some useful expressions:
me interesa = *I'm interested in*
no me interesa = *I'm not interested in*

me importa = *it matters to me*
no me importa = *I don't care*

me parece que sí = *I think so*
me parece que no = *I think not*

10.5 Expressing Reactions: More Verbs Like *gustar*

Like **gustar** and **encantar,** several other verbs also use indirect object pronouns.

dar miedo *to frighten*
dar rabia *to infuriate*
fascinar *to be fascinating; to love*
importar *to matter*
interesar *to be interesting*

llamar la atención *to attract attention*
molestar *to bother*
parecer *to seem like*
preocupar *to worry, be worrying*
urgir *to be pressing, really necessary*

The English equivalents of these verbs vary according to context.

—¿Qué **te interesa**?
—**Me interesa** la geografía porque **me fascina** viajar.

—What interests you?
—I'm interested in geography because I love to travel.

El paisaje es tan lindo que no **nos importa** si llueve.

The countryside is so pretty that it doesn't matter to us if it rains.

—Susana, ¿qué **te parece** un viaje
  a Chile y Bolivia?
—**Me parece** una idea fantástica.

*—Susana, what do you think about
  a trip to Chile and Bolivia?*
—It seems like a great idea to me.

The person whose opinion is described (**me, te, le, nos, os, les**) is usually mentioned first. The subject of this kind of sentence normally follows the verb. In the following sentence, *our* opinion (**nos**) is described, and the smoke (**el humo**) is the subject of the sentence. **Molesta** is singular because **el humo** is singular.

Nos molest**a** **el humo**. *The smoke bothers us.*

If the subject that follows the verb is a singular noun or an infinitive, the verb is singular. In the following sentence, the verb is followed by an infinitive, so the verb is singular.

Me import**a** **conservar** energía. *I care about conserving energy.*

In the next sentence, the subject (**las maletas**) is plural, so the verbs (**gustan/parecen**) are plural.

Me gust**an** **las maletas** que usted
compró; **me** parec**en** muy
prácticas.

*I like the suitcases you bought;
  they seem very practical to me.*

Ejercicio 7

Exprese su opinión usando la forma apropiada de los verbos indicados.

MODELO: La contaminación del aire...

     a. _____ (molestar)
     b. _____ (encantar)

     La contaminación del aire *me molesta.*

1. La conservación de nuestros
   recursos naturales...
   a. _____ necesaria.
     (parecer)
   b. no _____. (importar)
2. Los bosques y las selvas...
   a. _____. (fascinar)
   b. no _____. (interesar)
3. Vivir en un clima caluroso...
   a. _____. (encantar)
   b. no _____. (gustar)

4. El tránsito en las autopistas...
   a. _____. (molestar)
   b. no _____. (gustar)
5. Los ríos del mundo...
   a. _____. (importar)
   b. no _____. (preocupar)

De viaje

METAS

In **Capítulo 11** you will continue to talk about travel-related experiences: making plans, following directions, and reading maps. You will learn about travel in Spanish-speaking countries, including changing money, clearing customs, and finding lodging. You will also discover new places to visit in the Hispanic world.

Feria en Barrio Reus, por Jorge Pizzanelli (Uruguay)

Sobre el artista: Jorge Pizzanelli nació en Uruguay en 1945. En 1986 comenzó sus estudios de pintura. Tiene preferencia por el estilo impresionista y, como tema, prefiere los paisajes. Su obra se distingue por la capacidad para representar la luz natural. Desde 1987 ha expuesto en prestigiosas galerías de Montevideo y Punta del Este. Además, ha tenido exposiciones en Brasil, los Estados Unidos y Japón.

¡Conozca Uruguay!

Nombre del país: República Oriental del Uruguay

Ciudad capital: Montevideo

Ciudades principales: Salto, Paysandú, Maldonado, Colonia

Moneda: el peso uruguayo

Idiomas: el español (oficial), el portuñol

Población: 3.500.000

Día de la Independencia: el 25 de agosto

Fiestas típicas: el Desembarco de los 33 Orientales, el Día Internacional del Trabajo, la Batalla de las Piedras, la Jura de la Constitución

Comidas típicas: el asado, el chimichurri, el chivito, los canelones, los alfajores, el mate

Música típica: el candombe, las murgas

Gente famosa: Eduardo Galeano, Delmira Agustini, José Artigas, Tabaré Vázquez, Horacio Quiroga

Código del país por Internet: .uy

Voces uruguayas

agarrado/a	**tacaño/a**
un bondi	**un autobús**
estar del tomate	**estar loco/a**
las pavadas	**las tonterías**
un(a) pibe	**un(a) chico/a**
una pila de	**mucho**
tá	**está bien, de acuerdo**

¡Conozca Paraguay!

Nombre del país: República del Paraguay

Ciudad capital: Asunción

Ciudades principales: Ciudad del Este, San Lorenzo, Encarnación

Moneda: el guaraní

Idiomas: el español, el guaraní (oficiales)

Población: 6.700.000

Día de la Independencia: el 15 de mayo

Fiestas: el Día de los Héroes, el Día de la Paz del Chaco, la Fundación de Asunción, el Día de los Niños, el Día de la Virgen de Caacupé

Comidas típicas: la yuca, el maíz, la sopa paraguaya, la chipá, el borí borí

Música típica: la canción paraguaya o purajhei (polca), la guarania. El arpa y la guitarra son los instrumentos más populares en la música paraguaya.

Gente famosa: Augusto Roa Bastos, José Luis Chilavert, Alfredo Stroessner

Código del país por Internet: .py

Voces paraguayas

los championes	**los zapatos de tenis**
masiado	**mucho, bastante**
un mita'i (del guaraní)	**un niño**
¡ndera!	**¡no! (expresión de desilusión)**
un ñoño	**una botella de cerveza**
un péndex	**un joven**
vairo/a	**feo/a, mal educado/a**

En este capítulo…

MULTIMEDIA **ONLINE LEARNING CENTER** www.mhhe.com/dosmundos7

 CENTRO Your media center for languages   **DVD**

Actividades de comunicación y lecturas

Los viajes en automóvil

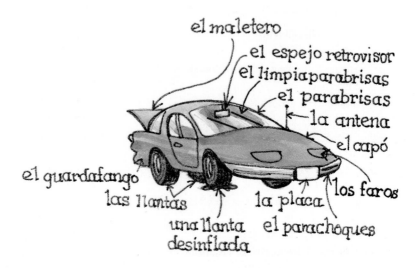

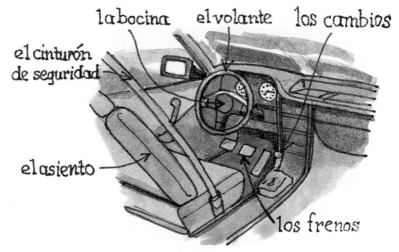

¡OJO!

Los viajes en automóvil son cómodos y divertidos, pero hay que recordar que el automóvil contribuye a la contaminación del medio ambiente. Por eso, este dato que apareció en la revista de la organización estadounidense Sierra Club resulta muy alentador: Si cada residente de una comunidad de 100.000 habitantes reemplaza un viaje en automóvil de 14.5 kilómetros (9 millas) con uno en bicicleta una vez al mes, se puede reducir la cantidad de emisiones de bióxido de carbono por 3.764 toneladas al año.

Actividad 1 Definiciones: Las partes del carro

1. _____ los frenos
2. _____ los limpiaparabrisas
3. _____ el volante
4. _____ la bocina
5. _____ la placa
6. _____ el parabrisas
7. _____ el cinturón de seguridad

a. Protege a los pasajeros del viento.
b. Se usa para mantener en el asiento a los pasajeros de un automóvil o un avión.
c. Se usan cuando llueve.
d. Se usan para parar el coche.
e. Se usa para manejar el coche.
f. Tiene los números para identificar el coche.
g. Se toca para llamar la atención de los peatones y otros choferes.

374

Actividad 2 Descripción de dibujos: Los letreros de la carretera

Diga cuál es la frase u oración que corresponde a cada número.

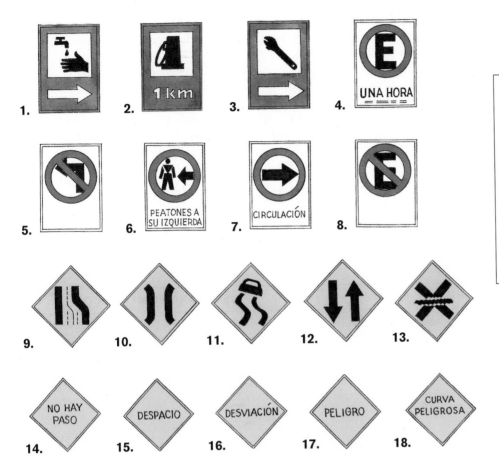

a. puente angosto
b. No doble a la izquierda.
c. tránsito de un solo sentido (una vía)
d. baños
e. gasolinera
f. ¡Cuidado! Puede haber personas a su izquierda.
g. mecánico
h. tránsito de doble sentido (vía)
i. estacionamiento de una hora

j. No se estacione.
k. tren
l. camino angosto
m. superficie resbalosa
n. prohibido el tránsito
o. Disminuya la velocidad porque hay una curva.
p. Tiene que ir por otro camino.
q. Disminuya la velocidad.
r. Tenga mucho cuidado.

Expresiones útiles

gastar gasolina
  (no) gasta...
tener la culpa
  yo (no) tuve la culpa
chocar
  choqué con...

Actividad 3 Entrevista: Tú y tu coche

1. ¿Tienes tu propio coche? ¿De qué marca es? ¿Cómo es tu coche? ¿Es práctico? ¿grande? ¿elegante? ¿Gasta mucha gasolina?
2. ¿Tienes seguro? ¿De qué compañía? ¿Es una compañía buena? ¿Por qué lo dices? ¿Es muy caro tu seguro?
3. ¿Te gusta manejar? ¿Cuántas millas manejas cada día, aproximadamente? ¿Cómo está el tránsito a la hora que sales para el trabajo? ¿Y cuando regresas a casa?
4. ¿Has tenido un accidente en tu coche? ¿Chocaste? ¿Con qué chocaste? ¿Quién tuvo la culpa? ¿Cuánto (tiempo) hace? ¿Fue un accidente serio o sin importancia?
5. ¿Has salido de vacaciones en tu coche? ¿Cuánto (tiempo) hace? ¿Adónde fuiste? ¿Con quién fuiste? ¿Cuántas horas tuviste que manejar? ¿Te gustó el viaje? ¿Por qué?

Palabras y frases útiles

el aceite
comprar
hacer las maletas
la llanta de repuesto
llevar
el radiador
reparar
revisar
el tanque

Actividad 4 Conversación: Un viaje en carro

Usted va a viajar de El Paso, Texas, a Barranca del Cobre en Chihuahua, México. Es una distancia de 500 kilómetros. Complete las siguientes dos listas con cinco tareas o más para cada lista.

ANTES DE SALIR	LISTA PARA EL MECÁNICO
Tengo que / Necesito:	Debe:
•	• Revisar…
•	•
•	•
•	•
•	•

La Barranca del Cobre, México

En busca de sitios

✳ **Lea Gramática 11.1.**

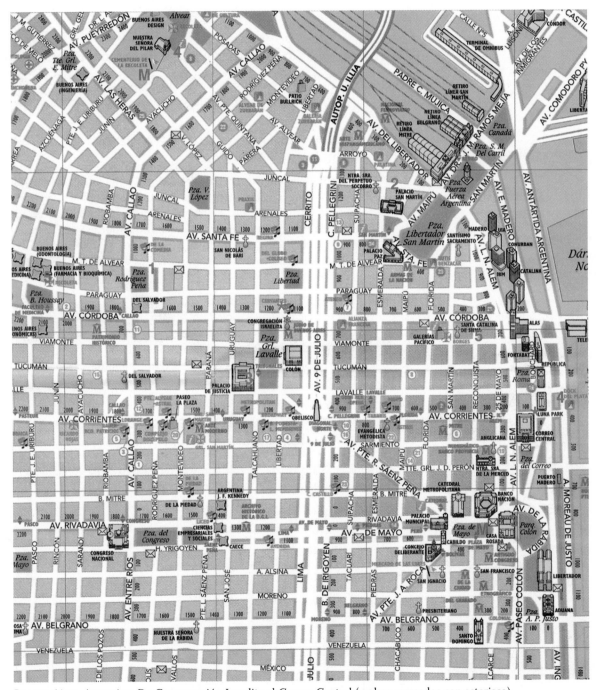

Buenos Aires, Argentina: De Congregación Israelita al Correo Central (ambos marcados con asterisco)

(Continúa)

TURISTA: Perdone, ¿puede decirme cómo llegar al Correo Central?

ADRIANA: Sí, por supuesto. Mire aquí en su plano. Salga de la Congregación Israelita por la calle Córdoba y camine dos cuadras hacia el este. En la Avenida 9 de Julio doble a la derecha. Camine cuatro cuadras por 9 de Julio y luego, en la glorieta del Obelisco, doble a la izquierda en la Avenida Corrientes. Camine siete cuadras hacia el este por Corrientes, cruce la Avenida L. N. Alem y ahí tiene usted el Correo Central.

TURISTA: Muchísimas gracias, señorita.

ADRIANA: Para servirle. Adiós.

Actividad 5   Conversación: La Ciudad de Buenos Aires

Mire el plano de la página anterior y explique cómo se va de una parte del centro de la ciudad a otra. (Los números en el plano van a ayudarle a encontrar los lugares mencionados.)

MODELO: del Cementerio de la Recoleta a la Plaza de Mayo (*Los dos están marcados con la* M *de* **Modelo.**) →

Salga del cementerio por la calle Junín y tome la calle Guido al sur. Camine once cuadras. En la Avenida Córdoba, doble a la izquierda y camine dos cuadras por esa avenida. Luego doble a la derecha en la Avenida 9 de Julio y camine nueve cuadras por esa calle tan ancha. Pase el Obelisco y siga hasta la Avenida de Mayo. Ahí doble a la izquierda. Camine cinco cuadras y ahí está la Plaza de Mayo, enfrente de usted.

1. de la Plaza Rodríguez Peña a la aduana
2. del Congreso Nacional al Palacio San Martín
3. del Palacio de Justicia a la Casa Rosada
4. de la iglesia de Nuestra Señora del Pilar a Luna Park
5. de la iglesia de Santa Catalina de Siena a (la facultad de) Farmacia y Bioquímica

Actividad 6   Del mundo hispano: Consejos para los viajeros

Lea los consejos de la izquierda. Luego, con un compañero / una compañera de clase, escriba otros dos o tres consejos útiles para los viajeros.

REFRÁN

Todos los caminos llegan a Roma.

(*All roads lead to Rome.*)

Cuando salga de VIAJE...

La misma atención que se pone para planear las vacaciones, se debe de tener para cuidar la casa antes de salir. Algunas sugerencias:

• Riegue las plantas antes de irse o pida a un vecino que lo haga.

• Pida a un vecino que recoja su correspondencia y el periódico.

• Avíseles a los vecinos que usted sale de vacaciones y deles el nombre y el número de teléfono de su hotel.

• Deje sus mascotas encargadas en casa de algún familiar o con su veterinario.

• Cubra su coche con una funda para protegerlo.

• Ponga las llaves en un lugar seguro de la casa.

Actividad 7 Del mundo hispano: El metro de Madrid

Dé instrucciones para ir de una estación del metro a otra. No olvide hacer los transbordos necesarios.

MODELO: De Atocha a El Carmen → Suba a un tren de la línea 1 en Atocha, dirección Plaza de Castilla, y baje en la Estación Sol. Allí suba a un tren de la línea 2, dirección La Elipa, y baje en la Estación Ventas. En Ventas, suba a un tren de la línea 5, dirección Canillejas, y siga hasta la primera estación. Bájese; allí es El Carmen.

1. de Puente de Vallecas a Ríos Rosas
2. de Tetuán a Sevilla
3. de Aluche a Goya
4. de Oporto a Portazgo
5. de Esperanza a Quintana

Enlace a la música

Susana Baca, cantante

La danza negra en Perú... ¡a bailar!

Al hablar de Perú, siempre mencionamos los Andes y el gran **Imperio** Inca, pero Perú tiene también una larga tradición africana. Como ocurrió en muchos otros países de América Latina, los españoles llevaron esclavos africanos a Perú para trabajar en las grandes plantaciones. Estos esclavos trajeron **consigo** las tradiciones musicales de **África occidental.** Cuando los españoles prohibieron el uso de los **tambores,** los africanos desarrollaron el uso del cajón, una **caja grande de madera,** como las que se usaban en la agricultura. Las formas musicales más conocidas de la danza negra son *el festejo, el landó, la zamba malató* y *el alcatraz.* El ritmo landó tiene sus orígenes en un baile de Angola llamado londu. Varias parejas participan en el baile del alcatraz, todos llevan velas y mueven las caderas al ritmo de los tambores. Este baile fue prohibido durante la época colonial por su sensualidad.

Por muchos años la danza negra **quedó en el olvido,** pero en 1969 se formó el grupo Perú Negro, con la meta de preservar el baile y la música de la gente negra de Perú. Una de las cantantes más famosas de la música afroperuana, Lucila Campos, empezó su carrera con este grupo. Actualmente hay muchos intérpretes de este estilo musical. En Lima, Susana Baca fundó el Centro Experimental de Música Negrocontinuo y se ha dedicado no sólo a cantar música negra sino a **difundir** esta tradición por todo el país. Baca ha grabado varios discos compactos de música afroperuana y en 2002 recibió un Premio Grammy por su disco *Lamento negro.* Eva Ayllón, conocida como «la voz de oro de Perú», **se destaca** con su versión del festejo, «Raíces negras». Ayllón incorpora palabras africanas al ritmo de su música.

Quien quiera escuchar esta música tan contagiosa puede ir al famoso club nocturno Manos Morenas en Lima donde tocan los artistas Arturo «Zambo» Cavero y el grupo Perú Negro. También puede visitar los sitios Web de los artistas aquí mencionados. ¡A bailar!

VOCABULARIO ÚTIL

el Imperio	*Empire*
consigo	*with them*
África occidental	*West Africa*
los tambores	*drums*
la caja grande de madera	*big wooden box*
quedó en el olvido	*was forgotten*
difundir	*to disseminate*
se destaca	*stands out*

Comprensión

1. ¿Con qué objetivo se formó el grupo Perú Negro?

2. ¿Cuál es la artista conocida como «la voz de oro de Perú»? ¿Qué incorpora ella en su música?

Los planes de viaje

✳ **Lea Gramática 11.2–11.3.**

hacer las reservaciones por Internet

¿Se necesitan vacunas?

LANCHILE.com
☐ boleto de ida
☑ boleto de ida y vuelta

el boleto

el pasaporte

el Consulado de Chile

la visa

la lancha

el barco

viajar en crucero

el equipaje (las maletas)

el aeropuerto

LANCHILE

el mostrador

Pedro y Andrea facturan el equipaje.

la clase turística

la primera clase

abordar el avión

la sala de espera

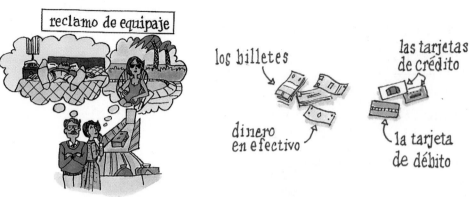

reclamo de equipaje

los billetes

dinero en efectivo

las tarjetas de crédito

la tarjeta de débito

la inmigración

← la cola →
hacer cola

—Su pasaporte, por favor.
—Aquí lo tiene.

Cuando lleguen al hotel, Pedro va a descansar y Andrea piensa sentarse al lado de la piscina.

—Permítame revisar su equipaje.

—Sí, como no. ¿La cámara también?

la aduana

revisar el equipaje

el contrabando

los derechos de aduana

Cuando Pedro y Andrea pasen por la aduana, el oficial va a revisar su equipaje.

el alojamiento

el gerente

el botones

la recepción

el ascensor (el elevador)

Cuando lleguen al hotel, van a hablar con el gerente.

¿Más?

CAJERO AUTOMÁTICO

Cuando Pedro necesite dinero puede ir al cajero automático.

la habitación

la camarera

la mesita de noche
la cama matrimonial

Andrea y Pedro quieren que la camarera les traiga toallas limpias.

la salida

TAXI

Hoy Pedro y Andrea regresan a México. Quieren que el botones ponga su equipaje en el maletero del taxi.

Actividad 8   Narración: El viaje de Carmen y Mónica

Carmen y Mónica quieren hacer un viaje a Chile. La profesora Martínez les hace estas sugerencias.

Primero les sugiero que _____[1] el viaje, que _____[2] el dinero necesario y _____[3] las reservaciones. Luego les sugiero que _____[4] los boletos y que _____[5] el pasaporte y la visa. Dos semanas antes de salir les sugiero que _____[6] ropa y otras cosas para el viaje. Con dos o tres días de anticipación, les sugiero que _____[7] las maletas y que _____[8] una copia de su itinerario con un amigo. El día de la salida, les sugiero que _____[9] al aeropuerto temprano. En el aeropuerto les sugiero que _____[10] dólares por pesos para tener pesos chilenos al llegar a Santiago. Y no olviden, ¡quiero que _____[11] español todos los días!

Actividad 9   Intercambios: Los paquetes turísticos

Mire estos paquetes turísticos ofrecidos por la aerolínea costarricense LACSA. Después, hágale preguntas a un compañero / una compañera.

Santiago de compras
4 noches / 5 días
Desde **$1899**

Incluye:
- **Boleto aéreo ida y vuelta** (sin impuestos).
- 4 noches de alojamiento en Hotel Galerías.
- Impuestos hoteleros.
- Traslado aeropuerto/hotel/aeropuerto.
- Desayuno buffet.
- Coctel de bienvenida.
- Tour de compras.

Barranquilla Ejecutivo
2 noches / 3 días
Desde **$686**

Incluye:
- **Boleto aéreo ida y vuelta** (sin impuestos).
- Dos noches de alojamiento con desayuno americano.
- Impuestos hoteleros.

Quito Ejecutivo
3 noches / 4 días
Desde **$1039**

Incluye:
- **Boleto aéreo ida y vuelta** (sin impuestos).
- Traslado aeropuerto/hotel/aeropuerto.
- 3 noches de alojamiento en hotel seleccionado.
- Impuestos hoteleros.

1. ¿Cuánto cuesta el paquete a Barranquilla? ¿Incluye los impuestos hoteleros?
2. ¿Qué más está incluido, además del alojamiento, en el paquete «Barranquilla Ejecutivo»?
3. ¿Está incluido un tour de compras en el paquete «Quito Ejecutivo»?
4. ¿Incluye el traslado del aeropuerto al hotel el paquete «Quito Ejecutivo»?
5. ¿Qué incluye el paquete «Santiago de compras» además del boleto, el alojamiento y los traslados del aeropuerto al hotel?
6. ¿Qué paquete prefieres tú? ¿Por qué?

Actividad 10 Intercambios: Las vacaciones ideales

A. Lea la descripción de cada persona que aparece abajo y luego escoja la excursión apropiada para cada una.

MODELO: A Pilar y Clara les recomiendo la gira de dos semanas por las capitales de Europa. En Londres, les sugiero que visiten la torre de Londres y en Roma les sugiero que vean el Coliseo. En París les sugiero que suban a la Torre Eiffel de noche.

Unas vacaciones de 6 noches y 7 días por las antiguas ciudades de Roma y Atenas. Excursiones al Partenón, la Basílica de San Pedro y otros lugares históricos. Alojamiento en hoteles de lujo.

Viaje de 5 noches y 6 días para acampar en las montañas al sur de Chile. Guía experto, caminatas de 10 kilómetros diarias, alojamiento en cabañas. Todo el equipo incluido.

CARIBE

Viaje en crucero de 6 noches y 7 días por el Caribe. Comida internacional, música y baile todas las noches. Piscina y cancha de tenis a bordo. Excursiones a mercados y sitios turísticos en cada puerto.

Gira de 8 noches y 9 días por la costa noreste de los Estados Unidos, incluyendo las ciudades históricas de Williamsburg, Jamestown, Boston, Baltimore y Charleston, terminando en Nueva York. Hoteles de precios módicos.

Dos semanas —13 noches y 14 días— en moderno club de vacaciones, en la península de Yucatán. Canchas de tenis, tres piscinas de agua dulce y una de agua salada. Clases de buceo, excursiones en barco de vela, campamento para niños.

Gira de dos semanas, 13 noches y 14 días, por las capitales de Europa: Londres, Roma, París, Estocolmo, Berlín y Viena. Excursiones en cada ciudad con guías expertos. Alojamiento en hoteles de precios módicos.

Una semana, 6 noches y 7 días, en un hotel en la Playa Dominical de Costa Rica. Restaurante, bar, dos piscinas, jacuzzi, canchas de tenis.

---

1. Adriana Bolini: Adriana es argentina, soltera, de 35 años. Ella es mujer de negocios. Le gusta mucho viajar y ha viajado por muchas partes de Europa.
2. Susana Yamasaki y sus hijos, Armando y Andrés (de 13 y 9 años, respectivamente): Susana es madre divorciada y trabaja de secretaria y también de guía de turistas para las ruinas de Machu Picchu. A Susana le gusta salir de vacaciones con sus hijos.
3. Raúl Saucedo: Raúl es estudiante de ingeniería en la Universidad de Texas, en San Antonio. Es muy aventurero y le gusta viajar porque le encanta conocer gente interesante.
4. Pilar y Clara: Clara está de visita en España por un año. Allí conoció a Pilar. Las dos son estudiantes y tienen un mes de vacaciones entre semestres.

B. Ahora dígale a sus compañeros / compañeras qué excursión le gustaría a usted y por qué. ¿Qué otras actividades piensa hacer durante sus vacaciones?

MODELO: A mí me gustaría la excursión de 5 noches y 6 días en Chile por que me gusta mucho caminar en las montañas. Pienso sacar fotos y hablar mucho español.

Actividad 11 Del mundo hispano: De viaje en Andalucía

Granada

HOTELES Y RESTAURANTES

HOTELES: Alhambra Palace. Caro. Hermoso palacio estilo morisco en la cumbre de la montaña Alhambra con magníficas vistas. Tel. 958-221-468. **Parador de Granada** San Francisco. Caro. Está en un antiguo convento de los muros de la Alhambra y es el parador más popular de España. Se requiere hacer reservación de 4 a 6 meses de anticipación. Tel. 958-222-264. **América.** Moderado. Encantador hotel dentro de los terrenos de la Alhambra. Es muy popular, reserve con anticipación. Tel. 958-227-471.

RESTAURANTES: La Yedra Real. Moderado. Cerca de la Alhambra. Gran variedad de comida típica española. Tel. 958-229-145. **Cunini.** Caro. Muy famoso por su pescado y comida marina. Tel. 958-267-587. **Colombia.** Caro-Moderado. En la montaña de la Alhambra con elegante decorado árabe, música de guitarra y espléndidas vistas. Muy turístico, pero divertido. Tel. 958-227-7433.

Sevilla ofrece a los visitantes hoteles de lujo, como el Alfonso XIII, un edificio de estilo morisco construido en 1929 para la Exhibición Mundial.

Sevilla

HOTELES Y RESTAURANTES

Todos los precios pueden duplicarse e incluso triplicarse durante la Semana Santa y los días que dura la Feria.

HOTELES: Alfonso XIII. De lujo. Construido en estilo morisco para la exhibición de 1929, es el hotel clásico de Sevilla lleno de belleza y encanto. Tel. 954-917-000. **Doña María.** Caro. Pequeño, con habitaciones de buen gusto amuebladas con antigüedades y piscina en la azotea con vista a la Giralda. Tel. 954-224-990. **Bécquer.** Moderado. Hotel agradable y moderno. Tel. 954-228-900. **Fernando III.** Moderado. A orillas del barrio Santa Cruz; piscina en la azotea. Tel. 954-220-246.

RESTAURANTES: Albahaca. Caro. Todos frecuentan este restaurante, hermosamente localizado en el corazón del viejo barrio judío; platos creativos. Tel. 954-220-714. **La Dorada.** Caro. Muy famoso por sus pescados y comida marina. Tel. 954-227-828. **Bodegón Torre del Oro.** Moderado. Atmósfera rústica, buena comida y popular entre turistas y locales. Tel. 954-220-880. **El Giraldillo.** Caro-Moderado. Restaurante y bar de tapas. Comida sevillana típica. Tel 954-214-525.

De estilo morisco, el Alhambra Palace es uno de los hoteles caros de Granada, con magníficas vistas desde la cumbre de la montaña.

EN GRANADA

1. Si usted necesita un hotel de precios módicos, ¿en dónde va a hospedarse?
2. ¿Cómo se llama un parador muy popular?
3. Si quiere comer en un restaurante de ambiente árabe, ¿en dónde va a cenar?
4. ¿En dónde va a cenar, si tiene ganas de comer mariscos?
5. Si desea cenar en un restaurante con gran variedad de comida española típica, ¿a cuál va a ir?

EN SEVILLA

1. Si desea cenar en un restaurante en el centro del barrio judío, ¿a cuál piensa ir?
2. Si busca un hotel elegante y clásico, ¿cuál va a escoger?
3. Si prefiere un hotel de precios módicos con piscina, ¿en dónde va a hospedarse?
4. Si desea comer tapas, ¿en qué restaurante puede hacerlo?
5. ¿Cómo se llama un restaurante de precios módicos y ambiente informal?

Las palabras nos transportan

Las diferencias de vocabulario entre los países hispanos son **comunes** y le dan al **lenguaje** de cada país un sabor **único**. Usted ya sabe que en México «el dormitorio» es «la recámara», que en Argentina las «fresas» son «frutillas» y que en España «el jugo» es «el zumo». **Al hacer un recorrido** de las palabras relacionadas con el transporte, vemos también diferencias muy interesantes. Por ejemplo, «autobús» es la palabra más usada para referirse al medio de transporte público que circula por las ciudades, pero en Puerto Rico, Cuba y la República Dominicana la palabra que más se usa es «guagua». En Argentina, Bolivia, Paraguay y Perú, se dice

Un camello es un tipo de autobús que circula en las grandes ciudades de Cuba.

«colectivo», en México es «el camión», mientras que en El Salvador es «el chuzón» y en Costa Rica es «la lata». Para referirse al transporte metropolitano la palabra «metro» es la más usada, pero en Buenos Aires se dice el «subte».

El automóvil también se conoce por muchos otros nombres. En España y en el centro y el sur de México es «coche», pero en el Caribe y Centroamérica se dice «carro». Existen otras palabras también, como «auto», que se usa en varios países. En España el carro puede ser un «buga» y en México y Centroamérica una «**nave**». Tanto en Argentina como en Uruguay el coche puede ser «el checo», que son las sílabas de *co-che* pronunciadas **al revés**. En México un carro muy viejo es una «carcacha». La placa del carro también tiene diferentes nombres: «la matrícula» en España, «la patente» en Argentina y «la chapa» en Cuba. Ponemos las maletas en «el maletero», pero en México las ponemos en «la cajuela» y en Argentina en «el baúl». Los españoles no «estacionan» el coche, lo «aparcan», mientras que los centroamericanos y los caribeños lo «parquean».

«El **monopatín**», tan popular entre los chicos, es «patineta» en México. Y «la bicicleta» es «bici» en muchos países, aunque en México y Perú puede ser «la bicla», mientras que en Costa Rica es una «cleta». En algunos países para hablar de una bicicleta se usa una palabra que se refiere a un animal: en Uruguay se dice «**chiva**» y en Cuba, «**chivo**».

A la hora de viajar, en España se hacen «las reservas» y se compran «los billetes» de avión, mientras que en los países de Hispanoamérica se hacen «las reservaciones» y se compran «los boletos». Para salir de viaje es necesario «hacer las maletas», pero en las Américas uno también puede «empacar». A propósito, la palabra «maleta» se usa en muchos países, pero en Argentina y en Uruguay se oye más «valija».

Con todas estas palabras diferentes es posible pensar que cada país tiene su propio idioma. Pero, en realidad los países hispanohablantes comparten mucho vocabulario y por suerte en todos se dice «¡Buen viaje!» de igual manera.

VOCABULARIO ÚTIL	
comunes	*common*
el lenguaje	*language*
único	*unique*
Al hacer un recorrido	*If we take a tour*
la nave	*ship, vessel*
al revés	*backwards*
el monopatín	*skateboard*
el chivo / la chiva	*goat*

Comprensión

1. ¿Qué otras palabras se usan para **coche** en el mundo hispano? ¿Cuál es el origen de la palabra argentina **checo**?

2. ¿Cuáles son otras dos palabras para decir **bicicleta**? ¿Cómo se dice **boleto** en España?

Actividad 12 **Del mundo hispano: La Barranca del Cobre en México**

Lea este artículo y luego hágale las siguientes preguntas a un compañero / una compañera de clase.

Barranca del Cobre
Una de las maravillas naturales de México

Visitar la Barranca del Cobre es una de las grandes experiencias que puede tener un viajero en México. Localizada en la Sierra Madre Occidental de Chihuahua, en un área de más de 35.000 km², es 1,5 veces más profunda y cubre cuatro veces la extensión de Gran Cañón en Arizona. Su vegetación y fauna desde el fondo de las barrancas —que en algunas zonas llegan a tener 3.000 metros de profundidad— hasta sus sierras nevadas en invierno son tan diversas, que nunca se acaban de admirar. En la región viven dispersos más de 50.000 indios tarahumaras descen-dientes de los indígenas uto-aztecas que anterior-mente habitaban gran parte del territorio occidental de América del Norte. Los tarahumaras se autodenominan rarámuri que en su idioma significa «gente de los pies ligeros» por su costumbre de correr largas distancias. Los hombres tarahumaras participan en un tipo de juego de pelota que puede durar varios días y en el cual los corredores descalzos corren hasta 300 kilómetros. Las mujeres también corren en una competencia con aros.

Quienes deseen conocer esta región, considerada por muchos la octava maravilla natural del mundo, pueden hacerlo en una de las excursiones de siete días organizadas por Ecovacaciones de México. Incluyen: organizador de grupo bilingüe, seis noches de hospedaje en hotel, transportación en autobús, lanchas, tren (desde donde se tienen vistas espectaculares atravesando puentes y túneles), camionetas, entradas a los sitios de interés, caminatas guiadas por los tarahumaras y diez alimentos. No incluye: transportación aérea, bebidas alcohólicas, gastos extras en el hotel (teléfono, lavandería, etc.).

Adulto doble: $8.369 (779 dólares), triple: $7.482 (696 dólares), sencillo: $9.353 (870 dólares), niño $4.249 (395 dólares). Los precios no incluyen IVA. Para mayores informes y reservaciones llame al 668-812-4356 o visite nuestro sitio Web: www.ecovacaciones.com.

1. ¿Dónde está la Barranca del Cobre?
2. ¿Es más grande o menos grande la Barranca del Cobre que el Gran Cañón de Arizona?
3. ¿Qué tribu de indígenas vive en esta región?
4. ¿Por qué razón son famosos estos indígenas?
5. ¿Cómo se llama la compañía que organiza las excursiones?
6. ¿Está incluido el vuelo en el precio de la excursión?
7. ¿Es necesario saber hablar español para ir en esta excursión?
8. ¿Cuánto cuesta una habitación doble, por adulto? ¿y una habitación sencilla?

Nuevos vuelos entre
Lima y Santiago

Los viajeros de negocios pueden ahora salir por la mañana de Lima para asistir a una reunión en Santiago y estar de regreso a la hora de la cena, gracias al nuevo vuelo que ofrece AeroPerú. Los vuelos que enlazan ambas ciudades operan miércoles, viernes y sábados en un Boeing 757. El vuelo 973 sale de Lima a las 8:35 a.m. y llega a Santiago a las 12:55 p.m.; el vuelo 972 sale de Santiago a las 6:00 p.m. y llega a Lima a las 8:35 p.m. El trayecto dura aproximadamente tres horas y media. ◑

Los sitios turísticos

✳ Lea Gramática 11.4–11.5.

Pedro y Andrea hicieron las reservaciones en la Agencia Universo el 6 de junio.

Pedro y Andrea llegaron a Madrid el 2 de julio.

Pedro y Andrea dormían cuando sonó el teléfono.

Estaban tomando un refresco en un café de la Gran Vía cuando vieron a un viejo amigo de Pedro.

A las 4:00 de la tarde Pedro y Andrea admiraban las pinturas de Goya en el Museo del Prado, cuando las luces se apagaron.

UN CHISTE

Conversación en un hotel

—¿Cuánto cuesta una habitación?

—En el primer piso, doscientos dólares.

—¿Y en el segundo?

—Ciento cincuenta.

—¿Y en el tercero?

—Cien.

—¿Y en el cuarto?

—No tenemos cuarto piso.

—Entonces, no me hospedo aquí.

—¿Pero por qué?

—¡Su hotel no es lo bastante alto para mí!

Actividad 13 Descripción de dibujos: El viaje de Virginia y Rubén a la Ciudad de México

Diga qué estaba pasando.

MODELO: A las 6:05 Virginia y Rubén estaban recogiendo (recogían) los boletos en la agencia de viajes.

¡OJO!

Hay un sólo lugar en América desde el cual se puede ver el Océano Atlántico y el Pacífico a la vez: desde el volcán Irazú de Costa Rica, que está a unos 11.200 pies de altura.

MODELO: Virginia y Rubén estaban paseando (paseaban) por el Paseo de la Reforma cuando dos carros chocaron.

Un conquistador original

ALVA NUÑEZ CABEZA DE VACA CROSSING THE GREAT AMERICAN DESERT.

El español Alvar Núñez Cabeza de Vaca (c.1490–c.1557) llegó al Nuevo Mundo como Hernán Cortés y Francisco Pizarro, para conquistar y colonizar a los indígenas. Pero pasó a la historia por razones muy diferentes. Cabeza de Vaca no colonizó grandes civilizaciones, **no se apoderó** de grandes extensiones de tierra. De hecho, en su primer viaje al nuevo mundo sufrió varios **naufragios.** La mayoría de sus compañeros **pereció** a causa de la sed o de los ataques de los nativos. Pero Cabeza de Vaca logró **sobrevivir** y, por años, exploró el sudeste de lo que ahora es los Estados Unidos en compañía de otros tres sobrevivientes.

La ruta de Cabeza de Vaca

Lo sorprendente de este «conquistador» que no conquistó nada es su adaptabilidad. Mientras era **esclavo** de los indígenas los observó, se adaptó a sus costumbres y aprendió mucho de ellos. Mientras viajaba en busca de otros españoles, para sobrevivir, comerciaba. Pero también trabajaba de **curandero;** era respetado y admirado por las muchas tribus que encontraba a lo largo de su camino.

Los diez años que Cabeza de Vaca pasó en el Nuevo Mundo estuvieron tan llenos de problemas que parecen más ficción que realidad. Los **relatos** en su libro, *La relación* (1542), demuestran cuán peligrosos eran los viajes en esa época. El libro describe sus aventuras, sus tragedias y su vida de esclavo. Hay información también sobre la vida y las costumbres de los indígenas del sur y sudeste, Texas y Florida especialmente. Su libro menciona, por ejemplo, que esas culturas amaban mucho a sus hijos y los trataban mejor que la gente de cualquier otra cultura. También da detalles sobre cómo los padres lloraban por todo un año la muerte de uno de sus hijos.

VOCABULARIO ÚTIL

no se apoderó	*did not seize*
los naufragios	*shipwrecks*
pereció	*perished*
sobrevivir	*to survive*
el esclavo	*slave*
el curandero	*healer*
los relatos	*accounts, stories*
el aliento	*breath*
las piedras	*pebbles, rocks*

Más interesante todavía, el libro revela información sobre los conocimientos de medicina natural de los indígenas y su manera de curar. Según Cabeza de Vaca, los indígenas le sacaban la enfermedad a una persona con el **aliento** y con las manos; asimismo, curaban el dolor pasando **piedras** calientes por el estómago del paciente. Además, estaban seguros de que todo lo que había en el campo tenía propiedades benéficas.

Al leer la historia de la conquista del Nuevo Mundo, descubrimos pasajes de mucha violencia y abuso. Pero, como lo demuestra la historia de Álvar Núñez Cabeza de Vaca, no todos los conquistadores llegaron para conquistar y controlar a los indígenas. Cabeza de Vaca se distingue como un hombre especial, único entre todos los demás.

Comprensión

1. ¿Cuál es la diferencia entre Cabeza de Vaca y Hernán Cortés o Francisco Pizarro?

2. En contraste con los otros conquistadores, ¿cómo se relacionó Cabeza de Vaca con los indígenas? ¿Qué pensaban ellos de él?

Actividad 14 Narración: De turistas en España

Diga qué hicieron Pedro y Andrea durante su viaje a España.

Actividad 15 Del mundo hispano: La ecología de Cuba

Lea el artículo y vea el mapa. Luego converse con un compañero / una compañera usando las preguntas debajo del mapa.

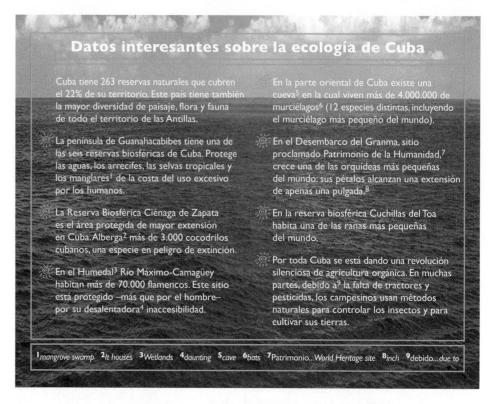

Datos interesantes sobre la ecología de Cuba

Cuba tiene 263 reservas naturales que cubren el 22% de su territorio. Este país tiene también la mayor diversidad de paisaje, flora y fauna de todo el territorio de las Antillas.

La península de Guanahacabibes tiene una de las seis reservas biosféricas de Cuba. Protege las aguas, los arrecifes, las selvas tropicales y los manglares[1] de la costa del uso excesivo por los humanos.

La Reserva Biosférica Ciénaga de Zapata es el área protegida de mayor extensión en Cuba. Alberga[2] más de 3.000 cocodrilos cubanos, una especie en peligro de extinción.

En el Humedal[3] Río Máximo-Camagüey habitan más de 70.000 flamencos. Este sitio está protegido —más que por el hombre— por su desalentadora[4] inaccesibilidad.

En la parte oriental de Cuba existe una cueva[5] en la cual viven más de 4.000.000 de murciélagos[6] (12 especies distintas, incluyendo el murciélago más pequeño del mundo).

En el Desembarco del Granma, sitio proclamado Patrimonio de la Humanidad,[7] crece una de las orquídeas más pequeñas del mundo: sus pétalos alcanzan una extensión de apenas una pulgada.[8]

En la reserva biosférica Cuchillas del Toa habita una de las ranas más pequeñas del mundo.

Por toda Cuba se está dando una revolución silenciosa de agricultura orgánica. En muchas partes, debido a[9] la falta de tractores y pesticidas, los campesinos usan métodos naturales para controlar los insectos y para cultivar sus tierras.

[1]mangrove swamp [2]It houses [3]Wetlands [4]daunting [5]cave [6]bats [7]Patrimonio...World Heritage site [8]inch [9]debido...due to

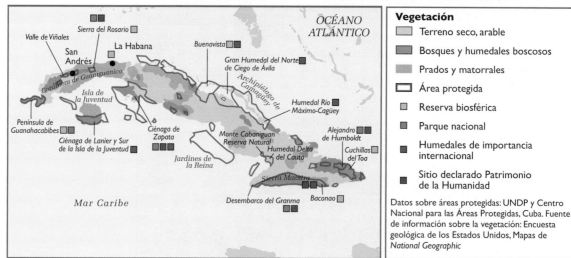

Vegetación
- Terreno seco, arable
- Bosques y humedales boscosos
- Prados y matorrales
- Área protegida
- Reserva biosférica
- Parque nacional
- Humedales de importancia internacional
- Sitio declarado Patrimonio de la Humanidad

Datos sobre áreas protegidas: UNDP y Centro Nacional para las Áreas Protegidas, Cuba. Fuente de información sobre la vegetación: Encuesta geológica de los Estados Unidos, Mapas de *National Geographic*

1. ¿Son extensas las reservas naturales de Cuba?
2. ¿Es variado el paisaje cubano? ¿y la flora y la fauna?
3. ¿Qué datos interesantes hay en relación con especies muy pequeñas de flora y fauna?
4. ¿Qué especie en peligro de extinción se protege en la Reserva Biosférica Ciénaga de Zapata? ¿Es pequeña esa reserva?
5. ¿Qué se protege en la península de Guanahacabibes?
6. ¿En qué consiste la nueva revolución cubana?
7. ¿Qué es lo que protege a los flamencos del Humedal Río Máximo-Camagüey?
8. ¿Ha visitado una reserva biológica? ¿Qué te llamó más la atención de ese lugar?

De todo un poco

A. Hable de sus viajes con un compañero / una compañera.

1. ¿Has visitado un país hispano? ¿Cuál? ¿Con quién fuiste? ¿Te gustó?

2. ¿A qué (otro) país hispano te gustaría viajar? ¿Por qué?

3. ¿Has tenido algún problema o una experiencia que no te permitió disfrutar de un viaje? ¿Dónde fue? ¿en el aeropuerto? ¿en aduana o inmigración? ¿en un restaurante?

4. Además de tu coche, ¿qué otros medios de transporte empleas tú aquí en este país? ¿Qué medios has empleado en otros países?

5. ¿Has hecho un viaje en un crucero? ¿Adónde fuiste? ¿Con quién? ¿Qué es lo que más te gustó? ¿Qué es lo que menos te gustó?

B. Con su compañero/a, prepare una de las siguientes situaciones.

1. Los planes de viaje: Usted va a salir de vacaciones con destino a Sudamérica. Hable por teléfono con el empleado / la empleada de la aerolínea para obtener la siguiente información: la hora de salida del avión, las escalas, la hora del almuerzo, la película y la hora de llegada del avión.

> EMPLEADO/A: Aeroméxico, a sus órdenes.
> USTED: Buenos días, señor(ita). Voy a viajar a Chile mañana y tengo algunas preguntas.
> EMPLEADO/A: Sí, dígame.
> USTED: ¿A qué hora sale el vuelo número _____?
> EMPLEADO/A: Ese vuelo sale a la(s) _____ de la _____.
> USTED: Otra pregunta, ¿... ?

2. En el hotel: Usted acaba de llegar a un hotel después de manejar ocho horas. Dígale al empleado / a la empleada lo que usted quiere y pídale la información necesaria (el precio, el tamaño de la cama, si tiene baño, teléfono, televisión, etcétera). Luego, decida si quiere la habitación o no.

> EMPLEADO/A: Buenas noches, señor/señora. ¿En qué puedo servirle?
> USTED: Quisiera una habitación con...

¡Dígalo por escrito!

Viajando por el mundo hispano

Prepare un folleto de turismo para viajeros que quieren visitar alguna ciudad o país del mundo hispano. El folleto debe incluir mapas, fotos o dibujos. Puede mencionar paisajes, excursiones, hoteles y restaurantes. Use mandatos como **camine, coma, conozca, descanse, disfrute, diviértase, vea, venga, viaje, visite,** etcétera.

¡Cuéntenos usted!

Cuéntenos sobre algo cómico o peligroso que le pasó en un viaje. ¿Adónde iba usted? ¿Con quién viajaba? ¿Qué pasó?

PISTAS PARA LEER
En esta **Lectura** se describe una de las regiones más hermosas de América Latina. ¿Qué tipo de lugar evocan las palabras del **Vocabulario útil**? ¿Es tropical, por ejemplo? Primero lea el texto selectivamente y visualice los sitios que se describen. Luego léalo en detalle y decida si quiere hacer un viaje a Mérida.

VOCABULARIO ÚTIL

primaveral	*spring-like*
la balsa	*raft*
los alrede-dores	*surround-ings*
los manantiales	*(water) springs*
las aldeas	*villages*
los trapiches	*sugar cane mills*
el guarapo	*sugar cane juice or liquor*
precolombinas	*from before Columbus*
el teleférico	*cable car*
la cima	*summit, top*

LECTURA

Mérida, ciudad en la montaña

Cuando pensamos en la belleza natural de Venezuela, generalmente evocamos sus playas, su clima tropical y su cultura caribeña. Es cierto que Caracas, la capital, es una de las ciudades más hermosas de la región del Caribe. Pero al suroeste de Caracas hay una zona montañosa que ofrece un ambiente muy diferente al del trópico. En esa región de Venezuela se encuentra una ciudad encantadora: Mérida.

La ciudad de Mérida está en el estado del mismo nombre, entre las montañas andinas, y tiene una de las dos universidades más antiguas de Venezuela: la Universidad de los Andes, fundada en 1785. El clima de Mérida es templado y **primaveral** casi todo el año, a pesar de estar en las montañas. La temporada lluviosa es de mayo a noviembre, pero llueve sólo muy temprano en la mañana. En el estado de Mérida hay doce parques nacionales, además de una increíble variedad de zonas geográficas: bosques, cascadas, lagos, montañas con picos nevados y hasta una playa, Palmarito, al sureste del Lago Maracaibo.

¿Se imagina todas las actividades que son posibles en el estado de Mérida? Allí puede hacer montañismo y ciclismo en Pico Bolívar y Pico Espejo; puede explorar los lagos en canoa y en **balsa**, nadar, pescar, dar largas caminatas por los

Pico Bolívar, Venezuela

bosques y observar una gran variedad de aves. En los **alrededores** de la ciudad de Mérida hay paisajes fantásticos, **manantiales** de agua caliente, pueblos que conservan intacta su arquitectura colonial y **aldeas** donde puede comprar bellas artesanías; también hay **trapiches** para observar cómo se hace el azúcar y probar el rico **guarapo,** una bebida que se prepara con el jugo de la caña de azúcar.

La ciudad de Mérida también tiene mucho que ofrecer. En febrero y marzo se celebra la Feria del Sol con bailes regionales. Pero si usted prefiere ir de compras y saborear los platos típicos, entonces debe visitar el mercado Principal de

Mérida, donde encontrará muchísimos restaurantes y tiendas. La Plaza Bolívar es el centro y corazón de la ciudad. Allí verá una imponente catedral, la Basílica Menor de la Inmaculada Concepción, varios museos importantes —como el Museo Arqueológico, donde se exhiben obras **precolombinas,** y el Museo de Arte Moderno— y la Casa de la Cultura, que muestra la obra de artesanos locales. Pero lo más emocionante de su visita a la ciudad de Mérida va a ser sin duda un paseo en **teleférico** a la **cima** de Pico Espejo. Es una subida de siete millas en el teleférico más largo y alto del mundo. Desde la cima de la montaña podrá admirar un paisaje maravilloso de valles y picos nevados.

Hay tantos lugares hermosos que visitar en América Latina, y entre todos está Mérida, encantadora ciudad en la montaña.

Comprensión

Complete las frases de la columna A con las frases de la columna B para hacer un resumen.

A	B
1. Entre los atractivos de la ciudad de Mérida...	**a.** para ver un paisaje fantástico de valles y picos nevados
2. Si usted quiere ver cómo se hace el azúcar,...	**b.** y probar la cocina venezolana, van al Mercado Principal de Mérida.
3. En el estado de Mérida uno puede disfrutar de varios deportes;...	**c.** una plaza, una catedral y varios museos.
4. En el centro de la ciudad de Mérida hay...	**d.** muy agradable, como de primavera, y tiene una temporada de lluvia.
5. Los turistas que quieren ir de compras...	**e.** debe visitar los trapiches, donde también hacen guarapo.
6. El clima de Mérida es...	**f.** está la Feria del Sol y un paseo en teleférico.
7. Vaya a la cima de Pico Espejo...	**g.** por ejemplo, el montañismo y la natación.

Un paso más... ¡a escribir!

Imagínese que usted está de vacaciones en Mérida (o en otra ciudad) y que va a mandarle una tarjeta postal a uno de sus amigos. Usando el siguiente modelo, mencione sus lugares favoritos en la ciudad o en la región y sus actividades más divertidas en esos lugares.

MODELO: Querido/a _____:
          Aquí estoy en (*ciudad*). Es una ciudad muy _____ y tiene
      _____. Mis lugares favoritos son _____ y _____. En esta ciudad
      uno puede hacer muchas actividades divertidas. Por ejemplo, el primer
      día yo (*actividad*) y (*actividad*). Ayer viajé con (*personas que viajan
      con usted*) por los alrededores de la ciudad y allí hicimos muchas
      cosas. Entre otras, (*actividades que hicieron*). Mañana vamos a...
          La foto en esta postal es de _____. ¿Qué te parece?
          Bueno, ¡hasta la próxima!
          Un abrazo,
              (*su firma*)

Vea el **Resumen cultural** en este capítulo del *Cuaderno de actividades.*

Vocabulario

El automóvil

The Automobile

abrocharse el cinturón de seguridad	to fasten one's seat belt
los cambios	gears
el capó	hood
el espejo retrovisor	rearview mirror
los faros	headlights
los frenos	brakes
el guardafangos	fender
el limpiaparabrisas	windshield wiper
la llanta (de repuesto / desinflada)	(spare/flat) tire
el maletero	trunk
el parabrisas	windshield
el parachoques	bumper
el peatón / la peatona	pedestrian
la placa	license plate
el seguro automovilístico	(automobile) insurance
tocar la bocina	to honk the horn
el tránsito	traffic
el volante	steering wheel

PALABRAS SEMEJANTES: la antena, la circulación, el radiador
REPASO: el aceite, el asiento, la autopista, la carretera, la rueda, el semáforo, la señal, el tanque

Los letreros en la carretera

Road Signs

el camino	road
despacio	slow
la desviación	detour
disminuya la velocidad	slow down
doble sentido (vía)	two-way
no hay paso	no entrance
el puente	bridge
un solo sentido (una sola vía)	one-way

PALABRA SEMEJANTE: la curva
REPASO: ¡Alto!, el peligro

Los viajes

Trips

la aduana	customs
el alojamiento	lodging
el barco de vela	sailboat
el botones	bellhop
la camarera	chambermaid
los derechos de aduana	customs duty, taxes

el destino	destination
la excursión	tour, field trip
la habitación	(hotel) room
sencilla	single occupancy
doble	double occupancy
los impuestos	taxes
las instrucciones	directions
la llegada	arrival
la maleta	suitcase
el mostrador	counter
la primera clase	first class
la recepción	lobby
la sala de espera	waiting room
la salida	departure; exit
la vacuna	vaccination, shot
el viajero / la viajera	traveler
el visado (la visa)	visa

PALABRAS SEMEJANTES: la agencia de viajes, la clase turística, el consulado, el contrabando, el itinerario, el turismo
REPASO: el crucero, la gira, el pasaje, el pasajero / la pasajera, el plano, el/la turista

El transporte aéreo

Air Travel

abordo	on board
el/la asistente de vuelo	flight attendant
el boleto	ticket
(de ida y vuelta)	round-trip
la escala	stopover
el reclamo de equipaje	baggage claim
el transbordo	transfer
el traslado de... a...	transportation from . . . to . . .
el vuelo	flight

PALABRAS SEMEJANTES: la aerolínea
REPASO: el aeropuerto, el avión

Los lugares

Places

la cabaña	cabin
el campamento	campground; camp
la corrida de toros	bullfight
la estación del metro	subway station
la glorieta	traffic circle
el parador	state (tourist) hotel
el puerto	port
la torre	tower

PALABRAS SEMEJANTES: el acueducto, el cementerio, la lancha, el monumento, el palacio, la plaza, la ruina

Los mandatos

Commands

baje(n) (bajar)	get off (to get off)
doble(n) (doblar)	turn (to turn)
haga(n) (hacer)	do; make (to do; to make)
salga(n) (salir)	leave (to leave)
siga(n) (seguir)	keep going (to keep going)
suba(n) (subir)	board (to board)
tome(n) (tomar)	(to take)

Los verbos

Verbs

abordar	to board
acabar de (+ *infin.*)	to have just done (*something*)
avisar	to advise; to warn
broncearse	to get a tan
caerse	to fall down
cambiar dólares por...	to exchange dollars for . . .
chocar (con)	to crash, run into (*something*)
disfrutar	to enjoy
estar de visita	to be staying
facturar el equipaje	to check baggage
gastar gasolina	to use (waste) gasoline
hacer clic en	to "click" on
hacer cola	to stand in line
hacer las maletas	to pack
olvidar	to forget
revisar	to check
sacar el pasaporte	to get a passport
salir de vacaciones	to go on vacation
sugerir (ie)	to suggest
tener la culpa	to be at fault

PALABRAS SEMEJANTES: admirar, anunciar, consistir (en), mantener, mencionar, organizar, planear
REPASO: estacionar el carro, hospedarse

Los sustantivos

Nouns

el agua dulce/salada	fresh/salt water
el billete	ticket
el cajero automático	ATM
la caminata	walk, hike
el consejo	advice

la cuadra	(*street*) block
el (dinero en) efectivo	cash (money)
el equipo	equipment
la esquina	corner
el este	east
el folleto	brochure
el lujo	luxury
la mesita de noche	night table, nightstand
el oeste	west
el paisaje	landscape; countryside
la pintura	painting
la superficie	surface
la tarjeta de débito	debit card, ATM card
la tribu	tribe

PALABRAS SEMEJANTES: el adulto, el ballet folclórico, el experto / la experta, el flamenco, la importancia, el kilómetro, la porcelana, la región, la revolución, la selección

Los adjetivos

Adjectives

ancho/a	wide
aventurero/a	adventurous
judío/a	Jewish
ofrecido/a	offered
resbaloso/a	slippery

PALABRAS SEMEJANTES: extenso/a, incluido/a, prohibido/a

Palabras y expresiones útiles

Useful Words and Expressions

además de	besides
Aquí lo tiene.	Here it is.
A sus órdenes	How may I help you?; At your service
a última hora	last minute
¿Cómo se va de... a... ?	How does one get from . . . to . . . ?
¡Cuidado!	Careful! Watch out!
Para servirle.	You are welcome.
permítame	allow me
por supuesto	of course
Sí, como no.	Yes, of course.

PALABRA SEMEJANTE: ¡Qué coincidencia!
REPASO: a la derecha / a la izquierda

Gramática y ejercicios

¿RECUERDA?

In **Gramática A.5** you learned that singular commands (to one person) end in **-a** or **-e.** Plural commands (to more than one person) end in **-an** or **-en.**

Polite commands:
-ar verbs take **-e(n)** endings: **hable** (usted), **tomen** (ustedes)
-er/-ir verbs take **-a(n)** endings: **coma** (usted), **escriban** (ustedes)

11.1 Giving Instructions: Polite Commands

A. Polite singular commands (a command you would make to a person you address with **usted**) are formed by changing **-ar** verb endings to **-e;** **-er** and **-ir** endings change to **-a.** (Informal commands are presented in **Gramática 14.3.**)

-ar: Lleve el paquete.	*Take the package.*
-er: Coma cereal por la mañana.	*Eat cereal in the morning.*
-ir: Abra la ventana, por favor.	*Open the window, please.*

B. To give polite commands to more than one person, add **-n.***

No bail**en** más de dos horas.	*Don't dance more than two hours.*

C. If a verb stem is irregular in the **yo** form of the present tense, it usually has the same irregularity in the command form: **yo pongo → ponga.**

Venga(n) temprano, por favor.	*Come early, please.*
Salga(n) inmediatamente.	*Leave immediately.*

Here are some common irregular commands based on the **yo** form.

conozca	(conocer)	*know*		tenga	(tener)	*have*
diga	(decir)	*say*		traiga	(traer)	*bring*
haga	(hacer)	*do; make*		vea	(ver)	*see*
oiga	(oír)	*hear*		venga	(venir)	*come*

Tengan cuidado en la autopista.	*Be careful on the freeway.*
Traiga sus documentos mañana a la oficina de la aduana.	*Bring your documents tomorrow to the customs office.*

D. The following irregular command forms do not match the first-person singular forms.

dé	(dar)	*give*		sepa	(saber)	*know*
esté	(estar)	*be*		vaya	(ir)	*go*
sea	(ser)	*be*				

Sepa muy bien lo que quiere decir antes de hablar.	*Know well what you want to say before speaking.*
Si quiere reservar un asiento para diciembre, **vaya** ahora mismo a la agencia de viajes.	*If you want to reserve a seat for December, go to the travel agency right away.*

---

*In Spain the **vosotros/as** command form is used for plural *informal* commands. See the section on **vos** and **vosotros** in the **Expansión gramatical** at the end of the *Cuaderno de actividades.* In most of Latin America, however, the plural polite command is used to give a command to more than one person, whether one normally addresses them politely or informally.

E. Verbs with vowel changes in the present indicative stem show the same changes in the polite command forms.

piense	pensar (ie)	*think*	**cie**rre	cerrar (ie)	*close*
duerma	dormir (ue)	*sleep*	**vue**lva	volver (ue)	*return*
sirva	servir (i)	*serve*	con**si**ga	conseguir (i)	*get*

Duerma por lo menos ocho horas cada noche.	*Sleep at least eight hours every night.*
Cierre la maleta.	*Close the suitcase.*
Sirva los refrescos.	*Serve the refreshments.*

F. Object pronouns and reflexive pronouns are attached to affirmative commands and precede negative ones.

Tráigale café, por favor; **no le traiga** té.	*Bring her coffee, please; don't bring her tea.*
Dígame la verdad; **no me diga** que no la sabe.	*Tell me the truth; don't tell me that you don't know (it).*
Espere, **no lo haga** ahora; **hágalo** más tarde.	*Wait, don't do it now; do it later.*
Levántese temprano; **no se pierda** las noticias de las seis.	*Get up early; don't miss the six o'clock news.*

Ejercicio 1

Imagínese que usted es agente de viajes. Conteste las preguntas de sus clientes con un mandato lógico. Si es necesario, use un pronombre de complemento directo (**lo, la, los** o **las**).

MODELOS: ¿Tengo que pagar el pasaje hoy? →
Sí, *páguelo* hoy, por favor.

¿Necesito ir al consulado mañana? →
Sí, *vaya* mañana por la mañana.

1. ¿Debo hacer las reservaciones inmediatamente?
2. ¿Tengo que comprar ya los pasajes?
3. ¿Tengo que traer el dinero mañana?
4. ¿Necesito recoger los pasajes la semana que viene?
5. ¿Debo llegar al aeropuerto dos horas antes de la salida de mi vuelo?
6. ¿Necesito conseguir otro pasaporte?

Ejercicio 2

Sus primos dicen que no saben si deben hacer las siguientes cosas. Déles mandatos directos. Si es necesario, use un pronombre de complemento directo (**lo, la, los** o **las**).

MODELOS: Debemos llamar a Jorge. → *¡Llámenlo!*

Debemos volver antes de septiembre. →
Sí, *vuelvan* antes de septiembre.

1. Debemos preparar el itinerario.
2. Debemos conseguir los pasaportes.
3. Debemos limpiar las maletas.
4. Debemos hacer las maletas esta noche.
5. Debemos dormir antes de salir.
6. Debemos salir inmediatamente.

¡OJO!

Remember to attach pronouns to the end of affirmative command forms.

mañana por la mañana
= *tomorrow morning*

conseguir = *to get, obtain*

11.2 Softening Commands: The Present Subjunctive following *querer* and *sugerir*

Gramática ilustrada

> Paula nos sugiere que compremos los boletos hoy.

> Hijos, estamos de vacaciones. Quiero que coman con nosotros; quiero que comamos todos juntos.

> ¡Ay, pero... estamos en los Estados Unidos! ¡Queremos comer en Burgerland!

> Andrea y Pedro quieren que el empleado les revise el boleto.

Softened commands = command forms after **querer que** and **sugerir que**:

Quieren que yo termine el trabajo.
(*They want me to finish the job.*)

Quiero que tú comas con nosotros.
(*I want you to eat with us.*)

Les sugerimos que tomen una clase de español.
(*We suggest that you take a Spanish class.*)

Les sugiero que hagan un viaje a Costa Rica.
(*I suggest that you take a trip to Costa Rica.*)

A. You already know the Spanish verb forms used to give direct commands: for example, **siéntese, escriba, camine.** Rather than give a direct command, a speaker may prefer to use a "softened" expression, such as *I want you to . . .* A softened expression is used to talk about what one person wants another to do: *My parents want me to . . . , Our professor suggests that we . . .*

—¿Qué **quiere** el inspector de aduanas?
—**Quiere** que abramos todas las maletas.

—*What does the customs inspector want?*
—*He wants us to open all of our suitcases.*

—¿Qué nos **sugiere** la profesora de español?
—Ella nos **sugiere** que lleguemos temprano al aeropuerto.

—*What does our Spanish professor suggest that we do?*
—*She suggests that we arrive at the airport early.*

In Spanish, the verb in the clause that follows softened expressions like **quiero que...** or **le(s) sugiero que...** has the same form as a command, but because these softened commands can be addressed to anyone, the second verb changes endings to indicate who is to do the action. These forms are called the *subjunctive mood.* You will learn more about the subjunctive in **Capítulos 12, 14,** and **15.**

Quiero que {
vayamos al museo primero.
tú **te quedes** con Adriana.
Carla nos **compre** los boletos.
}

I want {
us to go to the museum first.
you to stay with Adriana.
Carla to buy us the tickets.
}

Rogelio y Marta quieren que Carla les **compre** los boletos.

El agente de viajes nos sugiere que **saquemos** el pasaporte con varias semanas de antelación.

Rogelio and Marta want Carla to buy them the tickets.

Our travel agent suggests that we apply for a passport several weeks ahead of time.

> Here are the present-tense forms for the verb **sugerir**:
> (yo) sugiero
> (tú) sugieres
> (usted, él/ella) sugiere
> (nosotros/as) sugerimos
> (vosotros/as) sugerís
> (ustedes, ellos/ellas) sugieren

B. The forms of the present subjunctive are the same as the **usted** command forms plus the person/number endings: **hablar → hable + -s, -mos, -éis,* -n.** Thus, the endings contain a different vowel from the present tense (which we will call *present indicative* when we want to contrast it with the present subjunctive).

INFINITIVE	PRESENT INDICATIVE	PRESENT SUBJUNCTIVE
hablar	habla	hable
comer	come	coma
escribir	escribe	escriba

Here are the rest of the present subjunctive forms.†

	-ar	-er	-ir
(yo)	hable	coma	escriba
(tú)	hables	comas	escribas
(usted, él/ella)	hable	coma	escriba
(nosotros/as)	hablemos	comamos	escribamos
(vosotros/as)	habléis	comáis	escribáis
(ustedes, ellos/as)	hablen	coman	escriban

> Present subjunctive forms = polite command forms with person/number endings:
> coma viaje
> comas viajes
> coma viaje
> comamos viajemos
> comáis viajéis
> coman viajen

—¿Qué quiere la mesera?
—Quiere que **paguemos**‡ en la caja a la salida.
—¿Qué les sugiere Pedro a Marisa y Clarisa?
—Les sugiere que **se vistan** después de desayunar.

—*What does the waitress want?*
—*She wants us to pay at the cash register when we leave.*
—*What does Pedro suggest that Marisa and Clarisa do?*
—*He suggests that they get dressed after eating breakfast.*

C. Although pronouns are attached to affirmative commands (**cómalo**), they are placed before negative commands and conjugated verbs. (Pronouns are also attached to infinitives and present participles.)

—¿Qué quiere el agente de viajes?
—Quiere que **lo llamemos** mañana.
—Bueno, llámelo. Pero **no lo llame** muy temprano.

—*What does the travel agent want?*
—*He wants us to call him tomorrow.*
—*OK, call him. But don't call him too early.*

---

*Note that the **vosotros/as** form drops the **-e** of the **usted** command form.
†Recognition: **vos hablés, comás, escribás**
‡See Appendix 3 and the *Cuaderno de actividades*, **Capítulo 11**, for an explanation of spelling changes in the present subjunctive.

Ejercicio 3

Raúl invita a Esteban a pasar la Navidad en México con su familia. Quiere que Esteban disfrute de su viaje. ¿Qué sugerencias le hace Raúl a Esteban? Use estos verbos: **aprendas, comas, hables, saques, subas, veas, visites.**

MODELO: Te sugiero que *veas* los murales de Diego Rivera en el Palacio Nacional.

1. Esteban, quiero que _____ los platillos mexicanos que prepara mi abuela.
2. También quiero que _____ mucho español.
3. Te sugiero que _____ el Museo Nacional de Antropología.
4. También quiero que _____ las pirámides de Teotihuacán.
5. Te sugiero que _____ muchas fotos de tu viaje.
6. Quiero que _____ algo sobre la historia y la cultura de México.

Ejercicio 4

Aquí tiene usted algunas sugerencias del agente de viajes de Rubén y Virginia Hernández. Ahora Virginia está repitiéndole la información a una vecina. Use el subjuntivo en todos los casos.

MODELO: Lleguen al aeropuerto con una hora de anticipación. →
Nuestro agente de viajes nos sugiere que *lleguemos* al aeropuerto con una hora de anticipación.

1. Recojan sus boletos pronto.
2. Escriban una lista de lo que van a necesitar.
3. No lleven demasiadas cosas en las maletas.
4. Traigan su tarjeta de débito.
5. Coman en restaurantes buenos; no coman en la calle.
6. Lleguen al aeropuerto temprano.
7. Beban refrescos o agua mineral; no beban el agua.

> Verbs in **Ejercicio 4** are all regular. (There are spelling changes in **recoger** and **llegar;** see *Cuaderno de actividades.*) Change verbs from third-person to first-person plural.

11.3 Expressing Indefinite Future and the Present Subjunctive of Irregular Verbs

Gramática ilustrada

Pedro y Andrea van a viajar a Europa cuando tengan suficiente dinero.

Cuando Pedro llegue al aeropuerto va a cambiar dinero.

A. When the action or state described in a clause that begins with **cuando** refers to a habitual action, the present indicative is used.

Cuando papá llega a casa,
cenamos todos juntos.
Mis primos **siempre** van a la
costa **cuando viajan.**

When Dad gets home, we all
eat dinner together.
My cousins always go to the
coast when they travel.

On the other hand, when the action or state described in a clause that begins with **cuando** refers to the future, the subjunctive form of the verb is used.

Vamos a facturar el equipaje
cuando revisen el boleto.
Pedro va a hacer las reservaciones
cuando hable con Andrea.

We are going to check in the bags
when they check the ticket.
Pedro is going to make the
reservations when he speaks
with Andrea.

Cuando lleguemos a Madrid,
quiero ver el Museo del Prado.

When we get to Madrid, I want
to see the Prado Museum.

Subjunctive is used after **cuando** when referring to the future:
Cuando salga de viaje, voy a...
(*When I leave on my trip, I'm going to . . .*)

B. Verbs that have different stems in the **yo** forms of the present indicative have those same stems in the present subjunctive (as they do in the command forms).

The subjunctive takes a long time to acquire. You will hear it and read it extensively before you are able to produce it comfortably.

conocer	conozco	conozca, conozcas, conozca, conozcamos, conozcáis, conozcan
construir	construyo	construya, construyas, construya, construyamos, construyáis, construyan
decir	digo	diga, digas, diga, digamos, digáis, digan
hacer	hago	haga, hagas, haga, hagamos, hagáis, hagan
oír	oigo	oiga, oigas, oiga, oigamos, oigáis, oigan
poner	pongo	ponga, pongas, ponga, pongamos, pongáis, pongan
recoger	recojo	recoja, recojas, recoja, recojamos, recojáis, recojan
salir	salgo	salga, salgas, salga, salgamos, salgáis, salgan
tener	tengo	tenga, tengas, tenga, tengamos, tengáis, tengan
traer	traigo	traiga, traigas, traiga, traigamos, traigáis, traigan
venir	vengo	venga, vengas, venga, vengamos, vengáis, vengan
ver	veo	vea, veas, vea, veamos, veáis, vean

Cuando **recojamos** los boletos,
le vamos a preguntar al agente
si necesitamos vacunas.

When we pick up the tickets,
we'll ask the agent if we need
vaccinations.

C. Verbs that end in **-oy** in the **yo** form, as well as the verb **saber,** have irregular stems in the present subjunctive.*

dar	doy	dé, des, dé, demos, deis, den
estar	estoy	esté, estés, esté, estemos, estéis, estén
ir	voy	vaya, vayas, vaya, vayamos, vayáis, vayan
ser	soy	sea, seas, sea, seamos, seáis, sean
saber	sé	sepa, sepas, sepa, sepamos, sepáis, sepan

*Recognition: **vos des, estés, vayás, seás, sepás**

Cuando **llegues** a Barcelona, quiero que me **llames.**

When you arrive in Barcelona, I want you to call me.

La profesora nos sugiere que **hagamos** todos estos ejercicios para el martes.

The professor suggests that we do all these exercises by Tuesday.

D. The present subjunctive forms of stem-changing verbs are as follows.

Group I. Verbs with stem-vowel changes **e → ie** and **o → ue** in the present indicative keep those changes in the present subjunctive. The stems of verbs like **pensar** and **volver** always change except for the **nosotros/as** and **vosotros/as** forms.*

INDICATIVE	SUBJUNCTIVE	INDICATIVE	SUBJUNCTIVE
pienso	piense	vuelvo	vuelva
piensas	pienses	vuelves	vuelvas
piensa	piense	vuelve	vuelva
pensamos	pensemos	volvemos	volvamos
pensáis	penséis	volvéis	volváis
piensan	piensen	vuelven	vuelvan

No quiero que tú **pienses** mal de mí.

I don't want you to think badly of me.

El presidente del Banco de Guadalajara quiere que sus empleados **vuelvan** al trabajo a las 2:00.

The president of the Bank of Guadalajara wants his employees to return to work at 2:00.

Group II. Verbs like **pedir** and **servir**, whose stems show an **e → i** change in the present indicative (except for the **nosotros/as** and **vosotros/as** forms†), have the same stem-vowel change in *all* the present subjunctive forms.

INDICATIVE	SUBJUNCTIVE	INDICATIVE	SUBJUNCTIVE
pido	pida	sirvo	sirva
pides	pidas	sirves	sirvas
pide	pida	sirve	sirva
pedimos	pidamos	servimos	sirvamos
pedís	pidáis	servís	sirváis
piden	pidan	sirven	sirvan

Use this section as a reference; don't try to memorize all these forms!

EL PARADOR DE ZAFRA

Cuenta la historia que en un castillo de la localidad de Zafra habitó Hernán Cortés antes de partir para conquistar Méjico. Hoy, ese castillo ofrece todo el encanto de un cómodo Parador Nacional disponible para todos los que, sin sentirse héroes de grandes hazañas, están dispuestos a trasladarse hasta el siglo XV y revivir glorias pasadas. El Parador Hernán Cortés está acondicionado con todo tipo de comodidades. Destaca su restaurante especializado en platos típicos de la zona. Por su situación privilegiada, es la base

perfecta para recorrer los alrededores, que ofrecen pueblos medievales de gran interés cultural. Precio: 200€ euros habitación doble. Parador Hernán Cortés. Zafra, Badajoz.

*Recognition: **vos pensés, volvás**
†Recognition: **vos pidás, sirvás**

Papá nos sugiere que todos **pidamos** un sándwich.

Cuando **se sirva** el pastel, vamos a cantarle «Las Mañanitas» a Andrea.

Dad suggests that we all order a sandwich.

When the cake is served, let's sing "Happy Birthday" to Andrea.

Group III. Third-person changes: Verbs like **divertirse,** which show an **e → ie** change in the present indicative as well as an **e → i** change in the preterite, and verbs like **dormir,** which show an **o → ue** change in the present indicative and an **o → u** change in the preterite, maintain *both* changes in the present subjunctive.*

INDICATIVE	SUBJUNCTIVE	INDICATIVE	SUBJUNCTIVE
me divierto	me divierta	duermo	duerma
te diviertes	te diviertas	duermes	duermas
se divierte	se divierta	duerme	duerma
nos divertimos	nos divirtamos	dormimos	durmamos
os divertís	os divirtáis	dormís	durmáis
se divierten	se diviertan	duermen	duerman

Todos quieren que **nos divirtamos** mucho en el viaje.

Quiero que **duermas** ahora, porque el viaje mañana va a ser difícil.

Everyone wants us to have a lot of fun on the trip.

I want you to sleep now, because the trip tomorrow is going to be difficult.

Ejercicio 5

Escoja el verbo que mejor corresponda al contexto.

MODELO: Voy a darte tu boleto cuando *subamos/subimos* al avión.

1. Voy a mandarte una tarjeta postal cuando *llegue/llego* al hotel.
2. Cuando *viajemos/viajamos* a Argentina, siempre nos hospedamos en el Hotel Río Plata.
3. Todos los días la asistente de vuelo sirve las bebidas cuando los pasajeros *suban/suben* al avión.
4. Voy a saber más de los mayas cuando *lea/leo* estos libros sobre su cultura.
5. José y Pilar van a pagar en la caja cuando *terminen/terminan* de cenar.

In **Ejercicio 5,** you will need to decide whether **cuando** signals a habitual action (present indicative) or a future action (present subjunctive) and choose the appropriate verb form. Watch out for habitual action markers such as **siempre, todos los días,** etc.

caja = *cash register*

---

*Recognition: **vos te divirtás, durmás**

Ejercicio 6

Usted va a ir de excursión a México con un grupo de estudiantes de su clase de español. El agente de viajes le ha hecho una lista de recomendaciones para el viaje. Ahora sus padres le repiten estas recomendaciones.

MODELO: No salga sin los boletos. →
Hijo/a, no queremos que *salgas sin los boletos.*

1. Haga las maletas un día antes de la salida.
2. Duerma ocho horas la noche anterior a la salida.
3. Lléve ropa para ocho días.
4. Vaya directamente a la estación de autobuses.
5. Ponga el dinero en un lugar seguro.
6. Dele su pasaporte al profesor.
7. Vuelva con buenos recuerdos del viaje.
8. No pida comida norteamericana en los restaurantes.
9. Diviértase mucho y traiga regalos para toda la familia.
10. Dígale «Adiós» a su familia.

seguro = *safe*

¡OJO!

In **Ejercicio 7,** provide the correct subjunctive forms in both clauses and then match clauses logically to form sentences.

Ejercicio 7

Primero escriba las formas apropiadas de los verbos indicados. Luego señale la frase que mejor complete cada oración.

MODELO: Mi profesora quiere que yo *me divierta* (divertirse) cuando *salga* (salir: yo) de vacaciones.

1. Mis padres quieren que los _____ (llamar: yo)...
2. Queremos que Juan, el mesero más guapo, nos _____ (servir)...
3. Quiero que _____ (oír: tú) mi nuevo disco compacto...
4. Alberto quiere que nosotros le _____ (traer) regalos...
5. Quiero que _____ (sacar: tú) muchas fotos...

a. cuando _____ (estar: tú) en México.
b. cuando _____ (venir: tú) a visitarme.
c. cuando _____ (llegar: yo) a mi destino.
d. cuando _____ (ir: nosotros) al restaurante argentino.
e. cuando _____ (volver: nosotros) de Madrid.

11.4 Talking about Past Actions in Progress: The Imperfect Progressive

Gramática ilustrada

Ayer, a las 4:00 de la tarde,...

Andrea estaba descansando al lado de la piscina.

Pedro estaba escribiendo una carta.

Marisa y Clarisa estaban paseando en el parque con su abuela.

To describe an action that was taking place at some past moment, use the imperfect tense of **estar** (**estaba, estabas, estaba, estábamos, estabais, estaban**), followed by a present participle.

—¿Qué **estabas haciendo** a las 4:00?
—Creo que **estaba viendo** la televisión.

—*What were you doing at 4:00?*
—*I think I was watching television.*

—Rubén, ¿qué **estabas haciendo** ayer cuando te llamé?
—¡**Estaba durmiendo,** por supuesto!

—*Rubén, what were you doing yesterday when I called?*
—*I was sleeping, of course!*

¿RECUERDA?

In **Gramática 5.3** you learned how to use a present-tense form of **estar** with a present participle (the **-ando/-iendo** form of the verb) to talk about actions currently in progress. Review that section now, if necessary.

Ejercicio 8

Usando el participio del presente de **asistir, dormir, estudiar, leer** y **ver**, diga qué estaba haciendo y qué no estaba haciendo usted ayer.

Ayer a las 4:00 de la tarde estaba...

	SÍ	NO
1. _____ una siesta.	☐	☐
2. _____ a una clase.	☐	☐
3. _____ la televisión.	☐	☐
4. _____ la lección de español.	☐	☐
5. _____ el periódico.	☐	☐

Ahora diga qué estaban haciendo las siguientes personas. Use el verbo apropiado: **comer, dar, hacer, limpiar, preparar.**

6. Mi profesor(a) _____ la clase de español.
7. Mi mejor amigo/a _____ la tarea.
8. Dos compañeros de clase _____ en un restaurante.
9. Mis padres _____ la casa.
10. El presidente de los Estados Unidos _____ un discurso.

un discurso = *a speech*

11.5 Telling What Was Happening: The Imperfect in Contrast to the Preterite

Gramática ilustrada

Era un día de primavera. Hacía sol y hacía un poco de fresco. Pedro y Andrea estaban sentados en un café de la Gran Vía cuando de repente Pedro vio a un viejo amigo de la universidad. Pedro se levantó, corrió hacia él, lo saludó y lo invitó a tomar un refresco con él y Andrea. Los tres tomaron refrescos y charlaron.

Some review:
preterite = action was completed
imperfect = action went on over time in past
imperfect progressive = action was going on at a particular time in the past

Although the imperfect and the preterite both describe past actions or states, their uses are not the same. As you know, the preterite is used with verbs of action to emphasize that a past event was completed.

—¿Qué **hiciste** ayer?   —*What did you do yesterday?*
—**Visité** el Museo del Prado.   —*I visited the Prado Museum.*

The imperfect, on the other hand, is chosen if the speaker wishes to emphasize that an action happened repeatedly in the past.

Cuando **íbamos** de vacaciones a Acapulco, siempre nos **quedábamos** en el Hotel Condesa del Mar.   *When we were on vacation in Acapulco, we would always stay at the Condesa del Mar Hotel.*

—¿Qué **estabas haciendo** cuando te llamé?   —*What were you doing when I called?*
—**Estaba bañándome.**   —*I was taking a bath.*

Similarly, you can use the simple imperfect to describe an action that was in progress in the past when something else interrupted it. The interrupting action is expressed in the preterite tense.

¿RECUERDA?

In **Gramática 11.4,** you learned that the imperfect progressive can be used to indicate that something was happening at a particular time in the past.

Caminaba por la calle cuando **vi** al agente de policía.

I was walking down the street when I saw the policeman.

Descansaba en mi cuarto cuando **sonó** el teléfono.

I was resting in my room when the phone rang.

Salía de la casa cuando me **gritó** la vecina.

I was leaving (the house) when the neighbor yelled to me.

Llegábamos a Madrid cuando **se descompuso** el motor.

We were arriving in Madrid when the engine broke down.

> **action in progress** = imperfect
> **interrupting action** = preterite

> Imperfect is used for past habitual action:
> **De joven, *vivía* en México.**
> or past action in progress:
> ***Caminaba* por la plaza cuando oí la música.**

Ejercicio 9

Escriba la forma apropiada de los verbos entre paréntesis. Luego indique si eso le ha pasado a usted alguna vez.

MODELO: El profesor *hablaba* (hablar) cuando me dormí en clase.

	SÍ	NO
1. _____ (manejar: yo) en la autopista cuando dos carros chocaron.	☐	☐
2. _____ (ver: yo) mi programa favorito cuando sonó el teléfono y no contesté.	☐	☐
3. _____ (caminar: yo) por la calle cuando vi un accidente.	☐	☐
4. Mi profesor _____ (hablar) cuando entré tarde a la clase.	☐	☐
5. _____ (bañarse: yo) cuando entró un amiguito de mi hijo.	☐	☐

Ejercicio 10

Pilar habla de sus vacaciones. Lea toda la historia primero y luego escoja entre el imperfecto o el pretérito, según el contexto.

Cuando *era/fui*[1] niña, todos los años mi familia y yo *íbamos/fuimos*[2] a las islas Baleares. Siempre *alquilábamos/alquilamos*[3] una casa con vista al mar. De día *buceábamos/buceamos*[4] y nos *bañábamos/bañamos*.[5] De noche *salíamos/salimos*[6] a cenar a un restaurante elegante y luego *caminábamos/caminamos*[7] por la plaza.

Una tarde de verano, cuando mi hermano menor, Felipe, *tenía/tuvo*[8] 8 años, él y yo *íbamos/fuimos*[9] solos a la playa. Nuestros padres *dormían/durmieron*[10] todavía. Mi hermanito *jugaba/jugó*[11] en el agua y yo *hablaba/hablé*[12] con unos chicos que ya *conocía/conocí*[13] de otros veranos. Después de unos minutos *miraba/miré*[14] hacia donde *jugaba/jugó*[15] mi hermanito y no lo *veía/vi*.[16] Mis amigos y yo nos *levantábamos/levantamos*[17] y *corríamos/corrimos*[18] al agua para buscarlo. No lo *encontrábamos/encontramos*.[19] Lo *buscábamos/buscamos*[20] por toda la playa y no lo *podíamos/pudimos*[21] encontrar. Yo *estaba/estuve*[22] desesperada. Por fin *regresábamos/regresamos*[23] adonde *teníamos/tuvimos*[24] las toallas... allí *estaba/estuvo*[25] mi hermanito, comiendo sandía. «¿Adónde *ibas/fuiste*?[26]» le *gritaba/grité*.[27] Él no me *contestaba/contestó*,[28] pero yo *estaba/estuve*[29] tan contenta de verlo que no me *enojaba/enojé*[30] demasiado con él.

CAPÍTULO 12

La salud y las emergencias

METAS

In **Capítulo 12** you will talk about health-related situations, including keeping healthy and fit. You will also talk about experiences with illnesses and accidents.

El niño enfermo, por Pedro Lira (Chile)

Sobre el artista: Pedro Lira nació en Santiago en 1845. Estudió humanidades en el Instituto Nacional y más tarde se recibió de abogado. Viajó a Francia para ampliar sus conocimientos de la pintura europea. Organizó las primeras exposiciones de arte en Chile. Lira se considera uno de los grandes maestros de la pintura chilena.

¡Conozca Chile!

Nombre del país: República de Chile

Ciudad capital: Santiago

Ciudades principales: Valparaíso, Viña del Mar, Concepción, Temuco, Antofagasta

Moneda nacional: el peso chileno

Idiomas: el español (oficial), el mapudungun (idioma de los mapuches), el quechua, el rapa nui, el aimara

Población: 16.300.000

Día de la Independencia: el 18 de septiembre

Fiestas típicas: el Día de las Glorias Navales, el Día de San Pedro y San Pablo, el Día de la Asunción de la Virgen, el Día del Descubrimiento de Dos Mundos

Comidas típicas: el curanto, el pastel de choclo, las empanadas, los alfajores, el mote con huesillos

Música típica: la cueca, la tonada, el rock chileno

Gente famosa: Gabriela Mistral, Pablo Neruda, Salvador Allende, Augusto Pinochet, Violeta Parra, Víctor Jara

Código del país por Internet: .cl

Voces chilenas

al tiro	inmediatamente
bacán	maravilloso
cachar	entender
la guagua	el/la bebé
el/la pololo/a	el/la novio/a
pololear	to have a serious relationship
el taco	traffic jam

En este capítulo...

ACTIVIDADES DE COMUNICACIÓN

- El cuerpo humano y la salud
- Las enfermedades y su tratamiento
- Las visitas al médico, a la farmacia y al hospital
- Los accidentes y las emergencias

EN RESUMEN

LECTURAS Y CULTURA

- **Ventanas culturales**
  Nuestra comunidad: La música, nuestra mejor medicina
- **Ventanas al pasado**
  La medicina en la España árabe
- **Enlace al cine**
  El cine del Cono Sur (Argentina y Chile)
- **Lectura**
  El recetario de la abuela

GRAMÁTICA Y EJERCICIOS

12.1 Expressing Existence: **haber**

12.2 Expressing Changes in States: *become, get*

12.3 Making Requests: Indirect Object Pronouns with Commands and the Present Subjunctive

12.4 Relating Unplanned Occurrences: **se**

12.5 Narrating Past Experiences: The Present Perfect, Imperfect, and Preterite

El cuerpo humano y la salud

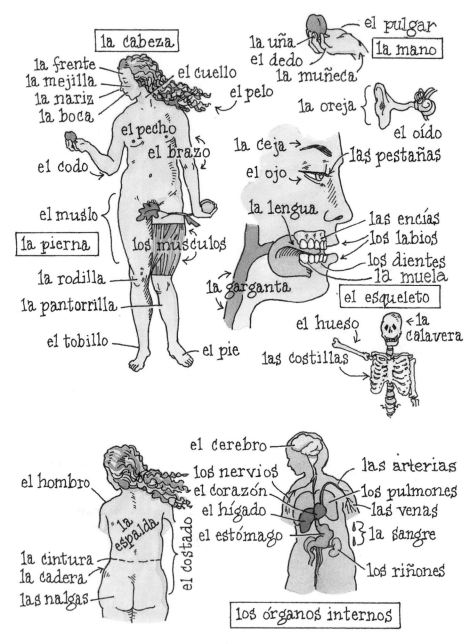

la cabeza

la frente
la mejilla
la nariz
la boca

el cuello
el pelo

el pecho
el brazo

el codo

el muslo

la pierna

los músculos

la rodilla

la pantorrilla

el tobillo

el pie

la uña
el dedo
la muñeca

el pulgar
la mano

la oreja

el oído

la ceja
el ojo

las pestañas

la lengua

las encías
los labios

los dientes
la muela

la garganta

el esqueleto

el hueso
la calavera

las costillas

el hombro

la espalda

el costado

la cintura
la cadera
las nalgas

el cerebro
los nervios
el corazón
el hígado
el estómago

las arterias
los pulmones
las venas
la sangre

los riñones

los órganos internos

REFRÁN

Ojos que no ven, corazón que no siente.

(*Out of sight, out of mind.* Literally, *The heart can't feel what the eyes can't see.*)

412

Actividad 1 Asociaciones: Las funciones de las partes del cuerpo

¿Para qué usamos estas partes del cuerpo?

MODELO: E1: ¿Para qué usamos *la boca?* →
E2: Usamos la boca *para comer* y *para hablar.*

1. los dientes	**a.** caminar
2. las piernas	**b.** tocar
3. los ojos	**c.** abrazar
4. los brazos	**d.** besar
5. los labios	**e.** oír
6. la nariz	**f.** ver
7. los oídos	**g.** oler
8. los dedos	**h.** morder

Actividad 2 Definiciones: Los órganos internos

1. los pulmones	**a.** Órganos internos que se usan para respirar.
2. el cerebro	**b.** Parte interior del cuello.
3. el corazón	**c.** Órgano que se usa para hablar y comer.
4. la garganta	**d.** Lo que usamos para percibir los sonidos.
5. los músculos	**e.** Órgano del pensamiento que forma parte del sistema nervioso.
6. la sangre	**f.** Órgano principal de la circulación de la sangre.
7. los oídos	**g.** Sus contracciones permiten los movimientos del cuerpo.
8. la lengua	**h.** Líquido rojo que circula por las venas y las arterias.

Actividad 3 Encuesta: ¿Es bueno para la salud?

Diga si estas actividades son beneficiosas o dañinas para la salud y para mantenerse en buena condición física. Explique por qué.

¿Es beneficioso...

1. comer carne con frecuencia?
2. tomar el sol tres horas o más diariamente?
3. hacer ejercicio cada día?
4. trabajar diez horas al día?
5. tomar vino con la cena?
6. dormir siete horas o más cada noche?
7. tomar refrescos dietéticos?
8. tomar café todas las mañanas?
9. beber seis vasos de agua o más diariamente?
10. tomar muchas vitaminas?
11. comer comidas con mucha grasa?
12. ¿ ?

Actividad 4 Del mundo hispano: Consejos para la salud

Lea los siguientes consejos de una revista hispana y luego hágale las preguntas que aparecen abajo a un compañero / una compañera de clase.

Consejos...

Ejercicios: Los músculos fríos se lastiman con el estrés del ejercicio. Todas las investigaciones muestran que calentar los músculos antes de ejercitarse evita lesiones.

La regla de los 3/4: Ésta es la proporción de legumbres, granos y frutas que tiene que haber en su plato. El 1/4 restante debe dedicarlo a carne, pollo o pescado.

Dieta: Si ingiere más panes de granos enteros, arroces y pastas, consumirá más fibra y carbohidratos complejos, lo cual mejorará su dieta.

Legumbres verdes: ¿Sabía usted que mientras más oscuro sea el verde de las hojas de las legumbres, más nutritivas son? En este sentido, las espinacas, el berro, etcétera, resultan inmejorables.

Sueño: ¿Es malo dormir con la TV o la radio puestas toda la noche? Sí, el ruido puede hacer su sueño menos profundo y también interferir con las fases más relajadoras del sueño, de acuerdo con un estudio de la Universidad de Florida.

La papaya, si se come diariamente, normaliza la digestión, desinflama los intestinos y ayuda al tratamiento de úlceras del estómago. Las semillas pulverizadas son beneficiosas en caso de disentería causada por amebas.

1. ¿Por qué se recomienda calentar los músculos antes de hacer ejercicio?
2. Según este artículo, ¿se recomienda dormir con la televisión y la radio puestas (encendidas)? Explique.
3. ¿Cómo se puede obtener más fibra en la dieta?
4. ¿A qué se refiere la regla de los ¾?
5. ¿Cuáles son las legumbres verdes que contienen más vitaminas y minerales?

PREGUNTAS PERSONALES

1. ¿Duermes con la radio o la televisión puesta (encendida)?
2. ¿Haces ejercicio todos los días? ¿Calientas los músculos antes de empezar?
3. ¿Observas la regla de los ¾? ¿Cuántas porciones de legumbres y frutas comes al día? ¿Qué frutas prefieres?
4. ¿Qué legumbres verdes (verduras) te gustan? ¿Las comes con frecuencia?
5. ¿Qué otros consejos tienes para mantener la salud?

Las enfermedades y su tratamiento

★ **Lea Gramática 12.1–12.2.**

un dolor de estómago

un dolor de muelas

un dolor de cabeza

¡Salud!

estornudar (el estornudo)

un dolor de garganta

la tos

la fiebre

el catarro — la gripe —

enyesado/a

el brazo fracturado

está inconsciente (se desmayó)

la presión
el pulso→

la nariz tapada (congestionado/a)

la cicatriz

una alergia (alérgico/a)

una herida

se torció el tobillo; tiene un esguince.

las muletas

El marañon es una fruta tropical. Contiene cinco veces más vitamina C que la naranja; cura eczema, diabetes y enfermedades de la piel; alivia reumas y cansancio; abre la memoria y estimula el cerebro. La almendra del marañon (*cashew*) es deliciosa y contiene proteína, fósforo y hierro.

Es peor el remedio...
Sabemos lo recomendable de hervir el agua antes de beberla. El otro día, cuando mi hijo Eduardo (7 años) llegó corriendo y se fue a la llave a beber, le dije que no lo hiciera, que había que hervirla para matar los microbios. El puso una cara muy rara y me dijo: «Pues qué asco, beberse luego los microbios muertos.»

Estrella Serrano

Actividad 5 Preferencias: Cuando me siento mal...

Exprese su opinión usando **siempre, generalmente, a veces** o **nunca.**

MODELO: Cuando tengo dolor de estómago generalmente tomo té caliente y a veces me acuesto.

1. Cuando tengo fiebre...
2. Cuando tengo dolor de cabeza...
3. Cuando tengo tos...
4. Cuando tengo gripe...

Posibilidades

consulto con el médico	llamo a mi mamá	tomo jarabe
corro	me acuesto	tomo muchos líquidos
descanso	me pongo algo frío en la frente	tomo el sol en la playa
escucho música clásica		tomo té caliente
hago ejercicio	me quedo en la cama	trabajo en el jardín
leo	tomo aspirinas	voy al trabajo

Y tú ¿qué dices?

Yo también.	Yo prefiero...
Yo no.	Es mejor...

Actividad 6 Intercambios: Doctor, ¿qué debo hacer?

Trabaje con un compañero / una compañera. Uno de ustedes debe hacer el papel de paciente y el otro el de doctor(a). El doctor / La doctora debe escoger el consejo o remedio adecuado para los síntomas del / de la paciente.

MODELO: PACIENTE: Doctor(a), *tengo el tobillo hinchado.*
DOCTOR: Si tiene el tobillo hinchado, *póngalo en agua fría.*

1. Tengo resfriado.
2. Tengo una herida en el brazo.
3. Me duele la cabeza.
4. Me corté el dedo.
5. Me duele la garganta.
6. Tengo la nariz tapada.
7. Tengo fiebre.
8. Tengo un esguince en el tobillo.
9. Tengo dolor de muelas.
10. Tengo diarrea.

a. beba muchos líquidos y descanse
b. póngase gotas
c. consulte con el dentista
d. póngase una curita
e. use muletas o no camine
f. póngase un vendaje
g. coma arroz y puré de manzana
h. haga gárgaras de agua con sal
i. tome aspirinas u otro analgésico
j. tome vitamina C
k. ¿ ?

REFRÁN

No hay mal que dure cien años, ni cuerpo que lo resista.

(*Nothing bad lasts forever.* Literally, *There is no ailment that can last a hundred years, nor body that can withstand it.*)

Actividad 7 Encuesta: Los estados de ánimo

¿Es usted irritable? ¿tranquilo/a? Conteste estas preguntas.

	SÍ	NO	A VECES
1. Me pongo muy nervioso/a cuando tengo un examen.	☐	☐	☐
2. Me vuelvo loco/a con las presiones de la vida moderna.	☐	☐	☐
3. Me pongo molesto/a cuando mi familia quiere que haga algo que no quiero hacer.	☐	☐	☐
4. Me enojo si pierdo algo valioso.	☐	☐	☐
5. Me pongo de mal humor cuando hay mucho tránsito y no puedo llegar a tiempo a una cita.	☐	☐	☐

VALOR DE SU RESPUESTA

sí = 2 puntos   **a veces** = 1 punto   **no** = 0 puntos

De 9 a 10 puntos = Usted es una persona extremadamente irritable. Tanta tensión es muy mala para la salud. ¡Contrólese!

De 7 a 8 puntos = Usted es una persona irritable. Esto afecta la salud.

De 5 a 6 puntos = Usted es una persona de un estado de ánimo normal.

De 3 a 4 puntos = Usted es una persona tranquila.

De 0 a 2 puntos = Usted es una persona demasiado calmada. ¡Sea más animado/a!

Actividad 8 Entrevistas: La salud física y mental

LAS MEDICINAS Y LOS REMEDIOS

1. ¿Qué medicinas buenas hay para el dolor de cabeza? ¿para el dolor de estómago? ¿para la tos? ¿la gripe?
2. ¿Había medicinas buenas para estas dolencias hace 100 años?
3. ¿Crees que algún día va a haber una vacuna contra el VIH? ¿Hay algún tratamiento o medicina ahora para los que ya sufren del SIDA?
4. ¿Crees que los científicos van a descubrir un nuevo antibiótico? ¿Crees que sea necesario tener más antibióticos? ¿Por qué?

LOS ESTADOS FÍSICOS Y ANÍMICOS

1. ¿Cuándo estás más contento/a? ¿Te sientes feliz cuando estás solo/a? Explica tus respuestas.
2. ¿Te sientes cansado/a frecuentemente? ¿Qué actividades te cansan?
3. ¿Te enojas con frecuencia? ¿Qué te hace enojar? ¿Qué cosas te entristecen? ¿Te entristeces fácilmente?
4. Cuando hay muchas presiones en tu vida, ¿qué síntomas tienes? ¿Sientes mareo? ¿comezón? ¿dolor de estómago?

UN CHISTE

Un señor está tosiendo mucho. Un amigo le dice:

—¿Oye, quieres jarabe para la tos?

—No, no. ¡Ya tengo tos!

VENTANAS CULTURALES Nuestra comunidad

La música, nuestra mejor medicina

La famosa cantautora colombiana Soraya **luchó** por mucho tiempo para curarse de su **cáncer de seno,** y lamentablemente murió de esta enfermedad en 2006, a la edad de 37 años. Pero esta talentosa artista nos dejó un testimonio valioso: su música. Sus hermosas canciones le ayudaron a Soraya a **soportar** el dolor y el sufrimiento. Y para sus muchos *fans*, esas canciones expresan la pasión por la vida que tenía Soraya. Como ella, mucha gente ha sobrevivido serios problemas de salud gracias a la música. La cantante cubanoamericana Gloria Estefan, por ejemplo, se recuperó de un terrible accidente automovilístico en 1990, gracias, en parte, a las canciones que escuchaba y las que escribía para su próximo álbum, *Into the Light*.

Gloria Estefan escribía canciones para recuperarse.

Hay canciones que nos transportan, que evocan recuerdos y experiencias vividas. Algunas piezas clásicas o instrumentales nos alivian el estrés, nos calman y nos ayudan a concentrarnos en el trabajo o el estudio. Además, la música es buena terapia. Por ejemplo, tocar el piano puede mejorar las **habilidades motoras y cognoscitivas** de personas que han sufrido un **derrame cerebral,** y componer canciones puede ser útil para expresar las emociones.

Hace 2.000 años que el filósofo griego Demócrito* escribió por primera vez sobre el poder **curativo** de la música. Ya en esa época, se consideraba que la música tenía una función curativa, y esta función se ha hecho muy evidente en nuestros días. La terapia musical se usa hoy en el tratamiento de muchas enfermedades como el autismo, el cáncer, el trauma emocional y los problemas de impedimento auditivo y visual. Hoy sabemos por cierto que Demócrito tenía razón: la música sí puede curarnos.

VOCABULARIO ÚTIL	
luchó	*struggled*
el cáncer	*breast*
de seno	*cancer*
soportar	*to endure*
habilidades	*motor and*
motoras y	*cognitive*
cognoscitivas	*skills*
el derrame	*stroke*
cerebral	
curativo	*healing*

Comprensión

1. ¿En qué manera le ayudaron a Soraya sus canciones?
2. Mencione tres enfermedades en las que se usa la terapia musical.

---

*Demócrito nació en 460 a.C. En su tratado (*treatise*) sobre infecciones fatales, se refiere específicamente al poder curativo de la música de flauta. Demócrito fue también el primero en postular la existencia del átomo.

Las visitas al médico, a la farmacia y al hospital

✳ Lea Gramática 12.3.

La enfermera atiende a los pacientes.

El dentista le examina los dientes a su paciente.

La farmacéutica surte las recetas médicas.

La paciente está embarazada. La doctora la está examinando.

La psiquiatra (psicóloga) cuida de la salud mental de sus pacientes.

El cirujano opera a los pacientes.

El veterinario cura a los animales.

El paciente tuvo un infarto (ataque al corazón).

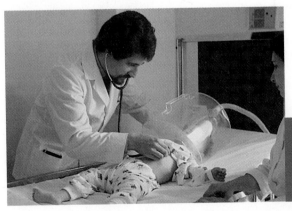

Este doctor especialista en pediatría revisa el aparato de oxígeno de su pequeño paciente (Bogotá, Colombia).

Actividad 9 Del mundo hispano: El médico recomienda...

Lea estas recomendaciones de un médico que aparecieron en una revista hispana. Con un compañero / una compañera, conteste las preguntas a continuación y luego háganse las preguntas personales.

El médico recomienda

Resfriado	Tos	Fiebre del heno	Pulmonía
QUÉ HACER: • Tome aspirina o paracetamol para bajar la fiebre. • Utilice descongestionantes para reducir la inflamación y destapar la nariz. • Quédese en casa uno o dos días; esto le ayudará a recuperarse más rápidamente. • Cuide el resfriado. Si no, puede abrirle la puerta a una enfermedad más grave. **QUÉ NO HACER:** • No tome antibióticos, ya que no tienen efecto sobre el virus. • No les dé aspirinas a los niños menores de 6 años.	**QUÉ HACER:** • Insista en que los niños se suenen la nariz frecuentemente. • Beba gran cantidad de líquido. • Inhale vapor. • Acuda al doctor / a la doctora si las secreciones son verdes, si la tos provoca dolor en el pecho o si sube la fiebre. **QUÉ NO HACER:** • No fume. • No tome antibióticos si no hay infección bacteriana.	**QUÉ HACER:** • Consulte con el doctor / la doctora y aplíquese inyecciones preventivas. • Utilice descongestionantes por períodos breves. • Evite la exposición al polen. • Evite el contacto con la hierba recién cortada. **QUÉ NO HACER:** • No use los descongestionantes por períodos prolongados (mucho tiempo).	**QUÉ HACER:** • Acuda al doctor / a la doctora para que le haga un diagnóstico con la ayuda de radiografías. • Tome antibióticos en caso de infección bacteriana. • Beba grandes cantidades de líquidos para evitar la deshidratación. • Haga inhalaciones de vapor. • Quédese en cama una semana o más. **QUÉ NO HACER:** • No impida la tos; es aconsejable que se expulsen libremente las secreciones. • No fume.

¡OJO!

- Cuba manda médicos a todas partes del mundo para ayudar en los barrios pobres y después de los desastres naturales.
- En Cuba la carrera de medicina es gratuita para todos los cubanos y el gobierno establece convenios con otros países para que sus jóvenes estudien medicina en Cuba.
- La biotecnología y la industria farmacéutica contribuyen tanto ingresos como prestigio. En Cuba los científicos han desarrollado medicamentos nuevos y sus equivalentes genéricos que se pueden vender a bajos precios en los países en vías de desarrollo. Entre los medicamentos más importantes se encuentran una medicina contra la malaria y una vacuna contra la meningitis.

CONVERSACIÓN

1. ¿Se debe tomar antibióticos si uno tiene tos o resfriado? ¿Por qué? Explique su respuesta.
2. ¿Por qué es recomendable cuidar un resfriado (resfrío)?
3. Si uno tiene tos, ¿qué síntomas indican que uno debe ir al médico / a la doctora?
4. ¿Para qué se recomienda el uso de descongestionantes?
5. Si uno tiene fiebre del heno, ¿qué debe evitar?
6. ¿Es recomendable tomar antibióticos para la pulmonía?
7. ¿Para qué enfermedades se recomienda la inhalación de vapor?

PREGUNTAS PERSONALES

1. ¿Te resfrías con frecuencia? ¿Cuáles de estas recomendaciones sigues?
2. ¿Cuándo tomas antibióticos?
3. ¿Consultas siempre al médico / a la doctora si estás enfermo/a?
4. ¿Padeces de fiebre del heno? ¿Qué síntomas tienes? ¿Consultas al/a la alergista?
5. ¿Has tenido pulmonía alguna vez? ¿Fuiste al médico / a la doctora? ¿Te dolían los pulmones? ¿Cuánto tiempo tardaste en recuperarte?

VENTANAS AL PASADO

La medicina en la España árabe

Los árabes **gobernaron** la mayor parte de España durante más de siete siglos, de 714 hasta 1492 d.C. Mientras el resto de Europa pasaba por la oscura **Edad Media,** en la España árabe **florecían** la arquitectura, las ciencias y la medicina. Los árabes tradujeron muchas de las grandes obras de filosofía y ciencias griegas: Aristóteles, Galeno, Hipócrates, y así las preservaron para futuros científicos. Pero los árabes no sólo se basaban en las obras de los antiguos griegos: varios hispanoárabes escribieron sus propios textos médicos. Abulcasis, nacido en Córdoba en 936, fue un cirujano muy importante de la época. Escribió una enciclopedia médica en la cual describe el uso del **yeso** para **tratar** las fracturas. Ibn Wafid, nacido en Toledo en 1008, **abogó** por tratamientos por medio de la dieta en vez de usar drogas y escribió un texto sobre la terapia del baño. Avenzoar, nacido en Sevilla en 1091, escribió sobre el uso de agua fría para bajar la fiebre y siempre recomendaba usar los medicamentos en la dosis más pequeña que fuera eficaz. El nombre más célebre entre los médicos hispanoárabes es el de Averroes. Nació en Córdoba en 1126 y escribió varios textos dedicados a la anatomía, la fisiología, la higiene y los medicamentos.

La Casa del Rey Moro, Ronda, España

VOCABULARIO ÚTIL

gobernaron	*governed*
la Edad Media	*Middle Ages*
florecían	*flourished*
el yeso	*(plaster) cast*
tratar	*to treat*
abogó	*advocated*
eficaz	*effective*
heredó	*inherited*
el alcanfor	*camphor*
el algodón	*cotton*
ojalá	*I hope; I wish*
si Dios quiere	*may God grant*
Hoy en día	*Nowadays*
¡Ojalá que te mejores pronto!	*I hope you get well soon!*

Averroes. Filósofo y médico andaluz; maestro de filosofía, leyes islámicas, matemáticas y médicina.

(Continúa)

El español **heredó** del idioma árabe muchas palabras que están relacionadas con la ciencia o la medicina, entre otras, alcohol de *al kohól*, **alcanfor** de
al kafûr, jarra de *yárra*, jarabe de *sharâb*, **algodón** de *al qutn*, álgebra de *al
yebr* y almanaque de *al manâh*. Una de las palabras de origen árabe usada en
español es **«ojalá»,** la cual se refiere a Alá, nombre que dan los musulmanes a
Dios. La palabra «ojalá» viene del árabe *«wa šá lláh»* que en español quiere
decir **«si Dios quiere». Hoy en día** «ojalá» no tiene significado religioso. Si un
amigo está enfermo, podemos decirle **«¡Ojalá que te mejores pronto!».**

Comprensión

1. Empareje estas palabras árabes *al barqûq, al birká, al mihádda, al qutn, al
súkkar, al zeit* y *sharâb,* con la versión moderna en español: **aceite, albaricoque, alberca, algodón, almohada, azúcar, jarabe.**
2. Nombre varios tratamientos de los cuales escribieron los médicos
hispanoárabes.

Actividad 10 Narración: Silvia tiene bronquitis

LOS SÍNTOMAS

ESE MISMO DÍA

AL DÍA SIGUIENTE

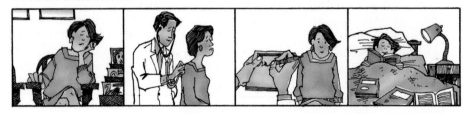

Actividad 11 **Entrevista: Historial clínico**

1. De niño/a, ¿te enfermabas con frecuencia? ¿Cuáles de estas enfermedades tuviste: las paperas, la varicela, el sarampión, gripe o resfriados, infecciones de los oídos?
2. ¿Tenías miedo de ir al médico cuando eras niño/a? ¿Por qué?
3. Cuenta alguna experiencia cómica o interesante relacionada con el consultorio del médico o con el hospital.
4. ¿Tienes miedo ahora cuando te ponen una inyección? ¿Y cuando te sacan sangre para un análisis?
5. ¿Has estado internado alguna vez en un hospital? ¿Qué tenías? ¿Fue una experiencia desagradable? ¿Por qué? Explica.

¡OJO!

En muchos países hispanos —México y Guatemala, por ejemplo— los estudiantes de medicina pasan un año trabajando en zonas rurales. Este trabajo es parte de su entrenamiento y de su servicio social.

Enlace al cine

El cine del Cono Sur (Argentina y Chile)

¿Sabía usted que en 1898 un médico cirujano de Argentina empezó a filmar y exhibir sus propias operaciones quirúrgicas? Se llamaba Alejandro Posadas (1870–1902) y era un médico de gran talento. Pasó a la historia del cine al filmar la primera película argentina, una operación del pulmón, reconocida en París como el primer documento fílmico de una cirugía. El Dr. Posadas murió muy joven, pero su carrera profesional estuvo llena de éxitos.

Como el Dr. Posadas, muchos argentinos se entusiasmaron con el cine desde sus comienzos. En 1897 se filmó en Argentina la primera «película», un corto sobre la bandera argentina. Después se hicieron otras películas mudas,[1] pero la verdadera industria cinematográfica comenzó en 1933, con el cine sonoro.[2] Se exportaron películas a toda la América Latina, algunas basadas en obras de escritores bien conocidos como Jorge Luis Borges y Julio Cortázar. En esta época se hizo famosa la gran actriz y cantante Libertad Lamarque, conocida por todo el mundo hispano. Desde los sesenta hasta ahora, ha habido grandes éxitos cinematográficos como *La historia oficial* (1985, Luis Puenzo), *Nueve reinas* (2000, Fabián Bielinski) y *El hijo de la novia* (2001, Juan José

El director argentino Juan José Campanella

Campanella). *La historia oficial* critica la dictadura de Jorge Videla* y, de todas, es la que capta mejor su momento histórico. Trata de una niña quien vive con sus padres adoptivos hasta que surgen rumores de que, como tantos otros niños, es huérfana[3] porque el gobierno militar asesinó a sus verdaderos padres.

En Chile el cine mudo presentó la primera película nacional, *Manuel Rodríguez*[†] en 1910 y la primera película sonora fue *Norte y sur* (1934). Más tarde se crearon películas chilenas con temas extranjeros[4] para no limitar al público a lo nacional: en la India *El diamante del Maharajá*, en Inglaterra *La dama de la muerte*.

[1]*silent* [2]*cine... talkies* [3]*orphan* [4]*foreign*

(Continúa)

---

*Jorge Rafael Videla (1925), ex militar y dictador argentino de 1976 a 1981. Después de la restauración de la democracia en 1983 fue juzgado y condenado a prisión perpetua por los crímenes cometidos durante su gobierno.
†Manuel Rodríguez (1785–1818) fue un líder guerrillero de la Independencia de Chile.

Después del golpe de estado[5] del general Pinochet* en 1973 se quemaron muchas películas, se cerraron los departamentos y escuelas de cine y se exiliaron cineastas y actores. Pero desde el exilio se hicieron películas para contarle al mundo lo sucedido en Chile: *Llueve sobré Santiago* de Helvio Soto, *Actas de Marusia* de Miguel Littin y *Ardiente paciencia* de Antonio Skármeta entre otras. En los últimos años han surgido películas excelentes de temas variados. *El chacotero sentimental* (1999, Cristián Galaz) se basa en un programa de radio al que la gente llama para contarle sus problemas sentimentales al locutor.[6] Esta película muestra la vida del chileno medio[7] con autenticidad. Otra excelente película, *Machuca* (2004, Andrés Woods), refleja el fin del gobierno socialista de Allende† y el principio de la dictadura de Pinochet. Narra la amistad llena de descubrimientos y sorpresas entre un niño pobre, Pedro Machuca, y un niño de clase alta.

El cine es un pasatiempo favorito de chilenos y argentinos. Sus películas abordan temas serios sin hacer proselitismo pero profundizando en el tema y en la humanidad de los personajes. Nos presentan una manera agradable de aprender más sobre la gente, su historia y su cultura. Nos ofrecen también una oportunidad de escuchar el español del Cono Sur en un contexto interesante. ¡Vale la pena verlas!

Comprensión

1. ¿Por qué pasó el Dr. Posadas a la historia del cine?
2. ¿Por qué se hicieron películas chilenas en el extranjero después de 1973?

[5]golpe... *coup d'état*   [6]*radio show host*   [7]chileno... *average Chilean*

---

*Augusto Pinochet (1915–2006), dictador de Chile, 1973–1990, tras el golpe de estado contra Salvador Allende.
†Salvador Allende (1908–1973), médico y presidente socialista de Chile, 1970–1973.

Los accidentes y las emergencias

✳ Lea Gramática 12.4–12.5.

Esteban subía la escalera cuando tropezó y se le cayeron los lentes.

—Sí, señor, iba despacio, pero se me descompusieron los frenos y no pude detener el coche.

—¿Tomaste la medicina esta
mañana?
—¡Ay! Se me olvidó en casa. La
voy a tomar cuando vuelva
esta tarde.

Andrea se siente muy frustrada.
Se le perdió una medicina. La ha
buscado por todas partes, pero no
la encuentra.

Nora iba a esquiar con sus
amigos este fin de semana,
pero no pudo porque se le
rompieron los esquíes.

Actividad 12   Descripción de dibujos: Los accidentes

Escuche a su profesor(a) mientras describe los siguientes dibujos. Señale el dibujo que mejor corresponda a cada descripción.

Actividad 13   Narración: El accidente de Guillermo

Actividad 14 Conversación: **Las confesiones**

MODELO: Una vez, en un restaurante de servicio rápido, mientras esperaba con mi padre para pedir la comida, se me cayeron los pantalones. Sentí mucha vergüenza.

1. Una vez, en la escuela primaria...
2. Una vez, en la escuela secundaria...
3. Una vez, en un restaurante...
4. Una vez, en una fiesta...
5. Una vez, cuando estaba de vacaciones...

Actividad 15   Entrevista: **Los accidentes**

1. Háblame de algún pequeño accidente de tu niñez.
2. ¿Se te descompuso el carro en la autopista alguna vez? ¿Tuviste miedo? ¿Qué hiciste?
3. ¿Se te ha perdido algo valioso? ¿Qué se te perdió? ¿Lo encontraste?
4. ¿Cuántas veces has ido a la sala de emergencias? ¿Cuándo fue la última vez? ¿Qué te pasó? ¿Fue grave? ¿Te atendieron rápidamente? ¿Tenías seguro médico?
5. ¿Has sufrido un accidente automovilístico? ¿Fue serio? ¿Cómo ocurrió? ¿Quién tuvo la culpa?

Palabras útiles

me atropelló un(a)...
me metí un(a)... en
  la nariz / un oído
me quemé
  salté de... y me
  rompí un(a)...

En resumen

De todo un poco

Cuadros de preferencia

A. Aquí tiene algunos remedios del libro *Las hierbas medicinales de más eficacia*, publicado en Barcelona, España. Complete el siguiente cuadro según las costumbres de su familia.

DOLENCIA	REMEDIO CASERO	REMEDIO QUE USA MI FAMILIA
el dolor de estómago	tomar té de manzanilla	
el dolor de garganta	hacer gárgaras de agua con sal	
el dolor de muelas	masticar un clavo (de especia)	
la quemadura	aplicarse un ungüento de áloe	
la sinusitis	inhalar vapores de eucalipto o pino	
la tos	tomar té caliente con miel y limón	
los vómitos	tomar té de albahaca, menta y canela	

B. Ahora charle con un compañero / una compañera sobre sus remedios preferidos.

E1: ¿Qué usa tu familia para el dolor de estómago?
E2: En mi casa usamos/tomamos _____.
E1: ¿Y para la quemadura?
E2: Preferimos ponernos _____.

¡Dígalo por escrito!

Los recuerdos

Describa un accidente que usted tuvo o una situación en la cual usted sintió mucho miedo. Si describe un accidente, hable de los daños y de quién tuvo la culpa. Si habla de una situación que le dio miedo, describa el lugar y cómo reaccionó usted.

MODELO: Recuerdo que una vez, cuando tenía _____ años, yo iba a _____ cuando de repente _____.

¡Cuéntenos usted!

Cuéntenos de una experiencia suya en el hospital o cuéntenos de una enfermedad infantil. ¿Cuántos años tenía? ¿Tuvo una enfermedad o sufrió un accidente?

Conexión a la comunidad

Averigüe si hay una clínica u hospital en su ciudad o condado que atienda a mucha gente hispana. Ofrézcase de voluntario/a.

 LECTURA

El recetario de la abuela

E l uso de la medicina natural es un aspecto esencial de la cultura hispana; en este contexto, la palabra «natural» se refiere a los medicamentos obtenidos directamente de la naturaleza: todos preparados con una variedad de hierbas. En general, estos remedios deben combinarse con un tratamiento médico. Pero hay hispanos que prefieren curarse con el «**recetario** de su abuela» exclusivamente. La frase se refiere a las «recetas» que pasan de generación a generación: de las abuelas a sus nietos, por ejemplo. Para estas personas, las curas tradicionales son más **eficaces** que la medicina moderna.

Dos de las regiones hispanas más ricas en el cultivo de remedios naturales son el sur y el sureste de México. Las culturas que **se desarrollaron** en esa zona —la olmeca, la maya, la mixteca y la zapoteca— tienen prácticas médicas avanzadas. Entre los médicos indígenas están los hierberos, que conocen la flora medicinal de la región, y las parteras, que ayudan a las mujeres embarazadas con el cuidado de su **embarazo** y también supervisan el **parto**: por eso se les llama *parteras*.

Durante largo tiempo, los métodos naturales de curación no fueron reconocidos por la institución médica: se les consideraba parte del pasado. Pero la opinión oficial está cambiando. En los Estados Unidos, un 25% de los medicamentos recetados contienen ingredientes basados en plantas; muchos estadounidenses están utilizando derivados de hierbas en vez de medicinas sintéticas. En todo el mundo está aumentando el número de personas que se cura con remedios naturales. De hecho, las plantas medicinales son los medicamentos principales de dos tercios (⅔) de la población mundial.

Entre las plantas medicinales más populares en los Estados Unidos está la equinacia, que **fortalece** el sistema inmunológico. La equinacia ayuda a prevenir los resfríos y a aliviar los síntomas de la gripe y las alergias. ¿Conoce usted otras plantas con **poder curativo**? Hay muchas: el **jengibre**, por ejemplo, es ideal para el mareo y el vértigo; la pasiflora sirve para quitar el insomnio; la planta áloe se usa para las quemaduras de primer y segundo grados; y el pimiento puede eliminar los dolores musculares.

No debemos recomendar el uso exclusivo de esas plantas u otros remedios naturales. Lo ideal es consultar con un doctor o una doctora, combinando la información científica con el «recetario de la abuela». En todo caso, la naturaleza nos ofrece una abundancia de medicinas.

PISTAS PARA LEER

Descubra aquí todo tipo de información sobre las plantas medicinales y los remedios naturales. Cada párrafo tiene un tema específico. Por ejemplo, el tema del primero es la medicina natural. Después de leer toda la **Lectura,** apunte el tema de cada párrafo y subraye las palabras que correspondan a ese tema.

VOCABULARIO ÚTIL

el recetario	*recipe book*
eficaces	*efficient*
se desarrollaron	*developed*
embarazo	*pregnancy*
el parto	*childbirth*
fortalece	*strengthens*
el poder curativo	*healing power*
el jengibre	*ginger*

(Continúa)

Comprensión

Busque la definición de las siguientes palabras.

1. la partera
2. los hierberos
3. la equinacia
4. el sur y el sureste de México
5. el jengibre
6. la medicina natural

a. Región que tiene una rica tradición relacionada con los remedios naturales.
b. Planta que se usa en casos de gripe o resfrío.
c. Ayuda a las mujeres embarazadas durante el parto.
d. Esta planta alivia el mareo.
e. Es una hierba que cura el dolor de garganta.
f. Estas personas conocen las plantas medicinales de su región.
g. Remedios obtenidos directamente de la naturaleza.

Un paso más... ¡a conversar!

1. ¿Prefiere curarse solamente con los medicamentos que le receta su doctor(a)? ¿Utiliza también remedios naturales cuando se enferma? Si los utiliza, diga cuáles son. ¿Para qué sirven?
2. ¿Cree usted que debemos saber más acerca de los remedios naturales en nuestra sociedad? Explique.

Vea el **Resumen cultural** en este capítulo del *Cuaderno de actividades.*

Un curandero en Chichimila, Yucatán, México

Vocabulario

These words come from the *Actividades de comunicación*. You are not expected to memorize the entire list. Your instructor may tell you which sections he or she wants to emphasize. Be patient; you will be familiar with most of these words by the end of the chapter.

El cuerpo humano

The Human Body

la cadera	hip
la calavera	skull
la ceja	eyebrow
el cerebro	brain
la cintura	waist
el codo	elbow
el corazón	heart
el costado	side
la costilla	rib
el dedo	finger
el diente	tooth
las encías	gums
la frente	forehead
la garganta	throat
el hueso	bone
el labio	lip
la lengua	tongue
la mejilla	cheek
la muela	molar (tooth)
la muñeca	wrist
el muslo	thigh
la nalga	buttock
el oído	(inner) ear
la pantorrilla	calf
el pecho	chest
la pestaña	eyelash
el pulgar	thumb
el pulmón	lung
el riñón	kidney
la rodilla	knee
la sangre	blood
el tobillo	ankle
la uña	fingernail

PALABRAS SEMEJANTES: la arteria, el esqueleto, el músculo, el nervio, el órgano interno, la vena

REPASO: la boca, el brazo, la cabeza, la cara, el cuello, la espalda, el estómago, el hígado, los hombros, las manos, la nariz, los ojos, las orejas, el pelo, las piernas, los pies

Las enfermedades y las dolencias

Illnesses and Ailments

el ataque al corazón	heart attack
la comezón	rash, itch
el estornudo	sneeze
la fiebre del heno	hay fever
el infarto	heart attack
el mareo	nausea, seasickness
las paperas	mumps
la pulmonía	pneumonia
el resfriado	cold
el resfrío	cold
el sarampión	measles
el SIDA	AIDS
la varicela	chicken pox
el VIH	HIV

PALABRAS SEMEJANTES: la alergia, la bronquitis, el cáncer

Los síntomas y los estados físicos

Symptoms and Physical States

¿Cómo se siente?	How are you (*pol. sing.*) feeling?
estar...	to be . . .
embarazada	pregnant
hinchado/a	swollen
internado/a (en el hospital)	hospitalized
mareado/a	dizzy, seasick, nauseous
estar resfriado/a	to have a cold
me/le duele *la espalda*	My/Your/His/Her *back* hurts
tener...	to have . . .
calentura	a fever
catarro	a cold
diarrea	diarrhea
fiebre	a fever
gripe	the flu
la nariz tapada	a stuffy nose
tos	a cough
tener dolor de...	to have a . . .
cabeza	headache
estómago	stomachache
garganta	sore throat
muela	toothache
tener náuseas	to be nauseous

La salud, las medicinas y los remedios

Health, Medicines, and Remedies

el agua con sal	salt water
la curita	Band-Aid; adhesive bandage
las gotas (para la nariz)	(nose) drops
el jarabe (para la tos)	(cough) syrup
la píldora	pill
el puré de manzana	apple sauce
la receta (médica)	prescription
el remedio casero	household remedy
el tratamiento	treatment
el vendaje	bandage

PALABRAS SEMEJANTES: el analgésico, el análisis, el antibiótico, la aspirina, la inhalación de vapor, la inyección

Las profesiones médicas

Medical Professions

el cirujano / la cirujana	surgeon
el/la socorrista	paramedic, emergency responder

PALABRAS SEMEJANTES: el/la alergista, el farmacéutico / la farmacéutica, el/la psiquiatra, el/la veterinario
REPASO: el/la dentista, el doctor / la doctora, el enfermero / la enfermera, el médico, el/la paciente, el psicólogo / la psicóloga

Los accidentes y las emergencias

Accidents and Emergencies

atropellar	to run over with a car
la camilla	gurney
el choque	crash
la cicatriz (las cicatrices)	scar
detener(se)	to stop (oneself)
el esguince	sprain
la herida	wound
el herido	wounded (person)
la lesión	injury
la muleta	crutch
la quemadura	burn
los rayos equis (rayos X)	X-rays
la sala de emergencias	emergency room
¡Socorro!	Help!
sobrevivir	to survive
el/la testigo	witness

PALABRA SEMEJANTE: ambulancia
REPASO: ¡Auxilio!, la clínica

Los verbos

Verbs

abrazar	to hug; to embrace
aplicarse un ungüento	to apply (put on) ointment
atender (ie)	to assist
besar	to kiss
cansar	to make tired
cansarse	to get tired
consultar con	to consult
cortarse	to cut oneself
desmayarse	to faint
doler (ue)	to hurt, ache
enojar	to make angry
entristecerse	to become sad
estornudar	to sneeze
evitar	to avoid
haber	to be (to exist)
había	there was/were
habrá (va a haber)	there will be
hay	there is, are
haya	there might be
hacer el papel (de)	to play the role (of)

hacer gárgaras	to gargle
mandar	to send; to order
mantenerse	to maintain oneself
masticar	to chew
meterse... en...	to put . . . in . . .
morder (ue)	to bite
mover	to move
oír	to hear
oler (ue)	to smell
huele / huela	it smells / smell (command)
padecer	to suffer
percibir	to perceive
recetar	to prescribe
resfriarse	to catch a cold
respirar	to breathe
surtir (una receta)	to fill (a prescription)
tardar	to take time
tener la culpa	to be guilty; to be to blame
tocar	to touch
torcerse	to twist, sprain
toser	to cough
tragar	to swallow
tropezar (ie)	to trip
volverse (ue) loco/a	to go crazy

PALABRAS SEMEJANTES: circular, controlarse, curar, indicar, inhalar, operar, reaccionar, recuperarse, responder
REPASO: chocar, enfermarse, enojarse, ponerse (+ adj.), quemar(se), sentirse (ie, i), sufrir

Accidentes y casos imprevistos

Accidents and Unforeseen Occurrences

caerse	to fall down
se le cayó/cayeron	[something (sing. or pl.)] fell (from your/his/her hands)
se me cayó/cayeron	[something (sing. or pl.)] fell (from my hands)
descomponerse	to break down
se me/le descompuso/ descompusieron	[something (sing. or pl.)] broke down (on me/you/ him/her)
escaparse	to escape, run away
se me/le escapó/ escaparon	[something/someone (sing. or pl.)] escaped (from me/you/him/her)
olvidarse	to forget
se me/le olvidó/ olvidaron	[something (sing. or pl.)] slipped my/your/his/her mind
perderse (ie)	to get lost
se me/le perdió/ perdieron	I/you/he/she lost [something (sing. or pl.)]
quedarse	to stay, remain; to get left behind
se me/le quedó/ quedaron	I/you/he/she left [something (sing. or pl.)] behind
romperse	to break
se me/le rompió/ rompieron	[something (sing. or pl.)] broke (on me/you/him/ her)

Los sustantivos

Nouns

la bocacalle	intersection
la cita	appointment; date
la cruz	cross
el dolor	pain
la fibra	fiber
el florero	vase (for flowers)
el historial clínico	medical history
la llave	key
la regla	rule; ruler (measurement)
la salud (mental)	(mental) health
el seguro médico	medical insurance
el sonido	sound
el suelo	ground
el valor	value

PALABRAS SEMEJANTES: la comunidad, la conexión, la contracción, el descongestionante, la dieta, la función, la infección, el movimiento, el narcótico, la presión, el pulso
REPASO: el consejo, el globo

Los adjetivos

Adjectives

adolorido/a	painful
animado/a	cheerful
calmado/a	calm
débil	weak
enyesado/a	in a cast
feliz	happy
inconsciente	unconscious
molesto/a	upset
puesto/a	turned on (*appliance*)
torcido/a	twisted, sprained
valioso/a	valuable

PALABRAS SEMEJANTES: adecuado/a, alérgico/a, beneficioso/a, congestionado/a, dietético/a, frustrado/a, grave, interior, irritable, tranquilo/a
REPASO: dañino/a

Palabras y expresiones útiles

Words and Useful Expressions

al día siguiente	on the next day
de repente	suddenly
en vías de desarrollo	developing (countries)
iba a (+ *verb*)	I (You [*pol. sing.*], He/She) was (were) going to (+ *verb*)
por lo menos	at least
por todas partes	everywhere
¡Salud!	To your health!; Bless you!
tener vergüenza	to be ashamed; to be embarrassed

Gramática y ejercicios

12.1 Expressing Existence: *haber*

The verb that signals existence in Spanish is **haber** (see **Gramática B.2**). It has only singular forms when used in this manner.

hay	there is/are
hubo, había	there was/were
va a haber	there is/are going to be
tiene que haber	there has/have to be, there must be
cuando haya	when there is/are

Hay 118 pacientes en el hospital.
There are 118 patients in the hospital.

Ayer **hubo** un accidente en la calle Octava.
Yesterday there was an accident on Eighth Street.

¿**Había** mucha gente allí cuando llegaste?
Were there many people there when you arrived?

¿**Va a haber** mucha gente en el consultorio?
Are there going to be many people at the doctor's office?

Tiene que haber varios médicos, no uno sólo.
There must be several doctors, not just one.

Avíseme **cuando haya** una enfermera disponible.
Let me know when there is a nurse available.

Ejercicio 1

Complete lo siguiente con **hay, tiene que haber, había, haya** o **va a haber.**

1. Ayer me sentía mal. A las 11:30 hablé con la recepcionista de la doctora Estrada y le dije: «Señorita, me siento muy mal. ¡_____ una buena medicina para mis dolores!»
2. Ella me dijo: «Necesita ver a la doctora. _____ una hora libre esta tarde, de las 2:00 a las 3:00.»
3. Yo le dije que por la tarde no podía ir. Luego le pregunté si _____ muchos pacientes esperando en este momento.
4. Ella me contestó: «No, solamente _____ dos ahora, pero seguramente _____ más a la hora del almuerzo. ¡_____ una epidemia de gripe!»
5. Yo tosía y me quejaba. Entonces ella me dijo que la doctora podía verme esa mañana, que los casos de gripe no toman mucho tiempo. Yo le dije: «Vivo muy cerca del consultorio. Por favor llámeme cuando no _____ nadie esperando.»

---

hay = *there is/are*

Hay cien centavos en un dólar.
There are a hundred cents in a dollar.

---

hubo = *there was/were*

Ayer hubo un terremoto en Chile.
Yesterday there was an earthquake in Chile.

---

había = *there was/were*

Después del terremoto, había mucha gente en las calles.
After the earthquake, there were a lot of people in the streets.

---

va a haber = *there is/are going to be*

Mañana va a haber una conferencia sobre el SIDA.
There is going to be a conference on AIDS tomorrow.

---

haya = *there might be*

Llámeme cuando haya una camilla disponible.
Let me know when there is (might be) a gurney available.

12.2 Expressing Changes in States: *become, get*

Gramática ilustrada

Esteban se puso nervioso cuando daba un informe en su clase de historia.

Después de muchos años de estudios, Luis Ventura se hizo médico.

Mamá, ¿dónde están mis pantalones negros?

Mamá, ayúdame, por favor. No comprendo la lección de matemáticas.

Mami, ¿qué hay de comer?

A veces Estela se vuelve loca con todas las presiones de los niños y la casa.

A. **Ponerse, hacerse,** and **volverse** describe changes in states when followed by adjectives and certain nouns.

Use **ponerse** with	most adjectives, such as **contento/a, de mal (buen) humor, furioso/a, molesto/a, nervioso/a, serio/a, triste,** and so on.
Use **hacerse** with	**bueno/a, malo/a, rico/a;** all professions (**abogado/a** and so on); religions and political affiliations (**católico/a** and so on).
Use **volverse** with	**antipático/a, desobediente, loco/a.**

Me puse muy contenta cuando leí tu carta.

I became very happy when I read your letter.

Adela estudió mucho y **se hizo profesora** en tres años.

Adela studied a lot and became a professor in three years.

Alberto va a **volverse loco** con todo el trabajo que tiene.

Alberto is going to go crazy with all the work that he has.

B. Some adjectives have corresponding verb forms that express *become* + the adjective. In these cases, either the verb form or the expression **ponerse** + adjective can be used.

ponerse alegre	= alegrarse		ponerse enojado/a	= enojarse
ponerse delgado/a	= adelgazar		ponerse gordo/a	= engordar
ponerse enfermo/a	= enfermarse		ponerse triste	= entristecerse

> **ponerse:** *signals a change in condition*
> **hacerse:** *signals a more permanent change of being*
> **volverse:** *Use* **volverse** *with* **antipático/a, desobediente, loco/a.**
>
> **Al oír la mala noticia, se puso triste.** (*On hearing the bad news, he became sad.*)
> **Después de tres años de estudios, se hizo abogada.** (*After three years of study, she became a lawyer.*)
> **A los trece años, mi hija se volvió muy desobediente.** (*At the age of thirteen, my daughter became very unruly.*)

Cuando Estela leyó la noticia de la muerte de su primo, **se entristeció.**	When Estela read the news of her cousin's death, she became sad.
Ernesto **se enojó** cuando le contaron la historia del accidente.	Ernesto got angry when they told him the story of the accident.
Diego **engordó** mucho el verano pasado porque no hizo bastante ejercicio.	Diego became very fat last summer because he didn't exercise enough.

Ejercicio 2

Indique la respuesta lógica.

MODELO: Ayer cuando salió el sol,...
  a. nos pusimos de buen humor.
  b. nos enfermamos.
  c. nos hicimos médicos. →
  Ayer cuando salió el sol, nos pusimos de buen humor.

1. Después de muchos años de estudio, Esteban...
   a. se puso muy nervioso.
   b. se hizo veterinario.
   c. se entristeció.
2. Cuando supieron los detalles del accidente de Amanda con el coche nuevo, sus padres...
   a. se pusieron molestos.
   b. se hicieron republicanos.
   c. se alegraron.
3. Cuando el héroe murió al final de la película, Graciela...
   a. se volvió loca.
   b. se puso triste.
   c. se hizo actriz.
4. Con tantos exámenes la semana pasada, los estudiantes...
   a. se volvieron locos.
   b. se pusieron contentos.
   c. se hicieron católicos.
5. Después de caminar algunos kilómetros bajo la lluvia, don Eduardo...
   a. se puso enfermo.
   b. se hizo rico.
   c. se puso alegre.

12.3 Making Requests: Indirect Object Pronouns with Commands and the Present Subjunctive

¿RECUERDA?

As you know from **Gramática 11.1** and **11.2**, object pronouns follow and are attached to affirmative commands but precede negative ones.

Muéstreme dónde le duele.	Show me where it hurts (you).
No **le** lleve la medicina al señor Ruiz hasta mañana.	Don't take the medicine to Mr. Ruiz until tomorrow.

Object pronouns also precede subjunctive verb forms.

El médico quiere que **le** ponga a la señora Silva una inyección de antibióticos.	The doctor wants you to give Mrs. Silva an injection of antibiotics.
Voy a comprar la medicina cuando mi esposo **me** dé el dinero.	I'm going to buy the medicine when my husband gives me the money.

Here are four additional verbs that can be used like **querer** and **sugerir** to give "softened" commands. It is necessary to use an indirect object pronoun with these verbs to point out to whom the command is given, even when the person or persons receiving the action are mentioned.

aconsejar   *to advise* (*someone to do something*)
decir   *to tell* (*someone to do something*)
pedir (i)   *to ask* (*that someone do something*)
recomendar (ie)   *to recommend* (*that someone do something*)

Los médicos siempre **les recomiendan** a los niños que no **coman** muchos dulces.
Voy a **pedirles** a las enfermeras que **estén** aquí a las 4:00.
Mi papá siempre **me dice** que **tenga** mucho cuidado en la autopista.
El psiquiatra **les aconseja** a muchos de sus pacientes que **tomen** unas vacaciones.

Doctors always recommend to children that they not eat a lot of candy.
I am going to ask the nurses to be here at 4:00.
My dad always tells me to be very careful on the freeway.
The psychiatrist advises many of his patients to take a vacation.

Object pronouns:
1) are generally placed before the first verb.
   El médico le recetó jarabe para la tos.
   (*The doctor prescribed cough syrup for him/her.*)
2) may optionally be attached to the end of an infinitive or present participle (**-ando/-iendo**).
   La doctora iba a ponerle una inyección. / La doctora le iba a poner una inyección.
   (*The doctor was going to give him/her a shot.*)
   ¿El paciente? Están examinándole la pierna ahora mismo. / ¿El paciente? Le están examinando la pierna ahora mismo. (*The patient? They are examining his leg right now.*)
3) *must* be attached to the end of affirmative commands.
   Póngale una curita.
   (*Put a Band-Aid on him/her.*)

Ejercicio 3

Usted no está de acuerdo. Haga negativos estos mandatos afirmativos.

MODELO: Hágale las preguntas a la dentista. →
No le haga las preguntas.

1. Muéstrele su pierna a la enfermera.
2. Dígame si le duele mucho.
3. Llévele estos papeles a la recepcionista.
4. Tráigale la comida al paciente.
5. Déle la receta al farmacéutico.

Ejercicio 4

Cambie estos mandatos negativos por mandatos afirmativos.

MODELO: No le muestre la herida a la enfermera. →
Muéstrele la herida a la enfermera.

1. No me llame el miércoles.
2. No nos traiga la medicina.
3. No le diga su nombre al médico.
4. No les lleve la receta a los pacientes.
5. No me dé la información.

Ejercicio 4. Only the position of the pronoun changes; the verb forms are the same in affirmative and negative **usted** commands.

Ejercicio 5

¿Qué les recomienda el doctor Sánchez a estas personas?

MODELO: Al paciente: Explíqueme sus síntomas. →
El doctor Sánchez le recomienda *al paciente* que *le explique* sus síntomas.

1. A la enfermera: Póngale la inyección a la paciente del cuarto número 408.
2. Al paciente: Pídame mañana los resultados del análisis de sangre.
3. A la enfermera: Explíquele los síntomas de la gripe a la señora López.
4. A la recepcionista: Lléveles a los señores Gómez estos papeles del seguro médico.
5. Al paciente: Cuéntele a la enfermera cómo ocurrió el accidente.

In negative commands and subjunctive forms, object pronouns precede the verb:
   No le ponga la inyección ahora.
   (*Don't give him/her the shot now.*)
   El médico recomienda que Andrea les dé la medicina a las niñas antes de la cena. (*The doctor recommends that Andrea give the girls their medicine before dinner.*)

This **se** construction will take some time to acquire, but it is very common. You will read and hear it often.

12.4 Relating Unplanned Occurrences: *se*

Use the pronoun **se** + a verb to describe unplanned occurrences such as forgetting, dropping, leaving behind, and breaking.

—¿Qué le pasó al coche?   —*What happened to the car?*
—**Se** descompuso.   —*It broke down.*
—¿Qué le pasó a la botella?   —*What happened to the bottle?*
—**Se** cayó y **se** rompió.   —*It fell and broke.*

If a person is involved, he or she is referred to with an indirect object pronoun: **me, te, le, nos, os,** or **les.**

Se me olvidó la medicina.   *I forgot the medicine.*
A Ernestito **se le** perdió el dinero.   *Ernestito lost the money.*

If the object involved is plural, the verb must also be plural.

Se me **quedaron los libros** en casa.   *I left my books at home.*

In **Ejercicio 5,** use both the indirect object pronoun and a prepositional phrase. Remember that object pronouns must precede conjugated verbs.

Ejercicio 6

Mire los dibujos y diga qué les pasó a estos objetos.

MODELO: —¿Qué le pasó al cajero automático?
           —¡Se descompuso!

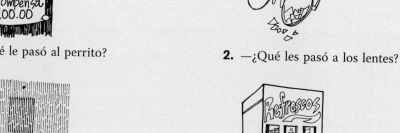

1. —¿Qué le pasó al perrito?

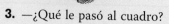

2. —¿Qué les pasó a los lentes?

3. —¿Qué le pasó al cuadro?

4. —¿Qué le pasó a la máquina de los refrescos?

Ejercicio 7

¿Qué les pasó a estas personas? Describa las escenas.

MODELO: romper / botella de jarabe para la tos / el
médico →
Al médico *se le rompió* la botella de jarabe para
la tos.

1. descomponer / carro / Lan

2. caer / espejo / dentista

3. olvidar / estetoscopio / en
su coche / doctor Rocha

4. quedar dentro de la casa /
llave / Ernesto y Estela

5. perder / vendajes / las
enfermeras

12.5 Narrating Past Experiences: The Present Perfect, Imperfect, and Preterite

Gramática ilustrada

1. Cuando el paciente llegó al consultorio del doctor Eloy Ovando, ya había tres pacientes. Todos esperaban con paciencia. Pero él no quería esperar.

2. Habló con la recepcionista y ella le dijo que el doctor no podía atenderlo porque no tenía cita y había muchos pacientes esperando. El paciente se puso furioso y dijo: —Siempre he venido sin hacer cita y el doctor siempre me ha atendido inmediatamente. ¡Eloy es mi mejor amigo!

3. El doctor salió a ver quién gritaba tanto. La recepcionista le dijo que un paciente insistía en entrar inmediatamente, pero que había llegado después de todos y no tenía cita.

4. Al ver al paciente, el doctor lo saludó cortésmente y le preguntó: —¿Se siente mal? ¿Tiene cita hoy? —Los pacientes y la recepcionista se pusieron contentos. Pero el paciente se puso más furioso todavía.

Tenses and examples:
present perfect: (**yo**) **he hablado** (*I have spoken*)
imperfect: (**yo**) **hablaba** (*I used to speak, was speaking*)
preterite: (**yo**) **hablé** (*I spoke* [completed event])

A. English and Spanish each have several verb forms from which to choose that relate past experiences. For example, the verb *to go* has the following past forms in English: *went, used to go, was going,* and *have gone.* Here are some guidelines to help you choose the Spanish form that will best convey the information you want to express.

PRESENT PERFECT
(See **Gramática 10.1.**) This tense is used to ask and answer a *Have you ever . . . ?* question. It has no reference to the specific time in the past when an event occurred.

—¿**Has escalado** una montaña alguna vez en tu vida?
—Sí, **he escalado** muchas montañas.

—*Have you ever in your life climbed a mountain?*
—*Yes, I've climbed many mountains.*

It also describes something you *have* or *have not yet* done.

Nunca **he montado** a caballo, pero mañana voy a aprender.

I have never ridden a horse, but tomorrow I am going to learn.

IMPERFECT

(See **Gramática 9.3–9.5.**) The imperfect tense describes things you *used to do* or *would always do.*

De niña, siempre **jugaba** con mis muñecas en el patio.

As a little girl, I always used to play with my dolls on the patio.

It commonly describes states in the past.

En el kínder, yo **era** una niña muy curiosa y nunca **tenía** miedo de nada.

In kindergarten, I was a very curious little girl and was never afraid of anything.

It also describes what someone was doing or what was happening when something else interrupted the action.

Caminaba tranquilamente por la calle cuando oí los gritos.

I was walking peacefully down the street when I heard the screams.

PRETERITE

(See **Gramática 6.3; 7.1–7.3.**) The preterite (simple past tense) is used to describe *completed events* that are isolated in the past.

Anoche **fui** al cine con mis amigos. **Vimos** una película muy aburrida. Después **comimos** pizza en un restaurante italiano.

Last night I went to the movies with my friends. We saw a very boring movie. Afterward we ate pizza in an Italian restaurant.

B. To tell a story or relate past events, the preterite forms are most frequently used: **fui, comí, salí, bailé, me divertí, dormí,** and so on. Imperfect forms usually describe the background or set the stage for the story: **vivía, jugaba, llovía, hacía calor.** In the following examples, the tenses in parentheses indicate in what tense the corresponding Spanish verb would be.

One night I was waiting (*imperfect*) at the bus stop on my way home from work. It was raining (*imperfect*) very hard, and I was (*imperfect*) very tired after a long, difficult day at work.

In most stories after the stage has been set with the imperfect, as in the preceding example, the story line is developed with the preterite.

Suddenly, I saw (*preterite*) the familiar face of my friend Ralph speed by in a new car. I waved (*preterite*) to him, but he didn't stop (*preterite*). He sped (*preterite*) on by without even a glance toward me. The bus arrived (*preterite*) within a few minutes, and I boarded (*preterite*).

Often in a story, description and narration of the main events are intermixed, so the tenses are, too.

I immediately noticed (*preterite*) that the bus was (*imperfect*) full and that I had to (*imperfect*) stand. Many other people were standing (*imperfect*), too. Buses were (*imperfect*) always so crowded during rush hour in San Francisco.

The preterite is often used to narrate the outcome of a story.

Finally we arrived (*preterite*) at my stop. I quickly got off (*preterite*) and walked (*preterite*) home. The house was (*imperfect*) dark, but when I opened (*preterite*) the door about fifty people, including Ralph, shouted (*preterite*) "Happy Birthday!" It turned out (*preterite*) to be a very good day indeed!

Nunca he hablado con el presidente.
I've never spoken with the president.

De niña, hablaba mucho en clase.
As a child, I talked a lot in class.

Ayer hablé con mi vecino.
Yesterday I talked with my neighbor.

To tell the action of a story, use the preterite: **fui, salió, comieron, bailaste, nos divertimos.**

To set the scene or describe the background for a story, use the imperfect: **Hacía sol... , Eran las 2:30... , Todos dormían...**

Ejercicio 8

En cada uno de los dibujos a continuación hay dos actividades: una interrumpe la otra. Describa cada dibujo, siguiendo el modelo.

MODELO: Amanda y Graciela *caminaban* por el parque cuando don Eduardo *tuvo* un infarto (ataque al corazón).

1. Estela y Ernesto

2. Ramón y Amanda

3. Andrea y Pedro

4. Ernesto

Ejercicio 8. For item 4 use **atravesar** (to cross) and **atropellar** (to run over); for item 6 use **terremoto** (earthquake).

5. Ernestito y sus amigos

6. Ernesto y Estela

Ejercicio 9

Aquí tiene usted lo que Paula le contó a su hermana Andrea anoche. Escoja la forma correcta de los verbos en letra cursiva.

Ayer *trabajé/trabajaba*[1] hasta las ocho de la noche. *Salí/Salía*[2] como de costumbre de mi oficina y *caminé/caminaba*[3] hasta la parada del autobús. *Hubo/Había*[4] poca gente que *esperó/esperaba*[5] porque ya *fue/era*[6] muy tarde. *Pensé/Pensaba*[7] en el proyecto para el día siguiente, cuando *vi/veía*[8] a una señora muy vieja que *caminó/ caminaba*[9] por la calle directamente enfrente de la parada donde yo *estuve/estaba*.[10] De repente, *llegó/llegaba*[11] un hombre, muy joven, y por supuesto, mucho más grande que la viejita, y le *robó/ robaba*[12] la bolsa a la señora. Ella *empezó/empezaba*[13] a gritar. El ladrón *desapareció/desaparecía*[14] rápidamente, pero cuando *llegó/ llegaba*[15] el policía, yo le *di/daba*[16] una descripción muy detallada del hombre y de su ropa. Por fin *llegó/llegaba*[17] el autobús y *llegué/llegaba*[18] a casa un poco antes de las diez.

De compras

In **Capítulo 13** you will talk about manufactured goods. You will also use numbers in the thousands and millions to describe buying and selling.

Domingo en la mañana, por Mihra (Perú)

Sobre la artista: Mihra es el seudónimo de Haydée Mendizábal. Esta artista nació en Lima, Perú, en 1948. Empezó sus estudios en la Escuela de Artes Plásticas en Lima en 1976. También estudió en Brasil y en los Estados Unidos. Sus obras reflejan la diversidad cultural que es Perú y se transmiten por medio de una paleta colorida y espontánea.

¡Conozca Perú!

Nombre del país: República del Perú

Ciudad capital: Lima

Ciudades principales: Cuzco, Iquitos, Arequipa

Moneda: el nuevo sol

Idiomas: el español (oficial), el quechua, el aimara y otras lenguas indígenas

Población: 28.700.000

Día de la Independencia: 28 de julio

Fiestas típicas: la fiesta inca del Inti Raymi, las Fiestas Patrias, la Fiesta de la Virgen de la Candelaria

Comidas típicas: las papas a la huancaína, los anticuchos, el cebiche, las humitas saladas, el tallarín saltado, la pachamanca, el cuy

Música típica: instrumentos tradicionales como la quena, la zampoña y la tinya; bailes folclóricos como la marinera, el tondero, la danza de las tijeras, el huayno

Gente famosa: Túpac Amaru, Atahualpa, Mario Vargas Llosa, César Vallejo

Código del país por Internet: .pe

Voces peruanas

una botánica	una botella
un cáncer	un cigarillo
la casaca	la chaqueta
un(a) choque	un(a) amigo/a
el/la cocho/a	el padre / la madre
una luca	un sol (moneda)
papear	comer

En este capítulo...

ACTIVIDADES DE COMUNICACIÓN

- Los productos y los materiales
- Los precios
- Comprando ropa
- Las compras y el regateo

EN RESUMEN

LECTURAS Y CULTURA

- **Ventanas al pasado**
  Los taínos, artesanos del Caribe
- **Enlace a la literatura**
  «Nada más», por María Elena Walsh
- **Enlace a la música**
  El nuevo flamenco
- **Lectura**
  «El potro del señor cura», por Armando Palacio Valdés

GRAMÁTICA Y EJERCICIOS

13.1 Describing People and Things: Adjectives Used as Nouns

13.2 Indicating Which One(s): Demonstrative Pronouns

13.3 Talking about Price, Beneficiary, and Purpose: **por** and **para** (Part 2)

13.4 Exchanging Items: Indirect Object Pronouns

13.5 Referring to People and Things already Mentioned: Using Indirect and Direct Object Pronouns Together

MULTIMEDIA    **ONLINE LEARNING CENTER** www.mhhe.com/dosmundos7

 C E N T R O   Your media center for languages   **DVD**

Actividades de comunicación y lecturas

Los productos y los materiales

✷ **Lea Gramática 13.1–13.2.**

Las tijeras son de acero.

El hilo es de algodón.

La caja es de cartón.

Los pantalones vaqueros son de mezclilla.

Las botas son de cuero.

El anillo es de diamantes.

Los suecos están hechos de goma.

La sartén es de hierro.

Las herramientas son de acero.

La chimenea es de ladrillo.

El suéter es de lana.

La mecedora es de madera.

El abrelatas está hecho de plástico.

Las joyas son de oro y plata.

La tabla es de fibra de vidrio.

Actividad 1 Definiciones: Los materiales

Lea las seis definiciones siguientes y diga qué material corresponde a cada descripción.

1. Es una piedra preciosa translúcida y muy valiosa. Sudáfrica exporta muchas de estas piedras.
2. Es la piel de un animal que se usa en la fabricación de botas, cinturones, bolsas y maletas.
3. Este material es como el papel, pero es más resistente. Se utiliza en la fabricación de cajas.
4. Este material se deriva del petróleo. Se usa para fabricar envases, botellas, bolígrafos, cepillos, aparatos domésticos y muchas cosas más.

446

5. Éstos son de un material derivado de la tierra. Vienen en varios colores naturales como rojo, café o beige. Se usan mucho en la construcción de edificios, chimeneas, asadores y patios.

6. Es una materia prima que viene de los árboles. Se usa en la construcción de casas y para fabricar muebles.

Actividad 2 Intercambios: Los productos, los materiales y sus usos

Diga para qué se usan estas cosas o materiales.

MODELOS: E1: ¿Para qué se usa *una computadora*?
                 E2: Se usa para *escribir cartas y para navegar por el Internet.*

                 E1: ¿Para qué se usa *la plata*?
                 E2: Se usa para *hacer anillos y otras joyas.*

1. una caja de cartón
2. las herramientas
3. un asador
4. un abrelatas
5. una licuadora
6. el acero
7. el algodón
8. la lana
9. el vidrio
10. la impresora

¿De qué están hechos los siguientes objetos?

MODELOS: E1: ¿De qué está hecha la mecedora?
                 E2: Está hecha de madera.

                 E1: ¿De qué están hechos los lentes?
                 E2: Están hechos de vidrio, plástico y metal.

1. la mesa
2. las tijeras
3. el anillo
4. el martillo
5. los zapatos
6. las llantas

Actividad 3 Intercambios: Las preferencias

Usted necesita comprar varios artículos para su casa. El dependiente / La dependienta (su compañero/a) le ha mostrado varios objetos de diferentes estilos. Diga cuál prefiere y por qué.

Palabras útiles

más elegante(s)	más bonito(s)/a(s)	más ligero(s)/a(s)
más práctico(s)/a(s)	más durable(s)	más pesado(s)/a(s)

REVISE SU CAMBIO ANTES DE SALIR

MODELO: DEPENDIENTE/A: ¿Prefiere usted el suéter grueso o el ligero?
                USTED: Prefiero el grueso porque es de lana.

1. la sartén de hierro o la de aluminio
2. las tijeras de acero o las de plástico
3. la calculadora pequeña o la grande
4. la mesa de madera o la de vidrio
5. el abrelatas eléctrico o el manual
6. los vasos de vidrio o los de plástico

Los taínos, artesanos del Caribe

Cuando Cristóbal Colón llegó a la isla de La Española en 1492, se encontró con los indígenas taínos, gente pacífica que ocupaba las islas que ahora se conocen como Puerto Rico, Jamaica, las Bahamas y parte de Cuba. El nombre «taíno» proviene de su propio idioma y significa «bueno» o «noble». Los taínos pertenecían al grupo de indígenas arahuaco, originario de Brasil y Venezuela.

Por más de 800 años los taínos vivieron en armonía con la naturaleza, cultivando **mandioca,** maní, calabaza, tabaco y algodón, pescando en las aguas del Caribe y **cazando** iguanas, tortugas y manatíes. Los pueblos taínos, llamados yucayeques, eran gobernados por un **cacique.** En el yucayeque había varios bohíos, casas **redondas** hechas de **hoja** de palma, organizados alrededor de una plaza central. Allí se presentaban areitos, ceremonias religiosas y culturales en las cuales recitaban su historia y rezaban a sus muchos **dioses** acompañados por la música de tambores.

Los taínos **esculpían** pequeños ídolos, los cemíes, que eran representaciones físicas de los dioses. Los cemíes, hechos de piedra, madera, hueso o **concha,** combinaban las formas del ser humano con las de un animal y algunos tenían ojos o dientes incrustados de oro. Pero el talento artístico de los taínos no se limitaba a estos pequeños ídolos; el arte era una parte íntegra de su vida diaria. Fabricaban dujos (duhos), sillas ceremoniales de madera o piedra; también **hilaban** hamacas, ropa y figuras de sus dioses de algodón y hacían recipientes de cerámica. Se pintaban el cuerpo, se decoraban con tatuajes religiosos y llevaban joyas de concha, hueso, piedras y plumas. Además construían grandes canoas de madera que usaban para hacer comercio con los mayas en Honduras, los mexicas en México y los caribes en la costa de Venezuela.

El final de los taínos fue trágico. Casi todos murieron durante la colonización española a causa del duro trabajo, el trato cruel que les dieron los españoles y las enfermedades que éstos trajeron. Pero en 2003 se publicaron los resultados de una investigación muy importante del genetista Juan Martínez Cruzado de la Universidad de Puerto Rico. El Dr. Martínez descubrió que el 61 por ciento de todos los puertorriqueños conserva **ADN**

El cemí era la representación física de un dios taíno.

VOCABULARIO ÚTIL

la mandioca	*manioc root, yucca*
cazando	*hunting*
el cacique	*tribal leader*
redondas	*round*
la hoja	*leaf*
dioses	*gods*
esculpían	*sculpted*
la concha	*seashell*
hilaban	*they wove*
el ADN	*DNA*
los campesinos	*rural farmers*
los antepasados	*ancestors*

de los indígenas. Además se sabe que muchos **campesinos** de Puerto Rico, la República Dominicana y Cuba todavía usan técnicas agrícolas y practican la medicina natural de sus **antepasados** taínos. La civilización taína desapareció pero su espíritu sigue vivo en la gente del Caribe.*

Comprensión

1. Mencione dos características de los taínos.

2. ¿Qué causó la desaparición de los taínos?

---

*Si usted viaja al Caribe puede visitar el Museo del Hombre Dominicano en Santo Domingo o el Museo de la Universidad de Puerto Rico; ambos tienen colecciones de arte taíno que demuestran la riqueza de su cultura.

Los precios

✳ **Lea Gramática 13.3.**

—¿Cuánto valen estas playeras?
—Pido sólo $115.00 pesos por cada una.
—¡Qué ganga!

—¿Cuánto cuesta esta chamarra de cuero?
—Cuesta $1075.00 pesos, señorita.
—¡Qué lástima! Sólo tengo $825.00.

—Compré una playera y una chamarra muy lindas hoy.
—¿Cuánto pagaste por la chamarra?
—Pagué $825.00 pesos ¡y ahora no tengo ni un centavo!

Actividad 4 Asociaciones: ¿Cuánto cuestan?

¿Cuánto cuestan los siguientes aparatos en los Estados Unidos? Haga una lista, empezando con el artículo más caro y terminando con el más barato. Luego decida cuáles considera usted más útiles y necesarios y explique por qué.

GRUPO A	GRUPO B
1. un televisor de pantalla plana	**1.** un radio-reloj despertador
2. un abrelatas eléctrico	**2.** un diccionario electrónico
3. una calculadora de bolsillo	**3.** una sartén eléctrica
4. un horno de microondas	**4.** una computadora con impresora a colores
5. una licuadora	**5.** un *iPhone*

Actividad 5 Del mundo hispano: Los artefactos del hogar

iPod nano 8 GB
Precio normal: Gs. 970.000
En oferta: Gs. 875.000
Aluminio anodizado, rueda de clic
Resolución 320 x 240
Video y podcasts

todoelectrónico.com
servicio electrónico de Electroguay, SA.

Teléfono inalámbrico Bell Phones
Precio normal: Gs. 645.275
En oferta: Gs. 568.715. IVA incluido
Color: Plateado y negro
Garantía oficial: 6 meses

Exprimidor de cítricos marca Oster
Precio normal: Gs. 188.400
En oferta: Gs. 131.800. IVA incluido
Garantía oficial: 12 meses

Aspiradora 1200W con bolsa de 3 litros
Precio normal: Gs. 876.150
En oferta: Gs. 773.400. IVA incluido
Garantía oficial: 12 meses
Cierre de seguridad. Enrollado automático de cable 9.5 mts.
Alto poder de succión
Soporte para enrollar el cable en la base de 9.5 mts

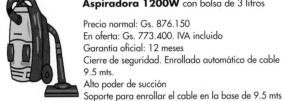

Televisor Sharp de pantalla plana, 20"
Cristal líquido
Precio normal: Gs. 7.100.000
En oferta: Gs. 5.650.000
Nuevo panel de LCD negro
Garantía oficial: 12 meses

Arrocera Oster de 1.8 litros
Precio normal: Gs. 217.385
En oferta: Gs. 193.235. IVA incluido
Garantía oficial: 12 meses
Color: Blanco

Heladera ejecutiva de 8.5 pies cúbicos
Marca LG
Precio normal: Gs. 2.825.000
En oferta: Gs.2.225.750. IVA incluido
Color: blanco
Sin escarcha
Garantía oficial: 12 meses

Horno de microondas Frigidaire de 1.8 pies cúbicos
Precio normal: Gs. 1.342.350
En oferta: Gs. 942.000. IVA incluido
Hecho de acero inoxidable
Garantía oficial: 12 meses

todoelectrónico.com
Pago del flete en destino

Trabajen en grupos de tres estudiantes. Miren los artefactos que se venden en **todoelectrónico.com,** un sitio Web de Paraguay, y conversen usando las siguientes preguntas como guía.

EL ARTEFACTO MÁS ÚTIL

1. En tu opinión, ¿cuál es el artefacto más útil?
2. ¿Cuánto cuesta en oferta? ¿Te ahorras mucho?
3. ¿Cómo es? ¿Por qué es el más útil?
4. ¿Necesitas comprarlo o ya tienes uno?

EL ARTEFACTO MENOS ÚTIL

1. ¿Cuál es el artefacto menos útil para ti?
2. ¿Cómo es el artefacto? ¿Por qué es el menos útil para ti?
3. ¿Cuál es su precio normal? ¿Te ahorras mucho si lo compras ahora?
4. ¿Has comprado algo que no necesitabas solamente porque estaba en oferta?

1000	mil
2000	dos mil
26.000	veintiséis mil
100.000	cien mil
500.000	quinientos mil
1.000.000	un millón (de)
3.700.000	tres millones, setecientos mil
150.000.000	ciento cincuenta millones (de)

Actividad 6 Intercambios: El precio de una casa

Pregúntele a un compañero / una compañera cuánto cuestan estas casas y luego dígale qué casa prefiere usted y por qué.

Viña del Mar, Chile
Villa estilo suizo, vista a la bahía
• 4 dormitorios • 3 baños •
cocina amplia • jardín grande
$535,658,000 pesos chilenos

Patagonia, Chile
Chalet pequeño en zona boscosa,
3 acres • dos dormitorios • un
baño • chimenea • cocina nueva
y amplia • sala mediana
$239,020,000 pesos chilenos

Región de los lagos, Chile
Casi mil acres, bosque • casa
pequeña, dos dormitorios • un
baño • cocina y sala
medianas • chimenea
$396,270,000 pesos chilenos

Marbella, España
Villa Tranquila • parcialmente
amueblada • 4 dormitorios • 3
baños • jardín grande • calefacción central • chimenea • cocina
amplia y comedor • terraza en la
azotea
525,000€

Fuengirola, España
Villa estilo mediterráneo • cerca
del mar • garaje para dos autos •
piscina • 5 dormitorios • dos
baños • cocina renovada •
chimenea
435,000€

Málaga, España
Villa en zona tranquila • 4
dormitorios • 3 baños •
garaje para 3 autos •
cocina con mucha luz •
hermosa vista al mar
645,850€

Enlace a la literatura

«Nada más», por María Elena Walsh

Selección de su libro *Tutú Marambá* (1996)

La escritora argentina María Elena Walsh (1930) es poeta, actriz y cantautora, y escribe teatro para niños. Walsh se enfoca en temas universales, pero también en cuestiones específicas de su país. Publicó su primer libro de poesía, *Otoño imperdonable*, a la edad de 17 años. En el hermoso poema que aquí incluimos, Walsh nos habla de las cosas que no podemos comprar con dinero.

Nada más

Con esta moneda
me voy a comprar
un ramo[1] de cielo
y un metro de mar,
un pico[2] de estrella,
un sol de verdad,
un kilo de viento,
y nada más.

Actividad creativa: Una moneda mágica

Usted tiene una moneda mágica con la que puede comprar cualquier cosa de la naturaleza. ¿Qué va a comprar? ¿Por qué? Escriba un poema para describir su compra.

[1]*un... a piece; lit., a bouquet [of sky]*   [2]*point*

SE VENDE

INFORMES:

_____

● **REFRÁN**

Lo barato cuesta caro.

(*You get what you pay for.* Literally, *What seems cheap costs more.*)

Comprando ropa

¡OJO!

En gran parte del mundo hispano los vecindarios son mixtos: Hay residencias y negocios en la misma zona. Así en vez de usar el carro, la gente camina para hacer las compras. Además, en muchas tiendas no les dan bolsas de papel o plástico a los clientes. Para hacer las compras es necesario que uno lleve su propia bolsa de lona, plástico u otro material.

Actividad 7   Definiciones: La ropa

1. la bufanda
2. el pijama
3. los calcetines
4. el cinturón
5. los guantes
6. la bata
7. la guayabera
8. el paraguas
9. las zapatillas
10. los aretes

a. Las mujeres y algunos hombres los llevan en las orejas.
b. Se usa después de bañarse.
c. Camisa que los hombres la llevan en los países tropicales.
d. Se usa para protegernos de la lluvia.
e. Se pone en el cuello cuando hace frío.
f. Se usa para sujetar los pantalones.
g. Se ponen en las manos cuando hace frío.
h. Se usa para dormir.
i. Se ponen en los pies, antes de ponernos los zapatos.
j. Las usamos para andar en casa, en vez de zapatos.

Actividad 8   Intercambios: Una venta

deTodo

San Francisco esquina Félix Cuevas

GRANDES OFERTAS

Para niñas
Camisetas de tirantes, de algodón y en los colores de la temporada. Tallas para niñas de 10 a 14 años.
De $95.00 a **$75.00**

Juego de falda y blusa, algodón, de Polo Ralph Lauren. Blusa blanca sin mangas, falda de varios colores. Tallas infantiles 8–16.
De $450.00 a **$399.00**

Para damas
Saco tres cuartos, en colores de moda; cinturón. Gabardina de lana, Calvin Klein. Tallas 6–14.
De $3.000.00 a **$2.599.99**

Bolsas estilo Prada con hebillas y bolsas pequeñas a los lados en los colores de moda.
De $900.50 a **$800.00**

Para niños
Mochilas Quicksilver en dos colores. Perfectas para actividades escolares; varios compartimientos.
De $500.00 a **$420.00**

Pantalón largo de niño para actividades desportivas; bolsillos laterales y cintura elástica.
De $320.00 a **$298.50**

Para caballeros
Camisa blanca estampada de manga larga. Muy fresca, en seda de la mejor calidad.
De $220.00 a **$189.99**

Bermudas de algodón marca Dustin disponibles en tres colores: beige, kaki y tostado, con bolsillos laterales y en la parte trasera.
De $500.00 a **$395.00**

deTodo *tiene* de todo
PARA TODA LA FAMILIA

NO USE EL ASCENSOR EN CASO DE TERREMOTO

MODELOS: E1: ¿Cuánto cuestan las mochilas?
E2: Cuestan cuatrocientos veinte pesos.

E1: ¿Cuánto costaban las camisetas de tirantes?
E2: Costaban noventa y cinco pesos.

E1: ¿Cuánto ahorras si compras la camisa blanca?
E2: Ahorro 30 pesos y un centavo.

Actividad 9 Intercambios: De compras

Trabaje con un compañero / una compañera. Imagínese que usted acaba de ir de compras a varias tiendas de ropa en México, D.F. Su compañero/a le pregunta qué cosas compró usted, dónde las compró, cuánto le costaron y de qué material son.

MODELO:
E1: ¿Qué compraste?
E2: *Una guayabera azul.*
E1: ¿Cuánto te costó?
E2: *Estaba rebajada a $350.00.*
E1: *¡Qué barata!* ¿De qué material es?
E2: Es de *algodón.*
E1: ¿Dónde *la* compraste?
E2: En *el Bazar de San Ángel.*

Expresiones útiles

Estaba rebajado/a
¡Qué barato/a!
¡Qué caro/a!
¡Qué ganga!

PRENDAS	MATERIALES	PRECIOS	TIENDAS
un suéter	de lana	$465.50	El Palacio de Hierro
una bufanda	de seda	$220.00	El Correo Francés
un par de guantes	de piel	$392.00	Safari Europeo
una cartera	de cuero	$440.00	Sanborn's
un pijama	de seda	$644.00	el Bazar de San Ángel
una bata	de algodón	$288.00	Milano: Ropa para Caballero
un sombrero color caqui	de lona	$528.75	la Zapatería Tres Estrellas
un vestido	de lino	$976.00	Trajes Suárez
un anillo	de plata	$120.75	Mercado de Artesanías
un pantalón	de mezclilla	$360.00	El Puerto de Liverpool
¿ ?	¿ ?	¿ ?	

Actividad 10 Diálogo abierto: De compras en San Juan

Imagínese que usted está de vacaciones en San Juan, Puerto Rico, y entra a una tienda de ropa. Todo le gusta; quiere comprar algo. Pruébese varias cosas y comente cómo le quedan. Trabaje con un compañero / una compañera. Uno de ustedes debe hacer el papel de dependiente/a y la otra persona, el de turista.

DEPENDIENTE/A: ¿En qué puedo servirle?
TURISTA: Quisiera probarme un(a) _____.
DEPENDIENTE/A: ¿Qué talla usa?
TURISTA: ¿Talla? Pues, creo que _____.
DEPENDIENTE/A: Aquí están los probadores. ¿Por qué no se prueba éste/a? Creo que le va a quedar bien.
TURISTA: A ver... Pues,... creo que me queda _____.
DEPENDIENTE/A: Entonces, pruébese éste/a.
TURISTA: ...

Expresiones útiles

(No) Me queda(n):
bien
apretado/a(s)
suelto/a(s)
grande(s)
pequeño/a(s)
largo/a(s)
corto/a(s)

Las compras y el regateo

✴ **Lea Gramática 13.4–13.5.**

Actividad 11 Asociaciones: Las tiendas en el mundo hispano

¿Dónde se compran estas cosas?

MODELO: el helado → El helado se compra *en la heladería.*

1. la fruta
2. la carne
3. un anillo (joya)
4. los zapatos
5. el pan
6. las tortillas
7. un reloj
8. un libro
9. los muebles
10. el perfume
11. las flores
12. los dulces

Ahora, entreviste a un compañero / una compañera.

1. ¿Cómo se llama tu zapatería favorita? ¿Por qué te gusta comprar los zapatos allí?
2. ¿Hay muchas librerías en tu ciudad? ¿Cuál prefieres? ¿Vas allí con frecuencia?
3. ¿Alquilas películas de un videocentro o las alquilas por Internet? ¿Compras canciones de *iTunes* o las bajas de otros sitios Web?
4. ¿Te gustan los dulces y los chocolates? ¿Cómo se llama la dulcería más famosa de tu ciudad?
5. ¿Compras el pan en el supermercado o vas a una panadería? ¿Hay una panadería buena en tu barrio? ¿Cómo se llama?

Actividad 12 Narración: Un día de compras

¿Qué hizo Amanda y qué compró? Narre las experiencias de Amanda en su día de compras.

Palabras útiles

primero	más tarde	también
luego	después	por fin

Actividad 13 Intercambios: Entre amigos

Usted vive en un apartamento y su amigo/a vive al lado. Él/Ella siempre le pide cosas prestadas. Trabaje con un compañero/a en esta situación.

HAGA COLA AQUÍ

HAGA SU APARTADO NAVIDEÑO

Expresiones útiles

¿Me prestas... ?	Con mucho gusto, te lo/la/los/las presto.
Lo siento, pero no tengo.	Lo siento, pero lo/la/los/las necesito hoy.

Palabras útiles

la cámara digital	el asador	el carro
el televisor	la sartén eléctrica	el diccionario electrónico

MODELO: E1: Se me descompuso el abrelatas. ¿Me prestas uno?
           E2: Sí, con mucho gusto te lo presto.

1. Quiero hacer una carne asada.
2. Mis amigos y yo queremos ver la Copa Mundial de Fútbol.
3. No encuentro mi diccionario y tengo que escribir una composición.
4. Se me descompuso el carro y tengo que ir a trabajar.
5. Salgo esta tarde para las montañas y quiero sacar fotos.
6. Mi estufa de gas no funciona.

Enlace a la música

El nuevo flamenco

El grupo Ojos de brujo

Al hablar de flamenco mucha gente piensa en bailarinas de hermoso traje, vivo **taconeo** y **palmadas**; también en canciones popularizadas por los Gypsy Kings. Pero en España el flamenco tiene una rica tradición de músicos serios y dedicados a su arte. Esta emocionante música nació en Andalucía, región al sur de España, con **raíces** en la cultura de los **moros** y los **gitanos**. En las ciudades sureñas —Cádiz, Jerez de la Frontera, Sevilla, Granada— la presencia del flamenco es constante. Los andaluces tienen una manera musical de expresarse, pero su canto también expresa dolor y sentimiento: la **queja** de los gitanos, gente pobre y **perseguida**.

VOCABULARIO ÚTIL	
el taconeo	*heel tapping*
las palmadas	*clapping*
las raíces	*roots, origin*
los moros	*Moors*
los gitanos	*Gypsies*
la queja	*protest, cry*
perseguida	*persecuted*
se remonta	*dates back*
los cantaores	*flamenco singers*
la mezcla	*mix*
emocionante	*exciting*

La historia del flamenco **se remonta** a los comienzos de la civilización ibérica. Este estilo de música y baile adquiere su forma contemporánea entre los años 1869 y 1910, en sitios muy populares que se llamaban «cafés cantantes». En el siglo XX surgieron grandes artistas de flamenco, entre ellos el guitarrista Paco de Lucía y los **cantaores** El Lebrijano, Camarón de la Isla y Enrique Morente. Y desde los años 70 el flamenco empieza a cambiar al recibir la influencia de otros estilos musicales como el son y el bolero de Cuba, el jazz, el blues y la música brasileña. El resultado de este cambio es lo que hoy llamamos nuevo flamenco o flamenco *fusión*.

Uno de los grupos más populares del nuevo flamenco es Ojos de Brujo, que se forma en Barcelona y combina hip-hop, salsa, rap, reggae y rock con ritmos flamencos en sus discos *Barí* (2004) y *Techarí* (2006).* El grupo Chambao, de Málaga, se ha hecho popular con el estilo *Flamenco Chill* de sus álbumes *Pokito a poko* (2005) y *Con otro aire* (2007). Y un dueto aclamado es el del pianista cubano Bebo Valdés y el cantaor madrileño Diego El Cigala, con su disco *Lágrimas negras* (2003). Hay también famosas bailarinas como Sara Baras y María Bermúdez que representan esta fusión cultural. Baras, una joven bailaora y coréografa de Cádiz, usa el flamenco para contar historias. Sus espectáculos como *Mariana Pineda* y *Carmen* combinan el flamenco tradicional con el teatro. Bermúdez, en cambio, es una bailarina mexicoamericana de Los Ángeles que lleva muchos años de triunfos en España. Vive y trabaja en Jerez de la Frontera,[†] hermosa ciudad donde se inicia el canto flamenco.

Algunos músicos lamentan la **mezcla** de estilos que caracteriza nuestra época. Otros ven en la transformación algo **emocionante** y necesario. En todo caso, los cambios son inevitables. Además, la música flamenca en su forma más pura no ha desaparecido, pues sigue tocándose en el sur de España. Allí, esa rica tradición sigue viva.

Comprensión

1. Describa el nuevo flamenco: ¿cuándo empieza? ¿qué influencias tiene?
2. Mencione el país o ciudad de origen de los siguientes artistas:
   a. Bebo Valdés   **b.** Ojos de Brujo   **c.** María Bermúdez   **d.** Diego El Cigala

---

[*]En caló, la lengua gitana, *barí* significa «alegría» o «la alegría de vivir.» Y *techarí* quiere decir «libre.»
[†]Allí se funda en 1993 El Centro Andaluz de Flamenco, dedicado a promover y celebrar esta tradición musical.

En resumen

De todo un poco

Traiga a clase dos o tres fotos de diferentes objetos (puede recortarlas de un periódico o revista, o sacarlas de Internet). En grupos de tres, escriban dos o tres anuncios comerciales para varias tiendas. Use las fotos para ilustrar la mercancía de estas tiendas. Incluya mandatos, los precios, los materiales u otra información pertinente. Luego compartan sus anuncios con la clase.

> **SOLICITE SU TARJETA DE CRÉDITO Y RECIBA UN DESCUENTO DEL 10% EN SU COMPRA DE HOY**

Vocabulario y expresiones útiles

frases: Está(n) a \$_____. Está(n) rebajado/a(s) a \$_____.
otras palabras: en oferta, especial, ganga, liquidación, venta
mandatos: aproveche, compre, dé, disfrute, muestre, vea, venga
materiales: acero, algodón, bronce, cartón, cristal, cuero, hierro, lino, madera, nilón, oro, plástico, plata, seda

¡Dígalo por escrito!

A. Diseñe el plano para un pequeño centro comercial en una comunidad. Incluya diez tiendas; póngales nombre y describa su mercancía. Sugerencias: un restaurante o café, una librería, un lugar para descansar, una tienda de ropa o un almacén, una zapatería, una joyería, etcétera.
B. Escoja tres de estas tiendas y haga una lista de algunos de sus productos, de qué materiales son y cuál es el precio de cada uno.

MODELO: En la mueblería «La Silla de Oro» hay sofás de cuero a \$2.000,00. Hay estantes de madera para libros a \$800.00. También hay lámparas de bronce muy elegantes a \$175.00 y...

¡Cuéntenos usted!

Describa una tienda que le gusta mucho. ¿Qué vende esa tienda? ¿Es grande o pequeña? ¿Cómo son los dueños/dependientes en esa tienda? ¿Es una tienda de Internet? ¿Son módicos los precios?

 Conexión a la comunidad

Averigüe si hay un programa para ancianos para ayudarles con las compras: recogerlos en el carro y acompañarlos a varias tiendas. Llame y ofrézcase para ayudar a una persona de habla hispana.

LECTURA

«El potro del señor cura», por Armando Palacio Valdés (1853–1938)

Parte 1

Don Pedro era el **cura** de un pueblo pequeño. Tenía dos animales, un perro y un caballo. Hacía más de veinte años que tenía el caballo. Quería mucho a su caballo porque era noble, paciente y muy inteligente. El caballo se llamaba Pichón porque era blanco. Tenía una memoria **prodigiosa:** sabía siempre hacia dónde iban y llevaba al señor cura por todos los caminos. El señor cura no tenía que dirigirlo. Además, cuando llegaban a un lugar, el caballo se paraba a la puerta y, cuando bajaba el señor cura, él solo se iba a la **cuadra.**

El señor cura estaba muy contento con su caballo, pero la gente del pueblo pensaba que el caballo ya estaba muy viejo. **Se burlaban** del pobre Pichón; lo llamaban «el **potro**». Un día el señor cura, cansado de escucharlos, decidió venderlo. Muy triste fue a la feria.

En la feria los caballos estaban muy baratos y Pichón era tan viejo que nadie quería comprarlo. Finalmente un hombre le ofreció setenta y cinco pesetas por él. El cura lo vendió por ese precio. Luego regresó muy triste a su casa.

Pronto se dio cuenta que necesitaba otro caballo porque no podía caminar tanto. Dos semanas después, volvió a la feria, pero ahora los caballos estaban muy caros. El señor cura pasó muchas horas buscando un caballo barato, regateando aquí y allá, pero no encontraba nada. Finalmente encontró un caballo joven y barato. Era de color tabaco y tenía ojos muy inteligentes. Costaba sólo trescientas pesetas. Al señor cura le pareció una ganga y lo compró. Regresó a su casa montado en él. Estaba contento con su compra y muy pronto se puso más contento. El caballo conocía perfectamente el camino a su casa. Al pasar por casa de su hermana, el caballo inmediatamente se paró. El cura, sorprendido, decidió saludar a su hermana. Se bajó y el caballo se fue a la cuadra. El cura dijo: —¡Qué inteligente es este animal!

Se quedó varias horas charlando con su hermana. Cuando salió, decidió regresar directamente a su casa, pero el caballo paró en casa de un amigo a quien el cura visitaba **siempre que** visitaba a su hermana.

—Prodigioso —dijo el cura y bajó para saludar a su amigo. El caballo se fue solo a la cuadra.

Parte 2

Llegó al pueblo de noche. Al siguiente día toda la gente del pueblo fue a ver al caballo nuevo en el establo. El señor cura lo presentó diciendo que se llamaba

PISTAS PARA LEER
El novelista español Armando Palacio Valdés escribía sobre las costumbres populares de Asturias, España. En este cuento, Valdés narra la historia de don Pedro, un cura que tenía un caballo muy viejo. Un día don Pedro vendió su caballo y compró otro más joven. ¡Entonces se llevó una tremenda sorpresa! Después de leer cada parte, haga un resumen. Luego narre todo el cuento.

VOCABULARIO ÚTIL

el cura	priest
prodigioso/a	excellent, wondrous
la cuadra	stable
Se burlaban	They made fun
el potro	colt
siempre que	whenever

León, por su color tabaco. Todos declararon que era un bello animal y **lo felicitaron** por su compra.

Por cinco o seis días no necesitó montar su nuevo caballo. Pero al séptimo, mandó al **criado** a limpiarlo pues pensaba salir y el animal tenía un poco de polvo. El criado lo llamó unos minutos después y le dijo:

—¿Sabe, señor cura? León tiene unas **manchas** blancas que no desaparecen.

—Límpialo bien —dijo el señor cura.

El criado lo limpió y lo limpió, pero las manchas no sólo no desaparecían sino que se hacían cada vez mayores.

—A ver, trae agua caliente y jabón —dijo el cura, cansado.

El agua **quedó teñida de rojo** inmediatamente y las manchas se extendieron hasta que casi le cubrían todo el cuerpo. El cura lo limpió tanto que en media hora había desaparecido el caballo color de tabaco y había aparecido uno blanco. El criado, sorprendido, exclamó:

—¡Caramba! ¡Es el Pichón!

El cura no podía creerlo pero, sí, ¡era su viejo caballo!

La gente empezó a llegar y a reírse del cura y de su «potro». Entonces el señor cura, enojado, les dijo: —¡Qué bien **merezco** todo esto **por hacerles caso** a unos tontos como ustedes! Si alguien se ríe otra vez de mi caballo o lo llama potro... ¡Voy a **romperle los huesos**!

Todos comprendieron que el cura **tenía razón** y se fueron en silencio a su casa. El cura entonces se acercó, feliz, a su caballo y le dijo: —¡Bienvenido a tu casa, Pichón!

VOCABULARIO ÚTIL

lo felicitaron	*they congratulated him*
el criado	*servant*
las manchas	*stains*
quedó teñida de rojo	*was tinted red*
merezco	*I deserve*
por hacerles caso	*for paying attention*
romperle los huesos	*break his bones*
tenía razón	*he was right*

Comprensión A

Narre el cuento con sus propias palabras, tomando en cuenta las siguientes sugerencias.

Parte 1: la descripción de don Pedro y Pichón, la decisión del cura, la feria, el nuevo caballo

Parte 2: la reacción de la gente del pueblo hacia el «nuevo» caballo, el séptimo día, la limpieza de León, la sorpresa

Comprensión B

1. ¿Piensa que hay un mensaje o una moraleja en este cuento? Explique.
2. ¿Cree usted que el señor cura aprendió una lección? ¿Cuál fue? ¿Fue una lección valiosa?

Vea el **Resumen cultural** en este capítulo del *Cuaderno de actividades.*

Un paso más... ¡a escribir!

¿Tiene usted una mascota que quiere mucho? ¿La vendería? Imagínese que alguien quiere comprarle su animal doméstico. Explíquele por escrito a esa persona por qué no puede vendérselo. O quizá usted decida vender su mascota por cierto precio...

Vocabulario

These words come from the *Actividades de comunicación*. You are not expected to memorize the entire list. Your instructor may tell you which sections he or she wants to emphasize. Be patient; you will be familiar with most of these words by the end of the chapter.

Los materiales

Materials

el acero (inoxidable)	(stainless) steel
el algodón	cotton
el cuero	leather
la fibra de vidrio	fiberglass
la goma	rubber
el hierro	iron
el hilo	thread; linen
el ladrillo	brick
la lana	wool
el lino	linen
la madera	wood
la materia prima	raw material
la mezclilla	denim
el oro	gold
la piedra (preciosa)	(gem)stone
la piel	skin, leather
la plata	silver
la seda	silk

PALABRAS SEMEJANTES: el aluminio, el bronce, el cristal, el diamante, el elástico, el gas, el metal
REPASO: el cartón, el plástico, el poliestireno, el vidrio

Las prendas de vestir y las joyas

Articles of Clothing and Jewelry

el anillo	ring
la bata	(bath)robe
la bolsa	purse
el bolsillo	pocket
la bufanda	scarf
los calcetines	socks
los calzoncillos	(men's) underpants
el camisón	nightgown
la cartera	wallet
la chamarra	jacket
el cinturón	belt
la combinación	(women's) slip
la gorra	cap
los guantes	gloves
la guayabera	*embroidered lightweight shirt worn in tropical climates*
la manga	sleeve
las medias	stockings
la moda	fashion
las pantaletas	women's underpants
las pantimedias	pantyhose
un par de...	a pair of . . .
el paraguas	umbrella
la playera	T-shirt (*Mex.*)
la ropa interior	underwear
el sostén	bra

los suecos	clogs
la tela	cloth, fabric
las zapatillas	slippers
los zapatos de tacón alto	high-heeled shoes

REPASO: la camiseta, los pantalones vaqueros, el pijama, el saco

De compras

Shopping

la calidad	quality
dárselo(s)/la(s) en: Se lo(s)/la(s) doy en...	I'll let you have it/them for . . .
¿De qué (material) es?	What (material) is it made of?
Es de...	It's (made) of . . .
¿De qué está hecho/a?	What is it made of?
Está hecho/a de...	It's made of . . .
dejárselo(s)/la(s) en: Se lo(s)/la(s) dejo en...	I'll let you have it/them for . . .
devolver (ue)	to return (*something*)
en oferta	on sale
¿En qué puedo servirle?	May I help you?
envolver (ue)	to wrap
¿Se lo/la/los/las envuelvo?	Shall I wrap it/them for you?
la fabricación	making, manufacture
fabricar	to manufacture, make
gastar	to spend (*money*)
hecho/a a mano	handmade
la liquidación	closing sale
llevarse	to take away
me lo/la llevo	I'll take (buy) it
la mercancía	merchandise
mostrar (ue)	to show
no tener ni un centavo	to be broke
el probador	dressing room
probarse (ue)	to try on
Pruébeselo/la/los/las.	Try it/them on.
el puesto	market stall, small shop
¡Qué ganga!	What a bargain!
¿Qué talla usa?	What size do you wear?
quedarle apretado/suelto	to fit tightly/loosely
Me quedan apretados estos pantalones.	These jeans are tight on me.
quedarle bien/mal	to look nice/bad on one
quedarle grande/pequeño	to be too big/small
Le queda muy grande ese abrigo.	That coat is big on him/her.
quedarle una cantidad de algo	to have a quantity of something left
Me quedan sólo cinco dólares.	I have only five dollars left.
rebajado/a	reduced (*price*)
rebajar (tanto)	to lower the price (so much)
regatear	to bargain
el regateo	bargaining

valer	to be worth
¿Cuánto vale?	How much is this (worth)?
la venta	sale

REPASO: el centro comercial, comprar, dinero (en efectivo), ofrecer, vender

Los verbos

Verbs

aprovechar	to take advantage of
bajar	to download
derivarse	to be derived from
entrar	to enter
funcionar	to work, function
imprimir	to print
licuar	to blend, liquefy
mezclar	to mix
pedir prestado/a(s)	to borrow
prestar	to lend
recortar	to cut out
sujetar	to hold up; to attach

PALABRAS SEMEJANTES: aceptar, exportar, ilustrar, utilizar

Las personas

People

el caballero	gentleman
la dama	lady
el vendedor / la vendedora	salesman/saleswoman

Los lugares

Places

la carnicería	meat market
la dulcería	candy store
la frutería	fruit store
la heladería	ice cream parlor
la joyería	jewelry store
la juguetería	toy store
el mercado al aire libre	open-air market

REPASO: la cafetería, la panadería, la papelería, la librería, el videocentro, la zapatería

Los aparatos domésticos

Household Appliances

el abrelatas	can opener
el asador	barbecue grill
la calefacción	heat(ing) system
el exprimidor	juicer
la licuadora	blender
el radio-reloj despertador	clock radio
el televisor de pantalla plana	flat-screen television

REPASO: la aspiradora, la calculadora, la impresora, la pantalla, la sartén

Los sustantivos

Nouns

el anuncio comercial	advertisement
la caja	box
la Copa Mundial	World Cup
los dulces	candy; sweets
las herramientas	tools
el hogar	home; hearth
el juego de	set of (*items*)
el martillo	hammer
la mecedora	rocking chair
el tamaño	size
las tijeras	scissors

PALABRAS SEMEJANTES: el artefacto, la cerámica, la construcción, el documento, el estilo, la garantía, el perfume, la vista

Los adjetivos

Adjectives

color caqui	khaki
(color) vivo	bright (color)
de cuadros	checkered, plaid
de lunares	polka-dotted
de moda	fashionable
de rayas	striped
estrecho/a	tight
grueso/a	thick, heavy
inalámbrico/a	wireless; cordless
pesado/a	heavy
plano/a	flat
renovado/a	remodeled

PALABRAS SEMEJANTES: derivado/a, durable, electrónico/a, enorme, manual, nilón, original, pertinente, resistente, translúcido/a
REPASO: cómodo/a, ligero/a, lleno/a, mediano/a

Palabras y expresiones útiles

Useful Words and Expressions

A ver	Let's see
lo siento	I'm sorry
¡Qué lástima!	That's too bad!
solamente	only

Los números

Numbers

| un millón (de) | a million (*of something*) |
| veintidós millones de pesos | twenty-two million pesos |

Gramática y ejercicios

13.1 Describing People and Things: Adjectives Used as Nouns

A. In English and Spanish, adjectives can be nominalized (used as nouns). To nominalize an adjective in Spanish, delete the noun to which it refers and use a definite or indefinite article before the adjective.

—¿Te gusta esta **blusa**?
—Sí, pero prefiero **la roja.**

—*Do you like this blouse?*
—*Yes, but I prefer the red one.*

—¿Quieres una **ensalada** grande
  o **una pequeña**?
—**Una grande,** por favor.

—*Do you want a large salad or
  a small one?*
—*A large one, please.*

Note that **uno** rather than **un** is used in nominalizations before masculine singular adjectives.

—¿Tienes un **coche** viejo o
  uno nuevo?
—Tengo **uno** muy **viejo.**

—*Do you have an old car or a
  new one?*
—*I have a very old one.*

B. The nominalization of adjectives is also possible in sentences that contain adjectival phrases using **de.**

Me gustan más los muebles de
  madera que **los de plástico.**
Carmen se compró una blusa de
  seda, pero yo me compré **una
  de algodón.**

*I like wood furniture more than
  plastic (furniture).*
*Carmen bought herself a silk blouse,
  but I bought myself a cotton one.*

C. To express an abstract idea using a nominalized adjective, use **lo** before the masculine singular form of the adjective: **lo atractivo, lo bueno, lo difícil, lo divertido, lo increíble, lo moderno, lo malo,** and so on.*

Hay muchas novelas buenas.
  Lo difícil es encontrar tiempo
  para leerlas.
Lo malo es que él nunca
  comprendió lo que hizo.
¡Qué mercado más lleno de
  gente! **Lo bueno** es que
  pudimos regatear y comprar
  varias cosas a precios bajos.

*There are many good novels.
  The hard part is finding time to
  read them.*
*The bad part (thing) is that he
  never understood what he did.*
*What a crowded market! The
  good thing is that we were
  able to bargain and buy some
  things at low prices.*

> **¿Cuál prefieres, la chaqueta roja o la amarilla?**
> *Which do you prefer, the red jacket or the yellow one?*
>
> **Prefiero la roja.**
> *I prefer the red one.*

> **Cuando compro ropa, nunca compro la de poliéster.**
> *When I buy clothes, I never buy polyester.*

> **Lo difícil es hacer paella; lo bueno es comérsela.**
> *The hard part is making paella; the good part is eating it.*

Ejercicio 1

Los estudiantes de la clase de español van a una fiesta, pero sus parientes no están de acuerdo con la ropa que ellos quieren llevar. Diga lo que prefiere cada persona.

****Lo que** corresponds to *what (that which)* in English.
  Rafael no sabe **lo que** quiere.
  Lo bueno es que Amanda nunca
    supo **lo que** pasó.

  Rafael doesn't know what (that which) he wants.
  *The good thing is that Amanda never found out what
    (that which) happened.*

465

MODELO: Carmen / las botas largas; su madre / las botas cortas
Carmen quiere llevar las botas largas, pero su madre prefiere
las cortas.

1. Nora / el vestido corto; su hermana / el vestido largo
2. Alberto / el abrigo de cuero; su hermano / el abrigo de lana
3. Pablo / el suéter ligero; su padre / el suéter grueso
4. Carmen / la falda vieja; su prima / la falda nueva
5. Esteban / la camisa de seda; su novia / la camisa de algodón

Ejercicio 2

Paula Saucedo y Armando, su novio, van a comprar cosas para su futura casa, pero no están de acuerdo en nada. Exprese lo que cada uno quiere/prefiere.

MODELO: Paula / una licuadora blanca; Armando / una licuadora negra
Paula quiere una licuadora blanca, pero su novio, Armando, prefiere
una negra.

1. Paula / un abrelatas manual; Armando / un abrelatas eléctrico
2. Paula / un asador pequeño; Armando / un asador grande
3. Paula / unos vasos de vidrio; Armando / unos vasos de plástico
4. Paula / unos muebles modernos para la sala; Armando / unos muebles antiguos
5. Paula / una computadora Dell; Armando / una computadora Mac

13.2 Indicating Which One(s): Demonstrative Pronouns

When a demonstrative adjective (**este, ese, aquel**) functions as a noun, it is called a *demonstrative pronoun.** As you saw in **Gramática 2.4,** there are three different demonstrative adjectives/pronouns to indicate distance from the speaker. Often you will hear these used in conjunction with adverbs of place that further clarify distance from the speaker.

este/a, estos/as... aquí (*nearest*)	ese/a, esos/as... allí	aquel/aquella, aquellos/as... allá (*farthest*)

—¿Quieres este reloj o **ése**? —*Do you want this watch or that one?*

—Prefiero **éste**. —*I prefer this one.*

—Estos vestidos son muy caros. —*These dresses are very expensive.*

—Sí, pero **aquéllos** no. —*Yes, but those aren't.*

---

*In *Dos mundos* and many other books you will see an accent on these pronouns because, until recently, they were always written with an accent mark to distinguish them from demonstrative adjectives.
Up-to-date usage suggests that the accent mark may be omitted when context makes the meaning clear.
Obviously, all books published before the rule was changed have accents on demonstrative pronouns.
Books published after this change may or may not use the written accent.

Ejercicio 3

Estas personas están tratando de decidir lo que quieren comprar. Mire los dibujos y use el adjetivo o el pronombre demostrativo en cada caso.

MODELO: Ayer me gustó *esta* blusa, pero ahora prefiero *ésa* que está allí.

1. Me gusta _____ bata, pero voy a comprar _____, la rosada.
2. No me gustan _____ guantes amarillos. Quiero comprar _____, los negros.
3. Creo que _____ tijeras funcionan bien, pero por favor muéstreme _____, las que cuestan más.
4. No me dé _____ martillo; es demasiado pequeño. Déme _____ que está aquí.
5. _____ pijama es caro. Prefiero comprar _____ de lunares porque tiene el precio rebajado.

¡OJO!

Pay attention to the distance of objects from the speaker. If there are only two objects, choose between **este/esta** and **ese/esa.**

13.3 Talking about Price, Beneficiary, and Purpose: *por* and *para* (Part 2)

A. You already know from **Gramática 10.3** that **por** is used as an equivalent for *through, by,* and *along* (**Caminamos por el río.**) and with time (**Esperamos por diez minutos.**). **Por** is also used with quantities and prices and corresponds to English (*in exchange*) *for.*

—Raúl, ¿cuánto pagaste **por** el suéter?

—Lo compré **por** sesenta pesos.

—*Raúl, how much did you pay for the sweater?*

—*I bought it for sixty pesos.*

> If a number is involved when you are choosing between **por** and **para** to express *for,* **por** is usually correct:
> **por 10 kilómetros**
> **por 250 pesos**
> **por 3 horas**
> **por 8 meses**
>
> **para** = *in order to, for* (recipient)

B. In addition to indicating destination (**Mañana salgo para Madrid.**) and deadlines (**La tarea es para el lunes.**), **para** can be followed by an infinitive to indicate function or purpose. In such cases **para** corresponds to English *(in order) to.*

—¿**Para** qué usan estos trapos? — *What do you use these rags for?*
—**Para** limpiar las ventanas. — *To clean the windows.*

Para coser su propia ropa, uno necesita mucha paciencia. — *In order to make your own clothes, you need a lot of patience.*

Para is also used to indicate the beneficiary or recipient of something.

—¿**Para** quién es este regalo? — *For whom is this gift?*
—Es **para** mi esposa. — *It's for my wife.*

Ejercicio 4

Indique la respuesta más lógica.

MODELO: ¿Para qué haces ejercicio? →
Para mantenerme en buena condición física.

1. ¿Para qué vas a la biblioteca?
2. ¿Para qué estás limpiando tu cuarto ahora?
3. ¿Para qué vas a usar la aspiradora?
4. ¿Para qué trajiste las herramientas?
5. ¿Para qué compraste el mantel rojo?

a. para limpiar la alfombra de la sala
b. para reparar el coche
c. para buscar un libro que necesito para una clase
d. para usarlo en la fiesta esta noche
e. para no tener que limpiarlo después

Ejercicio 5

Complete los diálogos entre Pilar y Clara con **por** o **para**.

—Mira, ¡qué blusa más bonita! Y la compré _____[1] solamente 30 euros.
—¿_____[2] quién es?
—Es_____[3] mi hermana, pero me gustaría comprar una _____[4] mí también.
—En El Corte Inglés vi unos pantalones Levi _____[5] 45,30 euros.
—Eso es un poco caro. Los míos los compré _____[6] 39,50.
—Acabo de comprar una bufanda de lana _____[7] 15,25 euros.
—¿_____[8] quién es?
—Es _____[9] mi abuela.
—Yo vi unas bufandas de seda muy lindas en Juvenil Cortefiel _____[10] solamente 10 euros.
—¿Bufandas de seda? ¿A ese precio? ¡Es una ganga! Tal vez compre una _____[11] mi mamá también.

13.4 Exchanging Items: Indirect Object Pronouns

Certain verbs describe the exchange of items between persons: **dar** (*to give [something to someone]*), **traer** (*to bring [something to someone]*), **llevar** (*to carry, take [something to someone]*), **prestar** (*to lend [something to someone]*), **devolver** (*to give [something] back [to someone]*), **regalar** (*to give [something] as a gift [to someone]*), and so forth.

Amanda me va a **traer** el disco compacto que le **presté.**	*Amanda is going to bring me the CD that I lent her.*
Guillermo me **devolvió** el dinero que me debía.	*Guillermo returned (to me) the money that he owed me.*

Normally these verbs are accompanied by indirect object pronouns (**me, te, le, nos, os,** and **les**) even when the person involved is specifically mentioned.

Le di el dinero **a mi hermano Guillermo.**	*I gave the money to my brother Guillermo.*
Ramón, ¿**le** llevaste **a tu novia** las flores que le prometiste?	*Ramón, did you take your girlfriend the flowers you promised her?*
Amanda, ¿qué **le** vas a regalar **a tu novio** para Navidad?	*Amanda, what are you going to give (to) your boyfriend for Christmas?*

Ejercicio 6

Llene cada espacio en blanco con el pronombre apropiado y luego indique la(s) respuesta(s) lógica(s).

MODELO: Este año mis padres *me* (a mí)...
    (a.) prestaron dinero.
    (b.) regalaron ropa nueva.
    (c.) trajeron comida cuando estaba enfermo/a.
    d. dieron una F en la clase de matemáticas.

Note: In **Ejercicio 6,** there will be more than one answer to each question.

1. La semana pasada la profesora _____ (a nosotros)...
   a. hizo muchas preguntas.
   b. dio buenas notas.
   c. explicó el subjuntivo muy bien.
   d. regaló carros nuevos.
2. La semana pasada yo _____ (a mi mejor amigo/a)...
   a. conté mis secretos.
   b. ofrecí un café.
   c. hice un regalo barato y feo.
   d. compré una casa en las Bahamas.
3. En la última clase de español yo _____ (a mis compañeros)...
   a. dije: —¡Hola!
   b. regalé camisetas viejas.
   c. contesté las preguntas de las entrevistas.
   d. presté mis herramientas para hacer la tarea.
4. Ayer, cuando fui de compras, la dependienta _____ (a mí)...
   a. atendió muy bien.
   b. sirvió la cena rápidamente.
   c. llevó ropa de mi talla al probador.
   d. preguntó: —¿En qué puedo servirle?

5. La última vez que yo fui al cine contigo _____ (a ti)...
   a. compré palomitas.
   b. presté mi diccionario.
   c. conté toda la historia de la película antes.
   d. pagué $1.000.00 por tu suéter favorito.

13.5 Referring to People and Things already Mentioned: Using Indirect and Direct Object Pronouns Together

Gramática ilustrada

When the context is clear, you will be able to understand speech with two object pronouns, but you may not be able to produce such sentences for a while.

A. Sometimes there is more than one object pronoun in a sentence. This is common if you want to *do something for someone, take something to someone, fix something for someone, buy something for someone,* and so forth. The indirect object (**me, te, le, nos, os,** or **les**) is usually the person *for whom* you are doing something, and the direct object (**lo, la, los,** or **las**) is the thing involved.

—¿Me compraste las pantimedias ayer?

—Sí, **te las** compré por la tarde.

—*Did you buy me the pantyhose yesterday?*

—*Yes, I bought them for you in the afternoon.*

—¿Quiere usted **el postre** ahora?

—Sí, tráiga**melo,** por favor.

—*Do you want the dessert now?*

—*Yes, bring it to me, please.*

B. Note the following possible combinations with **me, te, nos,** and **os.**

me lo(s) ⎫
me la(s) ⎭ *it/them to me*

te lo(s) ⎫ *it/them to you*
te la(s) ⎭ *(inf. sing.)*

nos lo(s) ⎫
nos la(s) ⎭ *it/them to us*

os lo(s) ⎫ *it/them to you*
os la(s) ⎭ *(inf. pl.)*

Pedro, si **te** falta **dinero,**
puedo prestár**telo.**

—¿**Me** lavaste las camisetas el
sábado?
—Sí, **te las** lavé; aquí están.

—Señores, ¿**les** preparo **la
cena** ahora?
—No, por favor, prepáre**nosla**
más tarde.

*Pedro, if you need money,
I can lend it to you.*

—*Did you wash my T-shirts on
Saturday?*
—*Yes, I washed them for you;
here they are.*

—*Gentlemen, should I prepare
dinner for you now?*
—*No, please prepare it for us
later.*

> Indirect object pronoun **(me, te, le, nos, os, les)** = person to or for whom you are doing something
>
> Direct object pronoun **(lo, la, los, las)** = the thing involved
>
> When two object pronouns are used together, the indirect object pronoun always precedes the direct object pronoun:
>> ***Me las* compró ayer.**
>> (*He bought them for me yesterday.*)
>
> The correct order of pronouns in a sentence is *indirect object + direct object.*
> Object pronouns:
> 1. are usually placed immediately before the verb.
> 2. may optionally be attached to the end of infinitives and present participles.
> 3. *must* be attached to the end of affirmative commands.

C. The indirect object pronouns **le** and **les** change to **se** when used together with the direct object pronouns **lo, la, los,** and **las.**

se lo	*it (m.) to you (pol. sing. or pl.), him, her, them*
se la	*it (f.) to you (pol. sing. or pl.), him, her, them*
se los	*them (m.) to you (pol. sing. or pl.), him, her, them*
se las	*them (f.) to you (pol. sing. or pl.), him, her, them*

All these combinations may look confusing in abstract sentences, but in the context of real conversations you will generally know to whom and to what the pronouns refer.

—Ernestito, ¿**le** llevaste a **papá**
sus zapatillas?
—Sí, ya **se las** llevé.

—Mamá, ¿**le** compraste una
camisa nueva a **papá**?
—Sí, **se la** compré hoy.

—Guillermo, ¿**les** diste los
dulces a las amigas de
Amanda?
—Sí, **se los** di esta mañana.

—Señor Saucedo, ¿**le** entregó
usted las llaves al **gerente**?
—Sí, **se las** entregué ayer.

—*Ernestito, did you take Dad
his slippers?*
—*Yes, I already took
them to him.*

—*Mom, did you buy Dad a
new shirt?*
—*Yes, I bought it for him today.*

—*Guillermo, did you give the
CDs to Amanda's friends?*

—*Yes, I gave them to them this
morning.*

—*Mr. Saucedo, did you hand in
the keys to the manager?*
—*Yes, I handed them in to him
yesterday.*

> **Le** and **les** become **se** when they precede **lo, la, los,** or **las.**

D. Remember that object pronouns can be attached to infinitives and present participles and are always attached to affirmative commands. When the verb form and the object pronouns are written together as one word, you must place an accent mark on the stressed syllable.

—Señorita López, en cuanto al informe para la señorita Saucedo, ¿va usted a **entregárselo** ahora?	—*Miss López, about that report for Miss Saucedo, are you going to give it to her now?*
—No, ya **se lo entregué** esta mañana.	—*No, I already turned it in to her this morning.*
—Adriana, necesito las listas de los clientes. ¿Vas a **prepararármelas** esta tarde?	—*Adriana, I need the lists of clients. Are you going to get them ready for me this afternoon?*
—No, estoy **preparándotelas** ahora mismo.	—*No, I'm getting them ready for you right now.*

Ejercicio 7

In **Ejercicio 7,** note that the verb in the answer is always a first-person form (**yo**) and that in items 1–5 the indirect object (**se**) is invariable: Only the direct object changes. In items 1–5 the past is used; in items 6–10 the informal future.

Hoy Ernestito le hace muchas preguntas a Guillermo. Conteste por Guillermo las preguntas en la página siguiente, según el modelo.

MODELO: ERNESTITO: ¿Ya le diste la revista a mamá? →
GUILLERMO: Sí, *se la di* ayer.

1. ¿Ya le entregaste la tarea de biología a la profesora?
2. ¿Ya le vendiste la patineta a Ramón?
3. ¿Ya le diste la carta a Amanda?
4. ¿Ya le prestaste la calculadora a Diego?
5. ¿Ya les llevaste la muñeca a las niñas?

Ahora Guillermo le hace a Ernestito algunas preguntas. Haga el papel de Ernestito y conteste según el modelo.

MODELO: GUILLERMO: ¿Cuándo me vas a mostrar tu nuevo iPod? →
ERNESTITO: Voy a *mostrártelo* mañana.

6. ¿Cuándo vas a prestarme las herramientas para reparar mi bicicleta?
7. ¿Cuándo vas a devolverme el suéter que te presté la semana pasada?
8. ¿Cuándo vas a traerme el videojuego que me prometiste?
9. ¿Cuándo vas a darme la carta que me escribió Raúl?
10. ¿Cuándo vas a mostrarme tus libros nuevos?

Ejercicio 8

La madre de Guillermo le hace algunas preguntas sobre lo que él va a hacer. Conteste por él, según el modelo.

MODELO: MADRE: ¿Les vas a mostrar tu nuevo teléfono celular a tus amigos? →
            GUILLERMO: Sí, voy a *mostrárselo* mañana.

1. ¿Le vas a pedir dinero a tu padre?
2. ¿Les vas a prestar los juegos de video a Ernestito y a sus amiguitos?
3. ¿Le vas a llevar las fotos a tu abuelita?
4. ¿Les vas a devolver las herramientas a tus tíos?
5. ¿Le vas a regalar un libro a Graciela?

In **Ejercicio 8,** although the indirect object in the question is sometimes **le** and sometimes **les,** the answer is invariable: **se.**

Ejercicio 9

Estela tiene mucha prisa y por eso le pide a Ernesto que haga algunas cosas. Conteste las preguntas, haciendo el papel de Ernesto.

MODELO: ESTELA: Sírveme el desayuno, por favor. →
            ERNESTO: *Te lo estoy sirviendo* ahora mismo.

1. ¿Puedes darme una servilleta, por favor?
2. No voy a tener tiempo de salir a almorzar. ¿Puedes prepararme unas tortas de jamón?
3. Ernesto, quiero ponerme una blusa limpia. ¿Puedes planchármela?
4. Ay, tengo prisa y no encuentro mi cinturón. ¿Puedes buscármelo?
5. Hoy trabajé mucho y estoy muy cansada. ¿Puedes buscarme las pantuflas (zapatillas)?

Ejercicio 10

Ernesto Saucedo le hace a Amanda varias preguntas sobre lo que van a hacer sus amigos, vecinos y familiares. Haga el papel de Amanda y conteste según el modelo.

MODELO: ERNESTO: ¿Te va a reparar Ramón tu cámara digital? →
            AMANDA: Ya *me la reparó* la semana pasada.

1. ¿Te va a regalar tu abuela una blusa nueva para tu cumpleaños?
2. ¿Te va a comprar Graciela un regalo para tu cumpleaños?
3. ¿Te va a prestar Guillermo su bicicleta para este fin de semana?
4. ¿Te va a traer Diego los libros de la escuela?
5. ¿Te va a dar tu madre el dinero para el cine?

In **Ejercicio 10,** the verb form in the answers will always be third-person singular (**él/ella**).

La familia y los consejos

METAS

In **Capítulo 14** you will have an opportunity to share your views on relationships, as well as on your own personal values. You will practice persuading others by giving commands, offering advice, and making suggestions. You will also talk about child rearing and social behavior.

Las meninas, por Diego Velázquez (España)

Sobre el artista: El pintor español Diego Rodríguez de Silva y Velázquez nació en Sevilla en 1599 y murió en 1660. Desde 1623 fue retratista de los reyes de España. Pintó *Las meninas* en 1656. Esta obra compleja es como una instantánea fotográfica. El espectador parece estar en el frente, pero dándole la espalda a los reyes, que se ven reflejados en el espejo.

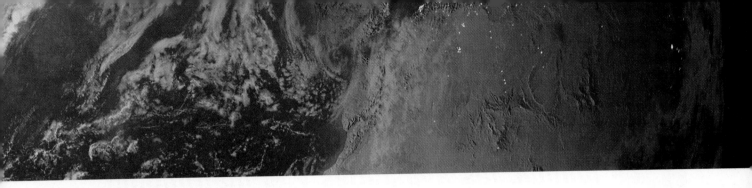

¡Conozca España!

Nombre del país: Reino de España

Ciudad capital: Madrid

Ciudades principales: Barcelona, Sevilla, Valencia, Bilbao

Moneda nacional: el euro

Idiomas: el español (castellano), el catalán, el vasco, el gallego (oficiales)

Población: ~ 40.500.000

Fiestas típicas: las Fallas de Valencia, la Feria de Abril, las Fiestas de San Fermín, la Tomatina

Comidas típicas: la paella, el gazpacho, la tortilla de patatas, el caldo gallego

Música típica: el cante hondo/flamenco (Andalucía), la jota (Aragón), la música de la gaita (*bagpipes*) (Galicia / Asturias y Cantabria)

Gente famosa: Fernando de Aragón e Isabel de Castilla, Pablo Picasso, Francisco de Goya, Federico García Lorca, Pedro Almodóvar, Rafael Nadal

Código del país por Internet: .es

Voces españolas

¡Qué guay!	How cool!
un(a) guiri	un(a) extranjero/a
majo/a	bonito/a, simpático/a
la marcha	la vida nocturna
un mogollón	mucho
un(a) tío/a	dude/chick
vale	está bien, de acuerdo

En este capítulo...

ACTIVIDADES DE COMUNICACIÓN

- La familia, las amistades y el matrimonio
- Las instrucciones y los mandatos
- Las órdenes, los consejos y las sugerencias
- La crianza y el comportamiento

 **EN RESUMEN**

LECTURAS Y CULTURA

- **Ventanas al pasado**
  Los logros de la mujer hispana
- **Enlace a la literatura**
  «Kinsey Report No. 6», por Rosario Castellanos
- **Ventanas culturales**
  Nuestra comunidad: El Ballet Folklórico de México: Un proyecto de familia
- **Lecturas**
  Los refranes
  «Lazarillo y el ciego»

GRAMÁTICA Y EJERCICIOS

14.1 Expressing *each other*: Reciprocal Pronouns

14.2 Describing: **ser** and **estar**

14.3 Giving Direct Commands: Polite and Informal

14.4 Using Softened Commands: The Subjunctive Mood

14.5 More Uses of the Subjunctive: Saying *Have someone else do it!*: **Que** + Subjunctive and Expressing *Let's* . . .

La familia, las amistades y el matrimonio

✷ **Lea Gramática 14.1–14.2.**

*Dora Muñoz de Saucedo y
Javier Saucedo González
participan a usted
el enlace matrimonial de su hija*
Andrea
con el señor
Pedro Ruiz Galván

*Y tienen el honor de invitarle
a la ceremonia religiosa
que se llevará a cabo
el 29 de junio a las 14:00
en la Iglesia San Bonifacio
Parroquia de San Agustín
Horacio 921, Colonia Polanco*

*Recepción en el Casino Español
Calle Isabel la Católica, Nº 4385
Comida 17:30–18:30
Baile 17:30–23:30*

Padrinos		Madrinas
Ernesto Saucedo	Velación	Estela de Saucedo
José Ortega	Anillos	Paula Saucedo Muñoz
Alejandro Estrada	Arras	Araceli Estrada
Benjamín Román	Copas	Blanca Velásquez
Manuel Muñoz	Cojines	Graciela Muñoz
Víctor Trujillo	Lazo	Leticia Saucedo
Joaquín Jiménez	Libro	Ángela Chávez
Ricardo Rubalcava	Pastel	Vanesa Zamora
Reynaldo Carrillo	Brindis	Julieta Quijada

La boda

Se conocen; se dan la mano. Se enamoran. Se quieren mucho y se abrazan. Se besan. Se casan.

los parientes — las madrinas — los padrinos

el hermano / la hermana — los cuñados — los padres / los suegros — la novia — el novio — los (bis)abuelos — el cura

REFRÁN

Antes que te cases, mira lo que haces.

(*Look before you leap.* Literally, *Before you get married, look at what you are doing.*)

Actividad 1 Definiciones: La familia y las amistades

1. el noviazgo
2. el compadre
3. la amistad
4. el bautizo
5. la hermanastra
6. el ahijado
7. el cura
8. la madrina

a. el hijo de un amigo de la familia, a quien usted lleva a bautizar; usted es responsable del bienestar del niño en caso de que los padres de él se mueran

b. dirige la ceremonia del matrimonio

c. el padrino de su hijo

d. la relación entre dos personas que están comprometidas para casarse

e. una amiga de la familia presente en el bautizo que debe criar al niño / a la niña si la madre no está

f. la hija de su madrastra o padrastro

g. la relación entre amigos

h. una ceremonia religiosa en la cual se le da un nombre al niño recién nacido / a la niña recién nacida

Actividad 2 Intercambios: La boda de Andrea

Mire la invitación a la boda de Andrea en la página anterior y, con un compañero / una compañera, contesten las siguientes preguntas.

1. ¿Dónde tuvo lugar la boda de Andrea?
2. Según la invitación, ¿crees que fue una boda formal o informal?
3. ¿Cómo se llamaban los padrinos de *arras*?
4. ¿Cómo se llamaba la madrina de *velación*?
5. ¿Cómo se llamaba el padrino de *brindis*?
6. ¿A que hora comenzó el baile?

Sugerencias

abrazarse

ayudarse

besarse

casarse

comprenderse

comunicarse

darse la mano

echarse de menos

enojarse

enviarse mensajes
 electrónicos

golpearse

gritarse

hablarse todas
 las noches por celular

insultarse

pedirse perdón

pelearse

textearse

verse

Esta familia disfruta de la playa.

Actividad 3 Asociaciones: Las relaciones personales

Trabaje con un compañero / una compañera para llenar los espacios en blanco.

1. Los señores Saucedo se llevan bien: *se abrazan,* _____ y _____.
2. Últimamente Nora y su novio no se llevan bien: _____, _____ y _____.
3. Marisa y Clarisa son hermanas; como todas las hermanitas, a veces _____ o _____.
4. Raúl estudia en la Universidad de Texas en San Antonio y su novia estudia en la Universidad Autónoma de México en el D.F. Ellos _____ y _____.
5. Ernesto y su compañero de trabajo han tenido problemas, pero ahora quieren resolverlos. Ellos _____ y _____.

Ahora hable de las relaciones entre usted y su novio/a, su esposo/a, su hermano/a o un compañero / una compañera.

Mi *novio/a* (*esposo/a*) y yo (no) nos llevamos bien; por eso siempre _____ y _____.

Mi *hermano/a* y yo (no) nos llevamos muy bien. Nosotros _____ y _____.

Un compañero / Una compañera de trabajo y yo (no) nos llevamos muy bien y por eso _____ y _____.

Actividad 4 Del mundo hispano: Familia numerosa, artículo de la revista española *Mía*.

Familia numerosa

Hace años, tener familia numerosa era un síntoma de prosperidad. Ahora, que los tiempos han cambiado, la gente se piensa un poco más eso de[1] tener hijos y más hijos, para lograr un premio de natalidad. ¿Es, pues, un beneficio o una desventaja la familia numerosa?

★★★★★ Félix Tabernero, médico: Estoy a favor de la familia numerosa, y de hecho yo tengo seis hijos. Sabiéndose administrar, uno no encuentra excesivos problemas para vivir desahogadamente.[2] Pero soy consciente de que al tener tantos hijos hay que estar dispuesto a renunciar[3] a muchas cosas, como salidas con los amigos, vicios mayores...

★★★★★ Ana Mérida, estudiante: No soy partidaria de[4] familias numerosas, tal y como funciona la sociedad española de hoy día. Ya es difícil sacar adelante[5] a un par de hijos, como para tener seis o siete.

[1]eso... *the idea of* [2]confortablemente [3]*give up* [4]partidaria... *in favor of* [5]sacar... *to raise*

COMPRENSIÓN

1. En el pasado, ¿de qué era símbolo el tener muchos hijos?
2. Según Félix Tabernero, ¿a qué deben estar dispuestos los padres que quieren tener muchos hijos?
3. ¿Está a favor o en contra de una familia numerosa Ana Mérida? ¿Por qué?

ENTREVISTA

4. ¿Con quién estás de acuerdo, con Félix o con Ana? ¿Por qué?

5. ¿Crees que es mejor para un niño criarse en una familia numerosa o en una de dos hijos? ¿Por qué?

6. ¿Qué opinas de la situación de un hijo único? ¿Qué ventajas o desventajas tiene?

7. ¿Qué oportunidades que tú no tuviste quieres darles a tus hijos?

Actividad 5   Entrevista: El buen carácter

1. ¿Qué características va a tener tu pareja? (¿Qué características valoras más en tu pareja?)

2. El 50 por ciento de los matrimonios en los Estados Unidos termina en divorcio. En tu opinión, ¿qué factores contribuyen al fracaso de tantos matrimonios?

3. ¿Qué características quieres que tengan tus amigos? ¿Cuál de estas cualidades son más importantes en los buenos amigos: la lealtad, la inteligencia, la comprensión o la ayuda incondicional? ¿Cuáles de estas cualidades les ofreces tú a tus amigos?

4. ¿Quiénes son más importantes en tu vida: tus amigos íntimos o los miembros de tu familia? ¿Por qué?

> **¡OJO!**
>
> Muchas familias hispanas se reúnen los domingos y los días de fiesta, aun en estos tiempos en que el cine, la televisión y las computadoras han cambiado muchas costumbres tradicionales. Los familiares comparten experiencias, cuentos, anécdotas. En estas reuniones todos se divierten juntos.

VENTANAS AL PASADO

Los logros de la mujer hispana

La situación de la mujer hispana en la sociedad ha cambiado mucho. Hoy la mujer participa **plenamente** en lo que antes era dominio exclusivo del hombre. Este progreso es evidente en todas las profesiones, incluso las que son tradicionalmente masculinas. Ahora la mujer está presente en los negocios, en el servicio militar, en la educación superior. Hay doctoras, ingenieras, arquitectas, abogadas, escritoras y grandes deportistas. En la política los logros son impresionantes: Violeta Chamorro fue presidenta de Nicaragua de 1990 a 1996, Mireya Moscoso gobernó Panamá desde 1999 a 2004 y María Teresa Fernández de la Vega es hoy vicepresidenta del gobierno español. En enero de 2006, el pueblo chileno **eligió** a Michelle Bachelet como presidenta, la primera mujer que logra ese **cargo** en Chile. Y en 2007, Cristina Fernández de Kirchner fue elegida presidenta de Argentina. Además, España y América Latina cuentan con un buen número de embajadoras, gobernadoras, **alcaldesas**, diputadas, ministras y senadoras.

No obstante, falta mucho para que exista una verdadera igualdad. La mujer no está ya relegada al trabajo doméstico, pero todavía no tiene las mismas prerrogativas y privilegios que tiene el hombre. Otro problema es que aun en países desarrollados como España, la mujer gana menos que el hombre. Sin embargo,

Michelle Bachelet, presidenta de Chile

VOCABULARIO ÚTIL

los logros	*achievements*
plenamente	*fully*
eligió	*elected*
el cargo	*post*
la alcaldesa	*female mayor*
No obstante	*Nevertheless*

(Continúa)

si vemos esta situación de manera global, tanto los logros como las dificultades de la mujer hispana son similares a las de sus hermanas en todo el mundo.

Comprensión

1. Mencione cinco mujeres hispanas en el mundo de la política y el país de cada una.
2. ¿Qué problemas hay todavía respecto a la igualdad entre los hombres y las mujeres?

Actividad 6 Del mundo hispano: Los recuerdos familiares

Trabaje con un compañero / una compañera. Lean el poema en voz alta, alternando estrofas. Luego háganse las preguntas que siguen.

«Las canciones de mi abuela»,
por Francisco Alarcón
(del libro *Jitomates risueños*)

compartían
el ritmo
de la lavadora

transformaban
la cocina
en una pista de baile[1]

consolaban
las sillas
patas arriba[2]

alegraban
los retratos colgados[3]
de la familia

arrullaban[4]
las sábanas[5]
en el tendedero[6]

les daban sabor
a los frijoles
de olla[7]

las canciones
que cantaba
mi abuela

eran capaces[8]
de hacer salir
a las estrellas

convertir
a mi abuela
en una joven

que de nuevo
iba por agua
al río

y hacerla
reír y llorar
a la vez

[1]pista... *dance floor* [2]patas... *placed upside down* [3]retratos... *hanging portraits* [4]*lulled to sleep* [5]*sheets* [6]*clothesline* [7]*cooking pot* [8]*capable*

1. ¿Dónde estaba la abuela cuando el poeta la recuerda en este poema?
2. ¿Qué efecto tenían las canciones de la abuela en la cocina? (Por ejemplo, las canciones de la abuela les daban sabor a los frijoles.)
3. ¿Qué otros efectos mágicos tenían las canciones de la abuela?
4. Mencione los quehaceres domésticos que hacía la abuela mientras cantaba.
5. ¿Por qué las canciones convertían a la abuela en una joven?

Ahora comparta con su compañero/a algunos de sus buenos recuerdos de un abuelo, una abuela, un(a) tío/a o su madre o padre.

Me acuerdo que mi *abuela* siempre...
Nunca voy a olvidar a mi *tío*, porque...
Mi *madre* era *la mujer* más...

Enlace a la literatura

«Kinsey Report No. 6», por Rosario Castellanos

Selección de su libro *Poesía no eres tú: Obra poética* (*1948–1971*)

Rosario Castellanos (1925–1974) fue una escritora mexicana de una obra muy rica y diversa. Castellanos recibió varios premios prestigiosos. Además de escritora, fue profesora y embajadora de México en Israel. Entre sus publicaciones se destacan la novela *Oficio de tinieblas* (1962) y el libro de poemas *Álbum de familia* (1971). En el interesante poema aquí incluido, habla una mujer que sueña con un «príncipe azul».

Kinsey Report No. 6

Señorita. Sí, insisto, Señorita.

Soy joven. Dicen que no fea. Carácter
llevadero.[1] Y un día
vendrá el Príncipe Azul,[2] porque se lo he rogado[3]
como un milagro[4] a San Antonio.[5] Entonces
vamos a ser felices. Enamorados siempre.

¡Qué importa la pobreza! Y si es borracho[6]
lo quitaré del vicio. Si es un mujeriego[7]
yo voy a mantenerme siempre tan atractiva,
tan atenta a sus gustos, tan buena ama de casa,
tan prolífica madre
y tan extraordinaria cocinera
que se volverá fiel[8] como premio a mis méritos
entre los que, el mayor, es la paciencia.

Lo mismo que mis padres y los de mi marido
celebraremos nuestras bodas de oro
con gran misa solemne.

No, no he tenido novio. No, ninguno
todavía. Mañana.

Actividad creativa: Carta a la señorita

En este poema hay una señorita que se describe a sí misma y describe su deseo de encontrar un «príncipe azul». Esta mujer quiere un matrimonio tradicional. ¿Qué le parecen a usted estos deseos? Imagínese que puede responder a la señorita del poema. Escríbale una carta breve dándole su opinión.

[1]*easygoing* [2]Príncipe... *Prince Charming* [3]se... *I have prayed for it* [4]*miracle* [5]santo que ayuda a las mujeres a encontrar esposo [6]*drunk* [7]*womanizer* [8]*faithful*

Las instrucciones y los mandatos

✴ **Lea Gramática 14.3.**

Los mandatos de los vecinos mexicanos

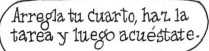

Actividad 7 **Identificaciones: Mandatos para Ernestito**

Si usted piensa un poco en su niñez, va a recordar que los niños pasan mucho tiempo escuchando órdenes. Ernestito tiene 8 años. ¿Quién le da los siguientes mandatos: la prima, la madre o la maestra?

	LA PRIMA	LA MADRE	LA MAESTRA
1. Haz la tarea antes de acostarte.	☐	☐	☐
2. Entrega la tarea a tiempo.	☐	☐	☐
3. Sal de mi cuarto.	☐	☐	☐
4. No toques mi muñeca.	☐	☐	☐
5. No grites; estoy hablando por teléfono.	☐	☐	☐
6. No escribas en tu pupitre.	☐	☐	☐
7. Juega conmigo, por favor.	☐	☐	☐
8. No me jales el pelo.	☐	☐	☐
9. Escribe las respuestas en la pizarra.	☐	☐	☐
10. Báñate y lávate los dientes.	☐	☐	☐

Actividad 8 Del mundo hispano: Consejos del veterinario

Lea esta columna y luego empareje a las amas con las recomendaciones del veterinario.

Consejos del veterinario

problema bacteriano o de hongos. Llévala al veterinario para que le haga un cultivo.

■ *Cambié a mi tortuga de hábitat y desde entonces casi ha dejado de comer, incluso después de regresarla a su lugar. ¿Por qué?*
Patricia Pidrahita
Las tortugas tienen menos apetito ahora porque están medio invernando. Vigila la temperatura (22º y 28º) y si pasado un tiempo no reacciona llévala al veterinario.

■ *Me gustaría saber por qué no crían mis dos parejas de periquitos.*
Rosario Pérez
Observa qué parejas se llevan mejor y júntalos en época de cría -primavera- en las mejores condiciones: un nido, tranquilidad, buena temperatura etc. Los periquitos son monógamos y tienen que "gustarse" para reproducirse.

■ *Mi perra de 13 años se fracturó la cadera, ¿debo sacrificarla?*
Ma. del Pilar Ansa
Depende de la fractura y su reparación. En principio es operable, pero hay que estudiar los riesgos de una operación en un animal tan mayor.

■ *A mi gata le salieron unas heridas, con caída de pelo, alrededor del cuello, ¿qué le pasa?*
Marisol Briviesca
Seguramente se trata de un

ENVIA TUS CARTAS A:
"Consejos del Veterinario" Revista **Clara**, Mier y Pesado 126, Col. del Valle. C.P. 03100.

1. al ama de la perra
2. al ama de los periquitos
3. al ama de la tortuga
4. al ama de la gata

a. «Cuida bien la temperatura.»
b. «Llévala al veterinario.»
c. «Obsérvalos bien. Si se llevan bien, ponlos juntos.»
d. «Opérale sólo si no hay muchos riesgos.»

Ahora, trabaje con un compañero / una compañera para inventar uno o dos problemas más que suelen tener los amos de las mascotas. Léanselos al resto de la clase para que los demás estudiantes respondan con unas recomendaciones lógicas.

Actividad 9 Descripción de dibujos: Mandatos para los muchachos Saucedo

Interprete los mandatos que sus padres y maestros les dan a Amanda, a Guillermo y a Ernestito.

Actividad 10 Intercambios: Consejos para los amigos

Con un compañero / una compañera, piensen en dos o tres buenos consejos para las siguientes personas. Luego, coméntenlos con la clase.

1. Un compañero: siempre llega tarde a clase.
2. Una estudiante en su clase de español: quiere sacar buenas notas.
3. Su hermana menor: tiene muchos problemas con sus padres; usted no fue un «ángel», pero nunca tuvo problemas con ellos.
4. Un amigo: tiene una ex novia que a él ya no le gusta, pero ella es muy insistente.
5. Una amiga: va a salir con un chico a quien no conoce.
6. Su papá/mamá: está preocupado/a por el precio de la matrícula de la universidad.

Juguetes sencillos para los bebés

Los bebés tratan de imitar todas las actividades que observan. Como ven a sus padres «jugando» con varios artículos domésticos, muchas veces ellos prefieren éstos a los juguetes caros. A continuación unas sugerencias para los bebés de 5 a 15 meses:

• Pelota de playa

• Sombreros
• Cucharas de plástico para medir
• Cucharas de madera
• Vasijas de plástico de varios tamaños y colores
• Botellas de plástico vacías
• Cartones de huevos
• Envases de plástico con etiquetas de colores y objetos que puedan colocar adentro

Las órdenes, los consejos y las sugerencias

✳ **Lea Gramática 14.4.**

Los consejos

Es necesario que terminemos este proyecto hoy.

Les prohíbo que se casen tan jóvenes.

Te recomiendo que no compres un coche deportivo.

Espero que recibas buenas notas este año.

Les ruego que no hagan tanto ruido. Estoy trabajando.

No tengo ganas... ¡Que los lave Amanda!

Actividad 11   Conversación: Consejos para una vida feliz

¿Qué importancia tienen estos consejos para tener una vida feliz?

> Para vivir feliz, es indispensable que uno... porque...
> es importante que uno... porque...
> no es necesario que uno... porque...

1. tenga paciencia
2. cuide su salud
3. visite a la familia y a los amigos con frecuencia
4. trabaje por el gusto de trabajar y no solamente para ganar dinero
5. duerma ocho horas diariamente
6. se case con una persona físicamente atractiva
7. no abuse de las drogas

© Joaquín Salvador Lavado, QUINO, Toda Mafalda, Ediciones de La Flor, 1993

Actividad 12   Descripción de dibujos: ¿Qué les aconseja?

¿Qué les aconseja usted a estos compañeros de la clase de la profesora Martínez?

MODELO: Le aconsejo / Le recomiendo *que llegue a clase a tiempo.*

Actividad 13   Entrevista: **Los consejos**

1. ¿Qué le aconsejas a un estudiante que no tiene dinero para comprar los libros para las clases de la universidad, pero va a comprar un coche nuevo? ¿Por qué?
2. ¿Qué le recomiendas a una estudiante de 18 años que quiere casarse en vez de seguir sus estudios? ¿Por qué?
3. ¿Qué le sugieres a un amigo que quiere dejar de fumar?
4. Un profesor está enojado porque los estudiantes siempre llegan tarde a clase. ¿Qué le recomiendas al profesor?
5. Un amigo tiene ya seis hijas, pero quiere un varón. ¿Qué le aconsejas? ¿Por qué?

La crianza y el comportamiento

✳ **Lea Gramática 14.5.**

Actividad 14 Asociaciones: Problemas y consejos

Trabaje con un compañero / una compañera para emparejar los deseos de los padres con los consejos del / de la pediatra. Después, inventen otros problemas y otras soluciones.

MODELO: —No queremos que nuestros hijos sean racistas.

—Les recomiendo que nunca hagan comentarios racistas delante de ellos.

LOS PADRES

1. Queremos que nuestro hijo sepa leer bien.
2. Queremos que los niños aprendan a comer comidas variadas.
3. No queremos que nuestro hijo sea violento.
4. Nuestro hijo llora mucho. No queremos que llore sin motivo.
5. Nuestra hija atormenta a su hermanita menor.
6. En el kínder hay un niño que muerde a mi hija.
7. Mi hijo de 8 años se chupa el dedo constantemente.
8. ¿ ?

EL/LA PEDIATRA

a. Les aconsejo que hablen con la maestra inmediatamente.
b. Les recomiendo que no le permitan ver programas violentos en la televisión.
c. Es necesario que vean a un psiquiatra lo más pronto posible.
d. Les sugiero que hablen con su hija y le pregunten por qué es tan cruel con su hermana.
e. Les aconsejo que le compren muchos libros y que lo lleven a la biblioteca pública.
f. Es importante que preparen comidas variadas en casa y que cuando ustedes salgan a cenar, lleven a los niños.
g. Les sugiero que hablen con el niño y le pregunten qué le pasa.
h. ¿ ?

Actividad 15 Descripción de dibujos: La crianza de los niños

¿Qué les recomienda usted a estos niños y jóvenes?

MODELOS: Le aconsejo que *limpie su cuarto.*

Le mando que *recoja sus juguetes y sus libros.*

1. viernes por la noche
2.
3. martes por la noche
4. lunes por la tarde — ... pero Papá, no tengo tarea hoy.
5. Graciela, 16 años / Felipe, 24 años
6.

VENTANAS CULTURALES   Nuestra comunidad

El Ballet Folklórico de México: Un proyecto de familia

El Ballet Folklórico es un **festejo** de movimiento y música que incorpora la rica tradición cultural de México. En sus danzas se combinan rituales indígenas con episodios del pasado mexicano y elementos de un folclor muy diverso. Esta compañía de fama internacional fue fundada por la **coreógrafa** Amalia Hernández en 1952. Desde que murió Amalia en el año 2000, sus hijas Norma López y Viviana Hernández, como también su nieto, Salvador López, han logrado mantener vivo el arte de la fundadora. Norma es la directora artística de la compañía; Viviana dirige su escuela y Salvador es su director ejecutivo. Los tres han coreografeado parte del repertorio de Amalia, produciendo numerosas obras en el Palacio de Bellas Artes de la ciudad de México y haciendo giras internacionales.

El talento de Amalia Hernández es un valioso **legado** de la gran coreógrafa. Como dijo ella, la cultura de México está hecha con sangre indígena, africana y europea. Y esta riqueza multicultural siempre fue parte de las obras que Amalia producía. Sus descendientes **heredaron** la visión artística de Amalia, aunque ellos también reflejan la cultura mexicana del momento presente. Gracias a esta familia, el Ballet Folklórico de México seguirá representando a su país por muchos años.

VOCABULARIO ÚTIL

el festejo	*celebration*
la coreógrafa	*choreographer*
el legado	*legacy*
heredaron	*they inherited*

Comprensión

1. ¿Qué elementos se combinan en las danzas del Ballet Folklórico de México?
2. ¿Por qué se considera el Ballet Folklórico de México un proyecto de familia?

Actividad 16 Conversación: El comportamiento social de sus hijos

Imagínese que usted es la madre o el padre de un niño / una niña de 4 años. ¿Qué hace o dice usted en las siguientes situaciones?

1. Su hijo/a no quiere jugar con el hijo / la hija de un amigo que ha llegado de visita.
2. Su hijo/a le pregunta si de veras existe Papá Noel. Sólo faltan seis semanas para la Navidad.

Ahora su hijo tiene 14 años. ¿Qué hace o dice usted en estas situaciones?

3. Su hijo/a está enamorado/a y pasa entre 4 y 5 horas cada noche texteándose con el novio / la novia.
4. Su hijo/a quiere hacerse un tatuaje de su grupo musical favorito.

¡OJO!

En la cultura hispana la celebración más importante para las muchachas es la fiesta de los quince años, que también se conoce como «la fiesta rosa». Este festejo representa la transición entre la vida de una niña y el mundo de una mujer. La quinceañera[1] tradicional lleva un vestido blanco o color de rosa elegante. La chica va acompañada de catorce amigas, que son sus «damas», y catorce muchachos, los «chambelanes». El padre de la novia baila el primer vals con su hija, presentándola así en la sociedad. La música sigue hasta tarde en la noche, y nunca faltan la comida rica y los regalos para la quinceañera.

[1]*girl turning 15*

Una quinceañera linda: la fiesta de los quince años es una de las celebraciones más importantes en la vida de toda jovencita hispana; es el momento en que pasa de niña a mujer. En la fiesta la acompañan sus padres, padrinos, damas y chambelanes.

En resumen

De todo un poco

A continuación tiene las opiniones de dos expertos en el campo de la psicología infantil sobre el uso del castigo corporal. Lea sus opiniones y luego hágale preguntas a un compañero / una compañera.

DOCTOR FÉLIX LEDESMA LUNA, PSICÓLOGO DE LA UNIVERSIDAD DE SANTIAGO EN CHILE	DOCTORA NATALIA TEVEZ BELTRÉ, PEDIATRA DE MONTEVIDEO, URUGUAY
• La violencia física nunca resuelve el mal comportamiento de un niño. • El castigo[1] corporal[2] muchas veces provoca acciones violentas por parte del niño. • Le recomiendo que mande a su hijo/a a su cuarto hasta que los dos se hayan calmado y usted le pueda hablar lógicamente sobre sus acciones. • En vez de golpear a su hijo, prívele[3] de sus actividades o cosas favoritas. • Recuerde que el mal comportamiento de su hijo siempre debe tener consecuencias; los niños quieren que los padres le pongan límites a su comportamiento.	• A veces es lo único que le hace poner atención al niño. • Les recomiendo a los padres que no les peguen[4] a sus hijos nunca en un momento de enojo; esperen hasta sentirse calmados. • Golpee[5] únicamente en las nalgas, nunca en las piernas, en la cabeza o en la espalda. • Después de la nalgada,[6] le aconsejo que mande a su hijo/a directamente a su cuarto para que piense en lo que él/ella hizo. • Después de una media hora, le sugiero que hable con su hijo y que le repita sus expectativas para el comportamiento de él/ella.

[1]punishment [2]physical [3]deprive him/her [4]hit [5]Strike [6]spanking

Preguntas sobre la lectura

1. ¿Dónde y cuándo dice la doctora Tevez que se debe de golpear al niño?
2. ¿Qué nos recomienda el doctor Ledesma en vez de las nalgadas?
3. ¿Qué nos aconseja la doctora Tevez para después de las nalgadas?
4. Según el doctor Ledesma, ¿es mejor no hacerle caso al niño cuando no se comporta bien?

Preguntas personales

1. ¿Con cuál de los dos expertos estás de acuerdo?
2. De niño/a, ¿te daban nalgadas tus padres?
3. ¿Golpeas a tus hijos? Si no tienes hijos ahora, ¿piensas golpear a tus hijos cuando los tengas?
4. ¿Estás de acuerdo con que la violencia física de parte de los padres provoca acciones violentas en los niños?

¡Dígalo por escrito!

Cartas a la pediatra Elsa Ríos

Lea las dos cartas que ha recibido la doctora Ríos. Luego, trabaje solo/a o con un compañero / una compañera o con un grupo. Haga(n) el papel de la pediatra y conteste(n) una de las cartas de los padres, dándoles consejos para resolver su problema. Recuerde(n) que debe(n) usar el subjuntivo después de frases como **le(s) recomiendo que, le(s) sugiero que, le(s) aconsejo que; es importante que, es necesario que.**

1.

Querida doctora Ríos:

Mi hijo Toño tiene cinco años. Mi esposo y yo creíamos que iba a ser hijo único pero, para nuestra sorpresa, estoy embarazada. Últimamente Toño, que antes era un niño alegre y obediente, literalmente un ángel, se ha vuelto un niño egoísta que siempre está de mal humor y llora por nada. ¿Qué podemos hacer para que Toño sea nuestro angelito otra vez?

Padres preocupados

2.

Estimada doctora Ríos:

¡Por favor ayúdenos! Mi esposo y yo ya no sabemos qué hacer. Tenemos dos hijas, una de seis años y una de cinco años. Se parecen mucho físicamente pero su personalidad es 100 por ciento distinta. Lilia, la de seis años, es una niña callada y tímida, pero obediente y estudiosa. Sus maestros la quieren mucho y siempre la ponen de ejemplo.

Su hermana Clarita es todo lo opuesto, sobre todo en la escuela. Todos los días recibimos quejas. En la escuela disfruta peleando con todos los niños y en casa atormenta a Lilia. Ya estamos cansados de decirle que debe ser como su hermanita. Ella sólo se enoja más y dice que preferimos a Lilia, que a ella no la queremos. Nada es eficaz: ni regaños ni castigos. ¿Qué nos aconseja? ¿Cómo podemos resolver este problema tan tremendo?

Padres frustrados y tristes

¡Cuéntenos usted!

Cuéntenos sobre un pariente con quien usted no se lleva muy bien. ¿Cuál es su parentesco? ¿Cómo se llama? ¿Dónde vive? ¿Cuántos años tiene? ¿Cómo es? ¿Por qué no se llevan bien?

 Conexión a la comunidad

Ofrézcase de voluntario/a en una escuela primaria o una guardería infantil a la cual asisten muchos niños de habla hispana. Léales un cuento en español o ayúdeles con algún proyecto.

LECTURA

Los refranes

Los refranes son una parte esencial de todo idioma. El origen de muchas de estas expresiones se encuentra en la literatura y el folclor. Estas frases populares expresan la actitud de los seres humanos hacia la vida y reflejan su cultura. Cuando una persona tiene un dilema difícil de resolver, por ejemplo, decimos que está «entre la **espada** y la pared». Si alguien ofrece su opinión abiertamente, con honestidad, esa persona llama «al pan, pan y al vino, vino»; o sea, que expresa la verdad. Y cuando se dice que una persona «pasó a mejor vida», quiere decir que murió.

La gente que se levanta muy temprano, tiene buena suerte. La razón es que «al que **madruga,** Dios lo ayuda». Si usted se enfrenta a una situación misteriosa, o si piensa que alguien **oculta** algo, puede comentar que «hay gato encerrado». Cuando una persona tiene un problema pero no **se da cuenta** de que lo tiene, entonces el problema no existe. Porque «ojos que no ven, corazón que no siente». ¿Es verdad que las cosas que no vemos no pueden afectarnos?

Muchos refranes expresan una **sabiduría** popular. Los siguientes **dichos,** por ejemplo, ofrecen algún tipo de consejo. Algunos son muy útiles.

«Más vale solo que mal acompañado»: es mejor estar solo que tener amigos malos. «Hay que consultarlo con la almohada»: es necesario pensarlo bien; siempre es mejor considerar las decisiones importantes y los problemas con calma, cuando uno se acuesta.

«Perro que **ladra** no **muerde**»: esto se dice de alguien que **amenaza** mucho, pero no **cumple** sus amenazas; es decir, que habla pero no hace nada.

«Más vale pájaro en mano que cien volando»: lo más seguro es lo que tiene ahora, no importa que sea poco; debemos estar contentos con lo que tenemos.

«El martes, ni te cases ni **te embarques**»: el martes es un día de mala suerte, como el viernes 13 en los Estados Unidos; no se debe hacer nada importante ese día.

«Más sabe el **diablo** por viejo que por diablo»: escuche los consejos de las personas mayores; éstas tienen mucha experiencia del mundo.

(Continúa)

VOCABULARIO ÚTIL

la espada	*sword*
madruga	*wakes up early*
oculta	*is hiding*
se da cuenta	*realizes*
la sabiduría	*wisdom*
los dichos	*sayings*
ladra	*barks*
muerde	*bites*
amenaza	*threatens*
cumple	*follows through*
te embarques	*embark on a journey*
el diablo	*the devil*
la riqueza	*wealth*
se arriesga	*takes a chance*
el desafío	*challenge*

«Entre más tienes, más quieres»: este refrán nos aconseja que no vivamos sólo para acumular **riqueza,** pues la ambición puede convertirse en una adicción destructiva.

«Quien no **se arriesga,** no gana»: si queremos triunfar en la vida, debemos buscar y aceptar los **desafíos.** Éste es uno de los consejos más útiles, ¿no cree usted?

Comprensión

Busque el equivalente en inglés de cada refrán.

1. ___d___ Cada loco con su tema.
2. ___a___ Al que le venga el saco, que se lo ponga.
3. ___b___ Dime con quién andas y te diré quién eres.
4. ___c___ Agua que no has de beber, déjala correr.
5. ___h___ Aunque la mona se vista de seda, mona se queda.
6. ___i___ Estar entre la espada y la pared.
7. ___f___ La mentira tiene las piernas cortas.
8. ___e___ Perro que ladra, no muerde.
9. ___g___ Llamar al pan, pan y al vino, vino.

a. *If the shoe fits, wear it.*
b. *Birds of a feather flock together.*
c. *Live and let live.*
d. *To each his own.*
e. *His bark is worse than his bite.*
f. *Oh, what a tangled web we weave . . .*
g. *Call a spade a spade.*
h. *You can't make a silk purse out of a sow's ear.*
i. *Between a rock and a hard place.*

Un paso más... ¡a escribir!

Imagínese que usted va a enseñarle un refrán o expresión coloquial de su idioma a un estudiante hispano o una estudiante hispana. Escriba un diálogo explicándole a esa persona lo que significa el refrán. Luego trate de darle un equivalente en español. Si quiere, puede ilustrar su refrán con un dibujo.

LECTURA

«Lazarillo y el ciego» Selección de *Lazarillo de Tormes* (1554)

Un campesino le dio al ciego un **racimo** de uvas y el ciego decidió compartirlas conmigo. Nos sentamos entonces a disfrutar del **banquete.** ¡Teníamos tanta hambre! Pero antes de empezar a comer, mi **amo** me dijo:

—Quiero que los dos nos comamos este racimo y que tú comas tantas uvas como yo. Tú tomarás una y yo otra. Pero debes prometerme que no vas a tomar más de una uva cada vez. Yo voy a hacer lo mismo, hasta que acabemos el

En resumen :: **495**

racimo y de esa manera no habrá **engaño**.

Hecho así el acuerdo, comenzamos a comer. Pero entonces el ciego empezó a tomar uvas **de dos en dos**. Como vi que él rompía nuestro **trato**, decidí hacer lo mismo que él. Pero no me contenté con tomar sólo dos uvas. ¡Empecé a tomarlas de tres en tres y a veces hasta más!

Cuando terminamos el racimo, el ciego levantó su **bastón** y, moviendo la cabeza, dijo:

—Lázaro, ¡**me has engañado**!

—¿Yo? ¡No, señor! —le respondí.

—Estoy seguro que tomaste tres uvas cada vez. ¡Y a veces más!

—No es verdad. ¿Por qué sospecha eso? —le pregunté.

Y el ciego **astuto** respondió:

—¿Sabes cómo lo sé? Porque cuando yo tomaba dos, tú no decías nada.

VOCABULARIO ÚTIL	
el pícaro	*rogue*
el ciego	*blind man*
el racimo	*bunch*
el banquete	*feast*
el amo	*master*
el engaño	*trick*
de dos en dos	*by twos*
el trato	*agreement*
el bastón	*cane*
¡me has engañado!	*you deceived me!*
astuto	*astute, clever*

Comprensión

1. ¿En qué consiste el acuerdo que propone el ciego?
2. ¿Quién rompió el acuerdo primero?
3. ¿Por qué empezó Lazarillo a tomar varias uvas a la vez?

Un paso más... ¡a escribir!

A. Narre el episodio tomando en cuenta los siguientes pasos:

1. el racimo de uvas
2. el trato (o acuerdo)
3. el banquete
4. el engaño

B. Escriba otro final para este episodio de *Lazarillo de Tormes* usando las siguientes preguntas como guía.

1. ¿Qué hace el ciego después de saber que Lazarillo lo engañó?
2. ¿Cómo reacciona Lazarillo?
3. ¿Serán amigos los dos después de este episodio?

Vea el **Resumen cultural** en este capítulo del *Cuaderno de actividades*.

Vocabulario

La familia, las amistades y el matrimonio

Family, Friends, and Marriage

el ahijado / la ahijada	godson/goddaughter
el amigo íntimo / la amiga íntima	close friend
la amistad	friendship
las arras	*coins given by a bridegroom to a bride as a token of his ability to provide*
el bautizo	baptism
el bisabuelo / la bisabuela	great-grandfather/ great-grandmother
la boda	wedding
el brindis	toast (drink or speech)
el compadre / la comadre	*what a child's parents and godparents call each other*
el cura	priest
el enlace	union, marriage; link
estar comprometido/a	to be engaged
el lazo	tie, bond
la luna de miel	honeymoon
la madrina	godmother; bridesmaid
la novia	bride
el noviazgo	courtship; engagement
el novio	groom
el padrino	godfather; best man in wedding
la velación	*ceremonial covering of the bride and groom with a veil during the nuptial mass*

REPASO: el hermanastro / la hermanastra, el hijo único / la hija única, la madrastra, los nietos, el padrastro, los primos, los sobrinos, los tíos

Acciones recíprocas (verbos)

Reciprocal Actions (Verbs)

abrazarse	to hug each other
besarse	to kiss each other
conocerse	to meet each other
darse la mano	to shake hands with each other
echarse de menos	to miss each other
enamorarse	to fall in love (with each other)
quererse (ie)	to love each other

PALABRAS SEMEJANTES: comunicarse, divorciarse, insultarse, textearse
REPASO: ayudarse, casarse, comprenderse, enojarse, gritarse, parecerse, pedirse perdón, pelearse

Los verbos

Verbs

aconsejar	to advise
acordarse (de) (ue)	to remember (*something/ someone*)
atormentar	to torment
bajarse	to get down
bautizar	to baptize
borrar	to erase
chuparse el dedo	to suck one's thumb (*finger*)
comenzar (ie)	to begin, commence
comportarse	to behave
criarse	to be brought up; to grow up
dejar de (+ *infin.*)	to stop (*doing something*)
enviar	to send
estar dispuesto/a a (+ *infin.*)	to be willing (*to do something*)
faltar... para...	The . . . is in . . .
Faltan tres días para la boda	The wedding is in three days
golpear	to beat, hit
hacer caso a	to pay attention to
jalar	to pull
mandar	to command; to order
opinar	to have an opinion about
pegar	to hit
poner atención	to pay attention, be alert
rogar (ue)	to beg
sacudir	to dust; to shake off
sentarse (ie)	to sit down, take a seat
soler (ue) (+ *infin.*)	to be accustomed to (*doing something*)
tener lugar	to take place
valorar	to value

PALABRAS SEMEJANTES: abusar de, calmarse, conservar, contribuir, existir, interpretar, prohibir, provocar, repetir, respetar
REPASO: compartir, consultar, cuidar, dirigir, entregar, estar de acuerdo, morir, olvidar, recomendar, recordar (ue), sugerir

Las personas

People

el amo / el ama	master/mistress
(el) Papá Noel	Santa Claus
el/la pediatra	pediatrician
el recién nacido / la recién nacida	newborn baby
el varón	male infant, male child

PALABRAS SEMEJANTES: el/la adolescente, el ángel

Los sustantivos

Nouns

el bienestar	well-being
el cariño	love
el castigo	punishment
el comportamiento	behavior
la comprensión	understanding, compassion
la crianza	upbringing
la cualidad	quality, trait
el enojo	anger
los estudios	studies
la expectativa	expectation
el fracaso	failure
el gasto	expense, waste
la lealtad	loyalty
la matrícula	(school) registration fees
el riesgo	risk
el ruido	noise
el sentido del humor	sense of humor
la sugerencia	suggestion
el tatuaje	tattoo
en voz (alta/baja)	in a (loud/soft) voice

PALABRAS SEMEJANTES: la acción, el carácter, la característica, el comentario, el divorcio, la droga, el efecto, el factor, la inteligencia, el kínder, el límite, el momento, el motivo, la oportunidad, las órdenes, el por ciento, el proyecto, las relaciones, el símbolo, la violencia

Los adjetivos

Adjectives

infantil	relating to children or childhood
recién casado/a	newlywed
tantos/as	so many

PALABRAS SEMEJANTES: cruel, incondicional, insistente, numeroso/a, racista, responsable, social

Los adverbios

Adverbs

ahora mismo	right now
únicamente	solely

PALABRAS SEMEJANTES: constantemente, directamente, físicamente

Frases impersonales

Impersonal Expressions

Es importante que... (+ *subjunctive*)	It's important that . . .
Es indispensable que... (+ *subjunctive*)	It's absolutely necessary that . . .
Es mejor que... (+ *subjunctive*)	It is better that . . .

REPASO: Es necesario que... (+ *subjunctive*), Es recomendable que... (+ *subjunctive*)

Palabras y expresiones útiles

Useful Words and Expressions

delante de	in front of, in the presence of
entre semana	on weekdays, during the week
por ejemplo	for example
por eso	for that reason, therefore

Gramática y ejercicios

¿RECUERDA?

In **Gramática 9.1** you saw how two common reflexive verbs, **parecerse** and **llevarse,** are used to express reciprocal actions, that is, actions *to each other.* Review that section now, if necessary.

14.1 Expressing *each other:* Reciprocal Pronouns

Gramática ilustrada

Se besaron.

Se abrazaron.

Se dieron la mano.

Se despidieron.

reciprocal (*each other*) = (same form as reflexive; see **Gramática 4.3**)

$$\left.\begin{array}{l} \textbf{nos} \\ \textbf{os} \\ \textbf{se} \end{array}\right\} + \text{verb}$$

Se besaron. (*They kissed each other.*)
Nos escribimos. (*We write [to] each other.*)

Reciprocal actions are expressed in Spanish with reflexive pronouns.

Los novios **se abrazaron** y luego **se besaron.**	*The bride and groom embraced (each other) and then kissed (each other).*
Nos vemos mañana en el bautizo de tu sobrino.	*We'll see each other tomorrow at the christening of your nephew.*

Context usually indicates whether the pronoun is reflexive (*self*) or reciprocal (*each other*).

Tenemos que **vestirnos** antes de ir a la boda.	*We have to get dressed before going to the wedding.*
Don Eduardo y don Anselmo **se reconocieron** en seguida y **se dieron** la mano.	*Don Eduardo and don Anselmo recognized each other at once and shook hands with each other.*

Some common reciprocal verbs:

abrazarse	darse la mano	quererse
besarse	divorciarse	reconocerse
comprenderse	mirarse	respetarse
conocerse	parecerse	verse

Ejercicio 1

Exprese las acciones recíprocas según el modelo.

MODELO: Yo quiero a mi esposo y mi esposo me quiere mucho también. →
Mi esposo y yo *nos queremos* mucho.

1. El señor Ruiz llamó a su suegra por teléfono y su suegra lo llamó
   a él también.
2. Mi ahijada me escribe a mí y yo le escribo a ella a menudo.
3. Amanda habla con su novio y él habla con Amanda todos los días.
4. Mi madre respeta mucho a mi padre y mi padre respeta mucho a
   mi madre.
5. El abuelo de Guillermo me conoce y yo lo conozco a él muy bien.

In **Ejercicio 1,** note:
quererse = *to love each other*

14.2 Describing: *ser* and *estar*

ser = inherent quality
estar = transitory state

¿Quién es... ?
(*Who is . . . ?*)

¿Dónde está... ?
(*Where is . . .* [*a person or thing*]*?*)

¿Dónde es... ?
(*Where is . . .* [*an event*]*?*)

¿Cómo es?
(*What is* [*someone or something*] *like?*)

¿Cómo está?
(*How is* [*someone or something*] *feeling?*)

Gramática ilustrada

1. Paula Saucedo es una mujer muy activa.
2. Esta semana Paula tuvo que trabajar horas
   extra y hoy está muy cansada.

1. Ernesto es un hombre muy feliz.
2. Hoy está deprimido porque no le aumentaron
   el sueldo.

A. To identify someone or something, use the verb **ser** followed by a noun.

—¿Quién **es** ese **muchacho**?	—*Who is that guy?*
—Es **Guillermo,** el primo de Marisa.	—*That's Guillermo, Marisa's cousin.*
—¿Y este vestido?	—*And this dress?*
—**Es** el **vestido** de novia que llevó mi abuelita.	—*It's the wedding dress that my grandmother wore.*

B. To form the progressive tenses, use **estar** with a present participle.

—¿Qué **estaban haciendo** el padrino y la madrina?	—*What were the best man and maid of honor doing?*
—**Estaban saludando** a los invitados que llegaban.	—*They were greeting the guests who were arriving.*

C. Use the verb **estar** to give the location of people or things.

—¿Dónde **está** el novio?	—*Where is the groom?*
—Creo que **está** en el baño.	—*I think he is in the bathroom.*

Use the verb **ser** to tell the location of an event.

—¿Dónde va a **ser** la ceremonia?	—*Where is the ceremony going to be (held)?*
—En la capilla.	—*In the chapel.*
—¿Dónde **es** la conferencia?	—*Where is the lecture?*
—En el salón 450.	—*In room 450.*

D. Although **ser** and **estar** are both used with adjectives to describe nouns, they are used in different situations. An adjective with **ser** tells what someone or something is like.

La novia **es** muy hermosa. **Es** alta, de pelo negro y **es** joven.	*The bride is very beautiful. She is tall, has black hair, and is young.*

An adjective with **estar** describes the condition of someone or something at a particular moment.

> **La clase de historia normalmente es aburrida, pero hoy está interesante.**
> *History class is usually boring, but today it's interesting.*

—¿Cómo **está** la novia?	—*How is the bride?*
—Ahora mismo **está** un poco nerviosa y cansada.	—*Right now she's a bit nervous and tired.*

In the following example, note that **ser** and **estar** can convey different meanings even when used with the same adjective. **Ser** emphasizes identification or normal characteristics; **estar** emphasizes the state of someone or something at a certain point in time.

—¿**Es** delgada la madre de la novia?	—*Is the bride's mother slender?*
—Sí, pero hoy parece que **está** aún más delgada porque estuvo enferma hace poco.	—*Yes, but today she looks even more slender because she was ill a short time ago.*

By using **estar** with an adjective usually associated with **ser,** we can emphasize how something is or looks *right now,* rather than how it is normally. Thus, the choice between **ser** + adjective and **estar** + adjective emphasizes the difference between the norm and variation from the norm.

Te juro que **generalmente** el mar aquí **es** tranquilo y limpio y las olas **son** pequeñas. Pero **hoy está** todo muy feo. Las olas **están** muy grandes y el mar **está** muy sucio por la tormenta de anoche.	*I swear to you that the ocean here is usually calm and clear, and the waves are small. But today everything is very ugly. The waves are very large, and the ocean is dirty due to last night's storm.*

Here are some other phrases that emphasize the differences in meaning between **ser** and **estar** with adjectives.

es bonito / está bonito	*is pretty / looks pretty*
es generoso / está generoso	*is generous / is being generous*
es nervioso / está nervioso	*is a nervous person / is nervous now*

In a few cases, the meaning of the adjective is quite different depending on whether it is used with **ser** or **estar.**

es listo / está listo	*is clever / is ready*
es aburrido / está aburrido	*is boring / is bored*
es verde / está verde	*is green / looks green; is unripe*

ser	estar
Identification	*Present Progressive*
Es hombre.	Está comiendo.
Location of Event	*Location of People, Things*
El baile es aquí.	El muchacho está aquí.
Description of Norm	*Description of State*
Es bonita.	Está enferma.

Ser:
- *Identification* = **ser** + noun
Es abogado.
Son los compadres de Ernesto.
- *Description* = **ser** + adjective
Soy entusiasta.
Eran ricos.
- *Location of an event* = **ser** + location
¿Dónde es la conferencia?
Los conciertos son en el salón 459.

Estar:
- *Current condition of someone or something* = **estar** + adjective
¿Estás triste?
Estaban enojados.
- *To be doing something* = **estar** + present participle
Estoy navegando por Internet.
A las 4:00 estaban nadando.
- *Location of someone or something* = **estar** + location
¿Dónde está la carta?
Mis hijos están en casa de los abuelos.

Ejercicio 2

Don Anselmo está de mal humor hoy y no está de acuerdo con nada de lo que le dice don Eduardo.

MODELO: DON EDUARDO: Doña Rosita es una persona muy activa. →
          DON ANSELMO: Pues, no está muy activa hoy.

1. Paula es muy amable con todos.
2. El clima de aquí es algo frío.
3. Normalmente este programa es muy cómico.
4. En la Tienda Miraflores la ropa es muy cara.
5. Ernesto es muy eficiente en su trabajo.

Ejercicio 3

¿Ser o **estar?** Lea el contexto con mucho cuidado.

1. —¿Te gusta la clase de biología?
   —No, _____ una clase muy aburrida.
2. —¿Tienes hambre? ¿Quieres comer un poco de fruta?
   —Gracias, pero toda la fruta _____ verde. No voy a comerla porque no quiero enfermarme.
3. Voy a llegar tarde a mi clase de las 9:00. ¡Ya son las 8:49 y yo todavía no_____ listo/a!
4. Pablo _____ muy aburrido porque esta película _____ aburridísima. ¡Prefiere estudiar!
5. ¡Ay! Estas manzanas no están buenas. _____ manzanas rojas pero todavía _____ verdes.
6. Los estudiantes _____ muy listos, pero hoy todavía no _____ listos para el examen final; necesitan estudiar más.

14.3 Giving Direct Commands: Polite and Informal

Gramática ilustrada

A. Polite commands are used to give a direct order to someone you address with **usted**. The forms of the polite commands were introduced in **Gramática 11.1**. They are also the same as the **usted** form of the present subjunctive (see **Gramática 11.2** and **11.3**).

A review of polite (**usted**) commands

INFINITIVE	PRESENT (yo/usted)	COMMAND (usted)	COMMAND (ustedes)
hablar	hablo/habla	hable	hablen
vender	vendo/vende	venda	vendan
escribir	escribo/escribe	escriba	escriban

Remember that **-ar** verbs take «**e**» endings; **-er/-ir** verbs take «**a**» endings:

hablar → **hable**
vender → **venda**
escribir → **escriba**

B. Singular informal commands are given to people you address with **tú** rather than **usted**—for example, your classmates or close friends.

Esteban, **trae** algunas bebidas para la fiesta.

Nora, no **mandes** los libros ahora, por favor.

Esteban, bring some drinks for the party.

Nora, don't send the books now, please.

affirmative **tú** commands = he/she form of present indicative

Él/Ella/Usted *come.* (*He/She eats; You [pol. sing.] eat.*) *Come* (**tú**). (*Eat [inf. sing.].*)

Él/Ella/Usted *arregla* **los papeles.** (*He/She straightens up the papers; You [pol. sing.] straighten up the papers.*) *Arregla* (**tú**) **los papeles.** (*Straighten up the papers [inf. sing.].*)

C. If the singular informal command is affirmative, it is identical to the *he/she* form of the present indicative.

Nora, **busca** las palabras en el diccionario y después **escribe** las definiciones.

Alberto, **come** temprano porque después vamos a la discoteca.

Nora, look up the words in the dictionary and afterward write down the definitions.

Alberto, eat early because afterward we're going to the discotheque.

D. If the informal command is negative, add **-s** to the **usted** command form.

No hables con ella; habla con Esteban.

No comas tanto, Luis, y come más despacio.

Don't talk to her; talk to Esteban.

Don't eat so much, Luis, and eat more slowly.

E. Here is a summary of the singular informal command forms.

negative **tú** commands = **usted** command form + **-s**

hable [usted]
no hables [tú]

coma [usted]
no comas [tú]

pida [usted]
no pidas [tú]

venga [usted]
no vengas [tú]

-ar VERBS		-er/-ir VERBS	
(-a)	(-es)	(-e)	(-as)
habla	no hables	come	no comas
canta	no cantes	escribe	no escribas
estudia	no estudies	pide	no pidas

F. Some verbs have an irregular affirmative informal command form; these verbs still take the regular forms in the negative.

The affirmative **tú** command of some verbs is irregular, but the negative command follows normal command/subjunctive rules:

ven / no vengas
di / no digas
pon / no pongas

INFINITIVE	tú (+)	tú (−)	
decir	di	no digas	*say / don't say*
hacer	haz	no hagas	*do / don't do*
ir	ve	no vayas	*go / don't go*
poner	pon	no pongas	*put / don't put*
salir	sal	no salgas	*leave / don't leave*
ser	sé	no seas	*be / don't be*
tener	ten	no tengas	*have / don't have*
venir	ven	no vengas	*come / don't come*

Ven ahora; no **vengas** mañana.

Come now; don't come tomorrow.

Ponlo en tu cuarto; no lo **pongas** en la cocina.

Put it in your room; don't put it in the kitchen.

G. Affirmative **vosotros/as** commands are derived from the infinitive by changing the final **-r** to **-d**. Negative **vosotros/as** commands use the subjunctive.

affirmative **vosotros/as** commands = change final **-r** of infinitive to **-d**

hablar → hablad
decir → decid

negative **vosotros/as** commands = subjunctive

hablar → no habléis
decir → no digáis

INFINITIVE	vosotros/as (+)	vosotros/as (−)	
hablar	hablad	no habléis	*speak / don't speak*
comer	comed	no comáis	*eat / don't eat*
escribir	escribid	no escribáis	*write / don't write*
decir	decid	no digáis	*say / don't say*
ir	id	no vayáis	*go / don't go*
venir	venid	no vengáis	*come / don't come*

H. Here is a summary of the polite and informal command forms.* Note that with the exception of the affirmative **tú** and **vosotros/as** commands, all commands use subjunctive forms.

usted(es)	tú (−)	tú (+)	vosotros/as (−)	vosotros/as (+)
(no) hable(n)	no hables	habla	no habléis	hablad
(no) coma(n)	no comas	come	no comáis	comed
(no) escriba(n)	no escribas	escribe	no escribáis	escribid
(no) diga(n)	no digas	di	no digáis	decid
(no) ponga(n)	no pongas	pon	no pongáis	poned

---

*Affirmative **vos** commands drop the **-r** of the infinitive and add an accent to the last vowel: **hablá vos, comé vos, escribí vos, decí vos, vení vos.** Negative **vos** commands are the same as the **tú** subjunctive forms, but these too add an accent to the last vowel: **no hablés vos, no comás vos, no escribás vos, no digás vos, no vengás vos.**

Ejercicio 4

Éstos son algunos de los mandatos que Estela le dio a Ernestito durante el día. Complételos con **acuéstate, apaga, bájate, dile, habla, haz, lee, levántate, sal, ten, ve** o **ven.**

In **Ejercicio 4,** read the informal commands and fit them logically into the sentences. Each answer can be used only once.

1. _____ rápido porque es muy tarde.
2. _____ conmigo a tu cuarto ahora.
3. _____ cuidado al cruzar la calle.
4. _____ de la casa por un ratito.
5. _____ de ese árbol ahora mismo.
6. _____ con tu papá si quieres una bicicleta nueva.
7. _____ en tu cama y _____ la luz.
8. _____ adiós a tu abuelita.
9. _____ a la sala y _____ uno de tus libros.
10. _____ tu tarea ahora y luego puedes ver la televisión.

Ejercicio 5

Nora y Esteban están de compras en un mercado en Nuevo Laredo. Ponga los infinitivos en el mandato (**tú/usted**) apropiado para el contexto.

In **Ejercicio 5,** look at the drawings and decide for each situation whether to use a **tú** or an **usted** command and then write in the correct form.

MODELO: Ay, Esteban, no *compres* dulces, *come* fruta. (comprar/comer)

1. _____ nos dos especialidades de la casa, por favor. (traer) No nos _____ la cuenta ahora. (dar)

2. _____ me éste, por favor. (mostrar) ¿Cuánto cuesta? Cuesta mil pesos, señorita. ¡No me _____ ! (decir)

3. Momentito, _____ me aquí. (esperar) Nora, quiero ver aquellas chaquetas de cuero. No _____ a otra tienda. (irse)

4. _____ me el precio, por favor. (rebajar) No me lo _____ . (subir)

5. _____ mi nueva chaqueta, Nora. (mirar) ¡Qué ganga! No me _____ que gasté demasiado dinero. (decir)

14.4 Using Softened Commands: The Subjunctive Mood

Spanish has two present tenses: the present indicative and the present subjunctive. The present indicative is used to ask questions and make statements. As you saw in **Gramática 11.2** and **11.3,** in Spanish the present subjunctive is used after the verb **querer** in softened commands and after **cuando** in statements about the future.

Cuando llegues al aeropuerto, llámame.	*When you get to the airport, call me.*
—¿Qué **quiere** Ramón?	*—What does Ramón want?*
—Quiere que yo **vaya** con él al Baile de los Enamorados.	*—He wants me to go with him to the Valentine's Day Dance.*

Gramática ilustrada

A. Like Spanish, English has a present subjunctive, but because most of its forms are identical to the infinitive, many speakers never notice them. Only in the singular *he/she* form in English is there a difference between the present indicative and the present subjunctive. Note the indicative *goes* and the subjunctive *go* in these examples.

Did you know that John *goes* to football practice after class?
Is it necessary that John *go* to football practice after class?

B. As you learned in **Gramática 11.2** and **12.3,** it is possible to give softened commands in Spanish with verbs like **querer** (*to want*), **sugerir** (*to suggest*), **aconsejar** (*to advise*), **recomendar** (*to recommend*), **decir** (*to say*), and **pedir** (*to ask for*) plus a present subjunctive verb form.

Diego, **te aconsejo que no comas** tantos dulces.	*Diego, I advise you not to eat so many sweets.*

> The present subjunctive is used to give softened commands:
> **Quiero que me digas la verdad.** (*I want you to tell me the truth.*)
> **Les aconsejo que no lo compren.** (*I advise you not to buy it.*)

Such sentences consist of two parts, or clauses. The first clause contains a verb or a verb phrase indicating a desire, a recommendation, or a suggestion. The second begins with the connector **que** (*that*) and contains a verb in the subjunctive.

Other, similar sentences may contain a personal verb phrase like **espero que** (*I hope that*) or an impersonal one like **es necesario que** (*it is necessary that*).

Espero que no nos llame nadie esta noche.
I hope (that) nobody calls us tonight.
Es necesario que llegues a tiempo para el banquete.
It is necessary that you arrive on time for the banquet.

Here is a list of typical phrases, both personal and impersonal, that are used with the present subjunctive to give softened commands.

PERSONAL

aconsejar que	*to advise (that)*	permitir que	*to permit that*
decir que	*to tell, order (that)*	preferir (ie) que	*to prefer that*
dejar que	*to allow (that)*	prohibir que	*to prohibit that*
desear que	*to desire (that)*	querer (ie) que	*to want that*
esperar que	*to hope (that)*	recomendar (ie) que	*to recommend (that)*
exigir que	*to demand (that)*	rogar (ue) que	*to beg, plead that*
mandar que	*to command (that)*	sugerir (ie) que	*to suggest (that)*
pedir (i) que	*to ask, request that*		

IMPERSONAL

es importante que	*it is important that*
es imposible que	*it is impossible that*
es mejor que	*it is better that*
es necesario que	*it is necessary that*
es preferible que	*it is preferable that*

¡OJO!
You may wish to review the forms of the present subjunctive in **Gramática 11.2** and **11.3** before doing the exercises that follow.

Ejercicio 6

La profesora Martínez requiere la participación de todos sus alumnos. Siguiendo el modelo, diga lo que quiere la profesora.

MODELO: Le *pide* a Luis que *borre* la pizarra. (pedir/borrar)

1. Le _____ a Alberto que _____ a clase a tiempo. (rogar/llegar)
2. _____ que todos _____ buenas notas en el examen. (esperar/sacar)
3. _____ que Esteban y Nora _____ las preguntas. (desear/contestar)
4. Le _____ a Pablo _____ en voz alta. (sugerir/leer)
5. Nos _____ que (nosotros) le _____ la tarea a tiempo. (recomendar/entregar)

In **Ejercicio 6,** note that **rogar** is a **ue** verb and, like **aconsejar,** it takes an indirect object pronoun: **le ruego que.** Also remember spelling changes in **llegar, sacar,** and **entregar.**

In **Ejercicio 7,** item 4, be careful with pronoun placement.

Ejercicio 7

Estela Saucedo les hace sugerencias a varias personas.

MODELO: a Ernesto: prefiero que / lavar el coche →
Ernesto, prefiero que tú *laves* el coche.

1. a Guillermo: es mejor que / hacer la tarea
2. a Graciela: quiero que / hablar con Amanda
3. a Amanda: es necesario que / llamar a Graciela
4. a Clarisa: es muy importante que / quedarse en el patio
5. a Marisa: sugiero que / jugar con tu hermanita

In **Ejercicio 8,** write the correct verb form, indicative or subjunctive, and then pick a logical response or responses. Remember spelling changes in **dormir, jugar, sacar,** and **almorzar.**

Ejercicio 8

En las siguientes situaciones unas personas quieren que otras hagan algo. Primero, llene cada espacio en blanco con la forma correcta del verbo indicado. Luego, indique las opciones más lógicas. Siga el modelo.

MODELO: Todos los días mi mamá me pide que...
- (a.) *saque* la basura. (sacar)
- **b.** *beba* licor en la autopista. (beber)
- (c.) *haga* mi tarea. (hacer)
- **d.** *regrese* muy tarde de las fiestas. (regresar)

1. Les sugiero a mis compañeros de clase que...
   - **a.** _____ conmigo a la biblioteca. (ir)
   - **b.** _____ a clase mucho. (faltar)
   - **c.** _____ español en clase. (hablar)
   - **d.** me _____ las respuestas durante el examen. (dar)
2. El médico nos aconseja que...
   - **a.** _____ muchos cigarrillos. (fumar)
   - **b.** _____ ocho horas. (dormir)
   - **c.** _____ al psiquiatra todos los días. (consultar)
   - **d.** _____ más legumbres. (comer)
3. Ernesto y Estela les dicen a sus hijos que...
   - **a.** _____ en la calle. (jugar)
   - **b.** _____ sus recámaras. (limpiar)
   - **c.** _____ galletitas todo el día. (comer)
   - **d.** _____ televisión toda la tarde. (ver)
4. Es importante que...
   - **a.** yo le _____ un regalo bonito a mi novio/a. (hacer)
   - **b.** mi hermano me _____ hoy. (llamar)
   - **c.** mis padres me _____ con los gastos de la matrícula. (ayudar)
   - **d.** yo _____ muy buenas notas en la clase. (sacar)
5. Quiero que tú...
   - **a.** _____ conmigo en la cafetería. (almorzar)
   - **b.** _____ a mi casa a estudiar esta noche. (venir)
   - **c.** me _____ un mensaje electrónico. (escribir)
   - **d.** _____ en la Plaza Central. (dormir)

14.5 More Uses of the Subjunctive: Saying *Have someone else do it!*: *Que* + Subjunctive and Expressing *Let's . . .*

Grámatica ilustrada

A. To form the indirect command *let/have someone else do it*, omit the initial verb of the softened command and start the sentence with **que**.

Quiero que manejen con cuidado.
¡Que manejen con cuidado!

I want them to drive carefully.
Have them drive carefully!

Sugiero que lo termine Carmen.
¡Que lo termine Carmen!

I suggest that Carmen finish it.
Have/Let Carmen finish it!

You can also use this form to express good wishes. As before, the initial verb is omitted. For example, to a sick person you might say the following.

Deseo que te mejores pronto.
¡Que te mejores pronto!

I hope you get well soon.
Get well soon!

¿Bróculi? ¡Que lo coma Jorge!
Broccoli? Let George eat it!

Here are other common good wishes.

¡**Que tenga** un buen viaje!	*Have a good (safe) trip!*
¡**Que les vaya** bien!	*I hope everything goes well for you!*
¡**Que pasen** buenas noches!	*Have a nice evening!*
¡**Que pases** un buen día!	*Have a nice day!*
¡**Que duermas** bien!	*Sleep well!*
¡**Que vuelvan** pronto!	*Come back soon!*

Ojalá que todo salga bien.
I hope everything goes well.

B. The word **ojalá** derives from an old Arabic expression that meant *May Allah grant that . . .* Today the expression **Ojalá (que)...** means *I hope (that) . . .* and is used with the present subjunctive.

Ojalá (que) no llueva.	*I hope it doesn't rain.*
Ojalá (que) me quiera.	*I hope that she loves me.*

C. To express *Let's* (let's do some activity) in Spanish, use the first-person plural of the present subjunctive.

Preparemos la cena ahora.	*Let's fix dinner now.*
No pongamos música clásica.	*Let's not put on classical music.*

With the verb **ir** the present indicative (**Vamos**) is used to express *Let's go* and the present subjunctive is used to express the negative (**No vayamos**).

Vamos a andar en bicicleta.	*Let's go out bike riding.*
No vayamos a la conferencia hoy.	*Let's not go to the conference today.*

In **Ejercicio 9,** watch for correct pronoun placement. Remember spelling changes in **pagar, jugar,** and **recoger.**

Ejercicio 9

Estela está muy cansada y no quiere hacer las siguientes cosas. Por eso sugiere que las hagan otras personas. ¿Qué dice Estela?

MODELO: preparar las enchiladas / Berta →
¿Las enchiladas? ¡*Que las prepare* Berta!

1. bañar al perro / Ernestito
2. barrer el patio / Guillermo
3. pagar las cuentas / Ernesto
4. cuidar a los niños / Ernesto
5. sacudir los muebles / Berta
6. arreglar el coche / Ernesto
7. enviar el paquete / Amanda
8. jugar con la gata / los niños
9. recoger la ropa / Ernestito
10. poner flores allí / Berta

Ejercicio 10

Lea las siguientes situaciones y escriba la respuesta apropiada.

MODELO: E1: ¡Adiós! Nos vemos el mes próximo.
E2: ¡*Que tengas buen viaje!*

1. Me voy a acostar. Hasta mañana.
2. Se me está haciendo tarde. Ya me voy al trabajo.
3. ¡Ay! Tengo un examen hoy.
4. Mi esposo está en el hospital y está muy grave (muy enfermo).
5. Mañana mis amigos y yo salimos para San Sebastián.

Ejercicio 11

Es su cumpleaños. Use **ojalá (que)** / **ojalá (que) no** para expresar lo que espera que ocurra.

MODELO: llover hoy → Ojalá (que) *no llueva hoy*.

1. recibir muchos regalos
2. hacer buen tiempo
3. tener que trabajar
4. estar enfermo/a
5. venir a visitarme mis amigos
6. ¿ ?

Ejercicio 12

Varios amigos están en su casa. Haga sugerencias negativas o afirmativas, según las actividades.

MODELO: llamar a Jorge → Llamemos a Jorge. (No llamemos a Jorge.)

1. escuchar música latina
2. trabajar en el proyecto
3. hacer ejercicio
4. ir al cine
5. alquilar una película

El porvenir

METAS

In **Capítulo 15** you will express your opinions and talk about future plans, goals, possibilities, and consequences. You will also talk about cultural diversity and other issues that affect modern society. In addition, you will discuss the role of technology in our lives.

Para la seguridad de todo obrero mexicano, por David Alfaro Siqueiros (México)

Sobre el artista: David Alfaro Siqueiros (1896–1974) nació en Chihuahua, México. En 1919 viajó a Europa para ampliar su formación artística. El arte de Siqueiros se destaca por sus colores vivos y la combinación de elementos precolombinos y surrealistas. Sus murales, casi todos con temas político-sociales, decoran muchos edificios en México.

¡Conozca México!

Nombre del país: Estados Unidos Mexicanos

Ciudad capital: México, D.F.

Ciudades principales: Guadalajara, Monterrey, Tijuana, Ciudad Juárez, León, Puebla

Moneda nacional: el peso mexicano

Idiomas: el español (oficial), el maya, el náhuatl y otras lenguas indígenas

Población: 110.000.000

Día de la Independencia: el 16 de septiembre

Fiestas típicas: el Día de Nuestra Señora de Guadalupe, las Posadas, el Día de los Muertos, la Guelaguetza

Comidas típicas: el pozole, el mole poblano, el tamal, la jamaica, el menudo, la barbacoa

Música típica: el mariachi, la música ranchera, el son jarocho, el jarabe tapatío, la música de banda

Gente famosa: Moctezuma Xocoyotzin, Sor Juana Inés de la Cruz, Miguel Hidalgo, Emiliano Zapata, Frida Kahlo, Octavio Paz, Carlos Fuentes, Lorena Ochoa

Código del país por Internet: .mx

Voces mexicanas

ándale pues	go ahead / come on / **está bien**
un(a) güero/a	**un(a) gringo/a**
güey	dude
¡Híjole!	**interjección de sorpresa**
¡No manches!	Stop kidding around!
¡Qué chido/a! /	Cool!
¡Qué padre!	
¿Qué onda?	**¿Qué pasa?, ¿Cómo estás?**

En este capítulo...

ACTIVIDADES DE COMUNICACIÓN

- El futuro y las metas personales
- Cuestiones sociales
- La tecnología: Posibilidades y consecuencias

EN RESUMEN

LECTURAS Y CULTURA

- **Enlace a la literatura**
  «Canción del día que se va», por Federico García Lorca
- **Ventanas culturales**
  Nuestra comunidad: La presencia hispana en los Estados Unidos
- **Ventanas culturales**
  La vida diaria: La divisoria tecnológica
- **Lecturas**
  «El eclipse», por Augusto Monterroso
  «La noche buena», por Tomás Rivera

GRAMÁTICA Y EJERCICIOS

15.1 Talking about the Future: The Future Tense

15.2 Talking about *when:* The Subjunctive in Time Clauses

15.3 Adding Details and Expressing *why* and *how:* More Uses of the Subjunctive

15.4 Expressing Opinions and Reactions: Indicative and Subjunctive

15.5 Expressing Hypothetical Reactions: The Conditional

15.6 Hypothesizing: *If* Clauses and the Past Subjunctive

 **MULTIMEDIA**   **ONLINE LEARNING CENTER** www.mhhe.com/dosmundos7

 C E N T R O Your media center for languages   **DVD**

El futuro y las metas personales

✳ **Lea Gramática 15.1–15.2.**

Éstos son los planes de
Amanda, Ernesto y Estela Saucedo.

1. Tan pronto como me gradúe, viajaré a Europa.
2. Cuando me case, iré a Chile de luna de miel.
3. Después de que nazca nuestro primer hijo, nos sentiremos orgullosos.

1. Cuando logre mis metas, seré feliz.
2. Si me cuido bien, viviré mucho tiempo y gozaré de la vida.
3. Después de que me jubile, realizaré mi sueño de vivir en las montañas.

1. En cuanto mi hijo menor termine la preparatoria, trabajaré para una empresa importante.
2. Cuando gane más de $890.000 pesos al año, me mudaré a un vecindario elegante.
3. Trabajaré hasta que tenga sesenta y cinco años.

Actividad 1 Encuesta: ¿Cómo será el mundo dentro de veinte años?

Indique si usted está de acuerdo o no con estas afirmaciones. Explique sus respuestas.

DENTRO DE VEINTE AÑOS	ESTOY DE ACUERDO.	NO ESTOY DE ACUERDO.
1. Ya no habrá guerras en el mundo. Gozaremos de paz.	☐	☐
2. Descubrirán una vacuna contra el SIDA.	☐	☐
3. Las computadoras podrán pensar como los seres humanos.	☐	☐

DENTRO DE VEINTE AÑOS	ESTOY DE ACUERDO.	NO ESTOY DE ACUERDO.
4. Usaremos coches híbridos solamente o el transporte público.	☐	☐
5. Todos nos comunicaremos por celular.	☐	☐
6. Habrá disminuido el calentamiento global.	☐	☐
7. Gracias a la tecnología, tendremos mucho más tiempo libre.	☐	☐
8. Ya no habrá reservas de petróleo. El mundo dependerá de la energía renovable.	☐	☐
9. Habrá un plan nacional de seguro médico en los Estados Unidos.	☐	☐
10. Será normal pasar las vacaciones en el espacio.	☐	☐

Actividad 2 Preferencias: El futuro, los sueños y las metas

Piense en su futuro y complete cada oración.

1. Me casaré tan pronto como....
2. Seré feliz en cuanto...
3. Compraré un coche de lujo cuando....

Frases útiles

...me gradúe en la universidad.   ...gane más de $7.000 al mes.
...empiece a trabajar.   ...compre la casa de mis sueños.
...me case y tenga hijos.   ....mejore la economía.
...tenga mi propio apartamento.   ...conozca a la persona perfecta.

4. ...después de que encuentre un buen empleo.
5. ...hasta que nazca mi primer hijo.
6. ...antes de que me muera.

"No te irás a casar conmigo por mi dinero, ¿verdad?"

Frases útiles

Me casaré   Iré a muchos conciertos
Compraré una casa en _____   Aprenderé a _____
Tendré una cabaña en las montañas   Viajaré por todo el mundo
Trabajaré 60 horas por semana   Seguiré estudiando

Actividad 3 Narración: El futuro de Adriana Bolini

Adriana consultó a una adivina. Narre la vida de Adriana según la adivina.

Actividad 4 Conversación: Las carreras y la felicidad

1. ¿Cuáles son sus metas en la vida? ¿Las podrá alcanzar sin un título universitario?
2. ¿Qué carrera quiere seguir usted? ¿Por qué la escogió?
3. ¿Qué conseguirá en su profesión? ¿dinero? ¿prestigio? ¿satisfacción personal? ¿aventuras? ¿Son importantes esas cosas para usted? Explique.
4. ¿Cree usted que trabajará toda la vida en la misma profesión? Explique.
5. ¿Tendrá usted su propio negocio algún día? ¿Qué clase de negocio le gustaría tener? ¿Piensa tener su oficina en su casa?
6. ¿En qué consiste la felicidad para usted? ¿Se puede comprar la felicidad?

Actividad 5 Entrevistas: Las metas

1. ¿Qué quieres hacer después de graduarte en la universidad? ¿Qué quieren tus padres que hagas?
2. Si vives ahora con tus padres, ¿quieres seguir viviendo con ellos por un tiempo? ¿Por qué? ¿Quieren tus padres que sigas viviendo con ellos?
3. ¿Qué es más importante, seguir los deseos de uno mismo o los de los padres?
4. Si no estás casado/a, ¿quieres casarte? ¿Quieren tus padres que te cases? ¿Por qué? Explica.
5. ¿Qué tipo de trabajo buscarás después de graduarte? ¿Por qué?
6. ¿Qué harás después de jubilarte? ¿Viajarás? ¿Tomarás clases? ¿Te irás a otro estado? ¿Cuál?

Enlace a la literatura

«Canción del día que se va», por Federico García Lorca

Selección del libro *Canciones* (1936)

El poeta y dramaturgo Federico García Lorca (1898–1936) es uno de los escritores más estimados y populares de España. Lorca murió joven, asesinado por el ejército fascista durante la Guerra Civil española, pero en su corta vida creó una obra muy rica. Todos sus dramas, como *Yerma* (1934), *Bodas de sangre* (1936) y *La casa de Bernarda Alba* (1936), se presentan en numerosos escenarios anualmente. Entre sus libros de poesía se destacan *Romancero gitano* (1928) y *Poeta en Nueva York* (1930). En el hermoso poema aquí incluido, el día se personifica, adquiriendo características humanas. El día es un ser inalcanzable,[1] pues, como el tiempo, siempre huye[2] de nosotros. El poeta lamenta el fin del día y su incapacidad para hacerlo durar más; es decir, la imposibilidad de detener el tiempo.

Canción del día que se va

¡Qué trabajo me cuesta[3]
dejarte marchar, día!
Te vas lleno de mí,
vuelves sin conocerme.
¡Qué trabajo me cuesta
dejar sobre tu pecho
posibles realidades
de imposibles minutos!

En la tarde, un Perseo[4]
te lima las cadenas,[5]
y huyes sobre los montes
hiriéndote[6] los pies.
No pueden seducirte
mi carne[7] ni mi llanto,
ni los ríos en donde
duermes tu siesta de oro.

Desde Oriente a Occidente
llevo tu luz redonda.
Tu gran luz que sostiene
mi alma,[8] en tensión aguda.[9]
Desde Oriente a Occidente,
¡qué trabajo me cuesta
llevarte con tus pájaros
y tus brazos de viento!

Actividad creativa

1. **¡Qué trabajo me cuesta!** ¿Hay actividades diarias o acciones que le cuestan mucho trabajo a usted? Escriba un poema sobre una de esas actividades o acciones difíciles. Comience así: *¡Qué trabajo me cuesta (actividad)!* Luego presente sus razones en forma poética.

2. **El mejor momento del día.** ¿Qué momento del día le gusta más a usted, el amanecer,[10] el atardecer[11] o el anochecer[12]? Escríbale un poema a ese momento especial. Si quiere, puede usar el siguiente modelo: *¡Qué hermoso es (momento del día)!/ Llega con...*

[1]*unreachable*   [2]*flees*   [3]¡Qué... ¡Qué difícil es...   [4]Se refiere a Perseo, semidiós de la mitología griega, quien liberó a la diosa Andrómeda de las cadenas (*chains*) que la aprisionaban.   [5]*te... files down your chains*   [6]*hurting, cutting*   [7]*flesh* [8]*soul*   [9]*sharp, acute*   [10]*dawn*   [11]*dusk*   [12]*nightfall*

Cuestiones sociales

✳ Lea Gramática 15.3–15.4.

«No conozco ninguna ciudad grande que no se enfrente diariamente con la cuestión de los desamparados.»

«Quiero vivir en un lugar donde pueda respirar aire puro y donde no haya tanta contaminación ambiental.»

«En el centro de muchas ciudades grandes se ha limitado el uso del automóvil para que disminuya el nivel de contaminación.»

«Espero que dejen de construir reactores nucleares antes de que ocurra un accidente grave.»

«La economía de México no será fuerte hasta que se reduzca la tasa del desempleo.»

NORA: Tenemos que ofrecer programas de educación sexual para que los jóvenes sepan las consecuencias de tener relaciones sin protegerse.

ALBERTO: Estoy de acuerdo, con tal de que los padres puedan participar en esos programas.

MÓNICA: Si se legalizan todas las drogas, las pandillas ya no podrán ganarse la vida traficando con drogas ilegales y habrá mucho menos crimen en las grandes ciudades.

ESTEBAN: Tal vez, Mónica. Pero si se legalizan, más jóvenes se harán drogadictos; ya tenemos demasiado con el abuso de drogas legales como el alcohol. Yo no creo que se deba aprobar el uso de ninguna droga.

Actividad 6 Preferencias: Condiciones y consecuencias

Seleccione todas las condiciones apropiadas.

MODELO: El problema de los desamparados será más grave cada día
a menos que…
a. el sueldo mínimo sea de $16.00 la hora.
b. se construyan más viviendas para los pobres.
c. se creen más trabajos para la gente desempleada.

El problema de los desamparados será más grave cada día a menos
que *se construyan más viviendas para los pobres.*

1. Debemos iniciar una campaña de educación sexual para que…
   a. no haya tantos abortos.
   b. no aumente el contagio del SIDA.
   c. haya menos madres adolescentes.
2. Vamos a destruir gran parte del medio ambiente a menos que…
   a. dependamos más del transporte público.
   b. controlemos la población mundial.
   c. desarrollemos más fuentes de energía renovable.
3. Es (im)posible eliminar las industrias que dañan el medio ambiente sin que…
   a. la economía sufra.
   b. aumente la tasa de desempleo.
   c. se aprueben nuevas leyes contra la contaminación.

4. Estoy de acuerdo con una reducción en el presupuesto federal con tal de que (no)...

   a. se reduzcan los fondos para la defensa del país.

   b. se reduzcan los fondos para la educación.

   c. se reduzcan los fondos para el bienestar social.

5. Busco una ciudad donde...

   a. haya un buen sistema de transporte público.

   b. se ofrezcan programas sociales para los pobres.

   c. la tasa de crimen sea baja.

6. Quiero vivir en una sociedad donde...

   a. todo ciudadano tenga seguro médico.

   b. se respeten los derechos civiles.

   c. haya gran diversidad cultural.

Actividad 7 Conversación: Sus predicciones

Escoja cuatro o cinco preguntas de las que aparecen a continuación y haga sus predicciones para el año 2030.

1. ¿Habrá otra guerra mundial? ¿Por qué? ¿Entre qué países?

2. ¿Existirá la carne clonada? ¿Será muy común o tendremos problemas con ella?

3. ¿Cómo será el transporte público? ¿y el transporte aéreo?

4. ¿Podrán los científicos crear seres humanos en el laboratorio? ¿Será legal hacerlo?

5. ¿Le pondrán a cada bebé recién nacido un chip de identificación nacional?

6. ¿Tomaremos vacaciones en el espacio o en otro planeta?

7. ¿Qué podrán hacer los médicos entonces? ¿Qué enfermedades (ya no) habrá en el 2030?

8. ¿Cuántas horas al día tendremos que trabajar?

9. ¿Seguirá el calentamiento global?

10. ¿Qué otras predicciones quiere usted hacer?

© Joaquín Salvador Lavado, (QUINO) Toda Mafalda—Ediciones de La Flor, 1993

Actividad 8 Intercambios: Un club que da miedo

NÚMERO DE CABEZAS NUCLEARES

Año	Estados Unidos	Rusia (URSS)	Reino Unido (Inglaterra)	Francia	China	Total*
1952	1.005	50	–	–	–	1.055
1962	27.297	3.322	205	–	–	30.823
1972	27.296	14.478	220	70	130	42.193
1982	22.937	33.952	335	275	360	57.859
1992	13.731	25.155	300	540	435	40.161
2002	10.640	8.600	200	350	400	20.190

*También Israel, India, Pakistán y Corea del Norte poseen arsenales nucleares. Se estima que Israel tiene entre 100 y 200, India y Pakistán entre 35 y 50 cada uno y Corea del Norte entre 1 y 10.

Fuente: National Resources Defense Council 25, noviembre de 2002. Para más información visite su sitio Web en español.

ARSENALES NUCLEARES

A. Mire la tabla **Número de cabezas nucleares.** Luego use las siguientes preguntas para conversar con un compañero / una compañera sobre el tema de las armas nucleares.

1. ¿Qué país tenía más cabezas nucleares en 1952? ¿Quién estaba en segundo lugar entonces? ¿En qué años tuvo más cabezas nucleares la Unión Soviética que los Estados Unidos?

2. Los políticos de varios países opinan que sin un arsenal nuclear su país queda vulnerable a ataques terroristas. En tu opinión, ¿es necesario tener un arsenal nuclear para asegurar la seguridad de un país? ¿Cuántas cabezas son suficientes? ¿Es eficaz un arsenal nuclear contra todo tipo de ataques?

3. ¿Crees justo que unos países tengan arsenales nucleares y a otros no se les permita tenerlos? ¿O crees que si todos los países tuvieran un arsenal nuclear sería más fácil lograr la paz mundial? Explica tus respuestas.

B. Un debate.

Trabajen en grupos de cuatro; dos estudiantes deben hablar a favor y dos en contra del armamento nuclear. Usen las preguntas 2 y 3 de arriba como guía para preparar sus argumentos. Piensen también en la posibilidad de terrorismo que estos arsenales implican.

Actividad 9 Intercambios: Problemas actuales

Lea estas afirmaciones sobre las cuestiones que la sociedad enfrenta actualmente. Decida si está de acuerdo o no y por qué. Luego comparta su opinión con otras tres o cuatro personas.

1. Es importante establecer buenas guarderías infantiles para que los padres puedan trabajar tranquilos.

2. No se acabará la pobreza en la América Latina hasta que las empresas internacionales establezcan más maquiladoras allí.

3. Es dudoso que la privatización de los sistemas del agua resuelva la escasez de agua potable.

4. Vamos a permitir el transporte de los desperdicios nucleares con tal de que se usen camiones seguros y choferes responsables.

5. Es importante que se eliminen los programas bilingües de las escuelas para que todos los niños aprendan bien el inglés.

6. Es urgente que se legalice a los inmigrantes indocumentados.

Actividad 10 Del mundo hispano: Los estereotipos en el trabajo

Hombre y mujer cuando de trabajo se trata

Observemos las distintas actitudes tomadas en situaciones iguales según el sujeto de la acción sea hombre o mujer.

Así le califican a él en la oficina	De esta manera a ella
Tiene colocadas[1] encima de su mesa las fotos de su esposa/esposo e hijos.	
Es un hombre responsable que se preocupa por su familia.	¡Um! Su familia tiene prioridad sobre su carrera.
Su escritorio está lleno de papeles.	
Se nota que es una persona ocupada, siempre trabajando.	Es una desordenada.
Está hablando con sus compañeros de trabajo.	
Seguro que está discutiendo nuevos proyectos.	Seguro que está cotilleando.[2]
Salió a almorzar con el jefe.	
Su prestigio aumenta.	Debe de tener un «affaire».
Le gritó a un empleado que no cumplió sus órdenes.	
Tiene carácter, sabe imponerse.	Está histérica.
Se va a casar.	
Eso le estabilizará.	Pronto quedará embarazada y dejará el trabajo.
Va a hacer un viaje de negocios.	
Es conveniente para su carrera.	¿Qué opina su marido?
Faltó al trabajo por enfermedad.	
Debe de encontrarse muy mal.	Tendrá un catarrito.[3]

[1]puestas [2]gossiping [3]un... *the sniffles*

1. Según este artículo, ¿cuál es el estereotipo de un hombre que tiene fotos de su familia sobre su escritorio? ¿Y cuando se trata de una mujer? ¿Cree usted que la familia debe tener prioridad sobre la carrera?

2. Si usted ve a un empleado / una empleada ante un escritorio lleno de papeles; ¿cómo lo/la caracteriza, como persona ocupada o desordenada?

3. ¿Cree que es verdad o que es una idea preconcebida que las mujeres chismean (cotillean) más que los hombres? ¿En qué se basa su opinión?

4. Según este artículo, ¿cuál es el estereotipo de la mujer que sale a almorzar con el jefe? ¿y el del hombre?

5. Si una jefa les gritara a sus empleados, ¿la consideraría usted una mujer histérica? ¿Y si fuera un hombre?

6. ¿Cuáles son algunos estereotipos negativos del hombre en el mundo del trabajo?

La presencia hispana en los Estados Unidos

La presencia hispana en los Estados Unidos data de los tiempos coloniales. Ya en 1513 estaba el español Ponce de León explorando la región que hoy forma el estado de Florida, buscando la legendaria «fuente de la juventud». Antes de llegar los primeros colonizadores ingleses, ya florecían en este continente varias comunidades hispanas como Santa Fe en Nuevo México. Esta ciudad fue fundada en 1609 y es la capital más antigua de los Estados Unidos.

Varios eventos han contribuido a aumentar la presencia hispana en este país. En 1848, por ejemplo, miles de ciudadanos mexicanos se hicieron estadounidenses al firmarse el Tratado de Guadalupe Hidalgo. Por medio de este **tratado,** los Estados Unidos le compraron a México el territorio de lo que hoy es California, Nevada, Utah, Arizona, Colorado, Nuevo México y Wyoming. Durante el siglo xx, muchos puertorriqueños formaron comunidades en el noroeste de los Estados Unidos. Y después de la Revolución Cubana de 1959, llegaron a este país millones de exiliados cubanos que se establecieron principalmente en Miami y Nueva Jersey. Muchos otros hispanos de América Central y Sudamérica han llegado a los Estados Unidos en busca de oportunidades económicas y también para escapar de gobiernos totalitarios y opresivos.

Hoy la población hispana en los Estados Unidos pasa de los 30 millones y se calcula que para el año 2010 los hispanos formarán el grupo minoritario más grande del país. Se trata de un grupo muy diverso, con gente de diferentes niveles socioeconómicos y de varios países, razas y generaciones. Los hispanos están presentes en todos los campos: el arte, **los medios de comunicación,** la política, los deportes, la ciencia y la literatura. **Aportan** sus costumbres y tradiciones a la sociedad estadounidense, transformando la vida cultural, económica y política de los Estados Unidos. De hecho, se han observado cambios en los patrones electorales de varios estados. Esto **se debe** al gran número de hispanos que votan hoy en día.

La presencia hispana en este país es cada día más fuerte. Y seguirá proyectándose a través de su larga historia, desde los tiempos coloniales hasta el presente y del presente hacia el futuro.

VOCABULARIO ÚTIL	
el tratado	*treaty*
los medios de comunicación	*the media*
aportan	*contribuyen*
se debe	*is due*

Comprensión

1. ¿Cuál es la capital más antigua de los Estados Unidos y cuándo fue fundada?
2. Mencione dos eventos que aumentaron la presencia hispana en los Estados Unidos.

Actividad 11 Entrevista: ¿El inglés o la lengua materna?

En varios estados de los Estados Unidos se han promulgado leyes declarando el inglés como lengua oficial. Hágale preguntas a un compañero / una compañera acerca de los siguientes aspectos de la inmigración y el uso del inglés.

1. ¿Habla más de una lengua tu familia? ¿y tus abuelos? ¿Cuál? ¿Qué beneficios hay en poder hablar más de una lengua?
2. Si tuvieras que emigrar a otro país en el cual no se hablara el inglés, ¿aprenderías el nuevo idioma? ¿Hablarías solamente ese idioma o hablarías inglés con tu familia y con tus amigos íntimos?
3. En tu opinión, ¿se debe enseñar a los niños pequeños en su lengua materna o en la lengua de la mayoría? ¿Por qué?
4. Si se ofreciera la educación bilingüe en una escuela cercana, ¿inscribirías allí a tus hijos, o preferirías mandarlos a una escuela donde la enseñanza fuera solamente en inglés? ¿Por qué?
5. ¿Crees que cada país debe tener un solo idioma oficial? ¿Por qué? Explica.

Actividad 12 Entrevista: Las drogas

1. ¿Dónde se producen las drogas? ¿Quiénes las producen (las cultivan)? ¿Por qué?
2. ¿Crees que deba legalizarse todo tipo de drogas? Explica. ¿Crees que la guerra contra las drogas reduce el narcotráfico?
3. ¿Para qué se usan las drogas? ¿Son drogas el alcohol, la nicotina y la cafeína? Describe los peligros de las drogas lícitas e ilícitas.
4. ¿Crees que el problema de la drogadicción ha llegado a un punto crítico en nuestra sociedad? ¿Por qué? ¿A qué se puede atribuir este problema?
5. ¿Crees que los estados deberían tener el derecho de legalizar la marihuana para usos medicinales? ¿Por qué?

La tecnología: Posibilidades y consecuencias

✴ **Lea Gramática 15.5–15.6.**

¿Qué haría Luis Ventura si se ganara $1.000.000 en la lotería?

Le daría una parte del dinero a su abuela.

Se compraría una computadora, una impresora con fax y un teléfono celular nuevos.

Establecería su propio negocio de importación de muebles.

Haría muchos viajes a Europa y América Latina.

Saldría a cenar con más frecuencia.

Tomaría vacaciones más a menudo.

Actividad 13 Preferencias: Las decisiones

¿Qué haría usted en las siguientes situaciones?

1. Si no fuera estudiante,...
   a. (no) trabajaría en el mismo lugar donde trabajo ahora.
   b. buscaría un empleo que pagara más.
   c. ¿ ?
2. Si me enamorara de una persona casada...
   a. (no) dejaría de verla.
   b. la obligaría a divorciarse para casarnos.
   c. ¿ ?

3. Si pudiera hablar con cualquier persona (viva o muerta) del mundo,...
   a. hablaría con _____, la famosa estrella de cine.
   b. hablaría con _____, el/la mejor atleta del mundo.
   c. ¿ ?
4. Si tuviera sólo un año de vida,...
   a. viajaría por todo el mundo.
   b. lo pasaría con mis seres queridos.
   c. ¿ ?
5. Si me ganara $50.000.000 en la lotería,...
   a. compraría varias casas.
   b. donaría dinero a _____.
   c. ¿ ?

Y tú, ¿qué dices?

Yo no, yo...	¿Por qué?	(No) Estoy de acuerdo.
¿De veras?	¡Qué buena idea!	¿Qué le dirías?
¡Yo también/tampoco!	Sería interesante.	¿Le pedirías algo?

Actividad 14 Encuesta: Las posibilidades del futuro

Haga la siguiente encuesta como proyecto de clase. Responda usando las siguientes letras: **D** = definitivamente; **TV** = tal vez; **N** = nunca.

1. Si subiera mucho más el precio de la gasolina,...
   _____ ¿comprarías un coche eléctrico?
   _____ ¿usarías el transporte público?
   _____ ¿caminarías o montarías en bicicleta?
2. Si se descubriera que los alimentos transgénicos causan alergias o cáncer,...
   _____ ¿protestarías para que el gobierno los prohibiera?
   _____ ¿los comerías de todos modos?
   _____ ¿sembrarías tus propias frutas y legumbres?
3. Si hubiera en la Tierra menos producción de alimentos y más contaminación ambiental,...
   _____ ¿te harías vegetariano?
   _____ ¿comerías insectos?
   _____ ¿vivirías en una colonia espacial?
4. Si fuera necesario,...
   _____ ¿compartirías tu vivienda con otra familia?
   _____ ¿compartirías tu vivienda con tus padres?
   _____ ¿vivirías en una comuna?
5. Si hubiera escasez de electricidad,...
   _____ ¿montarías paneles solares en el techo de tu casa?
   _____ ¿verías la televisión? ¿escucharías música?
   _____ ¿usarías la computadora?

Actividad 15   Narración: ¡Cómo cambiaría la vida de los Ruiz!

¿Qué harían los Ruiz si ganaran el premio gordo de la lotería?

Actividad 16   Conversación: La tecnología y los niños

1. ¿Le preocupa que los niños de hoy en día pasen demasiado tiempo ante la computadora? ¿Qué problemas cree usted que puedan surgir?
2. ¿Debemos permitir que los niños menores de cinco años utilicen las computadoras o los juegos electrónicos? ¿Por qué?
3. ¿Es muy importante, algo importante o poco importante que los niños sepan usar las computadoras? ¿Por qué?
4. ¿Qué ventajas tiene la tecnología (computadoras, teléfonos celulares, asistentes personales digitales [PDAs], teléfonos con Internet, etcétera) para los niños de hoy? ¿Hay desventajas también? ¿Cuáles son? ¿Le preocupa a usted la radiación que emiten estos aparatos? ¿Por qué?
5. ¿Cree usted que los niños deban tener su propia computadora (su propio televisor) en su cuarto? ¿Por qué? ¿Qué desventajas ve usted? ¿Considera necesario que tengan su propio teléfono celular? ¿Por qué?
6. ¿Qué actividades harán los niños del futuro por medio de la computadora? ¿Qué actividades hacen ellos hoy en la computadora que usted no hizo cuando era niño/a?

La divisoria tecnológica

Para muchos de nosotros es difícil imaginar nuestra vida diaria sin la tecnología que llena nuestro mundo, como el teléfono celular, la cámara digital, el DVD y el iPod, además de todos los servicios que nos ofrece el Internet. **A pesar de** los aspectos negativos de la computadora —*software* infectado por un virus, correo no deseado, o **buzenfia** adicción al correo electrónico— muchos pensamos que vale la pena ser parte de esta revolución tecnológica. Dependemos de la computadora para comunicarnos con amigos y familia, para hacer trabajo a distancia y para hacer estudios en línea. Esta tecnología es también una fuente de entretenimiento que pone a nuestro **alcance** una inmensa cantidad de información. Con la computadora hacemos búsquedas y **descargas** en el Internet, y nos mantenemos informados de las noticias más recientes.

Lamentablemente, todavía hay mucha gente que no tiene acceso a esta tecnología. Desde los años 80, cuando se hicieron populares las computadoras personales, ha estado surgiendo en los Estados Unidos una **divisoria** tecnológica. Esta frase se refiere a la línea que divide o separa a dos grupos de personas: las que se benefician de la tecnología digital y las que no pueden hacerlo. Según informes de la Administración de Telecomunicaciones e Información del Departamento de Comercio, hay razones socioeconómicas para explicar esta desigualdad, como el nivel de educación y el conocimiento del inglés. La población que no tiene acceso incluye a personas de bajos recursos, desempleados, incapacitados y muchos inmigrantes. En general, es gente que no puede **darse el lujo** de tener computadora en casa y pagar por conexión de **banda ancha,** un servicio muy caro. Y la falta de acceso significa desventaja y menos oportunidades de trabajo.

Para eliminar la divisoria tecnológica, tendríamos que ofrecer acceso universal al Internet, o por lo menos servicios **inalámbricos** más baratos y accesibles. Además, sería necesario realizar campañas de educación para familiarizar a millones de personas con el lenguaje del ciberespacio. Tendríamos que abrir las **infopistas** del Internet por completo para que todos pudiéramos viajar por ellas. Esto no es un sueño distante en el futuro sino una necesidad urgente, de nuestros días.

VOCABULARIO ÚTIL

a pesar de	*in spite of*
la buzonfia	*spam*
el alcance	*reach*
la descarga	*downloading*
la divisoria	*divide*
darse el lujo	*afford*
la banda ancha	*broadband*
inalámbrico	*wireless*
la infopista	*information highway*

Comprensión

1. Describa la divisoria tecnológica. ¿A qué se refiere?
2. ¿Quiénes no pueden beneficiarse de las computadoras y el Internet?

Actividad 17 Del mundo hispano: Explorando el Internet

En la siguiente tabla aparece una serie de palabras clave para buscar sitios Web. Escoja una categoría (OCIO, COMIDA, ESCUELAS, etcétera) y visite por lo menos un sitio relacionado con cada subcategoría. Traiga a la clase las direcciones de los sitios que visitó y la información que encontró. Usted debe estar preparado/a para hablar de los sitios que le gustaron más y explicar por qué le gustaron. Si no le gustó ninguno, también deberá explicar por qué. Luego comparta con la clase algo nuevo que aprendió de los sitios que exploró. **Sugerencia:** Use un buscador como *Google* o *Yahoo* y especifique que quiere ver sólo páginas en español.

PARA NAVEGAR EL INTERNET EN ESPAÑOL RECOMENDAMOS...

OCIO	COMIDA	ESCUELAS	DEPORTES	MUSEOS	VIAJES
Buscacine	Empanadas de carne, Argentina	Ideal Cuernavaca, México	Kayak Patagonia / Kayak Costa Brava	Museo del Prado	Aerolíneas argentinas
Cinépolis	Empanadas de papa, Chile	ICAI, Costa Rica	Buceo Isla Margarita	Museo Guggenheim	Aeroméxico
Ciudad futura	Pupusas, El Salvador	ILEE, Argentina	Trekking los Andes	Museo Nacional de Antropología	Aeroperú
Todo cine	Tapas, España	Sampere, Ecuador	Surf Perú / Surf Costa Rica	Museo Virtual de Arte	Iberia (España)
La música	Antojitos, México	Sampere, España	Esquí Chile / Esquí Argentina	Museo del Oro	TACA (Centroamérica)
Mundolatino	Sancocho, Puerto Rico	Nerja, España	Ala Delta Chile / Ala Delta Colombia	Museo Virtual Diego Rivera	LanChile

En resumen

De todo un poco

Diccionario cibernético

attachment	archivo adjunto
backup	copia de respaldo
blog	blog, bitácora
browser	navegador
bug	error, gazapo
chat	chatear; chateo
cookie	espía
download	bajar, descargar
file	archivo
firewall	cortafuegos
folder	carpeta
hacker	pirata
homepage	portada
icon	icono
information highway	infopista
junk mail	correo basura
keyboard	teclado
mail server	servidor de correo
online	en línea; conectado
password	contraseña
software	programas, software
spam	correo no deseado
upload	cargar, subir
username	nombre del usuario
worm	gusano

Fuente: R.F. Calvo, Copyright **www.ati.es**

A. Definiciones

Use el **Diccionario cibernético** si necesita ayuda para rellenar los espacios de las siguientes definiciones.

1. _____ propaganda masiva que nos llega al buzón de casa o al buzón electrónico
2. _____ un documento que se envía por correo electrónico, pero no en el mensaje mismo
3. _____ anglicismo (palabra adaptada del inglés) que quiere decir conversar por medios electrónicos
4. _____ algo que protege nuestra computadora de los virus
5. _____ pequeño programa que se mete dentro de nuestro sistema para espiar
6. _____ lo que necesitamos para ver una página de Internet
7. _____ el nombre que escribimos para entrar en nuestro buzón electrónico
8. _____ algo más que tenemos que escribir para tener acceso a nuestro correo electrónico
9. _____ lugar donde se ponen los archivos
10. _____ bombardeo publicitario; propaganda que se envía a muchos usuarios que no la desean

B. Las computadoras

Trabajen en grupos de cinco o seis personas. Anoten las respuestas en la hoja de cómputo y compartan sus respuestas con la clase.

1. ¿Para qué usas más la computadora? ¿para tus estudios? ¿para el trabajo? ¿para divertirte?
2. ¿Lees el periódico por Internet o prefieres leer el periódico tradicional? ¿Bajas música o podcasts del Internet? ¿Participas en un foro de discusiones por Internet?
3. ¿Usas mucho el correo electrónico? ¿A quiénes les mandas mensajes electrónicos? ¿a tus colegas en el trabajo o a tus familiares y amigos? ¿Prefieres comunicarte por correo electrónico o enviar mensajes de texto desde el celular?

4. ¿Tienes tu propia página Web, tu propio blog o una página en MySpace o Facebook? ¿Qué pones allí? ¿Es fácil mantenerla al corriente?

5. Si fuera posible, ¿te gustaría trabajar usando la computadora en tu hogar y no tener que ir al trabajo? Explica.

6. Si fuera necesario, ¿podrías vivir sin computadora? ¿sin televisor? ¿sin horno de microondas? ¿sin teléfono celular? ¿sin iPod? Explica.

7. ¿Crees que las computadoras nos ahorran mucho tiempo, o por el contrario, nos quitan tiempo? En general, ¿han mejorado o empeorado la condición humana? Menciona tres beneficios de esta invención. ¿Hay algunas desventajas también?

¡Dígalo por escrito!

Entreviste a un/una inmigrante de un país latinoamericano. Después de presentarse y saludarlo/la, hágale estas preguntas.

- ¿Cuándo llegó a este país? ¿Cómo llegó?
- ¿Dónde y cómo vive usted en los Estados Unidos? ¿Le gusta vivir allí o le gustaría vivir en otra parte? ¿Dónde?
- ¿Qué tipo de comida suele comer? ¿Es muy diferente su dieta a la que tenía en su país? Deme unos ejemplos.
- ¿Habla usted inglés? Si no lo habla, ¿está tomando clases? ¿Dónde? ¿Está aprendiendo mucho? ¿Por qué?
- ¿Con quién se asocia usted ahora? ¿Por qué? ¿Cómo son sus nuevos amigos?
- ¿Qué tipo de problemas ha tenido? ¿Cómo los ha resuelto o piensa resolverlos?
- ¿Piensa quedarse a vivir en los Estados Unidos? ¿Vino su familia con usted o van a venir a este país a vivir con usted? ¿Será fácil hacerlo? Explique por favor.

Ahora escriba un diálogo entre usted y el/la inmigrante basado en lo que el/ella le contestó.

¡Cuéntenos usted!

Háblenos sobre la cuestión social que más le preocupa a usted y díganos por qué. Díganos lo que usted cree que debemos hacer para remediar este problema o situación.

Conexión a la comunidad

Averigüe si hay un asilo para ancianos en su ciudad o condado. Ofrézcase para enseñarles destrezas computacionales a los asilados de habla hispana.

PISTAS PARA LEER

Augusto Monterroso publicó varias colecciones de cuentos. Sus cuentos son breves, satíricos e irónicos, y siempre sorprenden al lector. «El eclipse» presenta a un fraile español del siglo XVI solo ante un grupo de indígenas mayas. Al leer, tome en cuenta el título y fíjese en el motivo del eclipse de sol. ¿Cómo piensa utilizar el fraile este fenómeno natural? ¿Cómo resulta su plan?

VOCABULARIO ÚTIL

el fraile	friar, monk
fray	friar (used only before names)
lo había apresado	had trapped him
el celo	fervor, passion
redentora	redeeming
rodeado	surrounded
el rostro	face
impasible	expressionless
el lecho	bed, deathbed
el dominio	command
valerse	to make use of
engañar	to fool
se oscurezca	darken
el consejo	council
chorreaba	spurted
previsto	foreseen

LECTURA

«El eclipse», por Augusto Monterroso (Guatemala, 1921–2003)

Cuando **fray** Bartolomé Arrazola se sintió perdido, aceptó que ya nada podría salvarlo. La selva poderosa de Guatemala **lo había apresado,** implacable y definitiva. Ante su ignorancia topográfica se sentó con tranquilidad a esperar la muerte. Quiso morir allí sin ninguna esperanza, aislado, con el pensamiento fijo en la España distante, particularmente en el convento de Los Abrojos donde Carlos Quinto* condescendiera una vez a bajar de su eminencia para decirle que confiaba en el **celo** religioso de su labor **redentora.**

Al despertar se encontró **rodeado** por un grupo de indígenas de **rostro impasible** que se disponían a sacrificarlo ante un altar, un altar que a Bartolomé le pareció como el **lecho** en que descansaría, al fin, de sus temores, de su destino, de sí mismo.

Tres años en el país le habían conferido un mediano **dominio** de las lenguas nativas. Intentó algo. Dijo algunas palabras que fueron comprendidas.

Entonces floreció en él una idea que tuvo por digna de su talento y de su cultura universal y de su arduo conocimiento de Aristóteles.[†] Recordó que para ese día se esperaba un eclipse total de sol. Y dispuso, en lo más íntimo, **valerse** de aquel conocimiento para **engañar** a sus opresores y salvar la vida.

—Si me matáis —les dijo— puedo hacer que el sol **se oscurezca** en su altura.

Los indígenas lo miraron fijamente y fray Bartolomé sorprendió la incredulidad en sus ojos. Vio que se produjo un pequeño **consejo** y esperó confiado, no sin cierto desdén.

Dos horas después el corazón de fray Bartolomé Arrazola **chorreaba** su sangre vehemente sobre la piedra de los sacrificios (brillante bajo la opaca luz de un sol eclipsado), mientras uno de los indígenas recitaba sin ninguna inflexión de voz, sin prisa, una por una, las infinitas fechas en que se producirían eclipses solares y lunares, que los astrónomos de la comunidad maya habían **previsto** y anotado en sus códices sin la valiosa ayuda de Aristóteles.

---

*El emperador romano Carlos V (1500–1558) heredó un vasto imperio en Europa, el cual incluía el reinado español. Fue rey de España entre 1516 y 1556.
[†]Gran filósofo griego nacido en 384 a.C. Aristóteles escribió sobre una variedad de temas y campos de estudio: literatura, arte, ciencia, historia y filosofía, entre otros.

Comprensión

A. Complete cada oración con frases de la lista que aparece a la derecha.

1. Los indígenas ya tenían conocimiento...
2. Cuando fray Bartolomé se sentó a esperar la muerte...
3. El fraile les dijo a los indígenas...
4. Después de vivir tres años en Guatemala...
5. Fray Bartolomé quiso salvarse la vida...

a. que el eclipse iba a ocurrir en dos horas.
b. pensó en su país y en el convento donde el rey habló con él.
c. que podía predecir un eclipse de sol.
d. de cuándo ocurrirían todos los eclipses solares.
e. el fraile podía hablar un poco el idioma de los mayas.
f. por medio de un engaño.

B. Responda brevemente.

1. ¿Cuál es la cultura indígena que se describe en «El eclipse»? ¿Qué sabe usted de esta cultura?
2. ¿Qué idea se le ocurrió a fray Bartolomé para salvar su vida?
3. ¿Qué recita uno de los indígenas al final? ¿Por qué es tan importante esta recitación?
4. ¿Cuál es el mensaje o moraleja de «El eclipse»? ¿Piensa usted que es un mensaje valioso?

Un paso más... ¡a conversar!

¿Ha leído un cuento o una novela sobre el encuentro entre dos culturas o dos personas muy diferentes? Narre esa historia brevemente. ¿Tiene una moraleja o un mensaje?

LECTURA

«La noche buena», por Tomás Rivera (1935–1984)

Faltaban tres días para la nochebuena cuando doña María se decidió comprarles algo a sus niños. Ésta sería la primera vez que les compraría juguetes. Cada año **se proponía** hacerlo pero siempre terminaba diciéndose que no, que no podían. Su esposo de todas maneras les traía dulces y nueces a cada uno, así que racionalizaba que en realidad **no les faltaba nada.** **Sin embargo** cada navidad preguntaban los niños por sus juguetes. Ella siempre **los apaciguaba** con lo de siempre. Les decía que se esperaran hasta el seis de enero, el día de los reyes magos y así para cuando se llegaba ese día ya hasta se

(Continúa)

PISTAS PARA LEER
Tomás Rivera es uno de los escritores mexicoamericanos más reconocidos y apreciados. Poeta y novelista, Rivera también se destacó como profesor en varias universidades. Su obra más importante es ...*y no se lo tragó la tierra* (1971). Esta novela muestra las dificultades y esperanzas de una comunidad de obreros migratorios mexicanos en los años 50. En este fragmento de «La noche buena», selección de ...*y no se lo tragó la tierra*, vemos el deseo de una madre pobre de comprarles regalos de Navidad a sus hijos.

VOCABULARIO ÚTIL

se proponía	she intended
no les faltaba nada	they didn't lack anything
sin embargo	nevertheless
los apaciguaba	calmed them down, appeased them
la venida	arrival
el costal	sack
la máquina de coser	sewing machine
apoco cree (Mex.)	do you really think?
sino	rather
el mero (Mex.)	el correcto, el verdadero
a lo mejor	probablemente
pos (Mex.)	pues

les había olvidado todo a los niños. También había notado que sus hijos apreciaban menos y menos la **venida** de don Chon* la noche de navidad cuando venía con el **costal** de naranjas y nueces.

—Pero, ¿por qué a nosotros no nos trae nada Santo Clos?[†]

—¿Cómo que no? ¿Luego cuando viene y les trae naranjas y nueces?

—No, pero ése es don Chon.

—No, yo digo lo que siempre aparece debajo de la **máquina de coser.**

—Ah, eso lo trae papá, **apoco cree** que no sabemos. ¿Es que no somos buenos como los demás?

—Sí, sí son buenos, pero... pues espérense hasta el día de los reyes magos. Ése es el día en que de veras vienen los juguetes y los regalos. Allá en México no viene Santo Clos **sino** los reyes magos. Y no vienen hasta el seis de enero. Así que ése sí es el **mero** día.

—Pero, lo que pasa es que se les olvida. Porque a nosotros nunca nos han dado nada ni en la noche buena ni en el día de los reyes magos.

—Bueno, pero **a lo mejor** esta vez sí.

—**Pos** sí, ojalá.

Comprensión

A. Complete cada oración con la frase apropiada que aparece a la derecha.

1. Esta Navidad la madre...
2. El padre de los niños siempre...
3. La madre siempre les dice a sus hijos que....
4. Don Chon, un amigo de la familia,...
5. Los niños le preguntan a su madre...

a. si Santo Clos no les trae regalos porque no son buenos.
b. recibirán sus regalos el Día de los Reyes Magos.
c. viene con un costal lleno de frutas y nueces.
d. piensa comprarles juguetes a sus hijos.
e. les trae dulces y nueces que deja debajo de la máquina de coser.

B. Responda brevemente.

1. ¿Por qué no les ha comprado esta madre juguetes a sus hijos para la Navidad?
2. ¿Cómo apaciguaba siempre a sus hijos esta madre?
3. Al final del relato, ¿qué creen los niños?
4. ¿Qué puede hacer una familia pobre como ésta para disfrutar de la Navidad?

*Don Chon es un amigo de la familia.
[†]Esta pregunta la hacen los niños; el diálogo es entre la mamá y sus hijos.

Un paso más... ¡a escribir!

¿Recuerda usted alguna promesa que sus padres le hicieron cuando era niño o adolescente? Piense en algo que su mamá o su papá le prometió y describa este recuerdo en una página. ¿Cumplió (*Fulfilled*) él o ella la promesa? ¿Recibió usted lo que deseaba?

Vea el **Resumen cultural** en este capítulo del *Cuaderno de actividades.*

Vocabulario

Los sustantivos

Nouns

el analfabetismo	illiteracy
la bitácora	blog
el buscador	search engine
la buzonfia	spam
el camión	truck
el contagio	contagion
la costumbre	custom, habit
la cuestión	issue
los derechos (civiles)	(civil) rights
el desarrollo	development
la empresa	company, firm
la enseñanza	teaching
el estado	state
la felicidad	happiness
los fondos	funds
el foro	forum
la fuente de energía	energy source
la guardería infantil	childcare center
la guerra	war
la lengua materna	mother tongue, first language
la ley	law
la maquiladora	*large factory located in developing countries to take advantage of lower wages*
la mayoría	majority
la meta	goal
el negocio	business
el nivel	level
el ocio	leisure, free time
el orfanato	orphanage
la pandilla	gang
la paz	peace
la pobreza	poverty
el porvenir	future
el prejuicio	prejudice
el premio (gordo)	(grand) prize
el presupuesto	budget
la propiedad	property
la (sobre)población	(over)population
la tasa de desempleo	rate of unemployment
el término	term
el título	degree; title
el título de propiedad	property deed
la vivienda	housing

PALABRAS SEMEJANTES: el aborto, el abuso, el acceso, la actitud, el alcohol, el argumento, el armamento, las armas, el arsenal, el ataque, el beneficio, el blog, la cafeína, la colonia espacial, la comuna, el crimen, la decisión, la defensa, la dificultad, la discusión, la drogadicción, la educación (sexual), la importación, la institución, la invención, la lotería, la medicina, el narcotráfico, la nicotina, la opción, el panel solar, el planeta, la predicción, el prestigio, la prioridad, la privatización, el reactor nuclear, la reducción, las reservas, la satisfacción, la seguridad, la tecnología, el terrorismo, el/la terrorista

Las personas

People

el adivino / la adivina	fortune-teller
el desamparado / la desamparada	homeless person
el ser humano	human being

PALABRAS SEMEJANTES: el/la colega, el drogadicto / la drogadicta, el/la inmigrante, el político
REPASO: el jefe / la jefa

Las opiniones

Opinions

(no) creer que	to (not) believe that
(no) dudar que	to (not) doubt that
es dudoso que	it is doubtful that
esperar que	to hope that
qué bueno que	how great that
qué lástima que	it's too bad that

PALABRAS SEMEJANTES: (no) es (im)posible que

Las condiciones

Conditions

a menos que	unless
antes de que	before
con tal (de) que	as long as
de manera/modo que	so that, in a way that
después de que	after
en cuanto	as soon as
hasta que	until
para que	in order that
sin que	without
tan pronto como	as soon as

Los verbos

Verbs

acabar	to finish, put an end to
alcanzar	to reach
aprobar	to approve
asegurar	to assure
aumentar	to increase
chismear (cotillear)	to gossip
conseguir (i, i)	to obtain; to get
construir	to build
cuidarse	to take care of oneself
dañar	to damage
destruir	to destroy
disminuir	to diminish
empeorar	to worsen
enfrentarse con	to confront

ganar(se)	to win
ganarse la vida	to earn one's living
gozar de	to enjoy
implicar	to imply
inscribir(se)	to enroll (oneself)
irse	to go away, leave
jubilarse	to retire
lograr	to obtain, achieve
montar	to set up, assemble
nacer	to be born
promulgar	to enact, proclaim
proporcionar	to provide
proteger(se)	to protect (onself)
realizar su sueño	to realize/fulfill one's dream
soler (ue)	to be accustomed to
surgir	to arise
tener relaciones	to engage in sexual relations
tratarse de	to be about

PALABRAS SEMEJANTES: atribuir, caracterizar, continuar, declarar, depender de, donar, emitir, iniciar, legalizar, limitar, obligar, protestar, seleccionar, traficar, utilizar
REPASO: sembrar

Los adjetivos

Adjectives

actual	current
cierto/a	certain
clave	key; important
desempleado/a	unemployed
eficaz	efficient
igual	equal

(i)lícito/a	(il)legal
mundial	world (*adjective*)
orgulloso/a	proud
preconcebido/a	preconceived
transgénico/a	genetically modified
universitario/a	university (*adjective*)

PALABRAS SEMEJANTES: clonado/a, común, crítico/a, desordenado/a, distinto/a, federal, histérico/a, (i)legal, indocumentado/a, justo/a, nacional, oficial, potable, puro/a, racial, suficiente, urgente, vegetariano/a, vulnerable

Adverbios

Adverbs

actualmente	currently, nowadays
definitivamente	definitely

Palabras y expresiones útiles

Useful Words and Expressions

al corriente	up to date
ante	in front of
dentro de (+ *time*)	within, in (+ *time*)
de todos modos	anyway
hoy en día	nowadays
por medio de	through, by means of
tal vez	perhaps
todo el mundo	everyone
ya no	no longer

Gramática y ejercicios

¿RECUERDA?

In **Gramática 2.1** you learned to use the construction **ir a** + infinitive to express the "informal future":

Esta tarde voy a estudiar.

Spanish also has a future tense, with its own special set of endings. It is generally used to talk about long-term or important future events.

$$\text{future} = \text{infinitive} + \begin{cases} \text{-é} \\ \text{-ás} \\ \text{-á} \\ \text{-emos} \\ \text{-éis} \\ \text{-án} \end{cases}$$

15.1 Talking about the Future: The Future Tense

A. The future tense is formed by adding these endings to the infinitive: **-é, -ás, -á, -emos, -éis,** and **-án.***

FUTURE

(yo)	jugar**é**	*I will play*
(tú)	terminar**ás**	*you (inf. sing.) will finish*
(usted, él/ella)	escribir**á**	*you (pol. sing.) will write; he/she will write*
(nosotros/as)	lavar**emos**	*we will wash*
(vosotros/as)	comer**éis**	*you (inf. pl., Spain) will eat*
(ustedes, ellos/as)	dormir**án**	*you (pl.) will sleep; they will sleep*

Me jubilaré en dos años.
Los políticos nunca **cumplirán** con lo que prometen.

I will retire in two years.
The politicians will never carry out what they promise.

B. A few verbs have irregular stems to which the future-tense endings are attached.

caber	→	cabré	poner	→	pondré	decir	→	diré
haber	→	habré	salir	→	saldré	hacer	→	haré
poder	→	podré	tener	→	tendré			
querer	→	querré	valer	→	valdré			
saber	→	sabré	venir	→	vendré			

Mi hermana dice que **podrá** casarse cuando encuentre al hombre perfecto.

My sister says that she will be able to get married when she finds the perfect man.

C. For statements about future events, the **ir** + **a** + infinitive construction is more frequently used in conversation than are the future-tense verb forms.

Mañana **vamos a escuchar** el noticiero de las 6:00.

Tomorrow we are going to listen to the 6:00 news.

When there is doubt or speculation, however, especially in questions, the future tense is common. This is called the "future of probability."

¿A qué hora **llegarán**?

What time do you think they'll arrive? (I wonder what time they'll get here.)

---

*Recognition: **vos hablarás**

The future of probability may also refer to present conditions.

¿Qué **estarán haciendo** ahora?

What do you think they are doing now? (I wonder what they're doing now.)

¿Qué hora **será**? ¿**Serán** ya las 7:00?

What time do you think it is? (I wonder what time it is.) Do you think it's already 7:00?

Ejercicio 1

¿Qué pasará durante los próximos quince años?

	SÍ	NO
MODELO: La profesora Martínez *se jubilará* y *viajará* a Sudamérica. (jubilarse/viajar)	☐	☐
1. (Yo) _____ y _____ dos hijos. (casarse/tener)	☐	☐
2. Mi mejor amigo/a y yo _____ e _____ a Europa. (graduarse/ir)	☐	☐
3. Mis padres _____ y _____ en una isla tropical. (mudarse/vivir)	☐	☐
4. Mis compañeros de clase y yo _____ nuestras metas y _____ en la universidad en el año 2025. (lograr/reunirse)	☐	☐
5. El presidente _____ a cenar en mi casa y me _____ que le gustan mis ideas. (venir/decir)	☐	☐

15.2 Talking about *when:* The Subjunctive in Time Clauses

Gramática ilustrada

(Continúa)

Después de que Amanda y Graciela **terminen** la tarea, irán al cine.

A. As you know, Spanish requires subjunctive verb forms in time clauses whenever the time expressed is in the future (see **Gramática 11.3**). Present indicative forms are used to express habitual activities. (The word **siempre** often indicates a habitual activity, and therefore the indicative is used.)

Voy a ver las noticias cuando **termine** mi trabajo.
I am going to watch the news when I finish my work.
Yo siempre veo las noticias cuando **termino** mi trabajo.
I always watch the news when I finish my work.

> The subjunctive is used in clauses that begin with **cuando, hasta que, después de que, tan pronto como,** and **en cuanto** when they refer to the future. **Antes de que** is *always* followed by the subjunctive.

B. Although **cuando** is the most common word used to introduce time clauses, similar conjunctions are **hasta que** (*until*), **después de que** (*after*), **tan pronto como** (*as soon as*), and **en cuanto** (*as soon as*).

La madre estará nerviosa **hasta que** su hijo **llegue** de la escuela.
The mother will be nervous until her son arrives home from school.
La madre siempre está nerviosa **hasta que** su hijo **llega** de la escuela.
The mother is always nervous until her son arrives home from school.

C. The conjunction **antes de que** (*before*) is always followed by subjunctive verb forms, even when the activity described is habitual.

Voy a comprar un carro **antes de que suban** los precios.
I'm going to buy a car before the prices go up.
Cada mañana doy un paseo **antes de que** los niños **se despierten.**
Every morning I take a walk before the children wake up.

Ejercicio 2

¿Indicativo o subjuntivo? Siga el modelo.

MODELO: Algunos periodistas dicen que el presidente va a jubilarse cuando (cumple/<u>cumpla</u>) 65 años.

1. Toda mi familia va a dar una gran fiesta después de que (yo) me (gradúo/gradúe).
2. Estaremos muy contentos cuando no (hay/haya) más contaminación ambiental.
3. Raúl, ¿siempre hablas con tus abuelos cuando (tienes/tengas) tiempo libre?
4. Mis padrinos siempre preguntan por mí en cuanto (ven/vean) a mis padres.
5. Estaré dispuesto a ayudarte con la tarea esta tarde tan pronto como (llegas/llegues) a mi casa.
6. Voy a arreglar la casa antes de que (vienen/vengan) mis suegros.
7. Los empleados trabajarán hasta que (alcanzan/alcancen) las metas del jefe.
8. Mis primos siempre se pelean hasta que (vuelven/vuelvan) mis tíos del trabajo.
9. La profesora tiene que explicarnos la tarea antes de que (salimos/salgamos) del salón de clase.
10. Después de que me (saludan/saluden), mis tías siempre me invitan a comer.

15.3 Adding Details and Expressing *why* and *how*: More Uses of the Subjunctive

A. Adjective Clauses

1. Adjective clauses modify nouns, just as adjectives do. In English, adjective clauses usually begin with *that, which*, or *who*.

Give me the name of a country that welcomes immigrants in an era of economic decline.
The Spanish Civil War, which was fought in the 1930s, resulted in the loss of political freedom for the Spaniards.
This is the senator who proposed to negotiate a peaceful solution.

In Spanish, adjective clauses normally begin with the conjunction **que,** whether they refer to things or to people.

Señor Presidente, aquí está el grupo pro inmigrantes **que** viene a protestar contra la nueva ley.	*Mr. President, this is the pro-immigrant group that is here to protest against the new law.*
Benito Juárez fue el presidente mexicano **que** se opuso a la ocupación francesa.	*Benito Juárez was the Mexican president who opposed the French occupation.*

2. When an adjective clause is preceded by a preposition (**a, de, con, para**) and modifies a person, **quien** (not **que**) follows the preposition.

Aquí tienen ustedes un cuento escrito por el famoso escritor chicano de **quien** les hablé en la clase pasada.	*Here you have a short story written by the famous Chicano writer about whom I spoke to you in the last class.*

> Preposition + **que** becomes preposition + **quien** when referring to a person.

> If the person or thing is unknown or nonexistent, the verb in the adjective clause is in the subjunctive.

3. If the person, place, or thing the adjective clause modifies is unknown to the speaker, the verb in the adjective clause must be subjunctive.

Pedro compró **un libro** que **contiene** información sobre la diversidad cultural en México.	*Pedro bought a book that contains information about cultural diversity in Mexico.*
Pedro busca **un libro** que **contenga** buenos consejos para convivir con gente de otras culturas.	*Pedro is looking for a book that contains good advice about how to live peacefully with people from other cultures.*

The subjunctive is also used in adjective clauses if the person, place, or thing modified is nonexistent.

Hay varias regiones que **producen** grandes cantidades de café.	*There are several regions that produce large quantities of coffee.*
No hay ninguna región que **produzca** tanto café como ésta.	*There is no region that produces as much coffee as this one (does).*

B. Adverbial and Nominal Expressions

Following are some common adverbial and nominal expressions containing subjunctive verb forms, used when the speaker is in doubt about the wishes of the person being addressed.

Como usted quiera / tú quieras.	*However you want.*
Cuando usted diga / tú digas.	*Whenever you say.*
Donde usted quiera / tú quieras.	*Wherever you want.*
Lo que usted diga / tú digas.	*Whatever you say.*

—¿Cómo lo vamos a hacer?	—*How are we going to do it?*
—**Como tú quieras.**	—*However you want.*
—¿Cuándo nos vamos?	—*When are we leaving?*
—**Cuando usted quiera.**	—*Whenever you want.*
—¿Adónde vamos mañana?	—*Where are we going tomorrow?*
—**Adonde tú digas.**	—*Wherever you say.*
—¿Qué vamos a hacer ahora?	—*What are we going to do now?*
—**Lo que usted diga.**	—*Whatever you say.*

These expressions contain indicative verb forms if what is expressed in the second clause is already known.

Lo que tú **dices** es verdad.	*What you are saying is true.*

> The subjunctive *always* follows:
> **para que...**
> **con tal (de) que...**
> **sin que...**
> **de modo que...**
> **de manera que...**

C. Purpose Clauses

Spanish requires subjunctive verb forms in purpose clauses introduced by conjunctions such as **para que** (*so that, provided that*), **sin que** (*without*), **con tal (de) que** (*provided that*), and **de modo (manera) que** (*so that*).

¡La legislatura va a aprobar la nueva ley **sin que** los ciudadanos lo **sepan**! Es necesario reparar ese edificio **para que** no **se caiga** durante un terremoto.

The legislature is going to pass the new law without the citizens knowing it! That building needs to be repaired so that it won't collapse in an earthquake.

Ejercicio 3

Adriana y su futuro esposo, Víctor, están planeando su luna de miel. Escoja la forma correcta del verbo: el presente de indicativo o el presente de subjuntivo.

ADRIANA: Prefiero ir a un lugar que no _____[1] muy turístico. (es/sea)

VÍCTOR: Pero, Adriana, en agosto no hay ningún lugar que no _____[2] lleno de gente. (está/esté)

ADRIANA: Tienes razón, Víctor. También busco un lugar que _____[3] mucho para hacer, tanto de día como de noche. (ofrece/ofrezca)

VÍCTOR: Conozco varias ciudades de Europa que _____[4] muchas diversiones. (tienen/tengan)

ADRIANA: ¡Europa, sí! Quiero ir a un lugar donde se _____[5] mucha ropa elegante. (vende/venda)

VÍCTOR: Adriana, tú sabes que en París se _____[6] más ropa fina que en cualquier otra ciudad del mundo. (fabrica/fabrique)

ADRIANA: ¡Perfecto! París es una ciudad donde _____[7] mucha actividad cultural, además de tiendas elegantes. (hay/haya)

VÍCTOR: Pues Adriana, ¿por qué no hacemos una gira por Europa?

Ejercicio 4

Los estudiantes de la profesora Martínez expresan sus opiniones. Escoja entre el presente de indicativo y el presente de subjuntivo.

In each sentence of **Ejercicios 4** and **5,** you must determine whether the conjunction requires the subjunctive or the indicative and choose the appropriate verb form.

1. Es necesario construir más apartamentos para que _____ suficientes viviendas para todos. (hay/haya)
2. No podemos seguir usando tanta gasolina porque _____ la contaminación ambiental en nuestra ciudad. (aumenta/aumente)
3. Va a haber más crímenes violentos si no se _____ portar armas de fuego. (prohíbe/prohíba)
4. Voy a escribirle una carta al gobernador para que _____ a resolver el problema de las drogas en nuestro estado. (ayuda/ayude)
5. Seguirá el problema de la escasez de atención médica a menos que el gobierno _____ un plan nacional de seguro médico. (adopta/adopte)
6. Debemos controlar lo que los niños ven en la televisión porque _____ en su manera de pensar. (influye/influya)

portar armas de fuego = *to carry firearms (weapons)*

Ejercicio 5

Alberto y Carmen participan en una discusión en la clase de español. Están discutiendo la pena de muerte. Escoja la forma correcta entre el presente de indicativo y el presente de subjuntivo.

tasa de crímenes =
crime rate
pena de muerte =
death penalty
libertad provisional =
parole

ALBERTO: No podremos controlar la tasa de crímenes en este país a menos que se _____¹ en efecto la pena de muerte. (pone/ponga)

CARMEN: ¿Y tú crees que la pena de muerte resuelva el problema de la delincuencia? Si esperamos reducir la tasa de crímenes violentos en nuestra sociedad, tenemos que reformar nuestro sistema de educación de manera que todos _____² recibir instrucción escolar. (pueden/puedan)

ALBERTO: Es una propuesta excelente, y estoy de acuerdo, con tal de que ningún asesino _____³ derecho a la libertad provisional. (tiene/tenga)

PROFA MARTÍNEZ: Creo que todos queremos cambiar la sociedad para que _____⁴ menos violencia. (hay/haya)

15.4 Expressing Opinions and Reactions: Indicative and Subjunctive

A. The most common way to convey opinions is by asserting an idea directly. Assertion is expressed by indicative verb forms.

Los japoneses **son** muy trabajadores.

The Japanese are very hardworking.

Another way to convey opinions is to report others' assertions by using verb phrases such as **decir que** (*to say that*) and a second clause. Indicative verb forms are also used in such sentences.

Carmen **dice que** los latinoamericanos **son** optimistas.

Carmen says that Latin Americans are optimists.

In addition, it is possible to introduce assertions of opinion with verb phrases such as **creer que** (*to believe that*), **pensar que** (*to think that*), and **es verdad** (**cierto, seguro, indudable**) **que** (*it is true, [certain, sure, indubitable] that*). The verb in the second clause of such sentences is still indicative.

Creo que los inmigrantes **tienen** derecho a conservar su lengua y su cultura.

I believe immigrants have the right to keep their language and their culture.

Here are some useful short forms of verb phrases of opinion.

Creo que sí.	*I think/believe so.*	¡Ya lo creo!	*I should think so!*
Creo que no.	*I don't think/believe so.*	¡Es cierto!	*That's true!*
No lo creo.	*I don't believe it.*		

To assert, use the indicative. To deny or cast doubt, use the subjunctive:
Es verdad que muchos niños *ven* demasiada televisión.
Dudo que mis hijos *vean* demasiada televisión.

B. To deny a statement or to cast doubt on it, use a verb phrase like **no creer que** (*not to believe that*) or **dudar que** (*to doubt that*). In such statements, use a subjunctive verb form in the second clause. (See **Gramática 11.2, 11.3,** and **14.4.**)

No creo que los valores humanos **dependan de** una creencia en Dios.

I do not believe that human values are based on a belief in God.

Here are some verb phrases that require the use of the subjunctive in the second clause; they all express doubt or disbelief.

dudar que	*to doubt that*
no creer que	*not to believe that*
es dudoso que	*it's doubtful that*
es (im)probable que	*it's probable (unlikely) that*
es (im)posible que	*it's (im)possible that*
no es seguro que	*it's not certain that*

C. The following expressions are commonly used by Spanish speakers to react to information.

¡Qué bueno!	*How nice!*
(Eso) Es interesante.	*That's interesting.*
Me alegro.	*I'm glad.*
Estoy muy contento/a.	*I'm very happy.*
Lo siento mucho.	*I'm very sorry.*
(Eso) Me sorprende.	*That surprises me.*
¡Qué lástima!	*What a pity!*
¡Qué triste!	*How sad!*

These expressions can stand alone or be combined into longer sentences explaining what the speaker is reacting to. The conjunctions **y, pero,** and **porque,** followed by the indicative, can be used to link the two parts of the sentence.

> Expressions of reaction:
> Use indicative after **porque, y,** and **pero.**
> **Eso me sorprende, *porque* generalmente él *es* muy simpático.**
> Use subjunctive after **que.**
> **Me sorprende *que* él *sea* tan antipático.**

Estoy muy contenta **porque** mi familia **vive** en un barrio donde hay gente que habla varios idiomas distintos.	*I am very happy because my family lives in a neighborhood where there are people who speak several different languages.*
Lo siento mucho, **pero** el inglés **es** el idioma oficial de este país.	*I am very sorry, but English is the official language of this country.*

Another possibility is to join the two parts of the sentence directly with **que;** the verb in the second clause is then in the subjunctive.

Siento mucho **que tengas** esa opinión; a mí me gusta hablar con personas de otras culturas.	*I am very sorry that you have such an opinion; I like to speak with people from other cultures.*
Es una lástima que no **estemos** de acuerdo.	*It's a pity we do not agree.*

Ejercicio 6

Aquí tiene usted algunas opiniones y afirmaciones de varias personas. Seleccione el presente del indicativo o del subjuntivo para completarlas correctamente.

MODELO: ESTELA: La economía va de mal en peor pero no creo que *sea* culpa de los inmigrantes. (es/sea)

1. PEDRO: Es verdad que _____ inmigrantes árabes y judíos en México. (hay/haya)
2. ESTELA: Dudo que _____ más inmigrantes este año. (vienen/vengan)
3. ERNESTO: Es posible que algunos inmigrantes chinos indocumentados _____ al puerto de Ensenada. (llegan/lleguen)
4. ANDREA: Pero no es probable que el gobierno les _____ quedarse. (permite/permita)
5. ESTELA: Sí, pero es dudoso que los agentes de inmigración los _____. (encuentren/encuentran)
6. PEDRO: Tienes razón. Es verdad que nuestros agentes no _____ muy eficientes. (son/sean)
7. ESTELA: Es interesante que _____ eso; ¿no es agente de inmigración tu tío? (dices/digas)
8. PEDRO: Sí, mi tío Gilito es agente de inmigración, pero él trabaja en el aeropuerto; no es probable que _____ mucho de esto. (sabe/sepa)
9. ESTELA: Ay, bueno, cambiemos de tema; me niego a pensar que no _____ hablar de algo más agradable. (podemos/ podamos)
10. ANDREA: Bien. Además, es seguro que nosotros no _____ a resolver estos problemas. (vamos/vayamos)

me niego a pensar = *I refuse to believe*

Ejercicio 7

Seleccione el presente de indicativo o de subjuntivo para completar las oraciones correctamente.

MODELO: Es interesante que algunos grupos minoritarios *quieran* conservar su lengua y su cultura y otros no. (quieren/quieran)

1. ¡Qué triste que tanta gente _____ que dejar su propio país! (tiene/tenga)
2. Me sorprende que cada día _____ menos cursos de lenguas extranjeras en las universidades. (hay/haya)
3. Me alegro de que en mi barrio todos _____ amigos. (somos/seamos)
4. ¿Por qué? ¿_____ tus vecinos diferentes culturas? (Representan/Representen)
5. Sí, sé que allí _____ gente de cuatro culturas diferentes: mexicanos, japoneses, chinos y norteamericanos. (vive/viva)
6. Es una lástima que no _____ representadas también personas de las otras culturas. (están/estén)
7. Es verdad que no _____ a ningún iraní que viva en mi barrio. (conozco/conozca)

15.5 Expressing Hypothetical Reactions: The Conditional

A. The conditional is formed by adding these endings to the infinitive: **-ía, -ías, -ía, -íamos, -íais,** and **-ían.***

		CONDITIONAL	
(yo)	jugaría	*I would play*	
(tú)	comerías	*you (inf. sing.) would eat*	
(usted, él/ella)	dormiría	*you (pol. sing.) would sleep;*	
		he/she would sleep	
(nosotros/as)	tomaríamos	*we would drink*	
(vosotros/as)	jugaríais	*you (inf. pl., Spain) would play*	
(ustedes, ellos/as)	escribirían	*you (pl.) would write; they would write*	

conditional = infinitive +
- -ía
- -ías
- -ía
- -íamos
- -íais
- -ían

¡OJO!

In some areas of the Spanish-speaking world, the conditional is used very infrequently, being replaced by the imperfect subjunctive: **Si supiera, te lo dijera.** This use is not accepted by the Real Academia or by educational establishments, but it is widespread.

Yo **hablaría** con su familia primero.
I would speak with her family first.
A Alicia Márquez le **gustaría** ir de luna de miel a Cancún.
Alicia Márquez would like to go to Cancún on her honeymoon.

B. The verbs that have irregular stems in the future use the same stems in the conditional.

caber	→	cabría	poner	→	pondría	decir → diría
haber	→	habría	salir	→	saldría	hacer → haría
poder	→	podría	tener	→	tendría	
querer	→	querría	valer	→	valdría	
saber	→	sabría	venir	→	vendría	

—¡Yo no **sabría** qué decirle!
—I wouldn't know what to tell him!

—Pues yo le **diría** la verdad.
—Well, I would tell him the truth.

Ejercicio 8

Aquí aparecen algunas actividades que a los estudiantes de la Universidad de Texas en San Antonio les gustaría hacer en España. Escoja el verbo más lógico y dé la forma del condicional: **acostarse, caminar, comer, comprar, mandar, pasar, practicar, tomar, tratar, usar, visitar.**

1. Si tuvieran mucho tiempo libre, Esteban y Carmen _____ los sitios turísticos.
2. Alberto _____ de conocer a nuevos amigos.

---

*Recognition: **vos hablarías**

3. Si Nora tuviera mucho dinero, _____ zapatos españoles.
4. Pablo y Mónica _____ tapas y _____ cerveza por la tarde.
5. Todos _____ el español.
6. Esteban _____ por el parque del Retiro.
7. Pablo _____ mucho tiempo en el Museo del Prado.
8. Todos _____ el metro para ir de un lugar a otro.
9. Si Mónica y Nora no asistieran a clases, _____ a la 1:00 cada noche.
10. Luis les _____ mensajes electrónicos a sus amigos todos los días.

15.6 Hypothesizing: *If* Clauses and the Past Subjunctive

A. Statements of possibility introduced with the conjunction **si** (*if*) take indicative verb forms in both the *if* clause and the conclusion.

Si el gobierno **congela** los alquileres, **habrá** menos desamparados.	*If the government freezes rents, there will be fewer homeless people.*
Si hay poco trabajo, menos trabajadores sin documentos **cruzan** la frontera.	*If there is little work, fewer workers cross the border illegally.*

> In "contrary-to-fact" sentences, the verb in the **si** (*if*) clause is in the past subjunctive.

B. To imply that a situation is contrary to fact, however, another form, the past subjunctive, must be used in the *if* clause and a conditional verb form in the conclusion. (See **Gramática 15.5.**)

Si tuviera más dinero, **me jubilaría.**	*If I had more money, I would retire.*

Past subjunctive forms of both regular and irregular verbs are based on the stem of the preterite plus these endings: **-ara, -aras, -ara, -áramos, -arais, -aran** for **-ar** verbs and **-iera, -ieras, -iera, -iéramos, -ierais, -ieran** for **-er** and **-ir** verbs.*

PAST SUBJUNCTIVE

hablar	comer	tener
hablara	comiera	tuviera
hablaras	comieras	tuvieras
hablara	comiera	tuviera
habláramos	comiéramos	tuviéramos
hablarais	comierais	tuvierais
hablaran	comieran	tuvieran

---

*Recognition: **vos hablaras, comieras, tuvieras**

Si su madre **trabajara,** Marisa y
  Clarisa **tendrían que estar**
  todo el día en la guardería.

*If their mother worked, Marisa
  and Clarisa would have to be at
  the childcare center all day.*

Verbs like **decir** (**dij-**) and **traer** (**traj-**) differ somewhat from the pattern; they take endings without the initial **-i: dijera, trajera.**

Te sorprenderías si yo **te dijera**
  la verdad.

*You'd be surprised if I told you
  the truth.*

C. You can also use the expression **ojalá que** (*I wish that*) followed by the past subjunctive to express a desire that is contrary to fact.

Ojalá que **hubiera** menos
  contaminación.

I wish there were less pollution.

Ejercicio 9

Amanda está hablando de sí misma, de sus amigos y de sus vecinos. Complete las oraciones con la forma correcta del imperfecto de subjuntivo.

1. Si (yo) _____ este año, podría buscar un trabajo de jornada completa. (graduarse)
2. Si no _____ tan caro, mi padre compraría un coche eléctrico. (ser)
3. Si _____ (nosotros), no tendríamos que manejar distancias tan largas. (mudarse)
4. Si Guillermo y Rafael no _____ a tantas fiestas, sacarían mejores notas en el colegio. (ir)
5. Si más gente _____ la energía verde, no tendríamos que construir más reactores nucleares. (usar)
6. Si no _____ computadora, mi hermano Ernestito no podría usar el CD-ROM para aprender inglés y matemáticas. (tener)

Ejercicio 10

Escriba la forma correcta del verbo entre paréntesis.

1. Si cada persona _____ (tener) una computadora, muchos _____ (trabajar) en su casa en vez de ir a la oficina todos los días.
2. Si los jóvenes _____ (pasar) más tiempo navegando por Internet, _____ (ver) menos programas violentos en la televisión.
3. Si nosotros _____ (consultar) solamente sitios Web en español, _____ (aprender) mucho.
4. Si las computadoras no _____ (contaminar) el medio ambiente, yo _____ (estar) más contento/a de tenerlas.
5. Si los alimentos transgénicos no _____ (causar) problemas de salud, _____ (ser) la solución perfecta al problema del hambre en el mundo.
6. Pues... si el gobierno _____ (permitir) los alimentos transgénicos, probablemente _____ (haber) problemas ambientales muy graves.

Las fantásticas creaciones de Susana Buyo

Las creaciones de Susana Buyo son hermosas y tienen un nombre muy original: *alebrijes*.* La palabra describe perfectamente estas fantásticas figuras que representan dragones con cabeza de serpiente, sirenas con alas,[1] pájaros con dientes y muchas otras formas. Los alebrijes están

hechos de cartón y varios otros materiales. La artista los pinta con acrílico y los termina con laca.[2]

El gran artista mexicano Pedro Linares inventó los alebrijes en 1950. Esta invención hizo muy famoso a Linares, ganándole el Premio Nacional de Artes Tradicionales en 1990. Susana Buyo fue discípula del maestro por un tiempo y pronto se convirtió en una creadora extraordinaria de alebrijes.

Buyo es argentina, pero vive y trabaja en México. En México dirige varios talleres de artesanía[3] y ha tenido exposiciones en museos importantes.[†] Una de las metas profesionales de Susana Buyo es la de estimular el impulso creativo de sus discípulos. Por eso invita a los más talentosos a exponer su obra con ella.

¿Qué opina usted de los alebrijes? Mire las fotos. ¿Qué impresión le producen estas figuras? Para Susana Buyo, los alebrijes son la forma externa que toman sus sueños, la imagen de sus inseguridades[4] y preocupaciones. Gracias al don[5] artístico de esta creadora argentina, las imágenes que la asustan[6] cuando duerme se transforman en bellas criaturas. ■

[1]*sirenas… winged mermaids*   [2]*lacquer*   [3]*talleres… arts and crafts workshops*   [4]*insecurities*   [5]*gift, talent*   [6]la… *frighten her*

*La palabra *alebrije* se deriva del verbo *alebrarse*, que se refiere a la acción de tirarse al suelo, como lo haría un conejo con miedo.
[†]Por ejemplo, el Museo Soumaya de la Ciudad de México, el Museo Nacional de Culturas Populares y el Museo de la Ciudad de México. La obra de Buyo ha sido adquirida por coleccionistas de muchos países. Hay alebrijes en Copenhague, Estocolmo, Londres, Nueva York, Los Ángeles y Buenos Aires, entre otras ciudades.

Guinea Ecuatorial,
país hispano
de África

Territorio ecuatoguineano:[1] 28.051 kilómetros
cuadrados (17.433 millas cuadradas)

Población: 616.459 habitantes

Capital: Malabo (50.000 habitantes)

Idioma oficial: el español

Ubicación[2] geográfica: centro oeste de África

Guinea Ecuatorial es uno de los países más
nuevos del mundo, pues no recibió su nombre
hasta 1963 ni su independencia hasta 1968. Es
también el único país de cultura hispana en el
continente africano. En Guinea Ecuatorial se hablan
varios idiomas aborígenes,* pero una de las
lenguas oficiales es el español.

Esta pequeña nación africana está compuesta
de un territorio continental, el llamado Río Muni, y
cinco islas en el Océano Atlántico. Guinea Ecuatorial fue gobernada por Portugal de 1471 a 1778. La
primera expedición española llegó en 1778 y el país
fue colonizado por España poco después. Es por

La cantante Concha Buika

eso que hay tanta influencia hispana en muchos
aspectos de su sociedad.
La religión predominante,
por ejemplo, es la cató-
lica, aunque el gobierno
fomenta la libertad reli-
giosa.[†] Desde 1984, año
en que se celebró el Pri-
mer Congreso Cultural
Afrohispano, el gobierno
ecuatoguineano busca la
convivencia[3] de sus raíces
hispanas y africanas. Muchas personas de Guinea
Ecuatorial inmigran a España y tienen pocos problemas puesto que hablan el idioma. Entre ellas se
cuenta la familia de la famosa y talentosa cantante
Concha Buika. Sus padres son de Guinea Ecuatorial, pero ella nació en Palma de Mallorca, España, y
ahora vive y trabaja en Madrid.

La cultura de los grupos étnicos en Guinea
Ecuatorial es muy rica, especialmente su tradición
musical.[‡] El instrumento más popular del país es
un arpa que se hace con bambú. El arte de Guinea
Ecuatorial también es impresionante. Las máscaras[4]
de madera son las piezas más representativas del
arte ecuatoguineano. Se debe mencionar también
la cocina de Guinea Ecuatorial, que es sencilla pero
muy sabrosa. Muchos platillos llevan carne de res,
pollo o pescado, y todos se condimentan con espe-
cias que crecen en los bosques del país.[§]

El presidente de Guinea Ecuatorial, Teodoro
Obiang, tiene dos metas principales, que son mejorar
la economía y reformar el sistema educativo del país.
Entre sus proyectos culturales se encuentra la crea-
ción de museos para el arte tradicional y programas
de promoción de las lenguas aborígenes. Hasta
ahora los planes del presidente han dado fruto. El
país afrohispano prospera.

[1]*Equato-Guinean* [2]*Location* [3]*coexistence* [4]*masks*

NIGERIA

CAMERÚN

Malabo

GUINEA
ECUATORIAL

GABÓN

EL OCÉANO ATLÁNTICO

---

*Estos idiomas son, entre otros: fang, bubi, combe, bissio, annabonés y pichi (lengua basada en el inglés, *Pidgin English*).

[†]Existen más de veinte religiones, entre otras: la bautista, la evangélica, la adventista y la metodista. El gobierno también acepta la práctica de algunas creencias paganas.

[‡]Los tres grupos étnicos principales son el fang, el bubi y el ndow.

[§]Uno de los platillos que más se come es pollo con salsa de maní (cacahuate), el cual se sirve con plátano hervido y arroz.

Pablo Picasso (1881–1973) ha pasado a la historia como uno de los grandes genios del siglo XX. Su pintura es sinónimo de revolución y cambio. Desde su llegada a París en 1904, el pintor andaluz[1] comienza a explorar diferentes estilos. Surgen

Picasso y el *Guernica*

Autorretrato

entonces sus «épocas cromáticas»: la azul y la rosa. Picasso pasa luego al cubismo, un tipo de pintura geometrizada.

Durante toda su vida de artista, Picasso estuvo experimentando y cambiando de estilo. Hombre genial e incansable,[2] también se comprometió[3] políticamente. Apoyó la República[4] y en 1937 pintó el cuadro *Guernica,* haciendo así una fuerte denuncia de los crímenes del fascismo. El suceso[5] que inspiró esta obra fue un trágico episodio de la historia española. E1 28 de abril de 1937 las fuerzas fascistas alemanas bombardearon el pueblo de Guernica, situado al norte de España. Lo hicieron como experimento. Querían saber si un bombardeo aéreo podía destruir una población completa.

La famosa pintura de Picasso critica duramente la guerra y el tratamiento inhumano de los ciudadanos de Guernica. La masacre de este pueblo marca el comienzo de una de las más largas dictaduras de nuestro siglo: el *franquismo.* El general Francisco Franco, después de dirigir un golpe militar contra el gobierno español republicano, triunfó en 1939. Controló el destino de España hasta 1975, año de su muerte.

Picasso pidió en su testamento que el *Guernica* no se exhibiera en España hasta que su país tuviera

Guernica

un gobierno democrático. En 1981, los españoles eligieron un gobierno encabezado[6] por Felipe González, líder popular del Partido Socialista de España (PSOE). Ese mismo año, el *Guernica* fue trasladado por fin al Museo del Prado en Madrid. El pueblo español pudo admirar la obra por primera vez desde que Picasso la creó en 1937.

---

[1]de Andalucía, región al sur de España   [2]genial… *brilliant and tireless*   [3]se… *he was involved*   [4]partido que luchaba contra el general fascista Francisco Franco durante la Guerra Civil española (1936–1939)   [5]*event*   [6]*headed*

El nuevo espectáculo de son jarocho

La palabra «jarocho» se refiere a los habitantes del estado de Veracruz en México, pero también se asocia con un estilo de música y danza conocido como el «son jarocho», que ha sido parte de la cultura veracruzana desde hace más de 200 años. El son jarocho se baila zapateando[1] sobre una plataforma de madera llamada **tarima**; dos de sus instrumentos principales son el arpa y la jarana, que es un tipo de guitarra. El traje típico es blanco con motivos rojos. Entre los muchos espectáculos de son jarocho se encuentra «La Bamba», baile que se origina en el estado de Veracruz y es uno de los números más populares del Ballet Folklórico de México. Con «La Bamba», la cultura veracruzana y el son jarocho han llegado a conocerse a nivel internacional.

El estilo del son jarocho refleja una mezcla de influencias culturales al incorporar ritmos africanos, técnicas vocales indígenas y formas musicales españolas como el flamenco. Este estilo se hizo popular a comienzos del siglo XX y para mediados de siglo se había convertido en un producto cultural tan comercializado como el mariachi.

A partir de los años 70, surgió un grupo de músicos que se dedica a recuperar el son jarocho auténtico y a protegerlo de las influencias extranjeras. Pero las influencias y fusiones caracterizan nuestra época. De hecho, como el flamenco en España, el jarocho veracruzano está pasando por un momento de transformación inevitable. Para muchas personas, este cambio es dañino; para otras, es necesario. En todo caso, desde sus

comienzos el jarocho nace como fusión de estilos —africano, indígena, español— y esta fusión es característica de su historia.

Una de las nuevas representaciones del son jarocho es el espectáculo *Jarocho* que se estrenó[2] en Jalapa, Veracruz, en 2003. Su director, Richard O'Neal, es británico de raíces afrocaribeñas y se hizo famoso con su producción de *Riverdance*, el espectáculo de baile irlandés. Su nueva producción se propone contar la historia de Veracruz por medio de su música y su baile, incorporando otras formas musicales y siempre con una mirada hacia el futuro.

En los números de *Jarocho* se ve claramente la combinación de elementos tradicionales con otros nuevos. La fusión es evidente a nivel artístico: las selecciones musicales abarcan[3] piezas típicas del son jarocho, jazz y música afrocubana. Y el vestuario de los bailarines refleja esta diversidad. La

[1]*stamping or tapping with the feet* [2]*se... premiered* [3]*encompass*

fusión también se revela en la mezcla de orígenes del elenco[4] de *Jarocho*. O'Neal es ciudadano inglés cuya familia emigró del Caribe, y entre los coreógrafos hay un veracruzano, otras dos mexicanas, una española de las Islas Canarias y una afrocubana.

Desde su estreno, *Jarocho* ha provocado un debate acalorado.[5] Algunos críticos opinan que este espectáculo es una corrupción de la tradición y la esencia veracruzanas; otros piensan que es una expresión moderna de la cultura de Veracruz. Muchos señalan como sospechoso el parecido entre el tradicional «zapateado»[6] en *Jarocho* y el baile en línea emblemático de la obra irlandesa *Riverdance*. Parte del rechazo,[7] entonces, está relacionado con la idea de la apropiación cultural. Es decir, ¿cómo se atreve[8] un extranjero a interpretar la tradición veracruzana?

No debe sorprendernos el rechazo crítico cuando se trata de una interpretación nueva o moderna de la música, el baile o el arte tradicional de una región. El debate sobre la autenticidad cultural puede llegar a ser feroz cuando se percibe que hay riesgo[9] de perder o destruir la tradición. Lo interesante es que la obra *Jarocho* de Richard O'Neal sugiere una afirmación —y no una pérdida[10]— de la cultura veracruzana, ya que el encuentro multicultural ha sido parte íntegra de la historia de Veracruz. La música y danza de *Jarocho* son una manifestación del mestizaje[11] que comenzó hace más de 500 años. Este espectáculo es un vívido ejemplo del movimiento que caracteriza este milenio y que borra las fronteras entre las culturas y su expresión.

[4](theater) company [5]heated [6]heel-tapping [7]rejection [8]se... dares [9]risk [10]loss [11]mezcla de razas

VERBS

A. Regular Verbs: Simple Tenses

INFINITIVE / PRESENT PARTICIPLE / PAST PARTICIPLE	INDICATIVE PRESENT	IMPERFECT	PRETERITE	FUTURE	CONDITIONAL	SUBJUNCTIVE PRESENT	IMPERFECT	IMPERATIVE
hablar	hablo	hablaba	hablé	hablaré	hablaría	hable	hablara	
hablando	hablas	hablabas	hablaste	hablarás	hablarías	hables	hablaras	habla tú, no hables
hablado	habla	hablaba	habló	hablará	hablaría	hable	hablara	hable Ud.
	hablamos	hablábamos	hablamos	hablaremos	hablaríamos	hablemos	habláramos	hablemos
	habláis	hablabais	hablasteis	hablaréis	hablaríais	habléis	hablarais	hablad
	hablan	hablaban	hablaron	hablarán	hablarían	hablen	hablaran	hablen
comer	como	comía	comí	comeré	comería	coma	comiera	
comiendo	comes	comías	comiste	comerás	comerías	comas	comieras	come tú, no comas
comido	come	comía	comió	comerá	comería	coma	comiera	coma Ud.
	comemos	comíamos	comimos	comeremos	comeríamos	comamos	comiéramos	comamos
	coméis	comíais	comisteis	comeréis	comeríais	comáis	comierais	comed
	comen	comían	comieron	comerán	comerían	coman	comieran	coman
vivir	vivo	vivía	viví	viviré	viviría	viva	viviera	
viviendo	vives	vivías	viviste	vivirás	vivirías	vivas	vivieras	vive tú, no vivas
vivido	vive	vivía	vivió	vivirá	viviría	viva	viviera	viva Ud.
	vivimos	vivíamos	vivimos	viviremos	viviríamos	vivamos	viviéramos	vivamos
	vivís	vivíais	vivisteis	viviréis	viviríais	viváis	vivierais	vivid
	viven	vivían	vivieron	vivirán	vivirían	vivan	vivieran	vivan

B. Regular Verbs: Perfect Tenses

INDICATIVE PRESENT PERFECT		PAST PERFECT		PRETERITE PERFECT		FUTURE PERFECT		CONDITIONAL PERFECT	
he	hablado	había	hablado	hube	hablado	habré	hablado	habría	hablado
has	comido	habías	comido	hubiste	comido	habrás	comido	habrías	comido
ha	vivido	había	vivido	hubo	vivido	habrá	vivido	habría	vivido
hemos		habíamos		hubimos		habremos		habríamos	
habéis		habíais		hubisteis		habréis		habríais	
han		habían		hubieron		habrán		habrían	

SUBJUNCTIVE PRESENT PERFECT		PAST PERFECT	
haya	hablado	hubiera	hablado
hayas	comido	hubieras	comido
haya	vivido	hubiera	vivido
hayamos		hubiéramos	
hayáis		hubierais	
hayan		hubieran	

C. Irregular Verbs

INFINITIVE / PRESENT PARTICIPLE / PAST PARTICIPLE	INDICATIVE					SUBJUNCTIVE		IMPERATIVE
	PRESENT	IMPERFECT	PRETERITE	FUTURE	CONDITIONAL	PRESENT	IMPERFECT	
andar / andando / andado	ando	andaba	anduve	andaré	andaría	ande	anduviera	
	andas	andabas	anduviste	andarás	andarías	andes	anduvieras	anda tú, no andes
	anda	andaba	anduvo	andará	andaría	ande	anduviera	ande Ud.
	andamos	andábamos	anduvimos	andaremos	andaríamos	andemos	anduviéramos	andemos
	andáis	andabais	anduvisteis	andaréis	andaríais	andéis	anduvierais	andad
	andan	andaban	anduvieron	andarán	andarían	anden	anduvieran	anden
caer / cayendo / caído	caigo	caía	caí	caeré	caería	caiga	cayera	
	caes	caías	caíste	caerás	caerías	caigas	cayeras	cae tú, no caigas
	cae	caía	cayó	caerá	caería	caiga	cayera	caiga Ud.
	caemos	caíamos	caímos	caeremos	caeríamos	caigamos	cayéramos	caigamos
	caéis	caíais	caísteis	caeréis	caeríais	caigáis	cayerais	caed
	caen	caían	cayeron	caerán	caerían	caigan	cayeran	caigan
dar / dando / dado	doy	daba	di	daré	daría	dé	diera	
	das	dabas	diste	darás	darías	des	dieras	da tú, no des
	da	daba	dio	dará	daría	dé	diera	dé Ud.
	damos	dábamos	dimos	daremos	daríamos	demos	diéramos	demos
	dais	dabais	disteis	daréis	daríais	deis	dierais	dad
	dan	daban	dieron	darán	darían	den	dieran	den
decir / diciendo / dicho	digo	decía	dije	diré	diría	diga	dijera	
	dices	decías	dijiste	dirás	dirías	digas	dijeras	di tú, no digas
	dice	decía	dijo	dirá	diría	diga	dijera	diga Ud.
	decimos	decíamos	dijimos	diremos	diríamos	digamos	dijéramos	digamos
	decís	decíais	dijisteis	diréis	diríais	digáis	dijerais	decid
	dicen	decían	dijeron	dirán	dirían	digan	dijeran	digan
estar / estando / estado	estoy	estaba	estuve	estaré	estaría	esté	estuviera	
	estás	estabas	estuviste	estarás	estarías	estés	estuvieras	está tú, no estés
	está	estaba	estuvo	estará	estaría	esté	estuviera	esté Ud.
	estamos	estábamos	estuvimos	estaremos	estaríamos	estemos	estuviéramos	estemos
	estáis	estabais	estuvisteis	estaréis	estaríais	estéis	estuvierais	estad
	están	estaban	estuvieron	estarán	estarían	estén	estuvieran	estén
haber / habiendo / habido	he	había	hube	habré	habría	haya	hubiera	
	has	habías	hubiste	habrás	habrías	hayas	hubieras	
	ha	había	hubo	habrá	habría	haya	hubiera	
	hemos	habíamos	hubimos	habremos	habríamos	hayamos	hubiéramos	
	habéis	habíais	hubisteis	habréis	habríais	hayáis	hubierais	
	han	habían	hubieron	habrán	habrían	hayan	hubieran	
hacer / haciendo / hecho	hago	hacía	hice	haré	haría	haga	hiciera	
	haces	hacías	hiciste	harás	harías	hagas	hicieras	haz tú, no hagas
	hace	hacía	hizo	hará	haría	haga	hiciera	haga Ud.
	hacemos	hacíamos	hicimos	haremos	haríamos	hagamos	hiciéramos	hagamos
	hacéis	hacíais	hicisteis	haréis	haríais	hagáis	hicierais	haced
	hacen	hacían	hicieron	harán	harían	hagan	hicieran	hagan
ir / yendo / ido	voy	iba	fui	iré	iría	vaya	fuera	
	vas	ibas	fuiste	irás	irías	vayas	fueras	ve tú, no vayas
	va	iba	fue	irá	iría	vaya	fuera	vaya Ud.
	vamos	íbamos	fuimos	iremos	iríamos	vayamos	fuéramos	vayamos
	vais	ibais	fuisteis	iréis	iríais	vayáis	fuerais	id
	van	iban	fueron	irán	irían	vayan	fueran	vayan
oír / oyendo / oído	oigo	oía	oí	oiré	oiría	oiga	oyera	
	oyes	oías	oíste	oirás	oirías	oigas	oyeras	oye tú, no oigas
	oye	oía	oyó	oirá	oiría	oiga	oyera	oiga Ud.
	oímos	oíamos	oímos	oiremos	oiríamos	oigamos	oyéramos	oigamos
	oís	oíais	oísteis	oiréis	oiríais	oigáis	oyerais	oíd
	oyen	oían	oyeron	oirán	oirían	oigan	oyeran	oigan

C. Irregular Verbs (continued)

INFINITIVE / PRESENT PARTICIPLE / PAST PARTICIPLE	INDICATIVE					SUBJUNCTIVE		IMPERATIVE
	PRESENT	IMPERFECT	PRETERITE	FUTURE	CONDITIONAL	PRESENT	IMPERFECT	
poder pudiendo podido	puedo puedes puede podemos podéis pueden	podía podías podía podíamos podíais podían	pude pudiste pudo pudimos pudisteis pudieron	podré podrás podrá podremos podréis podrán	podría podrías podría podríamos podríais podrían	pueda puedas pueda podamos podáis puedan	pudiera pudieras pudiera pudiéramos pudierais pudieran	
poner poniendo puesto	pongo pones pone ponemos ponéis ponen	ponía ponías ponía poníamos poníais ponían	puse pusiste puso pusimos pusisteis pusieron	pondré pondrás pondrá pondremos pondréis pondrán	pondría pondrías pondría pondríamos pondríais pondrían	ponga pongas ponga pongamos pongáis pongan	pusiera pusieras pusiera pusiéramos pusierais pusieran	pon tú, no pongas ponga Ud. pongamos poned pongan
querer queriendo querido	quiero quieres quiere queremos queréis quieren	quería querías quería queríamos queríais querían	quise quisiste quiso quisimos quisisteis quisieron	querré querrás querrá querremos querréis querrán	querría querrías querría querríamos querríais querrían	quiera quieras quiera queramos queráis quieran	quisiera quisieras quisiera quisiéramos quisierais quisieran	quiere tú, no quieras quiera Ud. queramos quered quieran
saber sabiendo sabido	sé sabes sabe sabemos sabéis saben	sabía sabías sabía sabíamos sabíais sabían	supe supiste supo supimos supisteis supieron	sabré sabrás sabrá sabremos sabréis sabrán	sabría sabrías sabría sabríamos sabríais sabrían	sepa sepas sepa sepamos sepáis sepan	supiera supieras supiera supiéramos supierais supieran	sabe tú, no sepas sepa Ud. sepamos sabed sepan
salir saliendo salido	salgo sales sale salimos salís salen	salía salías salía salíamos salíais salían	salí saliste salió salimos salisteis salieron	saldré saldrás saldrá saldremos saldréis saldrán	saldría saldrías saldría saldríamos saldríais saldrían	salga salgas salga salgamos salgáis salgan	saliera salieras saliera saliéramos salierais salieran	sal tú, no salgas salga Ud. salgamos salid salgan
ser siendo sido	soy eres es somos sois son	era eras era éramos erais eran	fui fuiste fue fuimos fuisteis fueron	seré serás será seremos seréis serán	sería serías sería seríamos seríais serían	sea seas sea seamos seáis sean	fuera fueras fuera fuéramos fuerais fueran	sé tú, no seas sea Ud. seamos sed sean
tener teniendo tenido	tengo tienes tiene tenemos tenéis tienen	tenía tenías tenía teníamos teníais tenían	tuve tuviste tuvo tuvimos tuvisteis tuvieron	tendré tendrás tendrá tendremos tendréis tendrán	tendría tendrías tendría tendríamos tendríais tendrían	tenga tengas tenga tengamos tengáis tengan	tuviera tuvieras tuviera tuviéramos tuvierais tuvieran	ten tú, no tengas tenga Ud. tengamos tened tengan
traer trayendo traído	traigo traes trae traemos traéis traen	traía traías traía traíamos traíais traían	traje trajiste trajo trajimos trajisteis trajeron	traeré traerás traerá traeremos traeréis traerán	traería traerías traería traeríamos traeríais traerían	traiga traigas traiga traigamos traigáis traigan	trajera trajeras trajera trajéramos trajerais trajeran	trae tú, no traigas traiga Ud. traigamos traed traigan

C. Irregular Verbs (continued)

INFINITIVE / PRESENT PARTICIPLE / PAST PARTICIPLE	INDICATIVE					SUBJUNCTIVE		IMPERATIVE
	PRESENT	IMPERFECT	PRETERITE	FUTURE	CONDITIONAL	PRESENT	IMPERFECT	
venir viniendo venido	vengo vienes viene venimos venís vienen	venía venías venía veníamos veníais venían	vine viniste vino vinimos vinisteis vinieron	vendré vendrás vendrá vendremos vendréis vendrán	vendría vendrías vendría vendríamos vendríais vendrían	venga vengas venga vengamos vengáis vengan	viniera vinieras viniera viniéramos vinierais vinieran	ven tú, no vengas venga Ud. vengamos venid vengan
ver viendo visto	veo ves ve vemos veis ven	veía veías veía veíamos veíais veían	vi viste vio vimos visteis vieron	veré verás verá veremos veréis verán	vería verías vería veríamos veríais verían	vea veas vea veamos veáis vean	viera vieras viera viéramos vierais vieran	ve tú, no veas vea Ud. veamos ved vean

D. Stem-Changing and Spelling Change Verbs

INFINITIVE / PRESENT PARTICIPLE / PAST PARTICIPLE	INDICATIVE					SUBJUNCTIVE		IMPERATIVE
	PRESENT	IMPERFECT	PRETERITE	FUTURE	CONDITIONAL	PRESENT	IMPERFECT	
pensar (ie) pensando pensado	pienso piensas piensa pensamos pensáis piensan	pensaba pensabas pensaba pensábamos pensabais pensaban	pensé pensaste pensó pensamos pensasteis pensaron	pensaré pensarás pensará pensaremos pensaréis pensarán	pensaría pensarías pensaría pensaríamos pensaríais pensarían	piense pienses piense pensemos penséis piensen	pensara pensaras pensara pensáramos pensarais pensaran	piensa tú, no pienses piense Ud. pensemos pensad piensen
volver (ue) volviendo vuelto	vuelvo vuelves vuelve volvemos volvéis vuelven	volvía volvías volvía volvíamos volvíais volvían	volví volviste volvió volvimos volvisteis volvieron	volveré volverás volverá volveremos volveréis volverán	volvería volverías volvería volveríamos volveríais volverían	vuelva vuelvas vuelva volvamos volváis vuelvan	volviera volvieras volviera volviéramos volvierais volvieran	vuelve tú, no vuelvas vuelva Ud. volvamos volved vuelvan
dormir (ue, u) durmiendo dormido	duermo duermes duerme dormimos dormís duermen	dormía dormías dormía dormíamos dormíais dormían	dormí dormiste durmió dormimos dormisteis durmieron	dormiré dormirás dormirá dormiremos dormiréis dormirán	dormiría dormirías dormiría dormiríamos dormiríais dormirían	duerma duermas duerma durmamos durmáis duerman	durmiera durmieras durmiera durmiéramos durmierais durmieran	duerme tú, no duermas duerma Ud. durmamos dormid duerman
sentir (ie, i) sintiendo sentido	siento sientes siente sentimos sentís sienten	sentía sentías sentía sentíamos sentíais sentían	sentí sentiste sintió sentimos sentisteis sintieron	sentiré sentirás sentirá sentiremos sentiréis sentirán	sentiría sentirías sentiría sentiríamos sentiríais sentirían	sienta sientas sienta sintamos sintáis sientan	sintiera sintieras sintiera sintiéramos sintierais sintieran	siente tú, no sientas sienta Ud. sintamos sentid sientan

D. Stem-Changing and Spelling Change Verbs (continued)

INFINITIVE PRESENT PARTICIPLE PAST PARTICIPLE	INDICATIVE					SUBJUNCTIVE		IMPERATIVE
	PRESENT	IMPERFECT	PRETERITE	FUTURE	CONDITIONAL	PRESENT	IMPERFECT	
pedir (i, i) pidiendo pedido	pido pides pide pedimos pedís piden	pedía pedías pedía pedíamos pedíais pedían	pedí pediste pidió pedimos pedisteis pidieron	pediré pedirás pedirá pediremos pediréis pedirán	pediría pedirías pediría pediríamos pediríais pedirían	pida pidas pida pidamos pidáis pidan	pidiera pidieras pidiera pidiéramos pidierais pidieran	pide tú, no pidas pida Ud. pidamos pedid pidan
reír (i, i) riendo reído	río ríes ríe reímos reís ríen	reía reías reía reíamos reíais reían	reí reíste rió reímos reísteis rieron	reiré reirás reirá reiremos reiréis reirán	reiría reirías reiría reiríamos reiríais reirían	ría rías ría riamos riáis rían	riera rieras riera riéramos rierais rieran	ríe tú, no rías ría Ud. riamos reíd rían
seguir (i, i) (g) siguiendo seguido	sigo sigues sigue seguimos seguís siguen	seguía seguías seguía seguíamos seguíais seguían	seguí seguiste siguió seguimos seguisteis siguieron	seguiré seguirás seguirá seguiremos seguiréis seguirán	seguiría seguirías seguiría seguiríamos seguiríais seguirían	siga sigas siga sigamos sigáis sigan	siguiera siguieras siguiera siguiéramos siguierais siguieran	sigue tú, no sigas siga Ud. sigamos seguid sigan
construir (y) construyendo construido	construyo construyes construye construimos construís construyen	construía construías construía construíamos construíais construían	construí construiste construyó construimos construisteis construyeron	construiré construirás construirá construiremos construiréis construirán	construiría construirías construiría construiríamos construiríais construirían	construya construyas construya construyamos construyáis construyan	construyera construyeras construyera construyéramos construyerais construyeran	construye tú, no construyas construya Ud. construyamos construid construyan
producir (zc) produciendo producido	produzco produces produce producimos producís producen	producía producías producía producíamos producíais producían	produje produjiste produjo produjimos produjisteis produjeron	produciré producirás producirá produciremos produciréis producirán	produciría producirías produciría produciríamos produciríais producirían	produzca produzcas produzca produzcamos produzcáis produzcan	produjera produjeras produjera produjéramos produjerais produjeran	produce tú, no produzcas produzca Ud. produzcamos producid produzcan

E. Reflexive Verbs

INFINITIVE PRESENT PARTICIPLE PAST PARTICIPLE	INDICATIVE					SUBJUNCTIVE		IMPERATIVE
	PRESENT	IMPERFECT	PRETERITE	FUTURE	CONDITIONAL	PRESENT	IMPERFECT	
acostarse (ue) acostándose acostado	me acuesto te acuestas se acuesta nos acostamos os acostáis se acuestan	me acostaba te acostabas se acostaba nos acostábamos os acostabais se acostaban	me acosté te acostaste se acostó nos acostamos os acostasteis se acostaron	me acostaré te acostarás se acostará nos acostaremos os acostaréis se acostarán	me acostaría te acostarías se acostaría nos acostaríamos os acostaríais se acostarían	me acueste te acuestes se acueste nos acostemos os acostéis se acuesten	me acostara te acostaras se acostara nos acostáramos os acostarais se acostaran	acuéstate tú no te acuestes acuéstese Ud. acostémonos acostaos acuéstense
vestirse (i, i) vistiéndose vestido	me visto te vistes se viste nos vestimos os vestís se visten	me vestía te vestías se vestía nos vestíamos os vestíais se vestían	me vestí te vestiste se vistió nos vestimos os vestisteis se vistieron	me vestiré te vestirás se vestirá nos vestiremos os vestiréis se vestirán	me vestiría te vestirías se vestiría nos vestiríamos os vestiríais se vestirían	me vista te vistas se vista nos vistamos os vistáis se vistan	me vistiera te vistieras se vistiera nos vistiéramos os vistierais se vistieran	vístete tú no te vistas vístase Ud. vistámonos vestíos vístanse

Appendix Two

GRAMMAR SUMMARY TABLES

I. Personal Pronouns

SUBJECT	OBJECT OF PREPOSITION	REFLEXIVE	INDIRECT OBJECT	DIRECT OBJECT
yo	mí	me	me	me
tú	ti	te	te	te
usted	usted	se	le	lo/la
él	él	se	le	lo
ella	ella	se	le	la
nosotros/as	nosotros/as	nos	nos	nos
vosotros/as	vosotros/as	os	os	os
ustedes	ustedes	se	les	los/las
ellos	ellos	se	les	los
ellas	ellas	se	les	las

II. Possessive Adjectives and Pronouns

ADJECTIVES		PRONOUNS	
my	mi, mis	*mine*	mío/a, míos/as
your (inf. sing.)	tu, tus	*yours*	tuyo/a, tuyos/as
your (pol. sing.)	su, sus	*yours*	suyo/a, suyos/as
his	su, sus	*his*	suyo/a, suyos/as
her	su, sus	*hers*	suyo/a, suyos/as
our	nuestro/a, nuestros/as	*ours*	nuestro/a, nuestros/as
your (inf. pl.)	vuestro/a, vuestros/as	*yours*	vuestro/a, vuestros/as
your (pol. pl.)	su, sus	*yours*	suyo/a, suyos/as
their	su, sus	*theirs*	suyo/a, suyos/as

III. Demonstrative Adjectives and Pronouns*

MASCULINE AND FEMININE	ADJECTIVES AND PRONOUNS	NEUTER PRONOUNS
this, these	este/esta, estos/estas	esto
that, those *(not close to speaker)*	ese/esa, esos/esas	eso
that, those *(farther from speaker)*	aquel/aquella, aquellos/aquellas	aquello

IV. *Ser / estar*

ser		estar	
Description: inherent qualities, profession, religion	Yo soy un poco tímido. Nosotros somos médicos. Mi esposo es musulmán.	*Description of a condition, a transitory state*	Mis hijos estan enfermos. Yo estoy muy cansada.
Location of an event	¿Dónde es la clase? La fiesta es en el hotel Miramar.	*Location of object*	¿Dónde está el teatro? Está en la Avenida Bolívar.
Date (day, month) and telling time	Hoy es miércoles. ¿Qué hora es? Son las dos menos cuarto.	*Activities in progress* (**estar** + *gerund/present participle*)	Enrique, ¿qué estás haciendo ahora? Mi esposa y yo estamos viendo la televisión.
Origin, possession, and material (**ser de...**)	¿De dónde son ustedes? Somos de Perú. Los libros son de Carmen y Mónica. Las flores son de papel.	*Certain fixed expressions*	Estar de vacaciones. Estar de viaje. Estar de acuerdo. Estar de buen/mal humor.
Impersonal expressions	Es importante estudiar cada noche.	*Result of an action* (**estar** + *past participle*)	Los tacos ya están preparados.

V. *Por / para*

por		para	
Substitution for	Trabajo por Juan.	*Recipient*	Este regalo es para ti.
In exchange for/paying	por treinta pesos	*Employer*	Mi novio trabaja para la compañía de su padre.
Movement by, through, or along a place	por el parque	*Destination*	para Madrid
Length of time (may be omitted)	por doce horas	*Telling time*	Faltan diez para las once.
General time or area	por la noche	*Deadline*	para el viernes
Transportation	por avión	*Purpose*	Un lápiz es para escribir.

---

*In *Dos mundos* and many other books you may see an accent on these pronouns because, until recently, they were always written with an accent mark to distinguish them from demonstrative adjectives. Up-to-date usage suggests that the accent mark may be omitted when context makes the meaning clear. Obviously, all books published before the rule was changed have accents on demonstrative pronouns. Books published after this change may or may not use the accent.

VI. Past (Preterite) and Imperfect

PAST		IMPERFECT	
completed event	comí	*event in progress*	comía
completed state	estuve	*ongoing state*	estaba
completed series	bailé, canté	*"used to"*	bailaba, cantaba

VII. Indicative and Subjunctive

NOUN CLAUSES			
INDICATIVE		**SUBJUNCTIVE**	
assertion	es verdad que	*possibility*	es posible que
belief	creer que	*doubt*	dudar que
knowledge	saber que	*subjective reaction*	estar contento/a de que
		volition	querer que

ADJECTIVE CLAUSES	
INDICATIVE	**SUBJUNCTIVE**
known antecedent	*unknown antecedent*
Tengo un amigo que sabe…	Busco un amigo que sepa…
existent antecedent	*nonexistent antecedent*
Hay una persona que sabe…	No hay nadie que sepa…

ADVERBIAL CLAUSES: TIME	
INDICATIVE	**SUBJUNCTIVE**
cuando hasta que tan pronto como } + *habitual action* en cuanto después de que	cuando hasta que tan pronto como } + *future action* en cuanto después de que
Siempre cuando trabaja…	Mañana cuando trabaje…

Appendix Three

Syllabication

1. The basic rule of Spanish syllabication is to make each syllable end in a vowel whenever possible.

2. When attempting to divide a word into syllables, it is easier to look for the consonants and do the following:
   a. If the consonants in a word occur singly, each consonant should go with the following vowel: ca-sa, di-ga, ca-mi-na
   b. If there are two consecutive consonants, one will go with the preceding vowel and one with the following: al-co-hol, can-tan-te, es-cue-la, ac-ción, in-no-va-ción
   c. If there are three consecutive or more consonants, the first two will remain with the preceding vowel and the third (etc.) will go with the following vowel: obs-truc-ción, cons-cien-te
   d. The letter **h** always goes with the following vowel: al-co-hol, pro-hí-be
   e. The following consonant combinations are never divided: **br-, dr-, rr-, tr-, bl-, ll-**: a-bran, la-drón, bo-rra-dor, con-tra, ha-blar, man-te-qui-lla

3. Diphthongs (vowel combinations: two weak ones or a weak one and a strong one) are not divided, unless the weak vowel has an orthographic accent. Weak vowels: **i, u;** strong vowels: **a, e, o:** ciu-dad, sie-te, seis, cin-cuen-ta. But: re-ú-no, dí-a

Stress

How you pronounce a specific Spanish word is determined by two basic rules of stress. Written accents to indicate stress are needed only when those rules are violated. Here are the two rules of stress.

1. For words ending in a vowel, **n,** or **s,** the natural stress falls on the next-to-last syllable. The letter **y** is not considered a vowel for stress purposes.

   Es-**te**-ban   **blan**-co   es-**cu**-chen   **ro**-ja   es-**tu**-die

2. For words ending in *any other letter*, the natural stress falls on the last syllable.

   pa-**pel**   ciu-**dad**   es-cri-**bir**   re-**loj**   es-**toy**

   When these stress rules are violated by the word's accepted pronunciation, stress must be indicated with a written accent.

   in-**glés**   e-**léc**-tri-co   es-tu-**dié**   lla-ma-**rán**   sim-**pá**-ti-co
   ár-bol   **Ló**-pez   a-**zú**-car   **hués**-ped   a-**quí**

   Note that words that are stressed on any syllable other than the last or next-to-last will always show a written accent. Particularly frequent words in this category include adjectives and adverbs ending in **-ísimo** and verb forms with pronouns attached.

   gua-**pí**-si-mo   es-pe-**rán**-do-te   **pí**-de-se-las   de-**vuél**-van-se-la

   Written accents to show violations of stress rules are particularly important when diphthongs are involved. A diphthong is a combination of a weak (**i, u**) vowel and a strong (**a, e, o**) vowel (in either order), or of two weak vowels together. The two vowels are pronounced as a single sound, with one of the vowels being given slightly more emphasis than the other. In all diphthongs the strong vowel or the second of the two weak vowels receives this slightly greater stress.

   *a*i: b*a*ilar   i*a*: arteri*a*   u*e*: vu*e*lve   i*o*: vi*o*lento   u*i*: cu*i*dado

   When the stress in a vowel combination does not follow this rule, no diphthong exists. Instead, two separate sounds are heard, and a written accent appears over the weak vowel or the first of two weak vowels.

   a-í: país   ú-e: continúe   í-o: frío   í-a: tía   e-ú: reúnen   o-í: oído

Use of Written Accent as a Diacritic

The written accent is also used to distinguish two words with similar spelling and pronunciation but different meaning.

Nine common word pairs are identical in spelling and pronunciation; the accent mark is the only distinction between them.

dé	*give*	**de**	*of*	**sí**	*yes*	**si**	*if*
él	*he*	**el**	*the*	**sólo**	*only*	**solo**	*alone*
más	*more*	**mas**	*but*	**té**	*tea*	**te**	*you*
mí	*me*	**mi**	*my*	**tú**	*you*	**tu**	*your*
sé	*I know*	**se**	*(reflexive pronoun)*				

Diacritic accents are used to distinguish demonstrative adjectives from demonstrative pronouns. Although this distinction is disappearing in many parts of the Spanish-speaking world, you may find it in *Dos mundos* and in many other books.

aquellos países	*those countries*	**aquéllos**	*those ones*
esa persona	*that person*	**ésa**	*that one*
este libro	*this book*	**éste**	*this one*

Diacritic accents are placed over relative pronouns or adverbs that are used interrogatively or in exclamations.

cómo	*how*	**como**	*as, since*
dónde	*where*	**donde**	*where*
por qué	*why*	**porque**	*because*
qué	*what*	**que**	*that*
quién	*who (interrogative pronoun)*	**quien**	*who (relative pronoun)*
cuándo	*when (interrogative pronoun)*	**cuando**	*when (relative pronoun)*

—¿**Cómo** se llama? *What's his name?*
—No sé **cómo** se llama. *I don't know what his name is.*

Como es niño, tiene que acostarse temprano.
Since he's a child, he must go to bed early.

Spelling Changes

In general, Spanish has a far more phonetic system than many other modern languages. Most Spanish sounds correspond to just one written symbol. Those that can be written in more than one way are of two main types: those for which the sound/letter correspondence is largely arbitrary and those for which the sound/letter correspondence is determined by spelling rules.

A. In the case of arbitrary sound/letter correspondences, writing the sound correctly is mainly a matter of memorization. The following are some of the more common arbitrary, or *nonpatterned*, sound/letter correspondences in Spanish.

SOUND	SPELLING	EXAMPLES
/b/ + *vowel*	b, v	barco, ventana
/y/	y, ll, i + *vowel*	haya, amarillo, hielo
/s/	s, z, c	salario, zapato, cielo, hace
/x/ + e, i	g, j	general, jefe
		gitano, jinete

Note that, although spelling of the sounds /y/ and /s/ is largely arbitrary, two patterns occur with great frequency.

1. /y/   Whenever an unstressed **i** occurs between vowels, the **i** changes to **y.**

   leió → leyó   creiendo → creyendo   caieron → cayeron

2. /s/   The sequences **ze** and **zi** are rare in Spanish. Whenever a **ze** or **zi** combination would occur in the plural of a noun ending in **z** or in a conjugated verb (for example, an **-e** ending on a verb stem that ends in **z**), the **z** changes to **c.**

   luz → luces   voz → voces   empez + é → empecé   taza → tacita

B. There are three major sets of patterned sound/letters sequences.

SOUND	SPELLING	EXAMPLES
/g/	g, gu	**g**ato, pa**gu**e
/k/	c, qu	to**c**a, to**qu**e
/g^w/	gu, gü	a**gu**a, pin**gü**ino

1. /g/ Before the vowel sounds /a/, /o/, and /u/, and before all consonant sounds, the sound /g/ is spelled with the letter **g.**

   gato   **g**ordo   **g**usto   **g**ratis   **G**loria   lle**g**o

   Before the sounds /e/ and /i/, the sound /g/ is spelled with the letters **gu.**

   guerra   **gu**itarra   lle**gu**é

2. /k/ Before the vowel sounds /a/, /o/, and /u/, and before all consonant sounds, the sound /k/ is spelled with the letter **c.**

   casa   **c**osa   **c**urioso   **c**reer   **c**lub   lec**c**ión   to**c**o

   Before the sounds /e/ and /i/, the sound /k/ is spelled with the letters **qu.**

   queso   **qu**ímica   to**qu**é

3. /g^w/ Before the vowel sounds /a/ and /o/, the sound /g^w/ is spelled with the letters **gu.**

   guante   anti**gu**o

   Before the vowel sounds /e/ and /i/, the sound /g^w/ is spelled with the letters **gü.**

   bilin**gü**e   pin**gü**ino

These spelling rules are particularly important in conjugating, because a specific consonant sound in the infinitive must be maintained throughout the conjugation, despite changes in the stem vowels. It will help if you keep in mind the patterns of sound/letter correspondence, rather than attempt to conserve the spelling of the infinitive.

/ga/	= **ga**	lle**g**ar	/ge/	= **gue**	lle**gu**e (*present subjunctive*)
/ga/	= **ga**	lle**g**ar	/ge/	= **gué**	lle**gu**é (*preterite*)
/gi/	= **gui**	se**gu**ir	/go/	= **go**	si**g**o (*present indicative*)
/gi/	= **gui**	se**gu**ir	/ga/	= **ga**	si**g**a (*present subjunctive*)
/xe/	= **ge**	reco**g**er	/xo/	= **jo**	reco**j**o (*present indicative*)
/xe/	= **ge**	reco**g**er	/xa/	= **ja**	reco**j**a (*present subjunctive*)
/g^{w}a/	= **gua**	averi**gu**ar	/g^{w}e/	= **güe**	averi**gü**e (*present subjunctive*)
/ka/	= **ka**	sa**c**ar	/ke/	= **qué**	sa**qu**é (*preterite*)

Appendix Four

ANSWER KEY FOR GRAMÁTICA Y EJERCICIOS

PASO A

Ej. 1: 1. se llama 2. Me llamo 3. se llama 4. Se llama 5. Se llama 6. lleva 7. Lleva 8. llevan 9. Llevan 10. llevo **Ej. 2:** 1. a 2. b 3. a 4. a 5. a 6. a 7. a 8. a 9. b 10. a **Ej. 3:** 1. d 2. a 3. e 4. b 5. c **Ej. 4:** 1. Soy 2. es 3. son 4. Son 5. somos **Ej. 5:** 1. No, no es una chaqueta, es una camisa. 2. No, no es una mujer, es un hombre. 3. No, no es una falda, es un vestido. 4. No, no es un sombrero, es una blusa. 5. No, no es una naranja, es un reloj. **Ej. 6:** 1. La 2. El 3. La 4. El 5. El 6. La 7. La 8. El 9. La 10. El **Ej. 7:** 1. digan 2. escriba 3. cuenten 4. abran (cierren) 5. lea (estudie) 6. saque 7. lean (escriban) 8. abra (cierre)

PASO B

Ej. 1: 1. b 2. b 3. a 4. a 5. b **Ej. 2:** 1. Sí, hay libros en la mesa. 2. Sí, hay un reloj en la pared. 3. Hay un profesora en el salón de clase. 4. No hay un automóvil en el salón de clase. 5. No hay un profesor en el salón de clase. 6. Hay papeles en los pupitres. 7. Hay un bolígrafo en el pupitre de Alberto. 8. Hay muchos cuadernos en el salón de clase. 9. No hay una bicicleta en el salón de clase. 10. Hay una ventana en el salón de clase. **Ej. 3:** 1. En el salón de clase no hay diez pizarras. 2. Mónica no tiene el pelo negro. 3. Carmen no lleva una blusa muy fea. 4. Mi carro no es morado. 5. La profesora Martínez no tiene barba. **Ej. 4:** 1. Marisa tiene un par de zapatos, pero Clarisa tiene dos pares de zapatos. 2. Marisa tiene un perro nuevo, pero Clarisa tiene dos perros nuevos. 3. Marisa tiene una chaqueta roja, pero Clarisa tiene dos chaquetas rojas. 4. Marisa tiene un lápiz amarillo, pero Clarisa tiene dos lápices amarillos. 5. Marisa tiene una amiga norteamericana, pero Clarisa tiene dos amigas norteamericanas. **Ej. 5:** 1. Clarisa tiene un cuaderno pequeño, pero Marisa tiene dos cuadernos pequeños. 2. Clarisa tiene un gato negro, pero Marisa tiene dos gatos negros. 3. Clarisa tiene una fotografía bonita, pero Marisa tiene dos fotografías bonitas. 4. Clarisa tiene un reloj bonito, pero Marisa tiene dos relojes bonitos. 5. Clarisa tiene un libro difícil, pero Marisa tiene dos libros difíciles. 6. Clarisa tiene una amiga divertida, pero Marisa tiene dos amigas divertidas. **Ej. 6:** 1. d, i, k, n 2. b, e, i 3. g, h, 4. a, k, n 5. b, e, i, m 6. b, e, i, o 7. h, l **Ej. 7:** 1. Ashley y Mary Kate Olsen son ricas y bonitas. 2. Will Smith es delgado y elegante. 3. Hillary Clinton es inteligente y rubia. 4. Jennifer López es materialista y talentosa. 5. George Clooney es guapo y tímido. **Ej. 8:** 1. Los libros son difíciles y divertidos. Los libros difíciles son divertidos. 2. La chica es baja y tímida. La chica baja es tímida. 3. Las mujeres son tacañas y trabajadoras. Las mujeres tacañas son trabajadoras. 4. El amigo es inteligente y perezoso. El amigo inteligente es perezoso. 5. Los robots son fuertes y aburridos. Los robots fuertes son aburridos.

PASO C

Ej. 1: 1. tiene 2. tenemos 3. tienes 4. Tengo 5. tienen **Ej. 2:** 1. El carro es de la profesora Martínez. 2. La camisa es de Luis. 3. El perro es de Nora. 4. Los lentes son de Esteban. 5. El saco es de Alberto. 6. La bicicleta es de Carmen. **Ej. 3:** 1. su 2. sus 3. tu 4. mis 5. nuestros 6. sus; nuestras 7. su 8. su 9. tus 10. mi **Ej. 4:** 1. tu; mi 2. tus; mis 3. Su 4. sus; nuestros **Ej. 5:** 1. Adriana Bolini tiene 35 años. 2. Carla Espinosa tiene 22 años. 3. Rubén Hernández Arenas tiene 38 años. 4. Susana Yamasaki González tiene 33 años. 5. Doña María Eulalia González de Saucedo tiene 79 años. **Ej. 6:** 1. Don Eduardo Alvar tiene "X" años. 2. Estela Saucedo tiene "X" años. 3. Ernestito Saucedo tiene "X" años. 4. Amanda Saucedo tiene "X" años. 5. Doña Lola Batini tiene "X" años. **Ej. 7:** 1. Es española. 2. Son japoneses. 3. Es alemán. 4. Son francesas. 5. Son italianas. 6. Es china. 7. Es inglés. 8. Es iraní. 9. Son sirios. **Ej. 8:** 1. hablan 2. habla 3. hablan 4. hablas 5. hablo; hablo **Ej. 9:** 1. habla; español 2. hablan español 3. hablan chino 4. Hablan inglés 5. Hablan hebreo 6. hablas ruso

CAPÍTULO 1

Ej. 1: 1. mil ochocientos setenta y seis 2. mil quinientos ochenta y ocho 3. mil setecientos setenta y cinco 4. mil novecientos noventa y uno 5. dos mil seis 6. mil novecientos cuarenta y cinco 7. mil once 8. mil novecientos veintinueve 9. mil seiscientos quince 10. dos mil veinticinco **Ej. 2:** 1. leen 2. Lees 3. lee 4. Leo 5. lee **Ej. 3:** 1. vive 2. vivimos 3. viven 4. vivís 5. vivo 6. viven **Ej. 4:** 1. ¿Están casados Estela y Ernesto? 2. ¿Son inteligentes Marisa y Clarisa? 3. ¿Tiene un carro nuevo don Eduardo? 4. ¿Viven ustedes en Puerto Rico? 5. ¿Lee Pedro el periódico? **Ej. 5:** 1. ¿Dónde vive Rubén Hernández? 2. ¿Qué idioma habla Susana? 3. ¿Cuándo es la clase de español? 4. ¿Cuántos hijos tienen Ernesto y Estela? 5. ¿Cómo se llama el primer ministro de España? **Ej. 6:** 1. ¿Cuál es tu número de teléfono? 2. ¿Cómo se llama su esposa? 3. ¿Cuándo es el día de tu cumpleaños? 4. ¿Cuántos años tienen? 5. ¿Dónde viven? **Ej. 7:** 1. Son las cuatro y veinte. 2. Son las seis y cuarto. 3. Son las ocho y trece. 4. Es la una y diez. 5. Son las siete y siete. 6. Son las cinco y media. 7. Son las cuatro menos veinticinco. (Son las tres y treinta y cinco.) 8. Son las dos menos once. 9. Son las doce y media. 10. Son las cinco y cuarto. **Ej. 8:** 1. La clase de español es a las once. 2. El baile es a las nueve y media. 3. La conferencia es a las diez. 4. La clase de álgebra es a la una. 5. La fiesta del Club Internacional es a las siete y media. **Ej. 9:** 1. te, me 2. te, me 3. les, nos **Ej. 10:** 1. le, comer 2. le, cocinar 3. les, hablar por teléfono 4. le, leer 5. le, correr

CAPÍTULO 2

Ej. 1: 1.vas; Voy 2. van; va 3. va; va; vamos 4. vas; Voy 5. vas; Voy **Ej. 2:** 1. Ernesto 2. Estela 3. No, Guillermo es la cuarta (persona). 4. No, Amanda es la quinta (persona). 5. Sí. 6. Ramón 7. No, es la séptima (persona). 8. Ernesto 9. doña Lola 10. No, don Anselmo es el cuarto hombre. **Ej. 3:** 1. quiero; prefiere 2. quiere; prefiere 3. quiere; prefiero 4. quiere; prefieren 5. quiere; prefiere 6. quiere; prefiero 7. quiere; prefiere 8. quiere; prefiero 9. quieren; prefiero 10. quieren; prefiere **Ej. 4:** 1. Quiere jugar al béisbol. 2. Prefiero ver un partido de fútbol. 3. Quieren ir de compras. 4. Preferimos estudiar. 5. Prefieren levantar pesas. 6. Quiere viajar. **Ej. 5:** 1. Lan va a estudiar, pero prefiere charlar con sus amigas. 2. Carmen va a levantar pesas, pero prefiere hablar por teléfono. 3. Esteban va a escribir una composición, pero quiere tomar el sol en la playa. 4. Alberto va a montar a caballo, pero prefiere andar en motocicleta. 5. Pablo va a hablar con la profesora, pero prefiere hablar son su amiga. 6. Mi compañera va a hacer la tarea, pero quiere ¿ ?. 7. Yo voy a escuchar la actividades de comprensión, pero prefiero ¿ ?. **Ej. 6:** 1. Esta 2. Estos 3. Estos 4. Estas 5. Este **Ej. 7:** 1. Esas 2. Ese 3. Esa 4. Esos

5. Esos **Ej. 8:** 1. esa 2. este 3. esos 4. este 5. estas **Ej. 9:** 1. Estos 2. Aquellos 3. Esos 4. Esos 5. Aquellas 6. Estas **Ej. 10:** 1. Hace sol. 2. Llueve. 3. Hace frío. 4. Hace mal tiempo. 5. Hace mucho calor. 6. Nieva. **Ej. 11** 1. posible 2. posible 3. imposible 4. imposible 5. imposible

CAPÍTULO 3

Ej. 1: 1. b 2. d 3. f 4. c 5. a 6. e **Ej. 2:** 1. escribimos 2. lleva 3. limpiamos 4. desayunan 5. lee 6. comen 7. anda 8. hablo 9. asisten 10. escuchamos **Ej. 3:** 1. sale, salgo 2. juegas, juego 3. hace, hago 4. juegan, jugamos **Ej. 4:** 1. lo 2. la 3. los 4. las 5. la 6. las 7. los 8. lo **Ej. 5:** 1. Papá, ¿tomas mucho café en el trabajo? 2. Diego, ¿juegan tú y tus amigos al béisbol? 3. Graciela y Diego, ¿tienen ustedes una computadora? 4. Raúl, ¿haces ejercicio en un gimnasio? 5. Señor Ruiz, ¿trabaja usted por la noche? 6. Don Eduardo, ¿prepara usted café por la mañana? 7. Mamá, ¿cocinas por la mañana o por la tarde? 8. Clarisa, ¿ves la televisión por la noche? 9. Doña Rosita, ¿asiste usted a misa los domingos? 10. Doña Lola, ¿lava usted su ropa en casa o en una lavandería? **Ej. 6:** 1. ¿Dónde está su esposo? 2. ¿Cuándo es su cumpleaños? 3. ¿Qué tiene en su mochila? 4. ¿Cuál es la dirección de sus hermanos? 5. ¿Por qué no va(s) a jugar al tenis hoy? 6. ¿Cuánto cuesta el libro de química? **Ej. 7:** 1. estoy en 2. están en 3. estás en 4. estamos en 5. está en 6. estamos 7. estás 8. está 9. están en 10. estamos **Ej. 8:** 1. vamos a la 2. van al 3. vamos al 4. va a la 5. voy a la 6. voy a la 7. van al 8. va a la 9. vamos a la 10. vas al **Ej. 9:** 1. Ernesto y Estela (los esposos Saucedo) son de México pero ahora están en Roma. 2. Mayín Durán es de Panamá pero ahora está en Los Ángeles. 3. Rogelio y Carla son de Puerto Rico pero ahora están en Nueva York. 4. Pilar Álvarez es de España pero ahora está en Guatemala. 5. Ricardo Sícora es de Venezuela pero ahora está en España.

CAPÍTULO 4

Ej. 1: 1. Duermen; dormimos 2. Almuerzan; almorzamos 3. Vuelven; volvemos 4. Juegan; jugamos 5. Juegan; jugamos 6. Pierden; juegan; perdemos; jugamos 7. prefieren; preferimos 8. empiezan; empezamos **Ej. 2:** 1. traigo 2. pongo 3. digo 4. oigo 5. salgo 6. vengo 7. tengo 8. Hago **Ej. 3:** 1. d 2. b 3. f 4. e 5. c 6. g 7. a **Ej. 4:** 1. No, me baño a las ¿?:00. 2. No, me lavo el pelo con champú. 3. No, me afeito en el baño. 4. No, me levanto tarde los domingos. 5. No, me quito la ropa en mi dormitorio (recámara). 6. No, me peino en el baño. 7. No, me

maquillo en el baño / en casa. 8. No, me ducho en el baño. **Ej. 5:** 1. c 2. e 3. d 4. a 5. b **Ej. 6:** 1. c (e) 2. a (e) 3. a (e) 4. b 5. d (e) **Ej. 7:** 1. Después de hacer la compra, Estela prepara la comida. (Antes de preparar la comida, Estela hace la compra.) 2. Después de limpiar la casa, Pedro y Andrea invitan a unos amigos. (Antes de invitar a unos amigos, Pedro y Andrea limpian la casa.) 3. Después de dormir una siesta, Guillermo va al videocentro. (Antes de ir al videocentro, Guillermo duerme una siesta.) 4. Después de correr, te bañas. (Antes de bañarte, corres.) 5. Después de ponernos la ropa, salimos a bailar. (Antes de salir a bailar, nos ponemos la ropa.) **Ej. 8:** 1. c 2. a 3. d 4. f 5. e 6. b **Ej. 9:** 1. ¿Están tristes Clarisa y Marisa? 2. ¿Está enojado (irritado) Ernesto? 3. ¿Están enamorados Ramón y Amanda? 4. ¿Está ocupado Guillermo? 5. ¿Están contentos (enamorados) Silvia y Nacho? **Ej. 10:** 1. e 2. c 3. f 4. a 5. b **Ej. 11:** 1. tiene hambre 2. tienes frío 3. Tenemos calor 4. tengo sueño 5. Tengo prisa 6. tienen sed 7. tengo miedo 8. Tengo sed

CAPÍTULO 5

Ej. 1: 1. Les 2. les 3. le 4. nos 5. me; te 6. les 7. le; nos 8. me; te **Ej. 2:** 1. Frame 1: me; Frame 2: le; Frame 3: le, me; Frame 4: te; Frame 5: le, nos; Frame 6: nos, les **Ej. 3:** 1. sé 2. sabe 3. saben 4. sabes 5. sabemos **Ej. 4:** 1. Puedes 2. Pueden 3. puede 4. pueden 5. Podemos **Ej. 5:** 1. Está leyendo un libro. 2. Están pescando. 3. Está reparando un coche. 4. Está cocinando. 6. Están viendo/ mirando la televisión. 6. Está cuidando al paciente. (Está dándole medicina al paciente.) **Ej. 6:** 1. está calificando 2. está atendiendo 3. está sirviendo 4. está dando 5. está reparando 6. está vendiendo **Ej. 7:** 1. tiene que 2. tienen que 3. tengo que 4. tenemos que 5. tienes que **Ej. 8:** 1. debe 2. debo 3. debes 4. deben 5. debemos **Ej. 9:** 1. quisiera 2. quisiéramos 3. quisieran 4. quisieras 5. quisiera **Ej. 10:** 1. le 2. les 3. le 4. me 5. nos **Ej. 11:** 1. piensa 2. piensas 3. pensamos 4. piensan 5. pienso

CAPÍTULO 6

Ej. 1: 1. El sillón pesa más que la mesa. (La mesa pesa menos que el sillón.) 2. En mi casa viven más personas que en la casa de los vecinos. (En la casa de los vecinos viven menos personas que en mi casa.) 3. La casa de los López tiene más dormitorios que la casa de los vecinos. (La casa de los vecinos tiene menos dormitorios que la casa de los López.) 4. En nuestro patio hay más árboles que en el patio de mis abuelos. (En el patio de mis abuelos hay menos árboles que en

nuestro patio.) 5. En la casa de los Saucedo hay más dormitorios que en la casa de los Ruiz. (En la casa de los Ruiz hay menos dormitorios que en la casa de los Saucedo.) **Ej. 2:** (*Opinions may vary.*) 1. Vivir en el desierto es peor que vivir en el centro. 2. Vivir en una casa es mejor que vivir en un apartamento. 3. Un refrigerador es el más útil de todos. 4. Armando es mayor que Irma. 5. Mi hijo es menor que tu hija. 6. El Rolls Royce es el más caro de todos. **Ej. 3:** (*Answers may vary.*) 1. La piscina de los Lugo es tan bonita como la piscina de los Montes. 2. El edificio de la avenida Oriente no es tan alto como el edificio nuevo de la avenida del Libertador. 3. La lavandería vieja de la avenida Almendros no es tan limpia como la lavandería nueva de la calle Ebro. 4. Los condominios «San Juan» no son tan modernos como los condominios «Princesa». **Ej. 4:** 1. La sala de su casa no tiene tantas lámparas como la sala de nuestra casa. 2. La casa de los Ruiz no tiene tantos cuartos como la casa de los Saucedo. 3. La casa de los vecinos tiene tantos baños como la casa de mis padres. 4. El patio de don Anselmo no tiene tantas flores y plantas como el patio de doña Lola. **Ej. 5:** 1. Sí, (No, no) compré un espejo. 2. Sí, (No, no) comí en un restaurante. 3. Sí, (No, no) hablé por teléfono. 4. Sí, (No, no) escribí una carta. 5. Sí, (No, no) estudié por cuatro horas. 6. Sí, (No, no) abrí la ventana. 7. Sí, (No, no) visité a un amigo. 8. Sí, (No, no) corrí por la mañana. 9. Sí, (No, no) tomé un refresco. 10. Sí, (No, no) lavé los platos. **Ej. 6:** 1. Mi madre no charló con el presidente la semana pasada. 2. El presidente de México no comió tacos en la calle ayer. 3. La profesora de español no salió con Antonio Banderas anoche. 4. Yo no jugué al tenis con Rafael Nadal ayer a medianoche. 5. Hugo Chávez no visitó los Estados Unidos el mes pasado. **Ej. 7:** 1. ¿Conoce usted 2. ¿Conoce usted 3. ¿Sabe usted 4. ¿Sabe usted 5. ¿Conoce usted 6. ¿Conoce usted 7. ¿Sabe usted 8. ¿Sabe usted 9. ¿Sabe usted 10. ¿Conoce usted **Ej. 8:** 1. los 2. la 3. lo 4. los 5. lo 6. lo 7. la 8. los 9. lo 10. la

CAPÍTULO 7

Ej. 1: (1) se levantó a las 7:00. (2) Se bañó. (3) Se puso la ropa (se vistió). (4) Desayunó cereal con leche y fruta. (5) leyó el periódico. (6) Manejó el coche al trabajo. (7) Llegó al trabajo a las 8:30. (8) Almorzó con un amigo. (9) Comió una hamburguesa. **Ej. 2:** 1. llegaste 2. Llegué 3. llegamos 4. llegó 5. Leíste 6. leí 7. leyeron 8. leyó; leímos **Ej. 3:** 1. d 2. c 3. e 4. g 5. b 6. f 7. a; *Your list should have first-person plural forms* (nosotros) *such as* (Mi... yo) acampamos, viajamos, estudiamos, comimos, corrimos, escribimos, etc. **Ej. 4:** 1. dio 2. vinieron 3. traje 4. dijeron 5. vio 6. puso 7. hizo 8. fueron **Ej. 5:** 1. Fue; sus; Llegaron; descansó; Bucearon; vieron; hicieron; cocinaron; tocó; cantaron; bailaron 2. fue; su; Llegaron; entró, vio; estudió; saludó; salieron; bailó; tomó; Regresó **Ej. 6:** (1) Generalmente Pilar asiste a clase, pero ayer durmió toda la tarde y mañana va a visitar a una amiga. (2) Generalmente Andrea y Pedro almuerzan con sus hijas y ayer estuvieron en casa todo el día, pero mañana van a ir de compras. (3) Generalmente Adriana juega al tenis después de salir del trabajo, pero ayer tradujo un documento del italiano al español y mañana va a aprender a usar un nuevo programa de informática. (4) Generalmente doña Lola se queda en casa, pero ayer tomó café con sus amigas y mañana va a cocinar toda la tarde. (5) Generalmente Carla y Rogelio estudian en la biblioteca, pero ayer fueron a la playa y mañana van a lavar el carro. **Ej. 7:** 1. dormiste 2. Dormí 3. duermes 4. duermo 5. sientes 6. siento 7. sentiste 8. sentí 9. divertiste 10. divertí 11. divirtió 12. divirtió 13. mentiste 14. mentí 15. mintió **Ej. 8:** 1. me 2. dijiste 3. Te 4. dije 5. me 6. dijo 7. me 8. dijo 9. le 10. dijiste 11. le 12. dijiste 13. le 14. dije 15. le 16. dije **Ej. 9:** (After hace answers may vary.) 1. Pero, Estela, limpié el baño (lo limpié) ayer. 2. Pero, Estela, barrí el patio (lo barrí) hace una hora. 3. Pero, Estela, pasé la aspiradora (la pasé) hace dos días. 4. Pero, Estela, bañé al perro hace una semana. 5. Pero, Estela, te llevé a un restaurante elegante el mes pasado. **Ej. 10:** (Answers are for 2010; they will vary depending on the year the book is used.) 1. Alejandro G. Bell inventó el teléfono hace 134 años. 2. Gustave Eiffel construyó la Torre Eiffel hace 121 años. 3. Pancho Villa murió hace 87 años. 4. Colón llegó a América hace 518 años. 5. Francisco Franco murió hace 35 años. 6. Alemania se unificó hace 20 años. 7. Los países de la Unión soviética se independizaron hace 19 años.

CAPÍTULO 8

Ej. 1: 1. La... en el congelador. 2. Las compré en el supermercado. 3. Lo traje hace diez minutos. 4. La puse en la mesa. 5. Los puse en la alacena. 6. La vi en el restaurante. 7. Lo conocí ayer. 8. Sí, las llamé anoche. 9. Sí, la saludé hace cinco minutos. 10. Sí, los oí llegar a las 10:00 de la noche. **Ej. 2:** 1. la voy a poner / voy a ponerla 2. lo voy a preparar / voy a prepararlo 3. los estoy horneando / estoy horneándolos 4. lo está rallando / está rallándolo 5. las voy a abrir /

voy a abrirlas **Ej. 3:** 1. Te 2. me 3. ti 4. mí 5. le 6. él 7. mí 8. ti 9. te 10. mí 11. me **Ej. 4:** (Food items will vary.) 1. A mi mejor amigo/a le encanta(n)... 2. A mis padres les encanta(n)... 3. A mi profesor(a) le encanta(n)... 4. A mi novia (esposo/esposa) le encanta(n)... 5. A mí me encanta(n)... 6. A mi mejor amigo/amiga y a mí nos encanta(n)... **Ej. 5:** 1. nadie 2. nada 3. nunca 4. nadie 5. ninguna 6. nada 7. Nunca 8. ninguno **Ej. 6:** 1. A mí sí (me gustan). 2. A mí no (me gusta). 3. A mí sí (me gustan). 4. A mí tampoco (me gusta). 5. A mí tampoco (me gustan). 6. A mí también (me gustan). **Ej. 7:** 1. se cortan 2. se necesita 3. se lava; se pone 4. se preparan 5. se agregan 6. se necesitan 7. Se habla 8. Se baten **Ej. 8:** 1. pedir 2. pedir 3. sirven 4. pedir 5. pides 6. sirven 7. pido 8. pedir 9. pidieron 10. Pedimos 11. sirvieron 12. pedí 13. pidió 14. pediste 15. pedí 16. pidió 17. pidieron 18. pedimos 19. sirvió 20. sirvió

CAPÍTULO 9

Ej. 1: 1. se parece 2. se parecen; me parezco; te pareces 3. me parezco; me parezco 4. nos parecemos; se parece 5. se parece **Ej. 2:** 1. se llevan 2. te llevas; nos llevamos 3. nos llevamos; me llevo 4. se llevan 5. te llevas; nos llevamos **Ej. 3:** (After the first phrase, answers may vary.) 1. ¿Para ella? ¡No lo creo! 2. ¿Para mí? ¡Es muy pequeño! 3. ¿Para ellas? ¡No les gusta la música clásica! 4. ¿Para nosotros? No nos gusta leer. 5. ¿Para él? ¡No lo creo! 6. ¿Para ti? ¿Te gusta la cerveza? 7. ¿Para ella? ¿Le gustan? 8. ¿Para él? ¡No le gusta! **Ej. 4:** 1. conmigo; contigo 2. ti; mí 3. él 4. el 5. él; mí **Ej. 5:** 1. Guillermo andaba en bicicleta. 2. Amanda y yo jugábamos con muñecas. 3. Andrea leía las tiras cómicas del periódico los domingos. 4. Doña Lola y doña Rosita se bañaban en el mar en Acapulco. 5. Don Eduardo comía muchos dulces. 6. Estela limpiaba su recámara. 7. La familia Saucedo pasaba las vacaciones en Acapulco. 8. Pedro Ruiz escuchaba música rock. 9. Ernesto veía dibujos animados en la televisión. 10. El abuelo de Ernestito cuidaba el jardín. **Ej. 6:** 1. Andrea y Pedro; jugaban 2. Estela y Ernesto; iban 3. Estela; saltaba 4. Raúl; se peleaba 5. Andrea; lloraba 6. Raúl; se llevaba 7. Andrea y Paula; se parecían **Ej. 7:** 1. tenía 2. sabía 3. conocíamos 4. era 5. estaba **Ej. 8:** 1. tenía 2. era 3. conocía 4. queríamos; teníamos 5. estabas 6. tenía 7. supe 8. tuve 9. conocí 10. quise 11. pude **Ej. 9:** 1. Iba a venir, pero me quedé sin gasolina. 2. Iba a traer flores, pero la tienda cerró temprano. 3. Te iba a comprar un regalo, pero no tuve tiempo. 4. Iba a cenar con ustedes, pero cené en casa antes. 5. Iba a ir,

pero asistí a un concierto. 6. Te iba a decir, pero no pude. 7. Iba a llegar a tiempo pero, perdí mi reloj. 8. Iba a asistir, pero fui a ver a mi abuela enferma.

CAPÍTULO 10

Ej. 1: 1. hemos visto 2. ha escrito 3. he ido (viajado) 4. ha comprado 5. has comido 6. ha hablado 7. has viajado (ido) 8. han limpiado 9. has oído 10. han pasado **Ej. 2:** (Frequency will vary.) 1. ¿Cuántas veces has viajado a México? He viajado a México muchas veces. 2. ¿Cuántas veces has esquiado en un lago? Nunca he esquiado en un lago. 3. ¿Cuántas veces has subido a una pirámide? He subido a una pirámide una vez, en México. 4. ¿Cuántas veces has acampado en la montaña? He acampado en la montaña muchas veces. 5. ¿Cuántas veces has alquilado un coche? He alquilado un coche tres o cuatro veces. 6. ¿Cuántas veces has cocinado para diez personas? He cocinado para diez personas muchas veces. 7. ¿Cuántas veces has leído tres novelas en un día? Nunca he leído tres novelas en un día. 8. ¿Cuántas veces has corrido 5 kilómetros sin parar? He corrido 5 kilómetros sin para varias veces. 9. ¿Cuántas veces les has dicho una mentira a tus padres? ¡Nunca les he dicho una mentira! 10. ¿Cuántas veces has roto una vaso en un restaurante? He roto un vaso en un restaurante solamente una vez. **Ej. 3:** 1. ¡Qué país tan (más) interesante! 2. ¡Qué vuelo tan (más) largo! 3. ¡Qué montañas tan (más) altas! 4. ¡Qué selva tropical tan (más) verde! 5. ¡Qué arena tan (más) blanca! **Ej. 4:** 1. ¡Qué impresionantes son las ruinas de Machu Picchu! 2. ¡Qué grande es el lago Titicaca! 3. ¡Qué cosmopolita es la ciudad de Buenos Aires! 4. ¡Qué húmeda es la selva de Ecuador! 5. ¡Qué seco es el desierto de Atacama en Chile! 6. ¡Qué alta es la torre de la Giralda en Sevilla! 7. ¡Qué hermoso es el edificio del Alcázar en Segovia! 8. ¡Qué inmenso es el parque del Retiro en Madrid! 9. ¡Qué interesante es el Museo del Prado! 10. ¡Qué antiguo es el acueducto de Segovia! **Ej. 5:** 1. por 2. por 3. para 4. por 5. por 6. por 7. por 8. para **Ej. 6:** 1. rápidamente 2. cómodamente 3. puntualmente 4. constantemente 5. inmediatamente **Ej. 7:** (Answers will vary.) 1. a. me parece b. me importa 2. a. me fascinan b. me interesan 3. a. me encanta b. me gusta 4. a. me molesta b. me gusta 5. a. me importan b. me preocupan

CAPÍTULO 11

Ej. 1: 1. Sí, hágalas inmediatamente. 2. Sí, cómprelos ya. 3. Sí, tráigalo mañana. 4. Sí, recójalos la semana que viene. 5. Sí, llegue dos horas antes. 6. Sí, consiga otro. **Ej. 2:** 1. Sí, prepárenlo. 2. Sí, consíganlos. 3. Sí, límpienlas. 4. Sí, háganlas esta noche. 5. Sí, duerman antes de salir. 6. Sí, salgan inmediatamente. **Ej. 3:** 1. comas 2. hables 3. visites 4. veas 5. saques 6. aprendas **Ej. 4:** (Nuestro agente) sugiere que (no) 1. recojamos 2. escribamos 3. llevemos 4. traigamos 5. comamos 6. lleguemos 7. bebamos **Ej. 5:** 1. llegue 2. viajamos 3. suben 4. lea 5. terminen **Ej. 6:** Hijo/Hija, (no) queremos que hagas las maletas un día antes de la salida. 2. Hijo/Hija, (no) queremos que duermas ocho horas la noche anterior a la salida. 3. Hijo/Hija, (no) queremos que lleves ropa para ocho días. 4. Hijo/Hija, (no) queremos que vayas directamente a la estación de autobuses. 5. Hijo/Hija, (no) queremos que pongas el dinero en un lugar seguro. 6. Hijo/Hija, (no) queremos que le des tu pasaporte al profesor. 7. Hijo/Hija, (no) queremos que vuelvas con buenos recuerdos del viaje. 8. Hijo/Hija, (no) queremos que pidas comida norteamericana en los restaurantes. 9. Hijo/Hija, (no) queremos que te diviertas mucho y traigas regalos para toda la familia. 10. Hijo/Hija, (no) queremos que nos digas adiós / le digas adiós a la familia. **Ej. 7:** 1. c. llame; llegue 2. d. sirva; vayamos 3. b. oigas; vengas 4. e. traigamos; volvamos 5. a. saques; estés **Ej. 8:** (*Yes/no answers will vary.*) 1. durmiendo 2. asistiendo 3. viendo 4. estudiando 5. leyendo 6. estaba preparando 7. estaba haciendo 8. estaban comiendo 9. estaban limpiando 10. estaba dando **Ej. 9:** 1. Manejaba 2. Veía 3. Caminaba 4. hablaba 5. Me bañaba **Ej. 10:** 1. era 2. íbamos 3. alquilábamos 4. buceábamos 5. bañábamos 6. salíamos 7. caminábamos 8. tenía 9. fuimos 10. dormían 11. jugaba 12. hablaba 13. conocía 14. miré 15. jugaba 16. vi 17. levantamos 18. corrimos 19. encontramos 20. buscamos 21. pudimos 22. estaba 23. regresamos 24. teníamos 25. estaba 26. fuiste 27. grité 28. contestó 29. estaba 20. enojé

CAPÍTULO 12

Ej. 1: 1. Tiene que haber 2. Va a haber / Hay 3. había 4. hay; va a haber; Hay 5. haya **Ej. 2:** 1. b 2. a 3. b 4. a 5. a **Ej. 3:** 1. No le muestre su pierna. 2. No me diga si le duele mucho. 3. No le lleve estos papeles a la recepcionista. 4. No le traiga la comida al paciente. 5. No le dé la receta al farmacéutico. **Ej. 4:** 1. Llámeme el miércoles. 2. Tráiganos la medicina. 3. Dígale su nombre al médico. 4. Lléveles la receta a los pacientes. 5. Déme la información. **Ej. 5:** 1. Le recomienda a la enfermera que le ponga la inyección a la

paciente. 2. Le recomienda al paciente que le pida los resultados mañana. 3. Le recomienda a la enfermera que le explique los síntomas a la señora López. 4. Le recomienda a la recepcionista que le lleve estos papeles a los señores Gómez. 5. Le recomienda al paciente que le cuente a la enfermera cómo ocurrió el accidente. **Ej. 6:** 1. Se perdió. 2. Se rompieron. 3. Se cayó. 4. Se descompuso. **Ej. 7:** 1. A Lan se le descompuso el carro. 2. Al dentista se le cayó el espejo. 3. Al doctor Rocha se le olvidó el estetoscopio en su coche. 4. A Ernesto y a Estela se les quedó la llave dentro de la casa. 5. A las enfermeras se les perdieron los vendajes. **Ej. 8:** 1. Estela barría el patio cuando Ernesto se cayó de la escalera / del techo. 2. Ramón y Amanda patinaban cuando Amanda se cayó. 3. Andrea se maquillaba cuando Pedro se cayó en la bañera. 4. Ernesto manejaba cuando un perro atravesó la calle. Ernesto frenó y no lo atropelló. 5. Ernestito y sus amigos jugaban al béisbol cuando la pelota rompió la ventana. 6. Ernesto y Estela veían la televisión cuando ocurrió un terremoto. **Ej. 9:** 1. trabajé 2. Salí 3. caminé 4. Había 5. esperaba 6. era 7. Pensaba 8. vi 9. caminaba 10. estaba 11. llegó 12. robó 13. empezó 14. desapareció 15. llegó 16. di 17. llegó 18. llegué

CAPÍTULO 13

Ej. 1: 1. Nora quiere llevar el vestido corto, pero su hermana prefiere el largo. 2. Alberto quiere llevar el abrigo de cuero, pero su hermano prefiere el de lana. 3. Pablo quiere llevar el suéter ligero, pero su padre prefiere el grueso. 4. Carmen quiere llevar la falda vieja, pero su prima prefiere la nueva. 5. Esteban quiere llevar la camisa de seda, pero su novia prefiere la de algodón. **Ej. 2:** 1. Paula quiere un abrelatas manual; su novio, Armando, prefiere uno eléctrico. 2. Paula quiere un asador pequeño; Armando prefiere uno grande. 3. Paula quiere unos vasos de vidrio; Armando prefiere unos de plástico. 4. Paula quiere unos muebles modernos para la sala; Armando prefiere unos antiguos. 5. Paula quiere una computadora IBM; Armando prefiere una Mac. **Ej. 3:** 1. esta; ésa 2. estos; ésos 3. estas; aquéllas 4. aquel; éste 5. Ese; este **Ej. 4:** 1. c 2. e 3. a 4. b 5. d **Ej. 5:** 1. por 2. Para 3. para; para 5. por 6. por 7. por 8. Para 9. para 10. por 11. para **Ej. 6:** 1. nos, a, b, c 2. le; a, b 3. les; a, c 4. me; a, c, d 5. te; a; c **Ej. 7:** 1. Sí, se la entregué ayer. 2. Sí, se la vendí ayer. 3. Sí, se la di ayer. 4. Sí, se la presté ayer. 5. Sí, se la llevé ayer. 6. Voy a prestártelas / Te las voy a prestar mañana. 7. Voy a devolvértelo / Te lo voy a devolver

mañana. Voy a traértelo / Te lo voy a traer mañana. 9. Voy a dártela / Te la voy a dar mañana. 10. Voy a mostrártelos / Te los voy a mostrar mañana. **Ej. 8:** 1. Sí, se lo voy a pedir mañana. / Sí, voy a pedírselo mañana. 2. Sí, se los voy a prestar mañana. / Sí voy a prestárselos mañana. 3. Sí, se las voy a llevar mañana. / Sí, voy a llevárselas mañana. 4. Sí, se las voy a devolver mañana. / Sí, voy a devolvérselas mañana. 5. Sí, se lo voy a regalar mañana. / Sí, voy a regalárselo mañana. **Ej. 9:** 1. Te la estoy dando / Estoy dándotela ahora mismo. 2. Te las estoy preparando / Estoy preparándotelas ahora mismo. 3. Te la estoy planchando / Estoy planchándotela ahora mismo. 4. Te lo estoy buscando / Estoy buscándotelo ahora mismo. 5. Te las estoy buscando / Estoy buscándotelas ahora mismo. **Ej. 10:** 1. Ya me la regaló la semana pasada. 2. Ya me lo compró la semana pasada. 3. Ya me la prestó la semana pasada. 4. Ya me los trajo la semana pasada. 5. Ya me lo dio la semana pasada.

CAPÍTULO 14

Ej. 1: 1. El señor Ruiz y su suegra se llamaron. 2. Mi ahijada y yo nos escribimos a menudo. 3. Amanda y su novio se hablan todos los días. 4. Mi madre y mi padre se respetan mucho. 5. El abuelo de Guillermo y yo nos conocemos muy bien. **Ej. 2:** 1. Pues, no está muy amable hoy. 2. Pues, no está muy frío hoy. 3. Pues, no está muy cómico hoy. 4. Pues, no está muy cara hoy. 5. Pues, no está muy eficiente hoy. **Ej. 3:** 1. es 2. está 3. estoy 4. está; es 5. Son; están 6. son; están **Ej. 4:** 1. Levántate (Acuéstate) 2. Ven 3. Ten 4. Sal 5. Bájate 6. Habla 7. Acuéstate; apaga 8. Dile 9. Ve; lee 10. Haz **Ej. 5:** 1. Traiga; dé 2. Muestre; diga 3. espera (espérame); te vayas 4. Rebaje; suba 5. Mira; digas **Ej. 6:** 1. ruega; llegue 2. Espera; saquen 3. Desea; contesten 4. sugiere; lea 5. recomienda; entreguemos **Ej. 7:** 1. Guillermo, es mejor que hagas la tarea. 2. Graciela, quiero que hables con Amanda. 3. Amanda, es necesario que llames a Graciela. 4. Clarisa, es muy importante que te quedes en el patio. 5. Marisa, sugiero que juegues con tu hermanita. **Ej. 8:** 1. a. vayan b. falten c. hablen d. den; a, c 2. a. fumemos b. durmamos c. consultemos d. comamos; b, d 3. a. jueguen b. limpien c. coman d. vean; b 4. a. haga b. llame c. ayuden d. saque; a, b, c, d 5. a. almuerces b. vengas c. escribas d. duermas; a, b, c **Ej. 9:** 1. ¡Que lo bañe Ernestito! 2. ¡Que lo barra Guillermo! 3. ¡Qué las pague Ernesto! 4. ¡Que los cuide Ernesto! 5. ¡Que los sacuda Berta! 6. ¡Que lo arregle Ernesto! 7. ¡Que lo envíe Amanda! 8. ¡Que jueguen con la gata los niños! 9. ¡Que la recoja Ernestito! 10. ¡Que las ponga allí Berta! **Ej. 10:** (*Answers will vary.*) 1. ¡Que duermas bien! 2. ¡Que lo pases bien! 3. ¡Que tengas buena suerte! 4. ¡Que se mejore! 5. ¡Que tengan buen viaje! **Ej. 11:** 1. Ojalá (que) reciba muchos regalos. 2. Ojalá (que) haga buen tiempo. 3. Ojalá (que) no tenga que trabajar. 4. Ojalá (que) no esté enfermo/a. 5. Ojalá (que) vengan a visitarme mis amigos. **Ej. 12:** 1. (No) Escuchemos música latina. 2. (No) Trabajemos en el proyecto. 3. (No) Hagamos ejercicio. 4. (No) Vayamos al cine. 5. (No) Alquilemos una película.

CAPÍTULO 15

Ej. 1: 1. Me casaré; tendré 2. nos graduaremos; iremos 3. se mudarán; vivirán 4. lograremos; nos reuniremos 5. vendrá; dirá **Ej. 2:** 1. gradúe 2. haya 3. tienes 4. ven 5. llegues 6. vengan 7. alcancen 8. vuelven 9. salgamos 10. saludan **Ej. 3:** 1. sea 2. esté 3. ofrezca 4. tienen 5. venda 6. fabrica 7. hay **Ej. 4:** 1. haya 2. aumenta 3. prohíbe 4. ayude 5. adopte 6. influye **Ej. 5:** 1. ponga 2. puedan 3. tenga 4. haya **Ej. 6:** 1. hay 2. vengan 3. lleguen 4. permita 5. encuentren 6. son

7. digas 8. sepa 9. podamos 10. vamos **Ej. 7:** 1. tenga 2. haya 3. seamos 4. Representan 5. vive 6. estén 7. conozco **Ej. 8:** 1. visitarían 2. trataría 3. compraría 4. comerían; tomarían 5. practicarían 6. caminaría 7. pasaría 8. usarían 9. se acostarían 10. mandaría **Ej. 9:** 1. me graduara 2. fuera 3. nos mudáramos 4. fueran 5. usara 6. tuviera **Ej. 10:** 1. tuviera; trabajarían 2. pasaran; verían 3. consultáramos; aprenderíamos 4. contaminaran; estaría 5. causaran; serían 6. permitiera; habría

Spanish-English Vocabulary

This Spanish-English Vocabulary contains all of the words that appear in the text, with the following exceptions: (1) most identical cognates that do not appear in the chapter vocabulary lists; (2) conjugated verb forms, with the exception of certain forms of **haber** and expressions found in the chapter vocabulary lists; (3) diminutives in **-ito/a;** (4) absolute superlatives in **ísimo/a;** and (5) some adverbs in **-mente.** Active vocabulary is indicated by the number of the chapter in which a word or given meaning is first listed (A = **Paso A**); vocabulary that is glossed in the text is not considered to be active vocabulary and is not numbered. Only meanings that are used in this text are given.

The gender of nouns is indicated, except for masculine nouns ending in **-o** and feminine nouns ending in **-a.** Stem changes and spelling changes are indicated for verbs: **dormir (ue, u); llegar (gu).**

The following abbreviations are used:

abbrev.	abbreviation	*i.o.*	indirect object
adj.	adjective	*irreg.*	irregular
adv.	adverb	*m.*	masculine
Arg.	Argentina	*Mex.*	Mexico
coll.	colloquial	*n.*	noun
conj.	conjunction	*obj. of prep.*	object of preposition
def. art.	definite article	*pl.*	plural
d.o.	direct object	*pol.*	polite
f.	feminine	*poss.*	possessive
fig.	figurative	*p.p.*	past participle
gram.	grammatical	*prep.*	preposition
Guat.	Guatemala	*pron.*	pronoun
inf.	informal	*refl. pron.*	reflexive pronoun
infin.	infinitive	*sing.*	singular
interj.	interjection	*Sp.*	Spain
inv.	invariable	*sub. pron.*	subject pronoun

A

a to (1); at; **a la** to the (1); **al** *contraction of* **a** + **el** to the (1); **a cualquier hora** at any time (5); **a la derecha/izquierda de** to the right/left of (3); **a la parrilla** grilled, charbroiled (8); **a la vez** at the same time (5); **a menos que** unless (15); **a menudo** often (6); **a tiempo** on time (9); **a ver** let's see (13); **al corriente** up to date (15); **al día siguiente** the next day (12); **al horno** baked (8); **al lado de** to the side of (3); **al norte/sur** to the north/south (3); **al principio** at the beginning (3); **al punto** medium rare (8)

abajo *adv.* below (3)

abalorio glass bead

abeja bee (10)

abierto/a (*p.p. of* **abrir**) open (2); opened

abogado/a lawyer (5)

abordar to board (11)

abordo on board

aborto abortion (15)

abrazar (c) to hug, embrace (12); **abrazarse** to hug each other (14)

abrazo hug (3)

abrelatas *m.* can opener

abril *m.* April (1)

abrir (*p.p.* **abierto**) to open

absoluto/a absolute

absorber to absorb

absorción *f.* absorption

abstracto/a abstract

abuelo/a grandfather/grandmother; **abuelos** *pl.* grandparents

abundancia abundance (10)

abundante abundant (4)

aburrido/a boring; bored; **¡qué aburrido!** how boring! (1)

aburrimiento boredom

aburrirse to be bored

abusar de to abuse (14)

abusivamente abusively

abuso abuse (15)

acabar to finish, put an end to (15); **acabar de** (+ *infin.*) to have just done (*something*) (11)

academia academy

acampar to camp (1)

acceder to agree; to consent

acceso access

accidente *m.* accident (5)

acción *f.* action (3); **Día de Acción de Gracias** Thanksgiving (4)

aceite *m.* (olive) oil (8)

aceituna olive

acentuado/a accentuated

aceptable acceptable

aceptar to accept (7)

acero (inoxidable) (stainless) steel (13)

acerca de about (1)

acercarse (qu) (a) to approach, come near

acertar (ie) to guess right

acidez *f.* acidity

ácido/a acid; **lluvia ácida** acid rain

aclamar to acclaim, applaud

aclaración *f.* explanation
aclarar to explain
acomodar to accommodate
acompañar to accompany
acondicionador *m.* conditioner (4)
aconsejar to give advice, advise (14)
acontecimiento event, happening
acordar (ue) to agree; to resolve;
   acordarse de to remember (*something/*
   someone) (14)
acostarse (ue) to go to bed (4); **me acuesto**
   I go to bed (4); **se acuesta** he/she goes to
   bed, you (*pol. sing.*) go to bed (4)
actitud *f.* attitude (15)
activar to activate
actividad *f.* activity; **actividades auditivas**
   listening activities (5); **actividades del**
   tiempo libre leisure time activities (1);
   actividades diarias daily activities
activista *m., f.* activist (9)
activo/a active (5)
acto act
actor *m.* actor (1)
actriz *f.* actress (1)
actuación *f.* performance
actual present-day, current (15)
actualidad *f.* present, present-time
actualmente at present, nowadays (15)
actuar (yo actúo) to act (9)
acueducto aqueduct (11)
acuerdo: estar (*irreg.*) de acuerdo to
   agree (4)
acumular to accumulate
acumulativo/a cumulative
acusación *f.* accusation
acusado/a accused (5)
acusador(a) accusing
acusar to accuse
acusatorio/a accusatory
acústico/a acoustic
adaptar(se) to adapt oneself
adecuado/a adequate (12)
adelgazar (c) to lose weight
además moreover; **además de** besides (11)
adentro de inside (3)
aderezo (salad) dressing (8)
adherirse (ie) to stick to
adhesión *f.* adhesion, adherence
adiestramiento training, instruction
adivinador(a) fortune teller
adivinar to guess (5)
adjetival adjectival
adjetivo adjective
administrar to administer
admirar to admire (11)
admitir to admit
adolescente *m., f.* adolescent (14)
adolorido/a painful (12)
¿adónde? to where? (3)
adopción *f.* adoption
adoptar to adopt
adquirir to acquire

aduana *sing.* customs (11); **derechos de**
   aduana customs duty, taxes (11)
adulto adult (11)
aéreo/a pertaining to air (*travel*) (10);
   transporte (*m.*) aéreo air transport
aeróbico/a aerobic; **ejercicio aeróbico**
   aerobics
aerolínea airline (11)
aeropuerto airport (3)
aerosol *m.* aerosol
afectar to affect
afecto affection, fondness
afeitadora razor (4)
afeitarse to shave (4); **crema de afeitar**
   shaving cream
afición *f.* liking, love
afirmación *f.* statement (4)
afirmar to affirm
afortunado/a fortunate, lucky
africano/a African
africanocubano/a Afro-Cuban
afrontar to confront
afuera (de) outside (3)
agarrar to grasp, seize
agencia de viajes travel agency (11)
agenda electrónica PDA
agente *m., f.* agent (1); **agente de seguros**
   insurance agent (5)
agonizar (c) to be dying
agosto August (1)
agotado/a exhausted
agotarse to run out
agradable pleasant (6)
agradar to please
agradecer (zc) to thank
agrado pleasure
agrario/a agricultural
agregar (gu) to add (8)
agresivo/a aggressive
agricultor(a) farmer, agriculturalist
agricultura agriculture (10)
agua *f.* (*but* **el agua**) water (3); **agua con**
   sal salt water (12); **agua dulce** fresh
   water (11); **agua mineral** mineral water;
   agua salada salt water (11)
aguacate *m.* avocado (8)
águila *f.* (*but* **el águila**) eagle (10)
agujerear to make holes in
agujero hole; **agujero en la capa de**
   ozono hole in the ozone layer (10)
ahí there, over there (4)
ahijado/a godson/goddaughter (14)
ahora now; **ahora mismo** right now (14)
ahorrar to save (9)
ahuyentar to scare away; to drive away
aire *m.* air (10); **aire libre** outdoors (7);
   mercado al aire libre open-air market
aislar to isolate
ají *m.* (bell) pepper (8)
ajo garlic (8)
alacena kitchen cupboard (6)
alambre *m.* wire

alarmar to alarm, worry
albaricoque *m.* apricot (8)
alberca swimming pool (*Mex.*) (7)
alcance *m.:* **dar (*irreg.*) alcance** to catch
   up with
alcanzar (c) to reach (15)
alcohol *m.* alcohol (15)
alegrarse to be glad
alegre happy; **estar (*irreg.*) alegre** to be
   happy (4)
alejar to keep away
alemán, alemana *n., adj.* German
alentar (ie) to encourage
alergia allergy
alérgico/a allergic (12)
alergista *m., f.* allergist (12)
alfabetismo literacy
alfeizar *m.* windowsill
alfombra rug (6)
algo something (2)
algodón *m.* cotton (13)
alguien someone (6)
algún, alguno/a some; any (2); **algún día**
   someday; **alguna vez** once; ever;
   algunos/as some
alimentar to feed
alimento food, meal (8)
allá (over) there
allí there (3)
almacén *m.* department store (3)
almacenaje *m.* warehousing, storage
almacenar to warehouse, store
almeja clam (8)
almíbar *m.* syrup
almohada pillow (6)
almorzar (ue) (c) to eat lunch (2); **almorcé**
   I ate lunch (7); **almorzó** he/she/you
   (*pol. sing.*) ate lunch (7); **almuerza** he/
   she eats lunch, you (*pol. sing.*) eat lunch
   (3); **almuerzo** I eat lunch (3)
almuerzo lunch (2)
alojamiento lodging (11)
alquilar(se) to rent; to be rented (6); **se**
   alquila for rent (6)
alquiler *m.* rent (6)
alrededor de *prep.* around (3)
altar *m.* altar
alterado/a upset
alternativo/a alternative
¡alto! stop! (*Mex.*) (10)
alto/a tall; **clase (*f.*) alta** upper class; **voz**
   (*f.*) **alta** loud voice, out loud (14)
alucinado/a amazed, freaked out
aluminio aluminum (13)
alumno/a student
alzar (c) to raise, lift up
ama *f.* (*but* **el ama**) **de casa** housewife (3)
amante *m., f.* lover
amarillo/a yellow (A)
amasar to knead (8)
Amazonas *m.* Amazon (River)
Amazonia Amazon Basin (10)

ambición *f.* ambition
ambiental environmental; **contaminación** (*f.*) **ambiental** environmental pollution (10)
ambiente *m.* environment; atmosphere (8); **medio ambiente** environment (10)
ambos/as *pl.* both (10)
ambulancia ambulance
amenaza threat
amenazante threatening
amenazar (c) to threaten
América Central Central America (3)
América Latina Latin America (7)
americano/a American; **fútbol** (*m.*) **americano** football (1)
ametrallar to machine-gun
amigo/a friend; **amigo/a íntimo/a** close friend (14)
amistad *f.* friendship (14)
amnistía amnesty
amo/a master/mistress (14)
amor *m.* love
amoroso/a loving
ampliación *f.* enlargement
ampliar to broaden
amplio/a roomy (6)
amueblado/a furnished (6)
amuleto amulet
analfabetismo illiteracy
analgésico analgesic (12)
análisis analysis (12)
analítico/a analytical
analizar (c) to analyze
anaranjado/a orange (A)
ancho/a wide (11)
anciano/a elderly person
andar *irreg.* to walk; **andar en bicicleta** to ride a bicycle (1); **andar en motocicleta** to ride a motorcycle (2); **andar en patineta** to skateboard (1); **andar en velero** to go sailing (2)
anfitrión, anfitriona host, hostess
ángel *m.* angel (14)
anglohablante English-speaking person
anglosajón, anglosajona *n., adj.* Anglo-Saxon
anidar to nest (10)
anillo ring (13)
animado/a: cheerful (12); **dibujos animados** cartoons
animal *m.* animal (2); **amimal doméstico** pet (5)
animar to encourage
ánimo spirit, energy; **estado de ánimo** state of mind
aniversario anniversary; **aniversario de body** wedding anniversary (4)
anoche last night (6)
anotar to make note of; to jot down
ansia anxiety
ansiedad *f.* anxiety
ansioso/a anxious

antagónico/a antagonistic
antagonismo antagonism
antagonizar (c) to antagonize
Antártida Antarctica
ante before; faced with, in the presence of
anteayer day before yesterday (1)
antena antenna (11)
antepasado/a ancestor
anterior previous (1)
antes *adv.* before; **antes (de)** *prep.* before (4); **antes de que** *conj.* before (15)
antibiótico antibiotic (12)
anticientífico/a anti-scientific
anticipación *f.* anticipation
anticipar to anticipate (10)
antiguo/a old; antique
antisemítico/a anti-Semitic
antojito snack (*Mex.*) (8)
antónimo antonym
antónimo/a contrary, opposite
antro nightclub
antropología anthropology (2)
antropólogo/a anthropologist
anual annual
anular to annul; to nullify
anunciar to announce (11)
anuncio commercial (13); announcement (5)
añadir to add
año year; **a través de los años** through the years; **Año Nuevo** New Year (4); **cada año** every year; **cumplir años** to have a birthday (7); **de... a... años de edad** from . . . to . . . years old; **durante los años sesenta** during the sixties; **el año pasado** last year (6); **hace... años** . . . years ago; **los meses del año** the months of the year (1); **los próximos diez años** the next ten years; **por muchos años** for many years; **tener** (*irreg.*)**... años** to be . . . years old (C)
apaciguar to placate
apagar (gu) to turn off; to put out; **apagar incendios** to put out fires (5)
apalabrado/a agreed upon verbally
aparato appliance; **aparato doméstico** household appliance (6); **aparato eléctrico** electrical appliance (6)
aparecer (zc) to appear
aparición *f.* apparition
apariencia appearance
apartamento apartment (6)
apartar to remove; to separate
apasionado/a passionate
apasionamiento passion
apellido surname (1)
apenas barely
apetecer (zc) to long for; to crave
apio celery (8)
aplaudir to applaud
aplicarse (qu) a to be used; to apply (*something*) to, employ (*a remedy*);

aplicarse un ungüento to apply an ointment (12)
aportar to contribute
apoyar to support (6)
apoyo support
apreciar to appreciate
aprehender to apprehend
aprender to learn (5)
aprendizaje *n. m.* learning
apresar to take prisoner, capture
aprobar (ue) to pass; to approve (15)
apropiado/a appropriate
aprovechar(se) to take advantage of (13)
aproximadamente approximately (7)
aptitud *f.* aptitude, ability (5)
apuesto/a handsome, pretty
apuntar to note, jot down
apuntes *m. pl.* notes; **tomar apuntes** to take notes (4)
apuro difficult situation
aquejado/a suffering
aquel, aquella *adj.* that (over there); *pron.* that one (over there)
aquello that; that thing
aquí here (1); **aquí lo tiene** here it is (11)
árabe *n. m., f.* Arab; *n. m.* Arabic (language); *adj.* Arabic
araña spider
árbol *m.* tree (2); **árbol genealógico** family tree (9); **subirse a los árboles** to climb trees (9)
arbusto bush (6)
archivo file
arco arch; **arco iris** rainbow
arder to burn
área *f.* (*but* **el área**) area (2)
arena sand (7)
arepa thick corn cake
argentino/a *n., adj.* Argentine
argumento argument (15); reasoning
árido/a arid (10)
arma *f.* (*but* **el arma**) arm, weapon (15); **armas nucleares** nuclear weapons
armamento armament (15)
armario closet (6)
armonía harmony
arpillera sackcloth
arquitectura architecture
arras *coins given by a bridegroom to a bride as a token of his ability to provide* (14)
arrecife *m.* reef (10); **arrecife de coral** coral reef
arreglar to fix, repair (5) se — ready.
arrepentirse (ie) to repent
arrestar to arrest (7)
arresto arrest
arriba above (3)
arriesgado/a risky, hazardous
arriesgar (gu) to risk
arroba at (@)
arrodillarse to kneel down
arrogante arrogant

arroz *m.* rice (3); **arroz con leche** rice pudding
arruinar to ruin (7)
arsenal *m.* arsenal (15)
arte *m.* (*but* **las artes**) art (2); **bellas artes** fine arts; **Facultad de Bellas Artes** School of Fine Arts (3)
artefacto artifact (13)
arteria artery (12)
artículo article (10)
artista *m., f.* artist (3)
artístico/a artistic
arzobispo archbishop
asado/a roasted; **bien asado/a** well-done (8); **poco asado/a** rare (8)
asador *m.* barbecue grill (13)
asaltar to assault
asar to roast
ascendencia ancestry, origin
ascender to go up, rise
ascensor *m.* elevator (6)
asegurado/a insured
asegurar to assure (15); to insure
asemejarse to be similar to
asesinar to assassinate
asesino/a assassin, murderer
asfixiante suffocating
así thus, so, that way, this way (5)
Asia Asia (7)
asiento seat (10)
asignar to assign (5)
asimétrico/a asymmetrical
asimilación *f.* assimilation
asimilar(se) to assimilate
asistente *m., f.* assistant; **asistente de vuelo** flight attendant (11)
asistir (a) to attend (3)
asociación *f.* association
asociado/a associated (1)
asociar to associate (2)
asombrar to astonish
aspecto aspect (4); appearance
aspiración *f.* aspiration
aspiradora vacuum cleaner (6); **pasar la aspiradora** to vacuum (6)
aspirante *m., f.* candidate; applicant
aspirar to aspire
aspirina aspirin (12)
asunto subject, topic; matter, affair
asustado/a scared (7)
asustar to scare
atacar (qu) to attack
ataque *m.* attack (15); **ataque al corazón** heart attack
atar to tie (7)
ateísmo atheism
atención *f.* attention; **atención médica** health care; **llamar la atención (a)** to call attention (to) (10); **poner** (*irreg.*) **atención** to pay attention (5)
atender (ie) to wait on; to assist (12); **atender mesas** to wait on tables (5)

atentado attempted murder
atento/a attentive
ateo/a atheist
atestiguar to testify
Atlántico: Océano Atlántico Atlantic Ocean (3)
atleta *m., f.* athlete (9)
atmósfera atmosphere
atómico/a atomic
atormentar to torment (14)
atracción *f.* attraction
atractivo/a attractive
atraer (*like* **traer**) to attract
atrapar to catch (7); to trap (7)
atravesar (ie) to cross, go across
atreverse a (+ *infin.*) to dare to (*do something*)
atrevido/a bold, daring
atrevimiento boldness, daring
atribuir (y) (a) to attribute (*to*) (15)
atributo attribute
atropellar to run over with a car (12)
atún *m.* tuna (8)
auditorio auditorium
auge *m.* peak, climax
aula *f.* (*but* **el aula**) classroom
aullar to howl
aumentar to increase (15)
aumento raise, increase (10)
aun even
aún still, yet
aunque although
ausente absent
autobiografía autobiography
autobiográfico/a autobiographical
autobús *m.* bus; **terminal** (*m.*) **de autobuses** bus terminal
autodestructivo/a self-destructive
autógrafo autograph
automático/a automatic; **cajero automático** automatic teller machine
automatizar (c) to automate
automóvil *m.* automobile (11)
autonomía autonomy
autopista freeway, expressway (10)
autor(a) author
autoridad *f.* authority
autorización *f.* authorization
autorizar (c) to authorize
¡auxilio! help! (7)
avance *m.* advance
avanzar (c) to advance
avaricia greed
avaro/a greedy
ave *f.* (*but* **el ave**) bird; fowl; poultry (8)
avena oatmeal (8)
avenida avenue (3)
aventajar to come, finish ahead of
aventura adventure (7); **aventura extramarital** extramarital relationship
aventurero/a adventurous (11)

averiguar to verify; to find out
avión *m.* airplane (5); **por avión** by plane (10)
avisar to inform; to advise (11); to warn (11)
aviso (clasificado) (classified) ad (5)
ayer yesterday (1)
ayuda help
ayudar to help (5)
azar *m.* chance
azteca *n. m., f.; adj.* Aztec (7)
azúcar *m.* sugar (8)
azul blue (A)

B

bahía bay (10)
bailar to dance (1); **salir** (*irreg.*) **a bailar** to go out dancing (1)
bailarín, bailarina dancer
baile *m.* dance (4)
bajar to lower (10); to come down (10); **bajarse** to get down (14); **baje(n)** (*command*) get off (11); to download (13)
bajo *prep.* under
bajo/a short (*height*); low; **clase** (*f.*) **baja** lower class; **voz** (*f.*) **baja** soft voice (14)
balada ballad
balanza scale
balcón *m.* balcony (6)
ballena whale (10)
ballet *m.* **(folclórico)** (folkloric) ballet (11)
balón *m.* ball
baloncesto basketball (1)
bambú *m.* bamboo (10)
banana banana (8)
bancario/a *adj.* bank
banco bank (5); **banco de datos** data base
banda gang
bandera flag
bañarse to bathe (4)
bañera bathtub (6)
baño bathroom; bath; **traje** (*m.*) **de baño** bathing suit (7)
bar *m.* bar (3)
barato/a inexpensive, cheap (8)
barco boat (7); **barco de vela** (11)
barrer to sweep (6)
barrera barrier, obstacle
barril *m.* barrel
barrio neighborhood (9)
basarse (en) to be based (on) (9)
base *f.* base, foundation; **a base de** by; by means of
básico/a basic (1)
basílica basilica
basquetbol *m.* basketball (1)
bastante *adj.* enough (5); sufficient; **bastante** (+ *adj.*) quite (+ *adj.*) (5); *adv.* rather, quite
basura trash; **sacar (qu) la basura** to take out the trash (6)

basurero garbage can; dump
bata (bath)robe (13)
batalla battle (7)
bate *m.* bat
batido (de leche, de frutas) (milk, fruit) shake (8)
batir to beat (8)
baúl trunk
bautizar (c) to baptize (14)
bautizo christening ceremony, baptism (14)
beatitud *f.* beatitude; bliss
bebé *m., f.* baby
bebeleche *m.* hopscotch (*Mex.*); **jugar (ue) (gu) al bebeleche** to play hopscotch (*Mex.*) (9)
beber to drink (3)
bebida drink (8)
bebido/a *adj.* drunk
beca scholarship
béisbol *m.* baseball (1)
belleza beauty
bello/a beautiful (10); **bellas artes** fine arts; **Facultad de Bellas Artes** School of Fine Arts (3); **la Bella y la Bestia** Beauty and the Beast
bendición *f.* blessing
beneficencia charity; **organización (** *f.*) **de beneficencia** charitable organization
beneficiar to benefit
beneficio benefit (15)
beneficioso/a beneficial (12)
besar to kiss (12); **besarse** to kiss each other (14)
beso kiss (4)
bestia beast; **la Bella y la Bestia** Beauty and the Beast
Biblia Bible
biblioteca library (3)
bicarbonato de soda bicarbonate of soda (8)
bicicleta bicycle; **andar** (*irreg.*) **en bicicleta** to ride a bicycle (1)
biculturalismo biculturalism
bien *adv.* well; **bien asado/a** well-done (8); **bien cocido/a** well-done (8)
bienes *m. pl.* goods; **bienes raíces** real estate (6)
bienestar *m.* well-being
bienvenida *n.* welcome; **dar** (*irreg.*) **la bienvenida** to welcome (4)
bilingüe bilingual (5)
bilingüismo bilingualism
billete *m.* ticket (11)
biografía biography
biología biology (2)
biosfera biosphere (10)
bisabuelo/a great-grandfather/great-grandmother (14); **bisabuelos** *pl.* great-grandparents
bistec *m.* steak
bitácora blog
Blancanieves Snow White

blanco/a white (A); **espacio en blanco** blank space (3); **vino blanco** white wine (8)
bloque *m.* block
bocacalle *f.* intersection
bocina horn; **tocar (qu) la bocina** to honk the horn
boda wedding (14)
boleto ticket; **boleto de ida y vuelta** round-trip ticket (11)
boliche: jugar (ue) (gu) al boliche to bowl (2)
bolígrafo pen (B)
bolita little ball (*of material*) (8)
boliviano/a Bolivian
bolsa bag; purse (7); sack; **bolsa de lona** canvas bag (10); **bolsa de plástico** plastic bag
bolsillo pocket (13)
bolso purse
bombero, mujer (*f.*) **bombero** firefighter (5)
bordear to border
borracho/a drunk
borrador *m.* eraser; draft (*of written work*)
borrar to erase (14)
bosque *m.* forest (10)
bostezar to yawn
botánica drugstore
botella bottle (8)
botones *m. sing.* bellhop (11)
bozo fuzz; **apuntarle el bozo** to get fuzz on one's upper lip
brasa ember
brasileño/a *n, adj.* Brazilian
brazo arm
breve *adj.* brief
brillante bright
brindar to drink a toast
brindis *m.* toast (*drink or speech*) (14)
bróculi *m.* broccoli (8)
broma joke
bromear to joke
bromista *adj., m., f.* fond of joking
bronce *m.* bronze (13)
broncearse to get a tan (11)
bronquitis *f.* bronchitis (12)
bruja witch; **Día de las Brujas** Halloween (4)
brujería witchcraft
brusco/a brusque
bucear to skin dive or scuba dive (5)
buceo underwater swimming, diving (10)
bueno, bueno/a good (6); **buenas tardes/ noches** good afternoon/evening; **buenos días** good morning; **es bueno** it's good; **es una buena idea** it's a good idea; **estar** (*irreg.*) **de buen humor** to be in a good mood (4); **hace buen tiempo** the weather is fine; **qué bueno que...** how great that . . . (15); **sacar (qu) buenas notas** to get good grades (9); **tener** (*irreg.*) **buena suerte** to have good

luck; to be lucky; **traer** (*irreg.*) **buena suerte** to bring good luck
bueno... well . . .
búfalo buffalo
bufanda scarf (2)
buitre *m.* vulture
burbuja bubble
burlarse (de) to make fun (of)
burrito *rolled tortilla filled with meat, beans, and/or rice* (3)
buscador *m.* search engine (15)
buscar (qu) to look for (5); **buscó** he/she/ you (*pol. sing.*) looked for (7); **busqué** I looked for (7)
búsqueda search

C

caballero gentleman (13); knight
caballo horse; **montar a caballo** to ride a horse (2)
cabaña cabin (11)
caber *irreg.* to fit
cabeza head; **dolerle (ue) la cabeza** to have a headache; **tener** (*irreg.*) **dolor (** *m.*) **de cabeza** to have a headache (12)
cable *m.* cable; **sin cables** wireless
cacahuate *m.* peanut (8)
cachaza sluggishness, slowness
cacto cactus
cada *inv.* each, every; **cada año** every year; **cada día** every day; **cada vez** every time
cadera hip (12)
caerse *irreg.* to fall (11); **se me/le cayó/ cayeron** something (*sing. or pl.*) fell (from my/your/his/her hands) (12)
café *m.* coffee; café (3); **café Internet** Internet café; **tomar café** to drink coffee (2)
cafeína caffeine (15)
cafetera coffeepot (6)
cafetería cafeteria (3)
caimán *m.* alligator
caja box (13); cash register
cajero/a cashier (5); teller (*in a bank*); **cajero automático** automatic teller machine (ATM) (11)
calabacita zucchini (8)
calabaza pumpkin (8)
calavera skull (12)
calcetín *m.* sock (13)
calcio calcium (8)
calculador(a) calculating
calculadora calculator
calcular to calculate (8)
caldera de carbón coal-fired boiler
caldo broth; stock (8)
calefacción *f.* heating (system) (13)
calendario calendar
calentado/a heated
calentador heater (6)

calentamiento heating; **calentamiento global** global warming

calentar (ie) to warm up (6); **calienta** he/she warms up, you (*pol. sing.*) warm up (6); **caliento** I warm up (6)

calentura: tener (*irreg.*) **calentura** to have a fever (12)

calidad *f.* quality (13)

caliente hot (4); **perro caliente** hot dog (8); **té** (*m.*) **caliente** hot tea (8)

calificar (qu) to grade (5)

calle *f.* street (1)

calmado/a calm (12)

calmar to calm

calor *m.* heat; **hace (mucho) calor** it's (very) hot (2); **tener** (*irreg.*) **calor** to be hot (4)

caluroso/a warm, hot (10)

calvicie *f.* baldness

calvo/a bald

calzoncillos (men's) underwear (13)

cama (matrimonial) (double) bed (6); **quedarse en cama** to stay in bed; **tender (ie) la cama** to make the bed (6)

cámara (digital) (digital) camera (1)

camarera chambermaid (11)

camarón *m.* shrimp

cambiar to change (9); **cambiar dinero** to change/exchange money; **cambiar dólares por...** to exchange dollars for . . . (11)

cambio change; money exchange; **a cambio de** in exchange for; **en cambio** on the other hand

camello camel

camilla gurney (12)

caminar to walk (2)

caminata walk, hike (11)

camino road (11)

camión *m.* truck (15)

camisa shirt (A)

camisón *m.* nightgown (13)

campamento campground (11); camp (11)

campaña campaign

campeón, campeona champion

campesino/a peasant; field worker

campo country(side) (7); field (of study)

campus *m.* campus (2)

canadiense *n., adj.* Canadian

canal *m.* channel (1)

cancelar to cancel

cáncer *m.* cancer (10); **cáncer de la piel** skin cancer (10)

cancha de tenis tennis court (6)

cancillería chancellery

canción *f.* song

candidato/a candidate

cangrejo crab (8)

cansado/a tired

cansar to make tired (12); **cansarse** to get tired (12)

cantante *m., f.* singer (5)

cantar to sing (5)

cántaro pitcher

cantidad *f.* quantity

cañón *m.* canyon (10)

capa cape; **agujero en la capa de ozono** hole in the ozone layer (10); **capa de hielo polar** polar ice cap

capacidad *f.* capacity

capaz capable

capital *f.* capital city (3)

capó *m.* hood

captar to grasp, understand

capturar to capture

caqui: color (*m.*) **caqui** khaki (13)

cara face (B)

carácter *m.* character (14)

característica characteristic (14)

caracterizar (c) to characterize (15)

carbohidrato carbohydrate (8)

carbón coal; **caldera de carbón** coal-fired boiler

carbono carbon

carburo carbide; **carburo fluorado** fluorocarbon (10)

cárcel *f.* jail, prison

carecer (zc) to lack

carencia lack, shortage

cargo position (7); **cargo de conciencia** weight on one's conscience

Caribe *m.* Caribbean (3)

caribeño/a *n., adj.* Caribbean (10)

cariño affection; endearment; love (14)

carne *f.* meat (8); **carne de cerdo/puerco** pork (8); **carne de res** beef (8)

carnicería *f.* meat market

caro/a expensive (6)

carpintero/a carpenter

carrera career; course of study (5)

carretera highway (10)

carro car, automobile; **jugar (ue) (gu) con carritos** to play with little cars (9)

carta letter; card; menu (8); **cartas de tarot** tarot cards

cartel *m.* poster

cartera wallet (13)

cartón *m.* cardboard

casa house; **casa particular** private home (6)

casado *typical Costa Rican dish of white rice, black beans, meat, chicken, or fish and side salad or side of fried plantain* (8)

casado/a married (1); **recién casado/a** newlywed (14)

casarse (con) to get married (to) (7)

cáscara peel (8)

casco helmet (2); **casco urbano** city center

casero/a home, domestic

casi *inv.* almost (1); **casi nunca** almost never (3)

caso (criminal) (criminal) case (5); **caso imprevisto** unforeseen occurrence (12); **en caso de que** in case; **hacer** (*irreg.*) **caso a** to pay attention to (14)

castaño/a brown (*hair, eyes*)

castigar (gu) to punish (7)

castigo punishment (14)

castillo castle

casto/a chaste

casualidad *f.* coincidence

catalán *m.* Catalonian (*language*)

catalizador *m.* catalyst

catarata waterfall (10)

catarro cold; **tener** (*irreg.*) **catarro** to have a cold (12)

catástrofe *f.* catastrophe

cátedra chair (*of an academic department*)

categoría category

catolicismo Catholicism

católico/a *n., adj.* Catholic

catorce fourteen (A)

caudillo leader (7); strongman

causa cause: **a cause de** because of; **por causa de** because of

causar to cause (10)

caza hunt (10); hunting (10)

cebolla onion (8)

ceja eyebrow (12)

celebración *f.* celebration (4)

celebrar to celebrate (4)

célebre famous

célula cell

celular cellular; **(teléfono) celular** cell phone (1)

cementerio cemetery (11)

cena dinner (3)

cenar to dine, have dinner (1)

Cenicienta Cinderella

censura censorship

censurar to censor

centavo cent; **no tener un centavo** to be broke (13)

centenario centennial, centenary; **quinto centenario** five hundredth anniversary

centeno rye

central central (3); **América Central** Central America (3)

centro center; downtown (2); **centro comercial** shopping center (6); **centro estudiantil** student center (3)

Centroamérica Central America (10)

cepillo (de dientes) (tooth)brush (6)

cera wax

cerámica ceramics (13)

cerca *n.* fence (6)

cerca *adv.* near; **cerca de** *prep.* close to (3)

cercano/a near, close by

cerdo pig; **carne** (*f.*) **de cerdo** pork (8); **chuleta de cerdo** pork chop (8)

cereal *m.* cereal (2)

cerebro brain (12)

ceremonia ceremony (4)

cero zero

cerrar (ie) to close (2); to turn off (*appliance*); **cierra** he/she closes, you (*pol. sing.*) close (2); **cierro** I close (6)

certeza certainty
certidumbre *f.* certainty
cerveza beer (2)
cesación *f.* discontinuation, suspension
cesar to cease, stop, discontinue
césped *m.* lawn; **cortar el césped** to mow the lawn (6)
ceviche *m. Peruvian dish of raw fish marinated in lemon juice* (8)
chabacano apricot (*Mex.*) (8)
chamarra jacket (13)
champú *m.* shampoo (4)
charla chat
charlar to chat (2)
chatear to chat online (2)
cheque *m.* check; **cheque de viajero** traveler's check
chícharo green pea (*Mex.*) (8)
chile (*m.*) **relleno** stuffed pepper (8)
chileno/a *n., adj.* Chilean
chimenea fireplace (6)
chino *n.* Chinese (*language*); **chino/a** *n., adj.* Chinese
chisme *m.* gossip
chismear to gossip
chiste *m.* joke
chocar (**qu**) to crash into (7); to run into (*something*) (11)
chocolate *m.* chocolate (2)
chofer *m.* driver
choque *m.* crash (12)
chuleta (de cerdo/puerco) (pork) chop (8)
chuparse el dedo to suck one's thumb (*finger*) (14)
ciberespacio cyberspace
cibernauta *m., f.* person who surfs the Internet
cibernético/a cybernetic (3)
cicatriz *f.* (*pl.* **cicatrices**) scar (12)
ciclón *m.* cyclone (10)
cielo sky (10); heaven
cien, ciento one hundred; **por ciento** percent
ciencia science; **ciencia ficción** science fiction (3); **ciencias naturales** natural sciences; **ciencias sociales** social sciences (2); **Facultad** (*f.*) **de Ciencias Naturales** School of Natural Science (3); **Facultad** (*f.*) **de Ciencias Sociales** School of Social Sciences (3)
científicamente scientifically
científico/a *n.* scientist (9); *adj.* scientific
cierto/a certain; true (9)
cigarrillo cigarette
cigarro cigar
cigüeña stork
cinco five (A)
cincuenta fifty (B)
cine *m.* movie theater; **estrella de cine** movie star (7); **ir** (*irreg.*) **al cine** to go to the movies
cintura waist (12)

cinturón *m.* belt
circuito/a circuit
circulación *f.* circulation; traffic (11)
circular to circulate (12)
circunstancia circumstance
cirujano/a surgeon (12)
cita appointment (12); date (12)
ciudad *f.* city (2)
ciudadanía citizenship (1)
ciudadano/a citizen (10)
civil civil; **derechos civiles** civil rights; **estado civil** marital status; **guerra civil** civil war
civilización *f.* civilization
claridad *f.* clarity
claro of course; **claro que sí** of course
claro/a clear
clase *f.* class; type; **clase social** social class; **clase turística** tourist class (11); **primera clase** first class (11); **¿qué clase de... ?** what type of . . . ? (8)
clásico/a classic (2)
clasificación *f.* classification
cláusula clause
clave *adj. inv.* key (15)
clérigo priest, clergyman
cliente, clienta client (5)
clic: hacer (*irreg.*) **clic** to click on (11)
clima *m.* climate; weather (2)
climático/a climatic
clínica clinic (5)
clínico/a clinical; **historial** (*m.*) **clínico** medical history (12)
clonar to clone
cloro chlorine
clorofluorocarbón *m.* chlorofluorocarbon
club *m.* club (2); **club nocturno** nightclub (5)
cobrar to charge
cobrizo/a copper-colored
coche *m.* car, automobile; **coche eléctrico** electric car
cocido/a medium rare (8); **bien cocido/a** well-done (8); **poco cocido/a** rare (8)
cocina kitchen (5)
cocinar to cook (1)
cocinero/a cook
coco coconut; boogeyman
cóctel *m.* cocktail
códice *m.* codex
código code
codo elbow (12)
coger (**j**) to trap; to grab
cohete *m.* rocket
coincidir to coincide (4)
cola tail; line (11); **hacer** (*irreg.*) **cola** to stand in line (11)
colección *f.* collection
colectividad *f.* collectivity
colectivo/a collective
colega *m., f.* colleague (15)
colegio private school (3)

colesterol *m.* cholesterol
colgar (**ue**) (**gu**) to hang
coliflor *f.* cauliflower (8)
colina hill (10)
colindar to be adjacent; to adjoin
colocación *f.* placement
colocar (**qu**) to place, put
colombiano/a *n., adj.* Colombian
colonia cologne (4); colony; **colonia espacial** space colony (15)
colonista *m., f.* colonizer
colonización *f.* colonization
colonizador(a) colonizer
colonizar (**c**) to colonize
color *m.* color (A); **color caqui** khaki (13); **color vivo** bright color (13)
colorante *m.* coloring (8)
colorido/a colorful
columna column (2)
combinación *f.* women's slip (13)
combinar to combine (8)
combustibilidad *f.* combustion
combustibles fósiles fossil fuels
comedor *m.* dining room (6)
comentar to comment (6)
comentario comment (14)
comenzar (**c**) to begin (14); **comenzar a** (+ *infin.*) to begin to (*do something*)
comer to eat (1); **comer fuera** to eat out (8); **comerse las uñas** to bite one's (finger)nails (4); **dar** (*irreg.*) **de comer** to feed
comercial commercial; **centro comercial** shopping center (6)
comestibles *m. pl.* food; groceries (8)
cometa kite; **volar** (**ue**) **una cometa** to fly a kite (2)
cometer to commit
comezón *f.* rash; itch
cómico/a funny; **tiras cómicas** comic strips (9)
comida meal (8); food (8); **comida chatarra** junk food (8); **comida pre-elaborada** convenience food
comienzo beginning
comisión *f.* commission (5)
como as (2); as a; like (2); since; **tan pronto como** as soon as (15)
cómo: sí, cómo no of course (11)
¿cómo? how? what?; **¿cómo te llamas (tú)?** what is your (*inf. sing.*) name? (1)
cómoda chest of drawers (6)
cómodamente comfortably (10)
comodidad *f.* convenience, amenity
cómodo/a comfortable (10)
compacto: disco compacto compact disc (CD) (1); **poner** (*irreg.*) **discos compactos** to play CDs (3)
compadre/comadre *what a child's parents and godparents call each other* (14)
compañero/a companion; **compañero/a de clase** classmate

compañía company (5)
comparación *f.* comparison
comparar(se) to compare (2)
compartir to share (6)
compensar to compensate
competición *f.* competition (1)
competir (i, i) to compete
complemento: *gram.* **pronombre de complemento directo** direct object pronoun; *gram.* **pronombre de complemento indirecto** indirect object pronoun
completamente completely (10)
completar to complete, finish (3)
completo/a complete; **jornada completa** full time (5); **por completo** completely
complicar (qu) to complicate
cómplice *m., f.* accomplice
componente *m.* component
componer (*like* **poner**) to make up; to fix
comportamiento behavior (14)
comportarse to behave (14)
composición *f.* composition (4)
compostura composition, structure
compra purchase; **hacer** (*irreg.*) **la compra** to go shopping for food (3) **ir** (*irreg.*) **de compras** to go shopping (1)
comprar to buy (2)
comprender to understand
comprensible understandable
comprensión *f.* understanding
comprobar (ue) to prove
comprometido/a engaged (14)
computadora computer
computar to compute
común common
comuna commune (15)
comunicación *f.* communication
comunicar (qu) to communicate
comunidad *f.* community (12)
comunión *f.* communion; **primera comunión** first communion
comunista *n., adj.* communist
comunitario/a community
con with; **con cuidado** carefully (7); **con frecuencia** frequently (2); **con gusto** with pleasure (8); **con tal (de) que** as long as (15)
conceder to concede
concentración *f.* concentration (10)
concentrado/a concentrated (8)
concentrarse to concentrate
concepto concept
conciencia conscience
concienzudo/a conscientious
concierto concert; **entradas para un concierto** tickets for a concert (1)
concluir (y) to conclude
conclusión *f.* conclusion
concordancia agreement
concordar (ue) to agree
concreto/a concrete

concursante competitor; participant
concursar to compete
concurso contest
conde(sa) count(ess)
condenable condemnable
condenación *f.* condemnation
condenar to condemn
condición *f.* condition
condicional conditional
condimento condiment (8)
condominio condominium (3)
conducción *f.* conduction; driving
conducir *irreg.* to drive
conducta conduct
conductor(a) driver
conectarse (a) to connect (*to something*)
conejera rabbit warren
conejo rabbit; **conejo de la Pascua** Easter Bunny
conexión *f.* connection (12)
conferencia conference
confesar (ie) to confess
confesión *f.* confession (7)
confiado/a confident
confianza confidence
confiar (yo confío) to trust; to confide
confirmar to confirm
conflicto conflict
confundido/a confused
confundir to confuse
confusión *f.* confusion
congelado/a frozen
congestionado/a congested (12)
congregación *f.* congregation; group
congreso congress
conjetura conjecture
conjugación *f.* conjugation
conjugar (ue) (gu) to conjugate
conjunción *f.* conjunction
conjunto collection
conmemorar to commemorate
conmigo with me (3)
conmover (ue) to move (*emotionally*)
cono cone; area
conocer (zc) to meet; to know (6); **conoce** he/she knows, you (*pol. sing.*) know (6); **conocerse** to meet each other (14); **conozco** I know (6); **gusto en conocerlo/la** nice to meet you (*pol.*) (6)
conocimiento knowledge
conquista conquest
conquistador(a) conqueror
conquistar to conquer (7)
consecuencia consequence
consecuente consistent
conseguir (i, i) (g) to obtain, get (15)
consejero/a counselor
consejo advice (11)
consenso consensus
consentido/a spoiled
consentimiento consent
consentir (ie, i) to consent; to spoil

conservador(a) *adj.* conservative
conservante *m.* preservative (8)
conservar to preserve (14); to maintain
consideración *f.* consideration
considerar to consider (8)
consigo with him/her/you (*pol.*)
consistir (en) to consist (of) (15)
consolar to console
constante constant
constitución *f.* constitution
construcción *f.* construction (13)
construir (y) to build, construct
consulado consulate (11)
consultar to consult (4)
consultorio doctor's office (5)
consumidor(a) consumer
consumir to consume
consumo consumption (10)
contable *m., f.* accountant
contacto contact
contador(a) accountant (5)
contagio contagion (15)
contaminación (*f.*) **ambiental** environmental contamination (10)
contaminar to contaminate (10)
contar (ue) to count; to tell, narrate; **contar el dinero** to count money (5); **cuéntenos** (*command*) tell us
contemporáneo/a contemporary
contener (*like* **tener**) to contain (8)
contenido *sing.* contents
contento/a happy; **estar** (*irreg.*) **contento** to be happy (4)
contestación *f.* response, answer
contestador (*m.*) **automático** answering machine
contestar to answer (2)
contexto context
continente *m.* continent (7)
continuación: a continuación next, following; appearing below
continuar (yo continúo) to continue
contra against; **en contra de** against
contrabando contraband (11)
contracción *f.* contraction (12)
contradecir (*like* **decir**) to contradict
contraer (*like* **traer**) to contract (an illness)
contrariedad *f.* annoyance
contrario: al contrario on the contrary
contraseña password
contrastar to contrast
contribuir (y) to contribute (14)
control *m.* control
controlable controllable
controlar to control; **controlarse** to control oneself (12)
convencer (z) to convince
conveniencia convenience
conveniente convenient
convenir (*like* **venir**) to suit, be advisable
conversación *f.* conversation (2)

conversar to converse (3); **converse(n)** (*command*) converse
converso/a converted
convertirse (ie) to convert
convincente convincing
convivencia coexistence
convivir to live together (harmoniously); to coexist
coordinador(a) coordinator
copa wine glass (8); **Copa Mundial** World Cup (13)
copiar to copy; to cheat
coral: arrecife (*m.*) **de coral** coral reef
corazón *m.* heart (12)
cordillera (mountain) range (10)
Corea Korea
corona crown
correcto/a right
corredor *m.* corridor, hallway (6)
corregir (j) to correct (10)
correo mail; post office (3); **correo electrónico** e-mail (address) (1)
correr to run (1)
correspondencia correspondence (1)
corresponder to correspond; **corresponde** it corresponds (1)
correspondiente corresponding (3)
corrida de toros bull fight (11)
corriente *f.* current (10); **al corriente** up to date; **corriente de aire** air current
corromperse to become corrupt
corrosivo/a corrosive
corrupción *f.* corruption
cortar to cut; **cortar el césped** to mow the lawn (6); **cortar el pelo** to cut hair (5); **cortarse** to cut oneself (12)
cortina curtain (6)
corto/a short
cosa thing
coser to sew (2)
costa coast (10)
costado side (12)
costar (ue) to cost
costear to pay for; to defray the costs of
costilla rib (12)
costo cost
costumbre *f.* custom (15)
cotidianidad *f.* daily life
cotidiano/a *adj.* daily
cotillear to gossip (15)
crear to create (10)
creatividad *f.* creativity
creativo/a creative
crecer (zc) to grow (8); to grow up
creciente growing
crecimiento growth
creencia belief
creer to believe (5); **(no) creer que** to (not) believe that (15); **no lo creo** I don't believe it (1)
crema *n.* cream; *adj.* cream-colored; **crema batida** whipping cream; **crema**

de afeitar shaving cream; **crema hidratante** moisturizer
creyente *m., f.* believer
crianza upbringing (14)
criar(se) to bring up (be brought up) (14); to grow up; to raise (*children, animals*) (10)
crimen *m.* (*pl.* **crímenes**) crime (15); **crimen por odio** hate crime
crisis *f.* crisis
cristal crystal (13)
cristianismo Christianity
cristiano/a *n., adj.* Christian
criterio criterion
crítica criticism
criticar (qu) to criticize
crítico/a critical (15)
cronología chronology
cronológico/a chronological (6)
crucero cruise ship (10)
crudo/a raw
cruel cruel (14)
crueldad *f.* cruelty
cruz *f.* cross (12)
cruzar (c) to cross; **crucé** I crossed (7); **cruzó** he/she/you (*pol. sing.*) crossed
cuaderno notebook (B)
cuadra (*street*) block (11)
cuadro box, square; graph (3); picture (*on the wall*) (6); **de cuadros** plaid, checkered (13)
¿cuál? what?, which?; **¿cuáles?** which (ones)?
cualidad *f.* quality (14)
cualquier(a) any
cuando when; **de vez en cuando** from time to time (3)
¿cuándo? when? (1); **¿cuándo nació?** when was he/she born?, when were you (*pol. sing.*) born? (1)
cuanto: en cuanto as soon as (15)
¿cuánto? how much?; how long?; **¿cuánto cuesta?** how much does it cost? (B) **¿cuánto tiempo hace que... ?** how long has it been since . . . ? (7)
¿cuántos/as? how many?; **¡cuánto/a/os/ as... !** how many . . . ! (10)
cuarenta forty (B)
cuarto room (6); bedroom; fourth (2); **y/menos cuarto** quarter past/to (*time*) (1)
cuatrocientos/as four hundred (1)
cubano/a *n., adj.* Cuban
cubanoamericano/a *n., adj.* Cuban American
cubierto/a (*p.p. of* **cubrir**) covered (10); **cubiertos** utensils (8)
cubo cube
cubrir (*p.p.* **cubierto**) to cover (8)
cuchara spoon (8)
cucharada tablespoon (*measurement*) (8)
cucharadita teaspoon (*measurement*) (8)
cucharita teaspoon (8)

cucharón *m.* ladle
cuchillo knife (8)
cuenco large serving bowl
cuenta bill, check (8); **darse** (*irreg.*) **cuenta (de)** to realize
cuentista *m., f.* storyteller
cuento story; **cuento de hadas** fairy tale
cuero leather (13)
cuerpo body (12)
cuestión *f.* issue (15)
cuestionar to question
cuestionario questionnaire
cuidado care; **¡cuidado!** careful! watch out! (11); **con cuidado** carefully (7)
cuidar (de) to take care (of) (5); **cuidarse** to take care of oneself (15)
culpa guilt, blame; **tener** (*irreg.*) **la culpa** to be at fault (11); to be guilty, blame (12)
culpable guilty
cultivar to cultivate
cultivo cultivation
culto cult
cultura culture
cumpleaños *m. sing., pl.* birthday (1); **¿cuándo es el día de tu cumpleaños?** when is your (*inf. sing.*) birthday? (1); **¡feliz cumpleaños!** happy birthday! (1)
cumplir (con) to fulfill, carry out; **cumplir años** to have a birthday (7)
cuñado/a brother-in-law/sister-in-law (9)
cura *m.* priest (14); **cura** *f.* cure
curandero/a healer
curar to cure (12)
curiosear to poke one's nose into
curiosidad *f.* curiosity (1)
curioso/a curious
curita Band-Aid (12)
cursiva: letra cursiva italics
curso course (5)
curva curve
custodia custody
cuyo/a whose

D

dama lady (13)
dañar to hurt, harm (15)
dañino/a harmful (10)
daño harm; damage (10); **hacer** (*irreg.*) **daño** to harm
dar *irreg.* to give (4); **da** he/she gives, you (*pol. sing.*) give (4); **dar a conocer** to let something be known; **dar de comer** to feed (6); **dar gritos** to shout; **dar la bienvenida** to welcome; **dar permiso** to give permission (9); **dar por sentado/a** to take for granted; **dar un curso** to teach a class; **dar un ejemplo** to give an example; **dar un paseo** to go for a walk (2); **dar una fiesta** to give a party (2); **dar vueltas** to go around; **darse cuenta de** to

realize; **darse la mano** to shake hands with each other (14); **dárselo en...** to let it go for . . . (13); **di** I gave (7); **dio** he/she/you (*pol. sing.*) gave (7); **doy** I give; **se lo(s)/la(s) doy en...** I'll let you have it/them for . . . (13)

datos *pl.* data; **datos personales** personal data (1)

de *prep.* of, from; by; **del, de la** of the; **de las... a las...** from (*time*) . . . to (*time*) (3); **de lunes a viernes** Monday through Friday (4); **de manera/modo que** so that, in a way that (15); **de nuevo** again (8); **de pronto** suddenly (4); **de repente** suddenly (12); **de todos modos** anyway (15) **¿de veras/verdad?** really? (3); **de vez en cuando** from time to time (3)

debajo de under (3)

debate *m.* debate

deber *m.* duty

deber *v.* to owe; **deber** (+ *infin.*) should, ought to (*do something*) (5)

debido a due to

débil weak (12)

década decade

decaer (*like* **caer**) to decline, dwindle

decidir to decide (2)

décimo/a tenth (2)

decir *irreg.* to say, tell (5); **dice** he/she says, you (*pol. sing.*) say (5); **¡dígalo por escrito!** say it in writing! (1); **digo** I say (5); **dije** I said (7); **dijo** he/she/you (*pol. sing.*) said (7); **es decir** that is; **¡No me digas!** You can't be serious!; **y tú, ¿qué dices?** and you (*inf. sing.*); what do you say? (1)

decisión *f.* decision (15)

declaración *f.* declaration; statement

declarar to declare, state (15)

decoración *f.* decoration

decorado/a decorated (6)

decrecer (zc) to decrease

dedicación *f.* dedication

dedicar (qu) to dedicate

dedo finger (12)

defender to defend (5)

defensa defense (15)

defensor(a) defender

definición *f.* definition (2)

definir to define

definitivamente definitively (15)

deforestación *f.* deforestation

deforestar to deforest

dejar to leave; to let (8); **dejar de** (+ *infin.*) to stop (*stop something*) (14); **dejar en** to let go for . . . (13); **dejar una propina** to leave a tip (8); **se lo(s)/la(s) dejo en...** I'll let you have it/them for . . . (13)

del (*contraction of* **de** + **el**) of the; from the

delante de in front of, in the presence of (14)

delantero/a front

delfín *m.* dolphin (10)

delgadez *f.* slimness

delgado/a thin

delicioso/a delicious (3)

delincuencia delinquency

delincuente delinquent

delirio delirium

delito crime, offense

demanda demand

demás: lo demás the rest; **los/las demás** the rest, others (7)

demasiado *adv.* too much

demasiado/a *adj.* too much, too many (7)

democracia democracy

democrático/a democratic

demoledor(a) devastating

demoler (ue) to demolish

demostrar (ue) to demonstrate, show

denotar to denote

dentista *m., f.* dentist (5)

dentro inside (8); **dentro de** inside; within, in (*time*) (15)

denunciable accusable

denunciar to report, accuse

denunciatorio/a denunciatory, threatening, accusing

departamento apartment (*Mex.*) (6)

dependencia dependence

depender (ie) (de) to depend (on) (15); **depende (de)** (it) depends (on) (4)

dependiente (*m.*), **dependienta** clerk, salesperson (5)

deportación *f.* deportation

deporte *m.* sport (1); **practicar (qu) un deporte** to play a sport (1)

deportista *m., f.* athlete

deportivo/a sport related (2)

depositar to deposit

depresión *f.* depression

deprimido/a depressed; **estar** (*irreg.*) **deprimido/a** to be depressed (4)

deprimirse to get depressed

derecha *n.* right side; **a la derecha** to the right

derecho *n.* right (*legal*) (15); law; straight ahead; **derechos civiles** civil rights (15); **derechos de aduana** customs duty, taxes (11); **derechos humanos** human rights; **derechos legales** legal rights; **Facultad de Derecho** School of Law (3)

derivado/a derived (13)

derivarse (de) to be derived (from) (13)

derrocar (qu) to overthrow, bring down (from power)

derrochador(a) wasteful

derrochar to waste

derrota defeat

desacreditar to discredit

desacuerdo disagreement; **estar** (*irreg.*) **en desacuerdo** to disagree

desafortunadamente unfortunately

desagradable unpleasant (5)

desagradar to displease

desagrado displeasure

desamparado/a homeless person (15)

desanimar to depress

desaparecer (zc) to disappear

desaparición *f.* disappearance (10)

desapasionado/a dispassionate

desaprobar (ue) to disapprove

desarrollado/a developed; **país** (*m.*) **no desarrollado** undeveloped country

desarrollar to develop (10)

desarrollo development (15); **en vías de desarrollo** developing (15); in the process of developing (15)

desastre *m.* disaster (6); **desastre natural** natural disaster

desastroso/a disastrous (10)

desatinado/a rash, imprudent, unwise

desayunar to eat breakfast (2)

desayuno breakfast (3)

desbordamiento overflow (10)

descafeinado/a decaffeinated (8)

descansar to rest (2)

descanso rest; break (2)

descartar to discard

descender (ie) to descend

descomponerse (*like* **poner**) (*p.p.* **descompuesto**) to break down; to rot; **se me/le descompuso/descompusieron** something (*sing. or pl.*) broke down (on me/you/him/her) (12)

descomponible perishable

descompuesto/a (*p.p. of* **descomponer**) rotten; broken

desconectar to disconnect

desconfiado/a mistrusting

descongestionante *m.* decongestant (12)

desconocido/a unknown

describir (*p.p.* **descrito**) to describe (2); **describa(n)** (*command*) describe

descripción *f.* description (2)

descriptivo/a descriptive (1)

descrito/a (*p.p. of* **describir**) described

descriminatorio/a discriminatory

descubierto/a (*p.p. of* **descubrir**) discovered

descubrir (*p.p.* **descubierto**) to discover

descuidar to neglect

desde *prep.* from; **desde hace... años** for . . . years; **desde la(s)... hasta la(s)...** from . . . until . . . (*time*) (4)

desear to want, desire (8)

desechable disposable

desechar to discard, throw away

desembocar (qu) to flow; to run

desempeñar to play (a role, a part)

desempleado/a unemployed

desempleo unemployment

desempolvar to dust (6)

deseo wish; desire

desesperado/a desperate (7)

desgracia disgrace
desgraciadamente unfortunately
desgraciado/a unfortunate
deshacer (*like* **hacer**) to take apart; to destroy
desierto desert (10)
desigual unequal
desigualar to make unequal
desigualdad *f.* inequality
desilusionado/a disillusioned
desinfectante *m.* disinfectant
desintegrar to disintegrate
desmayarse to faint (12)
desnudar to undress; to strip
desnudez *f.* nudity
desnudo/a naked
desodorante *m.* deodorant
desorden *m.* disorder; mess
desordenado/a messy (15)
desordenar to make a mess
despacio *adj.* slow (11)
despasionado/a dispassionate
despectivo/a contemptuous
despedazar (c) to tear to pieces
despedir (i, i) to fire
desperdiciar to waste (10)
desperdicios (nucleares) (nuclear) waste (10)
despertador *m.* alarm (7); **reloj** (*m.*) **despertador** alarm clock (7)
despertar (ie) to wake; **despertarse** to wake up (4); **me despierto** I wake up (4); **se despierta** he/she wakes up, you (*pol. sing.*) wake up (4)
despistado/a absent-minded
desplazado/a moved, shifted
desplazar (c) to move, shift
despoblado/a depopulated
despreciar to despise
desprecio scorn; contempt; disdain
desprestigiar to discredit
desprestigio loss of reputation or prestige
después *adv.* after (2); **después de** *prep.* after (4); **después de que** *conj.* after; **poco después** a little later (7)
destacar (qu) to stand out
desterrar (ie) to banish, exile
destinado/a destined
destino destiny (11)
destrucción *f.* destruction (10)
destruir (y) to destroy (15)
desventaja disadvantage (10)
desvestido/a undressed
desviación *f.* detour
desviar to divert
detalle *m.* detail (1)
detectar to detect
detective *m., f.* detective
detener(se) to stop (oneself) (12)
detenido/a stopped; arrested
detergente *m.* detergent
determinar to determine (8)

detrás de behind (3)
devastación *f.* devastation
devastador(a) devastating
devolución *f.* return
devolver (ue) (*p.p.* **devuelto**) to return (13)
devorar to devour
devuelto/a (*p. p. of* **devolver**) returned
día *m.* day; **al día siguiente** on the next day (12); **cada día** everyday; **¿cuándo es el día de tu cumpleaños?** when is your (*inf. sing.*) birthday? (1); **Día de Acción de Gracias** Thanksgiving (4); **Día de la Independencia** Independence Day (4); **Día de la Madre** Mother's Day (4); **Día de las Brujas** Halloween (4); **Día de los Enamorados** Valentine's Day (4); **Día de los Muertos** All Souls' Day (4); **Día de los Reyes Magos** Epiphany, Day of the Magi (4); **Día de Todos los Santos** All Saints' Day (4); **Día del Padre** Father's Day (4); **día del santo** saint's day (4); **día feriado** holiday (4); **hoy (en) día** nowadays (15); **todo el día** all day (1); **todos los días** every day (3)
diablo devil
dialecto dialect
diamante *m.* diamond (13)
diariamente daily (10)
diario/a daily; **actividades** (*f. pl.*) **diarias** daily activities; **rutina diaria** daily routine (4)
diarrea diarrhea; **tener** (*irreg.*) **diarrea** to have diarrhea (12)
dibujante *m., f.* one who draws or sketches
dibujar to draw (5)
dibujo drawing
dicho saying
dicho/a (*p.p. of* **decir**) said
diciembre *m.* December (1)
dictador(a) dictator
dictadura dictatorship
diecinueve nineteen (A)
dieciséis sixteen (A)
diecisiete seventeen (A)
diente *m.* tooth (12); **lavarse los dientes** to brush one's teeth (4)
dieta diet (12); **estar** (*irreg.*) **a dieta** to be on a diet (8)
dietético/a diet (12)
diez ten (A); **los próximos diez años** the next ten years
diferencia difference
diferente different (3)
difícil hard, difficult
dificultad *f.* difficulty (15)
dificultar to make difficult
difundir to spread
difusión *f.* transmission; spreading
dimensión *f.* dimension
dinero money; **dinero en efectivo** cash (11)
dios *m.* god; **Dios** God
dióxido dioxide

diputado/a delegate
dirección *f.* address (1); direction; **¿cuál es tu dirección electrónica?** what is your (*inf. sing.*) e-mail (address)? (1)
directo/a directo; *gram.* **pronombre de complemento directo** direct object pronoun
director(a) director (6)
dirigente *m., f.* leader; manager
dirigir (j) to direct (7)
disciplinado/a disciplined
disco compacto compact disc (CD)
discordia discord
discoteca discotheque (2)
discriminación *f.* discrimination **discriminación sexual** sexual discrimination
discriminadamente offensively
discriminar to discriminate
discriminatorio/a discriminatory
disculpar to excuse; **disculpe(n)** (*command*) excuse me (7)
discurso speech
discusión *f.* discussion (15)
discutir to discuss (9); to argue (9)
diseñador(a) designer
diseñar to design (3)
diseño de la moda fashion design
disfrutar to enjoy (11)
disidente *m., f.* dissident
disminución *f.* decrease
disminuir (y) to decrease, diminish (15); **disminuya** (*command*) **la velocidad** slow down (11)
disposición *f.* disposition
disputa dispute, argument
distancia distance
distanciar to distance
distante distant
distinción *f.* distinction
distinguir (g) to distinguish
distintivo/a distinctive
distinto/a distinct, different (15)
distracción *f.* distraction (5)
distraer (*like* **traer**) to distract
distribuir (y) to distribute
diversidad *f.* diversity (10)
diversión *f.* entertainment (6)
diverso/a diverse
divertido/a fun; **¡qué divertido!** what fun! (1)
divertirse (ie, i) to have fun (5); **me divertí** I had fun (7); **se divirtió** he/she/ you (*pol. sing.*) had fun (7)
dividir to divide
divinidad *f.* divinity
divino/a divine
divisar to discern
división *f.* division
divorciarse to get divorced (15)
divorcio divorce (14)
divulgar (gu) to divulge

doblar to fold (8); to turn; **doble(n)** (*command*) turn (11)

doble double; **doble sentido (vía)** two-way (11); **habitación** (*f.*) **doble** double occupancy room (11)

doce twelve (A)

doctrina doctrine

documentar to document

documento document (5)

dogma *m.* dogma

dólar *m.* dollar; **cambiar dólares por...** to exchange dollars for . . . (11)

dolencia ailment (12)

doler (ue) to hurt; **me/le duele...** my/his/her/your (*pol. sing.*) . . . hurt(s) (12)

dolor *m.* pain, ache (12); **tener** (*irreg.*) **dolor de cabeza/estómago/garganta/muelas** to have a headache/stomachache/sore throat/toothache (12)

doméstico/a domestic; **animal** (*m.*) **doméstico** pet (5); **aparato doméstico** household appliance (6); **empleado/a doméstico/a** servant (6)

dominante dominant

dominar to dominate

domingo Sunday (1)

dominicano/a *n., adj.* Dominican

dominio authority; control

don *m. title of respect used with a man's first name*

donar to donate

¿dónde? where (1); **¿de dónde eres tú?** where are you (*inf. sing.*) from?, **¿de dónde es usted?** where are you (*pol. sing.*) from? (3); **¿de dónde es... ?** where is . . . from? (3); **¿dónde está... ?** where is . . . ? (3); **¿dónde vives tú?** where do you (*inf. sing.*) live?, **¿dónde vive usted?** where do you (*pol. sing.*) live? (1)

doña *f. title of respect used with a woman's first name*

dorado/a golden brown (8)

dormido/a asleep

dormir (ue, u) to sleep (1); **duerme** he/she sleeps, you (*pol. sing.*) sleep (4); **duermo** I sleep (4); **dormí** I slept (7); **durmió** he/she/you (*pol. sing.*) slept (7)

dormitorio bedroom (6)

dos two (A); **los/las dos** both

doscientos/as two hundred (1)

drama *m.* drama, play

drásticamente drastically

droga drug (14)

drogadicción *f.* drug addiction (15)

drogadicto/a drug addict

dualidad *f.* duality

dualismo dualism

ducha shower (6)

ducharse to shower (4)

duda doubt

dudable doubtful

dudar to doubt; **(no) dudar que** to (not) doubt that . . . (15)

dudoso/a doubtful; **es dudoso que...** it is doubtful that . . . (15)

dueño/a owner (6)

dulce *adj.* sweet (8); **agua** (*f.*) **dulce** fresh water (11)

dulcería candy store (13)

dulces *m. pl.* candy (13)

durable durable (13)

durante during

durar to last

durazno peach (8)

E

e and (*used instead of* **y** *before words beginning with* **i** *or* **hi**)

echar to throw, cast; **echar(se) de menos** to miss (each other) (14)

eclesiástico/a ecclesiastical

ecología ecology (10)

ecológico/a ecological (10)

ecologista *m., f.* ecologist

economía economy; economics (2)

económico/a economical

economizar (c) to economize

ecoturismo ecotourism

ecuatoriano/a *n., adj.* Ecuadorian

edad *f.* age

edificio building (3)

educación *f.* **(sexual)** (sex) education (15)

educado/a educated; well-mannered

educar (qu) to educate

EE.UU. (E.U.) (*abbrev. for* **Estados Unidos**) United States

efectivo: dinero en efectivo cash (*money*) (11)

efecto effect (14); **efecto invernadero** greenhouse effect

efectuar to carry out

eficacia effectiveness; efficiency

eficaz effective; efficient (15)

eficiente efficient (10)

ejecutivo/a executive

ejemplo example; **por ejemplo** for example (14)

ejercer (z) to practice; **ejercer los derechos** to excercise one's rights (15)

ejercicio exercise; **hacer** (*irreg.*) **ejercicio** to exercise

ejército army (10)

ejote *m.* green bean (*Mex.*) (8)

el *def. art. m.* the

él *sub. pron.* he

elaborar to elaborate

elástico elastic (13)

elección *f.* election

electricidad *f.* electricity (10)

electricista *m., f.* electrician

eléctrico/a electric (4); **aparato eléctrico** electrical appliance (6)

electrodo electrode

electrónico/a electronic (13); **correo electrónico** e-mail (1); **escribir mensajes electrónicos** to write e-mail (1)

elegante elegant (1)

elegido/a elected (7)

elegir (j) to elect

elemento element (8)

elevar to elevate

eliminar to eliminate (10)

elitista elitist

ella *sub. pron.* she

ellos/as *sub. pron.* they; *obj. of prep.* them

elote *m.* ear of corn (*Mex.*) (8)

eludir to elude

emancipación *f.* emancipation

embajada embassy

embarazada pregnant; **estar** (*irreg.*) **embarazada** to be pregnant (12)

embarcar (qu) to embark

embargo: sin embargo however

emblema *m.* emblem

emblematizar (c) to emblematize

emborracharse to get drunk

embotellado/a bottled; jammed, blocked

embotellar to bottle; to jam, block

emergencia emergency (12); **sala de emergencias** emergency room (12)

emigración *f.* emigration

emigrar to emigrate

emisión *f.* emission

emisora de radio radio station

emitir to emit (15)

emoción *f.* emotion (4)

emocionarse to get excited

empacar (qu) to pack

empanada turnover pie or pastry (8)

empaque *m.* packing

emparejar to match; **empareje(n)** (*command*) pair up (3)

empeñado/a vehement, heated

empeñarse (en) to strive (to)

empeorar to worsen (15)

emperador *m.* emperor

emperatriz *f.* empress

empezar (ie) (c) to start, begin (2); **empezar a** (+ *infin.*) to begin to (*do something*); **empecé** I started (7); **empezó** he/she/you (*pol. sing.*) started (7); **empiece(n)** (*command*) begin (3); **empiezo** I start; **empieza** he/she starts, you (*pol. sing.*) start

empleado/a employee (5); **empleado/a doméstico/a** servant (6)

empleo employment (5)

empresa company, firm (15)

en in; **en cuanto** as soon as (15); **en general** in general (2); **en medio de** in the middle of (3); **en oferta** on sale (13); **en orden lógico** in logical order (4); **en vez de** instead of (7); **en vías de**

desarrollo developing, in the process of developing (15)

enamorado/a: Día de los Enamorados Valentine's Day (4); **estar** (*irreg.*) **enamorado/a** to be in love (4)

enamorarse to fall in love (with each other) (14)

enano/a dwarf

encantado/a delighted (pleased) (to meet you) (6)

encantador(a) charming

encantar to delight, charm; **me encanta(n) el/la/los/las...** I really like . . . (8)

encarnar to incarnate

encendedor lighter

encender (ie) to turn on (4); to light (4); to set on fire; **encender la luz** to turn on the light; **enciende** he/she turns on, you (*pol. sing.*) turn on (4); **enciendo** I turn on (4)

encerrar (ie) to shut in; to lock up

enchilada *rolled tortilla filled with meat and topped with cheese and sauce, cooked in an oven* (8)

enchufar to plug in

encías *pl.* gums (12)

enciclopedia encyclopedia

encima de on top of (3); **por encima** above

encontrar (ue) to find (4); **encuentra** he/she finds, you (*pol. sing.*) find (4); **encuentro** I find (4)

encuentro encounter

encuesta poll (5)

enemigo/a enemy

energía energy; **energía renovable** renewable energy (10); **fuente** (*f.*) **de energía** energy source (15)

enérgico/a energetic

enero January (1)

énfasis *f.* emphasis; **hacer** (*irreg.*) **énfasis** to emphasize; **poner** (*irreg.*) **énfasis** to emphasize

enfatizar (c) to emphasize

enfermedad *f.* illness (12)

enfermero/a nurse (5)

enfermo/a sick (3)

enfocarse (qu) to focus

enfrentarse to face, confront (15)

enfrente *adv.* in front; **enfrente de** in front of (3)

engañar to deceive

enlace *m.* link; union, marriage (14)

enlatado/a canned

enlatar to can

enojado/a mad, angry; **estar** (*irreg.*) **enojado/a** to be mad (4)

enojar to anger (12); **enojarse** to get angry (7)

enojo anger (14)

enorme enormous (13)

enredar to tangle

ensalada salad (3)

ensayo essay

enseñanza teaching (15)

enseñar to teach (5)

entender (ie) to understand

enterado/a informed

enterarse to find out

entidad *f.* entity

entierro funeral, burial

entonces so, then (2)

entrada entrance (2); ticket; **entradas para un concierto** tickets for a concert (1)

entrar to enter (13); **entrar al trabajo** to start work (5)

entre between (3); among; **entre semana** on weekdays, during the week (14)

entrecruzarse to cross

entregar (gu) to hand in (9)

entretenerse (*like* **tener**) to pass the time; to amuse oneself

entretenido/a fun

entrevista interview

entrevistador(a) interviewer

entrevistar to interview (4)

entristecerse (zc) to become sad (12)

enumerado/a numbered

envasado/a in a container

envasar to package; to put in a container

envase *m.* container (10)

enviar to send (6)

envidia envy; **¡qué envidia!** what luck! (I envy you!) (7)

envoltorio wrapper

envolver (ue) to wrap (13); **¿se lo/la/los/ las envuelvo?** shall I wrap it/them for you? (13)

enyesado/a in a cast (12)

época era

equipaje *m.* baggage; **facturar el equipaje** to check baggage (11); **reclamo de equipaje** baggage claim (11)

equipo team (1); **equipo de música** stereo (1)

equitativo/a equitable, fair

equivalente equivalent

equivocado/a wrong

erosión *f.* erosion

errar to make a mistake

error *m.* mistake

escala scale; stopover (11)

escalar montañas to go mountain climbing (5)

escalera ladder (5); staircase (6)

escandaloso/a scandalous

escaparse to escape (9); to run away; **se me/le escapó/escaparon** something/ someone (*sing. or pl.*) escaped (from me/ you/him/her) (12)

escarcha frost (10)

escasez (*pl.* **escaseces**) *f.* scarcity, shortage

esclavitud *f.* slavery

esclavizar (c) to enslave

esclavo/a slave

escoba broom (6)

escoger (j) to choose (4); **escoge** he/she chooses, you (*pol. sing.*) choose (4); **escojo** I choose (4)

escoltar to escort

esconder to hide (something); **esconderse** to hide (oneself)

escondido/a hidden

escondite: jugar (ue) (gu) al escondite to play hide-and-seek (9)

escribir (*p.p.* **escrito**) to write (2); **escribir a máquina** to type (5); **escribir cartas** to write letters (2); **escribir mensajes electrónicos** to write e-mail (1)

escrito/a (*p.p. of* **escribir**) written; **¡dígalo por escrito!** say it in writing! (1)

escritor(a) writer (7)

escritura writing

escuchar to listen (1); **escuchar música** to listen to music (1)

escuela school (3); **escuela primaria** elementary school (7); **escuela secundaria** high school (7)

ese, esa *pron.* that (one); *adj.* that (2)

esencial essential

esfuerzo effort

esguince *m.* sprain (12)

esmog *m.* smog (10)

eso that, that thing, that fact; **por eso** for that reason, therefore (14)

Esopo Aesop

espacio space (10); **espacio en blanco** blank space (3)

espaguetis *m. pl.* spaghetti; pasta

espalda back

español *n. m.* Spanish (language)

español(a) *n.* Spaniard; *adj.* Spanish

espárragos *pl.* asparagus (8)

Espartaco Spartacus

especia spice (8)

especialidad *f.* major (2)

especialización *f.* major

especializarse (c) to major

especialmente especially (4)

especie *f. sing.* species (10)

específico/a specific

espectáculo show (7)

especulación *f.* speculation

espejismo mirage

espejo mirror (6); **espejo retrovisor** rearview mirror (11)

espejuelos eyeglasses, spectacles

esperar to wait; to hope; **esperar el autobús** to wait for the bus (3); **esperar que** to hope that (15)

espeso/a thick

espíritu *m.* spirit; soul

espiritual spiritual

espiritualidad *f.* spirituality

espliego lavender

espoleta wishbone

esponja sponge

esposo/a husband/wife

espuma foam
esqueleto skeleton (12)
esquiar to ski
esquíes *m. pl.* skis
esquina (*street*) corner
establecer (zc) to establish (10)
establecimiento establishment
estación *f.* station (3); season (1); **estación de metro** subway station (11)
estacionamiento parking lot (3)
estacionar to park (7)
estadio stadium (1)
estado state (15); **estado anímico** mental state (4); **estado civil** marital status (1); **estado de ánimo** mental state (4); **estado físico** physical state (4)
estadounidense *n. m., f.* United States citizen; *adj.* of, from, or pertaining to the United States
estallar to explode, blow up; to spark, trigger
estampilla (postage) stamp (3)
estandarte standard, banner
estante *m.* shelf
estar *irreg.* to be (4); **¿de qué está hecho/a?** what is it made of? (13); **está hecho/a de...** it's made of . . . (13); **estar a dieta** to be on a diet (8); **estar alegre** to be happy (4); **estar comprometido/a** to be engaged (14); **estar contento/a** to be happy (4); **estar de acuerdo** to agree (4); **estar de buen/mal humor** to be in a good/bad mood (4); **estar de visita** to be staying (11); **estar deprimido/a** to be depressed (4); **estar dispuesto/a a** (+ *infin.*) to be willing (*to do something*); **estar embarazada** to be pregnant (12); **estar enamorado/a** to be in love (4); **estar enojado/a** to be mad (4); **estar hinchado/a** to be swollen (12); **estar internado/a (en el hospital)** to be hospitalized (12); **estar mareado** to be dizzy, seasick, nauseous (12); **estar mejor** to be better; **estar muerto/a** to be dead (9); **estar ocupado/a** to be busy (4); **estar preocupado/a** to be worried (4); **estar resfriado/a** to have a cold (12); **estar solo/a** to be alone, lonely (4); **estar triste** to be sad (4); **estar vivo/a** to be alive (9); **estuve** I was (7); **estuvo** he/she was, you (*pol. sing.*) were (7)
estatua statue (6)
este *m.* east
este, esta *pron.* this (one); *adj.* this (2); **esta noche** tonight (2)
estéreo stereo
estereotipado/a stereotyped
estereotipo stereotype (2)
estilo style (13)
estima esteem, respect
estimular to stimulate
estímulo stimulus

esto this, this thing, this matter
estómago stomach; **tener** (*irreg.*) **dolor de estómago** to have a stomachache (12)
estorbar to hinder; to impede
estornudar to sneeze (12)
estornudo sneeze
estrategia strategy
estrecho/a tight (13)
estrella star; **estrella de cine/televisión** movie/television star (7); **estrella marina** starfish (10)
estresado/a stressed
estudiante *m., f.* student; **estudiante universitario/a** university student
estudiantil *adj.* student; **centro estudiantil** student center (3); **periódico estudiantil** student newspaper; **residencia estudiantil** student residence hall, dormitory (5)
estudiar to study
estudio study (14)
estudioso/a studious
estupendo/a stupendous
etcétera etcetera (4)
ético/a ethical
etiqueta label (8)
etnicidad *f.* ethnicity
étnico/a ethnic
E.U. (*abbrev. for* **Estados Unidos**) United States
euro euro, monetary unit of European Union (3)
europeo/a European (2)
evadir to evade
evaluar to evaluate
evento event
eventualmente eventually
evidencia evidence
evitar to avoid (12)
evolución *f.* evolution
exactamente exactly
exagerar to exaggerate
examen *m.* exam, test; **tomar un examen** to take a test (4)
examinar to examine (5)
excedente excess, surpass
excelente excellent (8)
excepcional exceptional
excepto except
excesivo/a excessive (10)
exceso excess; **exceso de velocidad** speeding (7)
excitar to excite
excluir (y) to exclude
exclusivo/a exclusive
excursión *f.* tour, field trip (11)
exhibición *f.* exhibition (3)
exigir (j) to demand
existencia existence
existir to exist (14)
éxito success; **tener** (*irreg.*) **éxito** to be successful

exitoso/a successful
expandir to expand
expectativa expectation (14)
experiencia experience (5)
experto/a expert (11)
explicar (qu) to explain (5)
exploración *f.* exploration
explorador(a) explorer (9)
explorar to explore; **explorar el Internet** to surf the Internet (1)
explotación *f.* exploitation (10)
explotar to exploit
exportación *f.* exportation (10)
expresar to express
expresión *f.* expression
exprimidor *m.* juicer (13)
expulsar to expel, throw out
extensión *f.* extension (10)
extenso/a extensive (11)
exterminación *f.* extermination
exterminar to exterminate
externo/a external
extinción *f.* extinction; **en peligro de extinción** in danger of extinction (10)
extinguible extinguishable
extinguir (g) to extinguish
extramarital: aventura extramarital extramarital relationship
extranjero abroad
extranjero/a foreigner
extraordinario extraordinary
extremista *m., f.* extremist
extremo/a extreme

F

fábrica factory
fabricación *f.* making, manufacture (13)
fabricar (qu) to manufacture, make
fábula fable
facción *f.* faction, feature
fácil easy
facilidad *f.* ease
facilitar to facilitate, make easy
fácilmente easily
facsimilar to fax
facsímile fax
factor *m.* factor (14)
facturar el equipaje to check baggage (11)
facultad *f.* school (*of a university*); **Facultad de Bellas Artes** School of Fine Arts (3); **Facultad de Ciencias Naturales** School of Natural Sciences (3); **Facultad de Ciencias Sociales** School of Social Science (3); **Facultad de Derecho** School of Law (3); **Facultad de Filosofía y Letras** School of Humanities (3); **Facultad de Medicina** School of Medicine (3)
falda skirt (A)
fallar to miss
fallecimiento death

falsificar (qu) to falsify
falso/a false (9)
falta lack
faltar to be missing, lacking (7); to be
 absent; **faltar... para...** it is . . . minutes
 til . . . (14)
fama fame
familia family (9)
familiar *m., f.* relative
famoso/a famous
fanático/a fanatic
fanatismo fanaticism
fantasma *m.* ghost
fantástico/a fantastic
farmacéutico/a pharmacist (12)
farmacia pharmacy (3)
faro headlight (11)
fascinado/a fascinated
fascinante fascinating
fascinar to fascinate
fastidiar to annoy; to upset, spoil one's
 plans
fauna fauna (10)
favor *m.* favor; **estar** (*irreg.*) **a favor de**
 to be in favor of; **en favor de** in favor
 of; **favor de** (+ *infin.*) please (+ *action*);
 por favor please
favorecer (zc) to favor
favorito/a favorite (1)
fe *f.* faith
febrero February (1)
febril feverish
fecha date; **fecha de nacimiento** date of
 birth (1)
federal *adj.* federal (15)
fehaciente authentic, reliable
felicidad *f.* happiness (15); **¡felicidades!**
 congratulations! (1)
feliz happy (12); **¡feliz cumpleaños!**
 happy birthday! (1); **¡feliz Navidad!**
 Merry Christmas!
femenino/a feminine
feminista *m., f.* feminist
fenómeno phenomenon
feo/a ugly
feria fair
fertilizante *m.* fertilizer
festejar to celebrate
festivo: día (*m.*) **festivo** holiday
fiarse to trust
fibra fiber (12); **fibra de vidrio**
 fiberglass (13)
ficción *f.* fiction
fideo noodle (8)
fiebre *f.* fever; **fiebre del heno** hay fever (12);
 tener (*irreg.*) **fiebre** to have a fever (12)
fiesta party (4); **dar** (*irreg.*) **una fiesta** to
 give a party (2)
figura figure
fila line, file, row
filosofía philosophy; **Facultad de Filosofía
 y Letras** School of Humanities (3)

filtro filter
fin end (4); **a fin de cuentas** in the end; **fin
 de semana** weekend (1); **por fin** finally (4)
final *n. m.* end; **al final** in the end
finalmente finally (3)
financiero/a financial
firma signature (1)
firmar to sign
firme firm (10)
física physics (2)
físico/a physical; **estado físico** physical
 state (4)
flamenco flamenco (dance) (11)
flan *m.* sweet custard (8)
flecha arrow
flor *f.* flower (2)
flora flora (10)
florero flower vase
flotar to float (10)
fluidez: hablar con fluidez to speak
 fluently
flúor fluorine
folklórico/a pertaining to folklore
folleto brochure (11)
fomentar to foster, encourage
fomento promotion, encouragement
fondo fund (15); **a fondo** deeply
forma form (10)
formación *f.* education, preparation
formar to form (8)
fórmula formula
foro forum
fortuito/a fortuitous, chance
fortuna fortune
fósil *m.* fossil; **combustible** (*m.*) **fósil**
 fossil fuel
foto(grafía) picture; **sacar (qu) fotos** to
 take photos
fotográfico/a photographic
fotosíntesis photosynthesis
fracasar to fail
fracaso failure (14)
fracturado/a fractured, broken
fragancia fragrance
francés, francesa *n., adj.* French
Francia France
frase *f.* sentence, phrase
fraternidad *f.* fraternity
frecuencia frequency; **con frecuencia**
 frequently (2)
frecuente frequent
frecuentemente frequently (8)
fregadero kitchen sink
freír (*p.p.* **frito**) to fry (8)
freno brake (11)
frente *m.* front; forehead (12); **frente a**
 adv. facing, in the face of; **hacerle**
 (*irreg.*) **frente** to face
fresa strawberry (8)
fresco/a fresh (8); **hace fresco** it's cool (2)
fricativo/a fricative
frijol *m.* bean (8)

frío cold; **hace (mucho) frío** it's (very)
 cold (2); **té** (*m.*) **frío** iced tea (8); **tener**
 (*irreg.*) **frío** to be cold (4)
frito/a (*p.p. of* **freír**) fried; **papas fritas**
 French fries (3); **pollo frito** fried chicken
frontera border, frontier
fronterizo/a of the border, frontier
frustrado/a frustrated (12)
fruta fruit (3); **batido de frutas** fruit
 shake (8)
frutería fruit store (13)
frutilla strawberry (*Arg.*) (8)
fuego fire; **fuegos artificiales** fireworks (4)
fuente *f.* source; fountain (3); **fuente de
 energía** energy source (15); **fuente de
 sopa** soup tureen (8)
fuerte strong
fuerza force
fuga escape
fulgor *m.* glow, brightness, sparkle
fumar to smoke
función *f.* function (12)
funcionar to function, work (13)
fundador(a) founder
fundamentalista *m., f.* fundamentalist
funeral *m.* funeral
furioso/a furious (7)
fútbol *m.* soccer (1); **fútbol americano**
 football (1)
futuro future (5)

G

gabinete *m.* cabinet
gafas *pl.* glasses; **gafas de sol** sunglasses
galardonar to reward
galería de arte art gallery
gallego *n.* Galician (*language*)
galleta cracker, cookie (3)
galletitas cookies (3)
ganado livestock, cattle
ganar to win (7); **ganar dinero** to earn
 money (5); **ganarse** to win something
 for oneself (15); **ganarse la vida** to earn
 one's living (15)
ganas: tener (*irreg.*) **ganas de** to feel like
 (*doing something*) (5)
ganga bargain; **¡qué ganga!** what a
 bargain! (13)
garaje *m.* garage (6)
garantía guarantee (13)
garantizar (c) to guarantee
garganta throat (12); **tener** (*irreg.*)
 dolor de garganta to have a sore
 throat (12)
gárgaras: hacer (*irreg.*) **gárgaras** to
 gargle (12)
gas *m.* gas (13)
gaseoso/a gaseous
gasolina gasoline (10); **gastar gasolina** to
 use (waste) gasoline (11)
gasolinera gas station (3)

gastar to spend (13); **gastar gasolina** to use (waste) gasoline (11)

gasto expense, waste (14)

gato cat; **jugar (ue) (gu) al gato** to play tag

genealógico/a genealogical; **árbol** (*m.*) **genealógico** family tree (9)

general *n.* general; *adj.* general; **en general** in general; **por lo general** generally (1)

generalización *f.* generalization

generalmente generally, usually (3)

generar to generate (10)

genocidio genocide

gente *f. s.* people (2)

geografía geography (2)

geográfico/a geographic

gerente *m., f.* manager (5)

gigantesco/a gigantic

gimnasio gymnasium (3)

Ginebra Geneva

gira tour; **hacer** (*irreg.*) **una gira** to take a tour (10)

giro turn

global: calentamiento global global warming

globalización *f.* globalization

globo balloon (4)

gloria glory (7)

glorieta traffic circle (11)

gobernar to govern (7)

gobierno government (10)

golfo gulf (10)

golpear to hit, beat (14)

goma rubber (13)

gordo/a fat; **premio gordo** grand prize (15)

gorguera ruff

gorila *m.* gorilla

gorra cap (2)

gota drop (10); **gotas para la nariz** nose drops (12)

gozar (c) de to enjoy

grabadora tape recorder

grabar to record

gracias thanks, thank you; **Día de Acción de Gracias** Thanksgiving (4); **gracias a** thanks to

grados (centígrados) degrees (centigrade) (2)

gradualmente gradually

graduarse (me gradúo) to graduate (5)

gráfico graphic (2)

grafología graphology

gramática grammar

gran, grande big, large (A)

granja farm

granjero/a farmer

grasa fat (8)

gratificar (qu) to gratify

grave serious (10)

griego/a *n., adj.* Greek

gripe *f.* flu; **tener** (*irreg.*) **gripe** to have the flu (12)

gris grey (A)

gritar to yell, scream

grito shout, scream (7); **dar** (*irreg.*) **gritos** to shout

grupo group (1); **trabajar en grupos** to work in groups

guacamayo parrot (10)

guajolote *m.* turkey (*Mex.*) (8)

guante *m.* glove (13)

guapo/a good-looking

guardafangos *m., sing.* fender

guardar to keep; to save; **guardar ropa** to put away clothes (6)

guardería infantil childcare center (15)

guatemalteco/a *n., adj.* Guatemalan

guayabera *embroidered lightweight shirt worn in tropical climates* (13)

guerra war (15); **guerra civil** civil war

guía *m., f.* guide

guiar (guío) to guide

guisante *m.* green pea (8)

guitarrista *m., f.* guitar player

gustar to be pleasing; **¿a quién le gusta... ?** who likes to . . . ? (1); **¿qué le/te/les gusta hacer?** what do you (*pol. sing./inf. sing./pl.*)/they like to do? (1); **le gusta...** he/she likes . . . , you (*pol. sing.*) like . . . (1); **les gusta...** they/you (*pl.*) like (to) . . . ; **(no) me gusta...** I (don't) like (to) . . . (1); **me (te/le/nos/os/les) gustaría** (+ *infin.*) I (you [*inf. sing.*]/you [*pol. sing.*]/he/she/we/you [*inf. pl. Sp.*]/you [*pl.*]/they would like (*to do something*) (5); **nos gusta...** we like (to) . . . (1); **te gusta...** you (*inf. sing.*) like (to) . . . (1)

gusto taste; pleasure, delight; **con gusto** with pleasure (8); **dar** (*irreg.*) **gusto** to be pleasing; **gusto en conocerlo/la** nice to meet you (*pol.*) (6)

gustoso/a pleasant; tasty

H

haber *irreg.* (*infin. of* **hay**) to have (*auxiliary*); to be; to exist; **había** there was/were (9); **habrá** there will be (12); **hay** there is / there are (B); **hay que** one has to (*do something*) (5); **no hay paso** no entrance (11)

habichuela green bean (8)

hábil skillful

habilidad *f.* ability (5)

habitación *f.* room (6); **habitación doble** double occupancy room; **habitación sencilla** single occupancy room (11)

habitante *m., f.* inhabitant

habitar to inhabit

hábitat *m.* habitat (10)

hábito habit

hablador(a) talkative

hablante *m., f.* speaker

hablar to speak, talk

hacer *irreg.* (*p.p.* **hecho**) to do; to make (1); **¿cuánto tiempo hace que... ?** how long has it been since . . . ? (7); **hace** (+ *time*) **que** + *present* (I) have been (*doing something*) for (+ *time*); it has been (+ *time*) since (7); **hace (muy) buen/mal tiempo** the weather is (very) fine/bad (2); **hace (mucho) calor/frío** it's (very) hot/cold (2); **hace fresco** it's cool (2); **hace más de...** it has been more than (+ *time*) (7); **hace sol** it's sunny (2); **hace (mucho) viento** it's (very) windy (2); **hacer caso a** to pay attention to (14); **hacer clic en** to click on (11); **hacer cola** to stand in line (11); **hacer daño** to harm; **hacer ejercicio** to exercise (1); **hacer el papel (de)** to play the role (of) (12); **hacer gárgaras** to gargle (12); **hacer huelga** to go on strike; **hacer las maletas** to pack (11); **hacer preguntas** to ask questions; **hacer una gira** to take a tour (10); **haga(n)** (*command*) do, make (11); **hágale preguntas a...** ask . . . questions (1); **hice** I did, made (7); **hizo** he/she/you (*pol. sing.*) did, made (7); **¿qué le/te/les gusta hacer?** what do you (*pol. sing./inf. sing./pl.*)/they like to do? (1); **¿qué tiempo hace?** what is the weather like? (2)

hacia toward (10); **hacia abajo** downward

hacienda ranch

hada fairy; **cuento de hadas** fairy tale

hallar to find

hambre *f.* (*but* **el hambre**) hunger; **tener** (*irreg.*) **hambre** to be hungry (4)

hamburguesa hamburger (3)

harina flour (8)

hasta *prep.* up to; until (2); *adv.* even; **desde la(s)... hasta la(s)...** from . . . to . . . (*time*); **hasta muy tarde** until very late; **hasta que** *conj.* until (15)

hecho *n.* fact; event (7); **de hecho** in fact; **¿de qué está hecho/a?** what is it made of? (13); **está hecho/a de...** it's made of . . . (13); **hecho/a a mano** handmade (13)

hecho/a (*p.p. of* **hacer**) made; **hecho de metal** made of metal

heladería ice cream parlor (13)

helado ice cream; **té** (*m.*) **helado** iced tea (8)

helicóptero helicopter

hemisférico/a hemispheric

hemisferio hemisphere (10)

heno: fiebre (*f.*) **del heno** hay fever (12)

heredar to inherit

herencia inheritance

herida wound (12)

herido/a wounded person (12)

herir (i, i) to wound

hermanastro/a stepbrother/stepsister (9)

hermano/a brother/sister; *pl.* siblings; **hermanito/a** little brother / little sister;

medio/a hermano/a half brother / half sister (9)

hermoso/a beautiful (7)

héroe *m.* hero (5)

heroico/a heroic (7)

herrador(a) blacksmith

herradura horse shoe

herraje *m.* ironwork

herramienta tool (13)

híbrido/a hybrid (10)

hielo ice; **capa de hielo polar** polar ice cap

hierba grass

hierro iron (13)

hígado liver (8)

hijastro/a stepson/stepdaughter (9)

hijo/a son/daughter; *pl.* siblings

hilo thread (13)

hinchado/a swollen; **estar** (*irreg.*) **hinchado** to be swollen (12)

hindú (*pl.* **hindúes**) *n., adj.* Hindu

hipótesis *f.* hypothesis

hipotético/a hypothetical

hispanidad *f.* Spanishness

hispano/a *n., adj.* Hispanic (1)

hispanohablante *m., f.* Spanish speaker

histérico/a hysterical (15)

historia history (2); story

historial (*m.*) **clínico** medical history (12)

histórico/a historical (7)

hogar *m.* home (13)

hoja leaf (10); **hoja de papel** sheet of paper (10); **trébol** (*m.*) **de cuatro hojas** four-leafed clover

hombre *m.* man; **hombre de negocios** businessman (3)

homicidio homicide

homofobia homophobia

homogeneidad *f.* homogeneity

homogéneo/a homogeneous, similar

homosexualidad *f.* homosexuality

hondo/a deep; **plato hondo** bowl (8)

hongo mushroom (8)

honor *m.* honor (7)

honrar to honor

hora time (1); hour (1); **¿a qué hora es... ?** what time is . . . ? (1); **a última hora** at the last minute (11); **horas de oficina** office hours; **horas pico** prime time; **¿qué hora es?** what time is it? (1); **¿qué hora tiene/tienes?** what time do you (*pol. sing.*)/(*inf. sing.*) have? (1); **seis horas al día** six hours a day

horario schedule (2)

horchata *sweet rice drink* (8)

hornear to bake (5)

horno (de microondas) (microwave) oven (6); **al horno** baked (8)

horóscopo horoscope (1)

horror *m.* horror (3); **historia de horror** horror story; **película de horror** horror movie

horrorizado/a horrified

horrorizar (c) to horrify

hospedarse to stay (*at a hotel*) (7)

hospital *m.* hospital (3)

hotel *m.* hotel (3)

hoy today (1); **hoy (en) día** nowadays

huelga strike; **hacer** (*irreg.*) **huelga** to go on strike

huellas digitales fingerprints

hueso bone (12)

huevo egg (3); **huevos fritos/cocidos** fried/hard-boiled eggs (8); **huevos rancheros** *eggs, usually fried or poached, topped with a spicy tomato sauce and sometimes served on a fried corn tortilla* (8); **huevos revueltos** scrambled eggs (3)

huida escape

humanidad *f.* humanity

humanizar (c) to humanize

humano/a human; **ser** (*m.*) **humano** human being (15)

humedad *f.* humidity (10)

húmedo humid (10)

humildad *f.* humility

humo smoke

humor *m.* humor; **sentido del humor** sense of humor (14)

huracán *m.* hurricane

I

Ibérica: Península Ibérica Iberian Peninsula

icono icon

ida: boleto de ida y vuelta round-trip ticket (11)

idealizar (c) to idealize

idéntico/a identical

identidad *f.* identity

identificación *f.* identification

identificar (qu) to identify

idioma *m.* language

idiomático/a idiomatic

idóneo suitable

iglesia church (3)

ignorar to ignore

igual equal (15)

igualar to equalize

igualdad *f.* equality

igualmente likewise

ilegal illegal

ilícito/a illegal

imagen *f.* image

imaginación *f.* imagination

imaginar to imagine; **imagínese** (*command*) imagine

imaginativo/a imaginative

impaciencia impatience (4)

impaciente impatient (4)

impacto impact

imparcial impartial

impedimento impediment

impedir (i, i) to impede

imperfecto *adj.* imperfect

imperialismo imperialism

imperio empire

implantar to implant

implicar (qu) to imply (15)

implícito/a implicit

imponer (*like* **poner**) to impose (10)

importación *f.* importation (15)

importancia importance (11)

importante important (2); **es importante que...** (+ *subjunctive*) it's important that . . . (14)

importar to matter, be important

imposible impossible (4)

imprescindible essential

impresión *f.* impression

impresionante impressive (10)

impresionar to impress

impreso/a (*p.p. of* **imprimir**) printed

impresora printer (10)

imprevisible unforeseeable, unpredictable

imprevisto/a unforeseen; **caso imprevisto** unforeseen occurrence (12)

imprimir (*p.p.* **impreso**) to print (13)

impuesto tax (11)

impulsar to impel, drive forward

impulsivo/a impulsive

impulso impulse

inalámbrico/a cordless

inca *n. m., f.* Inca; *adj.* Incan

incidencia incident (10)

incierto/a uncertain

incitar to incite

inclinación *f.* inclination

inclinado/a slanted

incluido/a included (11)

incluir (y) to include (6); **incluya(n)** (*command*) include

incompleto/a incomplete

incomprensible incomprehensible

incondicional unconditional (14)

inconfundible unmistakable

inconsciente unconscious (12)

incredulidad *f.* incredulity

incrédulo/a incredulous

increíble incredible

incrementar to increase

inculcación *f.* instillation

inculcar (qu) to instill

indemnización *f.* indemnification

independencia independence; **Día de la Independencia** Independence Day (4)

independiente independent

independizar (c) to free, make independent

indicar (qu) to indicate (12)

indicativo indicative

índice *m.* index

indiferente indifferent

indígena *n. m., f.; adj.* Indian; indigenous, native (7)

indio/a Indian

indirecto/a indirect; *gram.* **pronombre de complemento indirecto** indirect object pronoun

indiscreto/a indiscrete (7)

indispensable necessary; **es indispensable que...** (+ *subjunctive*) it's absolutely necessary that . . . (14)

individual individual (5)

individuo *n. m., f.* individual

indocumentado/a undocumented

indudable doubtless

industria industry (10)

inevitable unavoidable

infancia childhood

infantil relating to children or childhood (14); **guardería infantil** childcare center (15)

infección *f.* infection (12)

inferioridad *f.* inferiority

infinitivo infinitive

influencia influence

influir (y) to influence

información *f.* information (1)

informarse to inform oneself

informática data processing (2)

informativo/a informative

informe *m.* report

infundir to instill, infuse

ingeniería (mecánica) (mechanical) engineering (2)

ingeniero/a engineer (5)

Inglaterra England

inglés *n. m.* English (language)

inglés, inglesa *n., adj.* English

ingrediente *m.* ingredient (8)

ingresar to enroll, register

inhalación (*f.*) **de vapor** steam inhalation (12)

inhalar to inhale, breathe (12)

iniciador(a) initiator, pioneer

iniciar to initiate

injusticia injustice

injustificable unjustifiable

injusto/a unjust

inmediatamente immediately (7)

inmenso/a immense (10)

inmigración *f.* immigration (1)

inmigrante *m., f.* immigrant (15)

inmigrar to immigrate

inmóvil immobile

innato/a innate

innecesario/a unnecessary

inocente innocent (5)

inodoro toilet (6)

inolvidable unforgettable

inoxidable: acero inoxidable stainless steel (13)

inquietar to disturb; to worry

inquisición inquisition; **Inquisición Española** Spanish Inquisition

inscribir(se) to enroll (oneself) (15)

insecto insect

inseguro/a unsure

insensatez *f.* foolishness, stupidity

insinuar to insinuate

insistente insistent (14)

insistir to insist

insomnio insomnia

inspeccionar to inspect

inspiración *f.* inspiration

inspirar to inspire

instalación *f.* installation (5)

instantáneamente instantaneously

institución *f.* institution (15)

instrucción *f.* instruction; direction (11); **seguir (i, i) (g) las instrucciones** to follow directions (3)

instructor(a) instructor

instruir (y) to instruct

instrumento instrument

insuficiente insufficient

integración *f.* integration

integrado/a integrated

íntegro/a whole, complete; upright

intelectual intellectual

inteligencia intelligence (14)

inteligente intelligent

intención *f.* intention

intencionado/a deliberate

intensidad *f.* intensity

intensivo/a intensive (5)

intenso/a intense

intentar to try

intento attempt

interacción *f.* interaction

intercambiar to exchange

intercambio exchange

interés *m.* interest

interesante interesting

interesar to interest (10)

interfaz *f.* interface

interior interior (12); **ropa interior** underwear (13)

internacional international

internado/a: estar (*irreg.*) **internado/a (en el hospital)** to be hospitalized (12)

interpretación *f.* interpretation

interpretar to interpret (14)

interrupción *f.* interruption

intervenir (like venir) to intervene

íntimo/a close, intimate; **amigos íntimos** close friends

intolerancia intolerance

introducir (zc) to introduce

intuición *f.* intuition

intuir (y) to sense

intuitivo/a intuitive

inundación *f.* flood (10)

inútil useless

invadir to invade

invasión *f.* invasion

invención *f.* invention (15)

inventar to invent (9)

invento invention

inventor(a) inventor

invernadero greenhouse; **efecto invernadero** greenhouse effect

invernar to winter; to hibernate

inversión *f.* inversion

invertir (ie, i) to invest

investigación *f.* investigation

investigar (gu) to investigate

invierno winter (1)

invitación *f.* invitation (2)

invitar to invite (2)

inyección *f.* injection, shot (12); **poner** (*irreg.*) **una inyección** to give a shot

ir *irreg.* to go (1); **¿cómo se va de... a... ?** how does one get from . . . to . . . ? (11); **fue** he/she/you (*pol. sing.*) went (7); **fui** I went (7); **iba a** (+ *infin.*) I was going to (+ *infin.*) (12); **ir a** (+ *infin.*) to be going to (*do something*) (2); **ir a fiestas** to go to parties (1); **ir a la playa** to go to the beach (1); **ir al cine** to go to the movies (1); **ir al trabajo** to go to work (3); **ir de compras** to go shopping (1); **ir de vacaciones** to go on vacation (5); **irse** to go away, get away; **va a...** he/she is going to . . . , you (*pol. sing.*) are going to . . . (2); **voy a...** I am going to . . . (2)

Irak Iraq

Irlanda Ireland

irlandés, irlandesa *n.* Irishman/ Irishwoman; *adj.* Irish

irónicamente ironically

ironizar (c) to ridicule, treat ironically

irradiación *f.* irradiation

irreparablemente irreparably

irresponsable irresponsible

irritable irritable (12)

isla island (10)

itinerario itinerary (11)

izquierda *n.* left-hand side; **a/de la izquierda** to/from (on) the left

izquierdo/a *adj.* left

J

jabón *m.* soap (4)

jalar to pull (14)

jalea jelly

jamaica *sweet drink made with hibiscus flowers* (8)

jamás never

jamón *m.* ham (3)

Jánuca *m.* Hanukkah (4)

jarabe *m.* syrup; **jarabe para la tos** cough syrup (12)

jardín *m.* garden; **jardín zoológico** zoo (7); **trabajar en el jardín** to work in the garden (1)

jarra pitcher, jug (8)

jaula cage (5)

jefe, jefa boss, chief (5)

jeroglíficos hieroglyphics

jersey *m.* sweater
jornada: jornada completa full time (5); **media jornada** part-time (5)
joven *n. m., f.* youth (9); *adj.* young
joyería jewelry store (13)
jubilarse to retire
júbilo jubilation
judío/a *n.* Jewish person; *adj.* Jewish (11)
juego game (1); **juego de** set of (*items*) (13); **juegos de video** video games
jueves *m. sing., pl.* Thursday (1)
juez *m., f.* (*pl.* **jueces**) judge (5)
jugador(a) player (7)
jugar (ue) (gu) to play (1); **jugar a la / al** (+ *sport*) to play (*a sport*); **jugar a la lotería** to play the lottery; **jugar a la pelota** to play ball (9); **jugar a la rayuela (al bebeleche** [*Mex.*]) to play hopscotch (9); **jugar a las cartas** to play cards (3); **jugar al boliche** to bowl (2); **jugar al escondite** to play hide-and-seek (9); **jugar al gato** to play tag (9); **jugar al tenis** to play tennis (1); **jugar con carritos** to play with little cars; **jugar con muñecas** to play with dolls (9); **jugar en la nieve** to play in the snow (1); **jugó** he/she/you (*pol. sing.*) played (7); **jugué** I played (7)
jugo juice (3); **jugo de naranja** orange juice (3)
juguete *m.* toy (4)
juguetería toy store (13)
juicio judgment
julio July (1)
jungla jungle
junio June (1)
juntar to join
junto/a *adj.* together (3)
justicia justice (5)
justificar (qu) to justify
justo/a fair (15)
juvenil *adj.* juvenile
juventud *f.* youth (9)
juzgar (gu) to judge

K

kilómetro kilometer (7)
kínder *m.* kindergarten (14)

L

la *def. art. f.* the; *d.o.* her/it/you (*pol. sing.*)
labio lip (12)
laboratorio laboratory (2)
lado side; **al lado de** beside; **por otro lado...** on the other hand . . . ; **por un lado...** on one hand . . .
ladrillo brick (13)
ladrón, ladrona thief (4)
lago lake (2)
laguna lagoon (10)
lamentable unfortunate

lámpara lamp (6)
lana wool (13)
lancha launch (11)
langosta lobster (8)
lanzamiento launch
lapislázuli *m.* lapis lazuli
largo/a long
las *def. art. f. pl.* the; *d.o. f. pl.* them/you (*pol. pl.*)
lástima shame; **es una lástima** it's a shame; **¡qué lástima!** that's too bad! (13); **qué lástima que...** it's a shame that . . . (15)
lastimado/a injured, hurt (10)
lastimar to harm, injure
lata can (8)
latino/a *n., adj.* Latin
Latinoamérica Latin America
latinoamericano/a *n., adj.* Latin American (3)
lavabo bathroom sink (6)
lavadora washing machine (6)
lavandería laundromat (3)
lavaplatos *m. sing.* dishwasher (6)
lavar to wash (2); **lavar el carro** to wash the car (2); **lavar la ropa** to do laundry; **lavarse** to wash, bathe oneself; **lavarse el pelo** to wash one's hair (4); **lavarse los dientes** to brush one's teeth (4)
lazo tie
lealtad *f.* loyalty (14)
lección *f.* lesson (3)
leche *f.* milk (3); **arroz** (*m.*) **con leche** rice pudding (8); **batido de leche** milkshake (8)
lechuga lettuce (3)
lectura reading (1)
leer (y) to read; **leer el correo electrónico** to read one's e-mail; **leer el horóscopo** to read the horoscope; **leer el periódico** to read the newspaper (1); **leer revistas** to read magazines (1); **leí** I read (*past tense*) (7); **leyó** he/she/you (*pol. sing.*) read (*past tense*) (7)
legal legal (15)
legalizar (c) to legalize (15)
legislador(a) legislator
legislar to legislate
legumbre *f.* vegetable (3)
lejos de far from (3)
lengua tongue (12); language (15); **lengua materna** mother tongue (15)
lenguaje *m.* language
lentamente slowly (10)
lento/a slow
león, leonesa lion; **león marino** sea lion (10)
leopardo leopard (10)
lesbiana lesbian
lesión *f.* injury (12)
letal lethal
letra letter (*of the alphabet*) (10); **Facultad de Filosofía y Letras** School of Humanities (3); **letra cursiva** italics

letrero sign (10)
levantar to raise; **levantar pesas** to lift weights (2); **levantarse** to get up (4)
ley *f.* law (15)
leyenda legend
liberado/a liberated (2)
liberar to liberate, free
libertad *f.* liberty
libertador(a) liberator (7)
libra pound (8)
libre free; **actividades del tiempo libre** leisure-time activities (1); **aire** (*m.*) **libre** outdoors (7); **mercado al aire libre** open-air market (13)
librería bookstore (3)
libreta notebook
libro book
lícito/a lawful, legal (15)
licuadora blender
licuar to blend, liquefy (13)
líder *m., f.* leader
liderazgo leadership
lienzo canvas
ligero/a light (10)
limitar to limit (10)
límite *m.* limit (14)
limón lemon
limonada lemonade (4)
limpiaparabrisas *m. sing.* windshield wiper (11)
limpiar to clean (2)
limpieza cleaning; **productos de limpieza** cleaning products
limpio/a clean
linaje *m.* lineage
lindo/a pretty (7)
línea line
lingüístico/a linguistic
lino linen (13)
lío problem, trouble; **meterse en líos** to get into trouble (9)
liquidación *f.* closing sale (13)
líquido liquid (8)
lista list (B)
listeza cleverness
listo/a ready (5); prepared; **estar** (*irreg.*) **listo/a** to be ready; **ser** (*irreg.*) **listo/a** to be smart, clever
literatura literature (2)
llamada (telephone) call (4)
llamar to call (on phone) (4); **¿cómo te llamas (tú)?** what is your (*inf. sing.*) name? (1); **llamar la atención** to call attention (10)
llamativo/a showy; getting one's attention
llano plain (10)
llanta (desinflada) (flat) tire (11); **llanta de repuesto** spare tire (11)
llanura plain, prairie
llave *f.* key (12)
llegada arrival (11)

llegar (gu) to arrive (2); **llegar a ser** to become; **llegar a tiempo** to arrive on time; **llegar a una conclusión** to arrive at a conclusion; **llegar tarde** to arrive late; **llegó** he/she/you (*pol. sing.*) arrived (7); **llegué** I arrived (7)

llenar to fill; **llenar los espacios en blanco** to fill in the blank spaces (9)

lleno/a full (10)

llevar to wear (A); to take (*someone or something somewhere*) (3); to carry (3); **llevarse** to take away (13); **llevarse bien** to get along well (9); **me lo llevo** I'll take (buy) it (13)

llorar to cry (4)

llorón, llorona weeper

llover (ue) to rain (2); **llueve (mucho)** it's raining (a lot) (2)

llovizna drizzle (10)

lloviznar to drizzle (10)

lluvia rain (2)

lo *d.o. m.* him/it/you (*pol. sing.*); **lo que** that which, what (7); **lo siento** I'm sorry (13)

lobo wolf (10)

localizar (c) to locate

localmente locally

loco/a *n.* crazy person; *adj.* crazy; **volverse (ue) loco/a** to go crazy (12)

locomotora locomotive (10)

lógicamente logically (7)

lógico/a logical; **en orden lógico** in logical order (4)

lograr to achieve, obtain (15); **lograr (+ *infin.*)** to manage to (*do something*), succeed in (*doing something*)

logro achievement

lona canvas; **bolsa de lona** canvas bag (10)

lotería lottery (15); **jugar (ue) (gu) a la lotería** to play the lottery (15)

luchar to fight

luego then; later (1); **desde luego** of course; **hasta luego** see you later

lugar *m.* place (2); **lugar de nacimiento** birthplace (1); **lugar de origen** place of origin; **lugar de trabajo** workplace (5); **tener (*irreg.*) lugar** to take place (14)

lujo luxury (11)

lujoso/a luxurious

luminoso/a luminous

luna moon (10); **luna de miel** honeymoon (14)

lunares: de lunares polka-dotted

lunes *m. sing., pl.* Monday (1); **de lunes a viernes** Monday through Friday (4)

luz *f.* (*pl.* **luces**) light; electricity

M

macho *n.* male (2)

madera wood (13)

madrastra step-mother (9)

madre *f.* mother; **Día de la Madre** Mother's Day (4)

madrina godmother (14); bridesmaid (14)

madrugar (gu) to get up early

maduro/a ripe (8)

maestro/a teacher (5)

Magallanes Magellan

magia magic

mágico/a magic

maguey *m. cactus from which tequila is made*

maíz *m.* corn (8); **mazorca de maíz** ear of corn (8); **palomitas de maíz** popcorn (8)

mal *n. m.* evil; *adv.* badly; **estar (*irreg.*) de mal humor** to be in a bad mood (4); **hace mal tiempo** the weather is bad (2); **sentirse (ie, i) mal** to feel badly; to feel sick, ill

mal, malo/a *adj.* bad (4); **mal hábito** bad habit; **mala suerte** bad luck; **sacar (qu) malas notas** to get bad grades (9)

maldad *f.* evil, badness

maldecir (*like* **decir**) to curse

maldición *f.* curse

maleficencia wrongdoing

maléfico/a evil

maleta suitcase (11); **hacer (*irreg.*) las maletas** to pack (11)

maletero trunk (*automobile*) (11)

malgastar to waste

maltratar to mistreat

mamífero mammal (10)

mandamiento commandment

mandar to send (3); to order; to command (14); **mandar un mensaje por correo electrónico** to send an e-mail message

mandato command

mando a distancia remote control (*Sp.*)

manejar to drive (2)

manera manner, way; **de manera que** so that; in such a way that (15)

manga sleeve (13)

mango mango (8)

manifestación *f.* demonstration; **manifestación política** political demonstration

manifestante *m., f.* demonstrator

manifestar (ie) to demonstrate

mano *f.* hand (B)

mantel *m.* tablecloth (8)

mantener (*like* **tener**) to maintain (11); **mantenerse** to maintain oneself (12)

mantenimiento maintenance

mantequilla butter (3)

manual workbook; manual (13)

manzana apple (8); **puré (*m.*) de manzana** apple sauce (12)

mañana *n.* morning; tomorrow (1); **hasta mañana** see you tomorrow; **mañana por la mañana (la noche)** tomorrow morning (evening) (3); **pasado mañana** day after tomorrow (1); **por la mañana** in the morning (1)

mapa *m.* map

mapamundi *m.* world map

maquiladora *large factory located in developing country to take advantage of lower wages* (15)

maquillarse to put on make up (4)

máquina machine; **máquina de escribir** typewriter

mar *m., f.* sea, ocean (2)

marca brand (4)

marcado/a strong, pronounced

marcar (qu) to mark (5)

marcha march

mareado/a dizzy, seasick, nauseous; **estar (*irreg.*) mareado/a** to be dizzy, seasick, nauseous (12)

marearse to get seasick (10)

mareo nausea, seasickness (12)

margen *m.* margin

marginación *f.* marginalization

marginar to marginalize

marino/a marine, of the sea; **estrella marina** starfish (10); **león (*m.*) marino** sea lion (10); **tortuga marina** sea turtle (10)

mariposa butterfly (10)

mariscos *pl.* seafood

marrón brown

Marruecos Morocco

martes *m. sing., pl.* Tuesday (1)

martillo hammer (13)

marzo March (1)

más more; **el/la más (+ *adj.*)** the most (+ *adj.*); **más o menos** more or less (1); **más que (de)** more than (6); **más tarde** later (2)

masa dough (8)

mascota pet (C)

masculino/a masculine

mascullar to mumble, mutter

masticar (qu) to chew (12)

matar to kill

mate *f. an herbal tea typical of Argentina*

matemático/a mathematical

materia subject (*school*) (2); **materia prima** raw material (13)

material *m.* material (13); **¿de qué material es?** what material is it made of? (13)

materno/a maternal; **lengua materna** mother tongue (15)

matrícula (school) registration fees (14)

matricularse to enroll in (7)

matrimonio matrimony, marriage; couple; **contraer** (*like* **traer**) **matrimonio** to get married

máximo/a maximum; **temperatura máxima** maximum temperature (2)

maya *n. m., f.; adj.* Maya(n)

mayo May (1)

mayonesa mayonnaise (8)
mayor *adj.* older; oldest; major, main; greater
mayoría majority (15)
mazorca de maíz ear of corn (8)
mecánico/a mechanic (5)
mecedora rocking chair (13)
mecer (zc) to rock
medalla (de oro) (gold) medal
mediano/a medium (A); **de estatura mediana** of medium height
medianoche *f.* midnight (1)
mediante by means of
medias *pl.* stockings (13)
medicina medicine (7); **Facultad de Medicina** School of Medicine (3)
médico/a *n.* doctor (5); *adj.* medical
medida measurement (8)
medio/a *n. sing.* means; middle; half (8); **clase** (*f.*) **media** middle class; **es la una y media** it's one thirty (1); **media jornada** part-time (5); **medio ambiente** environment (10); **medio de comunicación** medium of communication; **medio/a hermano/a** half brother / half sister (9); **por medio de** by means of (15); **y media** half past (*time*) (1)
medioambiental environmental
meditación *f.* meditation
mejilla cheek (12)
mejor better; best (6); **el/la mejor** the best (6); **es mejor** it is better (4); **es mejor que...** (+ *subjunctive*) it's better that . . . (14); **mejor amigo/a** best friend
mejorar(se) to improve; to get better (9)
melodrama *m.* melodrama
melón melon
memorable memorable (7)
mencionar to mention (2) (11)
menesteroso/a needy, in want
menor younger; youngest
menos less; least; **a menos que** unless (15); **más o menos** more or less (1); **menos cuarto** quarter till (*time*) (1); **menos que (de)** less than (6); **por lo menos** at least (12)
mensaje *m.* message; **escribir mensajes electrónicos** to write e-mail (1)
mensajería transport service
mensajero/a messenger
mentalidad *f.* mentality
mente *f.* mind
mentir (ie, i) to lie
mentira lie
mentiroso/a liar; **¡qué mentiroso/a!** what a liar! (9)
mentón *m.* chin
menú *m.* menu (8)
menudo: a menudo often (6)
meñique little finger
mercader *m.* merchant

mercado market (3); **mercado al aire libre** open-air market (13)
mercadotécnia marketing (2)
mercancía merchandise (13)
merecer (zc) to deserve
merendar (ie) to have a picnic (2)
meridiano meridian
mermelada marmalade
mero/a mere; simple
merodear to prowl, plunder
mes *m.* month; **el mes pasado** last month (6)
mesa table (B)
mesero/a waiter/waitress (5)
mesita coffee table (6); **mesita de noche** night table, nightstand (11)
mestizaje the mixing of races
meta goal (15)
metal *m.* metal (13); **hecho/a de metal** made of metal
metálico/a metallic
meter to put; **meterse en** to get into; **meterse en líos** to get into trouble (9)
metódico/a methodical
método method
metodología methodology
metro subway (3); **estación** (*f.*) **de metro** subway station (11)
mexicano/a *n., adj.* Mexican
mexicanoamericano/a *n., adj.* Mexican American
mezcla mixture
mezclar to mix (8)
mezclilla denim (13)
mezcolanza mixture
mi *poss.* my
mí *obj. of prep.* me; **a mí también/ tampoco** I do too / I don't either (1)
miedo fear; **tener** (*irreg.*) **miedo** to be afraid (4)
miel *f.* honey (8); **luna de miel** honeymoon (14)
miembro member
mientras meanwhile (3); while; **mientras que** while
miércoles *m. sing., pl.* Wednesday (1)
mil thousand, one thousand; **mil millones** billion
milagro miracle
militar *n. m.* soldier; *adj.* military
milla mile (6)
millón *m.* million (10); **mil millones** billion; **un millón (de)** a million (*of something*) (13); **ventidós millones de pesos** twenty-two million pesos (13)
millonario/a millionaire (5)
mínimo minimum; **temperatura mínima** minimum temperature (2)
ministro minister
minoría minority
minoritario/a minority
minutos minute

mío/a *poss.* mine, of mine
mirar to look at, watch
misa mass (2)
misil *m.* missile (10)
misión *f.* mission
mismo/a *pron.* same (one); *adj.;* same; self; **ahora mismo** right now (14); **el/la mismo/a** the same (5); **sí mismo/a** oneself; **tú mismo/a** yourself (*inf. sing.*); **uno/a mismo/a** oneself; **usted mismo/a,** yourself (*pol. sing.*)
misterio mystery (3)
mitad *f.* half
mitología mythology
moda fashion (13); **de moda** fashionable (13); **diseño de la moda** fashion design (2)
modelo model
módem *m.* modem
moderno/a modern
modestia modesty
módico/a moderate (*in price*) (6)
modo way, manner; **de modo que** so that (15)
mojar to dip (8); to wet (8)
molestar to bother (10); **me molesta** it bothers me
molestia annoyance
molesto/a annoyed; upset (12)
molino de viento windmill
momento moment (14)
monarquía monarchy
monasterio monastery
moneda coin
monetario/a monetary
monja nun
monolingüe monolingual
montaña mountain (2)
montañoso/a mountainous
montar to ride; to set up, assemble; **montar a caballo** to ride a horse (2)
monte *m.* mount, mountain
monumento monument (11)
morado purple (A)
moralismo moralism
moralista moralistic
moralizar (c) to moralize
morder (ue) to bite (12)
moreno/a brown-skinned, dark-skinned
morfológico/a morphological
morir(se) (ue, u) (*p.p.* **muerto**) to die (7); **estar** (*irreg.*) **muerto** to be dead (9)
mosca fly (7)
mostaza mustard (8)
mostrador *m.* counter (11)
mostrar (ue) to show (13)
motivación *f.* motivation
motivar to motivate
motivo motive (14)
moto(cicleta) *f.* motorcycle; **andar** (*irreg.*) **en motocicleta** to ride a motorcycle (2)

mover(se) (ue) to move (12)
móvil mobile; **(teléfono) móvil** cell phone (1)
movimiento movement (12)
mozo/a boy/girl
muchacho/a boy/girl; young man / young woman
mucho *adv.* a lot; much
mucho/a *adj.* much; *pl.* many; **muchas gracias** thank you; **muchas veces** many times (5); **muchísimo/a** very much (7)
mudanza change; move (house)
mudarse to move (from one house to another) (9)
mueble *m.* piece of furniture; *pl.* furniture (6)
muela molar (tooth) (12); **tener** (*irreg.*) **dolor de muelas** to have a toothache (12)
muerte *f.* death
muerto/a (*p.p. of* **morir**) dead; **Día de los Muertos** All Soul's Day (4)
mujer *f.* woman; **mujer bombero** firefighter (5); **mujer de negocios** businesswoman (3); **mujer policía** policewoman (5); **mujer soldado** soldier; **mujer soltera** single woman
mulato/a mulatto
muleta crutch (12)
multa ticket, fine (7)
múltiple multiple; **opción** (*f.*) **múltiple** multiple choice
mundano/a worldly, of the world
mundial *pertaining to the world* (15); **Copa Mundial** World Cup (13); **Segunda Guerra Mundial** Second World War
mundo world; **todo el mundo** everyone (15)
municipal municipal (3)
muñeca doll; wrist (12); **jugar (ue) (gu) con muñecas** to play with dolls (9)
murciélago bat
músculo muscle (12)
museo museum (3)
música music; **equipo de música** stereo (1); **escuchar música** to listen to music (1)
musical *adj.* musical (3)
muslo thigh (12)
musulmán, musulmana *n., adj.* Muslim
mutuamente mutually

N

nacer (zc) to be born (2); **¿cuándo nació?** when was he/she born? when were you (*pol. sing.*) born? (1)
nacido/a born; **recién nacido/a** newborn (14)
nacimiento birth; **fecha de nacimiento** birth date (1); **lugar** (*m.*) **de nacimiento** birthplace (1)
nación *f.* nation
nacional national

nacionalidad *f.* nationality
nada nothing (4); **de nada** you are welcome; **no hacer** (*irreg.*) **nada** to do nothing
nadar (en una piscina) to swim (in a pool) (1)
nadie no one, nobody, not anybody (3)
náhuatl *m.* Nahuatl (*indigenous language of the Aztecs*)
nalga buttock (12)
narcótico narcotic, drug (12)
narcotráfico drug trafficking (15)
nariz *f.* nose; **gotas para la nariz** nose drops (12); **tener** (*irreg.*) **la nariz tapada** to have a stuffy nose (12)
narración *f.* narration (2)
narrador(a) narrator
narrar to narrate
narrativo/a narrative
natal *adj.* birth; **país** (*m.*) **natal** country of birth
natalidad *f.* birth rate (10)
nativo/a native
natural: desastre (*m.*) **natural** natural disaster
naturaleza nature
naturalización *f.* naturalization
náuseas: tener (*irreg.*) **náuseas** to be nauseous (12)
navaja razor (4); razor blade (4)
navegación *f.* navigation
navegante *m., f.* navigator (9)
navegar (gu) to navigate; **navegar el Internet** to surf the Internet
Navidad *f.* Christmas (4)
neblina fog (10)
necesario/a necessary (5)
necesidad *f.* necessity
necesitar to need (5); **necesitar** (+ *infin.*) to need to (*do something*)
negar (ie) (gu) to deny; to refuse
negativo/a negative
negocio business (15); **hombre** (*m.*) **de negocios, mujer** (*f.*) **de negocios** businessman/businesswoman (3)
negro/a black (A); **magia negra** black magic; **mercado negro** black market
nervio nerve (12)
nervioso/a nervous (4)
neurológico/a neurological
neutro/a neutral
nevar (ie) to snow (2); **nieva (mucho)** it's snowing (a lot) (2)
ni neither; nor; even; **ni... ni** neither . . . nor (1); **¡ni pensarlo!** don't even think of it! (4)
nicotina nicotine (15)
niebla fog
nieve *f.* snow (2); **jugar (ue) (gu) en la nieve** to play in the snow (1)
nilón *m.* nylon (13)
ningún, ninguno/a none, not any (2)

niñez *f.* childhood (9)
niño/a boy/girl; child; **de niño/a** as a child (9)
nivel *m.* level (15)
nivelación *f.* leveling
nivelar to level
no no; not
Nóbel: Premio Nobel Nobel Prize (7)
noche *f.* night; **de la noche** P.M.; **esta noche** tonight; **mañana por la noche** tomorrow evening (3); **por la noche** in the evening, at night (1)
Nochebuena Christmas Eve (4)
Nochevieja New Year's Eve (4)
nocividad *f.* harmfulness
nocivo/a harmful
Noel: Papá Noel Santa Claus
nombrar to name
nombre *m.* name
nominar to nominate
nopal *m.* type of cactus
norma rule, norm
normal normal (8)
normalmente normally
noroeste *m.* northwest
norte *m.* north
norteamericano/a *n., adj.* North American (2)
nos *d.o.* us; *i.o.* to/for us; *refl. pron.* ourselves
nosotros/as *sub. pron.* we; *obj. of prep.* us
nota grade (4); **sacar (qu) buenas/malas notas** to get good/bad grades (9)
notar to note
noticia(s) news (6)
noticiario newscast
noticiero newscast
notificar (qu) to notify
novecientos/as nine hundred (1)
novela novel (2)
novelar to convert into novel form
novelesco/a fictional
novelizar (c) to convert into novel form
noveno/a ninth (2)
noventa ninety
noviazgo courtship, engagement (14)
noviembre *m.* November (1)
novio/a boyfriend/girlfriend; fiancé(e); groom/bride (14)
nube *f.* cloud (10); **en las nubes** in the clouds; "out of it"
nuclear nuclear; **energía nuclear** nuclear energy; **planta nuclear** nuclear plant (10); **reactor** (*m.*) **nuclear** nuclear reactor (15)
nuera daughter-in-law (9)
nuestro/a *poss.* our
nueve nine (A)
nuevo/a new; **Año Nuevo** New Year (4); **de nuevo** again (8)
nuez *f.* (*pl.* **nueces**) nut
número number (A); **número ordinal** ordinal number (2)

numeroso/a numerous (14)
nunca never (3); **casi nunca** almost never (3)
nupcial nuptial, wedding
nutrición *f.* nutrition (8)

O

o or
obedecer (zc) to obey
obediente obedient
obispo bishop
objetividad *f.* objectivity
objetivo/a objective
objeto object (6)
obligación *f.* obligation (5)
obligar (gu) to obligate (15)
obligatorio/a obligatory
obra work; **obra de arte** work of art, art work
obrero/a (industrial) worker (5)
observador(a) observer
observar to observe (10)
obstáculo obstacle
obstante: no obstante nevertheless, however
obstinación *f.* stubbornness
obtener (*like* **tener**) to obtain, get (5)
obvio/a obvious
ocasión *f.* occasion (2)
ocasionar to cause
occidental western
occidente *m.* west
océano ocean; **Océano Atlántico** Atlantic Ocean (3); **Océano Pacífico** Pacific Ocean (3)
ochenta eighty (C)
ocho eight (A)
ochocientos/as eight hundred (1)
ocio leisure time
oclusivo/a occlusive
octavo/a eighth (2)
octubre *m.* October (1)
ocultar to hide
ocupado/a busy; **estar** (*irreg.*) **ocupado/a** to be busy (4)
ocupar to take up, occupy
ocurrencia: ¡qué ocurrencia! what a silly idea! (4)
ocurrir to occur (10)
odiar to hate
odio hate; **crimen** (*m.*) **por odio** hate crime
oeste *m.* west
ofender (ie) to offend
ofendido/a offended
ofensivo/a offensive
ofensor(a) offender
oferta offer; **en oferta** on sale (13)
oficial official (15); **idioma** (*m.*) **oficial** official language; **lengua oficial** official language

oficina office (3); **horas de oficina** office hours
oficio job, position (5)
ofrecer (zc) to offer (2)
ofrecido/a offered
oído inner ear (12)
oír *irreg.* to hear (12); **oí** I heard (7); **oyó** he/she/you (*pol. sing.*) heard (7)
ojalá (que) I hope (that)
ojo eye
ola wave (7)
oler (ue) to smell (12); **huele** it smells (12); **huela** (*command*) smell (12)
Olimpiadas *pl.* Olympics
olvidar(se) to forget (11); **se me/le olvidó/ olvidaron** something (*sing. or pl.*) slipped my/your/his/her mind (12)
once eleven (A)
onza ounce
opción *f.* option (15)
operar to operate (12)
opinar to think, believe (14)
opinión *f.* opinion
oponerse a (*like* **ponerse**) to oppose
oportunidad *f.* opportunity (14)
oposición *f.* opposition
opresión *f.* oppression
oprimir to oppress
optativo/a optional
optimista *n. m., f.* optimist; *adj.* optimistic
opuesto/a opposite
oración *f.* sentence (2)
oralmente orally
órbita orbit
orden (*pl.* **órdenes**) *m.* order (14); **a sus órdenes** how may I help you, at your service (11); **en orden lógico** in logical order (4); **orden cronológico** chronological order
ordenado/a orderly; in order, neat
ordenador *m.* computer (*Sp.*)
ordenar to arrange, put in order (6)
oreja (outer) ear
orfanato orphanage (15)
orgánico/a organic (10)
organismo organism (10)
organización *f.* organization
organizar (c) to organize (2)
órgano interno internal organ (12)
orgullo pride
orgulloso/a proud (15)
orientación *f.* orientation
oriental eastern
oriente *m.* east
orificio hole
origen origin
original original (13)
originalmente originally
originario/a originating
orilla shore, (river)bank (10)
oro gold (13)

os *d.o.* (*Sp.*) you (*inf. pl.*); *i.o.* (*Sp.*) to/for you (*inf. pl.*); *refl. pron.* (*Sp.*) yourselves (*inf. pl.*)
oscuro/a dark
oso (panda) (panda) bear (7)
ostras *pl.* oysters (8)
otoño fall, autumn (1)
otro/a other; another; **otra vez** again (5)
oxígeno oxygen
ozonización *f.* ozonization
ozono ozone; **agujero en la capa de ozono** hole in the ozone layer (10)
ozonósfera ozonosphere

P

pacer (zc) to graze
paciente *n. m., f.* patient (5); *adj.* patient (4)
Pacífico: Océano Pacífico Pacific Ocean (3)
padecer (zc) to suffer (from) (12)
padrastro stepfather (9)
padre *m.* father; priest; *pl.* parents; **Día del Padre** Father's Day (4)
padrino godfather (14); best man in a wedding (14)
paella valenciana *rice dish with meat, fish, or seafood and vegetables* (8)
pagar (gu) to pay (5)
página page
país *m.* country; **país de habla española** Spanish-speaking country; **país del tercer mundo** Third-World country
paisaje *m.* landscape (11)
pájaro bird (10)
palabra word
palabrear to agree verbally to
palabrería wordiness; hot air
palacio palace (11)
paletita *f.* lollipop, sucker
palma palm
palmera palm tree (7)
paloma dove; pigeon
palomitas (*pl.*) **de maíz** popcorn (8)
pan *m.* bread (3); **pan de maíz** corn bread; **pan tostado** toast (3)
panadería bakery (3)
Panamá *m.* Panama
panameño/a *n., adj.* Panamanian
panamericano/a Pan-American (1)
pandilla gang (15)
panecillo roll, bun (8)
panel (*m.*) **solar** solar panel (15)
pánico panic
panorama *m.* panorama
panqueque *m.* pancake (8)
pantaletas women's underpants (13)
pantalla screen (B)
pantalón, pantalones *m. sing., pl.* pants (A); **pantalones vaqueros** jeans (A)
pantimedias *pl.* pantyhose (13)
pantorrilla calf (12)

pañales *m. pl.* diapers
Papa *m.* Pope
papa potato (3); **papa al horno** baked potato (3); **papas fritas** French fries (3)
papá *m.* dad, father; **Papá Noel** Santa Claus (14)
papalote kite (*Mex.*); **volar (ue) un papalote** to fly a kite (9)
papaya papaya (8)
papel *m.* paper; role; **desempeñar un papel** to fulfill, play a role; **hacer** (*irreg.*) **el papel (de)** to play the role (of) (12); **hoja de papel** sheet of paper (10)
papelería stationery store (3)
paperas mumps (12)
paquete *m.* package (8)
par *m.* pair; **un par de...** a pair of ... (13)
para for (1); in order to; to (*in the direction of*) (10); **para que** in order that (15); **¿para qué sirve... ?** what is ... used for? (6); **para servirle** you are welcome (11); **salir** (*irreg.*) **para** to leave for (*a place*) (7)
parabrisas *m. sing.* windshield (11)
parachoques *m. sing.* bumper
parada del autobús bus stop (3)
parado/a stopped
parador *m.* state (*tourist*) hotel (11)
paraguas *m. sing.* umbrella (13)
paragüero umbrella stand
paraíso paradise
paralelo parallel
paramédico/a paramedic (12)
parapsicología parapsychology
parcial partial
parecer (zc) to look; to seem (10); **parecerle (a uno)** to seem (to one); **parecerse a** to look like (9); **¿qué te parece... ?** what do you think of ... ?
parecido/a similar to; **bien parecido/a** good-looking
pared *f.* wall
pareja couple, pair (6); **trabajar en parejas** to work in pairs
parentesco family relationship
paréntesis *m. sing., pl.* parentheses; **entre paréntesis** between parentheses
pariente, parienta relative (4)
París Paris
parque *m.* park (2)
párrafo paragraph
parral *m.* vine arbor
parrilla: a la parrilla grilled, char-broiled (8)
parrillada grilled meat (8)
parte *f.* part; **en parte** in part; **en todas partes** everywhere; **gran parte de** a large part of; **por todas partes** everywhere (12)
participante *m., f.* participant
participar to participate (5)
particular: en particular in particular

partida departure; **punto de partida** point of departure
partido game (in sports) (1), match (1); **partido de fútbol** soccer match; **ver** (*irreg.*) **un partido de...** to see a game of ... (1)
partir to leave; to divide
pasado past
pasado/a past, last; **el año pasado** last year (6); **el mes pasado** last month (6); **el siglo pasado** the last century; **la semana pasada** last week; **pasado mañana** day after tomorrow (1)
pasaje *m.* fare, ticket price (10)
pasajero/a passenger (10)
pasaporte *m.* passport (1); **sacar (qu) el pasaporte** to get a passport (11)
pasar to pass; to happen (10); to come in; to spend (*time*); **pasar la aspiradora** to vacuum (6); **pasar por** to go through; **pasar tiempo** to spend time (2); **¿qué pasa?** what's happening?
pasatiempo pastime (2)
Pascua Easter; **conejo de Pascua** Easter Bunny; **Pascua Judía** Passover (4)
pasear (por el parque) to go for a walk (1); to go for a walk (in the park) (2)
paseo walk; **dar** (*irreg.*) **un paseo** to go for a walk (2)
pasillo hall (6)
pasivo/a passive
paso step; **no hay paso** no entrance (11)
pastel *m.* pastry, cake (3)
pasto grass
pata foot (animal); **meter la pata** to commit a *faux pas*
patada kick
patalear to stamp; to kick
patear to kick
patín *m.* skate (2)
patinar (en el hielo) to skate (on ice) (1)
patineta skateboard; **andar** (*irreg.*) **en patineta** to skateboard (1)
patio de recreo playground (9)
patrón, patrona patron
pavo turkey (8)
paz *f.* peace
peatón, peatona pedestrian (11)
pecado sin
pecho chest (12)
pechuga breast
pediatra *m., f.* pediatrician (14)
pedir (i, i) to ask for (8); to request (4); to order food (8); **pedir prestado/a(s)** to borrow (13); **pide** he/she asks, you (*pol. sing.*) ask (4); **pido** I ask (4)
pegamento glue
pegar (gu) to hit (14); to glue
peinar(se) to comb one's hair (4)
pelar to peel (8)
pelear to fight (9)

película movie; **poner** (*irreg.*) **una película** to show a movie (3)
peligrar to peril, be in danger
peligro danger; **en peligro de extinción** in danger of extinction (10)
peligroso/a dangerous (5)
pelo hair; **lavarse el pelo** to wash one's hair (4); **pelo castaño** brown hair
pelota ball; **jugar (ue) (gu) a la pelota** to play ball (9)
peluquero/a hairdresser (5)
pena: vale la pena it's worth the trouble
penetrar to penetrate
península peninsula (10); **Península Ibérica** Iberian Peninsula
penitencia penitence
pensamiento thought (10)
pensar (ie) to think (5); **pensar** (+ *infin.*) to plan to (*do something*) (5); **pensar en** to think about (5); **¡ni pensarlo!** don't even think of it! (4)
penumbra *f.* semi-darkness
peor worse, worst; **es peor** it is worse (4)
pepino cucumber (8)
pequeño/a small (A)
pera pear (8)
percibir to perceive (12)
perder (ie) to lose; **perder el tiempo** to waste time; **perder peso** to lose weight; **perderse** to get lost; **se me/le perdió/ perdieron** I/you/he/she lost something (*sing. or pl.*) (12)
pérdida loss
perdonar to excuse
perdurar to last
Pérez: Ratoncito Pérez Tooth Fairy
pereza laziness
perezoso/a lazy
perfecto/a perfect (1)
perfil *m.* profile
perfumado/a perfumed
perfumar to perfume
perfume *m.* perfume; **ponerse** (*irreg.*) **perfume** to put on perfume
periferia periphery
periférico/a peripheral
periódico newspaper; **leer (y) el periódico** to read the newspaper (1)
periodista *m., f.* journalist (9)
perjudicar (qu) to harm, injure, cause damage to
permiso permission; **dar** (*irreg.*) **permiso** to give, grant permission (9)
permitir(se) to allow (9); **permítame** allow me (11)
pero but (1)
perpetrar to perpetrate
perro dog; **perro caliente** hot dog (8)
perseguir (i, i) to pursue, chase
persistencia persistence

persona person (15)
personaje *m.* character (*fictional*) (9)
personal personal; **libertad** (*f.*)
  personal personal liberty; **uso**
  personal personal use
personalidad *f.* personality
personalizar (c) to personalize
personalmente personally
personificar (qu) to personify
perspectiva perspective
persuadir to persuade
pertenecer (zc) to belong (8)
pertinente pertinent (13)
Perú *m.* Peru
pesado/a heavy
pesar to weigh; **a pesar de** *prep.* in spite of
pesca fishing; **red** (*f.*) **de pesca** fishing
  net (10)
pescado fish (*food*) (3)
pescar (qu) to fish (1)
pesimista *n. m., f.* pessimist; *adj.*
  pessimistic
peso weight; **perder (ie) peso** to lose weight
pestaña eyelash (12)
pesticida pesticide (10)
petróleo petroleum; oil (10)
pez *m.* (*pl.* **peces**) fish
piano piano (6)
picante hot (spicy) (8)
picar (qu) to prick; to itch
pícaro/a rascal; **¡qué pícaro/a!** what a
  rascal! (9)
picazón *m.* itch
pico point; **horas pico** prime time
pie *m.* foot; **estar** (*irreg.*) **de pie** to be
  standing; **pónga(n)se de pie** stand up
  (*command*)
piedra stone (13)
piel *f.* skin (13); leather (13); **cáncer** (*m.*)
  de la piel skin cancer (10)
pierna leg
pijama *m. sing.* pijamas
pila battery
píldora pill
piloto *m., f.* pilot (5)
pimentero pepper shaker (8)
pimienta pepper
pintar to paint (5)
pintor(a) painter
pintura paint; painting (11)
piña pineapple (8)
pionero/a pioneer
pirámide *f.* pyramid (7)
pirata *m., f.* pirate
piratear to pirate
piso story, floor (6); apartment (*Sp.*) (6)
pizarra chalkboard (B)
placa license plate (11)
placer *n. m.* pleasure
plan *m.* plan (2)
planear to plan (11)
planeta *m.* planet

planicie *f.* plain
plano map (of a room or city) (3)
plano/a flat (13)
planta plant; **planta nuclear** nuclear
  plant (10)
plantar to plant
plástico plastic (10)
plata silver (13)
plátano banana (8)
platillo saucer (8)
plato prepared dish (8); **plato hondo**
  bowl (8)
playa beach
playera T-shirt (*Mex.*)
plaza town square (11)
pleito lawsuit, case
plomero/a plumber (5)
pluma pen
pluscuamperfecto pluperfect
plutonio plutonium (10)
población *f.* population (15)
poblado/a populated
poblar to populate
pobre poor (A)
pobreza poverty (15)
poco/a little; *pl.* few (9); **poco a poco** little
  by little; **poco asado/a** rare (8); **poco**
  cocido rare (8); **poco después** a little
  later (7)
poder *n. m.* power
poder *v. irreg.* to be able to (5); **poder**
  (+ *infin.*) to be able to (*do something*);
  ¿en qué puedo servirle? how may I
  help you? (11)
poderoso/a powerful
poema *m.* poem
poesía poetry
polar: capa de hielo polar polar ice cap
policía, mujer policía *m., f.* policeman/
  policewoman (5); *f.* police force
poliestireno styrofoam
política *sing.* politics; policy
político/a *n.* politician (9) (15); *adj.* political
politizado/a politicized
pollo chicken (3); **pollo frito** fried
  chicken (3)
polo pole
polución *f.* pollution
polvo dust
pomelo grapefruit (*Sp., Arg.*) (8)
poner *irreg.* to put, place; to put on; to
  put up; **me puse** I got (+ *adj.*) (7);
  poner atención to pay attention, be
  alert; **poner discos compactos** to play
  CDs (3); **poner en peligro** to put in
  danger; **poner énfasis** to emphasize;
  poner la mesa to set the table (8);
  poner una película to show a movie (3);
  ponerse to get (+ *adj.*) (7); to become
  (+ *adj.*) (7); **ponerse perfume / la ropa**
  to put on perfume/clothes (4); **se puso**
  he got (+ *adj.*) (7)

popular popular (3)
por by; through (7); because of; for; per;
  around, about; on; on account of; **¿por**
  qué? why? (1); **dar** (*irreg.*) **por sentado/a**
  to take for granted; **mañana por la**
  mñana (la noche) tomorrow morning
  (evening) (3); **por ahora** for now; **por**
  avión/tren by plane/train (10); **por**
  causa de because of; **por ciento**
  percent; **por correo electrónico** by
  e-mail; **por debajo de** underneath; **por**
  ejemplo for example (14); **por el**
  contrario on the contrary; **por encima**
  above; **por eso** for that reason, therefore
  (14); **por favor** please; **por fin** finally (4);
  por la mañana/tarde/noche in the
  morning/afternoon/evening (1); **por lo**
  general generally (1); **por lo menos** at
  least (12); **por medio de** by means of
  (15); **por parte de** on behalf of; **por**
  razones de for reasons of; **por supuesto**
  of course (11); **por teléfono** by
  telephone; **por todas partes** everywhere
  (12); **por todos lados** everywhere;
  por un lado... por otro lado... on one
  hand . . . on the other hand . . .
porcelana porcelain (11)
porcentaje *m.* percentage
porcentual percentage
por ciento percent (8)
porche *m.* porch
porción *f.* portion (10)
pornografía pornography
portada cover
portar to carry; **portarse** to behave
portátil portable
portugués *m.* Portuguese (*language*)
portugués, portuguesa *n., adj.*
  Portuguese (3)
porvenir *m.* future (15)
poseer (y) to possess
posibilidad *f.* possibility (5)
posible possible (2); **es posible** it is
  possible; **todo lo posible** everything
  possible
posición *f.* position
positivo/a positive (10)
postergar (gu) to procrastinate
postre *m.* dessert (3)
postura posture
potable drinkable (15)
potencia *n.* power, strength, force
potencial potential
práctica practice
practicar (qu) to practice; **practicar un**
  deporte to play a sport (1)
preceder to precede
precepto precept
precio price
preconcebido/a preconceived (15)
predecir (*like* **decir**) to predict
predicción *f.* prediction

predominar to predominate
preferencia preference (1)
preferentemente preferably
preferible preferable (4)
preferido/a preferred (10)
preferir (ie, i) to prefer (2); **preferí**
    I preferred (7); **prefiere** he/she prefers,
    you (*pol. sing.*) prefer (2); **prefirió** he/
    she/you (*pol. sing.*) preferred (7)
pregunta question; **contestar una**
    pregunta to answer a question; **hacer**
    (*irreg.*) **una pregunta** to ask a question;
    hágale preguntas a... ask . . . questions (1)
preguntar to ask (questions); **pregúntele**
    (*command*) ask him/her (2)
prejuicio prejudice (15)
prejuicioso/a prejudiced
prejuzgar (gu) to prejudge
premiación *f.* awarding, granting
premiado/a awarded
premiar to award
premio award, prize; **premio gordo** grand
    prize (15); **Premio Nobel** Nobel Prize (7)
prender (la luz) to turn on (the light) (6)
prensa press
prensar to press
preocupación *f.* worry
preocupado/a worried; **estar** (*irreg.*)
    preocupado/a to be worried (4)
preocupar to worry (10); **preocuparse** to
    be worried
preparación *f.* preparation (8)
preparado/a prepared, ready
preparar to prepare (3)
preparatoria prep school; high school (2)
preposicional *gram.* prepositional
prerrogativa prerogative
presagiar to forebode
presagio omen
presencia presence
presentación *f.* presentation (5);
    introduction (6)
presentar to present; to introduce; **quiero**
    presentarle a... I want to introduce you
    (*sing. pol.*) to . . . (6); **quiero presentarte**
    a... I want to introduce you (*sing. inf.*)
    to . . . (6); **se presenta** is shown
presente present (2)
preservación *f.* preservation
preservar to preserve
presidencia presidency
presidencial presidential
presidente, presidenta president (1)
presión *f.* pressure (12)
prestado/a loaned; **pedir (i, i)**
    prestado/a(s) to borrow (13)
préstamo loan
prestar to loan
prestigio prestige
prestigioso/a prestigious (5)
presunto/a presumed, supposed
presupuesto budget (15)

pretender (ie) to seek, try for
pretérito preterite
prevalecer (zc) to prevail
prevenir (*like* **venir**) to prevent
previamente previously
previsible predictable
prima: materia prima raw material (13)
primaria: (escuela) primaria elementary
    school (7)
primavera spring (1)
primer, primero/a first (2); **en primer**
    lugar in the first place; **por primera**
    vez for the first time; **primera clase**
    first-class (11); **primera comunión**
    first communion; **primera persona** first
    person
primitivo/a primitive
principal main, primary (10)
principalmente principally
principio beginning; principle; **al**
    principio at the beginning
prioridad *f.* priority (15)
prisa: tener (*irreg.*) **prisa** to be in a
    hurry (4)
prisionero/a prisoner
privado/a private; deprived; **vida privada**
    private life
privatización *f.* privatization (15)
privilegiado/a privileged
privilegiar to grant a privilege to; to favor
privilegio privilege
probabilidad *f.* probability
probablemente probably
probador *m.* dressing room (13)
probar(se) (ue) to try (out); to prove; to
    taste; to try on (13); **pruébeselo/la/los/**
    las (*command*) try it/them on (13)
problema *m.* problem (10)
procedente coming from
procedimiento procedure, process;
    proceeding
procesar to process
proceso process
proclamado/a proclaimed
producción *f.* production (10)
producir (zc) to produce (10)
productivo/a productive
producto product (10)
productor(a) producer
profecía prophecy
profesar to profess
profesión *f.* profession (5)
profesor(a) professor
profeta *m., f.* prophet
profundidad *f.* depth
profundo/a deep (10)
programa *m.,* program (1); **programa de**
    entrevistas talk show; **programa de**
    estudio en el extranjero study abroad
    program; **programa de estudios**
    program of study; **programa de**
    reciclaje recycling program; **programa**

de salud health program; **programa**
    educativo educational program;
    programa televisivo television program
programador(a) programmer
programar to program (5)
progreso progress
prohibición *f.* prohibition
prohibido/a prohibited (11)
prohibir to prohibit, forbid (14)
prometer to promise
prominente prominent
promocionar to promote
promover (ue) to promote
promulgar (gu) to enact, proclaim (15)
pronombre *m.* pronoun; *gram.* **pronom-**
    bre de complemento directo direct
    object pronoun; *gram.* **pronombre de**
    complemento indirecto indirect object
    pronoun
pronosticar (qu) to forecast (*weather*)
pronóstico del tiempo weather forecast (2)
pronto soon (7); **de pronto** suddenly (4);
    tan pronto como as soon as (15)
pronunciación *f.* pronunciation
pronunciar to pronounce
propagar (gu) to spread, propagate
propicio/a favorable; suitable
propiedad *f.* property (15)
propina tip (8)
propio/a own (6); typical, characteristic
proponer (*like* **poner**) (*p.p.* **propuesto**) to
    propose
proporción *f.* proportion
proporcionar to provide (15)
propósito purpose
propuesto/a (*p.p. of* **proponer**) proposed
prosperidad *f.* prosperity
protagonista *m., f.* protagonist
protección *f.* protection
proteger (j) to protect (10)
protegido/a protected
proteína protein (8)
protesta protest
protestante *n. m., f., adj.* protestant
protestar to protest
provecho profit, benefit
provechoso/a beneficial
proveer to provide
providencia providence
provincia province
provocar (qu) to provoke (14)
próximo/a next (2); **los próximos diez**
    años the next ten years
proyecto project (14)
prudente prudent
prueba test
psicología psychology (2)
psicólogo/a psychologist (4)
psiquiatra *m., f.* psychiatrist (12)
psíquicamente psychically
publicación *f.* publication
publicar (qu) to publish

publicista *m., f.* publicist
publicitario/a publicity, advertising
público audience (5)
público/a public; **servicio público** public service; **vía pública** public way
pudrir(se) to rot
pueblo town (6); **pueblito** little town (9)
puente *m.* bridge (11)
puerco pig; **carne** (*f.*) **de puerco** pork; **chuleta de cerdo** pork chop (8)
puerta door
puerto port (11)
puertorriqueño/a *n., adj.* Puerto Rican
pues well, then (6)
puesto market stall, small shop (13)
puesto/a (*p.p. of* **poner**) placed; turned on (*appliance*) (12); **puesto que** *conj.* since, given that
pulgar *m.* thumb (12)
pulmón *m.* lung (12)
pulmonía pneumonia (12)
pulso pulse (12)
punta point, tip
punto point (8); **punto com** dot com
puntual punctual
puntualmente punctually (10)
pupusas *bean-stuffed cornmeal cakes from El Salvador* (8)
puré (*m.*) **de manzana** apple sauce (12)
puro cigar
puro/a pure (15); **por pura casualidad** purely by chance

Q

que that, which; than; **lo que** that which, what; **ya que** since
qué: qué bueno que... it's great that . . . (15); **qué lástima que...** it's too bad that . . . (15)
¿qué? what?; **¿en qué puedo servirle?** how may I help you? (11); **¿por qué?** why? (1); **¿qué clase de... ?** what type of . . . ? (8); **¿qué hora es?** what time is it? (1); **¿qué hora tiene/tienes?** what time do you (*pol. sing.*)/(*inf. sing.*) have? (1); **¿qué le/te/les gusta hacer?** what do you (*pol. sing./inf. sing./pl.*) like to do? (1); **¿qué pasa?** what's wrong? (7); **¿qué pasó?** what happened? (7); **¿qué talla usa?** what size do you (*pol. sing.*) wear? (13); **¿qué tiempo hace?** what is the weather like? (2); **y tú, ¿qué dices?** and you (*inf. sing.*), what do you say? (1)
¡qué! what!; **¡qué +** *noun* **+ tan/más +** *adj.* what a + *adj.* + *noun* (10); **¡qué aburrido!** how boring! (1); **¡qué bueno!** that's good!; **¡qué coincidencia!** what a coincidence! (11); **¡qué divertido!** how fun! (1); **¡qué envidia!** what luck! (I envy you!) (7); **¡qué ganga!** what a bargain! (13); **¡qué lástima!** that's too bad! (13); **¡qué mentiroso/a!** what a liar! (9); **¡qué**

ocurrencia! what a silly idea! (4); **¡qué pícaro/a!** what a rascal! (9)
quedar(se) to remain; to stay; to fit; to be situated; **me quedan sólo cinco dólares** I have only five dollars left (13); **quedarle bien/mal** to look nice/bad on one, to (not) fit well (13); **quedarle grande/pequeño** to be too big/small (13); **quedarle una cantidad de algo** to have left a quantity of something (13); **quedarse en cama** to stay in bed; **quedarse en casa** to stay at home (2); **se me/le quedó/quedaron** I/you/he/she left something (*sing. or pl.*) behind (12)
quehacer doméstico household chore (6)
quejarse to complain (7)
quemadura burn (12)
quemar to burn (7); **quemarse** to get burned (12)
querer *irreg.* to want (1); to love; **quererse** to love each other (14); **quieres** you (*inf. sing.*) want; **quiero** I want (1); **quise** I wanted (7); **quisiera** (*+ infin.*) I/he/she/you (*pol. sing.*) would like to (*do something*); **quiso** he/she/you (*pol. sing.*) wanted (7)
querido/a dear (3)
quesadilla *tortilla, filled with cheese, folded and grilled; (El Salvador, Honduras) cornmeal pie filled with cheese (Mex.)* (8)
queso cheese (3)
quien(es) who, whom
¿quién(es)? who? whom?; **¿a quién le gusta... ?** who likes to . . . ? (1); **¿de quién(es) es/son... ?** whose is/are . . . ?
química chemistry (2)
químico/a chemical; **residuo químico** chemical residue (10)
quince fifteen (A)
quinientos/as five hundred (1)
quinto/a fifth (2); **quinto centenario** five hundredth anniversary
quitar to take away (7); **quitarse (la ropa)** to take off (one's clothes) (4)
quizá(s) perhaps

R

rábano radish (8)
racial racial (15)
racionalmente rationally
racismo racism
racista *n. m., f., adj.* racist (14)
radiación *f.* radiation; **radiación ultravioleta** ultraviolet radiation
radiador *m.* radiator (11)
radiar to radiate
radio *f.* radio (*medium*) (2); *m.* (*appliance*); **radio-reloj** (*m.*) **despertador** alarm clock radio (13)
radioemisora radio transmitter

raíz (*pl.* **raíces**) root; **bienes** (*m. pl.*) **raíces** real estate (6)
rallado/a grated
rallar to grate (8)
Ramadán *m.* Ramadan (4)
rango rank
rápidamente quickly, rapidly
rápido/a *adj.* fast; quick (4); **restaurante de servicio rápido** fast-food restaurant (8)
raro/a rare, strange; **raras veces** rarely (5)
rasgo characteristic, feature, trait
ratificar (qu) to ratify
rato a while (7); little while, short time
ratón *m.* mouse; **Ratoncito Pérez** Tooth Fairy
raya stripe; **de rayas** striped (13)
rayo ray; **rayo ultravioleta** ultraviolet ray; **rayos equis** X-rays (12)
rayuela hopscotch; **jugar (ue) (gu) a la rayuela** to play hopscotch (9)
raza race
razón *f.* reason (8); **tener** (*irreg.*) **razón** to be right
razonable reasonable
razonamiento reasoning
razonar to reason
reacción *f.* reaction
reaccionar to react (12)
reactor (*m.*) **nuclear** nuclear reactor (15)
realidad *f.* reality
realismo realism
realista *n. m., f.* realist; *adj.* realistic
realización *f.* realization; fulfillment; achievement
realizar (c) to attain, achieve; to carry out; to realize; **realizar un sueño** to realize/fulfill one's dream (15)
reaparecer (zc) to reappear
rebajado/a reduced (price) (13)
rebajar (tanto) to lower a price (so much) (13)
rebanada slice (8)
rebelde rebellious
recado message
recámara bedroom (*Mex.*) (6)
recepción *f.* lobby (11)
recepcionista *m., f.* receptionist
receta recipe (8); prescription (12); **surtir una receta** to fill a prescription (12)
recetar to prescribe (12)
rechazar (c) to reject
rechazo rejection
rechinar to squeak; to creak
recibir to receive (2); **recibir regalos** to get gifts (4); **recibir visitas** to have company (2)
reciclable recyclable
reciclado/a recycled
reciclaje *m.* recycling (10)
reciclar to recycle (10)

recién recent; **recién casado/a** newlywed (14); **recién nacido/a** newborn (14)
reciente recent (7)
recipiente *m.* container (8)
reclamo de equipaje baggage claim (11)
recoger (j) to pick up, gather (3)
recomendable recommendable (4)
recomendación *f.* recommendation (8)
recomendar (ie) to recommend (8)
reconocer (zc) to recognize
recordar (ue) to remember (9)
recorrer to tour, travel across
recortar to cut out (13)
recreo recess, break (9); **patio de recreo** playground (9)
rectoría office of the (university) president (3)
recuerdo memory (7)
recuperarse to recover (12)
recurso resource; **recurso natural** natural resource (10)
red *f.* net; network; Internet; **red de pesca** fishing net (10)
redada roundup
reducción *f.* reduction (15)
reducido/a reduced
reducir (zc) to reduce (10)
reemplazar (c) to replace
reemplazo replacement
reescribir to re-write
referencia reference
referente *m.* reference
referir(se) a to refer to
reflejar to reflect
reflexivo/a reflexive
reforma reform
refrán *m.* saying (1)
refrescar (qu) to refresh
refresco soft drink (3)
refrigerador *m.* refrigerator (6)
regalar to give as a gift
regalo gift; **recibir regalos** to get gifts (4); **tienda de regalos** gift shop (3)
regar (ie) to water; **riega** he/she waters, you (*pol. sing.*) water (6); **riego** I water (6)
regateo bargaining (13)
regatear to bargain (13)
régimen *m.* (*pl.* **regímenes**) regime; diet
región *f.* region (11)
regionalismo regionalism
regionalización *f.* regionalization
regionalizar (c) to regionalize
regla rule (12)
regresar to return (3)
reguetón *m.* reggaeton
rehuir (yo rehuyo) to avoid, shun
reina queen
reino kingdom
reír(se) (río) (i, i) to laugh
relación *f.* relation (1); **tener** (*irreg.*) **relaciones** to engage in sexual relations (15)

relacionado/a related (5)
relacionarse to relate
relajación *f.* relaxation
relajado/a relaxed
relajamiento relaxation
relajarse to relax
relámpago lightning (10)
relatar to report, relate, recount
relato story; account
religión *f.* religion
religiosidad *f.* religiosity
religioso/a religious (4)
reloj (despertador) *m.* (alarm) clock (7); **radio-reloj** (*m.*) **despertador** clock radio (13)
remedio (casero) (home) remedy (12)
remitir to remit
remontar to go back (in time)
remoto/a remote
rencilla quarrel
renovado/a remodeled (13)
reparación *f.* repair
reparar to fix (2)
repartir to share; to hand out
repasar to review
repaso review
repeler to repel
repente: de repente suddenly (12)
repetición *f.* repetition
repetir (i, i) to repeat (14)
reportaje *m.* report (3)
reportero/a reporter
representación *f.* representation
representar to represent (2)
representativo/a representative
reprimir to repress
reprobable reproachable
reprobación *f.* reprobation, reproof
reprobador(a) reproachful
reprobar (ue) to reproach
reproducir (zc) to reproduce
repuesto: de repuesto spare (replacement)
reptil *m.* reptile (10)
república republic
reputación *f.* reputation
reputado/a famed, reputed
requerir (ie, i) to require (10)
res: carne (*f.*) **de res** beef (8)
resbaloso/a slippery
reserva reserve (15)
reservado/a reserved
reservar to reserve
resfriado/a: estar (*irreg.*) **resfriado/a** to have a cold (12)
resfrío cold (12)
residencia residence (6); **residencia estudiantil** university residence hall, dormitory (5)
residente *m., f.* resident
residir to reside
residuo químico chemical residue (10)
resistente resistant (13)

resistir to resist
resolver (ue) (*p.p.* **resuelto**) to resolve (10)
resonar to resound
respectivamente respectively
respecto: con respecto a with respect to; **respecto a** with respect to
respetar to respect (14)
respeto respect
responder to respond (12)
responsabilidad *f.* responsibility
responsable responsible (14)
respuesta answer (2)
restaurante *m.* restaurant (1); **restaurante de servicio rápido** fast-food restaurant (8)
restaurar to restore
resto rest; *pl.* remains
restricción *f.* restriction (10)
restringir (j) to restrict, limit (10)
resuelto/a (*p.p. of* **resolver**) resolved
resultado result; **como resultado** as a result
resultar to result
resumen *m.* summary
resumir to summarize
retar to challenge, dare
retener (*like* **tener**) to retain
retirar to remove; to draw back
retrato portrait
retrovisor: espejo retrovisor rearview mirror (11)
reunión *f.* meeting (3)
reunirse to get together (4); **me reúno** I get together (4); **se reúne** he/she gets together, you (*pol. sing.*) get together (4)
reutilizable reusable
reutilizar (c) to reuse
revelar to reveal
reventar to burst
revisar to check (11)
revisión *f.* revision
revista magazine; **leer (y) revistas** to read magazines (1)
revolución *f.* revolution (11)
revolucionario/a revolutionary
rey *m.* king; **Día de los Reyes Magos** Epiphany, Day of the Magi (4)
rezar (c) to pray (3)
rico/a rich (A); delicious (8)
ridiculez *f.* ridiculousness, absurdity
ridiculizar (c) to ridicule
ridículo/a ridiculous (7)
riesgo risk (14)
rigor *m.* severity, strictness, rigor
rincón *m.* corner (*of a room*)
riñón *m.* kidney (12)
río *m.* river (2)
risa laughter
rito ritual
rivalidad *f.* rivalry
robar to steal (7)
robo robbery, theft

robot *m.* robot
rocío dew (10)
rocoso/a rocky (10)
rodeado/a surrounded (10)
rodilla knee (12)
rogar (ue) (gu) to beg (14)
rojo/a red
romántico/a romantic (2)
romper(se) (*p.p.* **roto**) to break; **se me/le rompió/rompieron** something (*sing. or pl.*) broke (on me/you/him/her) (12)
ropa *sing.* clothes, clothing; **guardar ropa** to put away clothes (6); **lavar la ropa** to do laundry; **ponerse** (*irreg.*) **ropa** to put on clothes (4); **ropa interior** underwear (13)
rosa rose
rosado/a pink (A); **vino rosado** rosé wine (8)
rosario rosary
roto/a (*p.p. of* **romper**) broken
rubio/a blond(e)
rueda wheel (10)
ruido noise (7)
ruinas ruins (11)
Rusia Russia
ruta route; **en ruta** en route
rutina diaria daily routine (4)
rutinario/a routine

S

sábado Saturday (1)
sabelotodo know-it-all
saber *irreg.* to know (4); to find out about; **saber** (+ *infin.*) to know how to (*do something*) (5); **sabe** he/she knows, you (*pol. sing.*) know (4); **sé** I know (4)
sabido/a known
sabiduría wisdom
sabiendas: a sabiendas *adv.* knowingly, on purpose
sabor *m.* flavor (8)
sabroso/a delicious (8)
sacar (qu) to take out; to get, receive (*grade*); **sacar buenas/malas notas** to get good/bad grades (9); **sacar el pasaporte** to get a passport (11); **sacar fotos** to take pictures (1); **sacar la basura** to take out the trash (6); **sacar videos** to rent videos
sacerdote *m.* priest
sacrificio sacrifice
sacudir to dust, shake off (14)
safari *m.* safari
sal *f.* salt (8)
sala living room (6); **sala de emergencias** emergency room (12); **sala de espera** waiting room (11)
salado/a salty; **agua** (*f.*) **salada** salt water (11)
salchicha sausage (8)
salero salt shaker (8)

salida departure, exit (11)
salir *irreg.* to leave; to go out (1); **salir a bailar** to go out dancing (1); **salir a comer** to go out to eat; **salir bien** to do well; **salir de vacaciones** to go on vacation (11); **salir para** to leave for (*a place*) (7); **salga(n)** (*command*) leave (11)
salón (*m.*) **de clase** classroom
salsa salsa (8)
saltar to jump; **saltar la cuerda** to jump rope (9); **salte(n)** jump (*command*)
salud *f.* **(mental)** (mental) health (12); **¡salud!** to your health! (12); bless you (12); **buena salud** good health; **programa** (*m.*) **de salud** health program
saludable healthy (3)
salvar to save (10)
salvo que unless
san, santo/a saint; **Día de Todos los Santos** All Saints' Day (4); **día del santo** saint's day (4); **Semana Santa** Holy Week (4)
sandía watermelon (8)
sangre *f.* blood (12)
sarampión *m.* measles (12)
sartén *f.* frying pan
sátira satire
satírico/a satirical
satirizar (c) to satirize
satisfacción *f.* satisfaction (15)
satisfacer (zc) to satisfy
secador *m.* **(de pelo)** hair dryer (6)
secadora clothes dryer (6)
secarse (qu) el pelo to dry one's hair (4)
sección *f.* section
seco/a dry (8)
secretario/a (ejecutiva) (executive) secretary (5)
secreto secret
secuencia sequence
secundaria: escuela secundaria high school (7)
sed *f.* thirst; **tener** (*irreg.*) **sed** to be thirsty (4)
seda silk (13)
sedentario/a sedentary
sedentarismo sedentarism
segmento segment
segregación *f.* segregation
segregacionista *m., f.* segregationist
segregar (gu) to segregate
seguido/a followed
seguir (i, i) (g) to follow; to continue; **seguir + -ndo** to go on (*doing something*); **seguir las instrucciones** to follow directions (3); **siga(n)** (*command*) keep going (11)
según according to (1)
segundo *n.* second (2); *adv.* secondly
segundo/a *adj.* second; **Segunda Guerra Mundial** Second World War
seguridad *f.* security (15)

seguro insurance; **seguro automovilístico** (automobile) insurance (11); **seguro médico** medical insurance (12)
seguro/a sure; safe
seis six (A)
seiscientos/as six hundred (1)
selección *f.* selection (1)
seleccionar to select (15)
selva (tropical) (tropical) jungle (10)
semáforo signal (light) (10)
semana week; **entre semana** on weekdays, during the week (14); **fin** (*m.*) **de semana** weekend (1); **Semana Santa** Holy Week (4)
semanal weekly
sembrar (ie) to plant (10)
semejante similar
semestre *m.* semester (2)
semilla seed
senador(a) senator
sencillo/a simple; **habitación** (*f.*) **sencilla** single occupancy room (11)
sensación *f.* sensation
sensato/a sensible
sentarse (ie) to sit
sentencia ruling, sentence (legal)
sentido meaning; **doble sentido** two-way (11); **sentido del humor** sense of humor (14); **un solo sentido** one-way (11)
sentimiento *n.* feeling
sentir(se) (ie, i) to feel; **¿cómo se siente?** how are you (*pol. sing.*) feeling? (12); **lo siento** I'm sorry (13); **me sentí** I felt (7); **se sintió** he/she/you (*pol. sing.*) felt (7); **sentirse mal** to feel badly
señal *f.* sign; signal (10); **dar** (*irreg.*) **señal** to give a sign, indication
señalar to signal
señor (Sr.) *m.* man; Mr; **los señores...** Mr. and Mrs. . . .
señora (Sra.) woman; Mrs., Ms.
señorita (Srta.) young woman; Miss
separar to separate
septiembre *m.* (1)
séptimo/a seventh (2)
sequía drought (10)
ser *m.* being; **ser humano** human being (15); **ser querido** loved one; **seres vivos** living beings
ser *irreg.* to be; **¿a qué hora es... ?** what time is . . . ? (1); **¿cómo era... ?** what was/were . . . like? (9); **es...** it is . . . (1); **¿de dónde eres tú?** where are you (*inf. sing.*) from?, **¿de dónde es usted?** where are you (*pol. sing.*) from? (3); **¿de dónde es... ?** where is . . . from? (3); **es a las 8:30** it's at 8:30 (1); **es de...** he/she/you (*pol. sing.*) is from . . . (3); **es dudoso que...** it is doubtful that . . . (15); **es importante que...** (+ *subjunctive*) it's important that . . . (14); **(no) es (im)posible que** it is (not) (im)possible

that (15); **es indispensable que...** (+ *subjunctive*) it's absolutely necessary that . . . (14); **es la una y media** it's one thirty (1); **es mejor/peor** it is better/ worse (4); **es mejor que** (+ *subjunctive*) it's better that . . . (14); **fue** he/she/you (*pol. sing.*) was/were (7); **fui** I was (7); **llegar (gu) a ser** to become; **¿qué hora es?** what time is it? (1); **ser bilingüe** to be bilingual; **ser desechable** to be disposable; **ser estudiante universitario** to be a university student; **ser útil** to be useful; **son las nueve menos diez (minutos)** it is ten (minutes) to nine (1); **soy de...** I am from . . . (3)
serio/a serious (B)
serpiente *f.* snake (10)
servicial accommodating, helpful
servicio service; **restaurante de servicio rápido** fast-food restaurant (8); **Servicio de Inmigración y Naturalización** Immigration and Naturalization Service; **servicio militar** military service; **servicio público** public service
servilleta napkin (8)
servir (i, i) to serve (5); **¿en qué puedo servirle?** how may I help you? (11); **¿para qué sirve... ?** what is . . . used for? (6); **para servirle** you are welcome (11); **servir de** to serve as; **sirve** he/she serves, you (*pol. sing.*) serve (5); **serví** I served; **sirvió** he/she, you (*pol. sing.*) served; **sirvo** I serve (5)
sesenta sixty (B)
setecientos/as seven hundred (1)
setenta seventy (C)
sexismo sexism
sexista *adj.* sexist
sexo sex (1)
sexto/a sixth (2)
sexual sexual; **contenido sexual** sexual content; **discriminación** (*f.*) **sexual** sexual discrimination; **intolerancia sexual** sexual intolerance; **orientación** (*f.*) **sexual** sexual orientation
sexualmente sexually
si if (2)
sí yes; **sí, cómo no** yes, of course (11); **¡yo sí!** I do! (4)
Sicilia Sicily
SIDA *m. sing.* (*abbrev. for* **síndrome de inmunodeficiencia adquirida**) AIDS (12)
siempre always (3)
sierra mountains (10)
siervo/a servant; slave
siesta nap; **tomar una siesta** to take a nap (2)
siete seven (A)
siglo century (7); **siglo pasado** last century
significado meaning
significar (qu) to mean
siguiente following, next (1); **al día siguiente** the next day (12)

silencioso/a silent, quiet
silla chair
sillón *m.* easy chair (6)
simbólico/a symbolic
simbolismo symbolism
simbolizar (c) to symbolize
símbolo symbol (14)
simétrico/a symmetrical
simpatizar (c) to sympathize
simple simple, mere
simplemente simply
sin without (A); **sin duda** without a doubt; **sin embargo** however; **sin que** (*conj.*) without (15)
sincero/a sincere
sino but (rather), instead
sinónimo synonym
sintaxis *f.* syntax
sintético/a synthetic
síntoma *m.* symptom (12)
sistema *m.* system (10); **sistema de comunicación** communication system; **sistema de transporte público** public transportation system; **sistema neurológico** neurological system
sitio place, site; **sitio Web** website (3)
situación *f.* situation (4)
situado/a situated (10)
situar(se) (sitúo) to situate, be situated
sobre on; on top of (3); above (3); about (1); **sobre todo** above all, especially
sobrenatural supernatural
sobrepeso obesity
sobrepoblación *f.* overpopulation (15)
sobrevivir to survive (12)
sobrino/a nephew/niece
sociabilidad *f.* sociability
social social (14); **ciencias sociales** social sciences (2); **escala social** social scale; **nivel** (*m.*) **social** social level
socialismo socialism
socialista *n. m., f., adj.* socialist
sociedad *f.* society (9)
socio/a member (9)
sociohistórico/a socio-historical
sociología sociology (2)
socorrista *m., f.* paramedic, emergency responder (12)
¡socorro! help! (12)
sofá *m.* couch (6)
sol *m.* sun; **hace sol** it is sunny (2); **tomar el sol** to sunbathe (2)
solamente only (13)
solar: panel (*m.*) **solar** solar panel (15)
soldado, mujer (*f.*) **soldado** soldier
soleado sunny (10)
soledad *f.* solitude
soler (ue) (+ *infin.*) to be accustomed to (*doing something*) (14)
sólo *adv.* only
solo/a alone, lonely; **estar** (*irreg.*) **solo/a** to be alone, lonely (4); **un solo**

sentido one-way (11); **una sola vía** one-way (11)
soltero/a single, unmarried
solución *f.* solution (5)
solucionar to solve
sombra shadow
someter to subdue
sonar (ue) to ring, go off (*alarm*) (7)
sonido sound (12)
sonreír to smile (4)
soñador(a) *n., adj.* dreamer
soñar (ue) con to dream about (4)
sopa soup (3); **fuente** (*f.*) **de sopa** soup tureen (8)
soportar to stand, endure, put up with
sor sister (religious)
sorprendente surprising
sorprender to surprise
sorprendido/a surprised
sorpresa surprise
sospecha suspicion; **tener** (*irreg.*) **sospechas** to have suspicions
sospechoso/a suspicious
sostén *m.* bra (13)
sostener (*like* **tener**) to sustain
suavemente softly
suavizante *m.* softener; **suavizante de ropa** fabric softener
subir to go up (7); **suba(n)** (*command*) board (7); **subirse a los árboles** to climb trees (9)
subjetividad *f.* subjectivity
subjetivo/a subjective
subjuntivo subjunctive
subliminal: mensaje (*m.*) **subliminal** subliminal message
subordinación *f.* subordination
subrayado/a underlined
subterráneo/a subterranean (10)
subyacer to underlie
subyugación *f.* subjugation
subyugar (gu) to subjugate
suceso event, happening
sucio/a dirty
sucursal branch (*of an office*)
Sudamérica South America (3)
sueco clog (13)
suegro/a father-in-law/mother-in-law (9); *pl.* in-laws (9)
sueldo salary (5)
suelo floor; ground (12)
sueño dream; sleepiness; **realizar (c) un sueño** to realize/fulfill one's dream (15); **tener** (*irreg.*) **sueño** to be sleepy (4)
suerte *f.* luck; **tener** (*irreg.*) **buena/mala suerte** to have good/bad luck; **traer** (*irreg.*) **buena suerte** to bring good luck
suertudo/a lucky
suficiente sufficient (15)
sufrimiento suffering
sufrir to suffer
sugerencia suggestion (14)

sugerir (i, i) to suggest (11)
suicidarse to commit suicide
sujetar to hold up, attach (13)
suma sum
superficie *f.* surface (11)
superioridad *f.* superiority
supermercado supermarket (3)
superstición *f.* superstition
supersticioso/a superstitious
suplantar to supplant, take the place of
suplicar (qu) to implore, beseech, beg
suponer (*like* **poner**) (*p.p.* **supuesto**) to suppose
supuesto/a (*p.p. of* **suponer**) supposed; **por supuesto** of course (11)
sur *m.* south; **al sur** to the south
sureño/a southern
surfear to surf (2)
surgimiento emergence
surgir (j) to arise, emerge
surtido/a assorted
surtir una receta to fill a prescription (12)
suspensión *f.* suspension
suspicaz (*pl.* **suspicaces**) suspicious, distrustful
sustancia substance (10)
sustantivo noun (2)
sustituir (y) to substitute
susto fright
suyo/a *poss.* your, of yours (*pol. sing., pl.*); his, of his; her, of hers; their, of theirs

T

tabaco tobacco
tabla table (8); graph (8); **tabla de snowboard** snowboard
taco *rolled or folded tortilla filled with meat and beans* (*Mex.*) (3)
tal such, such a; **con tal (de) que** as long as (15); **¿qué tal?** how's it going?; how are you?; **tal vez** perhaps (15)
tala felling of trees
talar to cut, fell trees
talento talent (5)
talentoso/a talented
taller *m.* workshop, shop
tamal *m.* tamale (*dish of minced meat and red peppers rolled in cornmeal wrapped in corn husks or banana leaves*) (*Mex.*) (8)
tamaño size (13)
también also, too; **a mí también** I do too (1)
tampoco neither, not either; **a mí tampoco** I don't either (1)
tan so; **tan... como** as . . . as (6); **tan pronto como** as soon as (15)
Tánger Tangier
tanque *m.* tank (10)
tanto *adv.* so much; as much; **por lo tanto** therefore; **tanto como** as much as

tanto/a *adj.* so much; *pl.* so many (14)
tanto(s)/tanta(s)... como as many . . . as (6)
tapado/a covered; **tener** (*irreg.*) **la nariz tapada** to have a stuffy nose (12)
tapar to cover (8)
tapas *pl.* (*Sp.*) hors d'oeuvres (8)
tapiz (*pl.* **tapices**) *m.* tapestry
tardar to take time (12)
tarde *n. f.* afternoon (A); *adv.* late; **de la tarde** P.M.; **más tarde** later (2); **por la tarde** in the afternoon (1); **ya es tarde** it's late already (1)
tarea homework (3); task
tarjeta card; **tarjeta de crédito** credit card (8); **tarjeta de débito** bank card, ATM card
tarot *m.* tarot; **cartas de tarot** tarot cards
tarro jar (8)
tarta pastry
tasa rate, level; **tasa de deforestación** deforestation rate; **tasa de desempleo** unemployment rate (15)
tatuaje *m.* tattoo (A)
taxi *m.* taxi (10)
taza cup, mug
te *d.o.* you (*inf. sing.*); *i.o.* to/for you (*inf. sing.*); *refl. pron.* yourself (*inf. sing.*)
té *m.* tea; **té caliente/frío (helado)** (hot, iced) tea (8); **tomar té** to drink tea (2)
teatro theater (2)
techo roof
tecla key (*on a keyboard*)
teclado keyboard
técnica *n.* technique
tecnología technology (15)
tecnológico/a technological; **avance** (*m.*) **tecnológico** technological advance
tela cloth, fabric (13)
teleadicción addiction to television
telecomunicación *f.* telecommunication
telefonear to telephone
telefónico/a *adj.* telephone; **guía** (*f.*) **telefónico** telephone directory
teléfono telephone; **hablar por teléfono** to talk on the telephone; **número de teléfono** telephone number; **(teléfono) celular** cell phone (1); **(teléfono) móvil** cell phone (1)
teleguía *f.* television guide (1)
telenovela soap opera; **ver** (*irreg.*) **una telenovela** to watch a soap opera (1)
televidente television viewer
televisión *f.* television; **estrella de televisión** television star (7); **mirar la televisión** to watch television; **ver** (*irreg.*) **la televisión** to watch television (1)
televisivo/a *adj.* television; **concurso televisivo** television contest; **programa** (*m.*) **televisivo** television program
televisor *m.* television set (1)
tema *m.* theme (10)
temático/a thematic

temer to fear, be afraid of
temeroso/a frightful, fearful
temible frightening
temor *m.* fear
temperatura temperature; **temperatura máxima/mínima** maximum/minimum temperature (2)
templo temple
temporada season (of practice) (2)
temprano early (1)
tendencia tendency
tender (ie) la cama to make the bed (6); **tiende la cama** he/she makes the bed, you (*pol. sing.*) make the bed; **tiendo la cama** I make the bed (6)
tenedor *m.* fork
tener *irreg.* to have; **¿cuántos años tienes?** how old are you (*inf. sing.*)? (C); **no tener ni un centavo** to be broke (13); **¿qué hora tiene/tienes?** what time do you (*pol. sing.*)/(*inf. sing.*) have? (1); **tener... años** to be . . . years old (C); **tener buena/mala suerte** to have good/bad luck; **tener calentura** to have a fever (12); **tener calor** to be hot (4); **tener catarro** to have a cold (12); **tener confianza** to trust; **tener diarrea** to have diarrhea (12); **tener dolor de cabeza/estómago/garganta/muelas** to have a headache / stomachache / sore throat / toothache (12); **tener el derecho** to have the right; **tener fiebre** to have a fever (12); **tener frío** to be cold (4); **tener ganas de** to feel like (*doing something*) (5); **tener gripe** to have the flu (12); **tener hambre** to be hungry (4); **tener interés** to be interested in; **tener la certeza de que** to have the certainty that; **tener la culpa** to be at fault (11); to be guilty (12); **tener la nariz tapada** to have a stuffy nose (12); **tener lugar** to take place (14); **tener miedo** to be afraid (4); **tener náuseas** to be nauseous (12); **tener prisa** to be in a hurry (4); **tener que** (+ *infin.*) to have to (*do something*) (5); **tener que ver con** to have to do with; **tener razón** to be right; **tener relaciones** to engage in sexual relations (15); **tener sed** to be thirsty (4); **tener sueño** to be sleepy (4); **tener tiempo** to have time; **tener tos** to have a cough; **tener un aborto** to have an abortion; **tener un dolor de cabeza** to have a headache; **tener un horario** to have a schedule; **tener vergüenza** to be ashamed, embarrassed (12); **tuve** I had (7); **tuvo** he/she/you (*pol. sing.*) had (7)
tenis tennis; **cancha de tenis** tennis court (6); **jugar (ue) (gu) al tenis** to play tennis
tenista *m., f.* tennis player
tenso/a tense
teocracia theocracy

teoría theory

terapeuta *m., f.* therapist (5)

tercer, tercero/a third (2); **tercer mundo** Third World

terminal (*m.*) **de autobuses** bus terminal (9)

terminar to finish (5); **termine(n)** (*command*) finish

término term (15)

terraza terrace (6)

terremoto earthquake (10)

terreno ground, terrain

terrestre earthly

territorio territory

terrorismo terrorism (15)

terrorista *n. m., f., adj.* terrorist (15)

tesis *f.* thesis; **tesis doctoral** dissertation

testigo/a witness (12)

tetera teapot

textear to send a text message

ti *obj. of prep.* you (*inf. sing.*)

tibieza lukewarmness, tepidity

tibio/a warm

tiburón *m.* shark (10)

tiempo time; weather (2); **a tiempo** on time (9); **actividades del tiempo libre** leisure-time activites (1); **¿cuánto tiempo hace que... ?** how long has it been since . . . ? (7); **hace buen/mal tiempo** the weather is fine/bad (2); **llegar (gu) a tiempo** to arrive on time; **pasar tiempo** to spend time; **perder (ie) el tiempo** to waste time; **por mucho tiempo** for a long time; **pronóstico de tiempo** weather forecast (2); **¿qué tiempo hace?** what is the weather like? (2)

tienda store (3); **tienda de regalos** gift shop (3)

tierra earth; land (10)

tijeras scissors (13)

tímido/a timid, shy

tinto: vino tinto red wine (8)

tío/a uncle/aunt

típico/a typical (1)

tipo type, kind (3)

tiranía tyranny

tiránicamente tyrannically

tiranizar (c) to tyrannize

tirano/a tyrant

tirar to throw

tiras (*pl.*) **cómicas** comic strips (9)

titulado/a entitled

título degree; title (7)

toalla towel (4)

tobillo ankle (12)

tocador *m.* dresser

tocar (qu) to touch (12); to play (*musical instrument*) (1); **tocar la bocina** to honk the horn (11); **tocar madera** to knock on wood

tocino bacon (8)

todavía still, yet (2)

todo/a all; every (2); **Día de Todos los Santos** All Saints' Day (4); **de todos modos** anyway; **en todas partes** everywhere; **por todas partes** everywhere (12); **sobre todo** above all, especially; **toda la clase** the whole class; **toda la gente** everyone; **todo el día** all day (1); **todo el mundo** everyone (15); **todos los días** every day (3)

tolerar to tolerate

tomar to take; to drink; to eat; **tomar apuntes** to take notes (4); **tomar café/té** to drink coffee/tea (2); **tomar cartas en** to take a hand in; **tomar decisiones** to make decisions; **tomar el sol** to sunbathe (2); **tomar en cuenta** to take into account; **tomar un curso** to take a class; **tomar un examen** to take a test (4); **tomar una siesta** to take a nap (2); **tome(n)** (*command*) take (11)

tomate *m.* tomato (3)

tontería silly thing; foolishness

torcido/a twisted, sprained (12)

torero/a bullfighter

tormenta storm (10)

torneo tournament (7)

toro bull; **corrida de toros** bullfight (11)

toronja grapefruit (8)

torre *f.* tower

tortilla *thin bread made of cornmeal or flour;* **tortilla española** *Spanish omelet made of eggs, potatoes, and onions (Mex.)* (8)

tortuga tortoise (10); **tortuga marina** sea turtle (10)

torturar to torture

tos cough; **jarabe** (*m.*) **para la tos** cough syrup (12); **tener** (*irreg.*) **tos** to have a cough (12)

toser to cough (12)

tostada toast (*Sp.*) (8); *crispy tortilla with toppings (Mex.)* (8)

tostado: pan (*m.*) **tostado** toast (3)

tostador toaster (6)

total total (8)

totalitarismo totalitarianism

tóxico/a toxic (10)

trabajador(a) *n.* worker; *adj.* hardworking; **trabajador(a) social** social worker (5)

trabajar to work; **trabajar en el jardín** to work in the garden (1); **trabajar en grupos** to work in groups; **trabajar en parejas** to work in pairs; **trabaje(n)** (*command*) work

trabajo work; **compañero/a de trabajo** coworker; **ir** (*irreg.*) **al trabajo** to go to work

tradición *f.* tradition

tradicional traditional (2)

traducción *f.* translation

traducir (*like* **conducir**) to translate

traductor(a) translator

traer *irreg.* to bring (4); **trae** he/she brings, you (*pol. sing.*) bring (4); **traer buena suerte** to bring good luck; **traiga(n)** (*command*) bring; **traigo** I bring (4); **traje** I brought (7); **trajo** he/she/you (*pol. sing.*) brought (7)

traficar (qu) to traffic (15)

tráfico traffic

tragar (gu) to swallow (12)

trágico/a tragic

traje *m.* suit; **traje de baño** bathing suit (7)

trama plot

trampa trick; trap; **hacer** (*irreg.*) **trampa** to play a trick on, set a trap for

tranquilamente calmly (7)

tranquilo/a calm (12)

transbordador *m.* ferry (10)

transbordo transfer (11)

transferencia transfer

transformar to transform

transgénico/a genetically modified

transitado/a traveled (*street*)

transitar to go along, through streets

tránsito traffic (11)

translúcido/a translucent (13)

transmitir to transmit

transportador(a) transporting

transportar to transport (10)

transporte *m.* transportation (6); **transporte aéreo** air transportation (11); **transporte público** public transportation

tranvía *m.* cable car, streetcar (10)

trasero/a back

trasladarse to move

traslado de... a... transportation from . . . to . . . (11)

traspasar to go through

tratado treaty

tratamiento treatment (12)

tratar to treat; to deal with; **tratar de** (+ *infin.*) to try to (*do something*) (5); **tratarse de** to be about (15)

trato treatment

trébol clover; **trébol de cuatro hojas** four-leafed clover

trebolar *m.* clover field

trece thirteen (A)

treinta thirty (A)

tremendo/a tremendous

tren *m.* train (2); **por tren** by train (10)

trenza braid

trescientos/as three hundred (1)

tribu *f.* tribe (11)

tribunal court

trigueño/a olive-skinned

trimestre *m.* trimester (2)

triste sad; **estar** (*irreg.*) **triste** to be sad (4)

tristeza sadness

triunfante triumphant
triunfar to triumph
trolebús *m.* trolley bus
trono throne
tropas *pl.* troops
tropezar (c) to trip
tropical tropical (8); **bosque** (*m.*)
  tropical tropical forest
trotar to jog (1)
trozo piece, chunk (8)
trueno thunder (10)
tu *poss.* your (*inf. sing.*)
tú *sub. pron.* you (*inf. sing.*); **y tú, ¿qué
  dices?** and you (*inf. sing.*), what do you
  say? (1)
tubería *sing.* pipes (5)
turismo tourism (11)
turista *n. m., f.* tourist (1); **guía** (*m., f.*) **de
  turistas** tourist guide
turístico/a *adj.* tourist (8); **clase** (*f.*)
  turística tourist class (11)
tuyo/a *poss.* your, of yours (*inf. sing.*)

U

u or (*used instead of* **o** *before words
  beginning with* **o** *or* **ho**)
último/a last; latest; **a última hora** at
  the last minute (11); **la última vez** last
  time (7)
ultravioleta ultraviolet; **radiación** (*f.*)
  ultravioleta ultraviolet radiation; **rayo
  ultravioleta** ultraviolet ray
un, uno/a *indef. art.* a, an; one; *pl.* some
ungüento ointment; **aplicarse (qu) un
  ungüento** to apply an ointment (12)
únicamente solely (14)
único/a *adj.* only; unique
unidad *f.* unity
unido/a united; unified (10); connected
  (10); **Estados Unidos** United States
unión *f.* union
universidad *f.* university
universitario/a *of or pertaining to the
  university* (15)
uña fingernail (12)
uranio uranium (10)
urbanismo urbanism
urbanístico/a urban
urbanización *f.* urbanization
urbano/a urban; **casco urbano** city center
urbe *f.* large city
urgente urgent
urgir (j) to be urgent (10)
usado/a used (10)
usar to use (2); **use(n)** (*command*) use
uso use (10)
usted (Ud., Vd.) *sub. pron.* you (*pol. sing.*);
  obj. of prep. you (*pol. sing.*)
ustedes (Uds., Vds.) *sub. pron.* you (*pl.*);
  obj. of prep. you (*pl.*)

usuario/a user
utensilio utensil (6)
útil useful (6)
utilidad *f.* usefulness, utility
utilizar (c) to utilize, use (15)
uva grape (8)

V

vacaciones *f. pl.* vacation; **ir** (*irreg.*)
  de vacaciones to go on vacation (5);
  salir (*irreg.*) **de vacaciones** to go on
  vacation (11)
vacuna vaccination, shot (11)
vagón *m.* train car
vainilla vanilla (8)
valer *irreg.* to be worth (13); to cost;
  ¿cuánto vale? how much is this worth?
  (13); **vale la pena** to be worth the
  trouble
validez *f.* validity
válido/a valid
valiente brave
valioso/a valuable (12)
valle *m.* valley (10)
valor value (12)
valorar to value (14)
vapor *m.* vapor; steam; **vapor tóxico** toxic
  vapor
vaqueros: pantalones (*m. pl.*) **vaqueros**
  jeans (13)
variación *f.* variation
variante variant
variar to vary
varicela chicken pox (12)
variedad *f.* variety
varios/as *pl.* several (3)
varón *m.* male infant, male child (14)
vasija container
vaso (drinking) glass (4)
vecindario neighborhood (6)
vecino/a neighbor
vegetación *f.* vegetation (10)
vegetal *m.* vegetable
vegetariano/a vegetarian (8)
vehemente vehement
vehículo vehicle (10)
veinticinco twenty-five (A)
veintidós twenty-two (A); **veintidós
  millones de pesos** twenty-two million
  pesos (13)
veintitrés twenty-three (A)
vela candle (4)
velación *f.* ceremonial covering of the bride
  and groom with a veil; the nuptial mass
  (14)
velero: andar (*irreg.*) **en velero** to go
  sailing (2)
velocidad *f.* speed; **disminuya** (*command*)
  la velocidad slow down (11); **exceso de
  velocidad** speeding (7)

velorio wake
vena vein (12)
vencedor(a) conqueror, victor
vencer (zc) to conquer
vencimiento falling due; expiration
vendaje *m.* bandage (12)
vendedor(a) salesman/saleswoman (13)
vender to sell (5)
venir *irreg.* to come (4); **venga(n)**
  (*command*) come (5); **vengo** I come (4);
  viene he/she comes, you (*pol. sing.*)
  come (4); **vine** I came (7); **vino** he/she/
  you (*pol. sing.*) came (7)
venta sale (6)
ventaja advantage (10)
ventajoso/a advantageous
ventana window
ventilador *m.* fan (6)
ver *irreg.* (*p.p.* **visto**) to see; to watch (1); **a
  ver** let's see (13); **nos vemos** see you (2);
  tener (*irreg.*) **que ver con** to have to do
  with; **vamos a ver** let's see; **vea(n)**
  (*command*) see (1); **ver la televisión** to
  watch television (1); **ver un partido de…**
  to watch a game of . . . (1); **ver una
  telenovela** to watch a soap opera (1);
  verse to see oneself; to look, appear; **vi** I
  saw (7); **vio** he/she/you (*pol. sing.*) saw (7)
veracidad *f.* veracity, truthfulness
verano summer (1)
veras: ¿de veras? really? (3)
verbo verb
verdad *f.* truth; **¿de verdad?** really? (3);
  decir (*irreg.*) **la verdad** to tell the truth;
  (no) es verdad it is (not) true
verdaderamente truly
verdadero/a true, truthful, genuine
verde green (A)
vergüenza shame; **tener** (*irreg.*) **vergüenza**
  to be ashamed, embarrassed (12)
verificar (qu) to verify
versatilidad *f.* versatility
versión *f.* version
vestido dress
vestir (i, i) to dress; **vestirse** to get dressed
  (4); **me vestí** I got dressed (7); **me visto**
  I get dressed (4); **se viste** he/she gets
  dressed, you (*pol. sing.*) get dressed (4);
  se vistió he/she/you (*pol. sing.*) got
  dressed (7)
veterinario/a veterinarian (12)
vez *f.* (*pl.* **veces**) time; **a la vez** at the same
  time (5); **a veces** sometimes (C); **alguna
  vez** sometime; **cada vez** each time; **de
  vez en cuando** from time to time (3); **en
  vez de** instead of (7); **muchas veces**
  often (5); **otra vez** again (5); **raras veces**
  rarely (5); **tal vez** perhaps (15); **última
  vez** last time (7); **una vez** once
vía road; way; **doble vía** two-way (11); **en
  vías de desarrollo** developing; in the

process of developing; **una sola vía** one-way (11); **vía digital** digital passage; **vía pública** public way

viajar to travel

viaje *m.* trip (10); **agencia de viajes** travel agency (11)

viajero/a traveler (11); **cheque** (*m.*) **de viajero** traveler's check

viciar to corrupt

vicio vice, bad habit

vicioso/a depraved, addicted to vice

víctima *f.* victim

vida life (3); **ganarse la vida** to earn one's living (15)

vidente seer; sighted

video video; **sacar (qu) un video** to rent a movie

videocámara video camera

videocasete *m.* video

videocasetera VCR

videocentro video store (3)

videojuego video game

vidrio glass (*material*) (10); **fibra de vidrio** fiberglass (13)

viejo/a *n.* old person; *adj.* old

viento wind; **hace (mucho) viento** it's (very) windy (2); **molino de viento** windmill

viernes *m. sing., pl.* Friday (1); **de lunes a viernes** Monday through Friday (4)

VIH *m.* (*abbrev. for* **virus** [*m.*] **de la inmunodeficiencia humana**) HIV (12)

villano/a villain

vinagre *m.* vinegar (8)

vino (blanco, rosado, tinto) (white, rosé, red) wine (8)

violación *f.* violation; rape

violar to violate; to rape

violencia violence (14)

violento/a violent (2)

violín *m.* violin

violinista *m., f.* violinist

virgen *f.* virgin; **Virgen de Guadalupe** Virgin of Guadalupe; **Virgen María** Virgin Mary

virtud *f.* virtue

visa visa (11)

visado visa (11)

visión *f.* vision

visita visit; **estar** (*irreg.*) **de visita** to be staying (11)

visitar to visit (2)

vista view (6)

visto/a (*p.p. of* **ver**) seen

visualmente visually

vitamina vitamin (8)

vitorear to acclaim, applaud

vivienda housing (15)

vivir to live; **¿dónde vive usted?** where do you (*pol. sing.*) live?, **¿dónde vives tú?** where do you (*inf. sing.*) live? (1); **¡viva… !** long live . . . ! (9); **vivo en…** I live in/at . . . (1)

vivo/a alive; vibrant; **color** (*m.*) **vivo** bright color (13); **estar** (*irreg.*) **vivo/a** to be alive (9)

vocabulario vocabulary

volante *m.* steering wheel

volar (ue) to fly; **volar un papalote** to fly a kite (*Mex.*) (9); **volar una cometa** to fly a kite (2)

volcán *m.* volcano (10)

voleibol *m.* volleyball (3)

volumen *m.* volume

voluntad *f.* will

voluntariamente voluntarily

voluntario/a volunteer

volver (ue) (*p.p.* **vuelto**) to return, go back (4); **volverse loco/a** to go crazy (12); **vuelve** he/she returns, you (*pol. sing.*) return (4); **vuelvo** I return (4)

vos *sub. pron.* you (*inf. sing.*) (*Arg., Guat., Uruguay*)

vosotros/as *sub. pron.* you (*inf. pl.*) (*Sp.*); *obj. of prep.* you (*inf. pl.*) (*Sp.*)

votante *m., f.* voter

votar to vote

voto vote

voz *f.* (*pl.* **las voces**) (**alta/baja**) (loud/soft) voice (14)

vuelo flight (11); **asistente** (*m., f.*) **de vuelo** flight attendant (11)

vuelta turn; **boleto de ida y vuelta** round-trip ticket (11); **dar** (*irreg.*) **vueltas** to go around; **de(n) una vuelta** turn around (*command*)

vuelto/a (*p.p. of* **volver**) returned

vulnerable vulnerable (15)

Y

y and; **y cuarto** quarter past (*time*) (1); **y media** half past (*time*) (1); **y tú, ¿qué dices?** and you (*inf. sing.*), what do you say? (1)

ya already; **ya es tarde** it's late already (1); **ya no** no longer (15); **ya que** since

yerno son-in-law (9)

yo *sub. pron.* I; **¡yo sí!** I do! (4)

yogui *m.* yogi

yogur *m.* yogurt (3)

Yucatán *m.* Yucatan (10)

Z

zanahoria carrot (8)

zapatería shoe store (3)

zapatillas slippers (13)

zapato shoe; **zapato de tacón alto** high-heeled shoe (13); **zapatos de tenis** tennis shoes (A)

zona zone (8)

zoológico zoo (7)

Index

This index is divided into two parts. "Grammar" covers grammar, structure and usage; "Topics" lists cultural and vocabulary topics treated in the text. Topics appear as groups; they are not cross-referenced. In this index the abbreviation *f.n.* refers to a footnote. All other abbreviations are identical to those used in the end vocabulary.

GRAMMAR

a
   ¿a quién le gusta...?, 301–302
   + **el,** 149
   to express time, 81
   + infinitive, 108
   + noun or pronoun, to specify indirect
      object, 82–83, 186, 207, 300
   personal, 241
abstract ideas expressed by **lo,** 465
accent marks. *See also* Appendix 3
   with demonstrative pronouns, 466*f.n.*
   with interrogatives and exclamations, 79, 342,
      367–368
   with object pronouns, 436, 472
   in preterite, 240, 265
adjective clauses, 541–542
adjectives
   agreement of, 18, 52, 113
   defined, 18
   demonstrative, 113–114. *See also* Appendix 2
   descriptive, 3, 8, 26–27, 29, 499–501
   forms of, 52
   irregular comparative forms of, 237
   limiting, 35*f.n.*
   listed, 26–27, 29
   with **lo,** 465
   meaning after **ser** and **estar,** 160, 178, 499–501
   meanings changing with position, 114
   of nationality, 35*f.n.*, 42, 46, 53, 133
   nominalization (used as nouns), 465
   ordinal, 87, 90–91, 109
   position of, 35, 113, 114
   possessive (stressed). *See* Appendix 2
   possessive (unstressed), 49–50. *See also*
      Appendix 2
   regular comparative forms of, 236–237
adónde?, 148
adverbial clauses with subjunctive, 402–405,
   434, 506, 539–540, 541
adverbs
   defined, 370
   ending in -**mente,** 370
   of time, 74, 87, 168, 176
affirmative words, 303–304
age
   comparing, 237
   expressing, 41, 52
ago (with **hacer**), 255, 273
agreement
   of adjectives, 18, 52
   of articles, 17–19
   of demonstrative adjectives, 113
   of nouns, 17–19, 35
   of possessive adjectives, 49–50

   of possessive pronouns, 51–52
   of subject and verb, 12–13, 140
al, 149
allí/allá, 113
alphabet, Spanish, 14–15
andar (*irreg.*). *See* Appendix 1
animals, 18*f.n.*
apocopation, 304
aquel/aquellos/aquella(s), 113
aquí/acá, 113
articles
   definite, 18–19, 237, 465
   indefinite, 18–19, 465
   plural, 33–34, 237
-**ar** verbs
   commands, 6, 9, 397, 398–399, 502–504
   conditional, 525, 547
   future, 514, 538
   imperfect, 315, 320, 331–332. *See also*
      Appendix 1
   past participle, 367
   past (preterite), 225, 239–240, 246, 250, 264–
      266. *See also* Appendix 1
   past subjunctive, 548–549
   present, 54. *See also* Appendix 1
   subjunctive, 400–401. *See also* Appendix 1

become, 435–436
buen(o/a), 114*f.n.*

caber (*irreg.*), 538, 547
caer (*irreg.*). *See* Appendices 1 and 3
cardinal numbers, 5, 9–10, 25, 30, 41, 47, 76,
   449–450, 464
changes in state, expressing, 435–436, 499–501
clause
   defined, 507
comer, 140, 240, 265, 366, 503, 538, 547
commands
   singular and plural, 20
commands (imperative)
   defined, 398, 503
   formal (polite; **usted, ustedes**), 6, 398–399,
      502–503
   indirect, 400–401, 436
   informal (**tú**), 482, 502–504
   placement of object pronouns, 6, 399, 401,
      436–437, 470–472
   softened, 400–401, 437, 485, 506–507
   of stem-changing verbs, 399
   vosotros/as, 398*f.n.*, 504. *See also* Appendix 1
¿cómo?, in questions, 78–79, 146. *See also*
      Appendix 3
comparisons
   of equality, 238
   of inequality, 236–237

   of irregular adjectives, 237
   of nouns, 236–237
   of regular adjectives, 236–237
   superlatives, 237
conditional. *See also* Appendix 1
   forms, 525, 547
   regular and irregular, 525, 547
   uses of, 547
conditional perfect. *See* Appendix 1
conditional sentences, 525, 547
conducir (zc) (*irreg.*), 268
conjugate, defined, 54
conjunctions
   of purpose, 542–543
   of time, 539–540
   use of subjunctive after, 539–540, 542–543
conmigo, contigo, 330
conocer (zc), 241, 398, 403
   uses of, 241, 335
   versus **saber,** 241
construir (y), 403. *See also* Appendix 1
contractions
   al, 139
   del, 48
contrary-to-fact situations, 525, 548–549
countries, capitalizing, 53
¿cuál?, in questions, 79, 146. *See also*
      Appendix 3
¿cuándo?, in questions, 78–79, 146. *See also*
      Appendix 3
cuando, subjunctive after, 402–405, 434, 506,
   540, 542
¿cuánto?, ¿cuántos/as?
   to ask *how long . . . ?,* 273
   in exclamations, 342
   in questions, 79, 146. *See also* Appendix 3
¡cuánto!, ¡cuántos/as!
   in exclamations, 368

dar (*irreg.*), 268, 269, 398, 403, 469. *See also*
      Appendix 1
dates, expressing, 58
days of the week, 58, 74
de
   in adjectival phrases, 465
   + **el,** 48
   to express origin, 133, 147, 148
   + infinitive, 178
   nominalization of adjective phrases with
      de, 465
   + noun, 465
   with **salir,** 143
   to show possession, 48
   with superlative, 237
   used with prepositions, 126–127, 143, 178
deber, uses of, 211, 212

TOPICS

Credits

About the Authors

Tracy D. Terrell (*late*) received his Ph.D. in Spanish linguistics from the University of Texas at Austin and published extensively in the areas of Spanish dialectology, specializing in the sociolinguistics of Caribbean Spanish. Professor Terrell's publications on second language acquisition and on the Natural Approach are widely known in the United States and abroad.

Magdalena Andrade received her first B.A. in Spanish/French and a second B.A. in English from San Diego University. After teaching in the Calexico Unified School District Bilingual Program for several years, she taught elementary and intermediate Spanish at both San Diego State and the University of California, Irvine, where she also taught Spanish for Heritage Speakers and Humanities Core Courses. Upon receiving her Ph.D. from the University of California, Irvine, she continued to teach there for several years and also at California State University, Long Beach. Currently an instructor at Irvine Valley College, Professor Andrade has co-authored *Mundos de fantasía: Fábulas, cuentos de hadas y leyendas* and *Cocina y comidas hispanas* (McGraw-Hill) and is developing two other language books.

Jeanne Egasse received her B.A. and M.A. in Spanish linguistics from the University of California, Irvine. She has taught foreign language methodology courses and supervised foreign language and ESL teachers in training for the Department of Education at the University of California, Irvine. Currently, she is an instructor of Spanish and coordinates the Spanish language Program at Irvine Valley College. In addition, Professor Egasse serves as a consultant for local schools and universities on implementing Natural Approach in the language classroom. Professor Egasse is co-author of *Cocina y comidas hispanas* and *Mundos de fantasía: Fábulas, cuentos de hadas y leyendas* (McGraw-Hill).

Elías Miguel Muñoz is a Cuban American poet and prose writer. He has a Ph.D. in Spanish from the University of California, Irvine, and he has taught language and literature at the university level. Dr. Muñoz is the author of *Viajes fantásticos, Ladrón de la mente,* and *Isla de luz,* titles in the Storyteller's Series by McGraw-Hill. He has published five other novels, two books of literary criticism, and two poetry collections. His creative work has been featured in numerous anthologies and sourcebooks, including *Herencia: The Anthology of Hispanic Literature of the United States, The Encyclopedia of American Literature,* and *The Scribner Writers Series: Latino and Latina Writers.*

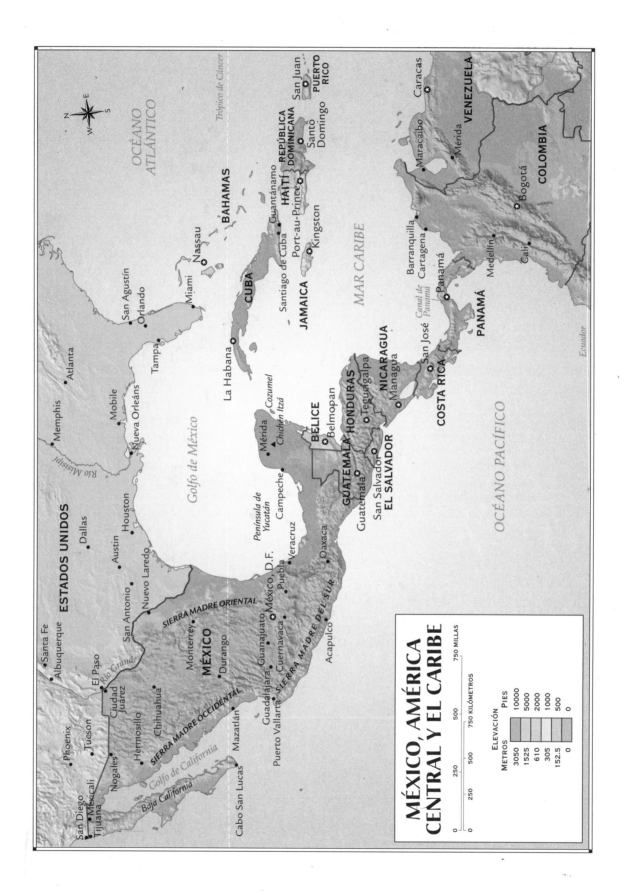

MÉXICO, AMÉRICA CENTRAL Y EL CARIBE

OCÉANO ATLÁNTICO

Trópico de Cáncer

BAHAMAS

Nassau

CUBA

La Habana

Santiago de Cuba

HAITÍ
Guantánamo
Port-au-Prince
JAMAICA
Kingston

REPÚBLICA DOMINICANA
Santo Domingo

San Juan
PUERTO RICO

MAR CARIBE

Caracas
VENEZUELA

Maracaibo
Mérida

Barranquilla
Cartagena
Panamá

COLOMBIA
Bogotá

Medellín
Cali

Ecuador

Canal de Panamá
PANAMÁ
Panamá

San José
COSTA RICA

NICARAGUA
Managua

Tegucigalpa
HONDURAS

Belmopan
BELICE

Cozumel
Chichén Itzá
Mérida

GUATEMALA
Guatemala
San Salvador
EL SALVADOR

Península de Yucatán

Campeche

Veracruz
Puebla
México, D.F.
Oaxaca
Acapulco

Golfo de México

ESTADOS UNIDOS

Atlanta
Memphis
Mobile
Nueva Orleáns

San Agustín
Orlando
Miami
Tampa

Río Misisipi

Santa Fe
Albuquerque
El Paso
Ciudad Juárez

Dallas
Austin
San Antonio
Nuevo Laredo

SIERRA MADRE ORIENTAL

Monterrey
MÉXICO
Durango

SIERRA MADRE OCCIDENTAL

Chihuahua
Hermosillo

Phoenix
Tucson
Nogales
Mexicali
Tijuana
San Diego

Guadalajara
Guanajuato
Cuernavaca
Puerto Vallarta
SIERRA MADRE DEL SUR

Mazatlán
Cabo San Lucas

Golfo de California
Baja California

OCÉANO PACÍFICO

OCÉANO ATLÁNTICO

N
E
W
S

ELEVACIÓN

METROS	PIES
3050	10000
1525	5000
610	2000
305	1000
152.5	500
0	0

0   250   500   750 KILÓMETROS
0   250   500   750 MILLAS